Contemporary Authors®

ISSN 0010-7468

Contemporary Authors®

A Bio-Bibliographical Guide to Current Writers in Fiction, General Nonfiction, Poetry, Journalism, Drama, Motion Pictures, Television, and Other Fields

volume *218*

GALE®

THOMSON

™

GALE

Detroit • New York • San Diego • San Francisco • Cleveland • New Haven, Conn. • Waterville, Maine • London • Munich

Contemporary Authors, Vol. 218

Project Editor
Jenai A.Mynatt

Editorial
Katy Balcer, Shavon Burden, Sara Constantakis, Natalie Fulkerson, Michelle Kazensky, Julie Keppen, Joshua Kondek, Mary Ruby, Lemma Shomali, Susan Strickland, Maikue Vang, Tracey Watson

Permissions
Lori Hines

Imaging and Multimedia
Lezlie Light, Kelly A. Quin

Composition and Electronic Capture
Carolyn A. Roney

Manufacturing
Lori Kessler

LIBRARY OF CONGRESS CATALOG CARD NUMBER 62-52046

ISBN 0-7876-6698-X
ISSN 0010-7468

Printed in the United States of America
10 9 8 7 6 5 4 3 2 1

Contents

Indexing note: All *Contemporary Authors* entries are indexed in the *Contemporary Authors* cumulative index, which is published separately and distributed twice a year.

As always, the most recent Contemporary Authors cumulative index continues to be the user's guide to the location of an individual author's listing.

Preface

Contemporary Authors (*CA*) provides information on approximately 115,000 writers in a wide range of media, including:

- Current writers of fiction, nonfiction, poetry, and drama whose works have been issued by commercial publishers, risk publishers, or university presses (authors whose books have been published only by known vanity or author-subsidized firms are ordinarily not included)

- Prominent print and broadcast journalists, editors, photojournalists, syndicated cartoonists, graphic novelists, screenwriters, television scriptwriters, and other media people

- Notable international authors

- Literary greats of the early twentieth century whose works are popular in today's high school and college curriculums and continue to elicit critical attention

A *CA* listing entails no charge or obligation. Authors are included on the basis of the above criteria and their interest to *CA* users. Sources of potential listees include trade periodicals, publishers' catalogs, librarians, and other users of the series.

How to Get the Most out of *CA*: Use the Index

The key to locating an author's most recent entry is the *CA* cumulative index, which is published separately and distributed twice a year. It provides access to *all* entries in *CA* and *Contemporary Authors New Revision Series* (*CANR*). Always consult the latest index to find an author's most recent entry.

For the convenience of users, the *CA* cumulative index also includes references to all entries in these Gale literary series: *Authors and Artists for Young Adults, Authors in the News, Bestsellers, Black Literature Criticism, Black Literature Criticism Supplement, Black Writers, Children's Literature Review, Concise Dictionary of American Literary Biography, Concise Dictionary of British Literary Biography, Contemporary Authors Autobiography Series, Contemporary Authors Bibliographical Series, Contemporary Dramatists, Contemporary Literary Criticism, Contemporary Novelists, Contemporary Poets, Contemporary Popular Writers, Contemporary Southern Writers, Contemporary Women Poets, Dictionary of Literary Biography, Dictionary of Literary Biography Documentary Series, Dictionary of Literary Biography Yearbook, DISCovering Authors, DISCovering Authors: British, DISCovering Authors: Canadian, DISCovering Authors: Modules* (including modules for Dramatists, Most-Studied Authors, Multicultural Authors, Novelists, Poets, and Popular/ Genre Authors), *DISCovering Authors 3.0, Drama Criticism, Drama for Students, Feminist Writers, Hispanic Literature Criticism, Hispanic Writers, Junior DISCovering Authors, Major Authors and Illustrators for Children and Young Adults, Major 20th-Century Writers, Native North American Literature, Novels for Students, Poetry Criticism, Poetry for Students, Short Stories for Students, Short Story Criticism, Something about the Author, Something about the Author Autobiography Series, St. James Guide to Children's Writers, St. James Guide to Crime & Mystery Writers, St. James Guide to Fantasy Writers, St. James Guide to Horror, Ghost & Gothic Writers, St. James Guide to Science Fiction Writers, St. James Guide to Young Adult Writers, Twentieth-Century Literary Criticism, 20th Century Romance and Historical Writers, World Literature Criticism,* and *Yesterday's Authors of Books for Children.*

A Sample Index Entry:

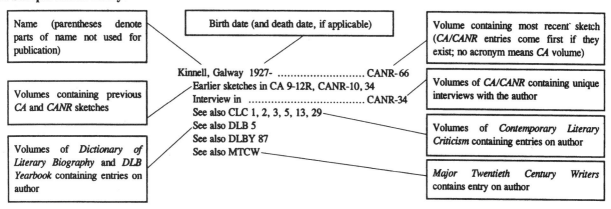

How Are Entries Compiled?

The editors make every effort to secure new information directly from the authors; listees' responses to our questionnaires and query letters provide most of the information featured in *CA*. For deceased writers, or those who fail to reply to requests for data, we consult other reliable biographical sources, such as those indexed in Gale's *Biography and Genealogy Master Index,* and bibliographical sources, including *National Union Catalog, LC MARC,* and *British National Bibliography.* Further details come from published interviews, feature stories, and book reviews, as well as information supplied by the authors' publishers and agents.

An asterisk (*) at the end of a sketch indicates that the listing has been compiled from secondary sources believed to be reliable but has not been personally verified for this edition by the author sketched.

What Kinds of Information Does An Entry Provide?

Sketches in *CA* contain the following biographical and bibliographical information:

- **Entry heading:** the most complete form of author's name, plus any pseudonyms or name variations used for writing

- **Personal information:** author's date and place of birth, family data, ethnicity, educational background, political and religious affiliations, and hobbies and leisure interests

- **Addresses:** author's home, office, or agent's addresses, plus e-mail and fax numbers, as available

- **Career summary:** name of employer, position, and dates held for each career post; resume of other vocational achievements; military service

- **Membership information:** professional, civic, and other association memberships and any official posts held

- **Awards and honors:** military and civic citations, major prizes and nominations, fellowships, grants, and honorary degrees

- **Writings:** a comprehensive, chronological list of titles, publishers, dates of original publication and revised editions, and production information for plays, television scripts, and screenplays

- **Adaptations:** a list of films, plays, and other media which have been adapted from the author's work

- **Work in progress:** current or planned projects, with dates of completion and/or publication, and expected publisher, when known

- **Sidelights:** a biographical portrait of the author's development; information about the critical reception of the author's works; revealing comments, often by the author, on personal interests, aspirations, motivations, and thoughts on writing

- **Interview:** a one-on-one discussion with authors conducted especially for *CA*, offering insight into authors' thoughts about their craft

- **Autobiographical essay:** an original essay written by noted authors for *CA*, a forum in which writers may present themselves, on their own terms, to their audience

- **Photographs:** portraits and personal photographs of notable authors

- **Biographical and critical sources:** a list of books and periodicals in which additional information on an author's life and/or writings appears

- **Obituary Notices** in *CA* provide date and place of birth as well as death information about authors whose full-length sketches appeared in the series before their deaths. The entries also summarize the authors' careers and writings and list other sources of biographical and death information.

Related Titles in the *CA* Series

Contemporary Authors Autobiography Series complements *CA* original and revised volumes with specially commissioned autobiographical essays by important current authors, illustrated with personal photographs they provide. Common topics include their motivations for writing, the people and experiences that shaped their careers, the rewards they derive from their work, and their impressions of the current literary scene.

Contemporary Authors Bibliographical Series surveys writings by and about important American authors since World War II. Each volume concentrates on a specific genre and features approximately ten writers; entries list works written by and about the author and contain a bibliographical essay discussing the merits and deficiencies of major critical and scholarly studies in detail.

Available in Electronic Formats

GaleNet. *CA* is available on a subscription basis through GaleNet, an online information resource that features an easy-to-use end-user interface, powerful search capabilities, and ease of access through the World-Wide Web. For more information, call 1-800-877-GALE.

Licensing. *CA* is available for licensing. The complete database is provided in a fielded format and is deliverable on such media as disk, CD-ROM, or tape. For more information, contact Gale's Business Development Group at 1-800-877-GALE, or visit us on our website at www.galegroup.com/bizdev.

Suggestions Are Welcome

The editors welcome comments and suggestions from users on any aspect of the *CA* series. If readers would like to recommend authors for inclusion in future volumes of the series, they are cordially invited to write the Editors at *Contemporary Authors*, Gale Group, 27500 Drake Rd., Farmington Hills, MI 48331-3535; or call at 1-248-699-4253; or fax at 1-248-699-8054.

Contemporary Authors Product Advisory Board

The editors of *Contemporary Authors* are dedicated to maintaining a high standard of excellence by publishing comprehensive, accurate, and highly readable entries on a wide array of writers. In addition to the quality of the content, the editors take pride in the graphic design of the series, which is intended to be orderly yet inviting, allowing readers to utilize the pages of *CA* easily and with efficiency. Despite the longevity of the *CA* print series, and the success of its format, we are mindful that the vitality of a literary reference product is dependent on its ability to serve its users over time. As literature, and attitudes about literature, constantly evolve, so do the reference needs of students, teachers, scholars, journalists, researchers, and book club members. To be certain that we continue to keep pace with the expectations of our customers, the editors of *CA* listen carefully to their comments regarding the value, utility, and quality of the series. Librarians, who have firsthand knowledge of the needs of library users, are a valuable resource for us. The *Contemporary Authors* Product Advisory Board, made up of school, public, and academic librarians, is a forum to promote focused feedback about *CA* on a regular basis. The six-member advisory board includes the following individuals, whom the editors wish to thank for sharing their expertise:

- **Anne M. Christensen,** Librarian II, Phoenix Public Library, Phoenix, Arizona.

- **Barbara C. Chumard,** Reference/Adult Services Librarian, Middletown Thrall Library, Middletown, New York.

- **Eva M. Davis,** Youth Department Manager, Ann Arbor District Library, Ann Arbor, Michigan.

- **Adam Janowski, Jr.,** Library Media Specialist, Naples High School Library Media Center, Naples, Florida.

- **Robert Reginald,** Head of Technical Services and Collection Development, California State University, San Bernadino, California.

- **Stephen Weiner,** Director, Maynard Public Library, Maynard, Massachusetts.

International Advisory Board

Well-represented among the 115,000 author entries published in *Contemporary Authors* are sketches on notable writers from many non-English-speaking countries. The primary criteria for inclusion of such authors has traditionally been the publication of at least one title in English, either as an original work or as a translation. However, the editors of *Contemporary Authors* came to observe that many important international writers were being overlooked due to a strict adherence to our inclusion criteria. In addition, writers who were publishing in languages other than English were not being covered in the traditional sources we used for identifying new listees. Intent on increasing our coverage of international authors, including those who write only in their native language and have not been translated into English, the editors enlisted the aid of a board of advisors, each of whom is an expert on the literature of a particular country or region. Among the countries we focused attention on are Mexico, Puerto Rico, Germany, Luxembourg, Belgium, the Netherlands, Norway, Sweden, Denmark, Finland, Taiwan, Singapore, Spain, Italy, South Africa, Israel, and Japan, as well as England, Scotland, Wales, Ireland, Australia, and New Zealand. The sixteen-member advisory board includes the following individuals, whom the editors wish to thank for sharing their expertise:

- **Lowell A. Bangerter,** Professor of German, University of Wyoming, Laramie, Wyoming.

- **Nancy E. Berg,** Associate Professor of Hebrew and Comparative Literature, Washington University, St. Louis, Missouri.

- **Frances Devlin-Glass,** Associate Professor, School of Literary and Communication Studies, Deakin University, Burwood, Victoria, Australia.

- **David William Foster,** Regent's Professor of Spanish, Interdisciplinary Humanities, and Women's Studies, Arizona State University, Tempe, Arizona.

- **Hosea Hirata,** Director of the Japanese Program, Associate Professor of Japanese, Tufts University, Medford, Massachusetts.

- **Jack Kolbert,** Professor Emeritus of French Literature, Susquehanna University, Selinsgrove, Pennsylvania.

- **Mark Libin,** Professor, University of Manitoba, Winnipeg, Manitoba, Canada.

- **C. S. Lim,** Professor, University of Malaya, Kuala Lumpur, Malaysia.

- **Eloy E. Merino,** Assistant Professor of Spanish, Northern Illinois University, DeKalb, Illinois.

- **Linda M. Rodríguez Guglielmoni,** Associate Professor, University of Puerto Rico—Mayagüez, Puerto Rico.

- **Sven Hakon Rossel,** Professor and Chair of Scandinavian Studies, University of Vienna, Vienna, Austria.

- **Steven R. Serafin,** Director, Writing Center, Hunter College of the City University of New York, New York City.

- **David Smyth,** Lecturer in Thai, School of Oriental and African Studies, University of London, England.

- **Ismail S. Talib,** Senior Lecturer, Department of English Language and Literature, National University of Singapore, Singapore.

- **Dionisio Viscarri,** Assistant Professor, Ohio State University, Columbus, Ohio.

- **Mark Williams,** Associate Professor, English Department, University of Canterbury, Christchurch, New Zealand.

CA Numbering System and Volume Update Chart

Occasionally questions arise about the *CA* numbering system and which volumes, if any, can be discarded. Despite numbers like "29-32R," "97-100" and "217," the entire *CA* print series consists of only 269 physical volumes with the publication of *CA* Volume 218. The following charts note changes in the numbering system and cover design, and indicate which volumes are essential for the most complete, up-to-date coverage.

CA First Revision	• 1-4R through 41-44R (11 books) *Cover:* Brown with black and gold trim. There will be no further First Revision volumes because revised entries are now being handled exclusively through the more efficient *New Revision Series* mentioned below.
CA Original Volumes	• 45-48 through 97-100 (14 books) *Cover:* Brown with black and gold trim. 101 through 218 (118 books) *Cover:* Blue and black with orange bands. The same as previous *CA* original volumes but with a new, simplified numbering system and new cover design.
CA Permanent Series	• *CAP*-1 and *CAP*-2 (2 books) *Cover:* Brown with red and gold trim. There will be no further Permanent Series volumes because revised entries are now being handled exclusively through the more efficient *New Revision Series* mentioned below.
CA New Revision Series	• CANR-1 through CANR-125 (125 books) *Cover:* Blue and black with green bands. Includes only sketches requiring significant changes; **sketches are taken from any previously published CA, CAP, or CANR volume.**

If You Have:	You May Discard:
CA First Revision Volumes 1-4R through 41-44R and *CA Permanent Series* Volumes 1 and 2	*CA* Original Volumes 1, 2, 3, 4 Volumes 5-6 through 41-44
CA Original Volumes 45-48 through 97-100 and 101 through 218	**NONE:** These volumes will not be superseded by corresponding revised volumes. Individual entries from these and all other volumes appearing in the left column of this chart may be revised and included in the various volumes of the *New Revision Series*.
CA New Revision Series Volumes CANR-1 through CANR-125	**NONE:** The *New Revision Series* does not replace any single volume of *CA*. Instead, volumes of *CANR* include entries from many previous *CA* series volumes. All *New Revision Series* volumes must be retained for full coverage.

A Sampling of Authors and Media People Featured in This Volume

Ann Brashares

Brashares is the author of the popular young-adult novel *The Sisterhood of the Traveling Pants*, a story about four teenage girls who agree to send a pair of secondhand jeans from friend to friend the first summer they are to be separated. Brashares continued the story with the publication of *The Second Summer of the Sisterhood* in 2003. In addition to her young adult fiction, Brashares has written two works of non-fiction which briefly detail the lives of the computer and software pioneers Steve Jobs and Linus Torvalds.

Nathan Englander

Englander was raised in an Orthodox Jewish home on Long Island in New York. However, after a life-changing trip to Israel during his junior year in college, he abandoned his religion and focused on a career as a writer. Englander completed a M.F.A. in creative writing at the Iowa Writer's Workshop and his first work *For the Relief of Unbearable Urges,* a collection of short stories, was published in 1999. The book features nine pieces written in the Jewish storytelling tradition of writers such as Bernard Malamud and Isaac Bashevis Singer.

Lillian Faderman

Faderman has written a number of books describing the minority experience in, and contribution to, the United States. Much of Faderman's work has been related to lesbian history and literature, culminating in the 1999 volume *To Believe in Women: What Lesbians Have Done for America-A History.* In 2003 her memoir *Naked in the Promised Land* was published. An autobiographical essay by Faderman is included in this volume of *CA.*

Michael J. Fox

Actor Fox, popular for his roles on television in *Family Ties* and *Spin City,* as well as his appearances in films, including *Back to the Future,* disclosed to the public in 1998 that he had been diagnosed with Parkinson&aps;s disease back in 1991. Fox's memoir *Lucky Man* was published in 2002 and, in addition to discussing his life and career as an actor, describes his struggles with the disease.

Morton Marcus

Marcus, a literature instructor for thirty years in California, is a poet whose work has been widely published in books, periodicals, and anthologies. Marcus&aps;s poetry has evolved over the years from traditional poetic structures to free verse and prose poetry. His most recent works include *Moments without Names: New & Selected Prose Poems* and *Shouting Down the Silence: Line Poems, 1988-2001,* both published in 2002. An autobiographical essay by Marcus is included in this volume of *CA.*

Rosie O'Donnell

O'Donnell is well known as a comedienne, actor, and host and executive producer of *The Rosie O'Donnell Show* for six years. She was the editorial director of the magazine *Rosie.* In addition to her charitable work on behalf of abused and neglected children, in 2002 O'Donnell published *Find Me,* a memoir which touches briefly on her own childhood abuse and her lesbian identity, but focuses on her relationship with a young woman with multiple personality disorder.

Jamie Oliver

Oliver, known as the Naked Chef, stands out among the latest generation of celebrity chefs as young, hip, energetic, and accessible. His moniker comes from his desire to reduce or "strip" food down to the basics. He is the host of a successful cooking show and his popular Web site includes recipes and a diary that updates Oliver's work and travel plans. His most recent publications include *Happy Days with the Naked Chef* and *Jamie's Kitchen: A Complete Cooking Course,* which appeared in 2003.

Leonid Tsypkin

Tsypkin, born in 1926 in the former Soviet Union, is the author of *Summer in Baden-Baden,* a novel about Dostoyevsky which imaginatively intertwines the story of an unnamed narrator and his admiration for the great Russian writer with an account of Dostoyevsk's time spent gambling in Baden-Baden in 1867. Pressured by Soviet officials following his son's immigration to the United States, Tsypkin had little hope of seeing the work published. It was smuggled out of the Soviet Union, however Tsypkin died shortly before it appeared in a Russian-language newspaper in New York City in 1982. *Summer in Baden-Baden* was published in English translation in 2001.

Acknowledgments

Grateful acknowledgment is made to those publishers, photographers, and artists whose work appear with these authors's essays. Following is a list of the copyright holders who have granted us permission to reproduce material in this volume of *CA*. Every effort has been made to trace copyright, but if omissions have been made, please let us know.

Photographs/Art

Joan Druett: All photographs reproduced by permission of the author.

Lillian Faderman: All photographs reproduced by permission of the author.

Text

Morton Marcus: Excerpt from interview in the *Bloomsbury Review,* March/April 2001. Reproduced by permission of Ray Gonzalez.

A

Indicates that a listing has been compiled from secondary sources believed to be reliable, but has not been personally verified for this edition by the author sketched.

ABHEDANANDA, Svami 1866-1939

PERSONAL: Born Kali Prasad Chandra, January 2, 1866, in Calcutta, India; died September 8, 1939, in Calcutta, India; son of Rasiklal (a teacher of English) and Nayantara (Devi) Chandra; name changed, 1886. *Education:* Studied with Sri Ramakrishna; studied Buddhism in Tibet.

CAREER: Initiated into *Sannyasa* order, 1886; joined monastery in Barangore, India, 1886; Vedanta Society, New York, NY, affiliate, 1894-96, preacher in London, England, 1896-97, and United States, 1897-c. 1910; independent Hindu preacher, c. 1910-21; member of Vedanta Society in Belur, India, 1921-c.1923. Founder of religious centers in Calcutta and Darjeeling, India, after 1923; lecturer in London, England, including appearance at Theosophical Society, 1896, and at U.S. institutions, including Brooklyn Institute of Arts and Sciences.

WRITINGS:

Vedanta Philosophy: Three Lectures by Svami Abhedananda on Reincarnation, Vedanta Society (New York, NY), 1899.
Vedanta Philosophy: Three Lectures by Svami Abhedananda on Spiritual Unfoldment . . . , Vedanta Society (New York, NY), 1901.
Vedanta Philosophy: Three Lectures by Svami Abhedananda on Philosophy of Work, Vedanta Society (New York, NY), 1902.

Vedanta Philosophy: Self-Knowledge, 1905, Kessinger Publishing Company (Whitefish, MT), 1998.
India and Her People: A Study in the Social, Political, Educational, and Religious Conditions of India (lectures), Vedanta Society (New York, NY), 1906, 6th edition, 1945, reprinted, Kessinger Publishing Company (Whitefish, MT), 1998.
(Editor) *The Gospel of Ramakrishna,* Vedanta Society (New York, NY), 1907.
Vedanta Philosophy: Five Lectures on Reincarnation (1908), Kessinger Publishing Company (Whitefish, MT), 1998.
Vedanta Philosophy; or, How to Be a Yogi (1908), Kessinger Publishing Company (Whitefish, MT), 2003.
Human Affection and Divine Love, 1911.
Paribrajaka Svami Abhedananda: Ka'smira, Amaranatha, o Tibhata bhramana (includes translation of *The Life of Saint Issa: The Best of the Sons of Men* by Nicolas Notovitch), [Calcutta, India], 1929, translation by Ansupati Dasgupta and Kunja Bihari Kundu published as *Journey into Kashmir and Tibet,* Ramakrishna Vedanta Math (Calcutta, India), 1987.
The Path of Realization, Ramakrishna Vedanta Math (Calcutta, India), 1939.
Lectures on Philosophy and Religion, Ramakrishna Vedanta Math (Calcutta, India), 1943.
How to Be a Yogi, Ramakrishna Vedanta Math (Calcutta, India), 1943.
Life beyond Death, Ramakrishna Vedanta Math (Calcutta, India), 1944, Vedanta Press and Bookshop (Hollywood, CA), 1986.
The Ideal of Education, Ramakrishna Vedanta Math (Calcutta, India), 1945.

Our Relation to the Absolute: A Study in True Psychology by Svami Abhedananda (lectures), Ramakrishna Vedanta Math (Calcutta, India), 1946, 3rd edition published as *True Psychology,* 1965.

Science of Psychic Phenomena, Ramakrishna Vedanta Math (Calcutta, India), 1946.

Spiritual Unfoldment, Ramakrishna Vedanta Math (Calcutta, India), 11th edition, 1946.

Attitude of Vedanta toward Religion, Ramakrishna Vedanta Math (Calcutta, India), 1947.

Vivekananda and His Work, Ramakrishna Vedanta Math (Calcutta, India), 3rd edition, 1950.

Reincarnation, Ramakrishna Vedanta Math (Calcutta, India), 6th edition, 1951, Kessinger Publishing Company (Whitefish, MT), 2003.

The Mystery of Death: A Study in the Philosophy and Religion of the Katha Upanishad, Ramakrishna Vedanta Math (Calcutta, India), 1953, Vedanta Press and Bookshop (Hollywood, CA), 1987.

Spiritual Teachings of Svami Abhedananda, translated by P. Seshadri Aiyer, Ramakrishna Vedanta Math (Calcutta, India), 1962.

Complete Works, ten volumes, Ramakrishna Vedanta Math (Calcutta, India), 1967.

Abhedananda in India in 1906, Ramakrishna Vedanta Math (Calcutta, India), 1968.

Bhagavad Gita: The Divine Message, two volumes, Ramakrishna Vedanta Math (Calcutta, India), 1969.

The Doctrine of Karma: A Study in Philosophy and Practice of Work, Vedanta Press and Bookshop (Hollywood, CA), 1975.

The Great Saviours of the World, Ramakrishna Vedanta Math (Calcutta, India), 4th edition, 1977, also published as *Great Saviors of the World,* Vedanta Society (New York, NY).

Kathaprasange Svami Abhedananda: Svami Pralnananananda bhumika sambalita; Svami Some'svarananda sankalita, Nababharata Pabali'sarsa (Calcutta, India), 1982.

Songs Divine: A Bouquet of Hymns to Sri Ramakrishna, Sri Sarada Devi, and Some Vedic Chants with English Translations (hymns in Sanskrit and English; originally published as *Stotraratnakara),* translated by P. Seshadri Aiyer, preface by Amiya Chakravarty, Ramakrishna Vedanta Math (Calcutta, India), 2nd edition, 1983.

Ramakrishna Kathamrita and Ramakrishna: Memoirs of Ramakrishna, Vedanta Press & Bookshop (Hollywood, CA), 1988.

Author of *The Complete Works of Swami Abheedananda,* Sri Ramakrishna Math (Mylapore, Madras,

India), beginning 1924. Author of tracts and pamphlets. Contributor to periodicals, including *Vedanta and the West.*

BIOGRAPHICAL AND CRITICAL SOURCES:

BOOKS

Ghosh, Ashutosh, *Swami Abhedananda, the Patriot-Saint,* Ramakrishna Vedanta Math (Calcutta, India) 1967.*

*   *   *

ABHEDANANDA, Swami
See ABHEDANANDA, Svami

*   *   *

ALEXANDER, Edward P(orter) 1907-2003

OBITUARY NOTICE—See index for *CA* sketch: Born January 11, 1907, in Keokuk, IA; died of a heart ailment July 31, 2003, in Chevy Chase, MD. Historian and author. Alexander, an authority on museums, was a former director of the Colonial Williamsburg Foundation. After earning his undergraduate degree from Drake University in 1928, he completed his master's degree at the State University of Iowa in 1931, and his Ph.D. at Columbia University in 1938. Beginning his career as a secondary-school teacher in Iowa and Minnesota during the late 1920s and early 1930s, Alexander eventually became executive director of the New York State Historical Association, where he worked from 1934 to 1941, and was supervisor of the Historical Records Survey for the state of New York from 1936 to 1938. During World War II Alexander resided in Wisconsin, where he directed the state historical society in Madison. Then, in 1946, he became director of interpretation at the Colonial Williamsburg Foundation, where he remained until 1972. The last years of his professional career were spent at the University of Delaware, where he was director of museum studies until his retirement in 1977. Alexander was the author of several history books, among them *A Revolutionary Conservative: James Duane of New York* (1938), *The Museum: A Living Book of History* (1959), and *The Museum in America: Innovators and Pioneers* (1997).

OBITUARIES AND OTHER SOURCES:

PERIODICALS

New York Times, August 16, 2003, p. A13.
Washington Post, August 10, 2003, p. C11.

*   *   *

ALEXANDER, Michael 1970-

PERSONAL: Born 1970. *Education:* University of Pennsylvania, B.A., 1992; Yale University, Ph.D., 1999.

ADDRESSES: Office—Department of History, University of Oklahoma, West Lindsey, Room 304A, Norman, OK 73019. *E-mail*—michael-alexander@ou.edu.

CAREER: University of Oklahoma, Norman, assistant professor of history and Judaic studies.

WRITINGS:

Jazz Age Jews, Princeton University Press (Princeton, NJ), 2001.

WORK IN PROGRESS: Research into a cultural history of Jews and money.

SIDELIGHTS: In *Jazz Age Jews,* Michael Alexander provides a study of three men who were born in the 1880s and grew up in Jewish ghettos before becoming middle class and marrying gentile women. All achieved fame during the period referred to as the Jazz Age, although for different reasons. Alexander questions the claim that Arnold Rothstein fixed baseball's 1919 World Series, an event known as the Black Sox scandal, and examines Felix Frankfurter's defense of Italian anarchists Sacco and Vanzetti. A *Publishers Weekly* contributor said Alexander's arguments about these cases "are dazzling." Alexander also writes of Al Jolson's appearance in *The Jazz Singer,* the first talking film, and how Jolson was instrumental in bringing jazz to Hollywood.

Additionally, *Jazz Age Jews* examines the feeling of marginality experienced by Jews and the era's link to anti-Semitism, as demonstrated by the negative portrait of a Jewish gangster in F. Scott Fitzgerald's *The Great Gatsby.* Alexander notes that auto tycoon Henry Ford's writings had racist themes, and that A. Lawrence Lowell attempted to institute quotas for Jewish admission to Harvard University. The author looks at the ways in which immigrant Jews melded into society, prospered, and became leaders in causes for social justice. The *Publishers Weekly* writer concluded by calling *Jazz Age Jews* "elucidating and insightful, an important contribution to both Jewish and cultural studies."

BIOGRAPHICAL AND CRITICAL SOURCES:

PERIODICALS

Publishers Weekly, September 17, 2001, review of *Jazz Age Jews,* p. 69.
Shofar, spring, 2003, Jeff Melnick, review of *Jazz Age Jews,* p. 203.*

*   *   *

ALI, Thalassa

PERSONAL: Born in Boston, MA; daughter of archaeologists; married, 1963 (husband died 1975); children: two. *Education:* Radcliffe College, B.A., 1962.

ADDRESSES:
Agent—c/o Author Mail, Random House, 1745 Broadway, New York, NY 10019.

CAREER: Writer. Stockbroker, 1975-83.

WRITINGS:

A Singular Hostage, Bantam Books (New York, NY), 2002.
A Beggar at the Gate, Bantam Books (New York, NY), 2003.

SIDELIGHTS: Author Thalassa Ali was born in Boston, Massachusetts, the daughter of two archeologists, one English and one American. She studied fine arts at Radcliffe College, earning a bachelor's degree in 1962. A year later she married a man from Pakistan, and moved to her husband's hometown of Lahore, where she lived for twelve years. When she was thirty-one years old, her husband died, and she remained in Pakistan for three more years to run his business.

In 1975 Ali returned to Boston with her two children and became a stockbroker. In 1993, after her children embarked on their own careers, she turned to writing, basing her work on her deep love for Pakistan and India. She had converted to Islam in 1984, during a visit to Pakistan, and became deeply interested in Sufism, a mystical branch of Islam; she is a member of Tauhidia, a Sufi brotherhood that is based in Karachi. While in Pakistan, Ali also began collecting books about nineteenth-century India, and when she began her first novel, she set it in that time and place.

A Singular Hostage is the first novel in a planned romantic trilogy. The story begins in 1838, when a young British woman, Mariana Givens, is sent to India in order to find a suitable husband. Spunky and intelligent, she is more interested in travel and military history than in mate-finding, despite her family's decree. She works as a translator, joining British Governor-General Lord Auckland as he travels across India with ten thousand troops to meet Ranjit Singh, maharajah of the Punjab. Auckland's mission is to negotiate an alliance with Singh that will place Afghanistan under British control.

Although Mariana has no shortage of suitors, she is more interested in the exotic culture she finds herself in, with its spicy foods, elephants that carry baggage, and interesting people, particularly Munshi Sahib, the wise tutor who is teaching her the local language and customs.

As Auckland negotiates the terms of his treaty, Givens becomes embroiled in a conspiracy involving a baby the maharajah is holding hostage: a boy named Saboor who is reputed to have mystical powers. When Saboor's mother is poisoned, Givens becomes his guardian, and she is entrusted to return him to his father, Hassan Sahib. She begins to feel romantic impulses toward Hassan, but the novel ends without resolving the issue, perhaps leaving this part of the story for the rest of the trilogy.

A *Publishers Weekly* reviewer praised Ali's use of history, comedy, and "compelling mysticism." In *Booklist,*

Shelley Mosley also complimented the author for weaving a tale of history, adventure, intrigue, and mysticism, calling the novel a "seductive tale."

BIOGRAPHICAL AND CRITICAL SOURCES:

PERIODICALS

Booklist, October 1, 2002, p. 299.
Kirkus Reviews, September 15, 2002, p. 1330.
Publishers Weekly, October 7, 2002, p. 52.
School Library Journal, April, 2003, Molly Connally, review of *A Singular Hostage,* p. 195.*

*   *   *

ALLAIRE, Bernard 1960-

PERSONAL: Born June 7, 1960, in Quebec City, Quebec, Canada; married (divorced); married Silvia Marzagalli (a historian and university teacher); children: Matteo, Elise. *Education:* Attended École des Hautes Etudes en Sciences Sociales, 1991-97; Laval University, graduated, 1995.

ADDRESSES: Agent—Gaston Deschênes, Edition du Septentrion, 1300 rue Maguire, Quebec City, Quebec G1T 1Z3, Canada. *E-mail*—b.allaire@wanadoo.fr.

CAREER: Academic and author. Researcher in Paris, France, 1990-94; research affiliate with Laval University, Quebec City, Quebec, Canada, and Canadian Museum, Ottawa, Ontario, Canada.

MEMBER: ARTAF (London, England), Historical Archaeology.

AWARDS, HONORS: J.-C. Falardeau prize, Humanities and Social Sciences Federation of Canada, 2000; Pelleteries award.

WRITINGS:

Meta Incognita: A Discourse of Discovery: Martin Frobisher Expeditions, 1576-1578, Canadian Museum of History (Ottawa, Ontario, Canada), 1998.

Pelleteries, manchons et chapeaux de castor: les four-rures Nord-Américaines à Paris 1500-1632, Septentrion (Quebec City, Quebec, Canada), 1999.

Editor of text for video documentary *Les essaise pyrométallurgiques,* Laval University, 1998.

WORK IN PROGRESS: Research on the voyage to Texas of French explorer Cavelier de la Salle (1684-87).

*   *   *

ALLEN, A(sa) A(lonzo) 1911-1970

PERSONAL: Born March 27, 1911, in Sulfur Rock, AR; died June 11, 1970, in San Francisco, CA; married, c. 1934; wife's name Lexia (divorced, 1967).

CAREER: Licensed preacher of Assemblies of God, beginning 1936; worked as traveling evangelist, 1936-47; pastor of church in Corpus Christi, TX, beginning 1947; Voice of Healing (ministry), traveling evangelist, c. 1950-55; A. A. Allen Revivals, Dallas, TX, founder and creator of *Allen Revival Hour* (radio program); founder of Miracle Revival Fellowship (later known as Miracle Life Fellowship International), 1956, and Miracle Valley (spiritual community), 1958.

WRITINGS:

The Price of God's Miracle Working Power, privately printed (Lamar, CO), 1950.
Power to Get Wealth: How You Can Have It!, A. A. Allen Revivals (Miracle Valley, AZ), 1963.
The Riches of the Gentiles Are Yours, A. A. Allen Revivals (Miracle Valley, AZ), 1965.
Witchcraft, Wizards, and Witches, A. A. Allen Revivals (Miracle Valley, AZ), 1968.
(With Walter Wagner) *Born to Lose, Bound to Win* (autobiography), Doubleday (Garden City, NY), 1970.

Other writings include *My Cross,* A. A. Allen Revivals (Miracle Valley, AZ). Founder of *Miracle* magazine.

BIOGRAPHICAL AND CRITICAL SOURCES:

BOOKS

Allen, A. A., and Walter Wagner, *Born to Lose, Bound to Win,* Doubleday (Garden City, NY), 1970.
Stewart, Don, *Man from Miracle Valley,* Great Horizons Co. (Long Beach, CA), 1971.

PERIODICALS

Look, October 7, 1939, William Hedgepath, "He Feels, He Heals, and He Turns You on to God," pp. 23-31.*

*   *   *

ALLEN, Ivan (Earnest), Jr. 1911-2003

OBITUARY NOTICE—See index for *CA* sketch: Born March 15, 1911, in Atlanta, GA; died July 2, 2003, in Atlanta, GA. Politician, businessman, and author. As mayor of Atlanta, Georgia, during the pivotal civil rights years, Allen became a nationally known political figure for his support of desegregation. The son of a state senator who owned an office supply store, Allen earned a bachelor's degree from the Georgia Institute of Technology in 1933 before joining his father's company. During World War II he served in the army's Quartermaster Corps stateside, returning home to take over presidency of the family business and increasing sales almost eightfold. His involvement in government began in 1945, when he worked for the governor of Georgia as an assistant for a year. Later, in 1957, he ran for the office himself. At the time, Allen was in favor of segregation, but this stand did not help him win his first run for office. Becoming president of the Atlanta Chamber of Commerce, he became involved in racial issues and eventually changed his stance on segregation. In 1961 Allen proved his support of African Americans by working to desegregate lunch counters throughout the city and to racially integrate schools. The result of this clear change of heart was that he gained the support of African-American voters and won the 1962 mayoral election, serving two terms in office. As mayor, Allen viewed desegregation as not only a social but also a practical issue, believing business stood to profit by welcoming rather than shunning black customers. His tenure oversaw many economic improvements for Atlanta, as he brought in more businesses, including sports franchises, by creating a positive economic atmosphere. While other cities lost population during this time, Atlanta saw its citizenry increase by almost one third. This is not to say that Atlanta was a peaceful place in the 1960s; race riots still occurred, but Allen faced the problem head-on, in 1966 walking into the middle of a riot without so much as a helmet on in an effort to show people he was on their side. In 1970 Allen retired from politics to return to his business, serving as chair of the board of directors of the Ivan Allen Co. The next year he published a book about his experiences in the turbulent 1960s titled *Mayor: Notes on the Sixties,* written with Paul Hemphill.

OBITUARIES AND OTHER SOURCES:

PERIODICALS

Chicago Tribune, July 4, 2003, section 1, p. 11.
Los Angeles Times, July 3, 2003, p. B14.
New York Times, July 3, 2003, p. A23.
Times (London, England), July 24, 2003.
Washington Post, July 3, 2003, p. B7.

*   *   *

ALLEN, Robert G. 1948-

PERSONAL: Born May 20, 1948, in Raymond, Alberta, Canada; son of John Leonard and May Leone (Judd) Allen; immigrated to United States c. 1970; naturalized U.S. citizen, 1974; married Daryl Elyse Lieurance, February 14, 1977; children: Aimee Elyse, Aaron, Hunter. *Education:* Attended Ricks College, Rexburg, ID, 1966-67; Brigham Young University, B.A. (magna cum laude), 1972, M.B.A., 197. *Religion:* Jesus Christ of Latter-Day Saints (Mormon).

ADDRESSES: Home—1696 Blackhawk Circle, Pleasant Grove, UT 84062.

CAREER: Writer. J.B. Realty, Provo, UT, employee, 1974-75; Lincoln Realty, Provo, realtor, 1975-77; Robert G. Allen Associates, Provo, president, 1977—.

WRITINGS:

Nothing Down: How to Buy Real Estate with Little or No Money Down, Simon & Schuster (New York, NY), 1980, revised as *Nothing down for the '90s: How to Buy Real Estate with Little or No Money Down,* Simon & Schuster (New York, NY), 1990.
Creating Wealth, Simon & Schuster (New York, NY), 1986.
The Challenge, Simon & Schuster (New York, NY), 1987.
Achieving Financial Liberty, Ranger Associates (Altamonte Springs, FL), 1995.
Multiple Streams of Income, Wiley (New York, NY), 2001.
Multiple Streams of Internet Income, Wiley (New York, NY), 2001.
(With Mark Victor Hansen) *The One-Minute Millionaire: The Enlightened Way to Wealth,* Harmony Books (New York, NY), 2002.

SIDELIGHTS: Robert G. Allen is the author of numerous books about making money. Allen was born in Canada, the younger of two children of an accountant father and a mother who died at his birth. He was raised as a Mormon, and spent two years as a missionary in Tahiti.

Allen studied in the United States, earned a bachelor's degree and an M.B.A. from Brigham Young University, and became a naturalized U.S. citizen in 1974. He worked in real estate, choosing that field because it was "one of the quickest ways to become rich," according to Edwin McDowell in the *New York Times Book Review.* However, he failed to become rich, and after a few years in real estate, he spent $6,000 to attend real-estate seminars throughout the United States, looking for answers. After attending, he decided that he didn't have to have cash or a good credit rating in order to make money, and he formed his own real estate company and began buying real estate. He then began writing his first book, *Nothing Down: How to Buy Real Estate with Little or No Money Down,* which shares some of the principles he has learned.

Allen told McDowell that he wrote an outline and several chapters of the book during a vacation in Hawaii, and then spent $1,000 to have the book edited before he submitted it to a commercial publisher. In

1978 he took the partly finished book to the American Booksellers Convention, where he went to a booth run by publisher Simon & Schuster. He had heard that this publisher had produced other finance-related books, and asked someone to point out the president of the company to him. It took Allen two days to work up the courage to speak to the company's president, who liked the book and said he would show it to his editors back in New York. A month later Allen received a contract.

In the book, Allen advises readers to use several unorthodox techniques; for example, he tells them to acquire as many credit cards as possible in order to get signature loans on a moment's notice. He also counsels about the use of "OPM" (Other People's Money), giving lenders fifty percent interest or less and keeping the balance, and advises buyers to look for people down on their luck, such as those who have recently experienced divorce, judgments, bankruptcies, foreclosures, deaths in the family, and probates, in order to find sellers who are desperate to unload their property.

In 1986 Allen published *Creating Wealth,* which lists seven steps to becoming rich, and also explores the value of a positive attitude. Many people, he notes, are "programmed" not to take risks, to remain poor, and to save rather than invest, all failings that will prevent them from becoming multimillionaires. A change in attitude can allow people to take risks and reach their true financial potential.

For *The Challenge,* Allen chose three unemployed people and taught them his techniques for buying property at below-market price from a seller who is highly motivated to get rid of the property. The challenge was for them to buy a residential rental property within 90 days and put $5,000 in the bank. The book describes the experiences of these protégés, all of whom bought property; only one succeeded in reaching the financial goal Allen set during the time allotted for the experiment.

Multiple Streams of Income provides ten methods for making over $100,000 a year by working from home, part-time, and with little or no investment. Allen also provides strategies for investment and tax shelters. In a similar volume, *Multiple Streams of Internet Income,* Allen advises readers on ways to make money through the Internet, including the use of niche marketing, auto responders, selling links, placing ads on a web page, net auctions, and selling client information.

In *The One-Minute Millionaire: The Enlightened Way to Wealth* Allen and coauthor Mark Victor Hansen provide what a *Publishers Weekly* reviewer called "a longwinded pep talk on how just about anybody can make big money." They offer affirmations, such as "You are your wealth," "I think like a millionaire," and "Clarity is power," as well as some broad suggestions for money making: write a book, buy and sell real estate, or start a company.

In addition to writing books on finance, Allen serves as a lay counselor for his Mormon parish, tithes ten percent of his income to the Church of Jesus Christ of Latter-Day Saints, and plans to leave the majority of his estate to the Mormons when he dies. According to Sally Jenkins in *People,* "He expects his children to create their own wealth, using his book as a guide." He has used the money he earned from his books and real estate ventures to buy a large estate in Provo, Utah, where he lives with his wife and three children. "The last thing that people want to hear is the plain simple fact that the rich think differently from the poor," Allen told Jenkins. "They have what I would call a wealthy mind-set."

BIOGRAPHICAL AND CRITICAL SOURCES:

PERIODICALS

Booklist, April 15, 1980, p. 1163; March 15, 1983, p. 929; March 15, 1987, p. 1076; November 1, 1990, p. 485; August, 2002, p. 1882.
Kirkus Reviews, December 1, 1979, p. 1404; February 15, 1983, p. 215.
Library Journal, February 15, 1980, p. 503; April 15, 1983, p. 820; July 1, 1986, p. 79; May 1, 1987, p. 65; May 1, 1990, p. 104; March 15, 2001, p. 44; April 15, 2001, p. 110; May 1, 2002, p. 150.
New York Times Book Review, May 25, 1980, p. 22.
People, August 22, 1983, p. 37.
Publishers Weekly, December 24, 1979, p. 47; March 13, 1987, p. 76; March 27, 2000, p. 69; May 7, 2001, p. 16; August 19, 2002, p. 76.
West Coast Review of Books, May, 1983, p. 43.

ONLINE

Robert G. Allen Home Page, http://www.robertgallen. com (October 14, 2003).*

*   *   *

ALLRED, Rulon C(lark) 1906-1977

PERSONAL: Born March 29, 1906, in Chihuahua, Mexico; murdered May 10, 1977, in Murray, UT; son of Byron Harvey Allred (a politician); married multiple times. *Education:* Attended a college of naturopathic medicine.

CAREER: Chiropractor and author. United Order Effort (fundamentalist, polygamist religious denomination; later renamed Apostolic United Order and Apostolic United Brethren), member, beginning c. 1933, ruling assistant, 1951-54, leader, 1954-77.

WRITINGS:

The Allred Family in America, (Salt Lake City, UT), 1965.
Treasures of Knowledge: Selected Discourses and Excerpts from Talks, two volumes, Bitterroot Publishing (Hamilton, MT), 1982.

BIOGRAPHICAL AND CRITICAL SOURCES:

BOOKS

Anderson, J. Max, *The Polygamy Story: Fiction and Fact,* Publishers Press (Salt Lake City, UT), 1979.
Bradlee, Ben, Jr., and Dale Van Atta, *Prophet of Blood,* Putnam (New York, NY), 1981.
LeBaron, Verlan M., *The LeBaron Story,* privately printed (Lubbock, TX), 1981.
Van Wagoner, Richard S., *Mormon Polygamy,* Signature Books (Salt Lake City, UT), 1986.*

*   *   *

AMES, Edward Scribner 1870-1958

PERSONAL: Born April 21, 1870, in Eau Claire, WI; died June 29, 1958, in Chicago, IL; son of Lucius Bowles (a minister) and Adeline (Scribner) Ames; married Mabel Van Meter, July 6, 1893; children: four.

Education: Drake University, B.A., 1889, M.A., 1891; Yale University, B.D., 1892, further graduate study, c. 1892-94; University of Chicago, Ph.D., 1895.

CAREER: Minister of Christian Church (Disciples of Christ); Butler College, professor of philosophy and religion, 1897-1900; University of Chicago, Chicago, IL, member of faculty of philosophy of religion, 1900-35, department chair until 1935; Disciples Divinity House (residence for seminarians), Chicago, dean, 1937-45. Harvard University, university preacher, 1912-14. University Church of the Disciples of Christ, pastor, 1900-c. 1940; Campbell Institute, associate.

WRITINGS:

The Psychology of Religious Experience, Houghton-Mifflin (Boston, MA), 1910.
The Divinity of Christ (sermons), New Christian Century (Chicago, IL), 1911.
The Higher Individualism (sermons), Houghton-Mifflin (Boston, MA), 1915.
The New Orthodoxy, University of Chicago Press (Chicago, IL), 1918.
(With others) *Experiments in Personal Religion,* American Institute of Sacred Literature (Chicago, IL), 1928.
Religion, Henry Holt (New York, NY), 1929.
Humanism, University of Chicago Press (Chicago, IL), 1931.
Letters to God and the Devil, Harper & Row (New York, NY), 1933.
Beyond Theology (autobiography), edited by Van Meter Ames, University of Chicago Press (Chicago, IL), 1959.
Prayers and Meditations of Edward Scribner Ames, edited by Van Meter Ames, 1970.

Author of pamphlets. Contributor to books, including *The Church at Work in the Modern World,* edited by William Clayton Bower, University of Chicago Press (Chicago, IL), 1935. Contributor to periodicals, including *Journal of Religion* and *International Journal of Ethics.* Editor, *Scroll,* 1903-51.

BIOGRAPHICAL AND CRITICAL SOURCES:

BOOKS

Ames, Edward Scribner, *Beyond Theology,* edited by Van Meter Ames, University of Chicago Press (Chicago, IL), 1959.

PERIODICALS

Encounter, fall, 1969, Harvey Arnold, "A Religion That Walks the Earth."*

* * *

ANDERSON, Atholl

PERSONAL: Male. *Ethnicity:* "Ngai Tahu Whanui through descent from Rakiura Maori." *Education:* University of Canterbury, B.A., M.A.; University of Otago, M.A.; Cambridge University, Ph.D.

ADDRESSES: Office—Department of Archaeology and Natural History, Research School of Pacific and Asian Studies, Australian National University, Canberra, Australian Capital Territory 0200, Australia; fax: 61 02 6249 4917. *E-mail*—aja@coombs.anu.edu.au.

CAREER: Educator and author. University of Otago, professor and head of department of anthropology; Australian National University, Canberra, Australia, professor of prehistory.

MEMBER: Society of Antiquaries of London (fellow); Royal Society, New Zealand (fellow).

AWARDS, HONORS: D.Sc., University of Cambridge.

WRITINGS:

(Editor) *Birds of a Feather: Osteological and Archaeological Papers from the South Pacific in Honour of R. J. Scarlett,* B.A.R. (Oxford, England), 1979.
When All the Moa Ovens Grew Cold: Nine Centuries of Changing Fortune for the Southern Maori, Otago Heritage Books (Dunedin, New Zealand), 1983.
Te Puoho's Last Raid: The March from Golden Bay to Southland in 1836 and Defeat at Tuturau, foreword by Angus Ross, Otago Heritage Books (Dunedin, New Zealand), 1986.
(Editor) *Traditional Fishing in the Pacific: Ethnographical and Archaeological Papers from the Fifteenth Pacific Science Congress,* Bernice Pauahi Bishop Museum (Honolulu, HI), 1986.

Prodigious Birds: Moas and Moa-hunting in Prehistoric New Zealand, Cambridge University Press (New York, NY), 1989.
(With Richard McGovern-Wilson) *Beech Forest Hunters: The Archaeology of Maori Rockshelter Sites on Lee Island, Lake Te Anua, in Southern New Zealand,* New Zealand Archaeological Association (Auckland, New Zealand), 1991.
Race against Time, Hocken Library, University of Otago (Dunedin, New Zealand), 1992.
(Editor) James Herries Beattie, *Traditional Lifeways of the Southern Maori: The Otago University Museum Ethnological Project, 1920,* University of Otago Press (Dunedin, New Zealand), 1994.
The Welcome of Strangers: An Ethnohistory of Southern Maori A.D. 1650-1850, Otago University Press (Dunedin, New Zealand), 1998.
(Editor, with Tim Murray) *Australian Archaeologist: Collected Papers in Honour of Jim Allen,* Coombs Academic Publishing (Canberra, Australian Capital Territory, Australia), 2000.
(Editor, with Ian Lilley and Sue O'Connor) *Histories of Old Ages: Essays in Honour of Rhys Jones,* Pandanus Books (Canberra, Australian Capital Territory, Australia), 2001.
(Editor, with G. R. Clark and T. Vunidilo) *The Archaeology of Lapita Dispersal in Oceania: Papers from the Fourth Lapita Conference, June 2000, Canberra, Australia,* Pandanus Books (Canberra, Australia), 2001.

Archeological consultant for *From the Beginning: The Archaeology of the Maori,* edited by John Wilson, Penguin, 1987.

SIDELIGHTS: Archaeologist and anthropologist Atholl Anderson has spent his life studying the prehistory of his native New Zealand and its indigenous inhabitants, the Maori. Anderson, himself a member of the Ngai Tahu tribe of the Maori, may be best known outside of New Zealand for his book *Prodigious Birds: Moas and Moa-hunting in Prehistoric New Zealand. Prodigious Birds* is a comprehensive study of moas, which were large flightless birds, and the interaction between the animals and the Maori who hunted them until the birds became extinct roughly four hundred years ago.

The first half of the book, which focuses on the natural history of the moa, "spans the entire spectrum of biology, from molecular evolution and systematics to plant evolution, biological anthropology, and even cryptozoology," Alan Feduccia explained in *Science*. "Anderson is first and formost an archeologist, but his grasp of biology leaves little to be desired," Agnar Ingolfsson commented in a review of *Prodigious Birds* for *Quarterly Review of Biology*. Then, in the second half of the book, Anderson discusses the methods with which the Maori hunted the moas, when and where they hunted them, and how they butchered and prepared the birds once they were killed. It is generally believed that the Maori hunted the moa to extinction. The extinction of the moas is "the most dramatic symbol of the devastation inflicted by the Polynesians in their trek through the South Pacific," Feduccia wrote; after *Prodigious Birds*, "no longer will there be the image of the 'noble savage' living in harmony with the environment."

BIOGRAPHICAL AND CRITICAL SOURCES:

PERIODICALS

Antiquity, March, 1988, Wilfred Shawcross, review of *Traditional Fishing in the Pacific: Ethnographical and Archaeological Papers from the Fifteenth Pacific Science Congress,* pp. 193-194; June, 1991, Matthew Spriggs, review of *Prodigious Birds: Moas and Moa-hunting in Prehistoric New Zealand,* pp. 422-423.
Archaeology in New Zealand, June, 1999, Nigel Prickett, review of *The Welcome of Strangers: An Ethnohistory of Southern Maori, A.D. 1650-1850,* pp. 178-179.
Archaeology in Oceania, July, 2002, Peter Veth, review of *Australian Archaeologist: Collected Papers in Honour of Jim Allen,* pp. 102-103.
Asian Perspectives, spring, 2003, J. Stephen Athens, review of *Australian Archaeologist,* pp. 181-183.
Choice, November, 1999, S. R. Martin, review of *The Welcome of Strangers,* p. 596.
Journal of Polynesian Society, June, 2000, Alan Ward, review of *The Welcome of Strangers,* pp. 199-201.
Landfall, May, 1999, Giselle Byrnes, review of *The Welcome of Strangers,* pp. 145-149.
New Zealand Journal of History, April, 1999, Michael P. J. Reilly, review of *The Welcome of Strangers,* pp. 111-112.
Quarterly Review of Biology, December, 1991, Agnar Ingolfsson, review of *Prodigious Birds,* pp. 503-504.
Science, May 17, 1991, Alan Feduccia, review of *Prodigious Birds,* pp. 1005-1006.

ONLINE

Centre for Archaeological Research, http://car.anu.edu.au/ (November 14, 2003), "Anderson, Professor Atholl."
Law Associates Consulting Engineers Web site, http://www.lawas.co.nz/ (April 15, 2003), "New Zealand Archaeological News."
New Zealand Books, http://www.nzbooks.com/ (November 14, 2003), "Atholl Anderson."
Research School of Pacific and Asian Studies, Australian National University, Web site, http://rspas.anu.edu.au/ (November 16, 2003), "Atholl Anderson's Home Page."*

*   *   *

ARCHER, Christon I(rving) 1940-

PERSONAL: Born August 24, 1940, in Victoria, British Columbia, Canada; married, 1965; children: two. *Education:* University of Victoria, British Columbia, B.A., 1965; State University of New York, Stony Brook, M.A., 1967, Ph.D., 1971.

ADDRESSES: Office—Department of History, University of Calgary, 2500 University Drive, N.W., Calgary, Alberta T2N 1N4, Canada. *E-mail*—archer@ucalgary.ca.

CAREER: University of Calgary, Alberta, Canada, assistant professor, 1969-73, associate professor, 1973-78, professor of history, 1978—.

MEMBER: American Historical Association, Conference on Latin American History, Canadian Association of Latin American Studies, Society for Spanish and Portuguese History Studies, Latin-American Studies Association.

AWARDS, HONORS: Canada Council, resident fellow, 1974-75, leave fellow, 1977-78; Hebert E. Bolton Prize, 1979; American Historical Association Prize, Pacific Coast Branch, 1979; Killam fellow, 1980; *Canadian Historical Review* annual prize, 1980.

WRITINGS:

The Army in Bourbon Mexico, 1760-1810, University of New Mexico Press (Albuquerque, NM), 1977.

(Editor, with Timothy Travers) *Men at War: Politics, Technology, and Innovation in the Twentieth Century,* Precedent (Chicago, IL), 1982.

(Editor) *The Wars of Independence in Spanish America,* Scholarly Resources (Wilmington, DE), 2000.

(With others) *World History of Warfare,* University of Nebraska Press (Lincoln, NE), 2002.

(Editor) *The Birth of Modern Mexico, 1780-1824,* Scholarly Resources (Wilmington, DE), 2003.

Contributor to periodicals, including *BC Studies, Journal of Latin-American Studies, Hispanic-American Historical Review,* and *Canadian Historical Review.* Contributor to *Rank and Privilege: The Military and Society in Latin America,* edited by Linda Alexander Rodríguez, 1994.

SIDELIGHTS: A professor of history at the University of Calgary, Christon I. Archer specializes in the areas of Mexican and Spanish history and military history. His publications have treated such subjects as the Mexican army during Bourbon rule, banditry and guerilla warfare, the fight for independence in New Spain, and Spanish maritime exploration.

In *The Army in Bourbon Mexico, 1760-1810* Archer exhibits extensive archival research on the Mexican colonial army under Bourbon rule during the period prior to independence. He shows the considerable hardships faced by Mexican soldiers, the difficulties the royal administration had in recruiting soldiers, and the fleeting autonomy of the army in New Spain. Reviewers described the book as a notable contribution to the period under study. In *Choice,* a reviewer called *The Army in Bourbon Mexico, 1760-1810* "handsome and important," and remarked that it is "likely to become the definitive work on the subject." Allan J. Kuethe noted in the *Hispanic-American Historical Review* that although he found it "often vague conceptually," Archer's is still "an important book." Kuethe explained, "Its strength is its vivid portrayal of the human side of the military reform and broader Mexican society." In the *American Historical Review,* Nettie Lee Benson called the book a "care-fully presented and thoroughly documented study" and said it "challenges many of the myths about the army in New Spain: its autonomy, its size, its *fuero,* the struggle between European Spaniards and *ciollos* for army commissions and so on."

Serving as editor of *The Wars of Independence in Spanish America,* Archer provides essays by established and new scholars to create a wide selection of perspectives on the wars against Spanish colonial forces. He also translates primary documents relating to these events. Critics commended the collection as a useful tool for understanding conflicts past and present. In the *Journal of Military History,* Kuethe credited Archer with an "insightful, provocative introduction" and remarked, "these essays go a long way toward showing why the odds for Spanish success in preserving the empire were so unfavorable." Peter Blanchard commented in the *Hispanic-American Historical Review* that the book is "a useful addition to [recent] reanalysis" of the independence period and features "a stimulating mix of primary and secondary materials." Blanchard concluded, "Archer has tried to force the reader to think, and for this—and his selection of readings—he is to be highly commended." In an online review for *H-Net,* Lance R. Blyth described the book's "major point" as being "that the rebellions, insurgencies, and counterinsurgencies that led to independence for Spanish America were wars in every sense of the word," and reflected that there are important similarities between these nineteenth-century events and the "low-intensity conflicts" and "ethnic" conflicts of contemporary times.

Archer's other works include collaborations with colleagues at the University of Calgary, the collection of essays titled *Men at War: Politics, Technology, and Innovation in the Twentieth Century,* and the textbook *World History of Warfare. Men at War* was described by Richard Nowicki in *Library Journal* as "a broad history of man at war" that used a "thoughtful, philosophical, multicultural" approach. Archer also edited *The Birth of Modern Mexico, 1780-1824,* which features essays on how the independence movement first took shape.

BIOGRAPHICAL AND CRITICAL SOURCES:

PERIODICALS

American Historical Review, February, 1979, Nettie Lee Benson, review of *The Army in Bourbon Mexico, 1760-1810,* p. 288.

Choice, July, 1978, review of *The Army in Bourbon Mexico, 1760-1810,* p. 745.

Hispanic-American Historical Review, February, 1979, Allan J. Kuethe, review of *The Army in Bourbon Mexico, 1760-1810,* p. 145; May, 2001, Peter Blanchard, review of *The Wars of Independence in Spanish America,* pp. 367-368.

Journal of Military History, July, 2001, Allan J. Kuethe, review of *The Wars of Independence in Spanish America,* pp. 794-795; April, 2003, Jeremy Black, review of *World History of Warfare,* pp. 544-545.

Library Journal, October 1, 2002, Richard Nowicki, review of *World History of Warfare,* p. 112.

ONLINE

H-Net, http://www.h-net/ (November, 2000), Lance R. Blyth, review of *The Wars of Independence in Spanish America.* *

* * *

ARNOLD, Tom 1959-

PERSONAL: Born March 6, 1959, in Ottumwa, IA; son of Jack and Linda (Collier) Arnold; stepson of Ruth Arnold; married Roseanne Barr (a comedian and actress), January 20, 1990 (divorced, 1994); married Julie Champnella (a hair stylist), July 22, 1995 (divorced, 1999); married Shelby Roos, 2001. *Education:* Attended Indian Hills Community College, Ottumwa, and University of Iowa.

ADDRESSES: Agent—Michael Gruber, William Morris Agency, 151 El Camino Dr., Beverly Hills, CA 90210-2775.

CAREER: Comedian, writer, actor, and producer. Appeared in television commercials for Sprint and Web TV. Worked in meat-packing plant, 1977-80; stand-up comedian and employed in various odd jobs, 1982-88; writer, actor, and co-executive producer of television shows, including *Rosanne,* 1988-94, and *Jackie Thomas Show,* 1992-93. Has acted in and directed various HBO specials and appeared in numerous TV series and movies, 1993—; *Best Damn Sports Show*

Period, Fox Sports Network, co-host, 2001—. Movie credits include supporting roles in *Freddy's Dead: The Final Nightmare, True Lies,* and *Nine Months.*

AWARDS, HONORS: CableACE Award, National Cable Television Association, 1992, for *Tom Arnold: The Naked Truth;* Vanguard Award (with Roseanne Barr), GLAAD Media Awards, 1993.

WRITINGS:

How I Lost Five Pounds in Six Years: An Autobiography, St. Martin's Press (New York, NY), 2002.

SIDELIGHTS: Propelled into the spotlight during his tempestuous marriage to—and very public divorce from—Roseanne Barr, Tom Arnold struggled to establish an independent identity with a number of movie appearances, including well-received co-starring roles opposite Arnold Schwarzenegger in *True Lies* and opposite Hugh Grant in *Nine Months.* A co-host of the hit cable show *Best Damn Sports Show Period,* Arnold has chronicled his development from a life of substance abuse and dead-end jobs to a successful show-business career in the memoir *How I Lost Five Pounds in Six Years: An Autobiography.* As Tacoma, Washington's *News Tribune* reporter Darrin Beene explained, "he got the inspiration for the book after watching the 'E! True Hollywood Story' about his stormy marriage to Barr and decided he didn't want his future children to think that's who he was."

The result is an "endearingly candid memoir—written as breezy correspondence to his wished-for child," in the words of a *Publishers Weekly* reviewer. His own childhood was a struggle in itself. Born the oldest of seven children to an alcoholic mother who abandoned the family when Arold was four years old, he had a difficult relationship with his stepmother, a proponent of corporal punishment. For solace, Arnold soon turned to drugs and alcohol, getting high regularly at the age of fourteen. After high school, he landed a rather miserable job at a Hormel meat-packing plant, where he sometimes had to shoot pigs in the head. He attended classes at the local community college, but without much hope that it would lead anywhere. Instead, he decided to attend the University of Iowa and hit on a novel way to raise the tuition. He enlisted friends to pledge a dollar a mile for him to walk twenty-five miles in 20-degree weather, in nothing but tennis shoes and a pair of boxer shorts. In addition to raising $2,500, Arnold got his first taste of the limelight. At the university, he saw some stand-up comics perform at a comedy showcase and decided that was the life for him.

Soon after, he moved to Minneapolis to do stand-up, taking odd jobs to stave off poverty. In 1983 he had the good fortune to open for up-and-comer Roseanne Barr, and the two developed a close friendship. Platonic at first, the friendship deepened into a romance when Barr divorced her husband in 1989. In addition to moral support, Arnold provided Barr with a number of jokes, and when Barr landed a new sitcom, she invited Arnold to come to Los Angeles as one of the writers. Before long, he was guest starring on the show as Arnie Thomas. The two had talked about marriage, but Barr had one condition first: Arnold had to go through a rehab program and kick his serious cocaine habit. He did so, and the two wed in January of 1990. Barr took Arnold's last name, and Arnold converted to Judaism. Arnold soon became co-executive producer of *Roseanne*, which was "heaven for Roseanne, hell for staffers fed up with his manic personality," according to *Entertainment Weekly* reporter Missy Schwartz. Barr also helped him garner his own series, the *Jackie Thomas Show*, which started well but soon tanked in the ratings.

The couple's exploits, such as mooning a World Series audience and a three-way "marriage" to Arnold's rumored mistress Kim Silva continually filled the tabloids. But despite all the controversy, Arnold and Barr seemed devoted to each other. Then "after she and he had grabbed five years of scandal-sheet headlines as a white-trash version of Taylor and Burton," in the words of *Time* magazine reporter Tom Elson, Barr grabbed even bigger headlines by filing for divorce, claiming physical and emotional abuse, and detailing her view of Arnold's deficiencies in numerous interviews. Not surprisingly, she also fired him from her show. Arnold denied the charges, but after another failed sitcom, *Tom,* he seemed destined for footnote status in the life of a true TV star.

Then came a lucky break in 1994, when director James Cameron cast him for a supporting role in *True Lies,* another mega-hit for Arnold Schwarzenegger. Arnold's memorable performance as the loud-mouthed best friend gave him newfound clout as a sought after

"second banana," and he went on to garner good reviews for his performance in *Nine Months*. A few award-winning Home Box Office specials also cemented his comic reputation, and in 2001 he was tapped by the Fox Sports Network to fill one of five host spots on its *Best Damn Sports Show Period,* a mix of "guy talk," sports updates and interviews, and humorous stunts that turned into a surprising hit for the network. His private life underwent a similar transformation. After marrying and divorcing Julie Champnella, a college student he met shortly after divorcing Barr, Arnold married Shelby Ross, a political consultant he met at a Democratic Party Convention. Indeed, he credits Ross with a part of his success, saying she was the one who insisted he audition for the sports show job.

Discussing *How I Lost Five Pounds in Six Years, Booklist* reviewer Brendan Dowling concluded, "The affable and self-deprecating tone will certainly satisfy his current following." And according to a *Kirkus Reviews* contributor, "readers may be surprised to find that the practitioner of generally dopey comedy can write frisky humor."

BIOGRAPHICAL AND CRITICAL SOURCES:

PERIODICALS

Booklist, November 15, 2002, Brendan Dowling, review of *How I Lost Five Pounds in Six Years,* p. 557.
Entertainment Weekly, January 25, 2002, Missy Schwartz, "Trash of the Titans," p. 110.
Kirkus Reviews, October 1, 2002, review of *How I Lost Five Pounds in Six Years,* p. 1437.
News Tribune (Tacoma, WA), November 15, 2002, Darrin Beene, "Fanfare: Media Watch—Sixteen Months and Counting for Arnold on FSN."
Publishers Weekly, October 28, 2002, review of *How I Lost Five Pounds in Six Years,* p. 63.
Time, August 14, 1995, Tom Elson, "Second Banana on Top," p. 71.

ONLINE

Tom Arnold Web site, http://tomarnoldonline.com (November 17, 2003).*

ARSENIEV, Vladimir K(lavdievich) 1872-1930

PERSONAL: Born September 10, 1872, in Russia; died 1930.

CAREER: Geographer, geologist, ethnographer, explorer, and writer.

WRITINGS:

With Dersu the Hunter: Adventures in the Taiga, adapted by Anne Terry White, Venture (New York, NY), 1941, published as *Dersu the Trapper: A True Account,* translated by Malcolm Burr, preface by Jaimy Gordon, McPherson & Co. (Kingston, NY), 1996.

ADAPTATIONS: Dersu the Trapper: A True Account was adapted as the film *Dersu Uzala,* directed by Akira Kurosawa, 1975.

SIDELIGHTS: Vladimir Klavdievich Arseniev was a Russian geographer, geologist, ethnographer, and explorer. He went on twelve major scientific expeditions between 1902 and 1930 in eastern Siberia. He authored sixty books from the geographical, geological, botanical, and ethnographic data he collected on his expeditions. He was well known for exploring the Krai and studying its indigenous people.

Arseniev's book *Dersu the Trapper: A True Account* is regarded as the Russian equivalent of *The Journals of Lewis and Clark* and the novels of early eighteenth-century American writer James Fenimore Cooper. In the book Arseniev recounts three of his expeditions in the great spruce forests of the eastern Siberian taiga along the Sea of Japan. During the first expedition, he meets an aboriginal hunter and member of the Gold tribe named Dersu, who becomes his guide. Arseniev discusses the hardships and dangers his team encountered during the expeditions, the land they were exploring, and the cross-cultural friendship that the two men formed. A reviewer for the *Washington Post Book World* wrote that the book "crackles with excitement," and in the *New York Times Book Review,* Robert Yale Libott deemed *Dersu the Trapper* "a book that, once read, will never be forgotten."

Arseniev's expeditions attracted additional notice in 1975, with the release of the acclaimed Akira Kurosawa film *Dersu Uzla,* based on the Russian geographer's book. The film won several international awards as well as an Academy Award for Best Foreign Film.

BIOGRAPHICAL AND CRITICAL SOURCES:

PERIODICALS

New Yorker, December 4, 1965, review of *With Dersu the Hunter: Adventures in the Taiga,* pp. 222-224.
New York Times Book Review, December 12, 1965, Robert Yale Libott, review of *With Dersu the Hunter,* p. 26.
Publishers Weekly, February 26, 1996, review of *Dersu the Trapper: A True Account,* p. 99.
Washington Post Book World, August 25, 1996, review of *Dersu the Trapper,* p. 12.

ONLINE

McPherson & Company Web site, http://www.mcphersonco.com/ (August 2, 2001), review of *Dersu the Trapper.*
Vladivostok News online, http://vn.vladnews.ru/ (August 2, 2001), Anatoly Medetsky, "Arseniev Fete Planned."
Washington State University Library Web site, http://www.wsublibs.wsu.edu/ (August 2, 2001), "4, Peter the Great Street."*

*   *   *

ASKEW, Amanda Jane 1955-
(Amanda Hemingway; Jan Siegel, a pseudonym)

PERSONAL: Born 1955.

ADDRESSES: Agent—c/o Author Mail, Del Rey, 1745 Broadway, New York, NY 10019.

CAREER: Writer. Worked variously as an untrained nurse, barmaid, secretary, lab assistant, actress, model, performance poet, and journalist.

WRITINGS:

AS AMANDA HEMINGWAY

Pzyche, Arbor House (New York, NY), 1982.
Tantalus, Arbor House (New York, NY), 1984.
Baccanal, Hamilton (London, England), 1987.
The Poison Heart, Simon & Schuster (New York, NY),
     1990, published as *The Viper's Heart,* Viking
     (London, England), 1990.
Soulfire, Warner (London, England), 1995.

"FERNANDA CAPEL" SERIES; UNDER PSEUDONYM JAN
SIEGEL

Prospero's Children, Voyager (London, England),
     1999, Del Rey (New York, NY), 2000.
The Dragon Charmer, Voyager (London, England),
     2000, Del Rey (New York, NY), 2001.
The Witch Queen, Del Rey (New York, NY), 2002.

Contributor to anthologies.

SIDELIGHTS: When Amanda Jane Askew first began
writing, she used her married name, Amanda
Hemingway. Her first novel, *Pzyche,* was science fiction, and her next four were thrillers. Beginning with
the first book of her fantasy trilogy featuring Fernanda
Capel, she used a pseudonym, Jan Siegel. Askew has
no children herself, but she is godmother to a number
of them, including the three children of artist Julian
Bell, whose great aunt was Virginia Woolf. On one
occasion when she was caring for them, they asked
her for a story, and she had to make one up that would
involve the three of them. This tale later evolved into
Prospero's Children, the first book of Askew's "Capel"
trilogy.

In an online interview with *Locus,* Askew explained
that she saw *Prospero's Children* as a "starting point"
and came up with a concept after reading the work of
writers including J. R. R. Tolkien, C. S. Lewis, and
Alan Garner. She said she had read all of the children's
classics but "what got me about those books is that
they always chickened out about what happened when
the people grew up. My whole idea, therefore, was to
start out a little bit at that level, with my protagonists
children or almost children, and then find out what

happens if you bring in the whole fantasy otherworld
when they're older and combine it much more with an
adult's real world." A writer for *Demensions* online,
who called *Prospero's Children* "a darn good read"
felt that, in this regard, the author has reached her
goal: "The book wavers just on the brink of being
truly adult but strays back into childhood on occasion.
At one moment, it feels like your old favorite bedtime
story; in the next paragraph, hard choices and very
grown-up power struggles take center stage."

The protagonist, Fernanda Capel, is sixteen years old,
and since the death of her mother, she has taken care
of her father, Robin, and her brother, Will. When
Robin inherits an old house in Yorkshire, Fern wants
to sell it, but her father convinces her that they should
at least go and look at it. When they do, she and Will
become drawn into a fantasy world that revolves
around the lost city of Atlantis and the death of a
mariner at the hands of a mermaid. At the beginning
of the story, Fern meets a wily art dealer named Javier,
and Alison, the woman who will replace her mother.
Roz Kaveney noted in the *Times Literary Supplement*
that "in a realist work, these two would represent the
pull of the sexual and the struggle for power that goes
with it. In Siegel's novel, they are there to help Fern
in her struggle with witches and old gods."

As one of Prospero's children, Fern must find the key
that will open the Gate of Death, a key hidden
somewhere in the old house that is being sought by an
evil witch who wants to unleash the destructive powers behind the door. Fern discovers she possesses powers—both telekinetic and telepathic—that can help her
accomplish this. Other characters include Ragginbone,
a kindly wizard-tramp, Lougarry the werewolf, a
unicorn, magicians, and talking statues.

Naomi de Bruyn, who reviewed *Prospero's Children*
for *Green Man Review,* online, called it "deep and
engaging, and the most riveting I have read in a long
time." *SF Site* reviewer Pat Caven wrote that "characterization is superb, right down to the bit players. . . .
Description, dialogue and humour are all managed
with subtle style and wit. . . . This is a fabulous
novel, and Jan Siegel is an astounding writer."

Askew's second "Capel" book, *The Dragon Charmer,*
opens some dozen years later, with Fern, now a public
relations consultant, trying to forget her magical pow-

ers and lead a normal life. She agrees to marry a man she doesn't love, but on the night before her wedding she falls into a coma and is taken to the hospital. Others would draw on her powers, including Morgus, the sorceress half-sister of King Arthur, who lives in purgatory beneath the Tree of Life and Death, the branches of which contain the last head of a dragon charmer and support the earth, and the roots of which penetrate into hell. In addition, Azmordis, a spirit from Atlantis who has taken over the body of medievalist Dr. Laye, wants to use Fern's gifts to control a dragon waiting to hatch in the basement of a college building, while Fern is fighting the forces of evil and protecting her friend, Gaynor Mobberley, and her brother.

A *Kirkus Reviews* contributor favored those parts of *The Dragon Charmer* "where Fern's adolescent brother Will, who fancies himself an artist, passes time with the house goblin, an irrepressible Scottish sprite name Bradachin, while Fern develops a passionate crush on Gaynor." *BookBrowser*'s Harriet Klausner cited *"The Dragon Charmer* as a strong fantasy novel because the story line ties the supernatural with the mundane in such a clever way that the otherworldly elements seem everyday and matter of fact." A *Publishers Weekly* contributor called it a "highly imaginative and darkly charming adult fantasy."

A *Kirkus Reviews* contributor commented that, with *The Witch Queen,* Askew's "by-now characteristic mix of Gothic fantasy and Bridget Jones-esque singles satire/farce survives the occasional patch of romance novel prose . . . concluding with Fern in love and all major plot threads neatly tied up." In this concluding novel of the trilogy, Morgus, who was not killed by Fern after all, is seeking control of the world and revenge on Fern, who is still being challenged by the evil Azmordis. "Infusions of Scottish lore, Arthurian legend, and the myth of Atlantis intensify an often spine-tingling story of a variety of mythical and mystical figures," wrote Sally Estes in *Booklist.*

BIOGRAPHICAL AND CRITICAL SOURCES:

PERIODICALS

Booklist, March 15, 2000, Sally Estes, review of *Prospero's Children,* p. 1335; June 1, 2001, Sally Estes, review of *The Dragon Charmer,* p. 1856; August, 2002, Sally Estes, review of *The Witch Queen,* p. 1937.

Kirkus Reviews, May 15, 2001, review of *The Dragon Charmer,* p. 715; July 1, 2002, review of *The Witch Queen,* p. 924.

Library Journal, July, 1990, A. M. B. Amantia, review of *The Poison Heart,* p. 131; April 15, 2000, Jackie Cassada, review of *Prospero's Children,* p. 126; August, 2002, Jackie Cassada, review of *The Witch Queen,* p. 151.

New Statesman, June 18, 1982, Marion Glastonbury, review of *Pzyche,* p. 22.

New Yorker, August 20, 1984, review of *Tantalus,* p. 92.

New York Times Book Review, September 23, 1984, David Evanier, review of *Tantalus,* p. 28.

Publishers Weekly, March 4,1983, review of *Pzyche,* p. 91; June 1, 1984, review of *Tantalus,* p. 56; June 29, 1990, review of *The Poison Heart,* p. 87; April 24, 2000, review of *Prospero's Children,* p. 67; June 11, 2001, review of *The Dragon Charmer,* p. 67; July 15, 2002, review of *The Witch Queen,* p. 60.

Times Literary Supplement, October 8, 1999, Roz Kaveney, review of *Prospero's Children,* p. 37.

ONLINE

BookBrowser, http://www.bookbrowser.com/ (August 16, 2000), Jill Kosmensky, review of *Prospero's Children;* (June 22, 2001) Harriet Klausner, review of *The Dragon Charmer;* (June 23, 2002) Harriet Klausner, review of *The Witch Queen.*

Demensions, http://www.demensionszine.com/ (October 22, 2002), review of *Prospero's Children.*

Green Man Review, http://www.greenmanreview.com/ (October 22, 2002), Naomi de Bruyn, review of *Prospero's Children.*

Locus, http://www.locusmag.com/ (March, 2002), interview with Askew.

SF Site, http://www.sfsite.com/ (January 13, 2003), Pat Caven, review of *Prospero's Children;* Victoria Strauss, review of *The Dragon Charmer.*

Writers Write, http://www.writerswrite.com/ (September, 2002), reviews of *The Dragon Charmer* and *The Witch Queen.**

*   *   *

ASTAFYEV, Victor 1924-2001

PERSONAL: Born 1924, in Ovsyanka, Siberia; died November 29, 2001, in Krasnoyarsk, Siberia; married; wife's name Maria; children: Irina.

CAREER: Writer. Worked as an ironworker. *Military service:* Russian Army, World War II; served in communications troops.

AWARDS, HONORS: State Prize of Russia, 1975, for *The Damned and the Dead;* named Hero of Socialist Labour.

WRITINGS:

The Crossing, 1959.
Tak Khochetsia Zhit': Povesti i Rasskazy, Izd-vo Knizhnaia Palata, 1966.
Krazha.—Gde-to Gremit Voina, Mol. Gvardiia, 1968.
Poslednii Poklon, Perm', Kn. izd., 1968.
Sinie Sumerki, 1968.
Der Diebstahl, Buchclub 65 (Berlin, Germany), 1969.
Starodub, 1969.
The Horse with the Pink Mane and Other Siberian Stories, translated by Robert Daglish, illustrations by B.A. Markevich, Progress Publishers (Moscow, USSR), 1970.
Izluchina: Rasskazy, Sovremennik, 1972.
Povesti o Moem Sovremennike, Mol. Gvardiia, 1972.
Zatesi. Kniga Korotkikh Rasskazov, Sov. Pisatel', 1972.
Iasnym li Dnem, 1973.
Gde-to Gremit Viona: Provesti i Rasskazy, Sovremennik, 1975.
Povesti, 1976.
Mal'chik v Beloi Rubakhe, 1977.
Povesti, Rasskazy, Zatesi, 1977.
The Horse with the Pink Mane = Kon's Rozovoi Grivoi, Progress Publishers (Moscow, Russia), 1978.
Strizhonok Skrip, Izd-vo Malysh, 1979.
Sobranie Sochinenii, Mol. Gvardiia, 1979-1981.
Tsar'-ryba: Provestvovanie v Rasskazakh, Sov. Pisatel', 1980.
Posokh Pamiati, Sovremennik, 1980.
Drevnee, Vechnoe, Sov. Rossiia, 1980.
Queen Fish: A Story in Two Parts and Twelve Episodes, Progress Publishers (Moscow, USSR) 1982.
(With others) *Sannyiput': Rasskazy,* Vostochno-Sibirshoe Izd-Vo, 1983.
Na Dalekoi Severnoi Vershine: Povesti, Rasskazy, Krasnoiarshoe Knizhnoe Izd-Vo, 1984.
Vsemu Svoi Chas, Molodaia Gvardiia, 1985.
Zhizn' Prozhit': Roman, Rasskazy, Sovremennik, 1986.
Padenie Lista: Roman, Rasskazy, Ocherki, Sov. Pisatel, 1988.

(With others) *15 Vstrech v Ostankine,* Izd-vo Polit. Lit-ry, 1989.
Takoe Dlinnoe, Dlinnoe Pis'mo Viktoru Astafiev i Drugie Poslaniia s Kartinkami v Cherno-Belom Tsvete, Ganatleba, 1989.
To Live Your Life and Other Stories, Raduga Publishers (Moscow, USSR), 1989.
Ulybka Volchitsy, Izd-vo Knizhnaia Palata, 1990.
Pechalnyi Detektive: Roman, (The Sad Detective), Profizdat, 1991.
Mnoiu Rozhdennyi: Roman, Povesti, Rasskazy, Khudozh Lit-ra, 1991.
Prokliaty i Ubity: Roman (title means "The Damned and the Slain"), Izd-Vo Riotio, 1993.
Russkii Almaz: Rasskazy, Zatesi, Iskusstvo, 1994.
The Condemned and the Killed, 1995.
Sobranie Sochinenii: V Piatnadtsati Tomakh, Ofset, 1997-1998.
Blagogovenie, IPK, 1999.
Veselyi Soldat, Limbus Press, 1999.
Povesti, Rasskazy, Esse, U-Faktoriia, 2000.
Proletnyigus': Rasskazy, Zatesi, Vospominaniia, Izdatel Skaia Gruppa Vektor, 2001.

Books translated into twenty-seven languages. Author of *Somewhere Sounds the War, The King Fish, How I Get Them and They Had Me, A Feast of Solidarity, I Want to Survive,* and *The Jolly Soldier.*

SIDELIGHTS: Viktor Astafiev's works are well known in his native Russia. Many have been translated into twenty-seven different languages. A contributor to the *Russian PEN Centre Web site* described Astafiev as "the mouthpiece of the nation." His books are about the various aspects of living in Russia and are now studied in Russian schools.

Astafiev's *Queen Fish* is a collection of twelve stories about life and surviving in Siberia's Yenisey territory. The characters in the stories are hunters, fishermen, and seasonal workers who must cooperate with others in order to meet their needs and survive. Along the way many of them learn valuable lessons. In a review for *World Literature Today,* Margot K. Frank claimed a "face-to-face encounter with the mystery and reality of creation."

In his book *The Jolly Soldier* Astafiev describes how, during World War II, young men were inadequately trained in the Soviet army and still sent into war. He also claims that some citizens of the Soviet Union were relieved when the Germans invaded because they hoped Stalin would be overthrown. Many of Astafiev's books have received high praise, but *The Jolly Soldier* did not. *UNESCO Courier* contributor Nick Holdsworth noted that Astafiev was "pilloried in the press and vilified by regional politicians."

BIOGRAPHICAL AND CRITICAL SOURCES:

PERIODICALS

Christian Science Monitor, October 8, 1987, Paul Quinn-Judge, "Kremlin Renews Its Attack on Brezhnev Years," pp. 9-10.
New York Times, December 3, 2001, "Viktor Astafyev, Who Wrote of Rural Russia, Dies at 77," p. F6.
Soviet Life, October, 1988, Valeri Demin, "The Writer and His Land," p. 28.
Times Literary Supplement, January 7, 1994, Alla Latynina, "The Russian Booker: Rewarding Reputation," p. 10; January 7, 1994, Geoffrey Hosking, ". . . Or a Final Reckoning?," p. 10.
UNESCO Courier, November, 2001, Nick Holdsworth, "Bound by Nostalgia," p. 33.
World Literature Today, spring, 1984, Margot K. Frank, review of *Queen Fish,* p. 288.

ONLINE

Pravda, http://english.pravda.ru/ (July 29, 2002), "Viktor Astafiev Died."
Russian PEN Centre Web site, http://www.penrussia. org/ (July 18, 2002), "Viktor Astafiev."
Voice of Russia, http://www.vor.ru/ (July 29, 2002), "The Russian Character."*

*   *   *

AXELROD, George 1922-2003

OBITUARY NOTICE—See index for *CA* sketch: Born June 9, 1922, in New York, NY; died of heart failure June 21, 2003, in Los Angeles, CA. Author. Axelrod was best known for *The Seven-Year Itch,* his play about sexual mores, and for adapting the novels *Breakfast at Tiffany's* and *The Manchurian Candidate* to film. A haphazard student growing up, he left high school before graduating to become an actor and stage

manager for summer stock theater. Soon, however, World War II came, and he spent the duration in the Army Signal Corps. With the war over, Axelrod established a successful career writing scripts for radio programs such as *The Shadow* and *The Grand Ole Opry.* He also began writing for television. His first play, *The Seven-Year Itch: A Romantic Comedy* (1952), became a huge hit in New York City, and he co-wrote the film version that starred actress Marilyn Monroe. Axelrod later expressed dismay that the then-puritanical mood in Hollywood—which prompted the removal of important parts of the storyline about a married man's affair with a young woman—damaged the integrity of the film version. Nevertheless, he went on to write another stage hit, *Will Success Spoil Rock Hunter? A New Comedy* (1955), which he also directed, and found great success adapting novels by other writers to film, among them *Bus Stop* (1956), *Breakfast at Tiffany's* (1961), and *The Manchurian Candidate* (1962). *Breakfast at Tiffany's,* based on the Truman Capote book, earned Axelrod an Academy Award nomination. In addition to writing for stage and screen, Axelrod produced and directed a number of productions during the 1950s and 1960s, including directing the plays *Goodbye Charlie* (1959), which he also wrote, and *The Star-Spangled Girl* (1966), and producing movies he wrote, such as *The Manchurian Candidate* (1962), *How to Murder Your Wife* (1965), and *The Secret Life of an American Wife* (1968). Although his output diminished in the 1970s and 1980s, he continued to write a few movies, including *The Holcroft Covenant* (1985) and *The Fourth Protocol* (1987). He was also the author of three novels: *Beggar's Choice* (1947), *Blackmailer* (1952), and *Where Am I Now When I Need Me?* (1971).

OBITUARIES AND OTHER SOURCES:

BOOKS

Contemporary Dramatists, sixth edition, St. James Press (Detroit, MI), 1999.
Contemporary Theatre, Film, and Television, Volume 22, Gale (Detroit, MI), 1999.

PERIODICALS

Los Angeles Times, June 22, 2003, p. B16.
New York Times, June 23, 2003, p. A23.
Times (London, England), June 25, 2003.
Washington Post, June 22, 2003, p. C10.

B

BABER, Asa 1936-2003

OBITUARY NOTICE—See index for *CA* sketch: Born June 19, 1936, in Chicago, IL; died of amyotrophic lateral sclerosis (Lou Gehrig's disease) June 16, 2003, in Chicago, IL. Educator and author. Baber was a former English and theater teacher who in the 1980s became well known for his regular *Playboy* magazine column, "Men," in which he stood up for the rights and dignity of men at a time when feminism was at its peak. After receiving a bachelor's degree from Princeton University in 1958, Baber joined the U.S. Marines and became a counterinsurgency specialist in Laos. He returned from Asia in 1961 and went back to school, earning a master's degree from Northwestern University in 1963. He then traveled to Istanbul to be an English and theater teacher. Again returning to the United States in 1966, he earned an M.F.A. from the prestigious Iowa Writer's Workshop in 1969 and in 1970 completed his novel *The Land of a Million Elephants,* which is based on his war experiences. He wrote the novel while on the faculty of the University of Hawaii, where he was an assistant professor of English until 1974. When he moved to Chicago in 1975, Baber began contributing stories and articles to *Playboy,* which had earlier serialized his novel. An article he wrote about his divorce led one of the editors to ask him to write a regular column, and this became "Men." The column advised male readers on such issues as how to deal with divorce, business and personal rejection, and depression. Selected columns were later published in *Naked at Gender Gap: A Man's View of the War between the Sexes* (1992). Baber was also the author of two short-story collections, *Tranquility Base and Other Stories* (1979) and *Papageno and Other Stories* (1993), as well as a musical, *Goslings* (1977).

OBITUARIES AND OTHER SOURCES:

BOOKS

Writers Directory, 17th edition, St. James Press (Detroit, MI), 2002.

PERIODICALS

Chicago Tribune, June 20, 2003, section 3, p. 11.
Los Angeles Times, June 20, 2003, p. B15.
Washington Post, June 23, 2003, p. B6.

*   *   *

BACEVICH, Andrew J. 1947-

PERSONAL: Born July 5, 1947, in Normal, IL; son of Andrew J. Bacevich (a physician) and Martha E. Greenis (a homemaker); married; wife's name Nancy Sue; children: Jennifer Maureen, Amy Elizabeth, Andrew John, Kathleen Therese. *Ethnicity:* "Lithuanian." *Education:* U.S. Military Academy, West Point, B.S.; Princeton University, M.A. (American history), Ph.D. (American diplomatic history). *Politics:* Independent. *Religion:* Roman Catholic.

ADDRESSES: Office—Boston University, Department of International Relations, 154 Bay State Road, Room 201, Boston, MA 02215. *Agent*—John Wright, JWWLitAgen@aol.com. *E-mail*—bacevich@bu.edu.

CAREER: U.S. Military Academy, West Point, NY, assistant professor of history, 1977-80; Johns Hopkins University, Baltimore, MD, professorial lecturer in strategic studies, 1992—, professorial lecturer in political science, 1995—; Foreign Policy Institute, Washington, DC, executive director, cofounder and executive director of Center for Strategic Education; Boston University, Boston, MA, professor of international relations, 1998—, director of Center for International Relations. *Military service:* U.S. Army, former officer.

AWARDS, HONORS: Fellowships at Johns Hopkins University's Paul H. Nitze School of Advanced International Studies, Harvard University's John F. Kennedy School of Government, and Council on Foreign Relations.

WRITINGS:

The Pentomic Era: The U.S. Army between Korea and Vietnam, National Defense University Press (Washington, DC), 1986.
(With others) *American Military Policy in Small Wars: The Case of El Salvador,* Pergamon-Brassey's (Washington, DC), 1988.
Diplomat in Khaki: Major General Frank Ross McCoy and American Foreign Policy, 1898-1949, University Press of Kansas (Lawrence, KS), 1989.
(With Michael Eisenstadt and Carl Ford) *Supporting Peace: America's Role in an Israel-Syria Peace Agreement,* Washington Institute for Near-East Policy (Washington, DC), 1994.
(With Eliot A. Cohen and Michael J. Eisenstadt) *Knives, Tanks, and Missiles: Israel's Security Revolution,* Washington Institute for Near East Policy (Washington, DC), 1998.
(Coeditor with Eliot A. Cohen) *War over Kosovo: Politics and Strategy in a Global Age,* Columbia University Press (New York, NY), 2001.
American Empire: The Realities and Consequences of U.S. Diplomacy, Harvard University Press (Cambridge, MA), 2002.
(Coeditor with Efraim Inbar) *The Gulf War of 1991 Reconsidered,* Frank Cass (Portland, OR), 2002.
(Editor) *The Imperial Tense: Prospects and Problems of American Empire,* Ivan R. Dee (Chicago, IL), 2003.

Contributor of articles and reviews to publications, including *Foreign Affairs, Journal of Military History, Diplomatic History, Wilson Quarterly, National Inter-* *est, Commentary, First Things, New Republic,* and *Weekly Standard.* Member of editorial advisory board, *SAIS Review: A Journal of International Affairs,* 1994—.

WORK IN PROGRESS: The New American Militarism.

SIDELIGHTS: Andrew J. Bacevich, a former U.S. army officer, teaches courses in U.S. foreign policy and security studies at Boston University, where he is also the director of the Center for International Relations.

In *Diplomat in Khaki: Major General Frank Ross McCoy and American Foreign Policy, 1898-1949* Bacevich discusses the life and military career of Major General Frank Ross McCoy. McCoy was an ordinary soldier, but he was involved in many U.S. military matters and served a number of well-known people. Some of McCoy's military duties included being a military aide to Theodore Roosevelt, gathering intelligence in China, Japan, and Colombia; serving as a commissioner to Calvin Coolidge; and serving as Harry S Truman's representative on the Far East Commission during the post-World War II period. *Historian* contributor Robert H. Ferrell found Bacevich's book "a delightfully written story of a man whose authority reached into many important U.S. matters of state." *American Historical Review* contributor Joyce S. Goldberg considered it "a most interesting and well-told story."

American Empire: The Realities and Consequences of U.S. Diplomacy compares the foreign and defense policies held by presidents George H.W. Bush and Bill Clinton, as well as those of George W. Bush during his first year in office. Bacevich argues that all three presidents worked to keep the United States as a supreme power in the world and as a protector. He shows that they wanted to open up trade and spread democracy to other areas of the world, and used military force when necessary to meet these goals. Bacevich goes into detail about the foreign and defense policies of these three presidents and compares them to the ideas of historians Charles Beard and William Appleton Williams. *Foreign Affairs* contributor Walter Russell Mead considered the book a "systematic, well-argued work."

BIOGRAPHICAL AND CRITICAL SOURCES:

PERIODICALS

American Historical Review, October, 1990, Joyce S. Goldberg, review of *Diplomat in Khaki: Major*

General Frank Ross McCoy and American Foreign Policy, 1898-1949, p. 1301.

Choice, February, 1990, C.W. Haury, review of *Diplomat in Khaki,* p. 998.

Commentary, October, 1998, Hillel Halkin, review of *Knives, Tanks, and Missiles: Israel's Security Revolution,* p. 58.

Foreign Affairs, May-June, 2002, Stephen Biddle, "The New Way of War? Debating the Kosovo Model," p. 138.

Historian, winter, 1991, Robert H. Ferrell, review of *Diplomat in Khaki,* p. 356.

Journal of American History, September, 1990, review of *Diplomat in Khaki,* p. 694.

Journal of Military History, April, 2002, Richard M. Swain, review of *War over Kosovo: Politics and Strategy in a Global Age,* p. 638.

Middle East Policy, June, 2000, Joshua Sinai, review of *Knives, Tanks, and Missles,* p. 176.

Orbis, winter, 1989, review of *American Military Policy in Small Wars: The Case of El Salvador,* p. 151.

Parameters, autumn, 2002, Jeffrey Record, review of *War over Kosovo,* p. 140.

Perspective, March, 1987, Garold W. Thumm, review of *The Pentomic Era: The U.S. Army between Korea and Vietnam,* p. 48.

Publishers Weekly, October 28, 2002, review of *American Empire: The Realities and Consequences of U.S. Diplomacy,* p. 61.

U.S. News & World Report, October 21, 2002, Jay Tolson, "World Disorder?," p. 56.

Wilson Quarterly, summer, 2000, "Fighting Bio-Terrorism," p. 98.

ONLINE

Boston University Web site, http://www.bu.edu/ (January 20, 2003), "Faculty: Andrew Bacevich."

Carnegie Endowment for International Peace Web site, http://www.ceip.org/ (January 20, 2003), Anatol Lieven, "The Dilemma of Sustaining an America Empire."

Foreign Affairs online, http://www.foreignaffairs.org/ (January 20, 2003), Walter Russell Mean, review of *American Empire.*

Washington Institute Web site, http://www.washingtoninstitute.org/ (January 20, 2003), review of *Knives, Tanks, and Missiles.*

Washington Times online, http://www.washtimes.com/ (January 20, 2003), "Are the Bush, Clinton Policies Similar?"

BAER, Morley 1916-1995

PERSONAL: Born April 5, 1916, in Toledo, OH; died of cancer, November 9, 1995; married, 1946; wife's name Frances M. *Education:* University of Michigan, B.A., 1936, M.A., 1937.

CAREER: Photographer for San Francisco and West Coast architects, architectural editors, and book publishers, beginning 1946; Ansel Adams Workshops, instructor, 1969-79. Taught photography classes at University of California Extension, Santa Cruz. *Exhibitions:* Work included in collections at New Orleans Museum of Art, San Francisco Museum of Modern Art, and M.H. de Young Museum, San Francisco, CA. *Military service:* U.S. Navy, photographer during World War II.

AWARDS, HONORS: Gold Medal in Photography, American Institute of Architects, 1965; fellow, American Academy in Rome, 1980.

WRITINGS:

(With Elizabeth Pomada and Michael Larsen) *Painted Ladies: San Francisco's Resplendent Victorians,* Dutton (New York, NY), 1978.

PHOTOGRAPHER

Augusta Fink and Amelie Elkinton, *Adobes in the Sun: Portraits of a Tranquil Era,* Chronicle Books (San Francisco, CA), 1972.

(With others) Sally Woodbridge, editor, *Bay Area Houses,* introduction by David Gebhard, Oxford University Press (New York, NY), 1976.

Mary Austin, *Room and Time Enough: The Land of Mary Austin,* introduction by Augusta Fink, Northland Press (Flagstaff, AZ), 1979.

David Rains Wallace, *The Wilder Shore,* foreword by Wallace Stegner, Sierra Club Books (San Francisco, CA), 1984.

Light Years: The Photography of Morley Baer, Photography West Graphics (Carmel, CA), 1988.

James Karman, editor, *Stones of the Sur,* poetry by Robinson Jeffers, Stanford University Press (Stanford, CA), 2001.

Bright Eastman, Patrick Jablonski, Frances M. Baer, *California Plain: Remembering Barns,* Stanford University Press (Stanford, CA), 2002.

Architectural photographer for magazines such as *House & Garden, House Beautiful,* and *Architectural Record.*

SIDELIGHTS: Photographer Morley Baer was known as the leading architectural photographer in Northern California, but his personal photography interests were of rural areas and the landscapes of California. *American Photographer* contributor Owen Edwards claimed, "What Baer represents is a generation or two of photographers whose aesthetic interest in the landscape was inseparable from their love of the land itself." Over the years Baer did not succumb to the advances in photography equipment. His main equipment during his entire career, which spanned forty-eight years, was an old wooden 8 x 10 Ansco view camera that weighed approximately fifteen pounds.

Two of Baer's influences were the photographers Edward Weston and Ansel Adams. He first came to California in 1939 in search of Weston, whose photographs he had first seen in a Chicago art gallery at the beginning of his career. Baer became a friend of Weston and learned a great deal from him. Baer is quoted in *Petersen's Photographic* as saying "A couple of things changed my life and my photography. One was meeting Edward Weston, who, I think, finally brought it home to me that photography is a very personal kind of expression that comes from your reactions to the world you live in and not a world you'd like to live in."

Baer provided the photographs and nature writer David Rains Wallace wrote the text to *The Wilder Shore.* Included are thirty-five color and forty black-and-white photographs that depict the varied landscapes found in California. Wallace's accompanying text describes those photographs and the natural history of California. "It is lovely," noted *AB Bookman's Weekly* contributor Franlee Frank. *Los Angeles Times Book Review* contributor David Graber described the book as "marvelous medicine for besieged lovers of the Golden State."

Before his death in 1995 Baer had been planning a book that combined his photographs of the Big Sur coast in California with the poetry the region's jagged rocks and cliffs inspired in Robinson Jeffers. *Stones of the Sur* was completed by James Karman and published after Baer's death. Included in the book are fifty of Baer's photographs of the Big Sur accompanied by some of Jeffers' poems. A *Virginia Quarterly Review* contributor claimed, "A haunting collection of image and verse that celebrates the intoxicating beauty of this region."

California Plain: Remembering Barns was also published after Baer's death. Baer's wife Frances was going through his things and came across a box of seventy-three black-and-white photographs, all depicting barns in California. Also included in the box was a note from Baer describing how he wanted to make a book featuring the barn photographs. That is just what his wife accomplished for him. Bright Eastman provides a essay on the history and styles of barns, and Patrick Jablonski, Baer's final assistant, describes the way Baer took his photographs and how he developed them. Frances Baer also provides her own essay on what it was like to be a student and wife of the noted photographer.

BIOGRAPHICAL AND CRITICAL SOURCES:

BOOKS

Browne, Turner, and Elaine Partnow, *Macmillan Biographical Encyclopedia of Photographic Artists and Innovators,* Collier Macmillan, 1987.

PERIODICALS

AB Bookman's Weekly, October 29, 1984, Franlee Frank, review of *The Wilder Shore,* p. 2998.

American Photographer, May, 1988, Owen Edwards, "Baer's Essentials," pp. 30-39, Evelyn Roth, "Simply Baer," p. 74.

Booklist, November 1, 1984, review of *The Wilder Shore,* p. 332.

Library Journal, December 15, 1978, Paul E. Bell, Jr., review of *Painted Ladies: San Francisco's Resplendent Victorians,* p. 2508; November 1, 2002, Joseph Hewgley, review of *California Plain: Remembering Barns,* p. 84.

Los Angeles Times Book Review, November 25, 1984, David Graber, review of *The Wilder Shore,* p. 8.

Modern Photography, February, 1985, Howard Millard, review of *The Wilder Shore,* p. 34.

Petersen's Photographic, January, 1986, "Meet the Masters: Morley Baer," pp. 26-27.

Science, November 9, 2001, "Browsings," p. 1289.

Virginia Quarterly Review, spring, 2002, review of *stones of the Sur,* p. 67.

ONLINE

Apogee online, http://www.apogeephoto.com/ (January 20, 2003), John Sexton, "John Sexton Remembers Morely Baer, 1916-1995."

Monterey Herald online, http://www.montereyherald.com/ (January 20, 2003), Lisa Crawford Watson, "Remembering Barns."*

*   *   *

BAISDEN, Michael 1963-

PERSONAL: Born June 26, 1963, in Chicago, IL; married (divorced); children: one daughter.

ADDRESSES: Home—Los Angeles, CA and Houston, TX. *Office*—Legacy Publishing Inc., P.O. Box 988, Colleyville, TX 76034. *E-mail*—mb@michaelbaisden.com.

CAREER: Writer, motivational speaker, and talk show host. Founder of Legacy Publishing and *Happilysingle.com.* Host of television talk show *Talk or Walk,* Tribune Broadcasting, 2001. Worked previously as route driver for Chicago Transit Authority and leather goods business owner.

WRITINGS:

Never Satisfied: How and Why Men Cheat, Legacy Publishing (Schaumburg, IL), 1995.

Men Cry in the Dark (novel), Legacy Publishing (Irving, TX), 1997.

The Maintenance Man: It's Midnight, Do You Know Where Your Woman Is? (novel), Legacy Publishing (Atlanta, GA), 1999.

God's Gift to Women (novel), Touchstone (New York, NY), 2002.

Men Cry in the Dark (play; adapted from his book), first produced in Dallas, TX, 2002.

The Maintenance Man (play; adapted from his book), first produced in Houston, TX, 2003.

ADAPTATIONS: The Maintenance Man was optioned for film by Reuben Cannon.

SIDELIGHTS: Novelist and motivational speaker Michael Baisden drove trains for the Chicago Transit Authority and ran a leather business before he started writing *Never Satisfied: How and Why Men Cheat* in 1993. Instead of listening to the large publishing houses that refused to publish his first book, Baisden used the whole of his financial and personal resources to self-publish and market the work through his own publishing company, Legacy Publishing, in 1995. Selling more than 50,000 copies in the first eight months, the book was on both *Essence* and *Emerge* bestseller lists during the same year. By touring around the country to promote *Never Satisfied,* Baisden was able to turn his book into a cultural phenomenon, attracting thousands of African Americans and others to his lectures. Focusing on the infidelities committed by a group of African-American men against their wives, the book attempts to tip women off to the signs of their husband's cheating. In addition to publishing several popular novels since his first book, Baisden has also created a Web site dedicated to African-American singles that promotes the interests of those who decide to stay single, and offers an online singles search service.

In *Men Cry in the Dark,* released in 1997, Baisden explores African-American relationships through the man's point of view. According to Baisden in an interview with *Black Book Network,* "Men Cry in the Dark was in many ways a reaction, or rebuttal, to *Waiting to Exhale.* At least, that's the way it started. I wanted to balance the portrayal of Black men—not reject hers and put mine out—but say, 'look at these positive brothers who have issues, too.' I wanted to show more positive portrayals of Black men and how we deal with relationships." Baisden adapted the book as a stage play in 2002. Baisden's popularity after the publication of *Men Cry in the Dark* was overwhelming, including appearances on numerous talk shows on radio and television. The author took advantage of the increased media attention by creating the *Love, Lust, and Lies* tour, in which he spoke of the difficulties of African-American relationships. He also videotaped these seminars, selling the tapes to those who could not attend. Baisden's unorthodox techniques for marketing his books have succeeded, based on book sales. As he admitted in an interview on the *Simon & Schuster Web site,* "I'm a straight up hustler. While most authors were sitting back waiting for their books to sell, I was out there peddling books at night clubs, restaurants, and hair salons."

Baisden's third book, the novel *The Maintenance Man: It's Midnight, Do You Know Where Your Woman Is?,* came out in 1999. The main character, Malcolm, is a male prostitute who finds that he is not satisfied with one-night stands, and looks for a more meaningful relationship with Toni, a classical dancer. Baisden describes Malcolm's character by asserting in an on-line interview with *Black Book Network* that "He is not happy with what he is doing. There are a lot of men who are playing the 'player' games and are not happy, at least not those with a conscience. So, he's representative of all the men who are players and really don't want to be." By giving his audience such a well-rounded character, an African-American male who is macho, but also sensitive and caring, Baisden has gained the readership of both male and female African Americans who are attracted to a more human picture of the battle between the sexes. The author uses the sensationalism of gratuitous sex and male sensuality in order to get the attention of his readers, while steadily building a backbone of morality and bringing a case for sexual fidelity to the story. *The Maintenance Man* was also adapted to the stage in 2003, and was also optioned for film.

Baisden's fourth book, *God's Gift to Women,* deals with similar issues, as a radio disc jockey who gives relationship advice takes advantage of one too many one-night stands, and finds himself the subject of a fatal attraction. When it was released in 2003, the novel quickly made the *New York Times* bestseller list. According to Binti L. Villinger in *Black Issues Book Review,* "With *God's Gift to Women,* Baisden presents a straightforward narrative filled with approachable, easy to relate to characters," which are qualities that must attract Baisden's many fans.

BIOGRAPHICAL AND CRITICAL SOURCES:

BOOKS

Contemporary Black Biography, Volume 25, edited by David G. Oblender, Gale (Detroit, MI), 2000.

PERIODICALS

Black Issues Book Review, January-February, 2001, Roger Waiter, review of *The Maintenance Man: It's Midnight, Do You Know Where Your Woman Is?,* p. 19; September-October, 2002, Binti L. Villinger, review of *God's Gift to Women,* p. 29.
Publishers Weekly, December 13, 1999, p. 37.

ONLINE

African American Kulture Zone, http://www.aakulturezone.com/ (July 4, 2003), Lena Williams, review of *God's Gift to Women.*
African American Literature Book Club, http://aalbc.com/ (April 8, 1998), Thumper, review of *Men Cry in the Dark.*
Black Book Network, http://www.blackbooknetwork.com/ (July 4, 2003), interview with Baisden; Betty Davis, "Michael Baisden"; review of *Men Cry in the Dark.*
Daughters of Eve Network, http://www.doenetwork.com/ (July 4, 2003), Pamela Jarmon, review of *God's Gift to Women.*
Exodus Newsmagazine Online, http://www.exodusnews.com/ (February 11, 2003), review of *Men Cry in the Dark.*
Happilysingle.com, http://happilysingle.com/ (July 8, 2003).
Look Online, http://www.lookmag.com/ (July 4, 2003), Cecil Cross, review of *God's Gift to Women.*
Michael Baisden Web site, http://www.michaelbaisden.com (July 4, 2003).
Simon and Schuster Web site, http://www.simonsays.com/ (July 4, 2003).*

*   *   *

BAKER, Howard (James) 1946-

PERSONAL: Born December 31, 1946, in London, England.

ADDRESSES: Agent—c/o Mainstream Publishing, 7 Albany St., Edinburgh EH1 3UG, Scotland. *E-mail*—howardjamesbaker@hotmail.com.

CAREER: Author of nonfiction.

WRITINGS:

Sawdust Caesar, Mainstream (Edinburgh, Scotland), 1999.
Enlightenment and the Death of Michael Mouse, Mainstream (Edinburgh, Scotland), 2001.

Contributor to *Esquire, Time Out, Property* (France), and *What's On* (London, England).

WORK IN PROGRESS: Freaks, about the Seventies' rural acid scene; feature-film scripts *Sawdust Caesar* and *Bed and Breakfast;* research on nineteenth- and twentieth-century rural life in England; research on France and Catharism.

SIDELIGHTS: Howard Baker told *CA:* "I write to entertain and inform, usually to throw new light upon an old subject (show me a new one), and to create a fuss among those who believe they know it all, I take a long look at the monitor, and hey, I start pressing the keys on the keyboard until something emerges on the screen. I go away. I come back and read what I've written and revise. This continues, day in and day out, until I've had enough; I'm rarely satisfied.

"*Sawdust Caesar* was written in response to the rubbish that was being spouted about the subject—I was there you see, and objected to those who knew nothing about the subject, warping it beyond recognition. History tends to come from the mouths of those who know nothing; those who have recycled the knowledge of others, and our kids grow up with a twisted view of the world. I object to this. *Sawdust Caesar* was a gritty book, so much so that some suggested I dumb down future works, but that just ain't my way. It's horses for courses as far as I'm concerned, and if the genre needs the muscle, so be it. Having said that, I can write pretty too."

BIOGRAPHICAL AND CRITICAL SOURCES:

ONLINE

Mainstream Publishing Web site, http://www.mainstreampublishing.com/ (November 15, 2003).

BALDWIN, Peter 1956-

PERSONAL: Born December 22, 1956, in Ann Arbor, MI; children: two. *Education:* Yale University, B.A., 1978; Harvard University, M.A., 1980, Ph.D., 1986.

ADDRESSES: Office—University of California, Los Angeles, Department of History, 6265 Bunche Hall, Mail Code: 147303, Box 951473, Los Angeles, CA 90095-1473. *E-mail*—pbaldwin@history.ucla.edu.

CAREER: Professor and historian. Harvard University, Cambridge, MA, assistant professor, 1986-90; University of California—Los Angeles, professor of history, 1990—.

AWARDS, HONORS: (As project director for the University of California) investigator award in health-policy research; Robert Wood Johnson Foundation award, 2000, for study *The Influence of History and Tradition on Public Health Strategies: A Nationally Comparative Approach to the AIDS Epidemic.*

WRITINGS:

The Politics of Social Solidarity: Class Bases of the European Welfare State, 1875-1975, Cambridge University Press (New York, NY), 1990.
(Editor) *Reworking the Past: Hitler, the Holocaust, and the Historians' Debate,* Beacon Press (Boston, MA), 1990.
Contagion and the State in Europe, 1830-1930, Cambridge University Press (New York, NY), 1999.

WORK IN PROGRESS: Research of the AIDS epidemic in historical perspective.

SIDELIGHTS: Peter Baldwin is a professor of history whose interests include modern Europe, Germany, France, and Scandinavia. As project director of a Robert Wood Johnson Foundation-funded project awarded to the University of California in 2000, Baldwin has studied the factors that have influenced AIDS responses in the United States, France, England, Germany, and Sweden. The study looks at social composition, local traditions, the political influence and clout of groups most severely affected by the AIDS epidemic, and other factors in determining how they impact, and to what degree, public health policy.

Baldwin's first volume, *The Politics of Social Solidarity: Class Bases of the European Welfare State, 1875-1975,* was called a "richly documented study" by *Choice* reviewer J. LaPalombara. Allan Mitchell noted in *American Historical Review* that because Baldwin studies five separate countries, "an exhaustive narrative of each over a full century is unfeasible. Accordingly, Baldwin adopts a typological approach that enables him to move deftly from one example to another. He is like a skillful juggler, forever attempting to keep several balls in the air at once while he handles the rest. It is a fiendishly difficult act to sustain, and the wonder is that he manages so well."

Pat Thane wrote in *Business History Review* that "Baldwin's interpretation is richly grounded in archival research in Danish, Swedish, German, and French, as well as in English, and he succeeds admirably in what he rightly describes as the difficult task of 'reconciling the social scientists' fondness for unimpededly logical argument with the historians' penchant for craggy detail'—a reconciliation that is obviously essential if we are ever to understand long-term process." Thane observed that "as Baldwin very clearly demonstrates, and as the politics of most developed nations daily show, social policy is the product of quite crude and open factional conflict and horse-trading among social groups with very real material interests at stake."

As editor of *Reworking the Past: Hitler, the Holocaust, and the Historians' Debate* Baldwin collected essays from Israeli, German, and English-speaking contributors to explore how the Holocaust period should be viewed—whether it should be historicized or set aside as something that can never be accepted or assimilated into history.

Contagion and the State in Europe, 1830-1930 is Baldwin's study of public health policies adopted in England, France, Germany, and Sweden, and the responses to such diseases as syphilis, smallpox, and cholera. It was during this period that the beginnings of current health policy were formed. On one hand, people were deciding how and to what extent government should be allowed to interfere in their private lives, and on the other, governments were determining

how far they could go before the people rebelled. Governments enforced policies that allowed the treatment of sick people against their will, that required physicians to report certain diseases, and that enlisted the public to take part in compulsory measures to contain disease. Baldwin looks at whether prevention in these countries was most influenced by politics or by more basic differences.

Conventional thought dictates that public health systems were created and run according to the political orientation of the governing body. Baldwin finds that this is not necessarily so. Liberal states did not always use liberal measures, nor did autocratic states always use conservative measures. They tried various approaches in an attempt to strike a balance between effective disease control and the public's acceptance of a measure that would provide protection with out too much inconvenience. Policy was also different in countries less affected by a particular disease and whose larger population centers could observe its devastation from a distance.

Times Literary Supplement reviewer James C. Riley felt that the parts of the book that deal with the implications of disease prevention are "the most successful and interesting." Baldwin considers how the treatment and prevention of cholera might be different from that of syphilis, a disease spread by "sin." Closing a country's borders in an attempt to stop the spread of disease also results in economic loss with reduced trade, as well as limiting personal freedom. Baldwin shows that none of three diseases could be prevented with measures that would have been acceptable.

Riley wrote that "Baldwin is a stylist as well as a deeply curious researcher. Some passages are beautifully written, terms have been artfully chosen, there is humour, amusing and effective anecdotes abound." Riley concluded by saying that "for most readers, brought up to believe that people learn from their mistakes, or that they might do so, this will be a disturbing book. Baldwin argues that we are bound up in all previous decisions made and the prejudices and preferences that we have had. It is a kind of epidemiologic path dependence, a term coined by economists to describe the degree to which previous decisions lock us into certain technologies or behaviours. Nevertheless, Baldwin remains hopeful."

BIOGRAPHICAL AND CRITICAL SOURCES:

PERIODICALS

American Historical Review, February, 1992, Allan Mitchell, review of *The Politics of Social Solidarity: Class Bases of the European Welfare State, 1875-1975,* pp. 185-186.

Business History Review, spring, 1992, Pat Thane, review of *The Politics of Social Solidarity,* p. 231.

Choice, April, 1991, J. LaPalombara, review of *The Politics of Social Solidarity,* pp. 1374-1375.

Michigan Quarterly Review, summer, 1991, Geoff Eley, review of *Reworking the Past: Hitler, the Holocaust, and the Historians' Debate,* pp. 488-505.

Times Literary Supplement, October 29, 1999, James C. Riley, review of *Contagion and the State in Europe, 1830-1930.**

*   *   *

BARQUIST, David L.

PERSONAL: Male.

ADDRESSES: Office—Yale University Art Gallery, P.O. Box 208271, New Haven, CT 06520-8271.

CAREER: Yale University Art Gallery, New Haven, CT, associate curator of American decorative arts, 1981—.

AWARDS, HONORS: Charles F. Montgomery Prize of the Decorative Arts Society, 1992, for *American Tables and Looking Glasses in the Mabel Brady Garvan and Other Collections at Yale University.*

WRITINGS:

American and English Pewter at the Yale University Gallery: A Supplementary Checklist, Yale University Gallery (New Haven, CT), 1985.

(Coauthor, with Patricia E. Kane and Aline H. Zeno) *American Silver from the Kossack Collection: A Checklist,* Yale University Art Gallery (New Haven, CT), 1988.

American Tables and Looking Glasses in the Mabel Brady Garvan and Other Collections at Yale University, essays by Elisabeth Donaghy and Gerald W. R. Ward, photographs by Charles Uht, Yale University Art Gallery (New Haven, CT), 1992.

Myer Myers: Jewish Silversmith in Colonial New York, with essays by Jon Butler and Jonathan D. Sarna, Yale University Press (New Haven, CT), 2001.

SIDELIGHTS: David L. Barquist has worked at the Yale Museum of Art since 1981 and has written extensively on colonial American decorative arts. In *American Tables and Looking Glasses in the Mabel Brady Garvan and Other Collections at Yale University,* Barquist presents a catalogue for museum curators, antique dealers, and collectors of Americana. In addition to Barquist's numerous catalogue entries on the objects, the book includes essays by other experts in the field. "Barquist translates the vocabulary of objects to the printed page and shares thousands of bits of information about construction techniques and materials," wrote Philip Zea in a review of the book for the *Journal of the Early Republic.* Zea went on to note that the book "is part of the tradition of education at Yale that reflects excellence in this field."

The book and catalogue *Myer Myers: Jewish Silversmith in Colonial New York* was written by Barquist as a result of research for his doctoral dissertation and to accompany a 2001 exhibition at the Yale University Art Museum focusing on the life and work of the first Jewish silversmith in New York. Considered one of New York's most productive silversmiths during the late colonial period, Myer Myers created silver pieces for wealthy patrons. "Myers success as a silversmith was the result of his talents not only as a craftsman but also as an entrepreneur who marshaled the skills of other craftsmen and specialist," noted Barquist in an article in the *Yale Bulletin & Calendar.*

The book features several essays on the craftsman's life and career and on colonial Judaism. Myers was born in New York City and worked there as a successful silversmith until 1776, when British troops attacked the city after George Washington had made it his headquarters during the Revolutionary War. Myers, who supported America's desire to be independent from Great Britain, moved to Norwalk, Connecticut, but the town was sacked and burned by the British in 1779. Myers lost his home, his studio, and all of his tools and moved to Stratford, Connecticut, and continued to work. Although he returned to New York immediately after the war, Myers's losses and the changing times—including new production techniques, a change from the Rococo style Myers specialized in to Neoclassicism, new artisans, and a troubled economy—were too great for Myers to overcome and rise once again to the status of an elite merchant-artisan. As Barquist commented of the Myers exhibition to Susan Emerling in the *Los Angeles Times,* "There is nothing else in American silver equal to this."

Writing in the *Library Journal,* Martin Chasin noted that Barquist's book is "a well-researched contribution on the work and life of the Jewish silversmith Myer Myers and an examination of the society in which he lived." A reviewer in *Publishers Weekly* called the book, which contains 200 photographs, "a fascinating scholarly look at a previously obscure aspect of pre-revolutionary America." In a review for *Choice,* W. Cahn stated that the book is "bound to remain the standard reference work on Myers for a long time."

BIOGRAPHICAL AND CRITICAL SOURCES:

PERIODICALS

Choice, May, 2002, W. Cahn, review of *Myer Myers: Jewish Silversmith in Colonial New York,* p. 1571.
Journal of the Early Republic, winter, 1993, Philip Zea, review of *American Tables and Looking Glasses in the Mabel Brady Garvan and Other Collections at Yale University,* pp. 548-549.
Library Journal, March 15, 2002, review of *Myer Myers,* p. 75.
Los Angeles Times, February 24, 2002, Susan Emerling, "An American Heritage Cast in Silver," pp. 65-66.
Publishers Weekly, September 17, 2001, review of *Myer Myers,* p. 74.
Yale Bulletin & Calendar, September 14, 2001, "Display Explores Life and Work of Colonial-Era Jewish Silversmith."*

*   *   *

BARR, Emily

PERSONAL: Married; husband's name James; children: Gabriel.

ADDRESSES: Home—Brighton, England. *Agent*—Jonny Gellar, Curtis Brown Ltd., Haymarket House, 28-29 Haymarket, London SW1Y 4SP, England.

CAREER: Columnist, travel writer, and novelist.

AWARDS, HONORS: Best New Talent, W. H. Smith Literary Awards, 2002.

WRITINGS:

Backpack, Hodder Headline (London, England), 2001.
Baggage, Hodder Headline (London, England), 2003.
Cuban Heels, Hodder Headline (London, England), 2003.

Contributor to periodicals, including *Guardian* and *Observer.*

WORK IN PROGRESS: A fourth novel.

SIDELIGHTS: Travel writer Emily Barr wrote her debut novel *Backpack,* which became a bestseller in England, after returning from her own trip around the world. *Booklist*'s Beth Warrell wrote that Barr "mixes many elements—adventure, romance, mystery—and successfully juggles them in a fast-paced and enjoyable tale."

The story is about Tansy Harris, a beautiful, blonde journalist living the good life in London, who has a couple of reasons for dropping out for a while. Her alcoholic mother has died, which, in a sense, frees Tansy, and her boyfriend Tom backs out of their planned trip together. She goes by herself, feeling that the trip will give her a chance to meditate, do her yoga, and wrestle with her own addictions to alcohol and drugs, particularly cocaine.

Tansy has a romantic picture of what the countries on her trip will be like, but those expectations are shattered when she visits such places as Vietnam, Laos, Thailand, and China. Amelia Morrey wrote in *New Statesman* that "seen through Tansy's eyes, everything is ugly, boring, and dirty. Barr might be making a point about the vulgarities of the new travellers, but it is hard to sympathise with such a self-important, intolerant protagonist." In her disappointment and loneliness, Tansy becomes friends with a group of backpackers she had initially found lacking in style. She also finds love with the generous and caring Max, who is very unlike her selfish boyfriend back in London.

Time International's Bryan Walsh wrote that Barr "loads *Backpack* with enough neurotic angst to fill a season's worth of *Ally McBeal*." Walsh called the subplot, a series of murders of blonde backpackers in the cities on Tansy's itinerary, "a diversion from a suddenly at-one-with-Asia Tansy looking down upon the 'tourists' in Bangkok or musing with unconscious irony upon 'deluded Westerners' at the base of Mount Everest."

A *Kirkus Reviews* contributor characterized the story as "the ever-churning mind of a bright and rebellious woman in flux." A *Publishers Weekly* reviewer wrote, "Caustically hilarious and entertaining, the novel carries emotional impact without schmaltz and rises above the usual Britpop fluff. Barr's is a welcome new voice."

BIOGRAPHICAL AND CRITICAL SOURCES:

PERIODICALS

Booklist, November 15, 2001, Beth Warrell, review of *Backpack,* p. 550.
Kirkus Reviews, November 15, 2001, review of *Backpack,* p. 1563; November 15, 2002, review of *Baggage,* p. 1635.
Library Journal, January, 2003, Karen Core, review of *Baggage,* p. 151.
New Statesman, February 19, 2001, Amelia Morrey, "Home Bird," p. 51.
Publishers Weekly, November 5, 2001, review of *Backpack,* p. 39; January 13, 2003, review of *Baggage,* p. 43.
Time International, February 4, 2002, Bryan Walsh, "Traveling Lite: Emily Barr's *Backpack* Is a Jaded Take on Asia's Travelers' Circuit," p. 55.
Washington Post Book World, February 10, 2002, "Roughing It," p. T07.

ONLINE

Emily Barr Web site, http://authorpages.hoddersystems. com/EmilyBarr (September 30, 2003).*

BASKER, James G(lynn) 1952-

PERSONAL: Born August 28, 1952, in San Francisco, CA; son of James Wenzel and Anne Marlo (Glynn) Basker. *Education:* Harvard University, B.A., 1974; Cambridge University, B.A., M.A., 1976; Oxford University, Ph.D., 1983. *Hobbies and other interests:* Rare books, travel, international education.

ADDRESSES: Office—English Department, Barnard College, 3009 Broadway, New York, NY 10027. *E-mail*—jbasker@barnard.edu.

CAREER: English educator. Harvard University, Cambridge, MA, lecturer and senior tutor, 1982-84, assistant professor and senior tutor, 1984-87; Barnard College, New York, NY, associate professor of English, 1987—. Oxford University, director of Enrichment, summers 1985-89; Oxbridge Academy Programs, New York, NY, director and president, 1989; Stanford/ Harvard Alumni Association Seminar in Oxford, co-president, 1990.

MEMBER: Modern Language Association, American Society for Eighteenth-Century Studies, British Society for Eighteenth-Century Studies, Johnsonians, American Association of Rhodes Scholars, Gilder Lehrman Institute of American History (president), Lincoln and Soldiers Institute at Gettysburg College (president).

WRITINGS:

Tobias Smollett: Critic and Journalist, University of Delaware Press (Newark, NJ), 1988.
(Coeditor with S. J. Alvaro Ribeiro) *Tradition in Transition: Women Writers, Marginal Texts, and the Eighteenth-Century Canon,* Clarendon Press (Oxford, England), 1996.
(Editor) *The Critical Review, or, Annals of Literature: 1756-1763,* Pickering & Chatto Publishers (London, England), 2001.
(Editor) *Amazing Grace: An Anthology of Poems about Slavery, 1660-1810,* Yale University Press (New Haven, CT), 2002.

SIDELIGHTS: James G. Basker, an English professor at Barnard College, has a keen interest in eighteenth-century literature and the antislavery movement. His scholarly passions are reflected in such works as *Tobias Smollett: Critic and Journalist, Tradition in Transition: Women Writers, Marginal Texts, and the Eighteenth-Century Canon,* and *Amazing Grace: An Anthology of Poems about Slavery, 1660-1810.*

Tobias Smollett is based upon Basker's doctoral research about this prolific eighteenth-century journalist, editor, and critic. Smollett was the author of several novels, but Basker maintains that his most important literary achievement was that of founding and editing the *Critical Review* from 1756 to 1763. Smollett founded the journal in order to educate the British public on matters of literature and art, and, according to Basker, he was quite successful in achieving his goal. Nearly half of Basker's book is devoted to descriptions and analyses of Smollett's editorial and critical activities. These chapters are followed by a discussion of the effect which the *Critical Review* had upon writers, the reading public, and bookshops.

Basker's "study provides numerous original insights and suggests numerous avenues of inquiry heretofore unexplored," wrote Byron Gassman in *Modern Philology. Choice* reviewer D. L. Patey considered *Tobias Smollett* to be "an important book." "Basker convincingly argues his case for Smollett as an Enlightenment spokesman working his way to fulfillment through journalism," said Morris Golden in *Journal of English and Germanic Philology.* In a *Review of English Studies* article, J. A. Downie felt that *Tobias Smollett* demonstrates both the stronger and weaker aspects of an adapted doctoral thesis. Yet, this critic also noted that Basker's work "genuinely breaks fresh ground, offering new information on Smollett and his writings, and changing our perspective on the writer."

In *Tradition in Transition* Basker and coeditor S. J. Alvaro Ribeiro collect essays written by former students of Roger Lonsdale, a scholar and teacher who contributed to a greater understanding of the depth and breadth of eighteenth-century English poetry. According to Donna Landry in a review for *Eighteenth-Century Fiction,* contributor Christine Gerrard writes in this work that Lonsdale "taught us to expect the unexpected from eighteenth-century poetry," for he showed that this era of poetry was characterized not only by the more famous writers such as Boswell and Wordsworth, but also by writings from "women . . . farm labourers, Dissenters, and other previously marginalized writers."

"This volume offers some powerful reappraisals of canonical figures in addition to bringing new subjects to light," Landry remarked. She also wrote that it "is all the more persuasive about the scholarly worth of its project for being understated in its ambitions and conclusions." Karen O'Brien praised *Tradition in Transition* in a *Review of English Studies* article. She noted that Basker and Alvaro Ribeiro have selected essays that "reflect the broad range of Professor Lonsdale's influence and work." O'Brien called the book "an eclectic and lively volume."

Amazing Grace, published in 2002, is a lengthy anthology of poetry written by a spectrum of writers ranging from hitherto unknown writers to more famous authors, such as Coleridge, Defoe, Wordsworth, and Johnson. In more than four hundred poems, the writers address the themes of enslavement, captivity, and occasional moments of freedom as experienced by Africans and African descendents in the English-speaking countries of the world. According to Renee Tawa in *Knox News,* "Barker said he wanted the anthology to address misconceptions that slavery was simply an American issue of the 1800s." Each of the poems is preceded by an introductory essay by Basker, in which he includes any biographical information he may have discovered about the poets.

A *Barnard News Center* writer described *Amazing Grace* as a "landmark anthology of poems" that "speak eloquently of the themes of slavery." In a *Publishers Weekly* review, a critic called *Amazing Grace* an "enormous . . . groundbreaking anthology."

BIOGRAPHICAL AND CRITICAL SOURCES:

PERIODICALS

Choice, July, 1988, D. L. Patey, review of *Tobias Smollett: Critic and Journalist,* p. 1692.

Eighteenth-Century Fiction, July, 1997, Donna Landry, review of *Tradition in Transition: Women Writers, Marginal Texts, and the Eighteenth-Century Canon,* pp. 516-518.

Journal of English and Germanic Philology, July, 1989, Morris Golden, review of *Tobias Smollett,* pp. 425-429.

Modern Philology, February, 1990, Byron Gassman, review of *Tobias Smollett,* pp. 311-313.

Publishers Weekly, September 23, 2002, review of *Amazing Grace: An Anthology of Poems about Slavery, 1660-1810,* p. 67.

Review of English Studies, November, 1990, J. A. Downie, review of *Tobias Smollett,* pp. 576-577; August, 1998, Karen O'Brien, review of *Tradition in Transition,* pp. 362-363.

ONLINE

Barnard News Center Web site, http://www.barnard. columbia.edu/ (January 17, 2003), description of *Amazing Grace.*

Knoxville News Sentinel online, http://www.knoxnews. com/ (January 14, 2003), Renee Tawa, review of *Amazing Grace.**

*   *   *

BASS, Amy

PERSONAL: Female. *Education:* Attended Williams College, 1991; Bates College, B.A., 1992; State University of New York, M.A./Ph.D., 1999.

ADDRESSES: *Office*—Plattsburgh State University, History Department, Champlain Valley Hall, 320, Plattsburgh, NY 12901. *E-mail*—bassab@plattsburgh. edu.

CAREER: Plattsburgh State University, Plattsburgh, NY, assistant professor of history. NBC research team member for Atlanta Olympics, 1996, Sydney Olympics, 2000, and Salt Lake City Olympics, 2002.

WRITINGS:

Not the Triumph but the Struggle: The 1968 Olympics and the Making of the Black Athlete, University of Minnesota Press (Minneapolis, MN), 2002.

WORK IN PROGRESS: A monograph that centers on W. E. B. Du Bois; an edited volume on ideas of race and sports.

SIDELIGHTS: In her book *Not the Triumph but the Struggle: The 1968 Olympics and the Making of the Black Athlete* historian Amy Bass examines the civil rights movement as it relates to sports. The specific focus is the 1968 Summer Olympics held in Mexico City, where Harry Edwards had called for African-American athletes to boycott the games to protest racism in the United States. Though the boycott failed to attract enough supporters, American track stars Tommie Smith and John Carlos, who won gold and bronze medals, respectively, made their point when they raised their black-gloved fists on the winners' podium in symbolic protest. Bass details the context of their controversial action and explains its impact on U.S. society and on the world of sports.

In a *Press Republican* online interview with Jeff Meyers, Bass explained, "It's not a book about sports. It's more about civil rights history more than anything else. Sports is an amazing venue to study the civil rights struggle, but this book is not confined to sports." The book describes the conditions in the United States that moved Smith and Carlos to take action, explains the Olympic Project for Human Rights and the Black Power Movement, and discusses what came to be seen as a politicization of sports following the protest. But as Daniel Caplice Lynch observed in the *Berkshire Eagle,* "Bass makes clear that the games have always been political." Praising the book's lucid prose and sophisticated analysis, *Philadelphia City Paper* contributor Cindy Fuchs commended *Not the Triumph but the Struggle* as an "absorbing and cogent" study that traces nothing less than the "'historical production of the black athlete.'"

BIOGRAPHICAL AND CRITICAL SOURCES:

PERIODICALS

Library Journal, November 1, 2002, R. C. Cottrell, review of *Not the Triumph but the Struggle: The 1968 Olympics and the Making of the Black Athlete* p. 97.

ONLINE

Berkshire Eagle online, http://www.berkshireeagle. com/ (March 20, 2003), Daniel Caplice Lynch, "New Book Explores the Role of Black Athletes in the U.S."

Philadelphia City Paper online, http://citypaper.net/ (March, 20, 2003), Cindy Fuchs, review of *Not the Triumph but the Struggle.*

Plattsburgh State University Web site, http://www.plattsburgh.edu/ (January 20, 2003), "Amy Bass."

Press Republican Web site, http://www.pressrepublican.com/ (March 20, 2003), Jeff Meyers, "A Moment That Changed Sports for Good."

University Press of Minnesota Web site, http://www.upress.umn.edu/ (January 20, 2003), review of *Not the Triumph but the Struggle.**

*   *   *

BAXT, George (Leonard) 1923-2003

OBITUARY NOTICE—See index for *CA* sketch: Born June 11, 1923, in Brooklyn, NY; died from complications after heart surgery June 28, 2003, in New York, NY. Author. Baxt was an author of horror and thriller film screenplays who also penned mysteries, most notably the novels featuring an openly gay African-American detective named Pharoah Love (the first name is deliberately misspelled). Born to immigrant parents, Baxt attended City College and Brooklyn College in New York before serving in the U.S. Army during World War II. Returning home, he took a job as a disc jockey before finding work as a casting agent. Early success led to his opening his own agency, but he lost money during the 1950s because so many of his clients were targets of Senator Joseph McCarthy's blacklist. Baxt weathered this setback by moving to England and writing episodes for a television series titled *Sword of Freedom* in 1958. He found historical drama boring, however, and began to write original horror and thriller scripts, starting with *City of the Dead* (1960), which was released in the United States as *Horror Hotel.* His next film, *Circus of Horrors* (1960), won a cult following; other films by Baxt include *Shadow of the Cat* (1961) and *Night of the Eagle* (1962), which was released in the United States as *Burn, Witch, Burn.* He was also an uncredited writer for the Vincent Price cult horror flick *The Abominable Dr. Phibes* (1971). Money problems during the 1960s again prompted Baxt to change his career path, and this time he began novel-writing. His first book, *A Queer Kind of Death* (1966), introduced Pharoah Love and caused a sensation among critics and readers alike. Love also appeared to critical acclaim in *Swing Low, Sweet Harriet* (1967) and *Topsy and Evil* (1968). Two

subsequent Love appearances—in *A Queer Kind of Love* (1994) and *A Queer Kind of Umbrella* (1995)—did less well, however, as the novelty of the character wore off. But Baxt also wrote other mystery and thriller novels, including a number of books that feature real-life celebrities in fictional situations, such as *The Dorothy Parker Murder Case* (1984), *The Alfred Hitchcock Murder Case* (1986), *The Mae West Murder Case* (1993), and his last novel, *The Clark Gable and Carole Lombard Murder Case* (1997). In all, Baxt published twenty-seven novels, as well as the play, *Spinechiller,* which was successfully produced in London in 1977.

OBITUARIES AND OTHER SOURCES:

BOOKS

Writers Directory, 18th edition, St. James Press (Detroit, MI), 2003.

PERIODICALS

Independent (London, England), July 10, 2003, p. 16.
Times (London, England), July 12, 2003, p. 42.

*   *   *

BAYAN, Matthew J. 1951-

PERSONAL: Born 1951; married.

ADDRESSES: Home—Reno, NV. *Agent*—Margret McBride Literary Agency, 7744 Fay Ave., Ste. 201, La Jolla, CA 92037. *E-mail*—Mattbayan@aol.com.

CAREER: Manager of public and private nutrition and health programs; author.

AWARDS, HONORS: Med411 Medical Award, 2000, for *HeartSavers Web site.*

WRITINGS:

Eat Fat, Be Healthy: Understanding the Heartstopper Gene and When a Low-Fat Diet Can Kill You, Scribner (New York, NY), 2000.

Contributor to *Online Journal of Issues in Nursing.*

SIDELIGHTS: Matthew J. Bayan thought he was practicing a healthy lifestyle by exercising, not smoking, and eating a low-fat diet. Healthy, he thought, until he had a massive heart attack at the age of forty-five and had to be revived over seventy times. Although he made a full recovery, Bayan learned that he has a gene, ApoB, which is present in some twenty percent of the population and which causes the body to produce excessive LDL—bad—cholesterol when a low-fat diet is consumed. Bayan claims that many people, including physicians, are unaware of this potential problem, and he has made it his goal to inform the general public of the danger those with this condition face by consuming too little fat. In an interview with *Palm Beach Post* contributor Carolyn Susman, Bayan stated, "I am on a mission. After the experience I had, I came to the conclusion I could save lives by getting this information out there." He also shared some good news: "This is very treatable, much more treatable than regular heart disease. If you know you have it, you can pretty much neutralize it."

In his book *Eat Fat, Be Healthy: Understanding the Heartstopper Gene and When a Low-Fat Diet Can Kill You* Bayan recounts his attack and shares information on how to identify the presence of the gene and the steps affected individuals can take for treatment. A reviewer for *Publishers Weekly* wrote that although "Parts of the memoir are overwritten . . . Bayan does a fine job translating medical terminology and, with a keen sense of humor, explaining how people can integrate healthy behavior into everyday life."

BIOGRAPHICAL AND CRITICAL SOURCES:

PERIODICALS

Austin American-Statesman, February 12, 2001, Kristi Kingston, review of *Eat Fat, Be Healthy: Understanding the Heartstopper Gene and When a Low-Fat Diet Can Kill You,* p. E8.
Palm Beach Post, April 21, 2000, Carolyn Susman, review of *Eat Fat, Be Healthy,* p. E3.
Publishers Weekly, January 3, 2000, review of *Eat Fat, Be Healthy,* p. 72.

ONLINE

HeartSavers Web site, http://www.eatfatbehealthy.com/ (June 18, 2003).*

BEARD, Julie

PERSONAL: Female. *Education:* Stephens College, Columbia, MO, B.F.A.; Northwestern University, M.A. (journalism), 1989.

ADDRESSES: Agent—c/o Jove Publicity, 375 Hudson St., New York, NY 10014. *E-mail*—juliebeard@aol.com.

CAREER: Writer and television journalist. Repertory Theatre of St. Louis, St. Louis, MO, actress; WFRV-TV, Green Bay, WI, and KSDK-TV, St. Louis, MO, reporter; WFLD-TV, Chicago, IL, writer and associate producer. Actor in television commercials.

AWARDS, HONORS: Romantic Times Reviewers' Choice Award for best medieval romance, 1996, for *A Dance in Heather.*

WRITINGS:

Lady and the Wolf, Diamond, 1994.
My Fair Lord, Diamond, 1994.
A Dance in Heather, Jove (New York, NY), 1996.
Falcon and the Sword, Jove (New York, NY), 1997.
Romance of the Rose, Berkley (New York, NY), 1998.
The Maiden's Heart, Jove (New York, NY), 1999.
Very Truly Yours, Jove (New York, NY), 2001.
The Duchess' Lover, Jove (New York, NY), 2002.

OTHER

(Editor and contributor) *The Christmas Cat* (stories), Berkley (New York, NY), 1996.
The Complete Idiot's Guide to Getting Your Romance Published, Alpha Books (Indianapolis, IN), 2000.

Work represented in the anthology *Charmed,* Berkley (New York, NY), 1999.

SIDELIGHTS: Julie Beard has written a number of historical romances, including *My Fair Lord.* In this Regency novel, Caroline Wainwright must marry before her twenty-fifth birthday or lose her inheritance. As she approaches the deadline, Caroline is still unmarried, in part because a ghost has driven away all her suitors. In desperation, she recruits a horse thief to be her husband with the help of Theodore Cavendish, an older friend just back from Africa. Lucas Davin, who is in fact the rejected son of an earl, goes along for the money but finds himself genuinely attracted to Caroline, who, with Uncle Teddy and friend Amanda Plumshaw, tutors him in the ways of a gentleman. When Lucas eventually becomes uncomfortable with the deception and wants to return to the London slums, Caroline must convince him to remain, not only because she loves him, but because otherwise she will lose her inheritance to her brother George. Reviewing the novel for *Romance Reader* online, Nancy J. Silberstein wrote that "at this point, the ghost of Lord Barrett takes a hand in the lovers' dispute—or is it a ghost? Perhaps there are natural explanations for what seems to be a supernatural phenomena. Clues abound for either interpretation."

A *Publishers Weekly* contributor called Beard's next novel, *A Dance in Heather,* a "rather gentle medieval romance." By royal decree, Lady Tess Farnsworth must marry Richard Avery, earl of Esterby, a man she hates because he refused to help her family when her father was burned at the stake as a Lollard heretic by Henry V. In addition, Tess is afraid of sex and childbirth, since her own mother died giving birth to her. *Library Journal*'s Mary Kay Chelton called the book "a nice interweaving of medieval British history, pageantry, and love."

Romance of the Rose, Beard's fifth book, features protagonist Lady Rosalind Carbery. After her father dies, the family estate, with the exception of Thornbury, the house Rosalind loves, reverts to Queen Elizabeth I. When a second will surfaces, the question arises of whether the house goes to Rosalind or to Mandrake Rothwell, the son of the man who built Thornbury, forcing them to cooperate in deciding the true heir or lose the house to the queen. *Romance Reader*'s Katy Cooper wrote that Beard "does a fine job of conveying the contrasts of the Elizabethan world, and she is to be commended for her handling of her two historical figures: Elizabeth the First and William Shakespeare. Shakespeare is clearly . . . a shrewd student of human nature, while Elizabeth is allowed the contradictions and complexity of her knotty personality."

In a *Romance Reader* review, Jean Mason noted that the premise of *The Maiden's Heart* is "a bit unusual.

How many romances are there where the heroine insists on a 'spiritual' marriage?" Sir Hugh de Grayhurst is a second son whose older brother inherits all of their father's property. At age thirty Hugh wants to marry and settle down but must find a wife who is not limited in her choice of husbands based on his finances. Nearby lives such a woman, Margrete Trewsbury, who has left the convent to handle her dying father's affairs. They marry, but for more than one reason, Margrete insists on a celibate marriage. Hugh is a good man who honors her wishes, but he is also very much in love with her. A *Publishers Weekly* contributor called *The Maiden's Heart* "engaging."

In *Very Truly Yours,* set during the Regency period, Liza Cranshaw meets Jack Fairchild and is so taken with him that she refuses all offers until the villainous Lord Barrington blackmails her into a promise of marriage. Years later Jack leaves London and a pile of debts to take over a law practice in Liza's village and ultimately saves her from Barrington. *Booklist* reviewer Patty Engelmann wrote of Liza and Jack that "these two charming characters make Beard's romance a true delight."

The Duchess's Lover, Beard's 2002 romance, takes place during the late Victorian era. Duchess Olivia Thorpe's abusive husband has died, killed with a letter opener. Soon after, Olivia shares a night with Will Barnes, an artist and garden designer, and this fact is used by her nephew in accusing her of the murder. Barnes is willing to give up everything to clear her name and find the real killer. The differences between the social classes of the time comprise a theme in the story, which also includes references to the plight of female factory workers. A *Publishers Weekly* reviewer called the novel "a multifaceted read that paints an accurate portrait of a bygone era while tugging on the reader's heartstrings."

BIOGRAPHICAL AND CRITICAL SOURCES:

PERIODICALS

Booklist, April 15, 2001, Patty Engelmann, review of *Very Truly Yours,* p. 1538; April 15, 2002, Lynne Wach, review of *The Duchess's Lover,* p. 1384.
Library Journal, May 15, 1996, Mary Kay Chelton, review of *A Dance in Heather,* p. 49.

Publishers Weekly, May 6, 1996, review of *A Dance in Heather,* p. 76; May 17, 1999, review of *The Maiden's Heart,* p. 76; May 29, 2000, review of *My Fair Lord,* p. 58; February 26, 2001, review of *Very Truly Yours,* p. 65; March 11, 2002, review of *The Duchess' Lover,* p. 57.

ONLINE

Julie Beard Web site, http://www.juliebeard.com (April 24, 2002).
Romance Reader, http://www.theromancereader.com/ (May 10, 1998), Katy Cooper, review of *Romance of the Rose;* (May 10, 1999) Jean Mason, review of *The Maiden's Heart;* (July 5, 2000) Nancy J. Silberstein, review of *My Fair Lord.**

*   *   *

BECKER, Abraham S(amuel) 1927-2003

OBITUARY NOTICE—See index for *CA* sketch: Born February 7, 1927, in New York, NY; died of leukemia July 5, 2003, in Los Angeles, CA. Economist and author. Becker was an expert on the Soviet economy and accurately predicted that the USSR's overspending on its military would cause an economic crisis there. A graduate of Harvard University, where he earned an A.B. in 1949, and Columbia University, where he received his master's degree in 1952 and a Ph.D. in 1959, Becker spent the mid-1950s as an economist for the Corporation for Economic and Industrial Research in Washington, D.C. He went on to spend most of his career with the RAND Corp., a think tank based in Santa Monica, California. Here he served as a senior economist and founded the RAND-UCLA Center for Soviet International Behavior in 1983; he was also associate program director of RAND's national security strategies program. Furthermore, in 1974 and 1976 he served as a U.S. representative to the United Nations, focusing on the issue of military budgets. Becker drew national attention in 1980, when he was quoted in the *New York Times* as predicting that the Soviet Union's expenditures on its military were overly burdensome and deprived the rest of that country's economy of precious natural resources. During his career, Becker published numerous books on economics, many of which concerned the Soviet Union. Among these are *Soviet National Income and Product in 1965: The Goals of the Seven-Year Plan* (1963), *Ruble Price Levels and Dollar-Ruble Ratios of Soviet Machinery in the 1960s* (1973), *The Burden of Soviet Defense: A Political-Economic Essay* (1981), and *Russia and Caspian Oil: Moscow Loses Control* (1998).

OBITUARIES AND OTHER SOURCES:

PERIODICALS

Los Angeles Times, July 16, 2003, p. B11.

*   *   *

BECKLES, Hilary McD(onald) 1955-

PERSONAL: Born 1955, in Barbados. *Education:* Hull University, Ph.D. (economic history).

ADDRESSES: Office—University of the West Indies, Cave Hill Campus, University Dr., Cave Hill, St. Michael, Barbados. *E-mail*—hbeckles@uwichill.edu. bb.

CAREER: University of the West Indies, professor of economic and social history, chair of Department of History, 1992-96, dean of Faculty of Humanities, 1995-98, director of the Centre for Cricket Research at Cave Hill Campus, pro-vice chancellor of the university. Coordinator of Annual Vice Chancellor XI Cricket Match; coordinator of Caribbean Community/ University of the West Indies Cricket Conference, 2000; chairman of the board of University of the West Indies Press; led Barbados delegation to Third United Nations World Conference against Racism, Durban, South Africa, 2001; Eric E. Williams Memorial Lecturer, Florida International University, 2002; director of Colonial Life Insurance Company Holdings, Barbados; consultant, principal writer, and committee member for United Nations Educational, Scientific, and Cultural Organization Slave Route Project. International Advisory Council, member of board of trustees of youth advocate program, 2003).

WRITINGS:

Black Rebellion in Barbados: The Struggle against Slavery, 1627-1838, Antilles (Bridgetown, Barbados), 1984.

Afro-Caribbean Women and Resistance to Slavery in Barbados, Karnak House (London, England), 1988.

Corporate Power in Barbados: The Mutual Affair; Economic Injustice in a Political Democracy, Lighthouse Communications (Bridgetown, Barbados), 1989.

Natural Rebels: A Social History of Enslaved Black Women in Barbados, Rutgers University Press (New Brunswick, NJ), 1989.

White Servitude and Black Slavery in Barbados, 1627-1715, University of Tennessee Press (Knoxville, TN), 1989.

A History of Barbados: From Amerindian Settlement to Nation-State, Cambridge University Press (New York, NY), 1990.

Bussa: The 1816 Revolution in Barbados ("Rewriting History" series), Department of History, University of the West Indies (Cave Hill, Barbados), 1998.

The Development of West Indies Cricket, Volume 1: *The Age of Nationalism,* Volume 2: *The Age of Globalization,* Press University of the West Indies (Barbados), 1998.

Centering Woman: Gender Discourses in Caribbean Slave Society, M. Wiener (Princeton, NJ), 1999.

Contributor of essays to anthologies, including *For Love of Country: The National Heroes of Barbados,* Foundation (St. Michael, Barbados), 2001.

EDITOR

(With Verene Shepherd) *Caribbean Slave Society and Economy: A Student Reader,* New Press (New York, NY), 1991, revised and expanded as *Caribbean Slavery in the Atlantic World,* M. Weiner (Princeton, NJ), 1999.

(With Verene Shepherd) *Caribbean Freedom: Society and Economy from Emancipation to the Present,* I. Randle (Kingston, Jamaica), 1993, published as *Caribbean Freedom: Economy and Society from Emancipation to the Present; A Student Reader,* M. Wiener (Princeton, NJ), 1996.

An Area of Conquest: Popular Democracy and West Indies Cricket Supremacy ("Studies in West Indies Cricket Culture" series), I. Randle (Kingston, Jamaica), 1994.

(With Brian Stoddart) *Liberation Cricket: West Indies Cricket Culture,* Manchester University Press (Manchester, England), 1995.

Inside Slavery: Process and Legacy in the Caribbean Experience (Elsa Goveia memorial lectures, 1987-93), foreword by Woodville K. Marshall, Canoe Press, University of the West Indies (Kingston, Jamaica), 1996.

Member of editorial boards of history journals, including *Journal of American History* and *Journal of Caribbean History.*

SIDELIGHTS: Barbadian history professor Hilary McD. Beckles has written widely on the subject of slavery, as well as both the exploitation and oppression of the people and economies that comprise the West Indies. He is also a well-known cricket historian. After receiving his Ph.D. in economic history at Hull University in England, Beckles returned to his native Barbados as one of the first professionally trained historians native to the island.

Beckles's 1989 book *White Servitude and Black Slavery in Barbados, 1627-1715* traces four stages in the formation of the British plantation system in the New World and the institution of "proto-slavery," necessary for the creation of wealth for plantation owners. At the core of the book is the little-known subject of the white English, Scottish, and Irish indentured servants—a mix of migrants, beggars, criminals, and those said to be possessed by spirits—who first cultivated the British colonial sugar cane plantations on Barbados during the early 1600s. Beckles tells of the rise and fall of this class of workers, from their important role carrying out the physical labor required on a plantation, to when they began to be replaced by African slaves during the 1660s, and their fall into poverty and redundancy as black slaves became more valuable by the early 1700s. His research shows that the white servants suffered the same ill treatment that African slaves would later suffer: they were kidnapped, bought and sold, transported under deplorable conditions, had no legal rights, were whipped and tortured, and received harsh treatment when finally freed.

R. T. Brown, in a review of *White Servitude* for *Choice,* wrote, "No other book has so thoroughly treated this important segment of British colonists in the 17th century." Kenneth Morgan, writing in the *English Historical Review,* pointed out that Beckles "tantalizingly suggests that there may have been separate urban and rural classes of servants, each with a different consciousness and outlook." Marcus Rediker, in a review for the *Journal of Social History,* noted that Beckles "makes indentured servants important actors in the unfolding contest of capital and labor in Barbados. He documents their malingering and marronage, their arson and armed revolts, noting the interracial nature of some of their struggles. . . . But in the end he does not directly connect the resistance of servants to the accelerated movement toward slavery, preferring instead the more neo-classical arguments about labor supply and market rationality." Franklin W. Knight, in the *Journal of American History,* found that the book "skillfully weaves in the long-term social, cultural, and psychological consequences of this revolutionary transition for the colony and commerce." Knight called the work "an important addition to the dynamic literature on the evolution of New World societies."

In *Natural Rebels: A Social History of Enslaved Black Women in Barbados* Beckles looks at the multiple roles that black slave women—who constituted the majority of the population on plantations—had to assume in Barbados in the early 1700s. Beckles shows that women, although sexually exploited and as ill treated as male slaves, played a central role in plantation culture. They were successful vendors in local markets, vocal participants in antislavery movements, bulwarks of slave families, and producers of the future supply of laborers. O. N. Bolland, in a review for *Choice,* praised Beckles's "extensive use of quotes from original sources, such as plantation records," and called the book "clearly written." Rediker, in the *Journal of Social History,* concluded that Beckles shows "slave women cannot in any way be considered marginal to the history of early Barbados; they were, rather, utterly central to it." Rediker said "Beckles has established himself as a serious, talented scholar and a major new voice in labor and social history."

Beckles's *A History of Barbados: From Amerindian Settlement to Nation-State* begins with the seldom-discussed period of the precolonial years, from 650 to 1540, when native Amerindian peoples inhabited the island. His historical narrative continues through the period of British colonization and slavery, through slave rebellions and emancipation, to the decline of the sugar plantations, the anticolonial movement, and independence in 1966. Beckles then discusses Barbados's culture and society in modern times.

Knight, in a review for *Choice,* found the book to be "highly readable," although "its breezy style tantalizes rather than satisfies." Edward L. Cox, writing in the *Journal of Southern History,* noted that Beckles "skillfully discusses the mechanisms" by which British colonizers exploited the Barbadians and their resources, even after slavery ended. Jay R. Mandle, in the *Journal of Economic History,* found the "tone of opposition" to the conservative leadership of Grantley Adams during the push for independence to be "jarring," saying he felt it was "ironic for a politically left historian such as Beckles" to attack the politician, whose regional integration goals matched those of the left today. Still, Mandle concluded that the book is "a valuable historical synthesis that will become the standard reference" on the island's history.

Developed as a history text for a course at the University of the West Indies, *Liberation Cricket: West Indies Cricket Culture,* is a collection of essays that explore the adoption of the British game by African West Indians and its evolution as a popular sport in the island's culture. The book also celebrates the work of the Trinidadian historian C. L. R. James, who wrote the definitive book on the history of West Indian cricket, *Beyond a Boundary* (1963). R. McGehee, in a review for *Choice,* commented that the book shows the paradox of cricket as "both a vehicle for breaking down class and race structures and a retained symbol of colonialism and British culture."

Beckles's 1999 work *Centering Woman: Gender Discourses in Caribbean Slave Society* tells the history of black and white women in Caribbean slave society. Thoroughly researched, using both primary and secondary sources, the book covers a wide range of topics, which are organized by chapter. Subjects covered include the exploitation of slaves, prostitution, the gendered division of labor, the racial differentiation of sexual identity, and the role of women as entrepreneurs. In a review for the *Journal of Commonwealth & Comparative Politics,* Georgina Waylen found the book to combine a "theoretically informed approach together with some detailed readings of primary sources . . . to produce a . . . scholarly volume." Bolland, reviewing the book for *Choice,* noted that Beckles "writes thoughtfully" about his subject and that his analysis of the lives of women "are excellent."

The two-volume *Development of West Indies Cricket* is a historical analysis of the sport in the region drawing on the work of C. L. R. James and others, as well as on Beckles's own extensive research. Beckles, a former cricket player, is both the founder and director of the Centre for Cricket Research at the University of the West Indies. In volume one, *The Age of Nationalism,* Beckles mentions the influence of famed players such as Clive Lloyd and Vivian Richards, women's cricket, and the effects of apartheid and colonialism on the sport. In volume two, *The Age of Globalization,* he explores the effects of globalism on West Indian cricket, showing how prospective players are lured by offers from U.S. universities to play basketball, football, and baseball instead. He also discusses how the sport has been affected by the declining West Indian economy and the lack of a West Indian federation. A contributor to the *Stylus Publishing Web site* called Beckles's history of the sport "lively, well-researched and thought-provoking" and "comparable to none other in the field." Laurie Taylor wrote in the Manchester, England, *Guardian* that Beckles has written "a widely praised inquiry into the cultural forces which have affected his nation's cricket fortunes." Huw Richards, also of the *Guardian,* wrote of Beckles: "A thwarted international cricketer he may be, but at 44 he is a test-class historian. His book was hailed by Scyld Berry—a cricket writer well qualified to judge—as the most important book ever written on the game's history."

BIOGRAPHICAL AND CRITICAL SOURCES:

PERIODICALS

Choice, February, 1990, R. T. Brown, review of *White Servitude and Black Slavery in Barbados, 1627-1715,* pp. 997-998; September, 1990, O. N. Bolland, review of *Natural Rebels: A Social History of Enslaved Black Women in Barbados,* p. 200; November, 1991, Franklin W. Knight, review of *A History of Barbados: From Amerindian Settlement to Nation-State,* p. 507; October, 1995, R. McGehee, review of *Liberation Cricket: West Indies Cricket Culture,* p. 332; November, 1999, O. N. Bolland, review of *Centering Woman: Gender Discourses in Caribbean Slave Society.*
English Historical Review, April, 1991, review of *White Servitude and Black Slavery,* pp. 401-402.
Guardian (Manchester, England), June 9, 1999, Laurie Taylor, review of *The Development of West Indies Cricket,* p. 7; June 13, 2000, Huw Richards, review of *The Development of West Indies Cricket,* p. 12.

Journal of American History, December, 1990, Franklin W. Knight, review of *White Servitude and Black Slavery,* pp. 988-989.
Journal of Commonwealth & Comparative Politics, November, 2000, Georgina Waylen, review of *Centering Woman,* p. 192.
Journal of Economic History, March, 1992, Jay R. Mandle, review of *A History of Barbados,* pp. 265-266.
Journal of Social History, fall, 1991, Marcus Rediker, reviews of *White Servitude and Black Slavery* and *Natural Rebels,* pp. 144-147.
Journal of Southern History, May, 1992, Edward L. Cox, review of *A History of Barbados,* p. 399.
New Statesman, June 2, 1995, Andrew Blake, review of *Liberation Cricket,,* p. 47.
Reference & Research Book News, August, 1997, review of *Caribbean Freedom: Economy and Society from Emancipation to the Present: A Student Reader,* p. 89.

ONLINE

Emancipation Support Committee of Trinidad and Tobago Web site, http://www.emancipationtt.org/ (October 15, 2003), "Hilary Beckles."
Florida International University Web site, http://www.fiu.edu/ (spring, 2002), "The Global Politics of Reparations: Before and after Durban."
Stylus Publishing Web site, http://styluspub.com/ (November 2, 2003), review of *The Development of West Indies Cricket.*
University of the West Indies, Cave Hill Campus Web site, http://www.cavehill.uwi.edu/ (November 2, 2003), "Beckles, Hilary McD."*

*   *   *

BEGLEY, Sharon (Lynn) 1956-

PERSONAL: Born June 14, 1956, in Englewood, NJ; daughter of John Joseph and Shirley (Wintner) Begley; married Edward Groth III, July 24, 1983; children: Sarah, Daniel. *Education:* Yale University, B.A., 1977.

ADDRESSES: Office—Wall Street Journal, World Financial Center, 200 Liberty St., New York, NY 10281. *E-mail*—Sharon.Begley@wsj.com.

CAREER: Journalist. *Newsweek,* New York, NY, editorial assistant, 1977-79, assistant science editor, 1979-80, associate science editor, 1980-83, general science editor, 1983-96, senior science editor, 1996-2002; *Wall Street Journal,* New York, NY, science editor, 2002—.

AWARDS, HONORS: Global Award for Media Excellence, Population Institute, and Benjamin Fine Award, National Association of Secondary School Principals, both 1990, both for "We Fowled Our Nest"; National Magazine Award nomination, American Society of Magazine Editors, 1991; Deadline Club Award for Public Service Reporting, 1991, for "How to Teach Our Kids"; Aviation/Space Writers Association Premier Award, 1993, for "Doomsday Science"; Educational Press Association's Distinguished Achievement Award, 1994, for "The Puzzle of Genius"; Clarion Award, Association for Women in Communications, for "Your Child's Brain."

WRITINGS:

(With Collette Dowling and Anne Marie Cunningham) *The Techno/Peasant Survival Manual,* Bantam Dell Publishing Group (New York, NY), 1980.
(Author of introduction) Michael Reagan, editor, *The Hand of God: Thoughts and Images Reflecting the Spirit of the Universe,* Templeton Foundation Press (Radnor, PA), 2001.
(Author of introduction) Michael Reagan, editor, *Inside the Mind of God: Images and Words of Inner Space,* Templeton Foundation Press (Radnor, PA), 2002.
(With Jeffrey M. Schwartz) *The Mind and the Brain: Neuroplasticity and the Power of Mental Force,* Regan Books (New York, NY), 2002.

SIDELIGHTS: Sharon Begley's articles and cover stories appeared in *Newsweek* for over a decade, and her scientific pieces frequently appear in *Wall Street Journal.* Begley is also the coauthor of several books, including *The Techno/Peasant Survival Manual* and *The Mind and the Brain: Neuroplasticity and the Power of Mental Force.*

Begley collaborated with Collette Dowling and Anne Marie Cunningham to produce *The Techno/Peasant Survival Manual,* which was published in 1980. This book is an early primer designed to aid the timid, uninformed majority of people—the "techno/peasants"—in understanding some aspects of the modern technological world, such as computers, genetic engineering, and nuclear fusion and weapons. In addition to a description of these technologies, the authors attempt to explain the scientific principles underlying them and to show the far-reaching social implications which might result from the use of such technologies.

A. Douglas Stone of *Technology Review* felt that the book "should be quite informative to the layperson" but would be "too superficial and imprecise" for someone with more scientific and technical knowledge. Stone concluded by calling *The Techno/Peasant Survival Manual* "amusing light reading on contemporary technology."

In 2002 Begley and Jeffrey Schwartz published their joint work, *The Mind and the Brain.* Schwartz, a psychiatrist, is an expert in the treatment of individuals suffering from obsessive compulsive disorder (OCD). He and Begley describe Schwartz's approach to treating OCD, which includes relabeling, reattributing, refocusing, and revaluing. The Buddhist principle of "mindful attention" also underlies this method. This four-step therapy has proven to be quite successful, and, according to William A. Dembski in a review for *First Things,* through it Schwartz learned that his patients were actually "able to reorganize their brains by intentionally modifying their thoughts and behaviors."

As the work progresses, the authors show how the traditional views of neuroplasticity are erroneous. For many years, scientists believed that a human being's neural circuitry was completely fixed during childhood, but more recent studies show that the brain retains its plasticity throughout its lifetime. This is an important discovery, inasmuch as it implies that it is possible to treat diseases previously considered to be incurable. "Schwartz and Begley's description of [neuroplastic research] . . . is worth the price of the book," Dembski wrote in *First Things.* The critic stated, "*The Mind and the Brain* is strongest where it reviews current neurological research." In a *Booklist* review, William Beatty called the work "a book that thoughtful readers will enjoy." A *Publishers Weekly* critic noted that the results of Schwartz's research "are exciting and deserve widespread attention."

BIOGRAPHICAL AND CRITICAL SOURCES:

PERIODICALS

Booklist, October 1, 2002, William Beatty, review of *The Mind and the Brain: Neuroplasticity and the Power of Mental Force,* p. 282.
First Things, May, 2003, William A. Dembski, review of *The Mind and the Brain,* pp. 58-63.

Publishers Weekly, September 23, 2002, review of *The Mind and the Brain,* p. 64.

Technology Review, July, 1981, A. Douglas Stone, review of *The Techno/Peasant Survival Manual,* pp. 17-18.

ONLINE

Templeton Foundation Press Web site, http://www.templetonpress.org/ (January 17, 2003).*

*   *   *

BEHLER, Deborah A. 1947-

PERSONAL: Born March 17, 1947, in Northhampton, MA; daughter of Thomas Kent and Muriel (a homemaker; maiden name, Barney) Bliss; married John L. Behler (a biologist), February 25, 1978. *Education:* Bates College, B.A., 1969.

ADDRESSES: Home—20 Elisha Purdy Rd., Amawalk, NY 10501. *Office*—Wildlife Conservation Society, Bronx, NY 10460. *E-mail*—dbehler@wcs.org.

CAREER: Writer and editor.

WRITINGS:

(With John L. Behler) *Alligators and Crocodiles,* Voyageur Press (Stillwater, MN), 1998.

The Rain Forests of the Pacific Northwest, Benchmark Books (New York, NY), 2001.

(With John L. Behler) *Snakes,* Benchmark Books (New York, NY), 2002.

SIDELIGHTS: Deborah A. Behler has written several books with her husband, John L. Behler. Her first solo book publication, *The Rain Forests of the Pacific Northwest* is a well-regarded introduction to the North American rain forest for middle and high school students. In this book, Behler examines plants and animals from the tops of the trees to the fertile forest ground. In addition, she chronicles plant and animal interactions with each other, with the environment,

and with humans, all in a way that is both interesting and informative for report-writers and other readers, according to Kathy Piehl in *School Library Journal.*

For more information on Deborah Behler's writings, see the entry for John L. Behler.

BIOGRAPHICAL AND CRITICAL SOURCES:

PERIODICALS

Horn Book Guide, spring, 2001, Erica L. Stahler, review of *The Rain Forests of the Pacific Northwest.*

School Library Journal, April, 2001, Kathy Piehl, review of *The Rain Forests of the Pacific Northwest,* p. 154.

*   *   *

BEHLER, John L. 1943-

PERSONAL: Born June 28, 1943, in Allentown, PA; son of John Luther and Mildred (a homemaker; maiden name, Ludwig) Behler; married Deborah A. Behler (a writer and editor), February 25, 1978; children: Cynthia Sibilia, David. *Education:* University of Miami, B.S.; East Stroudsburg University, M.Ed.

ADDRESSES: Home—20 Elisha Purdy Rd., Amawalk, NY 10510. *Office*—Wildlife Conservation Society, Bronx Zoo, Bronx, NY 10460-1099.

CAREER: Curator, naturalist, and writer. Wildlife Conservation Society, Bronx Zoo, Bronx, NY, curator of herpetology.

WRITINGS:

(With F. Wayne King) *The Audubon Society Field Guide to North American Reptiles and Amphibians,* Knopf (New York, NY), 1979, published as *National Audubon Society Field Guide to North American Reptiles and Amphibians,* 2000.

Familiar Reptiles and Amphibians: North America, Knopf (New York, NY), 1988.

(Editor) Massimo Capula, *Simon and Schuster's Guide to Reptiles and Amphibians of the World,* illustrated by Giuseppe Mazza, Simon & Schuster (New York, NY), 1989.

(With wife, Deborah A. Behler) *Alligators and Crocodiles,* Voyageur Press (Stillwater, MN), 1998.

National Audubon Society First Field Guide: Reptiles ("First Field Guide" series), Scholastic (New York, NY), 1999.

(With Deborah A. Behler) *Snakes,* Benchmark Books (New York, NY), 2001.

SIDELIGHTS: John L. Behler is a respected naturalist and curator at the Bronx Zoo who specializes in herpetology, the study of reptiles and amphibians. Out of his work he has produced several books, often in collaboration with other naturalists. With F. Wayne King, Behler produced *The Audubon Society Field Guide to North American Reptiles and Amphibians,* which was greeted by reviewers as a new standard for field guides, featuring clear photographs and illustrations and prose descriptions of each species marked by concision and interest. With his wife, Deborah A. Behler, Behler wrote *Alligators and Crocodiles,* and according to Michael A. Palladino in *American Biology Teacher,* "they do an excellent job of incorporating interesting and significant facts about the animals they study."

On his own, Behler authored *National Audubon Society First Field Guide: Reptiles,* part of the "First Field Guide" series produced by the National Audubon Society for young naturalists. The organization of the volume "make[s] it easy to identify each animal and its relatives," remarked Michele Snyder in *School Library Journal.* A contributor to *Appraisal,* in a review of the same book and three other works that launched the series, concluded that they were highly worthy additions to a library or nature lover's personal collection. "These little . . . books present a brief, competent, but interesting view with outstanding photography and descriptions," the reviewer concluded.

BIOGRAPHICAL AND CRITICAL SOURCES:

PERIODICALS

American Biology Teacher, May, 2000, Michael A. Palladino, review of *Alligators and Crocodiles,* p. 388.

American Reference Books Annual, 1981, Paul B. Cors, review of *The Audubon Society Field Guide to North American Reptiles and Amphibians,* pp. 676-677.

Appraisal, spring-summer-fall, 2000, review of *National Audubon Society First Field Guide: Reptiles,* p. 144.

Choice, April, 1980, review of *The Audubon Society Field Guide to North American Reptiles and Amphibians,* p. 243.

Library Journal, March 1, 1980, Katharine Galloway Garstka, review of *The Audubon Society Field Guide to North American Reptiles and Amphibians,* p. 623.

New Scientist, August 8, 1998, review of *Alligators and Crocodiles,* p. 46.

School Library Journal, July, 1999, Michele Snyder, review of *National Audubon Society First Field Guide: Reptiles,* pp. 103-104.

*   *   *

BEKOFF, Marc 1945-

PERSONAL: Born September 6, 1945, in Brooklyn, NY. *Education:* Washington University, A.B., 1967, Ph.D. (animal behavior), 1972; Hofstra University, M.A., 1968. *Hobbies and other interests:* Cycling, skiing, hiking, reading spy novels, cooking.

ADDRESSES: Home—296 Canyonside Dr., Boulder, CO 80302. *Office*—Department of EPO Biology, University of Colorado-Boulder, P.O. Box 334, Boulder, CO 80309-0334. *E-mail*—marc.bekoff@ colorado.edu.

CAREER: Educator, writer, and editor. University of Missouri, St. Louis, assistant professor of biology, 1973-74; University of Colorado-Boulder, professor of organismic biology. Coordinator of Jane Goodall's Roots and Shoots program; co-founder of Ethologists for the Ethical Treatment of Animals; affiliated with Science and the Spiritual Quest program and American Association for the Advancement of Science program on science, ethics, and religion. Member, board of directors, of Cougar Fund; member of advisory board, SINAPU.

MEMBER: Animal Behavior Society, American Society of Zoologists, American Society of Mammalogists.

AWARDS, HONORS: Guggenheim Memorial Foundation fellow, 1981; Exemplar Award, Animal Behavior Society, 2000, for major long-term contributions to the field of animal behavior.

WRITINGS:

(With Jim Carrier) *Nature's Life Lessons: Everyday Truths from Nature,* illustrated by Marjorie C. Leggitt, Fulcrum (Golden, CO), 1996.

(With Colin Allen) *Species of Mind: The Philosophy and Biology of Cognitive Ethology,* MIT Press (Cambridge, MA), 1997.

Strolling with Our Kin: Speaking for and Respecting Voiceless Animals (children's book), foreword by Jane Goodall, American Anti-Vivisection Society (Jenkintown, PA), 2000.

Minding Animals: Awareness, Emotions, and Heart, Oxford University Press (New York, NY), 2002.

(With Jane Goodall) *The Ten Trusts: What We Must Do to Care for the Animals,* HarperSanFrancisco (San Francisco, CA), 2002.

EDITOR

Coyotes: Biology, Behavior, and Management, Academic Press (New York, NY), 1978.

(With Gordon M. Burghardt) *The Development of Behavior: Comparative and Aspects,* Garland STPM Press (New York, NY), 1978.

(With Dale Jamieson) *Interpretation and Explanation in the Study of Behavior,* two volumes, Westview Press (Boulder, CO), 1990.

(With Dale Jamieson) *Readings in Animal Cognition,* MIT Press (Cambridge, MA), 1996.

(With John A. Byers) *Animal Play: Evolutionary, Comparative, and Ecological Perspectives,* Cambridge University Press (New York, NY), 1998.

(With Carron A. Meaney) *Encyclopedia of Animal Rights and Animal Welfare,* Greenwood Press (Westport, CT), 1998.

(With Colin Allen and George Lauder) *Nature's Purposes: Analyses of Function and Design Biology,* MIT Press (Cambridge, MA), 1998.

The Smile of a Dolphin: Remarkable Accounts of Animal Emotions, Discovery Books (New York, NY), 2000.

(With Colin Allen and Gordon M. Burghardt) *The Cognitive Animal: Empirical and Theoretical Perspectives on Animal Cognition,* MIT Press (Cambridge, MA), 2002.

Bekoff's children's book, *Strolling with Our Kin,* has been translated in Italian, German, and Chinese.

WORK IN PROGRESS: Wild Justice and Fair Play: Cooperation, Forgiveness, and Morality in Animals, a book on the evolution of cooperation and morality in animals; editor of three-volume *Encyclopedia of Animal Behavior.*

SIDELIGHTS: Dubbed by a reviewer for *Publishers Weekly* a "modern-day Dr. Dolittle who seeks to raise the level of human compassion toward animals," Marc Bekoff has authored or edited numerous books that help to prove that so-called lower animals exhibit what are thought of as human thought processes as well as emotions such as grief, fear, anger, love, and even compassion. "Basically, I am an animal rights advocate/activist with deep concerns about all animals, plants, bodies of water, the air we breathe, outer space, and inanimate landscapes," noted Bekoff on *AnaFlora. com.* Bekoff, a professor of organismic biology at the University of Colorado-Boulder, is a well-respected authority in his field who conducts research in animal behavior, cognitive ethology—the study of animal minds—and behavioral ecology. The author, coauthor, or editor of fourteen works on animal behavior and rights, as well as over 150 professional papers, Bekoff has had his work featured in national publications such as *Time* and *Life,* and on television programs from *Nature* to Discovery TV.

Born in Brooklyn, New York, in 1945, Bekoff earned his doctorate in animal behavior from Washington University. While taking up teaching duties at various universities, ultimately leading to his position as a professor at Colorado, he began publishing both articles and books on animal behavior and cognition. His first editorial effort, *Coyotes: Biology, Behavior, and Management,* collected a variety of articles on canid biology. A reviewer for *Choice* recommended the book for anyone wishing to "have an up-to-date encyclopedia on the coyote." Similarly, James Malcolm, reviewing *Coyotes* in *Science,* wrote that "both the authors and editor can be complimented on the consistently high standards of clarity and thoroughness maintained in the book."

Bekoff's subsequent editing tasks were likewise praised by critics. Reviewing his two-volume collection, *Interpretation and Explanation in the Study of*

Animal Behavior, Susan A. Foster, writing in *Quarterly Review of Biology,* noted that "it is my impression that the success of these volumes can be attributed, in large part, to the very high quality of editing." Foster went on to conclude, "The editors have done a fine job of compiling an interdisciplinary collection of essays on animal behavior." Many of the articles from those volumes were later collected in *Readings in Animal Cognition,* "a fine book, edited with care and comprised of thoughtful authors, each of whom argues compellingly for attention to major theoretical and practical issues," according to Craig Howard Kinsley in *Science Books and Films.* Herbert L. Roitblat, reviewing the collection in *American Journal of Psychology,* also found that "the book does an excellent job of presenting cognitive ethology in a way that makes clear its underlying assumptions and the issues that surround those assumptions." *Animal Play: Evolutionary, Comparative, and Ecological Perspectives* similarly won critical praise. This collection of studies on play behavior in a variety of animals, including man, was a "mental stimulus for students who are perhaps too narrowly entrenched in some research," according to F. S. Szalay in *Choice.* Summing up the thrust of the book in a *New Scientist* review, Gail Vines noted that "insights into the wellsprings of emotional health may come from a better understanding of how and why play has evolved in the animal kingdom." Peter H. Klopfer, however, reviewing *Animal Play* in *Quarterly Review of Biology,* faulted the contributors for not defining play. "Absent an all-encompassing and operational definition of play, there is little in this volume that offers the kind of evolutionary perspective that the editors desire to develop," Klopfer wrote. Lee C. Drickamer in *American Zoologist* was more positive, noting that the editors did a "commendable job" of stating the main themes, and that the book as a whole also "does a fine job of providing the reader with snapshots of where we stand with respect to key questions about play behavior."

With *Encyclopedia of Animal Rights and Animal Welfare,* Bekoff, in team with Carron A. Meaney, gathers 170 essays from a wide range of professional researchers in numerous fields to present a "welcome multidisciplinary approach that shows us the extensive roles nonhuman animals play in virtually all areas of our lives," according to *Library Journal*'s Peggie Partello. A *Booklist* contributor felt that, while "not encyclopedic," this volume "does have good descriptions of the animal rights movement, especially its impact on some types of medical research." *Choice*'s W. P. Hogan also found the book to be an "excellent contribution to the literature of animal rights and animal welfare."

The Smile of a Dolphin: Remarkable Accounts of Animal Emotions is another catalogue of animal behavior, in this case first-person accounts accompanied by "awe-evoking color photographs," as Karen Sokol described them in *School Library Journal,* which are intended to demonstrate that animals exhibit a wide range of emotional states. Sokol also called the text to the book a "treasure." Laura Tangley in *U.S. News and World Report* noted the evidence—both anecdotal and "hard" science—for the existence of animal emotions such as joy and grief, but also asked, rhetorically, "What difference does it really make?" Answering her own question, Tangley noted that "Bekoff, for one, hopes that greater understanding of what animals are feeling will spur more stringent rules on how animals should be treated, everywhere from zoos and circuses to farms and backyards."

As an author, Bekoff has also examined the emotional and cognitive states of animals. His *Species of Mind,* written with Colin Allen, is an argument for the existence of "conscious states to nonhuman organisms," according to Gary Purpura and Richard Samuels in *British Journal for the Philosophy of Science.* The same reviewers concluded that "there is much in *Species of Mind* that should be of interest to philosophers." In *Minding Animals: Awareness, Emotions, and Healing,* Bekoff tackles these subjects head on. "Bekoff has a talent for making his points by leading readers through the evidence for and against an issue and guiding them to a conclusion," noted *Booklist*'s Nancy Bent. Some, however, found Bekoff's anecdotal approach questionable. M. S. Grace, for example, writing in *Choice,* thought *Minding Animals* a "sickly sweet collection of stories." "Bekoff admits that his views are not held by the majority of scientists, but are gaining support," wrote a critic for *Science News.* Bekoff has also noted, as Tangley quoted, "'The plural of anecdote is data.'" E. S. Turner, writing in the *Times Literary Supplement,* acknowledged both sides of this critical divide, calling Bekoff's work an "oddly arranged, multifaceted book, stimulating and exasperating by turns." Rebecca Sanderman, reviewing *Minding Animals* in *M2 Best Books,* had more unqualified praise, calling it a "thoroughly engaging book about animals."

Bekoff has also teamed up with the well-known primatologist, Jane Goodall, to present a short course on what each individual can do to help treat animals better. Their *The Ten Trusts: What We Must Do to Care for the Animals We Love* is an "inspiring book," according to Partello in *Library Journal*. A reviewer for *Publishers Weekly* called the book a "prescriptive plan designed to protect animals as well as help educate people about the importance of saving both animals and the environment." Similarly, *Booklist*'s Donna Seaman found *The Ten Trusts* to be "an accessible, compelling, and important expose."

"Compassion begets compassion, cruelty begets cruelty," Bekoff told an interviewer for *AnaFlora.com*. "What we give we will ultimately receive. Nonhumans help make us human—they teach us respect, compassion, and unconditional love. When we mistreat animals we mistreat ourselves. When we destroy animal spirits and souls we destroy our own spirits and souls. The integrity and well-being of the universe depends on fostering and maintaining reciprocal and deep relationships and interconnections with all life."

BIOGRAPHICAL AND CRITICAL SOURCES:

PERIODICALS

American Journal of Psychology, winter, 1997, Herbert L. Roitblat, review of *Readings in Animal Cognition,* pp. 641-646.

American Scientist, January-February, 1999, Lee Alan Dugatkin, review of *Animal Play: Evolutionary, Comparative, and Ecological Perspectives,* pp. 86-87.

American Zoologist, December, 1998, Klaus Zuberbuhler, review of *Species of Mind: The Philosophy and Biology of Cognitive Ethology,* p. 983; April, 1999, Lee C. Drickamer, review of *Animal Play,* p. 463.

BioScience, March 1999, Laura Perini, review of *Nature's Purposes: Analyses of Function and Design Biology,* pp. 243-245.

Booklist, September 15, 1998, review of *Encyclopedia of Animal Rights and Animal Welfare,* p. 260; April 1, 2002, Nancy Bent, review of *Minding Animals: Awareness, Emotions, and Heart,* p. 1288; September 1, 2002, Donna Seaman, review of *The Ten Trusts: What We Must Do to Care for the Animals,* p. 3.

British Journal for the Philosophy of Science, June, 2000, Gary Purpura and Richard Samuels, review of *Species of Mind,* pp. 375-380.

Choice, September, 1978, review of *Coyotes: Biology, Behavior, and Management,* p. 901; November, 1998, W. P. Hogan, review of *Encyclopedia of Animal Rights and Animal Welfare,* p. 496; F. S. Szalay, review of *Animal Play,* p. 547; November, 2002, M. S. Grace, review of *Minding Animals,* p. 493.

Library Journal, April 15, 1998, Peggie Partello, review of *Encyclopedia of Animal Rights and Animal Welfare,* p. 68; November 1, 2001, John M. Kistler, review of *Strolling with Our Kin: Speaking for and Respecting Voiceless Animals,* p. 59; October 15, 2002, review of *The Ten Trusts,* p. 91.

M2 Best Books, October 18, 2002, Rebecca Sanderman, review of *Minding Animals.*

New Scientist, August 29, 1998, Gail Vines, review of *Animal Play,* p. 41.

Publishers Weekly, August 14, 2000, review of *Strolling with Our Kin,* p. 346; July 22, 2002, review of *The Ten Trusts,* p. 165.

Quarterly Review of Biology, March, 1992, Susan A. Foster, review of *Interpretation and Explanation in the Study of Animal Behavior,* pp. 67-68; March, 1997, Stephen J. Clark, review of *Readings in Animal Cognition,* p. 110; June, 1999, Peter H. Klopfer, review of *Animal Play,* p. 250; September, 1999, Heather Williams, review of *Species of Mind,* p. 367; December, 1999, Peter C. Wainwright, review of *Nature's Purposes,* p. 458.

School Library Journal, February, 2001, Karen Sokol, review of *The Smile of a Dolphin: Remarkable Accounts of Animal Emotions,* p. 144.

Science, October 27, 1978, James Malcolm, review of *Coyotes,* p. 424; August 14, 1998, R. McN. Alexander, review of *Nature's Purposes,* p. 924.

Science Books and Films, June, 1996, Craig Howard Kinsley, review of *Readings in Animal Cognition,* p. 135.

Science News, July 20, 2002, review of *Minding Animals,* p. 47.

Times Literary Supplement, October 11, 2002, E. S. Turner, review of *Minding Animals,* p. 32.

U.S. News and World Report, October 30, 2000, Laura Tangley, "Animal Emotions," p. 48.

ONLINE

AnaFlora.com, http://www.anaflora.com/ (March 26, 2003), interview with Bekoff.

Animal Protection Institute, http://www.api4animals. org/ (March 26, 2003), Camilla H. Fox, review of *Strolling with Our Kin.*

Cambridge University Press Web site, http://www.cup/ (March 26, 2003).

Ethological Ethics Web site, http://www. ethologicalethics.org/ (September 18, 2003).

Marc Bekoff Home page, http://www.literati.net/Bekoff (September 18, 2003).

Oxford University Press Web site, http://www.oup-usa. org/ (March 26, 2003).

Spirituality and Health Web site, http://www. spiritualityhealth.com/ (March 26, 2003), Frederic Brussart and Mary Ann Brussart, review of *The Ten Trusts.**

*   *   *

BELLONCI, Maria 1902-1986

PERSONAL: Born November 3, 1902 in Rome, Italy; died following a long illness, May 13, 1986, in Rome, Italy; daughter of Girolamo Vittoria (a professor of chemistry, University of Rome) and Felicita Bellucci Villavecchia; married Goffredo Bellonci (a journalist and critic), 1928.

CAREER: Journalist, reviewer, and author.

AWARDS, HONORS: Viareggio prize, 1939, for *Lucrezia Borgia.*

WRITINGS:

Lucrezia Borgia, la sua vita e i suoi tempi, Mondadori (Milan, Italy), 1939, translation by Bernard and Barbara Wall published as *The Life and Times of Lucrezia Borgia,* Grosset & Dunlap (New York, NY), 1939, reprinted, Phoenix Press (London, England), 2000.

Segreti dei Gonzaga (title means "Secrets of the Gonzagas"), Mondadori (Milan, Italy), 1947, translation by Stuart Hood published as *A Prince of Mantua: The Life and Times of Vincenzo Gonzaga,* Harcourt, Brace (New York, NY), 1956.

Milano Viscontea, Edizioni Radio Italiana (Turin, Italy), 1956.

Delitto di stato, Mondadori (Milan, Italy), 1961.

Pubblici segreti (title means "Public Secrets"), Mondadori (Milan, Italy), 1965.

(With Andrea Mantegna and Niny Garavaglia) *L'opera completa del Mantegna,* Rizzoli (Milan, Italy), 1967.

Piccolo romanzo di Dorotea Gonzaga, e altre prose, Mondadori (Milan, Italy), 1968.

(With Giuseppe Tomasi di Lampedusa) *Il gattopardo,* Club Degli Editori (Milan, Italy), 1969.

Come un racconto gli anni del Premio Strega (title means "The Years of the Strega Prize Told like a Story"), Mondadori (Milan, Italy), 1971.

Tu vipera gentile (title means "O, Noble Viper"), Mondadori (Milan, Italy), 1972.

(With Dell'Acqua Gian Alberto and Carlo Perogalli) *I Visconti a Milano,* Cassa di Risparmio delle Provincie Lombarde (Milan, Italy), 1977.

Rinascimento privato, Mondadori (Milan, Italy), 1985, translation by William Weaver published as *Private Renaissance,* Morrow (New York, NY), 1989.

Io e il Premio Strega, Mondadori (Milan, Italy), 1987.

Segni sul muro, Mondadori (Milan, Italy), 1988.

Pubblici segreti N.Z., Mondadori (Milan, Italy), 1989.

Opere, edited by Ernesto Ferrero, Mondadori (Milan, Italy), 1994.

(Author of introduction) Gaspara Stampa, *Rime,* Rizzoli (Milan, Italy), 1994.

TRANSLATOR

Emile Zola, *Nana,* Casini (Florence, Italy), 1955.

Stendhal, *Vanina Vanini e altre cronache italiane,* Mondadori (Milan, Italy), 1961.

Alexandre Dumas, *I tre moschettieri,* Giunti-Marzocco (Florence, Italy), 1977.

Marco Polo, *Il Milione ERI,* [Turin, Italy], 1982.

Jules Verne, *Viaggio al centro della terra,* Giunti-Marrocco (Florence, Italy), 1983.

Stendahl, *La duchessa di Paliano,* Mondadori (Milan, Italy), 1994.

Contributor to periodicals such as *Il Veltro, Nemla Italian Studie,* and *Lettere-Italiane.* Bellonci's works have been translated into a variety of languages, including Spanish, French, Polish, Japanese, and German.

ADAPTATIONS: Delitto di Stato was made into a film for television, directed by Guiseppe de Bosio, 1982.

SIDELIGHTS: Maria Bellonci was an Italian writer and translator who wrote fictional but historically accurate accounts of notable figures such as Lucrezia Borgia and Vincenzo Gonzaga. A lifelong resident of Rome, she was deeply involved in the literature of her time. Active during the years from 1930 to 1986, Bellonci furthered the pursuit of Italian literature with gatherings of dedicated writers and intellectuals. She helped found the premio Strega, Italy's prestigious literary prize, in 1944; Bellonci was herself the recipient of this honor in 1985.

Born Maria Villavecchia on November 3, 1902, in Rome, she was the oldest of four children of "a family of the upper bourgeoise that prided itself on its aristocratic roots," according to Angela M. Jeannet in the *Dictionary of Literary Biography.* "Bellonci's education was the standard one for many girls of her social class: excellent, thorough, and humanistic, with extensive grounding in the classics, music, and the arts," Jeannet wrote.

Bellonci began writing while relatively young, finishing a novel, later discarded, at age twenty. Her first published work was *Lucrezia Borgia, la sua vita e i suio tempi* (*The Life and Times of Lucrezia Borgia*), published in 1939. The book is a thoroughly researched, fact-based but fictionalized account of Borgia, the daughter of Pope Alexander VI. "Writing about Lucrezia, who lived from 1480 to 1519, Bellonci dissects the power struggles at the papal court with vivid detail, skillfully reconstructing the events and the passions that shaped the creation of the modern age," Jeannet wrote. Bellonci's novel recounts Borgia's life from a child already promised to more than one political marriage, to an adolescent used in a variety of political power plays by her father, to a mature woman of multiple marriages and mysteries. "Bellonci provides a documented rather than a mythical portrait of Lucrezia and thereby rescues her from the lurid legends her life inspired," Jeannet remarked.

In *Segreti dei Gonzaga,* published in 1947, Bellonci again uses a type of documentary fiction to write about Vincenzo Gonzaga, ruler of Mantua in the late sixteenth century. The three sections of the book chronicle Gonzaga's life from birth to his assumption of the crown and his death. Bellonci details the political intrigues, courtly maneuverings, territorial skirmishes, and power shifts inherent in a royal court and those specific to Gonzaga's rule.

Pubblici segreti, a collection of nonfiction pieces, was published in 1965. The book consists of book reviews, travel diaries, and essays Bellonci wrote for *Il Punto* from 1958 to 1964 that cover cultural events and contemporary issues. A second volume, *Pubblici segreti N.Z.,* published posthumously, collects her articles from *Il Messaggero* from 1964 to 1970. "Her concise pieces demonstrate her consummate skill, attention to detail, and control of her medium" Jeannet remarked. "Their broad range attests to her intellectual curiosity, vast culture, and enthusiasm for life. The entire spectrum of Italian cultural life opens up, drawn by the inimitable pen of a woman who was a close observer of and often a participant in the significant events that took place from the 1930s to the 1980s."

Bellonci's 1971 book, *Come un racconto gli anni del Premio Strega,* recounts her role in the creation and promotion of the Strega prize, a prestigious literary award in Italian letters. Toward the end of World War II, Bellonci and her husband, Goffredo, hosted regular Sunday gatherings of literary luminaries at their home. The effects of the war were still palpably visible in Rome, but the group continued to meet despite hardships, eventually coalescing into the original jury that selected exemplary works of fiction from submissions offered by publishers. The Belloncis formalized the prize with financing from the Alberti family, producers of Strega liqueur. Bellonci acted as manager and director of the prize for more than forty years. "The authors who vied for the Premio Strega include the most important names in contemporary Italian letters," Jeannet wrote. *Come un racconto gli anni del Premio Strega* traces the events leading up to the creation of the prize, including the inevitable feuds, rivalries, and triumphs. "Bellonci writes not only of the enthusiasm and energy that went into the establishment of a literary prize but also the fun that attended it," Jeannet observed. Bellonci's efforts to create the prize in the latter war years "made a crucial contribution to the revival of cultural life in Italy at a time when the country lay mortified by military defeat, torn by civil war, and weakened by physical devastation as well as economic ruin." Jeannet remarked.

Tu vipera gentile, published in 1971, contains three Bellonci novellas. In the first, *Delitto di stato* ("Crime for Reasons of State"), a royal courtier of the Gonzaga family arranges several murders to avoid the revelation of a shameful and lurid Gonzaga secret; in *Soccorso a Dorotea* ("Help for Dorotea") the title character is jilted by a royal suitor and dies in the humiliation of rejection; in the title novella, Bellonci relates the story of the various rulers of Milan from 1277 to 1447. "The novellas explore all aspects of our common human experience: love's secret passions, bound with political transgressions, the fleeting movements of feigned emotions, the pain held inside the face of pitiless onlookers, the questions asked in the secrecy of a conscience, and the mutual pacts made silently in conjugal love," Jeannet wrote.

Bellonci's final written work, *Rinascimento privato* ("Private Renaissance"), is another well-documented but fictionalized story, this one about Renaissance noblewoman Isabella d'Este. "Isabella appears briefly in every book Bellonci wrote," Jeannet observed, "and this last novel, Bellonci's most powerfully constructed and the most lovingly executed, is dedicated to her." Written in the form of a journal, the book explores d'Este's daydreams, doubts, and daily life. She is "depicted as a mature woman reflecting on her life and the events in which she played a large part," Jeannet stated. As she sits alone in the "Clocks Room" of her palace, each toll of the clocks peels back the years. She relives a life that brought her in contact with kings, popes, intellectuals, and scoundrels. "Again and again in Bellonci's account of her life, we see evidence of a powerful, synthesizing imagination that renders her worthy not only of the lucid intelligence embodied in Leonard da Vinci's famous portrait, but also of this lively and imaginative chronicle," wrote Rita Signorelli-Pappas in *World Literature Today.* Carol A. Crotta, writing in the *Los Angeles Times Book Review,* called the English translation of the book "a narrative of great energy and power," while Brad Hooper, in *Booklist,* wrote that *Rinascimento privato* is a "soundly prepared fathoming of past times and personalities." With the book, "Bellonci reaches the peak of her art, and Isabella reaches her fullest development," Jeannet remarked.

"Writing for Bellonci is a life passion," Jeannet observed, "literary creation is a willful construction; and literature is the field for the discovery of deep affinities among writers, across the centuries." Bellonci died on May 13, 1986, in Rome.

BIOGRAPHICAL AND CRITICAL SOURCES:

BOOKS

Dictionary of Literary Biography, Volume 196: *Italian Novelists Since World War II, 1965-1995,* Gale (Detroit, MI), 1999.

PERIODICALS

Booklist, September 1, 1984, review of *The Travels of Marco Polo,* pp. 18-19; February 15, 1989, Brad Hooper, review of *Private Renaissance,* p. 974; May 1, 1990, review of *Pubblici segreti,* pp. 1688-1689.
Geographical Journal, November, 1986, John Black, review of *The Travels of Marco Polo,* p. 415.
Library Journal, March 1, 1989, Jack Shreve, review of *Private Renaissance,* p. 87.
Los Angeles Times Book Review, June 4, 1989, Carol A. Crotta, review of *Private Renaissance,* p. 17.
Publishers Weekly, January 20, 1989, Sybil Steinberg, review of *Private Renaissance,* pp. 137-138.
Tribune Books (Chicago, IL), March 12, 1989, Constance Markey, review of *Private Renaissance,* p. 7.
West Coast Review of Books, January, 1985, review of *The Travels of Marco Polo,* p. 41.
World Literature Today, winter, 1987, Rita Signorelli-Pappas, review of *Rinascimento privato,* pp. 82-83.

OBITUARIES:

PERIODICALS

Times (London, England), May 16, 1986.*

*   *   *

BELLOSI, Luciano 1936-

PERSONAL: Born July 7, 1936, in Florence, Italy; son of Enrico (a gardener) and Maria (a domestic worker; maiden name, Cuccuini) Bellosi. *Education:* Attended University of Florence. *Religion:* Roman Catholic. *Hobbies and other interests:* Tennis.

ADDRESSES: Home—Via A. Manzoni 3, 50121 Florence, Italy. *Office*—University of Siena, Via Roma 56, 53100 Siena, Italy.

CAREER: Educator, historian, and author. Art historian and superintendent of art gallery in Florence, Italy, 1969-79; University of Siena, Siena, Italy, professor of history of medieval art, 1979—, director of department of archaeology and art history, 1983-86. *Military service:* Served in Italian armed forces, 1963-64.

MEMBER: Accademie degli Intronoti.

AWARDS, HONORS: Premio Viareggio, 1974.

WRITINGS:

Buffalmacco e il Trinfo della Morte, Einaudi (Turin, Italy), 1974.

Il museo dell'Ospedale degli Innocenti, Electa (Milan, Italy), 1977.

Giotto, Scala Books (New York, NY), 1981, published as *Giotto: Complete Works,* Riverside Book Co. (New York, NY), 1993.

La pecora di Giotto, Einaudi (Turin, Italy), 1985, translation published as *Duccio: The Maesta,* Thames & Hudson (New York, NY), 1999.

Cimabue, Federico Motta (Milan, Italy), 1998, translated by Jay Hyams, Alexandra Bonfante-Warren, and Frank Dabell, Abbeville Press (New York, NY), 1998.

Come un prato fiorito: studi sull'arte tardogotica, Jaca (Milan, Italy), 2000.

(Editor) *Le arti figuative nelle corti dei malatesti,* B. Ghigi (Rimini, Italy), 2002.

Contributor to exhibition catalogs and other reference books. Contributor to professional journals, including *Burlington.*

SIDELIGHTS: Luciano Bellosi told *CA:* "My primary motivation for writing is my great interest in the research on Italian Renaissance art. My work is particularly influenced by my master, the great Italian art historian Roberto Longhi.

"My writing process is to detect the many problems of Italian Renaissance art that are yet unsolved. It is like constructing a detective story. I use my eyes to understand and to 'read' the works of art, and then I confront them with the information we have about artists. I have to read many books and sometimes archival documents.

"The many works of art which reflect an 'environmental context' in the country where I live inspires me to write on the subjects that I choose."

BENNETT, Frederick 1928-

PERSONAL: Born October 10, 1928, in OH; married Margaret Bennett (an artist), 1972. *Education:* John Carroll University, B.A.; University of New Mexico, M.A.; University of Utah, Ph.D.

ADDRESSES: Home—770 Palm Ave., No. 401, Sarasota, FL 34236. *Office*—P.O. Box 3133, Sarasota, FL 34230. *E-mail*—bennett@fabenbooks.com.

CAREER: Author of nonfiction.

WRITINGS:

Computers as Tutors: Solving the Crisis in Education, Faban (Sarasota, FL), 1999.

*   *   *

BERGER, Todd R. 1968-

PERSONAL: Born January 11, 1968, in Madison, WI; son of Richard Berger (a law firm administrator) and Marjorie (Guelzow) Harris (a psychologist). *Ethnicity:* "White." *Education:* University of Wisconsin—Madison, B.A. (with distinction), 1991; attended Rheinische Friedrich-Wilhelms Universität (Bonn, West Germany), 1988-89; studied editing, University of Minnesota—Minneapolis, 1994. *Politics:* "Democratic." *Religion:* Lutheran. *Avocational interest:* Photography, wilderness travel, canoeing.

ADDRESSES: Home—1503 St. Clair Ave., Ste. 3, St. Paul, MN 55105. *Office*—Hazelden Information and Educational Services, P.O. Box 176, Center City, MN 55012. *E-mail*—tberger168@email.msn.com.

CAREER: Voyageur Press, Stillwater, MN, editorial associate, 1993-97, acquisitions editor, 1997-2000; Hazelden Information & Educational Services, Center City, MN, acquisitions editor, 2000—. Taught English and German to Trnava, Slovakia, high school students; news copywriter, interviewer, and announcer for two Madison, WI, commercial radio stations; KSKA Public Radio, production staff assistant.

MEMBER: North American Nature Photographers' Association, Dog Writers' Association of America, Professional Editors' Network—Minnesota Chapter.

WRITINGS:

EDITOR

Love of Labs, Voyageur Press (Stillwater, MN), 1997.
Love of Goldens, Voyageur Press (Stillwater, MN), 1998.
Majestic Elk, Voyageur Press (Stillwater, MN), 1998.
100 Years of Hunting: The Ultimate Tribute to Our Hunting Heritage, Voyageur Press (Stillwater, MN), 1999.
Love of German Shepherds, Voyageur Press (Stillwater, MN), 1999.
Majestic Mule Deer, Voyageur Press (Stillwater, MN), 1999.
Love of Dogs, Voyageur Press (Stillwater, MN), 1999.
Labs Afield, Voyageur Press (Stillwater, MN), 2000.
Love of Spaniels, Voyageur Press (Stillwater, MN), 2000.
Goldens Forever, Voyageur Press (Stillwater, MN), 2001.
Lighthouses of the Great Lakes, Voyageur Press (Stillwater, MN), 2002.

*   *   *

BESSIRE, Mark H. C. 1964-

PERSONAL: Born June 28, 1964; son of Henry (a management consultant) and Louise (a chaplain) Bessire; married August 12, 1991; wife's name Aimée (a professor of African art history); children: Blakey, Clay. *Education:* New York University, B.A., 1986; Hunter College of the City University of New York, M.A., 1992; Columbia University, M.B.A., 1994.

ADDRESSES: Home—20 Salem St., Portland, ME 04102. *Office*—Institute of Contemporary Art, Maine College of Art, 522 Congress, Portland, ME 04101. *E-mail*—mbessire@mcca.edu.

CAREER: Museum director, curator, and author. Whitney Museum of American Art, New York, NY, curatorial assistant, research assistant, then curator, 1987-89;

Hunter College of the City University of New York, curatorial assistant, 1990; Chase Manhattan Bank, New York, NY, registrar for Chase art program, 1991; Harvard University, Cambridge, MA, co-curator of exhibition at William Hayes Fogg Art Museum, 1996-2001, director of research, 1996-97, acting exhibitions coordinator for university art museums, 1997, academic dean and Allston Burr senior tutor, 1997-98; Maine College of Art, Portland, director of Institute of Contemporary Art, 1998—. Danforth Gallery, curator of "Generation X" at Maine Artists Space, 2000.

AWARDS, HONORS: Helena Rubinstein fellow, 1988; Fulbright fellow in Tanzania, 1995-96.

WRITINGS:

(With others) *The Sukuma,* Rosen Publishing (New York, NY), 1996.
Great Zimbabwe, Dillon Press (New Jersey), 1998.
Beyond Decorum: The Photography of Iké Udé, MIT Press (Cambridge, MA), 2000.
(Editor) *Wena Gu: Art from Middle Kingdom to Biological Millennium,* MIT Press (Cambridge, MA), 2003.

Author of exhibition catalogs and brochures. Contributor to periodicals, including *Art Journal, East African, Jambo, Museum International,* and *Boston Book Review.*

*   *   *

BILLHEIMER, John (W.)

PERSONAL: Born in WV; married; two children. *Education:* University of Detroit, B.S., 1961; Massachusetts Institute of Technology, M.S. (electrical engineering), 1962; Stanford University, Ph.D. (industrial engineering, operations research), 1971. *Hobbies and other interests:* Tennis, cinema.

ADDRESSES: Office—Systan, Inc., 343 Second St., P.O. Box U, Los Altos, CA 94022. *E-mail*—john@ systan.com.

CAREER: Engineer and novelist. Stanford Research Institute, Menlo Park, CA, senior operations analyst for management systems division, 1963-72; Systan,

Inc., Los Altos, CA, vice president, 1972—. California Motorcycle Safety Program, cofounder; member of California Transportation Research Board committee on traffic law enforcement, 1984—, committee on HOV lanes, 1993—, and chairman of committee on motorcycles and mopeds, 1994—.

AWARDS, HONORS: Pyke Johnson Award, Transportation Research Board, 1978, for outstanding paper published in the field of transportation systems planning and administration; *The Contrary Blues* named among ten best mysteries of 1998, *Drood Review.*

WRITINGS:

MYSTERY NOVELS

The Contrary Blues, St. Martin's Press (New York, NY), 1998.
Highway Robbery, St. Martin's Minotaur (New York, NY), 2000.
Dismal Mountain, St. Martin's Minotaur (New York, NY), 2001.
Drybone Hollow, St. Martin's Minotaur (New York, NY), 2003.

SIDELIGHTS: John Billheimer is the author of a series of mystery novels featuring fictional amateur sleuth Owen Allison. The "Allison" novels are set in West Virginia, where Billheimer was born and raised; the first, *The Contrary Blues,* takes place in the fictional town of Contrary. The action begins when the town is granted federal money for its bus system and mistakenly receives enough to maintain twenty buses rather than the two it owns. Instead of correcting the error, the townspeople decide to distribute the extra money around town. When a Department of Transportation auditor sent to check on the money winds up dead, a second federal auditor, Allison, is sent from Washington, D.C. to find out where the money has gone and how the first auditor died. "The plot is not the driving force behind the story, yet there is no shortage of action," noted observed Andy Plonka in *The Mystery Reader.* ". . . What compels the reader to pay attention is the description of the town itself and its inhabitants."

Allison returns to West Virginia in *Highway Robbery,* Billheimer's second novel, when a construction crew finds a skeleton Allison's mother believes may belong

to her late husband. While investigating this mystery, Allison uncovers many issues from his own past. *Drood Review* writer Craig Beresford described the book as "hugely successful, both as a mystery story and a novel." Reviewer Harriet Klausner also praised *Highway Robbery* in an online review for *Under the Covers,* calling the book "a delight due to the plausibility of the present and past killings, which allow the reader to further focus on Owen, who deserves future appearances."

In *BookReview.com,* Klausner described *Dismal Mountain* as "exciting" and noted that it "highlights the environmental vs. economy issue." In this book, Allison returns to West Virginia to defend his Aunt Lizzie against murder charges of which he knows she is innocent, despite her confession. The plot thickens with the addition of a corrupt hospital and disreputable construction company. *Booklist* contributor David Pitt observed that "Billheimer's characters are so vividly drawn they threaten to wander off the page and into the real world" and described the book as "a first-rate crime novel."

In *Drybone Hollow,* the fourth book to feature Allison, a dam breaks, filling the town of Contrary with coal sludge and killing four residents. When a mine owner asks Allison to investigate, he uncovers a story of corruption and greed. *Booklist's* David Pitt, again praised the author's work, writing: "In a genre laden with too many amateur sleuths, Allison is a fresh protagonist with an unusual pedigree." Remarked a *Kirkus* reviewer: "Soap opera aside, Billheimer constructs a puzzle so ingenious that . . . readers should a seen it coming—but they won't."

BIOGRAPHICAL AND CRITICAL SOURCES:

PERIODICALS

Booklist, May 15, 2001, David Pitt, review of *Dismal Mountain,* p. 1735; February 15, 2003, David Pitt, review of *Drybone Hollow,* pp. 1052-1053.
Kirkus Reviews, February 1, 2003, Ruth Cohen, review of *Drybone Hollow,* p. 185.
Palo Alto Weekly, October 7, 1998, Don Kazak, "A Swindle Unravels."
Publishers Weekly, April 6, 1998, review of *The Contrary Blues,* p. 62; January 31, 2000, review of *Highway Robbery,* p. 85; June 18, 2001, review of *Dismal Mountain,* p. 62; March 3, 2003, review of *Drybone Hollow,* p. 57.

ONLINE

Book Review.com, http://www.bookreview.com/ (June 3, 2003), Harriet Klausner, review of *Dismal Mountain.*

Drood Review, http://www.mysterynet.com/ (June 4, 2003), Craig Beresford, review of *Highway Robbery.*

John Billheimer Home Page, http://www.angelfire.com/ab6/ab664/ (June 4, 2003).

Mystery Reader, http://www.themysteryreader.com/ (June 4, 2003), Andy Plonka, review of *The Contrary Blues.*

Under the Covers, http://www.silcom.com/~manatee/ (November 28, 1999), Harriet Klausner, review of *Highway Robbery.**

* * *

BOYD, Greg 1957-

PERSONAL: Born March 8, 1957, in Utica, NY; son of Charles R. Boyd (a businessman) and Marjorie Pusateri Casey (a teacher); married 1982; wife's name Donna E.; children: Eric Benjamin. *Education:* California State University—Northridge, B.A. (English), 1979, M.A. (English), 1985.

ADDRESSES: Home—5847 Sawmill Road, Paradise, CA 95969. *E-mail*—asyarts@sunset.net.

CAREER: Writer and artist. California State University, Northridge, instructor of English, 1985-88; Unicorn Press, Greensboro, NC, artist-in-residence, 1988-89; Microwave Applications Group, Santa Maria, CA, technical publications specialist, 1990-92.

AWARDS, HONORS: Wormwood Award, 1982; Meritorious Performance and Professional Promise Award, California State University, 1986.

WRITINGS:

(Editor) *Circus Deluxe* (poems), Jump River Press (Prentice, WI), 1982.

(Translator, with Charles Baudelaire) *La fanfarlo* (fiction), Creative Arts (Berkeley, CA), 1986.

The Masked Ball (prose poems), Unicorn Press (Greensboro, NC), 1987

Balzac's Dolls, and Other Essays, Studies, and Literary Sketches, Legerete Press (Daphne, AL), 1987.

Puppet Theatre (prose poems), Unicorn Press (Greensboro, NC), 1989.

Water and Power (short stories), Asylum Arts (Santa Maria, CA), 1991.

(Editor) *Unscheduled Departures: The Asylum Anthology of Short Fiction,* Asylum Arts (Santa Maria, CA), 1991

Carnival Aptitude (short stories), Asylum Arts (Santa Maria, CA), 1993.

Sacred Hearts (novel), Hi Jinx Press (Davis, CA), 1996.

Modern Love and Other Tall Tales (short stories), Red Hen Press (Los Angeles, CA), 2000.

The Double: Doppelangelganger (novel), Leaping Dog Press (Chantilly, VA), 2002.

The Nambuli Papers, Leaping Dog Press (Chantilly, VA), 2004.

Editor, *Asylum* (later *Asylum Annual*), 1985-95.

* * *

BOYSSON-BARDIES, Bénédicte
  See de BOYSSON-BARDIES,Bénédicte de

* * *

BRADLEE, Frederic 1920-2003

OBITUARY NOTICE—See index for *CA* sketch: Born February 6, 1920, in New York, NY; died July 12, 2003, in New York, NY. Actor and author. Bradlee was an actor who appeared in a number of New York stage productions. Attending Harvard University and Columbia University prior to World War II, he served in the U.S. Army during the war, and returned to appear in Broadway, off-Broadway, and touring-company productions. Among his credits are theatrical productions of *A Winter's Tale, The Man Who Came to Dinner, Arms and the Man,* and *Second Threshold,* as well as the 1975 solo play *The Glory of Language.* In addition, Bradlee coedited the anthology *Vanity Fair*

(1961), with Cleveland Amory, and was the author of the novel *Esperie* (1967) and the memoir *A Lady in My Life* (1974). His later years were spent doing volunteer work for such organizations as the Opera Orchestra of New York, Reading for the Blind, and the International Council on Alcoholism.

OBITUARIES AND OTHER SOURCES:

PERIODICALS

New York Times, July 16, 2003, p. A16.
Washington Post, July 14, 2003, p. B4.

*   *   *

BRADLEY, Thomas Iver 1954-
(Tom Bradley)

PERSONAL: Born March 17, 1954, in Salt Lake City, UT; son of Iver Edwin (a professor) and Jane Frances (a teacher; maiden name, Glover) Bradley. *Ethnicity:* "Anglo-Saxon/Celtic." *Education:* University of Utah, Ph.D. (English literature).

ADDRESSES: Home—Nagasaki, Japan. *Agent*—c/o Author Mail, Infinity Publishing.com, 519 West Lancaster Ave., Haverford, PA 19041. *E-mail*—TBradley@ literati.net.

CAREER: Educator, novelist, author of short fiction, and musician. Worked as an English literature professor in Japanese and Chinese universities. Harpist, performing solo classical works.

MEMBER: PEN.

AWARDS, HONORS: Seaton Prize for Fiction, and AWP award finalist, both 1981; Editors Book Award nomination, and *Abiko Quarterly* Prize, both 1989, both for *Kara-Kun/Flip-Kun;* New York University Bobst Award nomination, 1992; HarperCollins/3AM Fiction award, 2002; several Pushcart Prize nominations for short fiction.

WRITINGS:

UNDER NAME TOM BRADLEY

Acting Alone (novel), Browntrout (San Francisco, CA), 1994.

The Spirit of Writing, J. P. Tarcher (New York, NY), 2001.
Kara-Kun/Flip-Kun, Infinity Press (Haverford, PA), 1999.
The Curved Jewels, Infinity Press (Haverford, PA), 2000.
Husting the East (contains *Kara-Kun/Flip-Kun* and *The Curved Jewels*), Xlibris (Philadelphia, PA), 2000.
Killing Bryce, Infinity Press (Haverford, PA), 2001.
Black Class Cur, Infinity Press (Haverford, PA), 2001.

Contributor to periodicals and Web zines, including *Salon.com, McSweeney's, Exquisite Corpse,* and *Poets & Writers.*

SIDELIGHTS: Tom Bradley told *CA:* "I have published five novels tracing the not-quite-career of a seedy member of the lumpen-intelligentsia named Sam Edwine. The first novel in the series, *Killing Bryce,* examines the disintegration of the Edwines, a family of gigantic Jack-Mormons. In *Acting Alone* Sam tries to get hired as ghost-writer for a recently released hostage of Islamic fundamentalists. *Black Class Cur* finds Sam in China in the halcyon days just before the student democracy movement gave the Party the excuse it needed to slam a lid on everything. *Kara-Kun/Flip-Kun* can be read as a portrait of contemporary Hiroshima, where Sam brings the expatriate community face to face with the Japanese mafia. *The Curved Jewels* shows the crown princess of Japan experiencing understandable second thoughts about being wed to the grandson of Hirohito, and fleeing the imperial palace with Sam's help."

Bradley's short stories have been nominated for Pushcart Prizes, and several of his works have been translated into Japanese.

BIOGRAPHICAL AND CRITICAL SOURCES:

ONLINE

Tom Bradley Web site, http://www.tombradley.org (November 20, 2003).

*   *   *

BRADLEY, Tom
See BRADLEY, Thomas Iver

BRAILSFORD, Dennis 1925-

PERSONAL: Born November 18, 1925, in Mansfield, Nottingham, England. *Education:* Cambridge University, M.A., 1953; University of Southampton, Ph.D., 1966.

ADDRESSES: Agent—c/o Author Mail, Lutterworth Press, P.O. Box 60, Cambridge CB1 2NT, England.

CAREER: Historian and author. North Worcestershire College, Worchestershire, England, former director; University of Birmingham, honorary research fellow. National Association of Citizens' Advice Bureau, England), chair, 1972-77.

WRITINGS:

Sport and Society: Elizabeth to Ann, Routledge and Kegan Paul (London, England), 1969.
Bareknuckles: A Social History of Prize-fighting, Lutterworth Press (Cambridge, England), 1988.
Sport, Time, and Society: The British at Play, Routledge (New York, NY), 1991.
British Sport: A Society History, Barnes and Noble (Lanham, MD), 1992, revised edition, Lutterworth Press (Cambridge, England), 1992.
A Taste for Diversions: Sport in Georgian England, Lutterworth Press (Cambridge, England), 1999.

Contributor of articles and reviews to periodicals.

BIOGRAPHICAL AND CRITICAL SOURCES:

ONLINE

Lutterworth Press Web site, http://www.lutterworth.com/ (November 16, 2003).

*　　*　　*

BRASHARES, Ann 1967-

PERSONAL: Born 1967, in Chevy Chase, MD; married Jacob Collins (an artist); children: Sam, Nathaniel, Susannah. *Education:* Attended Barnard College, studied philosophy.

ADDRESSES: Home—Brooklyn, NY. *Agent*—c/o Author Mail, Delacorte Press, 1540 Broadway, New York, NY 10036.

CAREER: Writer and editor.

AWARDS, HONORS: Best Book for Young Adults citation, American Library Association, and Book Sense Book of the Year, both 2002, both for *The Sisterhood of the Traveling Pants.*

WRITINGS:

The Sisterhood of the Traveling Pants, Delacorte (New York, NY), 2001.
Linus Torvalds: Software Rebel (nonfiction; "Techies" series), Twenty-first Century Books (Brookfield, CT), 2001.
Steve Jobs: Think Different (nonfiction; "Techies" series), Twenty-first Century Books (Brookfield, CT), 2001.
The Second Summer of the Sisterhood, Delacorte (New York, NY), 2003.

ADAPTATIONS: The Sisterhood of the Traveling Pants was been adapted for audiocassette by Listening Library, 2002, and film rights to the novel were purchased by Warner Bros.

SIDELIGHTS: Rule number one: "You must never wash the pants." Rule number two: "You must never double cuff the pants. It's tacky." Thus begin the ten commandments of *The Sisterhood of the Traveling Pants,* a young-adult novel penned by first-time novelist Ann Brashares and published in 2001. Rule number ten: "Remember: Pants equal Love. Love your pals. Love yourself." If there is a message in this "feel-good novel with substance," as a critic for *Kirkus Reviews* called the book, it is found in that final rule.

Long-time editor Brashares posits a new kind of sisterhood in her debut fiction bestseller, introducing four teenage girls who agree to send a pair of secondhand jeans from friend to friend the first summer they are to be separated. These traveling pants thus take on a metaphoric quality, uniting the best friends across the thousands of miles separating them.

Brashares, one of four children, grew up in Chevy Chase, Maryland, a very "Plain Jane" sort of place, as she noted in an autobiographical sketch on the Random House Web site. She and her three brothers attended Sidwell Friends, a Quaker school near Washington, D.C., and she was an avid reader, enjoying the works of Jane Austen, Charles Dickens, and other nineteenth-century writers. "When I was a kid, I had a scrapbook that I used to write letters in from places I wished I could have gone," Brashares noted on the Random House Web site. "I would imagine being in Argentina and then write about all the incredible things I was seeing there." Attending Barnard College, Brashares majored in philosophy and also met her future husband, artist Jacob Collins.

After graduation, Brashares took a year off before graduate school, planning to save money to pay for tuition. However, the job she took, working as an editor, was such a good fit that she never returned to school and instead made her career in publishing, working in children's books.

As an extension of her editorial work, Brashares gained authorial experience on two nonfiction titles, both published in 2001: *Steve Jobs: Think Different* and *Linus Torvalds: Software Rebel.* These books, Brashares related to Dave Weich in a *Powells.com* interview, "came out of an editing project." Brashares further explained, "I hadn't at any point considered myself an author of nonfiction. It was more a question of who was going to write those books, and I decided to try it. I was wearing a certain hat to do that project, and it was really fun, but I was functioning more as an editor, trying to come up with ideas for children's projects." Part of the "Techies" series for Twenty-first Century Books, Brashares's two nonfiction titles detail in brief format the lives of two computer and software pioneers.

Steve Jobs is a child of the 1960s who has become one of the most successful businessmen in the world, his name synonymous with Apple computers and Macintosh. Brashares traces Jobs's life from his youth traveling around the world in search of himself to his collaboration with Steve Wozniak during which the two made prototype PC's in a garage, to his departure and triumphant return to head Apple Computers. Linus Torvalds is the Finnish mastermind behind the open-source operating system known as Linux. His team-work approach to programming and the free access he

allows to his operating system have caused a revolution in computing. Reviewing *Steve Jobs* in *Voice of Youth Advocates,* Susan H. Levine praised the "breezy style, short length, large font, numerous photographs, and attractive page design" of the series. Similarly, Yapha Nussbaum Mason, writing in *School Library Journal,* found *Linus Torvalds* to be "fairly short and definitely accessible," with "appeal not only to report writers, but also to recreational readers."

While her nonfiction titles proved successful, Brashares always had the desire to write fiction. When she heard an appealing story about a traveling pair of pants, she saw the germ of an idea for a quirky novel. A woman Brashares worked with told her the story of one summer when she and her friends shared a pair of pants. Unfortunately, the pants were ultimately lost in Borneo. "My mind was immediately filled with all sorts of wonderful possibilities," Brashares noted on the Random House Web site. "I think pants have unique qualities, especially in a woman's life. Whatever bodily insecurities we have, we seem to take out on our pants. In high school, my friends would have their skinny pants and their fat pants. I like pants that allow women not to judge their bodies."

Brashares had also had another experience with shared clothing, as she recalled on the *BookBrowse* Web site. When she was planning her marriage, the sister of a friend offered her own bridal gown. Brashares at first turned down the offer, especially as the woman's own marriage had not been successful. Besides, she had envisioned the perfect gown for her and she was determined to find it. Then one night, this persistent donor came by with the wedding dress and Brashares discovered it was the exact dress she had been dreaming of. She wore it at her own wedding, and subsequently loaned it to other friends, creating a sort of "bond of the bridal gown." Taking these experiences together, as well as some of her own teenage angst and problems, Brashares came up with a fictional pair of pants that fit every body type and make the wearer feel loved. Brashares worked up a cast of characters to wear her magic pants, and an outline—a mixture of Greek myth and themes from movies such as *It's a Wonderful Life*—and then took the project to Random House, whose editors liked the idea.

The resulting book recounts the adventures of a group of girls who one summer decide to share a pair of jeans as a way of keeping their friendship alive. Carmen, Lena, Bridget, and Tibby are fifteen and have been best friends since childhood. Their mothers became friends when they enrolled in the same aerobics class together, and the four girls subsequently became bosom buddies, meeting periodically in the gym where their mothers had their classes. In the summer featured in *The Sisterhood of the Traveling Pants,* the friends will be separated for the first time: Carmen is planning to go to South Carolina and visit her divorced father; Lena is off to Greece to be with her grandparents; Bridget will be working out at a soccer camp in Baja California; and Tibby will stay at home in Washington, D.C., working in the local Wallman's drugstore. Before departure, Carmen has purchased a pair of jeans at a local thrift shop for less than four dollars. She decides to toss them, but when Tibby sees them she thinks she'd like them. Lena and Bridget also think they are fabulous. All the friends try on the pants, and they fit each in turn, even Carmen, who thinks she never looks good in anything. The friends decide these must be magic pants, for each of them has a distinctly different body type from the other girls. The night before departure they form the Sisterhood of the Traveling Pants, agreeing to a set of rules and behavior regarding the pants. (Rule number 4: "You must never let a boy take off the pants (although you may take them off yourself in his presence.)" Each friend will wear the pants for a week, and then send them on to the next wearer. The pants become a link between the members of the sisterhood.

If the pants seemed magical at first, the four girls soon realize they can not help them solve the problems each encounters that summer; such solutions must come from inner understanding. The pants, however, serve as a reminder that none of the friends are alone. Each learns to deal with individual problems and learn some elemental life lessons. Carmen's dream of spending time alone with her dad is thwarted when she discovers he is on the verge of marrying into a brand new family in South Carolina. Lena in Greece falls for Kostos, a family friend, but their relationship becomes marred when she accuses him, mistakenly, of spying on her while she is skinny dipping. Bridget also has romantic problems, falling in love with one of the counselors, something that is definitely off-limits at the camp. And Tibby, who has stayed home, becomes friends with a young girl, Bailey, who is suffering from leukemia. Together these two are making a documentary film about odd but interesting people, but when Bailey becomes so ill that she must go to the hospital, Tibby is confronted with the specter of death for the first time.

The pants connect the four friends, but they are not magic after all. "The pants are just pants," wrote Frances Bradburn in *Booklist,* "and life is just life, full of joys, sorrows, living, and dying. This is the charm of *The Sisterhood of the Traveling Pants.*" Brashares' unique coming-of-age novel won further critical praise from *New York Times* reviewer Christine Leahy, who called the characters "winning and precocious" and praised the narrative pace, noting that the "story zips along, bouncing faster than the jeans from girl to girl." Linda Bindner, reviewing the title in *School Library Journal,* also lauded Brashares's story-telling skills, remarking that the author "deftly moves from narrative to narrative, weaving together themes from the mundane to the profoundly important." Bindner further felt that Brashares created a "complex book about a solid group of friends." A contributor for *Kirkus Reviews* found that Brashares "renders each girl individual and lovable in her own right," while in *Horn Book* Jennifer M. Brabander praised the life lessons learned in this "breezy feel-good book." Reviewing the novel in *Voice of Youth Advocates,* teen critic Deana Rutherford mentioned that *The Sisterhood of the Traveling Pants* was "enjoyable and meaningful at the same time, and that's sometimes a hard thing to find in YA literature." And James Blasingame, writing in *Journal of Adolescent and Adult Literacy,* echoed something the book's sales figures had already established: "Ann Brashares's first fiction attempt is a successful one."

As Brashares noted on the Random House Web site, the characters in her book grew out of different parts of her own personality. "Carmen was the girl who said things I could never say and Bridget was the girl who did things I would never do." Speaking with Weich, Brashares also noted that she wanted to use the idea of the pants as a "repository of friendship—love, hope, challenges, all of those things." She also remarked to Weich that stay-at-home Tibby is the one who seems to grow and learn the most about herself during this one turbulent summer. "She's the one who's shaken up the most," Brashares commented. "The idea that that can happen at home was something I wanted to present." Brashares, the mother of three, has her own favorite pants: red ones that "make me feel loved even through major body transitions (like having a baby!)," as she remarked on the Random House site.

In a review of *The Sisterhood of the Traveling Pants,* a critic for *Publishers Weekly* called Brashares's novel an "outstanding and vivid book that will stay with readers for a long time." The same reviewer also noted that readers "will hope that Brashares chronicles the sisterhood for volumes to come." Brashares did exactly that, with the 2003 sequel, *The Second Summer of the Sisterhood.* In this take, the four girls are sixteen, and Bridget takes off for Alabama, Lena spends time with Kostos, Carmen is afraid her mother is going to make a fool of herself over a man, and Tibby takes a film course instead of spending another summer at Wallman's. Writing in *Horn Book,* Brabander suggested that "Fans of the first book . . . will eagerly travel with the sisterhood again." Offering warm words for the author's ability to present a realistic, "hopeful book, easy to read and gentle in its important lessons," *Booklist* critic Bradburn predicted that "readers will want" the girls to return for another season of shared sisterhood.

Like Brashares's earlier title, *The Second Summer of the Sisterhood* takes a lighthearted look at serious topics. "I feel as though there are a lot of books trying very hard to deal with social issues—illness or social ills, all kinds of shocking things—and in some part of my mind I knew that I didn't want to do that," the author told Weich. "I wanted to write a book that wasn't insubstantial but wasn't really issues-driven, either. I hope I did that." And writing on the Random House site, Brashares concluded about her "Sisterhood" books that she hopes they are the sort to "stick with [readers] a bit, the way books I liked when I was that age stuck with me. If there's a message, I guess it's just this: love yourself and your friends unconditionally."

BIOGRAPHICAL AND CRITICAL SOURCES:

BOOKS

Brashares, Ann, *The Sisterhood of the Traveling Pants,* Delacorte (New York, NY), 2001.

PERIODICALS

Booklist, August, 2001, Frances Bradburn, review of *The Sisterhood of the Traveling Pants,* p. 2106; January 1, 2002, review of *The Sisterhood of the Traveling Pants,* p. 764; April 15, 2003, Frances Bradburn, review of *The Second Summer of Sisterhood,* p. 1461.

Bookseller, March 15, 2002, Jennifer Taylor, "Strong Contenders," p. S31.

Horn Book, November-December, 2001, Jennifer M. Brabander, review of *The Sisterhood of the Traveling Pants,* pp. 741-742; May-June, 2002, Kristi Beavin, review of *The Sisterhood of the Traveling Pants* (audiobook), p. 353; May-June, 2003, Jennifer M. Brabander, review of *The Second Summer of Sisterhood,* p. 339.

Journal of Adolescent and Adult Literacy, September, 2002, James Blasingame, review of *The Sisterhood of the Traveling Pants,* pp. 87-88.

Kirkus Reviews, August 1, 2001, review of *The Sisterhood of the Traveling Pants,* p. 1117; July, 2002, Barbara Baskin, review of *The Sisterhood of the Traveling Pants* (audiobook), pp. 1866-1867.

New York Times, March 10, 2002, Christine Leahy, review of *The Sisterhood of the Traveling Pants,* p. 7.

Publishers Weekly, July 16, 2001, review of *The Sisterhood of the Traveling Pants,* p. 182; October 15, 2001, review of *The Sisterhood of the Traveling Pants* (audiobook), p. 26; December 24, 2001, Diane Roback, "Flying Starts," p. 30; March 25, 2002, Daisy Maryles, "A YA Debut Makes Five," p. 18; September 30, 2002, "Have Pants, Will Travel," p. 30; March 3, 2003, review of *The Second Summer of the Sisterhood,* p. 77.

School Library Journal, August, 2001, Linda Bindner, review of *The Sisterhood of the Traveling Pants,* p. 175; December, 2001, Yapha Nussbaum Mason, review of *Linus Torvalds: Software Rebel,* p. 153; May, 2003, Susan W. Hunter, review of *The Second Summer of Sisterhood,* p. 144.

U.S. News and World Report, May 12, 2003, Holly J. Morris, "Flying by the Seat of Her Pants," p. 8.

Voice of Youth Advocates, August, 2001, Susan H. Levine, review of *Steve Jobs: Think Different;* October, 2001, Dean Rutherford, review of *The Sisterhood of the Traveling Pants.*

Women's Wear Daily, June 6, 2002, Scott Malone and Julee Greenberg, "Denim Dish," p. 9.

ONLINE

BookBrowse, http://www.bookbrowse.com/ (February 2, 2003), "Ann Brashares."

Powells.com, http://www.powells.com/ (September 7, 2001), Dave Weich, "Author Interviews: Ann Brashares Embarks into Fiction."

Random House Web site, http://www.randomhouse.
com/ (February 2, 2003), "Teens@Random: Talking with Ann Brashares about the Sisterhood."*

*   *   *

BRAWNE, Michael 1925-2003

OBITUARY NOTICE—See index for *CA* sketch: Born May 5, 1925, in Vienna, Austria; died of cancer July 28, 2003, in Bath, England. Architect, educator, and author. Through his books, teaching, organization of exhibitions, and his own architectural projects, Brawne was a highly influential architect who made a mark on an entire generation of British architects. The son of an Austrian artist and a Croatian musician, he spent his early years speaking German, Croatian, and some Czech, a fact many of his colleagues were unaware of, given his excellent command of the English language. With the rise of the Nazi regime, his parents arranged for Brawne to be taken to England. During World War II his father, a Jew, was killed in a concentration camp; his mother, however, survived and joined her son following the war. Brawne attended the University of Edinburgh before enlisting in the British Royal Air Force (RAF) in 1943, receiving training in meteorology. When the war ended he remained in the military a while longer and was posted to Egypt, where he became familiar with the artifacts of that ancient land. He left the RAF in 1947, became a British citizen, and studied at the Architectural Association; he then traveled to the United States to attend the Massachusetts Institute of Technology, where he earned him master's degree in architecture in 1954. (Years later, in 1977, he earned a second master's degree from Cambridge University.) During the 1950s Brawne was employed at various architectural firms in San Francisco and London, and founded his own company, Michael Brawne & Associates, in 1963. Interested in the ways architecture can best serve society's needs, he primarily involved himself in designing public buildings, such as libraries, museums, and university structures. During the 1960s and 1970s he was also responsible for organizing exhibitions at such locations as the Tate Gallery, the Hayward Gallery, and the Royal Academy. Brawne was also highly regarded as a university lecturer; he taught at Cambridge University from 1964 to 1978, and at Bath University from 1978 until his retirement as professor emeritus in 1990. Among his many influential architecture books are *The New Museum: Architecture and Display* (1965),

The Museum Interior: Temporary and Permanent Display Techniques (1982), *From Idea to Building: Issues in Architecture* (1992), and *Architectural Thought: The Design Process and the Expectant Eye,* the last published posthumously.

OBITUARIES AND OTHER SOURCES:

BOOKS

Contemporary Architects, third edition, St. James Press (Detroit, MI), 1994.
Writers Directory, 18th edition, Gale (Detroit, MI), 2003.

PERIODICALS

Guardian (London, England), August 22, 2003.
Independent (London, England), August 16, 2003, p. 20.

*   *   *

BRISKIN, Alan 1954-

PERSONAL: Born February 8, 1954, in New York, NY; son of Samuel (an entrepreneur) and Rebecca Briskin; married Jane O'Brien (a teacher), July 10, 1987; children: Alex. *Education:* Goddard College, B.A. (education), 1974; Wright Institute, Ph.D. (psychology), 1984. *Religion:* "Jewish."

ADDRESSES: Agent—Sheryl Fullerton, 1095 Amito Dr., Berkeley, CA 94705. *E-mail*—albriskin@aol.com.

CAREER: Organizational consultant in Oakland, CA, 1985—.

MEMBER: Professional Associate, Grubb Institute, Fetzer Relationship Care Network.

AWARDS, HONORS: Humanistic Scholar award, Saybrook Graduate School, 1996, for *The Stirring of Soul in the Workplace.*

WRITINGS:

The Stirring of Soul in the Workplace, Jossey-Bass (San Francisco, CA), 1996.
(With Cheryl Peppers) *Bringing Your Soul to Work: An Everyday Practice,* Berrett Koehler (San Francisco, CA), 2000.

Author of *Centered on the Edge: Mapping the Field of Collective Intelligence and Spiritual Wisdom,* Fetzer Institute.

WORK IN PROGRESS: Research on collective intelligence.

SIDELIGHTS: Alan Briskin told *CA* that his goal is "To support spiritual development and articulate a new understanding of the relationship between inner knowing and outward action in the world."

*   *   *

BROWN, Timothy C(harles) 1938-

PERSONAL: Born June 9, 1938, in Anthony, KS; son of Gilbert E. (a minister of religion) and Frances (Shaw) Brown; married Leda Moraima Zúñniga Fernandez, September 11, 1958; children: Barbara Brown Peterson, Rebecca Zúñniga-Brown, Tamara E. Brown-Janick, Timothy Patrick Zúñniga-Brown. *Ethnicity:* "Caucasian." *Education:* University of Nevada, B.A., 1965; Foreign Service Institute of the U.S. State Department, M.A., 1974; New Mexico State University, Ph.D., 1997. *Politics:* "Non-partisan" *Religion:* Pentecostal Protestant. *Hobbies and other interests:* Reading, languages.

ADDRESSES: Office—Office of International Studies, Sierra Nevada College, Incline Village, NV 89451; Hoover Institution, Stanford University, Stanford, CA 94305. *Agent*—c/o University of Oklahoma Press, 1005 Asp Ave., Norman, OK 73019. *E-mail*—tcbrown@hoover.stanford.edu.

CAREER: Began career with U.S. Foreign Service, Department of State, 1965, and served in Israel, Spain, Vietnam, Mexico, France, and other nations; desk of-

ficer for Paraguay and Uruguay, 1978-80; desk officer for Organization for Economic Cooperation and Development, International Energy Agency, and European Community, 1980-81; deputy coordinator for Cuban affairs, Washington, DC, 1981-83; consul general in Martinique, 1983-87; senior liaison in Nicaragua, 1987-90; member of United Nations Cease-Fire Observation Force, 1989-90; New Mexico Development Institute, member of faculty, 1990-94; Border Research Institute, New Mexico State University, senior fellow, 1992-94; Hoover Institution, Stanford University, research fellow, 1994—; University of Nevada, Reno, adjunct professor, 1999—; Sierra Nevada College, chair of international studies, 2000—. Also served economic advisor to North Atlantic Treaty Organization, 1980-83. *Military service:* U.S. Marine Corps, 1954-64; served as Thai interpreter, Southeast Asia analyst, and posted to Central America; received from U.S. Department of State two Superior Honor Medals, Distinguished Honor Medal, two Meritorious Honor Medals, and Distinguished Service Award; received from U.S. Marine Corps two Meritorious commendations, two Campaign Medals, and additional honors.

AWARDS, HONORS: Foreign Policy Association Editor's Pick, 2000, for *When the AK-47s Fall Silent,* and 2003, for *The Real Contra War;* Commendation, U.N. International Peacekeeping Observer Force; named honorary comandante, Nicaraguan Democratic Resistance.

WRITINGS:

The Causes of Continuing Conflict in Nicaragua: A View from Radical Middle, Hoover Institution on War, Revolution, and Peace (Stanford, CA), 1995.
(Editor and translator) *When the AK-47s Fall Silent: Revolutionaries, Guerrillas, and the Dangers of Peace,* foreword by Cuauhtemoc Cardenas, Hoover Institution Press (Stanford, CA), 2000.
The Real Contra War: Highlander Peasant Resistance in Nicaragua, University of Oklahoma Press (Norman, OK), 2001.

Contributor to *Wall Street Journal, Policy Studies Review,* and *Annals of the American Academy of Political and Social Sciences,* among other publications.

WORK IN PROGRESS: A book on the internal organization of terrorist groups titled *Terror Incorpo-*

rated; research into organized armed political violence as described by former revolutionaries, terrorists, and guerrillas.

SIDELIGHTS: Since turning sixteen, Timothy C. Brown has had three distinctive careers involving international affairs, including ten years as a U.S. Marine, twenty-seven years as a diplomat, and eleven years as an academic and researcher. Twenty-nine of these years were served abroad, including Marine assignments in three countries and diplomatic assignments in eleven, spanning four continents. During most of those years Brown was subjected to terrorist threats from bombings and assassination attempts to involvement in armed conflicts, including the Vietnam War, the Thai Seri rebellion in northeast Thailand, Huk guerrilla warfare in the Philippines, the Sgt. Brunswyk uprising in Suriname from French Guiana, and Nicaragua's Contra War. These experiences have formed the primary foundation of his personal interests, concerns, research, and writing since he became an academic and professional researcher in 1992. Brown's published work draws heavily on his experiences and on contacts made during those years among former revolutionaries, terrorists, guerrillas, and government experts, and he concentrates on revealing the underlying causes of armed conflicts and how to resolve them.

As a Marine non-commissioned officer, Brown was posted to Nicaragua where he learned Spanish. He then went on to serve in the Fleet Marine Corps, Pacific after learning Thai at the Army Language School, and worked as an analyst of insurgency movements throughout Southeast Asia. Brown was a ten-year Marine Corps veteran by the time he graduated from the University of Nevada in 1965 and became an officer in the U.S. Foreign Service. He went on to serve as a Department of State diplomat for twenty-seven years. In 1987 Brown was named the State Department's senior liaison to the Resistencia Democratica Nicaraguense, popularly known as the Contras, a U.S.-supported insurgency movement battling to unseat Nicaragua's Marxist revolutionary government. In 1992 Brown retired from the Foreign Service and returned to school, earning a Ph.D. in political science, history, economics, and political psychology from New Mexico State University in 1997. He then returned home to Nevada and became the chair of international studies at Sierra Nevada College at Lake Tahoe, Nevada, where he is building a diplomatic academy.

Brown's three books focus on revolutionary violence and guerrilla warfare, and are based largely on the internal strife that plagued Central America from the 1950s through the 1980s. During his career Brown cultivated a wealth of contacts and expertise which he later mined for his published political analyses. His final overseas diplomatic assignment as senior liaison officer to the Nicaraguan Contras from 1987 to 1990, came during an unusually contentious period in U.S. foreign policy relations in the region. Many Americans were passionate in their support for the Nicaraguan Contras while others were equally passionate in their opposition to them and especially to U.S. support for the Contras via the Central Intelligence Agency. In his first book, *The Causes of Continuing Conflict in Nicaragua: A View from Radical Middle,* written after he left the Foreign Service and entered academe, Brown builds on his experience and subsequent research to explain that the Nicaraguan Contras were largely composed of Segovian central highlands peasants who took up arms against the Sandinista revolutionary government when it began a program of collectivization of their private farmlands and appropriating their crops and livestock.

In his second book, *The Real Contra War: Highlander Peasant Resistance in Nicaragua,* he directly challenges the conventional wisdom that the U.S. government, under President Ronald Reagan, instigated the Contra-Sandinista war in order to prevent communism from gaining a foothold in Central America. In addition to providing evidence that the first U.S. government approaches to the Contras actually took place during the Carter administration, Brown provides statistics to show that the Contras were indeed a mass popular movement whose resistance to the Sandinistas predated even this official U.S. involvement. He also explains Nicaraguan politics and history, pointing out that Contra rebels were from a region of the country with a tradition of resisting outsiders that dates from before the Spanish Conquest. "Brown makes the point that from both a geographic and ethnological point of view the Contra war was merely an extension of longer struggles in Nicaraguan history," wrote Mark Falcoff in a *World and I* review.

In writing *The Real Contra War* Brown interviewed several hundred former Contras, was given full access to their surviving archives, and used many recently declassified documents from U.S. government sources, some of which he himself had written while in government service. "The picture that emerges is vivid, detailed, and wholly at variance with the 'official' version," noted Falcoff. Only after 1986, when it was revealed that some American officials had been illegally selling arms to Iran in order to fund the Contra effort, did U.S. involvement wind down. The war ostensibly ended in 1990 with the election of president Violeta Chamorro and the defeat of the Sandinistas, but Chamorro was criticized for entering into a power-sharing arrangement with the vanquished. An official demobilization effort by the Organization of American States inadvertently provided some of the data that substantiates Brown's claims, revealing that the Contra army and its supporters were much larger than originally assumed, and had not diminished with the end of U.S. aid in 1987. "Brown makes an interesting case, but also neglects certain issues," noted a *Publishers Weekly* reviewer, citing human-rights abuses that occurred on both sides of the conflict. *Library Journal* critic James R. Holmes found Brown's tome a "meticulously researched work [that] promises to transform the historiography of the Contras' war."

Brown's third book, of which he is sole investigator, editor, and translator, is *When the AK-47s Fall Silent: Revolutionaries, Guerrillas, and the Dangers of Peace.* The volume collects the observations of participants in violent armed political movements in both Nicaragua and other parts of Latin America in the late twentieth century. The twelve essayists included several former leading communist revolutionaries from Mexico, El Salvador, Costa Rica, and Nicaragua, five former Nicaraguan Contras, a woman commando, and international peacemakers. These life-stories reveal how peace can emerge from war by documenting the personal transformations of once-violent armed revolutionaries, guerrillas, and terrorists into participants in the democratic processes within their respective countries. Brown includes analyses by international peacemakers who helped these individuals make their transitions. Leftist Mexican presidential candidate Cuauhtemoc Cardenas, a lifelong advocate of peaceful revolutionary change, contributed the foreword. The result is an unusual study that the Foreign Policy Association recommended as 'must' reading.

Brown's ongoing research and writing continues to be concentrated on better understanding what causes armed violence war because he considers gaining knowledge to be a condition precedent to building peace. Both *When the AK-47s Fall Silent* and *The Real Contra War* were two of only four books published about Latin America after 1997 that were recommended by the Foreign Policy Association.

BIOGRAPHICAL AND CRITICAL SOURCES:

PERIODICALS

Kirkus Reviews, February 1, 2001, review of *The Real Contra War,* p. 157.
Library Journal, March 15, 2001, James R. Holmes, review of *The Real Contra War,* p. 96.
Perspectives on Political Science, summer, 2002 Patrick D. Bernardo, review of *The Real Contra War,* p. 180.
Publishers Weekly, February 12, 2001, review of *The Real Contra War,* p. 197.
World and I, July, 2001, Mark Falcoff, "The War the Media Missed."*

*   *   *

BRUCE, William Cabell 1860-1946

PERSONAL: Born March 12, 1860, in Charlotte County, VA; died May 9, 1946; son of Charles (a tobacco planter, livestock breeder, and politician) and Sarah Alexander (Sedon) Bruce; married October 15, 1887; wife's name Louise E.; children: James, David K.E. *Education:* Attended Norwood College, 1875-78; attended University of Virginia, 1879-80; University of Maryland, LL.B.; Hampden-Sydney College, LL. D.; attended Loyola College, 1930. *Politics:* Democrat. *Religion:* Episcopalian.

CAREER: Attorney and politician. Fisher, Bruce & Fisher (law partner, 1887-1903, 1908-10; Maryland State Senate, elected member, 1894-96, president, 1896; Baltimore Law Department, head of department, 1903-08; Baltimore Charter Commission, member, 1910; Public Service Commission of Maryland, general counsel, 1910-22, 1929-35; U.S. Senate, elected member, 1923-29.

AWARDS, HONORS: Pulitzer Prize for biography, 1919, for *Benjamin Franklin, Self-Revealed.*

WRITINGS:

The Negro Problem, J. Murphy (Baltimore, MD), 1891.

Benjamin Franklin, Self-Revealed, G.P. Putnam's Sons (New York, NY), 1917.

Below the James: A Plantation Sketch, Neale Publishing Company (New York, NY), 1918.

John Randolph of Roanoke, 1773-1833, G.P. Putnam's Sons (New York, NY), 1922.

Selections from the Speeches, Addresses, and Political Writings of Wm. Cabell Bruce, Sun Book and Job Printing Office (Baltimore, MD), 1927.

Additional Selections from the Speeches, Addresses, etc. of Wm. Cabell Bruce, King Brothers (Baltimore, MD), 1928.

Seven Great Baltimore Lawyers, [(Baltimore, MD], 1931.

Recollections, King Brothers (Baltimore, MD), 1931.

Imaginary Conversations with Franklin, G.P. Putnam's Sons (New York, NY), 1933.

Latest Additional Selections from the Speeches, Addresses and Writings of Wm. Cabell Bruce, Press of the Daily Record Company (Baltimore, MD), 1934.

The Inn of Existence, King Brothers (Baltimore, MD), 1941.

SIDELIGHTS: William Cabell Bruce, a member of what was once one of Virginia's most wealthy and noted families, was a lawyer, biographer, and senator. During his career, he alternated regularly between a thriving law practice and serving in public office. It was during one of his public appointments, to the office of chief counsel to the Maryland Public Service Commission, that Bruce published two of his most noted works: *Benjamin Franklin, Self-Revealed* and *John Randolph of Roanoke. Benjamin Franklin, Self-Revealed* was awarded the Pulitzer Price in 1919 for biography.

Bruce grew up in a wealthy family. His father was a successful tobacco planter and livestock breeder, and served in the Virginia state senate for some years. The Bruce family estate, located in Charlotte County, Virginia, was one of the South's largest tobacco plantations, operating with 500 slaves. However, after a series of financial problems, Bruce's father, Charles Bruce, lost all of his property except for the Charlotte County land, which he passed on to William and his

two brothers. By all accounts, Bruce was well educated, both by private tutors and through formal education. He graduated with a law degree in 1882, and after passing the Maryland Bar that same year, began practicing in Baltimore. After five years he entered into a partnership with the law firm Fisher, Bruce & Fisher. William A. Fisher had been a former member of the supreme bench of Baltimore and Fisher's son, David Kirkpatrick Este Fisher, was also a member of the firm.

During his law career Bruce spent time away from this lucrative law practice to pursue public-service positions; as he wrote in his memoir, *Recollections,* "I had never intended always to give myself up so single-mindedly to the practice of law as to be unable to gratify my love of public life and letters." In 1893 Bruce was elected to the state senate, and in 1896 he became president of that same body. After serving his term, he returned to practice law at Fisher, Bruce & Fisher, but in 1903 resigned to accept an appointment as city solicitor. He left this office in 1908, returned once more to the law firm, and then was appointed by Governor Austin L. Crothers to the office of chief counsel to the Maryland Public Service Commission, where he served from 1910 to 1922.

It was during this time that Bruce became interested in historical writing and published *Benjamin Franklin, Self-Revealed* and *John Randolph of Roanoke.* Referencing *Benjamin Franklin, Self-Revealed,* a critic for the *Boston Transcript* applauded Bruce's "keen critical insight and deep understanding of human nature . . . fine sense of proportion, and a literary manner which renders the work eminently readable."

Bruce was elected from Maryland to the U.S. Senate in 1922 for one term. During his term in office he earned national acclaim for championing a crusade against the Ku Klux Klan, for advocating federal anti-lynching legislation, and for his fight against prohibition. Bruce lost his senate seat in 1928, and returned to Fisher, Bruce & Fisher. He formally retired from law in 1937 and his son David K. E. Bruce carried on his name in the political arena as a prominent statesman and diplomat, serving as ambassador to South Vietnam during the Vietnam War.

In addition to *Benjamin Franklin, Self-Revealed* and *John Randolph of Roanoke, 1773-1833* Bruce published other books, including biographies, autobiographies, fiction, drama, and nonfiction. He had several books privately printed, among these three individual collections of his public speeches, addresses, and writings.

BIOGRAPHICAL AND CRITICAL SOURCES:

BOOKS

Encyclopedia of American Biography, Volumes 4 and 5, American Historical Society (New York, NY), 1935.
Who Was Who in America, Volume 2: *1943-1950,* A.N. Marquia Company (Chicago, IL), 1963.*

*   *   *

BYLER, Stephen Raleigh 1970-

PERSONAL: Born May 24, 1970, in Lancaster, PA; son of Grace S. (Hurst) Byler. *Ethnicity:* "White." *Education:* Eastern Mennonite University, B.A.; Yale University, M.A.; Columbia University, M.F.A.

ADDRESSES: Home—1300 Newton Rd., Lancaster, PA 17603. *Agent*—Barbara Lowenstein, Lowenstein Associates, Inc., 121 W. 27th St.., Suite 601, New York, NY 10001. *E-mail*—stephenbyler@hotmail.com.

CAREER: Writer.

WRITINGS:

Searching for Intruders: A Novel in Stories, William Morrow and Co. (New York, NY), 2002.

WORK IN PROGRESS: A second novel.

BIOGRAPHICAL AND CRITICAL SOURCES:

PERIODICALS

Booklist, November 15, 2001, Brad Hooper, review of *Searching for Intruders: A Novel in Stories,* p. 550.
Kirkus Reviews, October 15, 2001, review of *Searching for Intruders,* p. 1443.
Library Journal, January, 2002, Edward B. St. John, review of *Searching for Intruders,* p. 148.
New York Times Book Review, December 30, 2001, Dwight Garner, review of *Searching for Intruders,* p. 6; January 6, 2002, review of *Searching for Introducers,* p. 18; June 2, 2002, review of *Searching for Intruders,* p. 24.
Publishers Weekly, November 12, 2001, review of *Searching for Intruders,* p. 34.

C

CALLENDAR, Newgate
See SCHONBERG, Harold C(harles)

*   *   *

CAMPOS, Augusto de 1931-

PERSONAL: Born 1931, in São Paulo, Brazil.

ADDRESSES: Agent—c/o Author Mail, Editora Perspectiva, AV. Brigadiero Luis Antonia, 3025/3025, São Paulo, 01401.000 Brazil.

CAREER: Poet, writer, translator, and critic.

WRITINGS:

O rei menos o reino, 1949-51, 1951.
(With Haroldo de Campos) *Sousândrade: o terremoto clandestino,* Ministerio de Educação e Cultura, Instituto Nacional do Livro (São Paulo, Brazil), 1960.
(With Haroldo de Campos) *Revisão de Sousândrade,* Edições Invenção (São Paulo, Brazil), 1964.
(With Haroldo de Campos and Décio Pognatari) *Teoria da poesia concreta; textos criticos e manifestos, 1950-1960,* Edições Invenção (São Paulo, Brazil), 1965.
(With Haroldo de Campos) *Traduzir & trovar (poetas dos séculos XII a XVII* Ediçoes Papyrus (São Paulo, Brazil) 1968.

Balanco da bossa; antologia critica da moderna música popular brasileira, Editoria Perspectiva (São Paulo, Brazil), 1968.
Re-visão de Kilkerry, Fundo Estadual de Cultura (São Paulo, Brazil), 1970.
Balanço da bossa e outras bossas, 1974.
Poesia, antipoesia, antropofagia, Cortez & Moraes (São Paulo, Brazil), 1978.
Verso, reverso, controverso, Editora Perspectiva (Sao Paulo, Brazil), 1978.
Poesia, 1949-1979, Livraria Dua Cidades (São Paulo, Brazil), 1979.
Pagu, Patricia Galvão, Brasiliense (São Paulo, Brazil), 1982.
Paul Valéry: a serpente e o pensar, Brasiliense (São Paulo, Brazil), 1984.
O anticritico, Editora Schwarcz (São Paulo, Brazil), 1986.
Linguaviagem, Cia. das Letras (São Paulo, Brazil), 1987.
A margem da margem, Companhia das Letras (São Paulo, Brazil), 1989.
Despoesia, Editoria Perspectiva (São Paulo, Brazil), 1994.
Os sertões dos Campos: duas vezes Euclides, Sette Letras (Rio de Janeiro, Brazil), 1997.
Música de invenção Editora Perspectiva (São Paulo, Brazil), 1998.
Galaxia concreta, Universidad Iberoamericana, Artes de México (Mexico), 1999.

TRANSLATOR

(With Haroldo de Campos and Décio Pignatari) Ezra Pound, *Cantares,* Ministerio de Educação e Cultura (São Paulo, Brazil), 1960.

e. e. cummings, *10 poemas,* Ministerio de Educação e Cultura (São Paulo, Brazil), 1960.

(With Haroldo de Campos) James Joyce and Lewis Carroll, *Panorama do Finnegans Wake,* Conselho Estadual de Cultura, Comissão de Literatura (São Paulo, Brazil), 1962.

(With Haroldo de Campos) Joaquin de Sousa Andrade, *Poesia,* AGIR (Rio de Janeiro, Brazil), 1966.

Poesia russa moderna, Civilização Brasileira (Rio de Janeiro, Brazil), 1968.

Louis Zukofsky, *A furia de Julia,* Macmillan (New York, NY), 1968.

(With José Paulo Paes) Ezra Pound, *ABC da literatura,* Editora Cultrix (São Paulo, Brazil) 1970.

(With Haroldo de Campos and Décio Pignatari) *Mallarmé,* Editora Perspectiva (São Paulo, Brazil), 1974.

e.e. cummings, *20 poemas,* Editora Noa Noa (Florianópolis, Ilha de Santa Catarina), 1979.

(With Haroldo de Campos) Ezra Pound, *Poesia,* Editora HUCITEC (São Paulo, Brazil), 1983.

Rilke: poesia-coisa, Imago (Rio de Janeiro, Brazil), 1994.

Hopkins: a beleza dificil, Editora Perspectiva (São Paulo, Brazil), 1997.

Coeditor of *Noigandres* (avant-garde magazine). Author's works have been translated into a variety of languages, including English, Portuguese, and Spanish.

ADAPTATIONS: Author's works and translations have been set to music by Brazilian musicians, including Caetano Veloso and Gal Costa.

SIDELIGHTS: Augusto de Campos is a Brazilian essayist, critic, translator, and author of experimental poetry. Campos was the founder of the concrete poetry movement at the Museum of Modern Art in São Paulo, Brazil, in December, 1956, along with his brother, Haroldo, and Décio Pignatari, the editors of the avant-garde magazine *Noigandres.* "In his poetry Augusto unites conquests of early twentieth-century poetry with an interest in the plastic arts, graphics, and experimental music," wrote Kenneth David Jackson in *World Literature Today.*

Concrete poetry emphasizes the visual arrangement of words and non-linguistic elements in the poem rather than the content. In a concrete poem the pattern of the words or the typeface contributes as much to the poem as the meaning of the words. Poems become objects in and of themselves, rather than arrangements of words that form meaning and images. Other types of concrete poetry are intended to be spoken rather than read, or performed by some type of action. Haroldo and Augusto de Campos defined and challenged concrete poetry in their manifesto *Teoria da poesia concreto,* written in 1965. The poem "Eye," for example, consists of a triangular arrangement of photographs of eyes and mouths. "Pentahexagram to John Cage" evolves from image of the musical staff containing four notes spelling CAGE into the Chinese *I Ching.* In "Luxo," repetitions of the tiny word "luxos," meaning luxury, combine to form another huge word: "lixo," meaning garbage.

Campos has also translated the work of numerous other poets and writers, including e.e. cummings, Rainer Maria Rilke, Ezra Pound, and Gerard Manly Hopkins.

BIOGRAPHICAL AND CRITICAL SOURCES:

BOOKS

Bush, Peter, and Kirsten Malmkjaer, editors, *Rimbaud's Rainbow: Literary Translation in Higher Education,* John Benjamins Publishing Company (Philadelphia, PA), 1998.

Cannibalism and the Colonial World, Cambridge University Press (Cambridge, England), 1998.

PERIODICALS

Brasil Brazil, 1997, George Monteiro, "Rose is a Rose is a Rose is a Rose as Poem: Stein, Hemingway, and Augusto de Campos," pp. 9-17.

Comparatist, May, 1982, "Concrete Poetry into Music," p. 3.

Harvard Library Bulletin, summer, 1992, Roland Green, "From Dante to the Post-Concrete," interview with Augusto de Campos, pp. 19-35.

Minas Gerais, Suplemento Literario September 29, 1984, "Entre a Palavra e o Silencio," p. 8.

Mester, spring, 1985, "Poetamenos," p. 55.

World Literature Today, winter, 1988, Kenneth David Jackson, review of *Poesia 1949-1979,* p. 108.*

CANNON, George Q(uayle) 1827-1901

PERSONAL: Born January 11, 1827, in Liverpool, England; immigrated to the United States, 1842; died of influenza May 12, 1901, in Monterey, CA; son of George and Ann (Quayle) Cannon; adopted son of John Taylor; married Elizabeth Hoagland, 1854; also married Jane Jenne, Eliza Lamercia Tenny, Martha Telle, and Caroline Young Croxall; children: (second marriage) Franklin Jenne. *Religion:* Church of Jesus Christ of Latter-Day Saints (Mormon).

CAREER: Missionary, author, and journalist. Church of Jesus Christ of Latter-Day Saints, missionary in California, 1849, and Hawaii, 1850, editor of *Western Standard,* mid-1850s, head of California Mission, 1856-58, leader of Eastern States Mission, 1858-60, ordained member of Council of Apostles, 1859, leader of European Mission based in England, 1860-c. 1864, personal secretary to Brigham Young, 1964-67, founder of *Juvenile Instructor,* 1866, general superintendent of Sunday School Union, 1867-1901, special counselor to First Presidency, 1873-1901. U.S. Congress, territorial delegate from Utah, 1872-c. 1881. Editor of *Millennial Star* (Liverpool, England), c. 1860, and *Deseret News,* beginning 1867; Utah Central Railroad, organizing member; Union Pacific Railroad, member of board of directors; also participated in business ventures in banking and the sugar industry.

WRITINGS:

Writings from the "Western Standard," G. Q. Cannon (Liverpool, England), 1864, reprinted, Paladin Press (New York, NY), 1969.
George R. Maxwell vs. George Q. Cannon, [Washington, DC], 1873.
My First Mission, Juvenile Instructor Office (Salt Lake City, UT), 1879.
A Review of the Decision of the Supreme Court of the United States in the Case of George Reynolds vs. the United States, Deseret News Printing and Publishing (Salt Lake City, UT), 1879.
The Life of Nephi, the Son of Lehi, Who Emigrated from Jerusalem, in Judea, to the Land Which Is Now Known as South America, Juvenile Instructor Office (Salt Lake City, UT), 1883.
The Latter-Day Prophet: Young People's History of Joseph Smith, Deseret Book (Salt Lake City, UT), 1914.

Gospel Truth: Discourses and Writings of George Q. Cannon, two volumes, edited by Jerreld L. Newquist, Zion's Book Store (Salt Lake City, UT), 1957-1974, 2nd edition published as *Gospel Truth: Discourses and Writings of President George Q. Cannon,* Deseret Book (Salt Lake City, UT), 1974.
The Journals of George Q. Cannon, Volume 1: *To California in '49,* edited by Michael L. Landon, Deseret Book (Salt Lake City, UT), 1999.

Shorter works include "Before Territorial Canvassers, Utah Territory," T. McGill and Co. (Washington, DC), 1881; and "The History of the Mormons," G. Q. Cannon and Sons (Salt Lake City, UT), 1891. Translator of Mormon books into the Hawaiian language.

BIOGRAPHICAL AND CRITICAL SOURCES:

BOOKS

Evans, Beatrice Cannon, and Janath Russell Cannon, editors, *Cannon Family Historical Treasury,* G. Q. Cannon Family Association (Salt Lake City, UT), 1967.

PERIODICALS

Pacific Historical Review, November, 1947, M. Hamlin Cannon, "Prison Diary of a Mormon Apostle," pp. 395-409.*

*   *   *

CAPELOTTI, P(eter) J(oseph) 1960-

PERSONAL: Born 1960. *Education:* University of Rhode Island, B.A., 1983, M.A., 1989; Rutgers University, Ph.D. 1996.

ADDRESSES: Office—Division of Social and Behavioral Sciences, Woodland 235B, Penn State University, Abington College, Abington, PA 19001. *E-mail*—pjc12@psu.edu.

CAREER: Professor of social and behavioral sciences. University of Rhode Island, lecturer, 1989-91; Holy Family College, Philadelphia, PA, adjunct professor;

Pennsylvania State University, Abington, lecturer in social sciences, 1997—. Member of advisory board for underwater and maritime archaeology, University of Hawaii, 1998—. *Military service:* U.S. Coast Guard Reserve, 1989—, attained rank of chief petty officer; called to active duty, 2001-03.

MEMBER: Council for Northeast Historical Archaeology, Sociedad Cubana de Historia de la Ciencia y la Tecnologia, Society for Industrial Archeology, Lighter-than-Air Institute; Association of Balloon and Airship Constructors, Explorers Club, North American Society for Oceanic History, Phi Kappa Phi.

AWARDS, HONORS: Named Explorer of the Year, Explorers Club, Philadelphia chapter, 1996.

WRITINGS:

Explorers Air Yacht: The Sikorsky S-38 Flying Boat, Pictorial Histories Publishing Co. (Missoula, MT), 1995.

By Airship to the North Pole: An Archeology of Human Exploration, Rutgers University Press (New Brunswick, NJ), 1999.

The Svalbard Archipelago: American Military and Political Geographies of Spitsbergen and Other Norwegian Polar Territories, 1941-1950, McFarland Publishers (Jefferson, NC), 2000.

Sea Drift: Rafting Adventures in the Wake of Kon-Tiki, Rutgers University Press (New Brunswick, NJ), 2001.

EDITOR

Our Man in the Crimea: Commander Hugo Koehler and the Russian Civil War, University of South Carolina Press (Columbia, SC), 1991.

Barry Jason Stein, *U.S. Army Heraldic Crests: A Complete Illustrated History of Authorized Distinctive Unit Insignia,* University of South Carolina Press (Columbia, SC), 1993.

Robert F. Bennett, *Sand Pounders: An Interpretation of the History of the U.S. Life-saving Service, Based on Its Annual Reports for the Years 1870 through 1914,* U.S. Coast Guard Historian's Office (Washington, DC), 1998.

Reviewer for *Polar Record* and *Public Historian;* contributor to journals and periodicals, including *Polar Record, Explorers Journal, Coast Guard, Crosscurrents, Rhode Island,* and *Air and Space Smithsonian* (magazine).

WORK IN PROGRESS: As editor, *Before the Airships Came: E. B. Baldwin's Journal of the Wellman Expedition to Franz Josef Land, 1898-1899.* Research on the archaeology and anthropology of American exploration, mass culture, technology, globalization, and theme parks; cultural development and diffusion in maritime and aerospace environments; historical and archaeological research and preservation of sites from polar and aeronautical history; Arctic (Svalbard); Indonesia (Irian Jaya); and Cuba.

SIDELIGHTS: A significant portion of P. J. Capelotti's research and teaching focuses on the archeological and anthropological study of American exploration. In his books he shares his findings and theories, most of which have been formed since embarking on his own expeditions near the North Pole, in Indonesia, and in the Caribbean.

By Airship to the North Pole: An Archeology of Human Exploration is a study of two explorers that is told in two parts. David W. Norton wrote in *Arctic* that Capelotti "tantalizes readers with his interdisciplinary subtitle." Capelotti's research in the Spitsbergen—called Svalbard by Norwegians—archipelago, less than a thousand miles from the North Pole, required an investigation of the artifacts left by the failed attempts to reach the Pole undertaken by Swedish explorer Salomon August Andrée and U.S. journalist Walter Wellman, both of whom made the attempt via airship.

Andrée was considered either mad or a fool for attempting the month-long voyage then deemed to be impossible owing to the fact that his craft could not hold its hydrogen for more than several days. His airship *Omen* ("Eagle") was lofted in 1897, and Andrée and his crew of two me disappeared soon thereafter. Thirty-three years passed before the remains of their camp were discovered on White Island. Wellman made three failed attempts in 1906, 1907, and 1909 to locate the missing explorer in his own dirigible, *America,* two modifications of which were paid for by his employer, the *Chicago Record-Herald.* The Frenchredesigned *America* was to be the first gasoline-powered airship to travel within the Arctic Circle, at a cost in modern dollars of between $10 and $15 million. Wellman was not thought to be a particularly able explorer, but he was an outstanding promoter and fundraiser.

Isis reviewer Geir Hestmark commented that Capelotti "tells the story well, pointing out all the bad planning, bad equipment, bad decision making, and bad luck that led to each disaster." Hestmark noted that the details of Andrée's trip are more well known, while those of Wellman's are less so, and felt that Capelotti's study "gives us the man more completely and also presents evidence that his intentions and preparations to reach the Pole were more serious and realistic than has usually been acknowledged."

The remains of these and other expeditions to the Virgo Harbor region, the departure point of both Andrée and Wellman, are examined by Capelotti in the second section of *By Airship to the North Pole,* which was described by a *Kirkus Reviews* contributor as "a nice job of historical reconstruction."

Capelotti's *The Svalbard Archipelago: American Military and Political Geographies of Spitsbergen and Other Norwegian Polar Territories, 1941-1950* studies the islands that were demilitarized in 1920, then mined by Norway and the Soviet Union until World War II. At that point the British, Canadians, and Norwegians exerted their power to prevent the Germans from occupying the islands and extracting their rich mineral deposits. The Germans did occupy the islands, however, and the Allies returned in 1943 to drive them out, whereupon two Allied ships were attacked and sunk from the air. The British returned to retrieve their wounded and attack the Germans, who fled but then returned in battleships, planning to destroy their coal-mining settlements. *History*'s Elizabeth B. Elliot-Meisel called *The Svalbard Archipelago* "an interesting assessment of the islands' strategic military, commercial, and geological value, providing a unique and important piece in the Arctic literature."

Sea Drift: Rafting Adventures in the Wake of Kon-Tiki is Capelotti's study of ocean expeditions by raft that have embarked since the famous voyages of Thor Heyerdahl, whose sea adventures led to the settlement of Easter Island. Heyerdahl's *Kon-Tiki* was a balsa-wood raft that drifted more than 4,000 miles from Peru to Polynesia and Heyerdahl's memoir of the trip sold twenty million copies in sixty-five languages.

Sea Drift documents the more than three dozen trans-oceanic raft expeditions that were carried out between 1947 and 2000, on crafts made from balsa, straw, plywood, or bamboo. Travelers include a Frenchman who squeezed fish to quench his thirst and an anthropologist who put six women and five men on a raft to determine how they would interact sexually.

American William Willis crossed the Pacific alone twice while in his sixties and seventies. During his first trip Willis imagined himself to be the sole survivor of a nuclear war that had killed everyone else on earth. "That is just terrific stuff," said Capelotti in an interview posted at the *Rutgers University Press Web* site. Capelotti was asked whether he ever thought of crossing the ocean himself. He said, "absolutely, yes. . . . I hope to accompany Phil Buck on at least a part of his around-the-world reed boat expedition. But of course my imagination has always been with explorers like Willis or Frenchman Alain Bombard, who made their voyages alone."

When asked why he thinks *Kon-Tiki* continues to be a popular book, Capelotti replied that he believes "adventure for adventure's sake is ultimately unsatisfying to the human soul. Humans require adventure as a component of our personalities—it is one of the traits that lead us even in childhood to new learning. But the actual triggers of new developments of the human brain, I believe, are the creative combination of adventure with the search for new knowledge. Nearly every expedition described in *Sea Drift* encompasses this idea pioneered by Thor Heyerdahl that science and adventure seem to be twin pillars of human development."

BIOGRAPHICAL AND CRITICAL SOURCES:

PERIODICALS

Arctic, December, 2002, David W. Norton, review of *By Airship to the North Pole: An Archaeology of Human Exploration,* p. 398.
Choice, November, 1999, R. E. Bilstein, review of *By Airship to the North Pole,* pp. 560-562; February, 2002, M. W. Graves, review of *Sea Drift: Rafting Adventures in the Wake of Kon-Tiki,* p. 1085.

History, fall, 2000, Elizabeth B. Elliot-Meisel, review of *The Svalbard Archipelago: American Political Geographies of Spitsbergen and Other Norwegian Polar Territories, 1941-1950,* p. 28.

Isis, March, 2001, Geir Hestmark, review of *By Airship to the North Pole,* p. 221.

Kirkus Reviews, June 1, 1999, review of *By Airship to the North Pole,* p. 847.

ONLINE

Rutgers University Press Web site, http://rutgerspress.rutgers.edu/ (May 5, 2003), interview with Capelotti.*

*   *   *

CARBERY, Mary 1867-1949

PERSONAL: Born 1867, in England; died 1949; married twice.

CAREER: Writer.

WRITINGS:

The Farm by Lough Gur, Longmans, Green (London, England), 1937, reprinted, Irish American Book Company (Lanham, MD), 1995.

Happy World: The Story of a Victorian Childhood, Longmans, Green (London, England), 1941.

(With Edwin Grey) *Hertfordshire Heritage: Ourselves and Our Words,* J. Green (London, Engalnd), 1948.

Mary Carbery's West Cork Journals (1898-1901); or, "From the Back of Beyond," edited by Jeremy Sandford, Lilliput (Dublin, Ireland), 1995.

SIDELIGHTS: Mary Carbery was born in England in 1867, but her work as a writer began after she had moved to West Cork, Ireland. There she married and made her home in Castle Freke, near the Ounahincha strand. Her Irish home and environs so enchanted Lady Carbery that only the accidental burning of the castle years after her husband's death persuaded her to leave.

Carbery loved the people of West Cork as well as the place. In her journals and her work of social history, *The Farm by Lough Gur,* she describes the local people

and their customs with tact and respect, while recording superstitions that must have struck her as strange. In one infanticidal superstition recorded in *Mary Carbury's West Cork Journal,* a woman who had just delivered a child refused to feed it because on the stormy night the child was born her husband neglected to untie the family's horse and donkey, and she herself had not had time to untie her hair before the child was born. These lapses were believed to result in a changeling, an idiot child substituted by the fairies for the one they had stolen.

Carbery brought alive the sadness of parents whose children had died or emigrated with characters like Mary Dinny, "a plain woman, with squinny eyes and snaggle teeth, whose children have all emigrated to America. While each had written home at first, one by one they left off writing." *Mary Carbury's West Cork Journal,* originally written in four volumes, was edited by screenwriter Jeremy Sandford, Carbery's grandson from her second marriage. Mary Kenny, in the *Times Literary Supplement,* recalled how Carbery recorded the people's sympathy for mental illness: "a local woman who has an obsession that a fox is eating her stomach is humoured in her mental malady rather than dismissed as demented." Kenny concluded that Carbery's journal is a "remarkable book" and Carbery herself a "matchless social observer."

BIOGRAPHICAL AND CRITICAL SOURCES:

PERIODICALS

Times Literary Supplement, October 30, 1998, p. 32.*

*   *   *

CARIAGA, Catalina 1958-

PERSONAL: Born 1958, in Los Angeles, CA. *Education:* Mount St. Mary's College, Los Angeles, B.A.; San Francisco State University, M.F.A.

ADDRESSES: Home—Oakland, CA. *Agent*—c/o Author Mail, 'A 'A Arts, 2955 Dole St., Honolulu, HI 96816.

CAREER: New College of California, San Francisco, adjunct faculty member of poetics program; writer.

WRITINGS:

Cultural Evidence (poetry), Subpress Collective (San Francisco, CA)/'A 'A Arts (Honolulu, HI), 1999.

Contributor of poetry to Nick Carbo, editor, *Returning a Borrowed Tongue: Poems by Filipino and Filipino American Authors;* and to periodicals, including *Chain, New American Writing,* and *Zyzzyva.*

SIDELIGHTS: Catalina Cariaga's poetry collection *Cultural Evidence* was the first release by the Subpress Collective of San Francisco, California, a group of writers who donate one percent of their yearly income toward the publication of books. In *Cultural Evidence* Cariaga offers the perspective of a Filipino American as she and her relatives assimilate into California communities. Through poems about the Philippines and in her depiction of her immediate family Cariaga casts light on the immigrant experience as "new" Americans come to understand how other Americans perceive them. A *Publishers Weekly* critic called the book a "vital first collection," adding that it is "a deep, occasionally tentative consideration of issues of nation and self-of belonging and exile."

BIOGRAPHICAL AND CRITICAL SOURCES:

PERIODICALS

Publishers Weekly, August 30, 1999, review of *Cultural Evidence,* p. 78.

ONLINE

Small Press Traffic, http://www.sptraffic.org/ (February 25, 2000), "Catalina Cariaga."*

*   *   *

CARL, Leo Darwin 1918(?)-2001

PERSONAL: Born c. 1918 in Brooklyn, NY; died of cancer, November 21, 2001, in McLean, VA; married Otilla "Tommie" Ewert; children: David. *Education:* Attended City College of New York; University of Maryland, B.A., M.A.; Defense Language Institute.

CAREER: Author, lexicographer, and linguist. U.S. Department of Defense, Washington, DC, civil servant, beginning 1968; International Defense Consultant Services, founder. *Military service:* U.S. Army, enlisted serviceman, 1930s; U.S. Air Force, intelligence officer, 1947-68; attained rank of colonel.

MEMBER: Association of Former Intelligence Officers.

WRITINGS:

The International Dictionary of Intelligence, Maven Books (McLean, VA), 1990, updated as *The CIA Insider's Dictionary of U.S. and Foreign Intelligence, Counterintelligence & Tradecraft,* NIBC Press (Washington, DC), 1996.

SIDELIGHTS: Leo Darwin Carl was a career military man who served most of his time as an intelligence officer. After retiring from the U.S. Air Force, Carl began his own company, International Defense Consultant Services, a publishing and database projects service. It was during these latter years of his life that he compiled two comprehensive dictionaries. The first, *The International Dictionary of Intelligence,* consists of almost five hundred pages with over six thousand entries. The second book, *The CIA Insider's Dictionary of U.S. and Foreign Intelligence, Counterintelligence & Tradecraft,* is actually an updated version of the first and includes more than seven hundred pages with nearly ten thousand entries. Carl spent most of his career, both in the military and as a civil servant, involved in intelligence work, and this gives his dictionaries special authority. It should be noted, however, that no classified information is included in either work, and as stated by a reviewer for *Booklist,* both dictionaries are "intended for use by students, professionals, and writers of spy fiction interested in intelligence, counterintelligence, and covert operations."

Carl was born in Brooklyn, New York, and after completing his college education, he began his long involvement with the military. He enlisted in the U.S. Army prior to World War II as a non-commissioned officer. Later he attended officer candidate school and upon completion was awarded a commission as an officer. During World War II he was stationed in England and after the war, in 1947, when the U.S. Air

Force became an independent branch of the military, Carl transferred there. With the U.S. Air Force he served in Japan and then later in Germany as an intelligence officer. In the late 1950s he returned to the United States and served on assignment with the Central Intelligence Agency. During his career with the Armed Forces, he was involved with the U.S. Air Force Office of Special Investigations and the army's Counterintelligence Corps, eventually reaching the rank of colonel. Upon retiring from the military in 1968, he worked at the Pentagon as a civil servant.

With this extensive background in intelligence, Carl undertook the task of compiling the vocabulary used not only by U.S. intelligence agencies but by foreign agencies as well. His dictionaries include the names of security organizations, state-sponsored terrorist groups, arms-control terminology, and types of weapons. Also incorporated in the books are appendixes, which some critics found to be the dictionaries' most interesting feature. One such index provides the names of the heads of Russian/Soviet security services. Also included are definitions of intelligence terms, code names, and the name of intelligence organizations throughout the world. J. D. Stempel, writing for *Choice,* called the more recent edition of Carl's dictionary "an essential reference book for any library or university that claims to cover intelligence."

Carl died of cancer on November 21, 2001.

BIOGRAPHICAL AND CRITICAL SOURCES:

PERIODICALS

Booklist, October 1, 1996, review of *The CIA Insider's Dictionary of U.S. and Foreign Intelligence, Counterintelligence and Tradecraft,* pp. 367-368.
Choice, November, 1996, J. D. Stempel, review of *The CIA Insider's Dictionary of U.S. and Foreign Intelligence, Counterintelligence, and Tradecraft,* p. 426.*

*　　*　　*

CARNEGIE, Dale 1888-1955

PERSONAL: Born November 23, 1888, in Marysville, MO; died November 1, 1955, in Forest Hills, NY; son of James Carnagey (a farmer); married Lolita Baucaire, 1921 (divorced); married Dorothy Prince Vanderpool,

1943; children: (second marraige) Donna Dale. *Education:* Warrensburg State Teachers College, received degree, 1908.

CAREER: Consultant, author, and speaker. Worked as a salesman for International Correspondence School and as a meat packing supply salesman for Armour Foods; Young Men's Christian Association, Harlem NY, instructor in public speaking until c. 1914; founder of Carnegie Institute and instructor in effective public speaking, beginning c. 1914; business manager for journalist Lowell Thomas. *Military service:* U.S. Army; served during World War I.

WRITINGS:

How to Win Friends and Influence People, Simon & Schuster (New York, NY), 1936, revised edition, 1981.
How to Stop Worrying and Start Living, Simon & Schuster (New York, NY), 1948, revised edition, edited by Dorothy Carnegie, 1984.

Also author of *The Art of Public Speaking,* 1915; *Lincoln the Unknown,* 1932; and *Little-known Facts about Well-known People,* 1934.

SIDELIGHTS: Dale Carnegie's *How to Win Friends and Influence People* made an incredible splash when it was first published in 1936. It is credited with creating a new genre in writing: the self-help book. Carnegie's most famous book, which is full of tips on becoming comfortable in social situations, remains an indispensable resource for individuals and business people who dread public speaking and shrink at the though of making small talk in social situations. Proof of its popularity can be found in the fact that it has been revised several times since its inception and has never been out of print. From the 1920s to the present day the Dale Carnegie teachings have continually been popular with companies and individuals alike.

Carnegie was born in rural Missouri in 1888, and he and his brother helped out on the family farm. As a young man, Carnegie was struck by the oratory prowess of the Chautauqua performers who stopped occasionally near his home, offering entertainment and education at local fairs. Soon his fascination led him to join and excel at the debate team in high school. Carnegie's widow, Dorothy, adeptly summed up his ambition in a 1987 *New York Times* article: "He was just a poor farm boy who wasn't good at athletics, but he wanted girls to notice him."

After graduating from Warrensburg State Teachers College in 1908, Carnegie ran through several jobs in quick succession, including selling correspondence courses and a position as a salesman for Armour Foods. Carnegie's first attempts at teaching were quite modest. After moving to New York City, he began teaching night-school classes in public speaking at the Young Men's Christian Association (YMCA) in Harlem. Around 1914 he left the YMCA and created his own school for effective public speaking. His business became so successful that in 1916 he rented out Carnegie Hall for one of his famous lectures. Carnegie served in the U.S. Army during World War I, and upon his return to civilian life he took a position as a business manager for a well-to-do radio personality. Around this time, he met and married his first wife, Lolita Baucaire. Unfortunately, they would divorce within ten years.

As the post-war economic boom took place, Carnegie was there, stressing the importance of personal-speaking and communication skills. Once again, his public-speaking business was in great demand and it made him a very wealthy man. In 1936, after being prodded to action by a Simon & Schuster editor, he published *How to Win Friends and Influence People,* which distills techniques gleaned from years of instructing at his public-speaking institute. Even during the darkest days of the Great Depression, it held its ground as a bestseller. The book advocates developing your listening skills, suggests six ways to get a person to like you, and instills a dozen ways to turn dissenters around to your opinion.

After the whirlwind success of *How to Win Friends and Influence People* Carnegie continued lecturing and operating his institute. At one lecture he met Dorothy Prince Vanderpool, who would become his second wife in 1943. The couple had one daughter, Donna Dale. In 1955 the international guru of public speaking died in Forest Hills, New York.

BIOGRAPHICAL AND CRITICAL SOURCES:

BOOKS

Contemporary Heroes and Heroines, Book 3, Gale (Detroit, MI), 1998.

PERIODICALS

Boston Transcript, January 2, 1937, p. 1.
New York Times, February 14, 1937, p. 12; December 13, 1987.
Saturday Review of Literature, January 30, 1937.
Springfield Republican, January 7, 1937, p. 8.*

ONLINE

Dale Carnegie Training Web site, http://www. dcarnegie.com/ (September 29, 2003).*

*   *   *

CHAFER, Lewis Sperry 1871-1952

PERSONAL: Born February 27, 1871, in Rock Creek, OH; died August 22, 1952, in Dallas, TX; son of Thomas Franklin (a Congregational minister) and Losi Lomita (Sperry) Chafer; married Ella Loraine Case, 1896. *Education:* Attended Oberlin College, 1889-92; studied theology privately.

CAREER: Ordained Congregational minister, 1900; ordained Presbyterian minister, 1907; assistant pastor of Congregational church in Painesville, OH, after 1896; pastor of Congregational church in Buffalo, NY; farmer and schoolteacher in Northfield, MA, beginning 1901; extension teacher for Bible correspondence school in New York, beginning 1915; pastor in Dallas, TX, 1920s; Evangelical Theological College (now Dallas Theological Seminary), founder, 1924, president and professor of systematic theology, 1924-52. Central American Mission, director; speaker at Bible conferences.

WRITINGS:

Elementary Outline Studies, [East Northfield, MA], 1907.
Satan: His Motive and Methods, Gospel Publishing House (New York, NY), 1909, revised edition, Sunday School Times (Philadelphia, PA), 1919, reprinted, Zondervan Publishing House (Grand Rapids, MI), 1977.

True Evangelism, Gospel Publishing House (New York, NY), 1911, revised edition published as *True Evangelism; or, Winning Souls by Prayer,* Zondervan Publishing House (Grand Rapids, MI), 1971.

The Kingdom in History and Prophesy, introduction by Cyrus I. Scofield, Fleming H. Revell (New York, NY), 1915.

Salvation, Dunham (Findley, OH), 1917, published as *Salvation: God's Marvelous Work of Grace,* Kregel Publications (Grand Rapids, MI), 1991.

He That Is Spiritual, 1918.

Grace, Sunday School Times (Philadelphia, PA), 1922.

Major Bible Themes, Representing Forty-nine Vital Doctrines of the Scriptures, Abbreviated and Simplified for Popular Use, Sunday School Times (Philadelphia, PA), 1926, revised edition published as *Major Bible Themes: Fifty-two Vital Doctrines of the Scripture Simplified and Explained,* edited by John F. Walvoord, Zondervan Publishing House (Grand Rapids, MI), 1974.

The Ephesian Letter Doctrinally Considered, Loizeaux Brothers, Bible Truth Depot (New York, NY), 1935, published as *The Epistle to the Ephesians,* Kregel Publications (Grand Rapids, MI), 1991.

Systematic Theology, eight volumes, Dallas Theological Seminary (Dallas, TX), 1947-1948, abridged edition by John F. Walvoord published in two volumes, Victor Books (Wheaton, IL), 1988.

Dispensationalism, 2nd edition, Dallas Seminary Press (Dallas, TX), 1951.*

*   *   *

CHURCH, Francis Pharcellus 1839-1906

PERSONAL: Born February 22, 1839, in Rochester, NY; died April 11, 1906; son of Pharcellus (a minister) and Emily (Conant) Church; married Mary Elizabeth Metcalf, 1863. *Education:* Columbia College, graduate (with honors), 1859.

CAREER: New-York Chronicle, New York, NY, chief assistant; *New York Sun,* New York, NY, editor, 1855-60 and 1874-1906; *New York Times,* New York, NY, war correspondent, 1862; also correspondent for *Army and Navy Journal,* during the Civil War; *Galaxy* (literary magazine), editor, 1866-72;. Also editor of *Internal Revenue Record and Customs Journal.*

MEMBER: Sons of the Revolution, National Sculptor Society, Century Club.

WRITINGS:

Is There a Santa Claus?, privately printed (Boston, MA), 1921, enlarged edition, Grosset & Dunlap (New York, NY), 1934.

SIDELIGHTS: "Yes, Virginia, there is a Santa Claus." That sentence is the touchstone line of what is arguably the best-known newspaper editorial ever published in America. The author of the five-hundred-word answer to a child's question was Francis Pharcellus Church, editor of the *New York Sun.* His unsigned editorial went on to have an existence that outlasted Church, his newspaper, and even the little girl who first posed the question, Virginia O'Hanlon.

The son of Baptist minister Pharcellus Church, "Frank" Church was an unlikely choice for journalistic prominence. His schooling centered not on writing but on math and foreign languages, and the younger Church terminated his formal studies at age fifteen to help care for his family after his father fell ill, although he would later go on to complete a college degree. Church worked as an assistant for his father's small religious paper, the *New-York Chronicle,* before finding his way to the *New York Sun.* That paper was something of a family affair as well; the *Sun* had been purchased by Church's brother, William Conant Church. The large metropolitan daily was notorious for publishing the scandalous and sensational, but William strove to make the *Sun* a religious publication instead. Under the direction of his brother, Frank Church was ordered to remove all advertising for liquor, cigars, and theater productions, and to give large editorial space to religious topics. Frank warned his brother that this was a recipe for financial disaster, and his prediction came to pass. In 1861 the Church family sold the *Sun* back to its original owner.

After serving in management positions at several periodicals, notably the *Galaxy,* launched in 1866 as a New York-based counterpart to Boston's established *Atlantic Monthly,* Church returned to the *New York Sun* in 1874 as an editor and writer under editor-in-chief Edward P. Mitchell. Church penned thousands of editorials for the publication, and "all but one have since been forgotten," as Ralph Frasca noted in a *Dictionary of Literary Biography* essay. The paper had received a letter from Virginia O'Hanlon, whose brief message began, "Dear Editor: I am 8 years old. Some of my little friends say there is no Santa Claus. Papa says, 'If you see it in the *Sun,* it's so.' Please tell me the truth, is there a Santa Claus?"

Church was given the task of answering this question. According to editor Mitchell, as quoted in a *Humanist* article by Champe Ransom, Church at first "bristled and pooh-poohed at the subject but he took the letter and turned with an air of resignation to his desk and in a short time produced the classic expression of Christmas sentiment."

"Virginia, your little friends are wrong," Church wrote. "They have been affected by the skepticism of a skeptical age." He argued that Santa, though he may never be seen, exists "as certainly as love and generosity and devotion exist, and you know that they abound and give your life its highest beauty and joy." His editorial's second-paragraph led with, "Yes, Virginia, there is a Santa Claus," and this became the signature line of the editorial, which was reprinted by the *Sun* annually for several decades. The famous rejoinder became part of pop culture, with generations of writers aping the "Yes, Virginia" theme in their own interpretations.

Despite its popularity, Church's editorial had its critics. One of them, Heywood Broun of the *New York World-Telegram,* lambasted Church in his 1934 editorial "There Isn't Any Santa Claus." In Broun's view, Church had encouraged children like Virginia to "maintain an illusion and discouraged the 'healthy skepticism' which she had expressed in her inquiry," according to Lana Whited in an online article for *Roanoke.com.*

Church continued with the *Sun* until his death in 1906. He had one posthumously published book, which is based on his most famous editorial.

BIOGRAPHICAL AND CRITICAL SOURCES:

BOOKS

Bigelow, Donald N., *William Conant Church and the Army and Navy Journal,* AMS Press (New York, NY), 1968.

Dictionary of Literary Biography, Volume 79: *American Magazine Journalists, 1850-1900,* Gale (Detroit, MI), 1989.
Mitchell, Edward P., *Memoirs of an Editor,* Scribner's (New York, NY), 1924.
Stedman, Laura, and George Gould, *The Life and Letters of Edmund Clarence Stedman,* two volumes, Moffat, Yard (New York, NY), 1910.

PERIODICALS

Atlantic, March, 1878, "To Old Friends and New," p. 272.
Humanist, November-December, 1997, Champe Ransom, "Yes, Virginia, There Probably Is No Santa Claus," p. 33.
Nation, April 26, 1866, pp. 534-535; May 30, 1867, pp. 432-433.

ONLINE

History Channel, http://www.historychannel.com/ (March 13, 2002), "Yes, Virginia."
Roanoke.com, http://www.roanoke.com/ (December 8, 1999), Lana Whited, "Yes, Roanoke, There Is a Santa Claus."*

*   *   *

CLAIR, Louis
    See COSER, Lewis A(lfred)

*   *   *

COELHO, Susie

PERSONAL: Born December 7, in Sussex, England; daughter of a college instructor; married Salvatore "Sonny" Bono, December 31, 1981 (divorced June 1, 1984); married Robert Rounds (an investment broker); children: Hutton (son), Hailey (daughter). *Education:* Attended American University.

ADDRESSES: Home—Los Angeles, CA. *Office*—Susie Coelho Enterprises, Inc., 466 Foothill Blvd., No. 203, La Canada, CA 91011.

CAREER: Decorating and lifestyle consultant and author. National Heart Institute, Bethesda, MD, secretary; model under contract with Eileen Ford Modeling Agency; Home Box Office, television news reporter; Bono Restaurants, co-founder with husband, Sonny Bono, c. 1982; A Star Is Worn (boutique), Beverly Hills, CA, founder, 1985; Susie Coelho Enterprises, Inc., founder. Host of television programs *On Stage America,* 1984, *Surprise Gardener,* 1998-2003, and *Outer Spaces,* HGTV, 2003. Actress in television films, including *Mysterious Island of Beautiful Women,* 1979, and *A Perfect Match,* 1980, and on television series *Police Story, Six-Million-Dollar Man,* and *C-16: FBI.*

WRITINGS:

Susie Coelho's Everyday Styling: Easy Tips for Home, Garden, and Entertaining, photography by Jennifer Cheung and Steven Nilsson, Simon and Schuster (New York, NY), 2002.
Susie Coelho's Styling for Entertaining: Twelve One-Day Makeovers in Eight Easy Steps, Simon and Schuster (New York, NY), 2003.

Contributor to periodicals, including *Cosmopolitan, Redbook, Woman's Day, Good Housekeeping,* and *Home;* columnist for *Palm Springs Life Magazine.*

SIDELIGHTS: Susie Coelho was born in Sussex, England of East Indian parentage, and lived in several large cities before her family moved to Washington, D.C. After she won the title of Ms. Photogenic at the Ms. D.C. Beauty Pageant, Coelho dropped out of college and moved to New York City to pursue a career in modeling. Within only a few years Coelho appeared on the covers of such magazines as *Guide, Big Valley, Vive,* and *Vogue Mexico.* Her modeling career also brought her into contact with several celebrities, including actress Rene Russo, hairdresser Jose Eber, and singer Sonny Bono, whom she married in 1981. Together, Coelho and Bono founded and ran the Bono Restaurants, and sponsored the Sonny and Susie Bono Pro-Celebrity Tennis Invitational. Meanwhile, Coelho began to establish a career as an actress in television. However, in 1984, Coelho and Bono divorced.

Mining her phone book full of celebrities, Coelho opened a boutique in Beverly Hills, California in 1985 that sold clothes and memorabilia formerly belonging to the rich and famous. The shop, called A Star Is Worn, donated a portion of its profits to charity. In 1998 she founded Susie Coelho Enterprises, Inc., a multimedia company focusing on gardening, cooking, style, and entertaining. Coelho's first gardening show on HGTV was *Surprise Gardener,* followed in 2003 by *Outer Spaces,* which focuses on creating "outdoor rooms."

Coelho's first book, *Susie Coelho's Everyday Styling: Easy Tips for Home, Garden, and Entertaining,* was published in 2002. The book features many of the tips presented on her television programs, taking the reader through the home-decorating process and the creative use of space, form, and function. *New York Times* contributor Mitchell Ownes claimed that "Coelho takes an infectious, gung-ho approach to low budget decors" that is "frolicsome, rather than egotistical," and a *Publishers Weekly* reviewer wrote that in the book's "200 full-color photos, rooms move and change taking on new character, as do outdoor areas and entrances. And it all looks like fun." In *Susie Coelho's Styling for Entertaining: Twelve One-Day Makeovers in Eight Easy Steps,* the author provides advice for creating what her Web site described as "settings for casual entertaining or extraordinary parties—with minimum effort to maximum effect." In addition to her work for television, Coelho regularly contributes to lifestyle, home, and garden magazines and Internet sites.

BIOGRAPHICAL AND CRITICAL SOURCES:

PERIODICALS

Dallas Morning News, March 1, 2002, Ellen Sweets, review of *Susie Coelho's Everyday Styling: Easy Tips for Home, Garden, and Entertaining.*
Fort Worth Star-Telegram, February 28, 2002, Alyson Ward, review of *Susie Coelho's Everyday Styling.*
New York Times, March 21, 2002, Mitchell Owens, review of *Susie Coelho's Everyday Styling,* p. 6.
Publishers Weekly, January 21, 2002, review of *Susie Coelho's Everyday Styling,* p. 84.
Toronto Star, March 10, 2002, review of *Susie Coelho's Everyday Styling,* p. 3F.
Washington Post, February 23, 2002, Barbara E. Martinez, "Convertible Coelho."

ONLINE

Susie Coelho Web site, http://www.susiecoelho.com (July 12, 2003).*

COFFEY, Wayne
(Eric Ryerson, a pseudonym)

PERSONAL: Male.

ADDRESSES: Home—Westchester County, NY. *Office*—c/o New York *Daily News,* 450 West 33rd St., Third Floor, New York, NY 10001.

CAREER: New York *Daily News,* New York, NY, sportswriter.

WRITINGS:

How We Choose a Congress (for juveniles), St. Martin's Press (New York, NY), 1980.

(With Michael Schatzki) *Negotiation, the Art of Getting What You Want,* New American Library (New York, NY), 1981.

303 of the World's Worst Predictions, illustrated by Steven DuQuette, Tribeca Communications (New York, NY), 1983.

All-Pro's Greatest Football Players (for young adults), Scholastic (New York, NY), 1983.

(Under pseudonym Eric Ryerson) *When Your Parent Drinks Too Much: A Book for Teenagers,* Facts on File (New York, NY), 1985.

Straight Talk about Drinking: Teenagers Speak out about Alcohol, New American Library (New York, NY), 1988.

(With Faye Young Miller) *Winning Basketball for Girls,* photographs by Don Haderman and others, Facts on File (New York, NY), 1992, third edition, 2002.

Jesse Owens (for juveniles), illustrated by Mike Eagle, Blackbirch Press (Woodbridge, CT), 1992.

Katarina Witt (for juveniles), illustrated by Mike Eagle, Blackbirch Press (Woodbridge, CT), 1992.

Kip Keino (for juveniles), illustrated by Richard Smolinski, Blackbirch Press (Woodbridge, CT), 1992.

Olga Korbut (for juveniles), illustrated by Ed Vebell, Blackbirch Press (Woodbridge, CT), 1992.

Jim Thorpe (for juveniles), illustrated by David Taylor, Blackbirch Press (Woodbridge, CT), 1993.

Carl Lewis (for juveniles), Blackbirch Press (Woodbridge, CT), 1993.

Wilma Rudolph (for juveniles), Blackbirch Press (Woodbridge, CT), 1993.

1980 U.S. Hockey Team (for juveniles), illustrated by Richard Smolinski, Blackbirch Press (Woodbridge, CT), 1993.

(With Filip Bondy) *Dreams of Gold: The Nancy Kerrigan Story,* St. Martin's Press (New York, NY), 1994.

The Kobe Bryant Story (for juveniles), Scholastic (New York, NY), 1999.

Meet the Women of American Soccer: An Inside Look at America's Team, photographs by Michael Stahlschmidt, Scholastic (New York, NY), 1999.

Winning Sounds like This: A Season with the Women's Basketball Team at Gallaudet, the World's Only Deaf University, photographs by Brian Morris, Crown (New York, NY), 2002.

SIDELIGHTS: Sports reporter Wayne Coffey has written several nonfiction books on prominent athletes and some on other topics, including the U.S. government and teen drinking. Many of his works are aimed at young people, such as his series of biographies of Olympic athletes. Some of the competitors profiled in this series are Jim Thorpe, Jesse Owens, Olga Korbut, and the 1980 U.S. men's hockey team. Concerning the biography *Jim Thorpe, School Library Journal* contributor Elaine Fort Weischedel observed that Coffey "does a good job" telling the story of this great multisport athlete's achievements, as well as of the career controversies and personal troubles that marked Thorpe's life. For instance, Coffey deals with Thorpe's drinking problem "briefly and compassionately," she wrote. Coffey's book *1980 U.S. Hockey Team,* meanwhile, "conveys a good sense of the near-hysteria" surrounding the team's gold medal win, Weischedel related.

Aimed at a general readership is another sports chronicle, *Winning Sounds like This: A Season with the Women's Basketball Team at Gallaudet, the World's Only Deaf University.* The book following the players through the 1999-2000 season, during which the team made it to the semifinals of its conference championship. Coffey demonstrates how deaf athletes differ from hearing ones and how they do not; their sign-language communications create what Coffey calls a surreal, silent world that may baffle their opponents, but the spirit of competition is the same among the deaf and the hearing. He also provides a history of education for the deaf and an exploration of deaf culture; he reports that the players and most of their fellow Gallaudet students do not mind not being able to hear—they do not see themselves as needing to be "fixed." The result is less a book about basketball than one about "trying, achieving and living with a condition most of us would consider a handicap but one that the athletes in question don't," wrote Dick Heller in the *Washington Times.* Indeed, commented a *Publishers Weekly* reviewer, Coffey makes deafness appear "less alien than the big egos of Division I and the salaries of the NBA." *Library Journal* critic Kathy Ruffle remarked that "readers come away with a great respect for these players," while a *Publishers Weekly* reviewer summed up the book as "a great story in a good storyteller's hands." Heller noted, "The word 'inspiring' is frequently overused, but no other serves as well to describe Wayne Coffey's *Winning Sounds like This.*"

Coffey's non-sports writings include *How We Choose a Congress* and *Straight Talk about Drinking: Teenagers Speak out about Alcohol,* both designed for young audiences. The former explains the electoral process "in simple terms, but not simplistically," in the opinion of *Booklist* contributor William Bradley Hooper. *Straight Talk about Drinking* features interviews with fifty teenagers who have a variety of perspectives on the subject: some drink, some do not, some have alcoholics in the family. Coffey, who describes himself as a moderate drinker, also writes about his experience of having an alcoholic mother and provides information generally aimed at helping teenagers make well-considered decisions about drinking. "The information is realistic—not all drinking is bad—but cautious," observed Martha Gordon in the *School Library Journal. Voice of Youth Advocates* reviewer Sue Rosenzweig noted that Coffey's call for responsible decision-making "is not preachy," and "will be listened to by the readers."

BIOGRAPHICAL AND CRITICAL SOURCES:

PERIODICALS

Booklist, June 1, 1980, William Bradley Hooper, review of *How We Choose a Congress,* p. 1392; September 15, 1988, Stephanie Zvirin, review of *Straight Talk about Drinking: Teenagers Speak out about Alcohol,* p. 146.

Kirkus Reviews, April 15, 1980, review of *How We Choose a Congress,* p. 547.

Library Journal, February 15, 2002, Kathy Ruffle, review of *Winning Sounds like This: A Season with the Women's Basketball Team at Gallaudet, the World's Only Deaf University,* p. 152.

Publishers Weekly, June 10, 1988, review of *Straight Talk about Drinking,* p. 85; February 25, 2002, review of *Winning Sounds like This,* p. 53.

School Library Journal, November, 1988, Martha Gordon, review of *Straight Talk about Drinking,* pp. 135-136; September, 1993, Elaine Fort Weischedel, review of *Jim Thorpe* and *1980 U.S. Hockey Team,* pp. 239-240.

Voice of Youth Advocates, April, 1984, Virginia Sankey, review of *All-Pro's Greatest Football Players,* p. 44; February, 1989, Sue Rosenzweig, review of *Straight Talk about Drinking,* p. 298.

Washington Times, April 1, 2002, Dick Heller, "Book on Gallaudet Inspirational Read," p. C4.*

*　　*　　*

COGLEY, Richard W. 1950-

PERSONAL: Born 1950. *Education:* Franklin and Marshall College, B.A.; Yale University, M.Div.; Princeton University, Ph.D.

ADDRESSES: Office—Southern Methodist University, 6425 Boaz Lane, Dallas, TX 75205. *E-mail*—rcogley@mail.smu.edu.

CAREER: Southern Methodist University, Dallas, TX, associate professor and chair of department of religious studies, 1999—. Visiting professor at North Carolina State University, Loyola Marymount University, and Reed College.

WRITINGS:

John Eliot's Mission to the Indians before King Philip's War, Harvard University Press (Cambridge, MA), 1999.

Contributor of articles and reviews to periodicals, including *William and Mary Quarterly.*

WORK IN PROGRESS: Research of early American Puritan eschatology.

SIDELIGHTS: Richard W. Cogley's many years of research into the conversion of Native Americans in Southern New England by the English during the seventeenth century led to his study *John Eliot's Mission to the Indians before King Philip's War.* The primary figure in the volume is John Eliot, who was involved in nearly every missionary effort in the area. Eliot is seen by Cogley as a man of pure intentions who delayed converting natives until they could observe the Christian practices of the colonists and voluntarily become members of the "praying towns" that were established for that purpose. According to Cogley, Eliot also waited until the demands of the Massachusetts settlement had been met, and he cites the language barrier and the Congregational Church's lack of a missionary arm as other factors. Eliot began his active missionary work with native people in 1646, after a number of sachems voluntarily submitted to English authority.

Choice reviewer T. D. Bozeman noted that Cogley takes issue with a number of previously held views, one being that Eliot's mission was the expansion of English imperialism and culture. Bozeman wrote that Cogley's argument "that the mission was more a way to counteract rather than to aid English domination will spark lively debate."

Jenny Hale Pulsipher reviewed the volume in the *Journal of Ecclesiastical History,* stating that Cogley "works to give the Indian perspective, noting ways they used the mission to advance their material well-being and authority within English and Indian cultures." Most of the settlements had populations of less than one hundred, but the native Americans who lived there had many advantages. They assimilated fastest as English settlement expanded, and they began cottage industries that produced needed materials, such as clapboard shingles. They learned other trades and often became apprentices. In addition, they were still self-sustaining, in that they continued to plant, hunt, and fish.

Eliot and others, in the work of converting native Americans, promoted the necessity of wearing English-style clothing and the adoption of a more European lifestyle, which included accepting more Puritanical sexual behaviors. On the other hand, Cogley points out that Eliot furthered the land rights of the tribes and encouraged them to continue their medical practices, which he also encouraged them to share with the settlers.

H. Roger Grant wrote in *Utopian Studies* that "Cogley's study is a masterpiece of scholarship. As any good historian should do, he has exploited a vast array of primary source materials and . . . pertinent secondary works. Although no study is ever 'definitive,' this one is close. Moreover, Cogley has wisely created several appendixes, including one on individual praying Indian settlements. Finally, Richard Cogley has presented John Eliot in a logical and readable fashion."

BIOGRAPHICAL AND CRITICAL SOURCES:

PERIODICALS

American Historical Review, June, 2000, Edward G. Gray, review of *John Eliot's Mission to the Indians before King Philip's War,* p. 917.
Catholic Historical Review, October, 1999, Neal Salisbury, review of *John Eliot's Mission to the Indians before King Philip's War,* p. 652.
Choice, November, 1999, T. D. Bozeman, review of *John Eliot's Mission to the Indians before King Philip's War,* p. 554.
Historian, fall, 2000, Robin Fabel, review of *John Eliot's Mission to the Indians before King Philip's War,* p. 140.
Journal of American History, September, 2000, Virginia DeJohn Anderson, review of *John Eliot's Mission to the Indians before King Philip's War,* p. 639.
Journal of Ecclesiastical History, July, 2000, Jenny Hale Pulsipher, review of *John Eliot's Mission to the Indians before King Philip's War,* p. 637.
Utopian Studies, spring, 2000, H. Roger Grant, review of *John Eliot's Mission to the Indians before King Philip's War,* p. 247.*

* * *

COHEN, Jayne 1949-

PERSONAL: Born February 5, 1949, in New York, NY; daughter of Max (an attorney) and Joan (an interior designer and entrepenur) Cohen; married; children: one daughter. *Ethnicity:* "Ashkenazi Jew." *Education:* City College of New York, B.A. (English literature), 1971; Pratt Institute, M.L.S., 1996; graduate coursework at Hunter College. *Politics:* Democrat. *Religion:* Jewish. *Hobbies and other interests:* Theatre, folktales and folklore, storytelling, everything to do with food, children's literature, languages, history, and travel.

ADDRESSES: Agent—Goodman Associates, 500 West End Ave., New York, NY 10024. *E-mail*—jcohen0205@aol.com.

CAREER: Author and food writer.

MEMBER: International Association of Culinary Professionals, New York Women's Culinary Association, New York Culinary Historians, Beta Phi Mu, Phi Beta Kappa.

AWARDS, HONORS: Pratt Circle Award for outstanding academic achievement in library science.

WRITINGS:

The Gefilte Variations: Two Hundred Inspired Recreations of Classics from the Jewish Kitchen with Menus, Stories, and Traditions for the Holidays and Year-Round, Scribner (New York, NY), 2000.

Contributor to periodicals, including *Bon Appetit, Los Angeles Times, Food and Wine, Gourmet, Cook's, New York Times, Boston Globe,* and *Newsday.*

WORK IN PROGRESS: The Ultimate Bar/Bat Mitzvah Celebration Book: A Guide to Inspiring Ceremonies and Joyous Festivities, for Clarkson Potter.

SIDELIGHTS: In her cookbook *The Gefilte Variations: Two Hundred Inspired Recreations of Classics from the Jewish Kitchen with Menus, Stories, and Traditions for the Holidays and Year-Round,* Jayne Cohen "brings a breath of fresh air to favorite Jewish dishes, from matzoh brei to noodle kugel," commented Judith C. Sutton in *Library Journal.* Florence Fabricant in the *New York Times* noted that the book "reveals the author's frequently playful approach to Jewish Food," but that "none of her clearly written recipes violate the spirit of Jewish cooking traditions. And they are strictly kosher."

Cohen told Matt Schaffer of the *Boston Herald* that "potchkehing—playing with—a recipe is what Jewish cuisine is all about." Kathleen Purvis in the *Pittsburgh Post-Gazette* added that "it's worth remembering that traditions are set in hearts, not in stone," and that *The Gefilte Variations* illustrates "that it's OK to adjust and to renew, as long as you do it with reverence and care."

The Gefilte Variations is the result of what Cohen views as a personal journey, what she described on the book's Web site as "the autobiography of one palate" as cuisine is examined through its associations with family and tradition. "These are the foods that were really made in the home, . . . not for kings or in the grandest restaurants," Cohen explained to Schaffer, describing the resulting recipes as components of "meals that you're going to share around a table with conversation."

The Gefilte Variations also includes information about Jewish culture and the history behind many Jewish dishes. Ronna Welsh, in a review of the book for the *Austin Chronicle,* concluded that *The Gefilte Variations* "is a worthy tribute and contribution to a continually evolving cuisine," while a *Publishers Weekly* contributor noted: "Few can explain the essence of Jewish food as charmingly and lyrically as . . . Cohen does in this outstanding debut."

Cohen told *CA:* "I've always considered myself a storyteller who often tells her tales through recipes."

BIOGRAPHICAL AND CRITICAL SOURCES:

PERIODICALS

Austin Chronicle, May 5, 2000, Ronna Welsh, review of *The Gefilte Variations: Two-Hundred Inspired Recreations of Classics from the Jewish Kitchen with Menus, Stories, and Traditions for the Holidays and Year-Round.*
Boston Herald, April 19, 2000, Matt Schaffer, review of *The Gefilte Variations,* p. 53.
Jerusalem Post, December 21, 2000, Linda Morel, review of *The Gefilte Variations.*
Library Journal, February 15, 2000, Judith C. Sutton, review of *The Gefilte Variations,* p. 191.
New York Times, April 5, 2000, Florence Fabricant, review of *The Gefilte Variations,* p. F5.

Pittsburgh Post-Gazette, April 13, 2000, Kathleen Purvis, review of *The Gefilte Variations,* p. E8.

Publishers Weekly, February 7, 2000, review of *The Gefilte Variations,* p. 81.

San Francisco Chronicle, April 5, 2000, Karola Saekel, review of *The Gefilte Variations.*

ONLINE

Bookpage, http://www.bookpage.com/ (March, 2000), review of *The Gefilte Variations.*

Gefilte Variations Web site, http://www.gefiltevariations.com/ (June 10, 2003).

*   *   *

COHEN, Misha Ruth 1951(?)-

PERSONAL: Born c. 1951. *Education:* Doctorate in Oriental medicine; Lincoln Medical and Mental Health Center, License in acupuncture.

ADDRESSES: Office—Quan Yin Healing Arts Center, 455 Valencia St., San Francisco, CA 94103. *E-mail*—TCMpaths@aol.com.

CAREER: Physician, researcher, and author. Quan Yin Healing Arts Center, San Francisco, CA, founder and educational research director; Chicken Soup Chinese Medicine, San Francisco, clinical director. Member, National Institute of Heath Office of AIDS Research ad hoc subpanel on alternative and complementary therapy research; member of board, National Conference on Women and HIV.

AWARDS, HONORS: National Institute of Health grant; named among fifty top AIDS researchers, *POZ* magazine, 1996; fellow of American Academy of Oriental Medicine.

WRITINGS:

(With Kalia Doner) *The Chinese Way to Healing: Many Paths to Wholeness,* Berkley Publishing Group (New York, NY), 1996.

(With Kalia Doner) *The HIV Wellness Sourcebook: An East/West Guide to Living Well with HIV/AIDS and Related Conditions,* Henry Holt (New York, NY), 1998.

(With Robert G. Gish and Kalia Doner) *The Hepatitis C Help Book: A Groundbreaking Treatment Program Combining Western and Eastern Medicine for Maximum Wellness and Healing,* St. Martin's Press (New York, NY), 2000.

SIDELIGHTS: Misha Ruth Cohen is a doctor of Oriental medicine whose books focus on the merger of Eastern and Western methods to provide the most effective medical treatment possible. She is especially well known for her research into the use of Chinese medicine in the treatment of HIV/AIDS. As William Beatty wrote in *Booklist,* Cohen's advice "demonstrates rational combination of Eastern and Western medicine in service to the needs of each particular patient."

As a child Cohen was introduced to alternative therapies by her grandmother, who was a practitioner of yoga and vegetarianism. Her interest was revived after injuries she received in a serious car accident were successfully treated using Japanese *shiatsu* massage. Cohen began to study shiatsu massage and acupuncture in the 1970s, when few opportunities existed to formally study traditional Chinese medicine in the United States. Her early studies were carried out in New York City at an acupuncture school affiliated with a drug treatment center whose purpose was to provide training in the use of Chinese remedies to help patients battle addiction. During her medical studies Cohen developed a special interest in gynecology, and especially in the treatment of HIV and AIDS.

Moving to San Francisco, Cohen founded the Quan Yin Healing Arts Center and began treating HIV-positive patients there in the mid-1980s. She explains her approach, which includes diet, herbal therapy, acupuncture, exercise, and meditation in *The HIV Wellness Sourcebook: An East/West Guide to Living Well with HIV/AIDS and Related Conditions.* This book is a result of Cohen's years in practice and her extensive research in the field. A grant from the National Institute of Health's Office of Alternative Medicine allowed her to formally study the use of a herbal formula in HIV patients. A reviewer for *Publishers Weekly* wrote, "Cohen carefully explains how Western and Eastern medical approaches differ and how they can be blended into a comprehensive and effective treatment program." In a review of *The HIV Wellness Sourcebook* for *Library Journal,* Charles Wessel noted that the book is an "informative resource for anyone seeking an understanding of Chinese medicine and its approach to HIV and AIDS."

Cohen's other books include *The Chinese Way to Healing: Many Paths to Wholeness,* which provides an overview of the ancient healing techniques of Chinese medicine, and *The Hepatitis C Help Book: A Groundbreaking Treatment Program Combining Western and Eastern Medicine for Maximum Wellness and Healing.*

BIOGRAPHICAL AND CRITICAL SOURCES:

PERIODICALS

Booklist, April, 1998, William Beatty, review of *The HIV Wellness Sourcebook: An East/West Guide to Living Well with HIV/AIDS and Related Conditions,* p. 1290.
Library Journal, June 1, 1998, Charles Wessel, review of *The HIV Wellness Sourcebook,* p. 141.
Publishers Weekly, April 20, 1998, review of *The HIV Wellness Sourcebook,* p. 61.

ONLINE

Doc Misha's Chicken Soup Chinese Medicine, http://www.docmisha.com (June 16, 2003).*

*   *   *

COHN, Leopold 1862-1937

PERSONAL: Born 1862, in Berezna, Hungary; immigrated to the United States, 1892; died December 19, 1937; married Rose Hoffman, 1880; children: Joseph Hoffman. *Education:* Attended New College of the Free Church, Edinburgh, Scotland.

CAREER: Founder of Christian mission in Brooklyn, NY, 1893; American Board of Missions to the Jews (originally Williamsburg Mission to the Jews), Brooklyn, NY, founder, 1896, board chair, 1896-1937. Beth Bar Shalom (Christian mission), founder, 1909.

WRITINGS:

A Modern Missionary to an Ancient People, American Board of Missions to the Jews (New York, NY), 1911, published as *To an Ancient People: The Autobiography of Dr. Leopold Cohn,* Chosen People Ministries (Charlotte, NC), 1996.
(Editor, with Joseph Hoffman Cohn) *The Chosen People Question Box: A Compilation of Bible Questions and Answers Which Appeared over . . . Forty Years in . . . The Chosen People,* American Board of Missions to the Jews (Brooklyn, NY), 1938.

Founder, *Chosen People,* 1898, and *Shepherd of Israel* (bilingual in Yiddish and English), 1920.

BIOGRAPHICAL AND CRITICAL SOURCES:

BOOKS

Cohn, Joseph Hoffman, *I Have Fought a Good Fight,* American Board of Missions to the Jews (New York, NY), 1953.
Cohn, Leopold, *A Modern Missionary to an Ancient People,* American Board of Missions to the Jews (New York, NY), 1911, published as *To an Ancient People: The Autobiography of Dr. Leopold Cohn,* Chosen People Ministries (Charlotte, NC), 1996.
Eichhorn, David Max, *Evangelizing the American Jew,* Jonathan David Publishers (Middle Village, NY), 1978.
Religious Leaders of America, 2nd edition, Gale (Detroit, MI), 1999.*

*   *   *

COLBY, William H. 1955-

PERSONAL: Born 1955; married; children: four.

ADDRESSES: Home—Kansas City, MO. *Agent*—c/o Author Mail, Hay House, P.O. Box 5100, Carlsbad, CA 92018-5100.

CAREER: Attorney and author. Kansas School of Law, visiting professor; Midwest Bioethics Center, fellow. Has appeared on national TV programs, including, *Good Morning, America, Today Show, CBS This Morning, MacNeil Lehrer Report,* and others.

WRITINGS:

Long Goodbye: The Deaths of Nancy Cruzan, Hay House (Carlsbad, CA), 2002.

SIDELIGHTS: Attorney and writer William H. Colby is the lawyer who successfully argued the first "right to die" case to come before the U.S. Supreme Court. In *Long Goodbye: The Deaths of Nancy Cruzan,* Colby recounts the tragic events leading up to the case, the legal process involved, and the profound effects that Nancy Cruzan's short life and lingering death had on her family and the world.

In the early 1980s, twenty-five-year-old Nancy Cruzan suffered a devastating automobile accident when her car left a Missouri highway and came to a crashing, rolling stop hundreds of yards away. Cruzan, having been thrown from the car, was left in a persistent vegetative state that required continuous life support and nourishment through a feeding tube. "Every part of her brain that made her uniquely Nancy was gone by the time [the emergency workers] got there," Colby was quoted as saying on the *Life's End Institute* Web site.

Early on, parents Joe and Joyce Cruzan hoped that their daughter might recover. For five years, Nancy Cruzan was kept alive by artificial means, though she showed no signs of recovery from the coma she had been in since the accident. Ultimately, according to Harry Charles in *Library Journal,* Joe and Joyce made the decision to remove their daughter's feeding tube and let her die "in peace." The Cruzan's decision ignited a furious controversy, involving vigorous opposition by right-to-life advocates, the Missouri legislature, Missouri Governor John Ashcroft, the media, and, finally, the Supreme Court. In a protracted legal battle before the high court, Colby argued that the Cruzans had the right to decide to withhold their daughter's life-sustaining treatment. His argument was based on the fact that Nancy's own wishes in the matter were unclear and she was incapable of making the decision herself. The court eventually agreed. Despite the unceasing media attention, the interminable legal pressure, and the violence threatened by protesters, Nancy Cruzan's feeding tube was removed. She died on December 26, 1990.

Using quotes from legal briefs, news stories, letters, and other documents, as well as reconstructions of conversations with family members, opposing lawyers,

government representatives, and judges, Colby's book provides a detailed, first-hand analysis of the landmark case. Charles called Colby's account of the case "thoughtful," adding, "the book is distinguished by the author's attention to detail and clear writing style." *Booklist* reviewer Vanessa Bush called the book "a truly riveting look at the case that sharpened public debate about the medical and legal issues surrounding brain death and the right to die with dignity."

Colby also emphasizes the deep impact the case had on Joe and Joyce Cruzan—the book begins and ends with Joe Cruzan's suicide note. "This blue-collar family keeps one goal from beginning to end—trying to do what they know in their hearts their loved one would want them to do," remarked a writer in a description of the book on the *Hay House Web site.* Elizabeth D. McCarter wrote on the *Missouri Bar* Web site, "Bill Colby revealed the deep anguish of the Cruzans . . . as parents suffering a non-ending nightmare: attempting for years to bring Nancy back, and finally fighting for years to give her peace."

BIOGRAPHICAL AND CRITICAL SOURCES:

PERIODICALS

Booklist, November 1, 2002, Vanessa Bush, review of *Long Goodbye: The Deaths of Nancy Cruzan,* pp. 453-454.

Library Journal, November 1, 2002, Harry Charles, review of *Long Goodbye: The Deaths of Nancy Cruzan,* p. 108.

New York Times, December 7, 1989, Linda Greenhouse, "Right-to-Die Case Gets First Hearing in Supreme Court," p. 1.

ONLINE

Hay House Web site, http://www.hayhouse.com/ (January 21, 2003).

Life's End Institute Web site, http://www.missoulademonstration.org/ (January 17, 2003), Ginny Merriam, interview with William H. Colby.

Missouri Bar Web site, http://www.mobar.org/ (January 21, 2002), Elizabeth D. McCarter, review of *Long Goodbye: The Deaths of Nancy Cruzan.**

COLE, Cornelius 1822-1924

PERSONAL: Born September 17, 1822, in Lodi, NY; died of pneumonia November 3, 1924, in Los Angeles, CA; son of David and Rachael (Townsend) Cole; married Olive Colegrove, 1853 (died, 1918); children: Seward, Schuyler, George T., Emma Brown, Lucretia Waring, Mrs. Reginald H. Jones, Mrs. James G. McLaughlin. *Education:* Attended Ovid Academy, Lima Seminary, and Hobart College; Wesleyan University, B.A., 1847; studied law in Auburn, NY, 1848, and at law offices of William R. Seward. *Politics:* Republican. *Religion:* Methodist.

CAREER: Politician and lawyer. Admitted to the Bar of New York State, 1848; gold miner in California, 1849-c.50; practiced law in San Francisco, CA, 1850-51, and in Sacramento, CA, beginning 1852; *Sacramento Daily Times,* editor, began 1856; Republican National Committee, elected member, 1856-60; City and County of Sacramento, district attorney, 1859-62; U.S. House of Representatives, at-large representative from California, 1863-65; U.S. Senate, senator from California, 1867-73, chairman of Committee on Appropriations, 1871-73; practiced law in California, 1873-c.1922. Central Pacific Railroad Company, Sacramento, organizer. *Military service:* Union Army, commissioned as a captain, 1863.

MEMBER: Sons of the American Revolution, Republican Party.

AWARDS, HONORS: Honorary LL.D., Wesleyan University, 1923.

WRITINGS:

Speech of Hon. Cornelius Cole, of California, on Arming the Slaves. Delivered in the House of Representatives, February 18, 1864, McGill & Witherow (Washington, DC), 1864.
Speech of Hon. Cornelius Cole, of California, on the China Mail Bill, Delivered in the House of Representatives, February 16, 1865, 1865.
Australian Mail Line: Speech of Hon. Cornelius Cole, of California, Delivered to the U.S. Senate, July 9, 1870, 1870.

Income Tax: Speech of Hon. Cornelius Cole, of California, Delivered January 26, 1871, 1871.
Annexation of Dominica: Speech of Hon. Cornelius Cole, of California, in the Senate of the United States, April 19, 1871, Congressional Globe Office (Washington, DC), 1871.
Speech of Senator Cole, on Pending Railway Legislation, Delivered at Platt's Hall, San Francisco, 1872, 1872.
California Three Hundred and Fifty Years Ago: Manuelo's Narrative, Translated from the Portuguese, by a Pioneer, Samuel Carson (San Francisco, CA), 1888.
Memoirs of Cornelius Cole, Ex-Senator of the United States from California, McLoughlin Brothers (New York, NY), 1908.
Ideals in Verse, Times-Mirror Press (Los Angeles, CA), 1924.

Numerous other brief congressional and senatorial speeches by Cole were issued as pamphlets by the Congress and its printers during his years in Washington.

SIDELIGHTS: When Cornelius Cole, a former Republican senator from California, died in 1924, the mayor of Los Angeles, George E. Cryer, said at Cole's funeral: "No man had been more closely identified with the city of Los Angeles for so many years than Senator Cole. To meet and talk with him about his early experiences in public affairs was like reading a lively chapter from the history of the past, for he could recount many interesting occurrences of the days of the Lincoln Administration, and the stirring periods preceding the Civil War."

Cole, a New York lawyer, first came to California during the gold rush of 1849. Unlike many other miners, Cole actually found gold, and with the proceeds he built himself a law office in San Francisco. When the law office burnt down in 1851, Cole relocated to Sacramento—which would become the capital of California in 1854—and opened another practice. Two years later, Cole became the first Californian to serve on the national committee of the newly formed Republican Party. He went on to serve in the Union Army during the U.S. Civil War, and in 1863 he was elected to the U.S. House of Representatives. During those years Cole became a friend of and adviser to the country's first Republican president, Abraham Lincoln.

Cole returned to Washington, D.C., as a senator after the 1866 elections. He only served one term, but for part of it he chaired the powerful Committee on Appropriations. After Cole lost his re-election bid in 1872, he returned to California and resumed his law practice. He bought a ranch in Hollywood in 1881 and until age 100 he commuted daily to his law office in Los Angeles.

BIOGRAPHICAL AND CRITICAL SOURCES:

BOOKS

Biographical Directory of the American Congress, 1774-1989, U.S. Government Printing Office (Washington, DC), 1989.

Cole, Cornelius, II, *Senator Cornelius Cole and the Beginning of Hollywood,* Crescent Publications (New York, NY), 1980.

Hart, James D., *A Companion to California,* Oxford University Press (New York, NY), 1978.

Johnson, Rossiter, editor, *The Twentieth-Century Biographical Dictionary of Notable Americans,* Biographical Society, 1904.

Lanman, Charles, *Biographical Annals of the Civil Government of the United States During Its First Century, from Original and Official Sources,* James Anglim (Washington, DC), 1876.

National Cyclopaedia of American Biography, James T. White & Co. (New York, NY), 1932.

Phillips, Catherine Coffin, *Cornelius Cole, California Pioneer and U.S. Senator,* J. H. Nash (San Francisco, CA), 1929.

Preston, Wheeler, *American Biographies,* Harper & Brothers (New York, NY), 1940.

Spalding, William A., *History of Los Angeles, City and County, California,* J. R. Finnell & Sons (Los Angeles, CA), 1931.

Wilson, James Grant, and John Fiske, editors, *Appleton's Cyclopaedia of American Biography,* D. Appleton (New York, NY), 1888-89.

PERIODICALS

Los Angeles Times, February 10, 1999, Richard Simon, "Few Remember Cornelius Cole but the Name Lives On," p. A13.

ONLINE

Biographical Directory of the United States Congress, 1774-Present, http://bioguide.congress.gov/ (March 8, 2003), "COLE, Cornelius, 1822-1924."

Political Graveyard, http://politicalgraveyard.com/ (March 8, 2003).

OBITUARIES:

PERIODICALS

Los Angeles Times, November 4, 1924, part 2, p. 2.*

*   *   *

CONASON, Joe 1954(?)-

PERSONAL: Born c. 1954; son of Emanuel V. and Eleanor L. Conason (owners of a contemporary design and crafts store); married Elizabeth Horan Wagley (a fund-raising consultant), October 12, 2002. *Education:* Received degree from Brandeis University.

ADDRESSES: Office—Salon.com, 22 Fourth St., 16th Floor, San Francisco, CA 94103. *E-mail*—jconason@ observer.com.

CAREER: Journalist and author. *East Boston Community News,* reporter; *Real Paper,* reporter; *Village Voice,* columnist, staff writer, and national correspondent, 1978-90; *New York Observer,* columnist, political editor, and national correspondent, 1992—; *Salon.com,* author of daily Web log "Joe Conason's Journal."

WRITINGS:

(With Gene Lyons) *The Hunting of the President: The Ten-Year Campaign to Destroy Bill and Hillary Clinton,* Thomas Dunne Books (New York, NY), 2000.

Big Lies: The Right-Wing Propaganda Machine and How It Distorts the Truth, Thomas Dunne Books (New York, NY), 2003.

SIDELIGHTS: Author, editor, and journalist Joe Conason is a columnist for the Internet magazine *Salon.com* and is the national correspondent for the liberal *New York Observer.* He wrote, with Gene Lyons, *The Hunting of the President: The Ten-Year Campaign to Destroy Bill and Hillary Clinton,* and is the solo author of *Big Lies: The Right-Wing Propaganda Machine and How It Distorts the Truth.*

The Hunting of the President is a detailed account of what former U.S. first lady Hillary Clinton once called the "vast, right-wing conspiracy" directed at her and her husband, former president Bill Clinton. Robert F. Nardini, a reviewer for *Library Journal,* said Conason and Lyons's reporting is "thickly documented" and "makes a firm case" for their allegations. The book begins with Clinton's 1989 gubernatorial reelection campaign in Arkansas and ends with the 1998 Monica Lewinsky scandal. The authors discuss difficult times the Clinton presidency endured, such as the Whitewater real estate investigation, the Arkansas Project, the Paula Jones lawsuit, and the Lewinsky scandal. A *Publishers Weekly* contributor found that the authors' "cast of characters is enormous, and their research overwhelming," yet noted that the book would help readers "gain a considerably more balanced and complex picture of the road to impeachment."

James Bowman commented in the *Washington Post* that "if even a fraction of the allegations against President Clinton laboriously charted by Conason and Lyons are indeed as false and fanciful as . . . represented . . . here, then there is a powerful evidence that the siren song of a possible 'cover-up' enticed a great many journalists, politicians and others into error." Joshua Micah Marshall, in the *American Prospect,* wrote: "The book does a masterful job of mixing investigative revelations and political analysis with unflinching attacks on those who deserve them. Nowhere will a reader find a more detailed and instructive survey of the origins of the Clinton scandals or a more systematic refutation of the many inaccuracies that still plague the story."

Noting the wealth of new books by both conservative and liberal authors, Ilene Cooper, in *Booklist,* called Conason's second book, *Big Lies,* "More raw meat for the lions of the Left and the Right to devour." In the book Conason sets out to refute what right-wing conservatives often remark are the hallmarks of liberal politics, ideas propagated by the right through books, television, and radio talk shows. Points heavily contested are: that liberals are unpatriotic, soft on crime, "politically correct," fiscally irresponsible, raise taxes, promote immorality, and that that the media is liberally biased. Jill Ortner, writing in *American Libraries,* noted that Conason "methodically presents evidence to the contrary while showing how conservatives/Republicans fail to measure up" to their own standards.

A contributor to *Kirkus Reviews* said that in *Big Lies* Conason "flushes the hypocrisy out of conservative rants and jibes at liberals." *Washington Post* contributor Steve Weinberg noted that "Conason deserves high marks for the book's organization. . . . He deserves praise as well for allowing that Republicans and/or conservatives can be good human beings. . . . His thinking often transcends glib and clever to warrant the phrase 'downright deep.'" *New York Times Book Review* contributor Michael Janeway wrote, "His chapter on 'crony capitalism'—the web of deals, ventures and profiteering on the part of President Bush, his family members and their allies—is worth the price of the book," even though it is drawn from other sources. William O'Rourke, writing in the *Chicago Sun-Times,* described Conason as "straight out of the liberal muckraker tradition, a journalist . . . who sets out to expose corruption in big business and government." *Big Lies,* noted O'Rourke, "is a rigorous and devastating portrait of the last three Republican administrations."

BIOGRAPHICAL AND CRITICAL SOURCES:

PERIODICALS

American Libraries, September, 2003, Jill Ortner, review of *Big Lies: The Right-Wing Propaganda Machine and How It Distorts the Truth.*
American Prospect, July 17, 2000, Joshua Micah Marshall, "Clinton-Hating," pp. 43-44.
Booklist, February 15, 2000, Ilene Cooper, review of *The Hunting of the President: The Ten-Year Campaign to Destroy Bill and Hillary Clinton,* p. 1050; August, 2003, Ilene Cooper, review of *Big Lies,* p. 1946.
Boston Globe, April 30, 2000, Scott Alarik, "The Endless Campaign against the Clintons," p. J3.
Chicago Sun-Times, August 17, 2003, William O'Rourke, "Thunder from the Left: Journalist Conason Takes on Mudslinging Ranters of the Right," p. 11.

Economist, July 29, 2000, "Moreover: Washington, Babylon?," pp. 81-82.

Kirkus Reviews, June 15, 2003, review of *Big Lies,* p. 843.

Library Journal, February 15, 2000, Robert F. Nardini, review of *The Hunting of the President,* p. 182.

New York Times, October 5, 2003, Emily Eakin, "Among Best-Selling Authors the Daggers Are Out," p. 4.

New York Times Book Review, April 9, 2000, Neil A. Lewis, "Conspiracy Theories"; August 31, 2003, Michael Janeway, "Propaganda Machinists versus Carping Harpies," pp. 11-12.

Nieman Reports, fall, 2000, Michael Gartner, "An Indictment of the Washington Press," pp. 68-69.

Publishers Weekly, January 24, 2000, review of *The Hunting of the President,* p. 301; June 23, 2003, review of *Big Lies,* p. 58; September 1, 2003, Daisy Maryles and Dick Donahue, "Two Rights Make a Wrong," p. 18.

St. Louis Post-Dispatch, August 31, 2003, Jane Henderson, "Ideologies Battle in Fall's Nonfiction," p. F1.

Telegram & Gazette (Worcester, MA), October 2, 2003, Pamela H. Sacks, "*Big Lies* Author on Tap Tonight," p. C5.

USA Today, September 4, 2003, Clara Frenk, "Conason's *Big Lies* Serves up Red Meat for Hungry Liberals," p. D5.

Washington Post, March 29, 2000, James Bowman, "The President, Right or Wrong," p. C11; September 24, 2000, Ellen Nakashima, "Clinton Plans No Book on His Impeachment," p. A21; August 31, 2003, Steve Weinberg, "Going to Extremes," p. T4.

ONLINE

Salon.com, http://www.salon.com/ (May 18, 2000).*

*   *   *

CONLAN, Kathleen Elizabeth 1950-
(Kathy Conlan)

PERSONAL: Born June 30, 1950, in Ottawa, Ontario, Canada; daughter of Lloyd M. (an anesthetist) and Jean K. (a homemaker) Hampson; married Glenn Conlan (in business), May 24, 1974; children: Janelle, Mike. *Education:* Carleton University, Ph.D., 1988.

ADDRESSES: Office—Canadian Museum of Nature, P.O. Box 3443, Station D, Ottawa, Ontario K1P 6P4, Canada. *E-mail*—kconlan@mus-nature.ca.

CAREER: Canadian Museum of Nature, Ottawa, Ontario, Canada, research scientist, marine biologist, scuba diver, and photographer.

AWARDS, HONORS: Science in Society Children's Book Award, Canadian Science Writers Association, 2002, for *Under the Ice.*

WRITINGS:

(And photographer; as Kathy Conlan) *Under the Ice* (nonfiction), Kids Can Press (Toronto, Ontario, Canada), 2002.

Also author of several scientific works in the area of marine biology.

BIOGRAPHICAL AND CRITICAL SOURCES:

PERIODICALS

Booklist, November 1, 2002, Carolyn Phelan, review of *Under the Ice,* p. 486.

Canadian Geographic, November-December, 2002, Carol Hilton, review of *Under the Ice,* p. 98.

Canadian Materials, May 9, 2003, Tom Chambers, review of *Under the Ice.*

Childhood Education, summer, 2003, Irene A. Allen, review of *Under the Ice,* p. 244.

Resource Links, December, 2002, Jennifer Batycky, review of *Under the Ice,* p. 38.

School Library Journal, December, 2002, Susan Scheps, review of *Under the Ice,* p. 120.

ONLINE

Canadian Museum of Nature Online!, http://www.nature.ca/museum/press/ (December 12, 2002), "Cool Adventures! Museum Scientist Pens Children's Book about Diving in the Arctic and Antarctic."

Natural Resources Canada, http://nrcan-rncan.gc.ca/echo/ (May 3, 2002), "Woman at the Bottom of the Sea."

*   *   *

CONLAN, Kathy
    See CONLAN, Kathleen Elizabeth

*   *   *

CONSOLMAGNO, Guy J. 1952-

PERSONAL: Born September 19, 1952, in Detroit, MI. *Education:* Massachusetts Institute of Technology, B.S., 1974, M.S. (earth and planetary sciences), 1975; University of Arizona, Ph.D. (planetary science), 1978; Loyola University, Chicago, IL, studied philosophy and theology; University of Chicago, studied physics. *Religion:* Jesuit.

ADDRESSES: Home—Tucson, AZ, and Castel Gandolfo, Italy. *Agent*—The Barry Swayne Agency, LLC, 4 Manitou Rd., Garrison, NY 10524. *E-mail*—gjc@as.arizona.edu.

CAREER: Author, lecturer, and researcher. Harvard College Observatory, postdoctoral fellow and lecturer, 1978-80; Massachusetts Institute of Technology, Cambridge, postdoctoral fellow and lecturer, 1980-83; U.S. Peace Corps, Kenya, Africa, teacher of physics and astronomy, 1983-85; Lafayette College, Easton, PA, assistant professor of physics, 1985-89; entered Society of Jesus (Jesuit) order, 1989, took vows as Jesuit brother, 1991; Vatican Observatory, Castel Gandolfo, Italy, researcher, 1993—, curator of meteorite collection, 2000—. Loyola College, Baltimore, MD, visiting professor of physics and astronomy; Loyola University, Chicago, IL, visiting professor of physics and astronomy; Goddard Space Flight Center, visiting scientist.

AWARDS, HONORS: MacLean Chair for visiting Jesuit scholars, St. Joseph's University, Philadelphia, PA, 2000; asteroid named in his honor in recognition of his work in asteroid and meteorite studies (4597 Consolmagno), International Astronomical Union, 2000.

WRITINGS:

(With Dan M. Davis) *Turn Left at Orion: A Hundred Night Sky Objects to See in a Small Telescope and How to Find Them,* illustrations by Karen Kotash Sepp and Anne Drogin, Cambridge University Press (New York, NY), 1989, revised 3rd edition, 2000.
(With Martha W. Schaefer) *Worlds Apart: A Textbook in Planetary Sciences,* Prentice Hall (Englewood Cliffs, NJ), 1994.
The Way to the Dwelling of Light, Libreria Editrice Vaticana, (Rome, Italy), 1998.
Brother Astronomer: Adventures of a Vatican Scientist, McGraw-Hill (New York, NY), 2000.

Author of several dozen scientific publications.

SIDELIGHTS: Guy Consolmagno became an astronomer and professor of astronomy before deciding, in 1983, to join the Peace Corps as a way to contribute to the world outside the confines of a university. He was assigned to teach astronomy to university students in Kenya, but he often found himself admiring the night sky through a telescope with ordinary Kenyans during his time off. In 1989 he returned to his devout Catholic upbringing and an early desire to join the Roman Catholic order of the Society of Jesus (the Jesuits); he took his vows in 1991. Two years later he was called to the Vatican Observatory at Castel Gandolfo, Italy—the pope's summer home—to do astronomical research. A specialist in meteorites, he became curator of the Vatican's meteorite collection, one of the world's largest. Consolmagno divides his time between Castel Gandolfo and the Vatican's observatory on Mount Graham, near Tucson, Arizona, where he studies the Edgeworth-Kuiper Belt of planetoids. Often referring to himself as a "missionary of science," he travels widely, has written several books, and was part of an expedition to Antarctica to collect meteorite specimens. An asteroid named for him in honor of his contribution to asteroid and meteorite studies, 4597 Consolmagno, is also known as "Little Guy."

Turn Left at Orion, written by Consolmagno and Dan M. Davis and first published in 1989, is a beginner's guide to finding celestial objects with a small telescope. It breaks the sky into sections visible during specific seasons and uses bright and easily identifiable objects as guideposts for finding nearby stars, nebulae, planets, and galaxies. The moon is featured prominently in the book, since it is the object most easily studied with a small telescope. Each object is illustrated in black and white—as it would appear through a telescope—and glossy white pages make it easy to read at night. Devon G. Crowe, writing in *Science Books & Film,* noted that the book "will do more" toward providing a good experience for students and amateur astronomers "than the more common approaches using constellations and coordinates on the celestial sphere." William Bruce Weaver, in a review of the second edition for *Science Books & Films,* concluded that "for many—including casual amateurs—this book will be all they need for several years." Donna Popowich, in the *Science Teacher,* observed, "This would . . . be the ideal book for schools that conduct viewing sessions with middle or high school students."

Brother Astronomer: Adventures of a Vatican Scientist, published in 2000, is a collection of Consolmagno's papers, lectures, and memoirs arranged into twenty essays organized into four main sections: a discussion of meteorites, including his work with the Vatican's meteorite collection; the science-religion conflict in modern culture, with an essay about the early astronomer Galileo's work and his relationship to the Catholic Church; a discussion of the author's own religious beliefs and his theories about extraterrestrial life and the possibility of life-sustaining conditions on other planets and moons; and a humorous account of the author's trip to Antarctica to collect some four hundred new meteorite specimens.

A contributor to *Publishers Weekly,* although finding some of the scientific discussions "rather technical" and the story of the Antarctica trip lacking "alert wordsmithery," concluded, "There's not a whit of posturing in his words, but, instead, a sincerity and enthusiasm that are consistently congenial and infectious." Martha Downs, in the *Chronicle of Higher Education,* noted that "woven through [the essays] are his convictions that science can help to reveal the complexities of faith and that religion enlivens the pursuit of science." Ray Olson, of *Booklist,* noted, "Consolmagno contributes vitally to the rapprochement of science and faith." Edwin L. Aguire, writing in *Sky and Telescope,* found the book's sections to be "woven into a light-hearted, witty, and delightfully entertaining style" that makes for "good, thought-provoking reading during cloudy (or even clear) nights."

In an interview with Richard Vara of the *Houston Chronicle,* Consolmagno said, "When you peer into a telescope, you are looking into a mirror. . . . Someone who has the light of God in his soul can't help but see the light of God in the universe." Talking with Dorothy Crawford of the *Harvard-Smithsonian Center for Astrophysics* for the film *Cosmic Questions,* Consolmagno said, "If there's a limit to what is possible to know we haven't bumped up anywhere close to it yet. . . . Somebody once described knowledge as being like an island. The more you know the bigger the island gets. The bigger the island gets the longer the shoreline. . . . The more you know the more you realize there is to learn. And if you love learning that's why learning more is so much more fun."

BIOGRAPHICAL AND CRITICAL SOURCES:

PERIODICALS

Booklist, March 1, 2000, Ray Olson, review of *Brother Astronomer: Adventures of a Vatican Scientist,* p. 1182.

Chronicle of Higher Education, July 28, 2000, Martha Downs, review of *Brother Astronomer,* p. A21.

Houston Chronicle, May 8, 1999, Richard Vara, "Astronomer Looks at the Stars, Sees God," Religion section, p. 1.

Library Journal, March 1, 2000, Michael D. Cramer, review of *Brother Astronomer,* p. 121.

Los Angeles Times, August 24, 2003, Nicole Winfield, "Vatican's Stargazers Place Faith in Science," p. A3.

Publishers Weekly, November 22, 1999, review of *Brother Astronomer,* p. 47.

Science Books & Films, September-October, 1990, Devon G. Crowe, review of *Turn Left at Orion: A Hundred Night Sky Objects to See in a Small Telescope and How to Find Them,* p. 47; January-February, 1996, William Bruce Weaver, review of *Turn Left at Orion,* p. 10.

Science News, August 26, 1995, Cait Anthony, review of *Turn Left at Orion,* p. 130; April 8, 2000, Cait Goldberg, review of *Brother Astronomer,* p. 226.

Science Teacher, November, 2001, Donna Popowich, review of *Turn Left at Orion,* p. 84.

Sky and Telescope, July, 1995, Stuart J. Goldman, review of *Turn Left at Orion,* p. 57; November, 2000, Edwin L. Aguire, "Confessions of a Vatican Astronomer," p. 77.

U.S. Catholic, December, 2002, Cathy O'Connell-Cahill, "Putting Faith in the Universe," pp. 26-30.

ONLINE

Barry Swayne Agency Web site, http://www.swayneagency.com/ (October 22, 2003), "Brother Guy Consolmagno, S.J."

Brother Guy J. Consolmagno's Home Page, http://homepage.mac.com/brother_guy/ (May 6, 2002), Dorothy Crawford, "Edited Interview with Guy Consolmagno for National Science Foundation-sponsored film *Cosmic Questions.*"

Vatican Observatory Web site, http://clavius.as.arizona.edu/ (October 22, 2003), "Guy J. Consolmagno, S.J."*

*   *   *

COOTE, Cathy 1977-

PERSONAL: Born 1977. *Education:* Attended Narrabundah College and Australian National University.

ADDRESSES: Agent—c/o Cameron Cresswell Management, 5/2 New McLean St., Edgecliff, Sydney 2027, Australia.

CAREER: Writer.

AWARDS, HONORS: Sydney Morning Herald Young Writer of the Year, 1995; *Canberra Times* Young Writer of the Year, 1993 and 1995.

WRITINGS:

Innocents, Grove Press (New York, NY), 1999.

Columnist for *Sun Herald,* 1996; writing also published in *Canberra Times* and *Sydney Morning Herald.*

WORK IN PROGRESS: The Red Queen.

SIDELIGHTS: Cathy Coote wrote her debut novel, *Innocents,* at the age of nineteen. The disturbing tale of a sixteen-year-old Australian schoolgirl who seduces her high school English teacher, *Innocents* received critical acclaim both in Australia and in the United States. Erika Krouse wrote in the *New York Times Book Review* that "Coote is a natural, wryly dissecting the workings of human desire. She damns and absolves her characters in the space of a minute. Her touch is a ruthless finger in a wound."

Coote, who grew up in Australia, the daughter of two doctors, told the *ACT Writers Centre:* "I have [been writing] ever since I was old enough to hold a pencil." While still in her teens, she received three Young Writer of the Year Awards—one from the *Sydney Morning Herald* and two from the *Canberra Times*—and had stories and columns published in other Australian newspapers.

In *Innocents* Coote's schoolgirl narrator, who remains unnamed, has always felt herself to be different from her peers. Caught drawing masochistic, degrading sketches of her female classmates, the girl seeks the friendship of her teacher—also unnamed—and thus sets in motion the relationship at the center of what Krouse called "a vivid and uncomfortable book."

The epistolary form of the novel—the text is simply one long letter to her teacher—allows the reader to remain in the claustrophobic world of the narrator's mind. A writer for *Kirkus Reviews* commented that Coote "excels at describing the infinite small ways in which the girl manipulates every aspect of her life" in order to remain sexually attractive to her teacher; she sucks her thumb, wears childish clothes, colors with crayons. In enacting the sexual role-play of a father-daughter relationship, Coote's narrator is deliberately conscious of Freudian theory. But she is also careful to point out that she is *not* the victim of sexual abuse or any other emotionally scarring childhood trauma—she's simply an orphan girl with a twisted mind, brought up by her aunt and uncle and (thus far) successfully maintaining a wholesome outward appearance. (Her teacher, in an unusual twist, has a more unhappy history: he was abused as a child, and his wife left him.) Although some critics, such as *San Francisco Chronicle's* David Hill, felt that Coote's "narrator is more convincing as troubled teen than cold-blooded sexual predator," most reviewers appreciated the calculated complexity of the narrator.

As the months go by, the illicit relationship develops between the narrator and her teacher, forcing the narrator continually to construct more devices to keep her lover trapped by his desire. She snoops in his personal papers and spies on him, collecting information which she uses to her advantage. When the teacher finally resigns from the school, they move together to another town and live under the rather implausible guise of uncle and niece. The stakes get higher and higher in their game of sexual manipulation, however, as the narrative begins to point towards what Krouse called a "devastating" climax.

The relationship between the schoolgirl and her thirty-four-year-old teacher has necessarily elicited comparisons with Vladimir Nabokov's novel *Lolita,* although most critics have found Coote's novel to be an exploration—and in fact a reversal—of the dynamic found in *Lolita.* A *Publishers Weekly* reviewer wrote: "The rejection of sentimentality and the carefully calibrated knowingness make this more than just another Nabokov knockoff." Coote's book seems to call into question the assumed roles of victim and perpetrator; the narrator's calculated manipulations place her in the position of the seducer, whereas her defenseless teacher appears to be the "innocent." Indeed, despite all of her sexual manipulation, the narrator doesn't really enjoy the act of sex; the game is simply about power. *Absolute Write* online reviewer Amy Brozio-Andrews wrote that "*Innocents* chronicles a young woman's exercise in power. Powerless in her family and social circle, she is intrigued at her newfound dominance over a man, eighteen years her senior—a 'grownup.'" Mark Rozzo, writing for the *Los Angeles Times,* noted how well the book, "written by a teenager, portrays adult, innocence-ending consequences."

BIOGRAPHICAL AND CRITICAL SOURCES:

PERIODICALS

Bulletin with Newsweek, November 23, 1999, Judith White, review of *Innocents,* p. 8.
Kirkus Reviews, July 1, 2002, review of *Innocents,* p. 899.
Los Angeles Times, September 29, 2002, Mark Rozzo, review of *Innocents,* p. R14.
New York Times Book Review, November 3, 2002, Erika Krouse, review of *Innocents,* p. 29.
Publishers Weekly, July 15, 2002, review of *Innocents,* p. 52.

San Francisco Chronicle, November 2, 2002, David Hill, review of *Innocents,* p. 4.

ONLINE

Absolute Write, http://www.absolutewrite.com/ (May 28, 2003), review of *Innocents.*
ACT Writers Centre, http://www.actwriters.org.au/ (May 28, 2003), interview with Coote.*

*   *   *

COPE, Stephen

PERSONAL: Male. *Education:* Obtained M.S. in social work.

ADDRESSES: Office—Kripalu Center for Yoga and Health, P.O. Box 793, West St., Route 183, Lenox, MA 01240.

CAREER: Licensed social worker and psychotherapist in Boston, MA; Kripalu Center for Yoga and Health, Lenox, MA, senior teacher. Lecturer on yoga and meditation. Featured in video, *Kripalu Yoga Dynamic.*

WRITINGS:

Yoga and the Quest for the True Self, Bantam (New York, NY), 1999.
Will Yoga and Meditation Really Change My Life?: Personal Stories from America's Leading Teachers, Kripalu Center for Yoga and Health (Lenox, MA), 2003.
Yoga for Emotional Flow: Free Your Emotions through Yoga Breathing, Body Awareness, and Energetic Release (audio book), 2003.

SIDELIGHTS: Stephen Cope is a former psychotherapist who teaches and writes about Kripalu Yoga, a practice that combines physical exercise with spiritual uplift. With his background in Western psychotherapeutic techniques, Cope brings a different perspective to the study of yoga and meditation, and his book *Yoga and the Quest for the True Self* offers advice and anecdotes tailored to an American readership. Barb

Bindon in *Lambda Book Report* particularly appreciated Cope's approach, calling *Yoga and the Quest for the True Self* an "unexpectedly accessible and engaging read." A *Publishers Weekly* critic likewise felt that the work "lights up a notoriously arcane subject for Western readers." Cope's book also focuses upon the ways in which yoga can lead to psychological as well as physical health. According to Rebecca Miller in *Library Journal*, "few other accessible books provide as good an overview of the spirituality of yoga."

BIOGRAPHICAL AND CRITICAL SOURCES:

PERIODICALS

Booklist, October 15, 1999, Donna Seaman, review of *Yoga and the Quest for the True Self,* p. 396.
Lambda Book Report, February, 2000, Barb Bindon, review of *Yoga and the Quest for the True Self,* p. 31.
Library Journal, August, 1999, Rebecca Miller, review of *Yoga and the Quest for the True Self,* p. 99.
Publishers Weekly, August 30, 1999, review of *Yoga and the Quest for the True Self,* p. 74.

ONLINE

Kripalu Center for Yoga and Health, http://www.kripalu.org/ (October 23, 2003).
Yoga Journal, http://www.yogajournal.com/ (October 23, 2003), Richard Rosen, review of video, *Kripalu Yoga Dynamic.**

*   *   *

CORAM, Robert

PERSONAL: Born in Edison, GA; married Jeanine Addams (a business owner). *Hobbies and other interests:* Flower gardening, fly fishing.

ADDRESSES: Home—Atlanta, GA. *Agent*—c/o Author Mail, Warner Books, 1271 Avenue of the Americas, New York, NY 10020. *E-mail*—rbc@robertcoram.com.

CAREER: Writer. Journalist for *Atlanta Journal* and *Atlanta Constitution;* press secretary for Georgia governor Carl Sanders; writer for McGraw-Hill publications; journalism instructor at Emory University. Worked variously as a house-sitter and park ranger.

AWARDS, HONORS: Pulitzer Prize nomination for *Atlanta Constitution* stories about drug smuggling and the development of Georgia's Cumberland Island.

WRITINGS:

Narcs, New American Library (New York, NY), 1988.
Narcs II: Drug Warriors, New American Library (New York, NY), 1989.
Narcs III: America's Heroes, New American Library (New York, NY), 1990.
Running Dead, Signet (New York, NY), 1993.
Caribbean Time Bomb: The United States' Complicity in the Corruption of Antigua, Morrow (New York, NY), 1993.
(With Christina Noble) *Nobody's Child: A Woman's Abusive Past and the Inspiring Dreams That Led Her to Rescue the Street Children of Saigon,* Grove Press (New York, NY), 1994, published as *Bridge across My Sorrows: The Christina Noble Story,* J. Murray (London, England), 1994.
Kill the Angels, Signet (New York, NY), 1996.
Atlanta Heat, Signet (New York, NY), 1997.
(With Shaw E. Grigsby) *Bass Master Shaw Grigsby: Notes on Fishing and Life,* National Geographic Society (Washington, DC), 1998.
Dead South, Signet (New York, NY), 1999.
Boyd: The Fighter Pilot Who Changed the Art of War, Little, Brown (Boston, MA), 2002.

Contributor to periodicals, including *Esquire, New Yorker, Atlanta, New York Times, Sports Illustrated,* and aviation publications.

SIDELIGHTS: Robert Coram is a novelist and journalist who has covered issues such as the civil rights movement in the 1960s, the overdevelopment of natural lands, and drug trafficking in South America and the United States. His reporting has earned him two Pulitzer Prize nominations, and his work has appeared in magazines across the United States.

Coram became a reporter for the *Atlanta Journal* during his sophomore year in college. After serving an apprenticeship writing features, book reviews, aviation articles, and general assignment pieces, Coram started freelancing for *Atlanta* magazine and a number of national periodicals. When he tried to organize the *Atlanta Journal*'s staff into a union, he was fired. Coram considered his firing "the most painful moment of his life, first because he had been fired from what he considered the best job in the world and, second, because the newspaper said the real reason he was fired was that he tricked a prominent politician into telling the truth about a controversial news issue," a biographer wrote on Coram's Web site.

After several years writing for McGraw-Hill publications, a year as press secretary to then-governor Carl Sanders, and four years on staff at *Atlanta,* Coram moved to Cumberland Island, off Georgia's coast. There he worked as a house sitter and ranger for the National Park Service, and freelanced for *Sports Illustrated* and the Sunday *New York Times.* He returned to Atlanta in the mid-1970s and continued freelancing.

A series of articles on narcotics trafficking in *Esquire* led to a job offer at the *Atlanta Constitution.* There, Coram was nominated for a Pulitzer Prize for his reporting on drug smuggling. A pilot himself, Coram flew among British islands such as the Turks and Caicos and became acquainted with another pilot who provided the main transportation for a group of smugglers. Coram's stories inspired the British government to clean up the drug trade on the islands, which led to a large bounty being placed on Coram's head "just to bring him back to the islands," wrote Adam Feuerstein in *Atlanta Business Chronicle.* Eventually, Coram abandoned reporting on the drug trade "after being shot at by drug smugglers in Bimini in 1980," Feuerstein wrote.

Coram also received a Pulitzer nomination for a series of *Atlanta Constitution* articles on development of his former home, Cumberland Island. After three years on staff at the paper, he was fired "because his interviewing techniques were too aggressive," wrote the biographer on Coram's Web site. "Coram now had the unique distinction of having been fired from both the *Atlanta Journal* and the *Atlanta Constitution.* The two papers later merged and then the *Journal* was rendered extinct, so his feat can never be duplicated."

For twelve years Coram worked as a journalism instructor at Emory University. He continued freelancing for national magazines, and in 1998, his first novel, *Narcs,* was published. Based on the in-depth knowledge he had gained during his reporting years, *Narcs* and its two sequels are thrillers about drug smuggling.

Four other novels—*Running Dead, Kill the Angels, Atlanta Heat,* and *Dead South*—are police procedurals set in Atlanta.

Coram also writes nonfiction books along with his novels. *Caribbean Time Bomb: The United States' Complicity in the Corruption of Antigua* is a "candid account, scrupulously researched" that "focuses on the excesses of Antiguan Prime Minister Vere Cornwall Bird and his sons, who run the island nation like feudal lords," engaging in a variety of unscrupulous and possibly illegal activity, wrote a *Kirkus Reviews* critic. The Bird family endured scandals and accusations of arms dealing, favor-selling, and financial misdeeds. Coram examines the involvement of the United States in the Birds' activities. The book relates "plenty of crimes to leave the readers thoroughly disgusted with the Birds and with U.S. involvement with them" and their supporters, wrote Anita L. Cole in *Library Journal.*

Nobody's Child: A Woman's Abusive Past and the Inspiring Dream That Led Her to Rescue the Street Children of Saigon, is the autobiography of Christina Noble, written with assistance from Coram. Following a childhood of abuse, poverty, family problems, and homelessness in Dublin, Ireland, Noble finds herself incarcerated in a Galway girls' school. Gang-raped at age sixteen, she is forced to give up her son. A subsequent marriage is abusive and leads to divorce. After spending some time in mental hospitals, she remarries. Despite these traumas, in 1989 Noble went to Ho Chi Minh City (formerly Saigon), to work with orphans and street children, helping them avoid facing same type of future as her. "This is a deeply moving story that should appeal to a wide readership," wrote Arla Lindgren in *Library Journal.* A *Publishers Weekly* reviewer noted that, "Along with freelancer Coram, Noble has written a painfully frank and at times riveting autobiography."

With his 2002 biography, *Boyd: The Fighter Pilot Who Changed the Art of War,* Coram rekindled his longtime interest in aviation and aviation history. John Boyd, a colonel in the U.S. Air Force, was known as "Forty-second Boyd." His standing bet with any pilot, at any level of skill, from any branch of the military, was that he could out-maneuver them in simulated air-to-air combat and have them in his gunsights, ready for the "kill," in forty seconds or less. Boyd never lost a single bet.

Boyd joined the U.S. Air Force in 1951 and honed his skills in Korea. He developed a functional theory of aerial attack and put into writing a series of effective maneuvers and counter maneuvers for combat pilots. He created the "Energy-Maneuverability" theory, which "enabled fighter pilots to evaluate their energy potential at any altitude and at any maneuver. And, perhaps more importantly, the energy potential of their adversary," Coram wrote on the *Aviation History* Web site. "It changed forever the way aircraft are fought in combat."

Some of Boyd's most hard-fought battles were waged against friendly forces on the ground. Boyd was a keen analyst who detested obstruction, obfuscation, and pettiness and fought with superiors, subordinates, and civilians over inefficiency, waste, and unthinking adherence to tradition. *Washington Post* reviewer Jason Vest wrote, "As Coram's book shows, Boyd gave no quarter in his various battles to prove just how right he was about the stifling, self-serving features of military bureaucracy." But to his equally loyal supporters, according to Coram, Boyd was a savior. "America has dominated the skies for the past thirty years because of John Boyd," the author remarked on the *Aviation History Online Museum.*

Boyd is a "worthy biography" and "deeply researched and detailed," observed a *Publishers Weekly* reviewer. "Coram does not shy away from Boyd's often self-defeating abrasiveness and the neglect and treatment of his long-suffering wife and children, and keeps the story of a unique life moving smoothly and engagingly." "Overall, Coram has done a great service by introducing Boyd to the American public," noted Joseph Neff in *Raleigh News & Observer.* A writer for *Kirkus Reviews* called the book "required reading for frustrated innovators, aviation buffs, and Horatio Algers intent on improving the world against the best efforts of ever-prevailing deal-busters and naysayers."

BIOGRAPHICAL AND CRITICAL SOURCES:

PERIODICALS

Atlanta Business Chronicle, January 22, 1990, Adam Feuerstein, profile of Coram, p. A16.
Booklist, October 15, 2002, Roland Green, review of *Boyd: The Fighter Pilot Who Changed the Art of War,* p. 367.

Kirkus Reviews, June 1, 1993, review of *Caribbean Time Bomb: The United States' Complicity in the Corruption of Antigua,* p. 693; October 15, 2002, review of *Boyd,* p. 1513.
Library Journal, July, 1993, Anita L. Cole, review of *Caribbean Time Bomb,* p. 100; February 1, 1995, review of *Nobody's Child: A Woman's Abusive Past and the Inspiring Dreams That Led Her to Rescue the Street Children of Saigon,* p. 91.
Los Angeles Daily Journal, August 15, 1989, Bill Carbine, review of *Narcs II: Drug Warriors,* p. 7.
Publishers Weekly, October 28, 1988, review of *Narcs,* p. 73; June 28, 1993, review of *Caribbean Time Bomb,* pp. 65-66; December 19, 1994, review of *Nobody's Child,* p. 43; June 10, 1996, review of *Kill the Angels,* p. 96; October 20, 1997, review of *Atlanda Heat,* p. 73; October 14, 2002, review of *Boyd,* p. 78.
Raleigh News & Observer, January 19, 2003, Joseph Neff, review of *Boyd.*
Washington Post Book World, January 12, 2003, Jason Vest, review of *Boyd,* p. 7.

ONLINE

Aviation History Online Museum, http://www.aviation-history.com (January 21, 2003).
Bookbrowser, http://www.bookbrowser.com (January 21, 2003), Harriet Klausner, review of *Atlanta Heat.*
Defense and the National Interest Web site, http://www.d-n-i.net/ (May 25, 2003).
Robert Coram Home Page, http://www.robertcoram.com (January 21, 2003).*

*   *   *

COSER, Lewis A(lfred) 1913-2003
(Louis Clair, Europicus)

OBITUARY NOTICE—See index for *CA* sketch: Born November 27, 1913, in Berlin, Germany; died July 8, 2003, in Cambridge, MA. Sociologist, educator, and author. Coser was a prominent sociologist with leftist leanings and was a cofounder of the important journal *Dissent.* Born Ludwig Cohen, his family changed its surname to shield themselves from the anti-Jewish sentiment growing in Germany. With Adolph Hitler's ascension to power, Coser fled to Paris, France, where he worked odd jobs, became active in socialist politics, and attended the Sorbonne. When World War II erupted, he was sent to an internment camp because he was German, even though he opposed the Nazis. Coser was fortunate, however, to obtain a passport to the United States in 1941, and, arriving in New York City, changed his first name to Louis. In America he worked at various jobs, some of which were government-related, and began contributing articles to *Partisan Review, Politics, Nation,* and other publications under the pseudonyms Louis Clair and Europicus. He then enrolled at Columbia University, where he earned his Ph.D. in sociology in 1954, four years after becoming a U.S. citizen. Along with Irving Howe, in 1954 he founded *Dissent,* an anti-establishment journal that remains in publication. During the 1950s and 1960s he taught sociology at Brandeis University, where he founded the department of sociology; he then moved to the State University of New York at Stony Brook in 1968, where he remained until his retirement in 1987. Although Coser was definitely a socialist, he was not afraid to criticize the communists any more than he was afraid to attack greedy capitalist practices. He tried to remain neutral in his writings, which were often preoccupied with themes relating to the intellectual's role within society. In his later life he often fretted that the influence of intellectuals would diminish as scholars became increasingly absorbed into government and corporate organizations. After becoming professor emeritus Coser continued to teach as an adjunct professor of sociology at Boston College. Among his publications are *The Functions of Social Conflict* (1954), *Men of Ideas: A Sociologist's View* (1965), *Masters of Sociological Thought* (1970), and *Refugee Scholars in America: Their Impact and Their Experiences* (1984).

OBITUARIES AND OTHER SOURCES:

BOOKS

World of Sociology, Gale (Detroit, MI), 2001.
Writers Directory, 18th edition, St. James Press (Detroit, MI), 2003.

PERIODICALS

Chicago Tribune, July 14, 2003, section 1, p. 14.
New York Times, July 12, 2003, p. A21.

COTTON, John 1925-2003

OBITUARY NOTICE—See index for *CA* sketch: Born March 7, 1925, in London, England; died March 20, 2003, in Hemel Hempstead, Hertfordshire, England. School administrator and author. Cotton was a respected poet who, in his work, reflected on themes relating to the disparity between reality and personal desires. He attended Acton Technical College, and during World War II was an officer with the Royal Naval Commandos, seeing action in the Far East. Upon his return to England, he completed his bachelor's degree at Birkbeck College, London. From 1947 to 1957 he taught English in Middlesex, followed by six years as head of the English department at Southall Grammar Technical School. He next became headmaster of Highfield Comprehensive School in Hemel Hempstead, where he remained until his retirement in 1985. Cotton's first attempts at writing were novels, but after realizing no success in publishing them he switched his emphasis to poetry. Cofounding the literary magazine *Priapus* with fellow poet Ted Walker, Cotton eventually helped organize Priapus Press, through which he published his first verse collection, *Fourteen Poems,* in 1967. His first great success with poetry came when the Poetry Society recommended his 1971 collection *Old Movies and Other Poems,* which also won a publication award from the Arts Council of Great Britain. His *Kilroy Was Here* (1974) was a Poetry Society selection a few years later. While both these collections were published by Chatto & Windus, Cotton never managed to duplicate these successes, and the remainder of his verses were published by smaller, less-prestigious presses. Nevertheless, Cotton was content to continue publishing his works while earning a living as a headmaster. Some of his later works include *The Totleigh Riddles* (1981), *The Crystal Zoo* (1985), *Here's Looking at You Kid* (1992), and the children's-verse collection *Oscar the Dog and Friends* (1994). He was also active in literary societies, serving as a chairman and council member in the National Poetry Society and as a president of Ver Poets and the Toddington Poetry Society. His honors include being appointed deputy lieutenant of the county of Hertfordshire in 1989. At the time of his death, a new book of poems, *Out There in Rows,* was in press.

OBITUARIES AND OTHER SOURCES:

BOOKS

Contemporary Poets, seventh edition, St. James Press (Detroit, MI), 2001.

Writers Directory, 18th edition, St. James Press (Detroit, MI), 2003.

PERIODICALS

Independent (London, England), March 24, 2003, p. 20.
Times (London, England), March 31, 2003, p. 28.

*   *   *

COUGHLIN, Con 1955-

PERSONAL: Born 1955.

ADDRESSES: Office—Sunday Telegraph, Telegraph Group, 1 Canada Square, Canary Wharf, London E14 5DT, England.

CAREER: Journalist and editor. *Daily Telegraph,* London, England, reporter; *Sunday Telegraph,* London, editor.

WRITINGS:

Hostage: The Complete Story of the Lebanon Captives, Warner Books (London, England), 1993.
A Golden Basin Full of Scorpions: The Quest for Modern Jerusalem, Warner Books (London, England), 1998.
Saddam: King of Terror, Ecco (New York, NY), 2002, published as *Saddam: The Secret Life,* Macmillan (London, England), 2003.

SIDELIGHTS: British journalist Con Coughlin writes on the Middle East. His books have examined political and social efforts to create a modern Jerusalem, the ordeal of hostages in Lebanon, and the rise and rule of Iraqi ruler Saddam Hussein.

In *Hostage: The Complete Story of the Lebanese Captives,* Coughlin provides a "persuasive and readable study" of the Lebanese hostage crisis, wrote Stephen Smith in *London Review of Books.* "Economically turned, Coughlin's bulletin is a sample of the bracingly low opinion in which its author holds most of

the hostages," Smith remarked. Coughlin narrowly escaped becoming one of the hostages himself, but this fact "failed to leave him noticeably forgiving of expats less blessed than himself," Smith observed. The hostages, in Coughlin's view, were "asking for it"; by "deciding to stay on in Beirut because of the dissolute thrills of life near the city's notorious dividing line, they had simply relinquished their common sense."

However, "Coughlin's greatest scorn is reserved for Terry Waite," Smith remarked. Despite Waite's efforts in securing the release of the hostages, "Coughlin's allegations are that Waite was in it for the publicity, with the freedom of the hostages a happy by-product," Smith commented. Coughlin, Smith remarked, feels that Waite took credit where it was not due, and held up the release process with his celebrity and ties to Oliver North. Even in the face of Waite's success, much about his role in the hostage crisis "remains to be explained," wrote a reviewer in the London *Observer.*

Coughlin explores the history, development, and condition of present-day Jerusalem in *A Golden Basin Full of Scorpions: The Quest for Modern Jerusalem.* "Coughlin's pragmatic approach to Jerusalem's 3,000-year-long convoluted history is to start with the Bible, where it all began, and then hop deftly over much of the intervening millennia of Crusader conquest and Ottoman control, to contemplate Jerusalem in the twentieth century," wrote Natasha Fairweather in the London *Observer.*

Coughlin describes a Jerusalem "that has known destruction and mayhem any number of times—invasions, earthquakes, plagues, famines, and crusades—but that . . . mysteriously survives," wrote A. N. Wilson in the *Spectator.* But, Coughlin observes in the book, "There is not much that one can say is good about the modern city." Religious extremists vie for control, craving a Holy war and seeking to impose their own version of God on the country. "Bigotry, zealotry, and ideological intransigence" create unprecedented suffering, Fairweather observed. Coughlin considers the Netanyahu government "a disaster," and explains that the territorial demands of the Likud party do not conform with borders determined by international law or with the possibility of peace with the Arabs. Coughlin "knows the place well, and he has done his homework on the historical background thoroughly," Wilson observed. Fairweather called *A*

Golden Basin Full of Scorpions "a very accessible and lively account of life in a city which has always taken itself too seriously."

In *Saddam: King of Terror*–published in England as *Saddam: The Secret Life*–Coughlin examines the life and reign of Iraq's Saddam Hussein. *Saddam: King of Terror* is "a timely, detailed portrait of the Iraqi dictator–though not one that fully supports the subtitle's implied link to al-Quaeda," wrote a reviewer in *Publishers Weekly.* Beginning with Hussein's lower-class birth in a mud hut in a small town on the Tigris, Coughlin chronicles the dictator's early days, the events that set him on the path to Iraqi rule, and his rise to power. Throughout the decades from the 1950s to the 1960s, Hussein rose through a series of assassinations, coups, and skillful political maneuverings to become second in command of Iraq's ruling Revolutionary Command Council. Throughout the early 1970s, Hussein enjoyed the privileges of power. "Coughlin does a fine, creepy job of evoking the gangster ambience of 1970s Iraq, in which the nouveau riche Hussein cultivated a taste for fancy cars, expensive suits, American-style barbecue ribs, race-track gambling, married blondes, and sickly sweet Portuguese rose wine," wrote Warren Bass in *New York Times.* In 1979, Hussein seized full control of Iraq and instituted his oppressive, violent, totalitarian regime.

Using a combination of institutionalized violence, social programs, and "cult of personality," Saddam remained fully in control of Iraq, gathering intense popular support among the country's residents, the *Publishers Weekly* critic wrote. Even after debacles such as Iraq's war with Iran in the early 1980s, Iraq's expulsion from Kuwait in Operation Desert Storm, and the decade of deprivation and sanctions following the Gulf War, Hussein's grip on power did not slip. Coughlin "gives a horrifying account of Saddam's numerous purges, tortures, and mass murders," wrote a reviewer in the *Economist,* but even these atrocities did nothing to endanger Hussein's position in Iraq.

Coughlin also suggests that Iraq knew about, or was involved in, the 9/11 attacks on the United States, although Bass expresses some doubts about the credibility of such charges. "It's a shame Coughlin overdoes the King of Terror theme, both because his book features some good, gory detail and because one can make a case for toppling an uncommonly vicious thug like Hussein without overblowing Iraq's link to the war on terrorism," Bass wrote. Coughlin's *Saddam* depicts Hussein as a vicious and bloody dictator, but also highlights the modern elements of his rule and the technological aspects of the regime. "Coughlin has competently put together such evidence as there is [to explain the Hussein regime], quite enough to shock him," wrote David Pryce-Jones in the *Spectator.* In Coughlin's analysis, Hussein "proved to be too limited and brutal a character for the complexities of his position," Pryce-Jones observed. "In Coughlin's opinion, Saddam's single-minded concentration of power has increasingly detached him from reality." In Bass's view, "Regime change, readers . . . will surely agree, couldn't happen to a more deserving guy."

BIOGRAPHICAL AND CRITICAL SOURCES:

PERIODICALS

Economist, April 18, 1998, review of *A Golden Basin Full of Scorpions: The Quest for Modern Jerusalem,* pp. S3-S4; November 9, 2002, review of *Saddam: King of Terror.*
London Review of Books, December 3, 1992, Stephen Smith, review of *Hostage: The Complete Story of the Lebanon Captives,* p. 22.
Los Angeles Times, April 3, 2003, review of *Saddam: King of Terror,* p. A-20.
New Statesman, December 9, 2002, Richard Gott, review of *Saddam: The Secret Life,* pp. 46-48.
New York Times, December 15, 2002, Warren Bass, review of *Saddam: King of Terror,* p. 20.
Observer (London, England), July 4, 1993, review of *Hostage: The Complete Story of the Lebanon Captives,* p. 61; December 7, 1997, Natasha Fairweather, review of *A Golden Basin Full of Scorpions,* pp. 15-16.
Publishers Weekly, October 28, 2002, review of *Saddam: King of Terror,* p. 61.
Spectator, February 14, 1998, A. N. Wilson, review of *A Golden Basin Full of Scorpions,* pp. 26-27; November 30, 2002, David Pryce-Jones, review of *Saddam: The Secret Life,* p. 52.
Times Literary Supplement, February 7, 2003, review of *Saddam: The Secret Life,* p. 8.

ONLINE

Los Angeles Times Calendarlive, http://www.calendarlive.com/ (November 3, 2002), Andrew Cockburn, review of *Saddam: King of Terror.*

National Public Radio Web site, http://www.npr.org/
(November 8, 2002), transcript of *All Things Considered* interview with Coughlin.
Washington Post online, http://www.washingtonpost.
com/ (December 6, 2002).*

*   *   *

COX, James Middleton 1870-1957

PERSONAL: Born March 31, 1870, near Dayton,
Ohio; died July 15, 1957; son of Gilbert and Eliza
Cox; married Mayme L. Harding, 1893 (divorced,
1910); married Margaretta Parker Blair, 1917; children
(first marriage) James, John, Richard; (second
marriage) Anne, Barbara. *Education:* Earned a teaching certificate.

CAREER: Cincinnati Enquirer, reporter, 1892-95;
secretary to U.S. Representative Paul J. Sorg, 1895;
bought controlling interest in Dayton, Ohio, *Evening
News,* 1898; formed News League of Ohio. U.S.
Representative for Third Congressional District, Ohio,
1908-12; Ohio governor, 1912-14 and 1916-20;
Democratic candidate for president, 1920. Founder,
Cox Enterprises (media company).

AWARDS, HONORS: Pulitzer Prize for journalism,
1927, for articles exposing city government corruption
in Canton, Ohio.

WRITINGS:

Journey through My Years (autobiography), Simon &
Schuster (New York, NY), 1946.

SIDELIGHTS: James Middleton Cox worked his way
up from a position working as a janitor to newspaper
mogul to Ohio governor, then to presidential nominee.
Cox, the youngest of seven children in a farming family, dropped out of high school after two years, but
earned his teaching certificate. Later he founded the
company that became Cox Enterprises, a top U.S.
media outlet.

Working for a printer in 1892, Cox discovered a career
opportunity as a reporter. He covered railroad news at
the *Cincinnati Enquirer*—"magnificent training," as he

called it. By 1895 he was married and working in
Washington as a secretary to Ohio Democratic
Congressman Paul J. Sorg. But newspapering remained
in Cox's blood. At age twenty-eight, backed by a
$6,000 loan from Sorg, Cox bought the Dayton, Ohio,
Evening News. The *Dayton Journal* was skeptical.
"The *Evening News* has been sold and will hereafter
be a Democratic paper," one of its writers said.
"Democratic papers have never paid in Dayton and
never will. Four of them have failed."

Though he would later describe himself as "too young
to be running a newspaper," Cox revived the struggling daily, adopting wire services to provide domestic
and global updates, using state-of-the-art photography,
and adding a local society column. "He developed a
reputation for aggressive, reform journalism, characterizing the *News* as 'the People's paper,'" Gregory C.
Lisby wrote in the *Dictionary of Literary Biography.*

A friend of labor and an enemy of prohibition, Cox
often found himself and his paper under fire. But he
chose not to resort to mudslinging; in the midst of a
rumor-fueled controversy, he instructed his staff not to
discuss competitors publicly. By the end of 1900 the
News was one of the country's top newspapers. A few
years later Cox formed the News League of Ohio after
acquiring the Springfield *Press-Republic.*

Twice elected to represent Ohio's third congressional
district, Cox was elected governor in 1912. He was
the first Democrat to serve three two-year terms and,
as Lisby wrote, he "left a legacy of reform legislation
that included a direct-primary law, public-school and
prison reforms, state court reorganization, extension of
the civil-service law, authorization of a budget commission and a roads program." Democratic party
stalwarts nominated Cox for president at its 1920
national convention in San Francisco. Choosing Franklin D. Roosevelt as his running mate, Cox campaigned on a platform supporting Woodrow Wilson's
League of Nations. Republican Warren G. Harding
soundly defeated the Democrats–the electoral vote
was 404-127–after which Cox resolved "never again
to seek or to accept a public office," as he was quoted
in *Dictionary of Literary Biography.* "I had my
newspapers."

Cox vigorously resumed his publishing career,
purchasing the *Miami Metropolis* and the *Atlanta Constitution,* among other papers, and in 1934 entered the

broadcasting business when his son, James, established Dayton's first radio station. Though he no longer ran for elective office, Roosevelt after becoming president appointed Cox to the American delegation to the London World Monetary and Economic Conference.

Cox's memoirs, published as *Journey through My Years,* drew mixed critical reaction, ranging from "neither informative nor entertaining," as a *Kirkus Reviews* writer said, to "full of shrewd insights and ripe wisdom," from Allan Nevins of *Saturday Review of Literature.* According to Nevins, Cox produced "one of the best books of political reminiscences in many years; a book valuable for its inside story of important transactions, its many anecdotes and sketches of people, and its personal record—but most of all, valuable for its animating spirit."

BIOGRAPHICAL AND CRITICAL SOURCES:

BOOKS

Babson, Roger, W., *Cox—The Man,* Brentano's (New York, NY), 1920.
Dictionary of Literary Biography, Volume 127: *American Newspaper Publishers, 1950-1990,* Gale (Detroit, MI), 1993, pp. 54-58.
Stone, Irving, *They Also Ran: The Story of Men Who Were Defeated for the Presidency,* Doubleday (Garden City, NY), 1966.

PERIODICALS

Kirkus Reviews, August 1 1946, review of *Journey through My Years.*
New Republic, December 23, 1946, R. L. Strout, review of *Journey through My Years.*
New York Times, December 8, 1946, Karl Schriftgiesser, review of *Journey through My Years.*
Saturday Review of Literature, January 4, 1947, Allan Nevins, review of *Journey through My Years.*

ONLINE

Cox Enterprises Web site, http://www.coxenterprises.com/ (January 26, 2004).*

COX, Michael 1948-

PERSONAL: Born 1948.

ADDRESSES: Office—Oxford University Press, Great Clarendon Street, Oxford OX2 6DP, England.

CAREER: Oxford University Press, Oxford, England, senior commissioning editor of reference books.

WRITINGS:

AS EDITOR

(With R. A. Gilbert) *The Oxford Book of English Ghost Stories,* Oxford University Press (New York, NY), 1986.
(And author of introduction) M. R. James, *The Ghost Stories of M. R. James,* illustrated by Rosalind Caldecott, Oxford University Press (New York, NY), 1986.
(And author of introduction) M. R. James, *Casting the Runes, and Other Ghost Stories,* Oxford University Press (New York, NY), 1987.
(And author of introduction) J. S. Le Fanu, *The Illustrated J. S. Le Fanu: Ghost Stories and Mysteries by a Master Victorian Storyteller,* Equation (Wellingborough, Northamptonshire, England), 1988.
(And author of introduction, with R. A. Gilbert) *Victorian Ghost Stories: An Oxford Anthology,* Oxford University Press (New York, NY), 1991.
(And author of introduction) *Victorian Tales of Mystery and Detection: An Oxford Anthology,* Oxford University Press (New York, NY), 1992.
(With Jack Adrian) *The Oxford Book of Historical Stories,* Oxford University Press (New York, NY), 1994.
The Oxford Book of Spy Stories, Oxford University Press (New York, NY), 1996.
The Oxford Book of Twentieth-Century Ghost Stories, Oxford University Press (New York, NY), 1996.
(And author of introduction) *Twelve Victorian Ghost Stories,* Oxford University Press (New York, NY), 1997.
(And author of introduction) *Twelve Tales of the Supernatural,* Oxford University Press (New York, NY), 1997.

(And author of introduction) *Twelve English Detective Stories,* Oxford University Press (New York, NY), 1998.

(And adapter) *Top Ten Ghost Stories,* illustrated by Michael Tickner, Scholastic (New York, NY), 2001.

A Dictionary of Writers and Their Works, Oxford University Press (New York, NY), 2001, second edition published as *Who Wrote What: A Dictionary of Writers and Their Works,* 2002.

The Oxford Chronology of English Literature, two volumes, Oxford University Press (New York, NY), 2002.

(With R. A. Gilbert) *The Oxford Book of Victorian Ghost Stories,* Oxford University Press (New York, NY), 2002.

The Concise Oxford Chronology of English Literature, Oxford University Press (New York, NY), 2003.

OTHER

M. R. James: An Informal Portrait (biography), Oxford University Press (New York, NY), 1983.

Mysticism: The Direct Experience of God, Aquarian Press (Wellingborough, Northamptonshire, England), 1983.

Handbook of Christian Spirituality, Harper (San Francisco, CA), 1985.

SIDELIGHTS: Michael Cox, long an editor with Oxford University Press, has focused much of his work on the literature of the supernatural. He is a biographer of English ghost-story writer M. R. James and the editor or coeditor of several collections of ghost stories, encompassing the work of James and others. He has "splendid credentials" as an expert on the genre, noted a *Washington Post Book World* contributor in a review of *The Oxford Book of Twentieth-Century Ghost Stories,* edited by Cox.

These credentials include the biography *M. R. James: An Informal Portrait.* James, born in 1862, was a scholar of the Bible and the Middle Ages and provost of Cambridge University and Eton College in addition to being one of the top authors of ghost stories in his day. He published four volumes of these stories between 1904 and 1925. Many of the stories take place in estates, cathedrals, or libraries, settings he researched thoroughly. James's ghostly tales have remained popular and well regarded, and they are his most famous work. Cox's book seeks to enlighten readers about the other aspects of James's career and life. The volume "is both familiar and respectful, warm, and accomplished in its admitted informality," commented a *Choice* reviewer.

Fifteen of James's spectral stories are collected in *The Ghost Stories of M. R. James,* to which Cox provides a "thought-provoking and informative" introduction, offering information about James's life and the ghost-story genre in general, related Sam Pickering in *Sewanee Review.* James is also among the authors anthologized in *The Oxford Book of English Ghost Stories,* which Cox edited with R. A. Gilbert and which features both British and American writers. This is "a rich collection of tales," Pickering remarked. It includes James's "Oh, Whistle, and I'll Come to You, My Lad" and W. W. Jacobs's "The Monkey's Paw"—both "undoubted masterpieces," a *Washington Post Book World* reviewer observed—as well as stories by Sir Walter Scott, E. Nesbit, Henry James, W. Somerset Maugham, Edith Wharton, and several others.

Cox and Gilbert's follow-up to this volume is *Victorian Ghost Stories: An Oxford Anthology,* which includes works by Rudyard Kipling, Charles Dickens, Rhoda Broughton, Elizabeth Gaskell, J. S. Le Fanu, and many others. The editors note that ghost stories were a way for Victorian-era writers and readers to project their fears about social, economic, and political upheaval. With selections from diverse voices of the era, Cox and Gilbert have assembled a "superior anthology," commented a *Publishers Weekly* critic. *New York Times Book Review* contributor Jack Sullivan, meanwhile, pronounced the collection "splendid" and "uncommonly imaginative."

The Oxford Book of Twentieth-Century Ghost Stories, like the volumes covering the Victorians, features some writers not usually associated with the genre, such as F. Scott Fitzgerald, Graham Greene, Fay Weldon, and Alison Lurie, in addition to those well known for scary stories, including Robert Aickman and L. P. Hartley. "Cox is a clear-headed editor, and this is an intriguing collection, which takes in a good range of tones," remarked Patricia Craig in the *Times Literary Supplement.* Celia Wren, however, writing in *Commonweal,* thought the modern settings of the tales "disappointingly flat," although she noted that Cox's introduction does make a case for the modern ghost story, using as an example Fritz Leiber's "Smoke

Ghost," which gives a detailed and gritty urban background to its hauntings and is "one of the book's more successful stories," in Wren's opinion. A *Washington Post Book World* reviewer praised the anthology generally, calling it "appealingly eclectic."

Cox has also edited anthologies covering other genres of fiction, such as detective stories and espionage tales. *Victorian Tales of Mystery and Detection* features works by Edgar Allan Poe, Arthur Conan Doyle, Wilkie Collins, and other famous and lesser-known writers. "There's great variety in these stories," noted *Washington Post Book World* contributor Pat Dowell, who also related that Cox's introduction "helpfully charts the progress of the detective short story" and "delineates the detective's place within the larger world of Victorian sensation fiction." *The Oxford Book of Spy Stories,* with authors including Edgar Wallace, Len Deighton, Graham Greene, Baroness Orczy, Ambrose Bierce, John Galsworthy, and James Bond creator Ian Fleming, is a "diverse and entertaining" collection, in the view of *Magpies* reviewer John Murray.

Cox's reference works on literature have won praise as well. *A Dictionary of Writers and Their Works,* listing more than 3,000 American and European authors and 25,000 of their writings, "will prove a blessing to countless students and readers," observed a *Contemporary Review* commentator. *The Oxford Chronology of English Literature* offers information on about 4,000 writers, mostly from the British Isles, and 30,000 works published from 1474, when printing-press technology began to be used in England, to 2000. The volume has "breadth and depth," remarked Kevin O'Kelly in *Library Journal,* while *Choice* contributor W. S. Brockman thought "the authority, accuracy, and comprehensiveness of the work done by Cox" and his colleagues will make the book "a fundamental reference work in the field."

BIOGRAPHICAL AND CRITICAL SOURCES:

PERIODICALS

Choice, March, 1984, review of *M. R. James: An Informal Portrait,* p. 974; January, 2003, W. S. Brockman, review of *The Oxford Chronology of English Literature,* p. 796.

Commonweal, December 20, 1996, Celia Wren, "Boo-Hoo," pp. 20-21.
Contemporary Review, July, 2001, review of *A Dictionary of Writers and Their Works,* p. 61.
Library Journal, October 15, 2002, Kevin O'Kelly, review of *The Oxford Chronology of English Literature,* p. 62.
Magpies, September, 1996, John Murray, review of *The Oxford Book of Spy Stories,* pp. 38-39.
New York Times Book Review, March 8, 1992, Jack Sullivan, "A Tomb with a View," p. 12.
Publishers Weekly, July 21, 1991, review of *Victorian Ghost Stories: An Oxford Anthology,* p. 38.
Sewanee Review, winter, 1988, Sam Pickering, "Ghostly Occasions," pp. xiii-xv.
Times Literary Supplement, December 6, 1996, Patricia Craig, "Pregnant Phantoms," p. 25.
Washington Post Book World, November 5, 1989, review of *The Oxford Book of English Ghost Stories,* p. 16; October 18, 1992, Pat Dowell, "Terror by Gaslight," p. 9; October 27, 1996, review of *The Oxford Book of Twentieth-Century Ghost Stories,* p. 13.*

* * *

COYNE, Tami 1960-

PERSONAL: Born March 9, 1960; married; children: a daughter. *Education:* Smith College, A.B.

ADDRESSES: Home—New York, NY. *Agent*—c/o Author Mail, Red Wheel/Weiser, P.O. Box 612, York Beach, ME 03910-0612. *E-mail*—info@spiritualchicks.com.

CAREER: Marketing, management, and executive recruiter; spiritually oriented career and life coach; author. Featured essayist on *Managementgeneral.com.*

WRITINGS:

Your Life's Work: A Guide to Creating a Spiritual and Successful Work Life, Berkley (New York, NY), 1998.
(With Karen Weissman) *The Spiritual Chicks Question Everything: Learn to Risk, Release, and Soar,* Red Wheel/Weiser (York Beach, ME), 2002.

SIDELIGHTS: Tami Coyne authored her first book, *Your Life's Work: A Guide to Creating a Spiritual and Successful Work Life,* when she discovered that people who love their work and those who don't project distinct differences in their attitudes. Her second book, *The Spiritual Chicks Question Everything: Learn to Risk, Release, and Soar,* was born from a serendipitous meeting with coauthor Karen Weissman at a course in metaphysics, a subject that probes the connection between spirituality and science. In association with her writings, Coyne has led seminars, presented lectures, hosted online chats for *iVillage.com,* made guest appearances on radio shows and online with *WellNet,* and been a featured essayist on *managementgeneral.com.*

A *Publishers Weekly* reviewer pointed out that, in her first book, Coyne combines her spiritual and vocational experience to examine how one's spirituality affects one's work life. She begins with the premise that we are all spiritual beings who, in conjunction with divine energy, create our own future. She then explains that all aspects of one's job, like them or hate them, "are merely the appropriate response of 'Spirit' to one's own conscious and unconscious requests."

Coyne's second book, coauthored with Weissman, took birth when she signed up for a 1994 course called "Concept Therapy." The course focused on the underlying similarity between spirituality and science-areas of inquiry that appear, on the surface, to be almost diametrically opposed. When she began the course, little did she know it would bear fruit in the forms of a friendship, a Web site, and a book. Coyne and Weissman ended up in the same tiny classroom in Brooklyn and discovered they lived just a block from each other in Greenwich Village. The women admit to having entirely different personalities, and they come from entirely different backgrounds: Coyne, a right-brained, passionate, and highly motivated woman, is a French literature major; Weissman, a left-brained, analytical woman who thoroughly think things through, has a Ph.D. in engineering. However, they discovered during long sidewalk conversations that they had similar philosophies to life and the concept of spirituality.

From those sidewalk conversations grew a friendship, and from friendship a collaboration. Self-confirmed spiritual women, they decided to call themselves the "Spiritual Chicks." They began contributing essays to

a lifestyle Web 'zine in 1999 and, after the Web site's demise, collected their articles and sent them to Red Wheel as a book proposal. The proposal was accepted, but the Spiritual Chicks needed more material to make their work book length. In the process of writing additional essays and articles, they started their own Web site, *www.spiritualchicks.com,* to field-test their new material. The book was written with the deliberate intent of relating to the real-life experiences of its audience.

The basis of *The Spiritual Chicks Question Everything* is the "One Life Principle," the idea that a single universal power manifests in all things and holds the universe together at the same time. Coyne and Weissmann formatted their book in a question-and-answer style, with short essays on real-life experiences wherever they felt it necessary to bring an answer to life. Those essays may be hard hitting, or humorous, just as real-life experiences are. Many answers, however, have no corresponding essay, the reason being—according to the authors—that readers need the opportunity to apply their own life experiences rather than just reading those of the authors. "Otherwise it would just read like the 'Tami and Karen show!'" the authors commented on an online interview for *Girlposse.com.*

In her review in *Awareness,* Maryel McKinley described *The Spiritual Chicks Question Everything* as "a refreshing, if not mind-blowing, book that will open your heart and help you dispose of junk thoughts one might be holding onto unnecessarily." Leslie Gilbert Elman, in *Healing Retreats and Spas,* called the book "savvy, affirming and enjoyable," and a *Girlposse.com* contributor dubbed it "Sassy, saucy and completely insightful." Jan Suzukawa in *Science of Mind* described the work as a "delightful and irreverent book" that counsels its readers to "(1) question everything; (2) condemn nothing; (3) and then, align ourselves with what we want."

Concluding their online interview with *Girlposse.com,* the authors wrote: "Questioning what we believe invites life to bring us answers to even our most troubling issues. Not condemning—our beliefs or anyone else's—makes us open to new perspectives and new experiences, and allows us to align ourselves with, and get, what we really want. The spiritual process is about learning that we are the masters of our own destinies—and, if you want to have a great life, there's nothing better than knowing that."

BIOGRAPHICAL AND CRITICAL SOURCES:

PERIODICALS

Healing Retreats and Spas, November-December, 2002, review of *The Spiritual Chicks Question Everything: Learn to Risk, Release, and Soar.*

Publishers Weekly, March 9, 1998, review of *Your Life's Work: A Guide to Creating a Spiritual and Successful Work Life,* p. 61; September 30, 2002, p. 66.

Science of Mind, February, 2003, Jan Suzukawa, review of *The Spiritual Chicks Question Everything.*

ONLINE

Girlposse.com, http://www.girlposse.com/ (May 8, 2003), review of *The Spiritual Chicks Question Everything: Learn to Risk, Release, and Soar;* "The Fifteen-Question E-Mail Interview with 'The Spiritual Chicks', Tami Coyne and Karen Weissman."

Spiritual Chicks Web site, http://www.spiritualchicks. com (May 8, 2003).

*   *   *

CRAIN, William C(hristopher) 1943-

PERSONAL: Born December 23, 1943, in Los Angeles, CA; son of William Willis and Kay Crain; married Ellen V. Fairweather, March 18, 1966; children: Adam, Thomas, Sarah. *Ethnicity:* "White." *Education:* Harvard University, A.B., 1965; University of Chicago, Ph.D., 1969. *Politics:* Democrat.

ADDRESSES: Home—801 West End Ave., Apt. 2B, New York, NY 10025. *Office*—Psychology Department, Office 7/317, City College of the City University of New York, 138th St. and Convent Ave., New York, NY 10031. *E-mail*—billcrain@aol.com.

CAREER: City College of the City University of New York, assistant professor, 1970-78, associate professor, 1979-88, professor of psychology, 1988—. Consulting psychologist, St. Luke's-Roosevelt Hospital Center, 1976-95.

MEMBER: American Psychological Association.

AWARDS, HONORS: Special resolution, City University of New York, in recognition of work on open meetings and open access, 1998; Edpress Award finalist, 1998, for essay, "How Nature Helps Children Develop."

WRITINGS:

Children's Role-taking as Participants and Observers (Ph.D. thesis), University of Chicago (Chicago, IL), 1969.

Theories of Development: Concepts and Applications (textbook), Prentice-Hall (Englewood Cliffs, NJ), 1980, 4th edition, 2000.

Reclaiming Childhood: Letting Children Be Children in an Achievement-oriented Society, Times Books/ Holt (New York, NY), 2003.

Contributor to journals, including *Academe, New York Times,* and *Montessori Life.*

WORK IN PROGRESS: Fifth edition of *Theories of Development;* editing the journal *Encounter: Education for Meaning and Social Justice.*

SIDELIGHTS: William C. Crain is a developmental psychologist who is concerned with how children's minds and personalities evolve. His *Theories of Development: Concepts and Applications* is a major textbook in the field, while *Reclaiming Childhood: Letting Children Be Children in an Achievement-oriented Society* is geared toward a more general audience and questions the assumption that the major task of parents and educators is to prepare children for the future. Adults, Crain argues, must begin to appreciate the special qualities of childhood and give children a chance to develop these qualities. He emphasizes children's natural dramatic, artistic, poetic, and linguistic capacities and their sensitivity to nature.

Theories of Development provides a sampling of theories from a diverse group of thinkers, including Sigmund Freud, Jean Piaget, Maria Montessori, and even Enlightenment philosophers John Locke and Jean-Jacques Rousseau. It also discusses how these theories may be put into practice in schools, the home, and other environments. Some critics have praised Crain's work for covering such a variety of theorists. "Crain spreads his net widely and some of his most interesting material is about theorists who usually do not figure much in books about developmental psychology," commented P. E. Bryant in a review of the second edition for *Nature*. Bryant thought Crain sometimes "rather too uncritical" of the various theories, but the reviewer still found the book "clear, enthusiastic and erudite." A *Choice* contributor called *Theories of Development* "interesting and well-documented."

Reclaiming Childhood addresses a modern trend in child-rearing, at least among middle- and upper-class families: the tendency of parents to fill children's time with lessons and other organized activities and of schools to emphasize test preparation, all with an eye on children's future educational and occupational success. Crain argues that adults are so busy preparing children for a competitive future that they are robbing children of the chance to develop fully as children. He urges adults to give children opportunities for spontaneous play, exposure to the arts, and the exploration of nature, and describes children's spontaneous achievements in these areas. "Crain supports child-centered education wherein children evolve on their own," noted Charity Peak in *Library Journal*. She observed that he "takes a proactive stance, offering numerous helpful strategies" that grew out of his interviews with parents and children. The result, according to *Booklist* contributor Vanessa Bush, is a "valuable resource for parents and teachers looking for alternative approaches to education." A *Publishers Weekly* reviewer further described the book as "a thoughtful plea for parents to focus on the quality of life that children can have now rather than on their future achievements."

In a positive review of *Reclaiming Childhood, Montessori Life* editor Joy Turner wrote, "This delightful book offers powerful support for children, as well as the discovery of a true friend and mentor for their parents and teachers."

Crain told *CA:* "I have always tried to translate ideas into action. From 1988 to 1997, I served as an elected member of the Teaneck, New Jersey school board, where I promoted child-centered education and fought against the growing testing movement and race-based academic tracking. I became deeply involved in civil rights issues and the protection of nature in Teaneck. These experiences have informed my writings.

"I also have been active in the effort to maintain open access to the City University of New York–to make sure that low-income students, recent immigrants, and students of color continue to have the opportunities that were won in the open admissions struggle of 1969. I have described the issues in an article, 'Open Admissions at the City University of New York,' in the July-August 2003 issue of *Academe*."

In 2002 Crain became the editor of the journal *Encounter: Education for Meaning and Social Justice*. In 2003 he joined the board of "The Alliance for Childhood," a coalition of professionals trying to protect childhood in today's high-pressured society.

BIOGRAPHICAL AND CRITICAL SOURCES:

PERIODICALS

Booklist, January 1, 2002, Vanessa Bush, review of *Reclaiming Childhood: Letting Children Be Children in an Achievement-oriented Society*, p. 824.
Choice, July-August, 1980, review of *Theories of Development: Concepts and Applications*, p. 728.
Institute for Waldorf Education Research Bulletin, June, 2003, Ed Miller, review of *Reclaiming Childhood*, p. 53.
Library Journal, January, 2003, Charity Peak, review of *Reclaiming Childhood*, p. 146.
Montessori Life, summer, 1991, "Passion Is the Key: An Interview with William C. Crain," pp. 22-26; spring, 2003, Joy Turner, review of *Reclaiming Childhood*, p. 13.
Nature, February, 1986, P. E. Bryant, review of *Theories of Development*, p. 797.
Publishers Weekly, November 4, 2002, review of *Reclaiming Childhood*, p. 81.

*　　*　　*

CROUCH, Austin 1870-1957

PERSONAL: Born July 13, 1870, in Carrolton, MO; died after a car crash, August 28, 1957, in Nashville, TN; son of Elbert Hildebrand and Adelaide (Newell) Crouch; married Arianna Hill, 1900 (deceased); married Myrtle Oldham, 1946. *Education:* Baylor University, A.B., 1898; attended Southern Baptist Theological Seminary, 1898-1900; Howard College (now Stanford University), M.A., 1906.

CAREER: Ordained Baptist minister, 1893; pastor of Baptist churches in Alabama, Arkansas, Mississippi, Tennessee, and Texas; Southern Baptist Convention, superintendent of church extension for Home Mission Board, then executive secretary-treasurer of executive committee, 1927-46; preacher and writer, 1946-57.

WRITINGS:

The Plan of Salvation, [Nashville, TN], 1924.
The Progress of the Christian Life, Sunday School Board of the Southern Baptist Convention (Nashville, TN), 1949.
How Southern Baptists Do Their Work, Broadman Press (Nashville, TN), 1951.
Is Baptism Essential to Salvation?, 1953.

Also author of "The Bright Side of Death," Broadman Press (Nashville, TN), 1951.

BIOGRAPHICAL AND CRITICAL SOURCES:

BOOKS

Religious Leaders of America, 2nd edition, Gale (Detroit, MI), 1999.*

* * *

CROWDER, Stephanie R. Buckhanon 1969-

PERSONAL: Born April 23, 1969, in TN; married William E. Crowder, Jr.; children: William Rowland-Jackson. *Ethnicity:* "African American." *Education:* Howard University, B.S.; United Theological Seminary, M.Div.; Vanderbilt University, Ph.D.

ADDRESSES: Home—7916 Amber Hills Lane, Nashville, TN 37221; fax: 615-277-1778.

CAREER: American Baptist College, Nashville, TN, assistant professor, 2000—. Also works as Baptist and Disciples of Christ minister. Program coordinator for HIV/AIDS Network; Nashville READ, member of board of directors.

MEMBER: Society of Biblical Literature.

AWARDS, HONORS: Fellow of Wabash Center for Teaching, 2002-03.

WRITINGS:

Simon of Cyrene: A Case of Roman Conscription, Peter Lang Publishing (New York, NY), 2002.

Contributor to books, including *The African American Pulpit,* Judson Press, 2002.

WORK IN PROGRESS: Race, Ethnicity, and Power in the New Testament, for Chalice Press, completion expected in 2004; "The Gospel of Luke," to be included in *African-American New Testament,* Abingdon Press (Nashville, TN), 2004.

SIDELIGHTS: Stephanie R. Buckhanon Crowder told *CA:* "My writing is influenced by my call to a preaching and teaching ministry. I want to bridge the gap between what happens in the academy and the church. My writing allows me to help lay persons who serve in the church to access scholarship in universities and colleges for the purpose of spiritual development."

* * *

CROWNER, David 1938-

PERSONAL: Born September 17, 1938, in Brainerd, MN; son of Louis Carl (a Lutheran pastor) and Linnea Marie (a homemaker and church volunteer) Crowner; married August 17, 1963; wife's name Pat (a special education teacher); children: Michael, Karen, Matthew. *Education:* Pacific Lutheran University, B.A., 1961; Rutgers University, M.A., Ph.D., 1966. *Politics:* Democrat. *Religion:* Lutheran. *Hobbies and other interests:* Sailing, soccer, working on a sister-city project.

ADDRESSES: Home—160 Gordon Ave., Gettysburg, PA 17325. *E-mail*—pcrowner@netrax.net.

CAREER: Hartwick College, Oneonta, NY, instructor in German language and literature, 1964-66; Gettysburg College, Gettysburg, PA, began as assistant professor, became professor of German language and literature, 1967-2001, professor emeritus, 2001—, also served as faculty director of service-learning.

MEMBER: American Council of Teachers of Foreign Languages, American Association of Teachers of German, Torch International.

WRITINGS:

German for Mastery, D. Van Nostrand (New York, NY), 1980.

(With K. Lill) *Impulse: Kommunikatives Deutsch für die Mittelstufe,* Houghton Mifflin (Boston, MA), 1995, 2nd edition, 1999.

Spirituality of the German Awakening, Paulist Press (Mahwah, NJ), 2002.

*   *   *

CUMMINS, Joseph

PERSONAL: Born in Detroit, MI; married Dede Kinerk (an actress); children: Carson. *Education:* Attended John Carroll University; Columbia University, M.F.A. (writing), 1970.

ADDRESSES: Home—New Jersey. *Agent*—c/o Akashic Books, P.O. Box 1456, New York, NY 10009. *E-mail*—jscummins@earthlink.net.

CAREER: Writer.

WRITINGS:

(Editor) *Cannibals: Shocking True Tales of the Last Taboo on Land and Sea* (nonfiction), Lyons Press (Guilford, CT), 2001.

The Snow Train (novel), Akashic (New York, NY), 2001.

(Editor and author of introduction) *The Greatest Search and Rescue Stories Ever Told* (nonfiction), Lyons Press (Guilford, CT), 2002.

SIDELIGHTS: Joseph Cummins's debut novel, *The Snow Train,* is written in the voice of three-year-old Robbie O'Conor, and convincingly so according to

critics. It is 1952, and Robbie lives in Michigan with his parents and his beloved older sister, Rosemary. Their father sells cars and their mother writes poetry, so the two children are often left to amuse themselves. Everything about the O'Conors suggests the possibility for a happy life, until eight-month-old Robbie is discovered to have a skin disease that soon takes control of his life.

At about this time, Rosemary dies in an accident, and Robbie realizes with alarming clarity that his parents are too deep in their grief to care about or for him as they should. Where once he relied upon his sister for compassion and understanding, young Robbie must now face his tormented life without his champion. How he handles the grief of losing Rosemary and the burden of his disfiguring disease is what lies at the core of *The Snow Train.*

Cummins's novel moves between Rosemary's death and the time, five years later, when Robbie enters the hospital for experimental treatment of his condition. By seeing through Robbie's eyes, the reader is taken back to the Technicolor world of childhood. What Cummins ultimately presents is a realistic portrait of the terrors and insecurities that pave the path of a child's earliest memorable years.

The Snow Train has been favorably compared to Harper Lee's *To Kill a Mockingbird* and Dorothy Allison's *Bastard out of Carolina* in its ability to articulate the thoughts and concerns of a young child without seeming manipulative. "Throughout," wrote Debbie Bogenschutz in *Library Journal,* "Cummins inhabits the mind of a child and gives him voice as few writers could."

BIOGRAPHICAL AND CRITICAL SOURCES:

PERIODICALS

Library Journal, July, 2001, Debbie Bogenschutz, review of *The Snow Train,* p. 121.

Publishers Weekly, September 24, 2001, review of *The Snow Train,* p. 68.

ONLINE

Akashic Books, http://www.akashicbooks.com/ (January 8, 2002), review of *The Snow Train.*

Book Muse, http://www.bookmuse.com/ (March 7, 2002), review of *The Snow Train.*

Pop Matters, http://www.popmatters.com/ (January 8, 2002), Aaron Beebe, "How Did This Happen? When Did We Meet?"*

*   *   *

CURNUTT, Jordan 1958-

PERSONAL: Born September 15, 1958, in Tucson, AZ; married November 26, 1994; wife's name, Rosemarie (an archivist); children: Gabriel Puerta, Miranda Esperanza. *Education:* University of Arizona, Ph.D., 1991.

ADDRESSES: Office—Department of Philosophy, St. Cloud State University, St. Cloud, MN 56301-4498. *E-mail*—jcurnutt@stcloudstate.edu.

CAREER: St. Cloud State University, St. Cloud, MN, professor of philosophy, 1992—.

WRITINGS:

(With John W. Dienhart) *Business Ethics: A Reference Handbook,* American Bibliographical Center-Clio Press (Santa Barbara, CA), 1999.

Animals and the Law: A Sourcebook, American Bibliographical Center-Clio Press (Santa Barbara, CA), 2001.

Contributor to books, including *Contemporary Moral Problems,* edited by James E. White, 5th edition, West Publishing (St. Paul, MN), 1996; and *Ethics for Everyday,* edited by David Benatar, McGraw-Hill (New York, NY), 2002. Contributor to periodicals, including *Journal of Social Philosophy* and *Religious Studies.*

WORK IN PROGRESS: Editing *Contemporary Readings in Animal Ethics;* research on moral and legal perspectives on American Indian whaling.

BIOGRAPHICAL AND CRITICAL SOURCES:

PERIODICALS

Booklist, February 15, 1999, Mary Ellen Quinn, review of *Business Ethics: A Reference Handbook,* p. 1092; March 1, 2002, Mary Ellen Quinn, review of *Animals and the Law: A Sourcebook,* p. 1175.

Library Journal, February 1, 1999, Steven Silkunas, review of *Business Ethics,* p. 103.

*   *   *

CYMBALA, Carol Joy 1947-

PERSONAL: Born December 28, 1947, in Chicago, IL; daughter of Clair Dean (a minister) and Wilma Viola (Arn) Hutchins; married James Roger Cymbala (a minister), January 11, 1969; children: Christine Cymbala Toledo, Susan Cymbala Pettrey, James. *Religion:* Christian.

ADDRESSES: Home—25-31 West Dr., Douglaston, NY 11363. *Office*—17 Smith St., Brooklyn, NY 11201; fax: 718-783-6380. *E-mail*—ccymbala@brooklyntabernacle.org.

CAREER: Brooklyn Tabernacle, Brooklyn, NY, music director of Brooklyn Tabernacle Choir, c. 1973—.

MEMBER: American Society of Composers, Authors, and Publishers, National Academy of Recording Arts and Sciences, GMA.

AWARDS, HONORS: Four Grammy awards, National Academy of Recording Arts and Sciences; several Dove Awards.

WRITINGS:

(With Ann Spangler) *He's Been Faithful: Trusting God to Do What Only He Can Do,* Zondervan (Grand Rapids, MI), 2001.

*   *   *

CZAJKOWSKI, Chris(tine) 1947-

PERSONAL: Surname is pronounced Chy-*koff*-ski; born August 7, 1947, in England; immigrated to Canada, 1979; daughter of Edmund Jan (an antique restorer) and Edith May (Rumbold) Czajkowski. *Ethnicity:* "Caucasian." *Education:* Studley College, diploma in agriculture. *Politics:* "Pro-environment."

ADDRESSES: Home—c/o General Delivery, Nimpo Lake, British Columbia, Canada V0L 1R0. *E-mail*—nuktessli@coyote.chilcotin.bc.ca.

CAREER: Worked in agriculture at various sites around the world, prior to 1979; farmer in Canada, 1979-82; writer and operator of "eco-tours," 1982—.

AWARDS, HONORS: Nomination for Canadian National Magazine Award, for an article published in *Harrowsmith*.

WRITINGS:

AUTHOR AND ILLUSTRATOR

To Stalk the Oomingmak: An Artist's Arctic Journal, Aquarelle Publishing (Baton Rouge, LA), 1990.
Cabin at Singing River: Building a Home in the Wilderness, Camden House (Camden East, Ontario, Canada), 1991.
Diary of a Wilderness Dweller, Orca (Custer, WA), 1996.
Nuk Tessli: The Life of a Wilderness Dweller (sequel to *Diary of a Wilderness Dweller*), Orca (Custer, WA), 1999.
Snowshoes and Spotted Dick: Letters from a Wilderness Dweller, Harbour Publishing (Medeira Park, British Columbia, Columbia, Canada), 2003.

Contributor of articles, photographs, and drawings to periodicals, including *Harrowsmith* and *Wildflower.*

WORK IN PROGRESS: Lonesome: Diary of a Wilderness Dog, for Raincoast Book Distribution (Vancouver, British Columbia, Canada).

SIDELIGHTS: Chris Czajkowski told *CA:* "The primary motivation for writing is my life. I live in an exciting environment: a high-altitude lake in British Columbia's Coast Mountains that can be reached only by float plane or on foot. I, a middle-aged woman, built my first two cabins single-handedly, felling the trees myself and dragging them to the site with a come-along. I live alone, and I guess a desire to share my beautiful world with friends and strangers has led me to write about it in various ways. I've always loved creating things—paintings, buildings, fabric from raw, natural fibers—consequently I love the actual craft of writing.

"My work is obviously influenced by my environment. I'm also a painter, printmaker, photographer, and a self-taught botanist: my visual art has a heavy botanical bias. From my remote cabin I run an eco-tour business for hikers and naturalists. During the spring and fall, I give slide shows about my world, often speaking to audiences of several hundred people. Everything in my life is tied together.

"To write, I have an eleven-year-old Mac Classic computer. Because of my remote existence, it is operated by solar power. As I do most of my writing in winter when I have few tourists, and have only a very small solar system, I must conserve power. I usually, therefore, do a very rough first draft in longhand. The second draft often bears very little relationship to the first, but without the initial scribbling I spend long, unproductive hors staring at the screen, and power is wasted. If I want to do a lot of computer work I cannot spare enough power for electric lights, so I must illuminate the keyboard by candlelight or coal oil lamps.

"I find it best to put a draft of a manuscript aside for several months to get a more balanced look at it. The other occupations in my life (tourists, slide show and book tours) in fact force me to do this. Being the kind of person who likes to completely finish a job once it is started, I always find the interruptions irritating, but they are the best thing that could happen to the manuscript."

BIOGRAPHICAL AND CRITICAL SOURCES:

ONLINE

Nuk Tessli Alpine Experience, http://www.chilcotin.bc.ca/nuktessli/ (November 16, 2003).

D

DAM, Satyabrata 1965-

PERSONAL: Born February 13, 1965, in Kanpur, Uttar Pradesh, India; son of D. P. and Sabita Dam. *Education:* D.A.V., B.Com, 1989. *Religion:* Agnostic. *Hobbies and other interests:* Mountaineering, sky diving, water sports, painting, saxophone, magic.

ADDRESSES: Home—C-1/1599, Fasant Kunj, New Delhi 110070, India. *E-mail*—satyabratadam@yahoo.com.

CAREER: Mountaineer and fiction writer.

MEMBER: Himalayan Club (secretary, 1999-2001).

WRITINGS:

Eyewitness and Other Tales of Detection, Minerva Press (London, England), 2001.

Contributor to periodicals, including *Himalayan Journal, Moutaineers, Climb,* and *High.* Editor, *Anil Aggrawal's Internet Journal of Book Reviews.*

WORK IN PROGRESS: Checkmate and More Tales of Detection; With Malice Aforethought; "research on Tibet, Egyptology, and Einstein's brain for a forthcoming book on adventure."

SIDELIGHTS: Satyabrata Dam told *CA:* "I write to revive the almost extinct genre of classic murder crime whodunits. I am mainly influenced by Arthur Conan Doyle and Austin Freeman. I write directly in Microsoft Word on my computer, and complete my research work before starting the main text. I am a forensic expert with an in-depth knowledge of forensic medicine, and I decided to share my knowledge with general readers through my writing."

A well-known mountaineer, Dam has climbed in the Himalayas, Alps, and Tien Shan ranges since beginning the sport in the 1980s.

BIOGRAPHICAL AND CRITICAL SOURCES:

ONLINE

Writers Net, http://www.writers.net/ (November 16, 2003), "Satyabrata Dam."

*   *   *

DANCHIN, Antoine 1944-

PERSONAL: Born May 7, 1944, in Besan, Doubs, France; son of Pierre and (Boutillier) Danchin; married Agnieszka Sekowska; children: Raphael, Coralie. *Ethnicity:* "Homo Sapien." *Education:* M.A. (mathematics), 1965; M.A. (physics), 1957; Ph.D., 1967; D.Sci., 1971.

ADDRESSES: Home—Pine Court Block 1, Flat A6, Pokfulam, Hong Kong, China. *Office*—Institut Pasteur, Unit of Genetics of Bacterial Genomes, Deptartment of Structure and Dynamics of Genomes, 28 rue du Docteur Roux, 75724, Paris Cedex 15, France. *E-mail*—adanchin@hkucc.hku.hk.

CAREER: Scientist, research director, and professor. École Normale Superieure Ulm, Paris, France, researcher, 1964-68; National Center for the Research of Science (CNRS), Paris, 1968—, began as researcher, became director of research, 1984; Pasteur Institute, Paris, head of research unit, 1986—, professor and former department head at Institut Pasteur, 2001—, head of Unit of Genetics of Bacterial Genomes, beginning 1993; HKU-Pasteur Research Centre, Hong Kong, China, cofounder and first director. Instructor and program organizer at universities in France, Italy, and the United States; advisor to, and committee and board member of, multiple scientific organizations and groups.

MEMBER: European Molecular Biology Organization, French Society for Microbiology, French Society for Molecular Biology, American Society for Microbiology.

WRITINGS:

Ordre et dynamique du vivant: chemins de la biologie moléculaire, Seuil (Paris, France), 1978.
L'oeuf et la poule: histoires du code génétique, Fayard (Paris, France), 1983.
(With Agnes Ullmann and others) *Régulation de l'expression génétique: rôle de l'AMP cyclique: microbiologie générale, protocoles expérimentaux,* edited by Francis Gasser, Hermann (Paris, France), 1986.
La barque de Delphes: ce que révèle le textes des génomes, Odile Jacob (Paris, France), 1998, translated by Alison Quayle as *The Delphi Boat: What Genomes Tell Us,* Harvard University Press (Cambridge, MA), 2002.

Contributor to periodicals and scientific journals.

SIDELIGHTS: Antoine Danchin was first a mathematician and physicist before becoming a geneticist. In 1985 he began a collaboration with computer scientists that explored the use of artificial intelligence techniques in the study of molecular genetics. Danchin felt

that the study of whole genomes should begin, provided that parallel advancements in computer science could also be initiated. His 1987 proposal that the genome of Bacillus subtilis be sequenced became a reality in 1988 when R. Dedonder began the European effort. Danchin contributed to the work with his colleagues in Europe and Japan.

Danchin's 1998 study was translated and published as *The Delphic Boat: What Genomes Tell Us.* The title refers to the question posed by the oracle at Delphi, who asked whether a boat is the same if, over time, every board rots away and is replaced. The answer is yes, because the boat is actually the relationship of its parts. Similarly, Danchin argues that life cannot be understood by a mere examination of its parts—DNA, genes, cells, etc.—as they have been mapped by the Human Genome Project, but by their relationships to each other. *Booklist's* Bryce Christensen noted that Danchin explains "that the genetic code functions not with the mechanical predictability of Newtonian physics but rather with the elusive suggestiveness of foreign metaphors."

The volume reveals that the evolution and survival of living organisms is an organized unfolding of a program shaped both by heredity and by the environment. A *Kirkus Reviews* contributor wrote that "Danchin's elaboration on this theme leads to daunting but fascinating discourses on information theory, entropy, chaos, and the creation of life," and concluded by calling *The Delphic Boat* "a rich Gallic feast of ideas to stimulate and savor."

Danchin's interests include philosophy and cultures, and in addition to his scientific articles he has written on a variety of other subjects, such as ethics and epistemology.

BIOGRAPHICAL AND CRITICAL SOURCES:

PERIODICALS

Booklist, December 1, 2002, Bryce Christensen, review of *The Delphic Boat: What Genomes Tell Us,* p. 636.
Kirkus Reviews, November 15, 2002, review of *The Delphic Boat,* p. 1670.

Library Journal, December, 2002, Margaret Henderson, review of *The Delphic Boat,* p. 168.

Nature, April, 2003, Axel Meyer, review of *The Delphic Boat,* pp. 564-565.

Publishers Weekly, November 25, 2002, review of *The Delphic Boat,* p. 51.

*   *   *

DANN, Kevin T. 1956-

PERSONAL: Born March 25, 1956, in New York, NY; son of Tyler and Catherine (Ellerkamp) Dann; married Joyce Macksoud, August 13, 1976 (divorced, February, 2001); children: Jordan (daughter). *Ethnicity:* "White." *Education:* Attended Dartmouth College; University of California—Santa Cruz, B.A., 1979; University of Vermont, M.A., 1984; Rutgers University, Ph.D., 1995.

ADDRESSES: Home—11A College Hill, Woodstock, VT 05091. *E-mail*—kdann@valley.net.

CAREER: Writer. Damaged Freight (string band), performer; leader of historical walking tours. Taught American history, environmental history, and environmental studies at University of Vermont, Rutgers University, University of Oklahoma, and Ramapo College of New Jersey. Director of Audubon Society wildlife refuge in Rhode Island, c. 1979.

WRITINGS:

Twenty-five Walks in New Jersey, Rutgers University Press (Piscataway, NJ), 1982, revised edition published as *Thirty Walks in New Jersey,* 1992.

Traces on the Appalachians: A Natural History of Serpentine in Eastern North America, Rutgers University Press (Piscataway, NJ), 1988.

Bright Colors Falsely Seen: Synaesthesia and the Modern Search for Transcendental Knowledge, Yale University Press (New Haven, CT), 1998.

Across the Great Border Fault: The Naturalist Myth in America, Rutgers University Press (Piscataway, NJ), 2000.

Lewis Creek Lost and Found, University Press of New England (Hanover, NH), 2001.

WORK IN PROGRESS: How Long? Henry David Thoreau and Nature's Nation, for Hill & Wang; *Water upon Stone,* "a personal adventure tale about contemporary Earth mysteries," for Lantern Books.

SIDELIGHTS: Kevin T. Dann told *CA:* "Just today, out on a midday run, it struck me that I began writing in wide-eyed wonder about the world beyond the senses, and now my writing is largely about the intersection of the two, and is driven largely by a sense that we are at this point in history destined to be a bit more awake than we seem to be to the Earth's and humanity's deeper mysteries."

*   *   *

DARLEY, Gillian

PERSONAL: Female.

ADDRESSES: Agent—Caroline Dawnay, Peters, Fraser & Dunlop Group Ltd., Drury House, 34-43 Russell St., London WC2B 5HA, England.

CAREER: Journalist, leturer, and writer on architectural subjects and the history of English architecture and land use. Has appeared on British Broadcasting Corporation (BBC) television and radio. Curator of museum exhibit "The Idea of the Village: An Illustrated Survey of the Planned Village," Architectural Association, London, 1976.

WRITINGS:

Villages of Vision, Architectural Press (London, England), 1975.

The National Trust Book of the Farm, Weidenfeld & Nicolson (London, England), 1981, Crescent Books (New York, NY), 1985.

Built in Britain, Weidenfeld & Nicolson (London, England), 1983.

(With Philippa Lewis) *Dictionary of Ornament,* Pantheon Books (New York, NY), 1986.

A Future for Farm Buildings, Save Britain's Heritage, 1988.

Octavia Hill: A Life, Constable (London, England), 1989.

(With Peter Hall and David Lock) *Tomorrow's New Communities,* Joseph Rowntree Foundation (York, England), 1991.

(With Andrew Saint) *The Chronicles of London,* St. Martin's (New York, NY), 1994.

John Soane: An Accidental Romantic, Yale University Press (New Haven, CT), 1999.

Factory (Objekt), Reaktion Books, 2003.

Contributor, Tony Rivers and Dan Cruickshank, editors, *The Name of the Room: A History of the British House and Home,* British Broadcasting Corporation (London, England), 1994. Contributor to newspapers and magazines, including *Financial Times, Times Literary Supplement, Architects's Journal, Architectural Review,* and *Country Life.* Former architectural correspondent, *Observer.*

SIDELIGHTS: Gillian Darley is a British author and journalist who has been writing on architectural topics for more than a quarter of a century. Darley has contributed columns to such publications as the *Financial Times* and London *Observer,* and her interests range from buildings to planned communities to factories and farmlands. She has also written biographies of Octavia Hill and John Soane.

John Soane: An Accidental Romantic is Darley's best known work in the United States. Soane, who died in 1837, was a prominent architect in eighteenth- and early nineteenth-century England who bequeathed his home in Lincoln's Inn Fields to the government for use as a museum. Darley's biography makes use of Soane's papers and other memorabilia from the Lincoln's Inn Fields house, as well as correspondence and public papers on his extraordinary, and contentious, life. In his critique of the book for *Architectural Review,* Gavin Stamp called *John Soane: An Accidental Romantic* "a most illuminating and riveting portrait both of Soane . . . and of his changing and complicated times." Darley's biography covers all aspects of Soane's life, from his pioneering work and artistic vision to his domestic troubles and bouts of mental instability. *New Republic* contributor Martin Filler praised the work as "definitive," adding that it "is not only the finest life-and-works of an architect to appear in many years, it is also a character study of the utmost understanding. Darley's panoramic approach places Soane in his times with a cultural authority and a wealth of erudition rarely encountered in

architectural writing today." *New Criterion* reviewer J. Duncan Berry wrote: "It is one of the great accomplishments of Gillian Darley's . . . biography that the full scope of Soane's life and works can be seen in exquisite detail, thus allowing a fresh perspective on this vexing figure and his ethereal aesthetic objectives."

BIOGRAPHICAL AND CRITICAL SOURCES:

PERIODICALS

Architectural Review, March, 2000, Gavin Stamp, review of *John Soane: An Accidental Romantic,* p. 96.

British Book News, February, 1982, G. E. Fussell, review of *The National Trust Book of the Farm,* p. 106.

Guardian (London, England), September 2, 2000, Vera Rule, review of *John Soane: An Accidental Romantic,* p. 11.

New Criterion, November, 1999, J. Duncan Berry, review of *John Soane: An Accidental Romantic.*

New Republic, February 7, 2000, Martin Filler, "On Architecture-Shafts of Light," p. 28.

New York Times Book Review, December 5, 1999, Martin Filler, review of *John Soane: An Accidental Romantic,* p. 40.

Observer, January 21, 1990, Penelope Fitzgerald, "The Poor of Paradise Place," p. 61.

Times Literary Supplement, March 12, 1976, David Watkin, "Worlds Apart," p. 281; November 5, 1999, David Watkin, "He Raised a Nest of Wasps," p. 12.*

*   *   *

DAVIES, Luke 1962-

PERSONAL: Born 1962, in Sydney, Australia. *Education:* Attended Sydney University.

ADDRESSES: Agent—c/o Author Correspondence, Allen & Unwin, P.O. Box 8500, St. Leonard's, New South Wales 1590, Australia.

CAREER: Writer. Has worked as a bartender, truck driver, editor, and teacher.

WRITINGS:

Four Plots for Magnets (poetry), Glandular Press (Australia), 1982.

Absolute Event Horizon: Poems, Angus & Robertson (Sydney, Australia), 1994.

Candy (novel), Ballantine Books (New York, NY), 1998.

Running with Light: Poems, Allen & Unwin (St. Leonard's, New South Wales, Australia), 1999.

Isabelle the Navigator (novel), Allen & Unwin (St. Leonard's, New South Wales, Australia), 2000, Berkley Books (New York, NY), 2002.

Contributor of poetry to periodicals, including *Weekend Australian.*

ADAPTATIONS: Candy was been optioned as a motion picture.

WORK IN PROGRESS: A novel.

SIDELIGHTS: Luke Davies is an Australian writer who has had success with both poetry and fiction. Davies's poetry is better known in Australia, but he has gained an international audience for his novels *Candy* and *Isabelle the Navigator.* Set in Sydney and Melbourne, *Candy* tells the harrowing story of a couple dragged into desperation by heroin addiction. The unnamed narrator describes his love affair with a young woman named Candy who, with his complicity, becomes addicted herself. The novel goes into great detail about the daily lives of addicts and their single-minded pursuit of the next fix. Candy descends into prostitution, and the narrator commits fraud and petty acts of robbery as he frantically searches his body for a vein he can prick. Although Davies has admitted that he used drugs in the past, he insists that *Candy* is fiction and that it bears no true resemblance to his life. As he put it in the Brisbane *Courier-Mail,* "I don't think there is anybody under 45 today who hasn't had some contact with drugs. Yet this is a fictional creation and hopefully what rings true is the emotional landscape that I have constructed."

Critics in Australia and America reacted positively to Davies's images in *Candy.* In the *Australian Book Review,* Jill Jones wrote: "This is a good book, a true

book, which left me feeling sad for some days. . . . Davies is a very good writer." *Rocky Mountain News* correspondent Gary Williams felt that the author's "soulful prose is the perfect antidote to the harsh realities of the underground world inhabited by these hopeless junkies." Williams concluded that Davies's portrayal of the addicted lifestyle "helps us understand a world most people are not familiar with." Reviewer Rosser Street in the *Weekend Australian* observed that the novel "is a timely window into the realities of heroin addiction. It is also something of a stylistic breakthrough in terms of our 'drug' literature. The nature of addiction is rendered clearly, precisely, often surprisingly. . . . This alone makes it valuable."

Davies's second novel bears no resemblance to his first. *Isabelle the Navigator* is a first-person account of a woman's grief over the loss of her lover and her father. As she reminisces about her past and deals with her present circumstances, Isabelle draws solace from wind charts and other navigational tools that she learns about in night classes. In a Brisbane *Courier-Mail* review, Rebekah Scott stated: "Isabelle's tale is a confessional, cross-generational, lyrical, nautical saga. . . . The imagery is elemental." *Seattle Times* contributor Clarence Brown deemed the title character "a consummately imagined young woman."

In an interview with the *Weekend Australian,* Davies said that he is grateful for the success of his fiction because it gives him more time to write poetry. This is no small consideration for a writer whose 1995 collection, *Absolute Event Horizon* was shortlisted for Australia's Trunbull Fox Phillips poetry prize. Davies told an online interviewer that his accomplishments have come because he is a survivor of drug abuse who feels inner contentment. "What's changed for me is that I spent my time as a drug addict wishing that I was someone else, somewhere else, some other time, and these days I'm really happy to be me. Glad to be who I am."

BIOGRAPHICAL AND CRITICAL SOURCES:

PERIODICALS

Australian Book Review, November, 1994, Peter Mitchell, "Colours of Poetry," p. 58; December, 1997/January, 1998, Jill Jones, "Addictive Genre," p. 46.

Booklist, July, 1998, Kevin Grandfield, review of *Candy,* p. 1857.

Courier-Mail (Brisbane, Australia), September 6, 1997, C. Bantick, "Sniff Today and Die," p. 7; October 7, 2000, Rebekah Scott, "On Women and the Wind," p. M5.

Publishers Weekly, June 8, 1998, review of *Candy,* p. 46.

Rocky Mountain News (Denver, CO), October 7, 1998, Gary Williams, "Soulful Prose Hooks Interest in Drug Odyssey," p. D10.

Seattle Times, September 29, 2002, Clarence Brown, review of *Isabelle the Navigator,* p. K9.

Weekend Australian (Sydney, Australia), October 11, 1997, Rosser Street, "Desperate Lives," p. R30; October 14, 2000, Sian Powell, "Risky Business," p. R10.

ONLINE

IAustralia, http://www.thei.aust.com/ (October 23, 2003), interview with Davies.*

*   *   *

DEAN, Ruth (Brigham) 1947-

PERSONAL: Born May 11, 1947, in Salem, MA; daughter of Richard B. (a lawyer) and Chloe Tyler (Walker) Johnson; married Jonathan Dean (an attorney), September 22, 1966; children: Ann C., Alexander J. *Education:* University of Akron, B.A. (summa cum laude), 1984, M.A. (English), 1987.

ADDRESSES: Office—The Writing Toolbox, 1221 West Market St., Akron, OH 44313. *E-mail*—rdean@ wtoolbox.com.

CAREER: Writer. University of Akron—Wayne College, Orville, OH, coordinator of Writing Center, 1986-91; Ryerson Management Associates, Akron, OH, senior technical writer, 1990-93; The Writing Toolbox, Akron, president, 1993—. President of Women's Endowment Fund of Akron Community Foundation.

WRITINGS:

(With Melissa Thomson) *Teen Prostitution,* Lucent Books (San Diego, CA), 1998.

(With Melissa Thomson) *Life in the American Colonies,* Lucent Books (San Diego, CA), 1999.

(With Melissa Thomson) *Women of the Middle Ages,* Lucent Books (San Diego, CA), 2003.

The Value of Integrity: A Memoir Celebrating the Ninetieth Anniversary of Buckingham, Doolittle & Burroughs, LLP, Buckingham, Doolittle & Burroughs, LLP (Akron, OH), 2003.

WORK IN PROGRESS: (With Melissa Thomson, Norma Rist, and Stephen Grant) *Ten Steps to a Great Business Name*; a history of Akron public schools' Head Start program.

SIDELIGHTS: Ruth Dean is a nonfiction writer who has teamed up with fellow writer Melissa Thomson to pen several young-adult titles for Lucent Books. Their *Life in the American Colonies* covers a myriad of topics, being careful to distinguish differences between the settlements in the north and south of the country in matters such as immigrant populations, ownership of slaves, organization of cities and towns, common professions, and relations with Native American groups. Other topics covered include the home, the frontier, farm life, science, health, and technology, as well as the life of children, men's and women's attire, and food and cooking. The result is "a clearly written and well-organized look at Colonial America," according to Debbie Feulner, a reviewer for *School Library Journal. Booklist* contributor Carolyn Phelan noted that "the text itself brings up many interesting points about the period," supported by quotes from original source material that is cited in a reference section.

Dean and Thomson have also collaborated on other books, including *Teen Prostitution,* which examines the extent of this social problem, several of its causes, and available resources for help, and *Women of the Middle Ages,* a work *School Library Journal* contributor Tina Cohen predicted would "fill . . . a gap" in many libraries.

"My 'writing career' didn't really have a starting point," Dean told *CA.* "I have been scribbling on bits of paper since I was old enough to hold a pencil. My family taught me to love books, plays, poems, and telling stories, and I have continued to work with words, as a reader and a writer, throughout my life.

"After seven years of teaching freshman composition courses at the University of Akron and its branch campus in Orville, Ohio, I got a job writing for a management consulting company. Here I learned how to write fast, to do spreadsheets and charts, and to create writing that would work in the world of business.

"In 1993, I established my own company, The Writing Toolbox. We focus on helping businesses and other organizations tell their stories, directly in the case of a history written for a law firm, or indirectly in the case of sales and marketing materials for businesses of all kinds. . . .

"When we were given the opportunity to write books for young people, we were delighted, although I must say that the only title then available in the Lucent series, *Teen Prostitution,* was a real challenge, both to research and to frame in the required 'balanced' terms. Balanced between what and what? We finally realized that we could frame this topic as a contrast between teen prostitutes as criminals and as victims of abuse. It was hard to face up to this material and hard to find ways to present it that might be appropriate for teen readers. I think the result was successful, though.

"*Life in the American Colonies* was much more fun to research, especially for [coauthor] Melissa, who was born in Dublin, Ireland, and therefore did not grow up learning about American history in school. We are especially pleased with the chapters on colonial technology and on Native Americans. We are very proud of the fact that this book was well reviewed in *Booklist.*

"It is difficult to work the research necessary to write a Lucent book into a very busy schedule, but when the *Women of the Middle Ages* title was offered, we could not resist. (I was a medievalist when I was in graduate school.) It was fascinating to see what has been learned about this topic as researchers have gone back over the available documents searching for women's names and information on their activities.

"Throughout my career as a teacher, writer, and business marketer, my focus really has been the same: to make information clear to a non-specialist. How can an American teenager come to understand what it was like to be a newlywed thirteen-year-old medieval duchess, who suddenly would have responsibility for managing six castles and hundreds of workers when her husband was called away to war? How does a teen runaway survive on the streets of an American city? What did the founders of the United States learn from Native American tribal governments that enabled them to establish one of the world's longest-lasting democracies?

"While it's unlikely that any of these books will be made into a major motion picture (or even a minor one), it is rewarding to see them on library shelves, and to talk to people who say, 'I never realized that!' about something I've written."

BIOGRAPHICAL AND CRITICAL SOURCES:

PERIODICALS

Booklist, May 1, 1999, Carolyn Phelan, review of *Life in the American Colonies,* p. 1592.
Horn Book Guide, fall, 1998, Carolyn Shute, review of *Teen Prostitution,* p. 357.
School Library Journal, July, 1999, Debbie Feulner, review of *Life in the American Colonies,* p. 105; August, 2003, Tina Cohen, review of *Women of the Middle Ages,* p. 172.

*   *   *

de BOYSSON-BARDIES, Bénédicte 1931-

PERSONAL: Born February 2, 1931, in Ismailia, Egypt; citizenship, French; children: Thierry, Olivier, Benoit. *Education:* Sorbonne, University of Paris V, doctorate (with honors), 1972. *Religion:* Roman Catholic.

ADDRESSES: Home—262 rue St. Jacques, 75005 Paris, France. *E-mail*—bbb@esct.jussieu.fr.

CAREER: Centre National de la Recherche Scientifique, Paris, France, director of research.

AWARDS, HONORS: Prix Jean Rostand.

WRITINGS:

Négation et performance linguistique, Mouton (Paris, France), 1976.

(Editor with others) *Developmental Neurocognition: Speech and Face Processing in the First Year of Life,* Kluwer Academic (Boston, MA), 1993.

Comment la parole vient aux enfants, Odile Jacob (Paris, France), 1996, translated by M. B. DeBevoise as *How Language Comes to Children: From Birth to Two Years,* MIT Press (Cambridge, MA), 1999.

Le langage, q'est-ce que c'est, illustrated by Tanitoc, Odile Jacob (Paris, France), 2003.

*　　*　　*

DeCURE, John

PERSONAL: Married; children: two sons. *Education:* California State University, Fullerton, B.A. (English); graduated from law school, 1990; studied creative writing at University of California, Irvine. *Hobbies and other interests:* Skateboarding, surfing.

ADDRESSES: Home—Long Beach, CA. *Agent*—c/o Author Mail, St. Martin's Press, 175 Fifth Ave., New York, NY 10010.

CAREER: Attorney and author. Motorola, San Jose, CA, salesman; called to the Bar of the State of California, 1990; juvenile dependency court attorney, 1991-93; California State Bar, Los Angeles, prosecuting attorney; Office of California Attorney General, prosecuting attorney.

WRITINGS:

Reef Dance, St. Martin's Minotaur (New York, NY), 2001.
Bluebird Rising, St. Martin's Minotaur (New York, NY), 2003.

Contributor to periodicals, including *Surfer* and *Surfer's Journal.*

SIDELIGHTS: John DeCure is a California attorney and mystery writer. His debut novel, *Reef Dance,* introduces readers to protagonist J. Shepard, a young West Coast lawyer who spends his days in court and his free time catching waves on his surfboard.

DeCure, an avid surfer, grew up in La Mirada, California. After receiving an undergraduate degree in English, he worked in sales for a copier company and then for Motorola before attending law school. He began his legal career in juvenile dependency court, a vocation his *Reef Dance* protagonist also shares. While still dedicated to practicing law, DeCure started to write in his sparc time and began studying creative writing in the evening. A year after accepting a position as a prosecutor for the State Bar of California, he began writing his first novel.

The title of *Reef Dance* comes from a surfing term used to indicate being stuck in one place, a situation in which DeCure's Shepard metaphorically finds himself. Shepard is frustrated in his personal life and overwhelmed by his caseload, until his work on a case involving a mother who has tried to sell her newborn child motivates him to explore the mysterious disappearance of his own mother when he was sixteen. Surfing plays a prominent role in the novel, and Joanne Wilkinson noted in *Booklist* that the "amply detailed surfing scenes and the rude, irreverent humor give this debut novel plenty of zip." A reviewer for *Publishers Weekly* dubbed *Reef Dance* an "edgy, in-your-face legal thriller," but added that "most readers . . . will find that surfing and detection make for an uneasy mix." David Olan in *Surfer* ranked the novel "with some of the best in surf fiction" and Rex E. Klett in *Library Journal* highly recommended the novel, writing that "surfing commentary, savory courtroom melodrama, and wry humor provide much attraction." DeCure's second J. Shepard novel, *Bluebird Rising,* was published in late 2003.

BIOGRAPHICAL AND CRITICAL SOURCES:

PERIODICALS

Booklist, August, 2001, Joanne Wilkinson, review of *Reef Dance,* p. 2095.
Library Journal, September 1, 2001, Rex E. Klett, review of *Reef Dance,* p. 237.
Publishers Weekly, August 6, 2001, review of *Reef Dance,* p. 65.
Surfer, May, 2003, David Olan, review of *Reef Dance,* p. S136.

ONLINE

John DeCure Web site, http://www.johndecure.com (June 17, 2003).*

DELANEY, Carol (Lowery) 1940-

PERSONAL: Born December 12, 1940 in New York, NY; married David Bangs (divorced 1967), children: Elizabeth Lowery Bangs. *Education:* Harvard Divinity School, M.T.S., 1976, University of Chicago, M.A., 1978, Ph.D. (anthropology), 1984. *Politics:* Democrat.

ADDRESSES: Office—Bldg. 110, Room 112 O, Stanford University, Stanford, CA 94305-2145. *E-mail*—cdelaney@Leland.stanford.edu.

CAREER: Harvard University Center for the Study of World Religions, Cambridge, MA, director, 1985-87; Stanford University, Stanford, CA, assistant professor, 1987-95, associate professor of cultural and social anthropology, 1995—.

MEMBER: American Anthropological Association, American Ethnological Society, American Academy of Religion, Middle East Studies Association.

AWARDS, HONORS: Galler prize, University of Chicago, 1985; Fulbright advanced research fellowship, 1984-85.

WRITINGS:

The Seed and the Soil: Gender and Cosmology in Turkish Village Society, University of California Press (Berkeley, CA), 1991.
(Editor, with Sylvia Yanagisako) *Naturalizing Power: Essays in Feminist Cultural Analysis,* Routledge (New York, NY), 1995.
Abraham on Trial: The Social Legacy of Biblical Myth, Princeton University Press (Princeton, NJ), 1998.

The Seed and the Soil was translated into Turkish.

WORK IN PROGRESS: Investigating Culture: An Experiential Introduction to Anthropology, Blackwell (Malden, MA), 2004.

SIDELIGHTS: Carol Delaney, a member of the anthropology faculty at Stanford University, has devoted her scholarly attention to the relation between gender and religion. She is the author of *The Seed and the Soil,* an exploration of life in a Turkish village, based on her fieldwork in a relatively remote Turkish village between 1980 and 1982. She also coedited *Naturalizing Power,* a book of essays on feminist cultural interpretation.

In *The Seed and the Soil* Delaney examines the symbolic structures rooted beneath the village society of Gokler in Turkey, concluding that patriarchal norms are inextricable from the monotheistic beliefs of the people and necessary to community cohesiveness. She organized her study along such subject lines as kinship, social geography, gender, procreation, and marriage customs. In a favorable notice in the *Whole Earth Review,* Mira Zussman concluded *The Seed and the Soil* offers "more than the title implies."

Abraham on Trial: The Social Legacy of Biblical Myth, published in 1998, was a finalist for the National Jewish Book Award. In this study Delaney examines the myth of Abraham and its interpretation in Judaism, Christianity, and Islam, and traces the myth's effect on the development of notions of paternal authority. Arguing that the myth should no longer be perpetuated, Delaney supportes her conclusions by drawing on sources from anthropological, religious, and psychological literature. In *Shofar* Gerald T. Sheppard noted that "at her best, Delaney surveys much of the evidence of how the story has been interpreted within each of the three religions." A *Library Journal* reviewer concluded that Delaney's study "offers a thought-provoking argument."

BIOGRAPHICAL AND CRITICAL SOURCES:

PERIODICALS

Choice, July-August, 1992, M. M. J. Fischer, review of *The Seed and the Soil: Gender and Cosmology in Turkish Village Society,* p. 1719.
Library Journal, October 1, 1998, Augustine J. Curley, review of *Abraham on Trial: The Social Legacy of Biblical Myth,* pp. 95-96.
MAN, March, 1994, June Starr, review of *The Seed and the Soil,* pp. 229-230.
Shofar, fall, 2001, Gerald T. Sheppard, review of *Abraham on Trial,* p. 142.
Theological Studies, September, 1999, Edward M. O'Flaherty, review of *Abraham on Trial,* p. 541.

Whole Earth Review, summer, 1995, Mira Zussman, review of *The Seed and the Soil,* p. 33.

ONLINE

Stanford University Web site, http://www.stanford.edu/ (September 23, 2003).

*   *   *

DINTER, Paul E(dward) 1944-

PERSONAL: Born December 13, 1944, in Port Chester, NY; married; children: two. *Ethnicity:* "Serbo-Croatian." *Education:* Attended St. Joseph Seminary; Union Theological Seminary, Ph.D. (Bible studies), 1980. *Politics:* Democrat. *Religion:* Roman Catholic.

ADDRESSES: Home—Cortlandt Manor, NY. *Agent*—c/o Author Mail, Farrar, Strauss & Giroux, 19 Union Square W., New York, NY 10003.

CAREER: Catholic chaplain at Columbia University, New York, NY, c.1970s-80s; currently associate director, Care for the Homeless (multiservice organization), New York, NY.

WRITINGS:

Beyond Naïve Belief: The Bible and Adult Catholic Faith, Crossroad (New York, NY), 1994.
The Changing Priesthood: From the Bible to the Twenty-first Century, T. More (Allen, TX), 1996.
The Other Side of the Altar: One Man's Life in the Catholic Priesthood, Farrar, Straus, & Giroux (New York, NY), 2003.

SIDELIGHTS: Paul Dinter is a resigned priest who, through his writing, has revealed the inner conflicts of Roman Catholic priests, who sometimes turn to alcohol and sexual abuse to cope with intense loneliness and sexual frustration. In his book, *The Other Side of the Altar: One Man's Life in the Catholic Priesthood,* Dinter vividly portrays the private life of a priest, a vocation whose requirement of celibacy he laid aside in 1994 amidst a rash of sex scandals within the church.

America reviewer Paul Wilkes described *The Other Side of the Altar* as a "searing, unblinking and perceptive look behind the shroud that once clouded our view of the priesthood." Wilkes added that "Dinter provides an achingly human and ultimately transcendent portrait of what the formation was like, how priests were at once revered (and sometimes tempted) by their flock."

Dinter became acquainted with the church after he became an altar boy in the 1950s. He entered the archdiocese of New York's St. Joseph Seminary in 1964 and served as a Catholic chaplain at Columbia University for fifteen years before resigning from the priesthood. Wilkes said that students at the seminary during Dinter's years were "disciplined to need neither to communicate nor to commune with others, a training that would follow them to their lonely rectories and, sadly, shape some of them into misanthropes whose typical subterfuges have been booze, boys, or the boob tube."

In addition to discussing the loneliness among priests, *The Other Side of the Altar* discusses the church's obsession with power. Dinter describes priests who arc often more loyal to their "brothers" in the priesthood than to parishioners. He cites several examples of priests being demeaned by their superiors. Wilkes described Dinter's portrayal of the dichotomy between the radically changing outside world and the church as "vivid" and noted that Dinter gives an excellent description of the church "whose hierarchal structures remained firmly rooted in principles of medieval autocracy."

The Other Side of the Altar is graphic and readers may find some description upsetting. John-Leonard Berg commented in *Library Journal,* "Some of the material is disturbing, as Dinter airs the church's dirty laundry, though most is nostalgic reminiscence. This honest portrayal of one man's struggle with celibacy, sexuality, and power is also a call for systematic change."

After leaving the priesthood, Dinter secured employment as director of a women's shelter operated by Care for the Homeless in New York City.

BIOGRAPHICAL AND CRITICAL SOURCES:

PERIODICALS

America, April 7, 2003, Paul Wilkes, "From Inside Out to Out," p. 28.

Booklist, February 1, 2003, June Sawyers, review of *The Other Side of the Altar: One Man's Life in the Catholic Priesthood,* p. 957.

Commonweal, March 10, 1995, Dennis O'Brien, review of *Beyond Naïve Belief: The Bible and Adult Catholic Faith,* pp. 20-22.

Library Journal, February 15, 2003, John-Leonard Berg, review of *The Other Side of the Altar,* p. 142.

Publishers Weekly, March 3, 2003, review of *The Other Side of the Altar,* p. 72.

Theological Studies, December, 1995, Richard J. Sklba, review of *Beyond Naïve Belief,* pp. 771-772.

*   *   *

DOBRIN, Sidney I. 1967-

PERSONAL: Born February 28, 1967, in Bowling Green, KY; son of Leonard (a professor of criminology) and Dora (a professor of human services; maiden name, Harbin) Dobrin. *Education:* Virginia Wesleyan College, B.A. (English), 1989; Old Dominion University, M.A. (English), 1991; University of South Florida, Ph.D. (composition and rhetoric), 1995. *Religion:* Jewish. *Hobbies and other interests:* Fishing, diving, spearfishing, hunting, drinking.

ADDRESSES: Office—University of Florida, Box 117310, Gainesville, FL 32611-7310. *E-mail*—sdobrin@English.ufl.edu.

CAREER: Willoughby Bay Marina, Norfolk, VA, dock master, 1984-89. University of Kansas, Lawrence, assistant professor, 1995-97; University of Florida, Gainesville, associate professor and director of writing programs, 1997—. Dive instructor at aquatic center, Gainesville, FL.

MEMBER: Conference on College Composition and Communication, Association for Study of Literature and Environment, Writing Program Administrators.

WRITINGS:

(Coeditor, with Gary A. Olson) *Composition Theory for the Postmodern Classroom,* State University of New York Press (Albany, NY), 1994.

Constructing Knowledges: The Politics of Theory-building and Pedagogy in Composition, State University of New York Press (Albany, NY), 1997.

(Coeditor, with Gary A. Olson and Lynn Worsham) *The Kinneavy Papers: Theory and the Study of Discourse,* State University of New York Press (Albany, NY), 2000.

Distance Casting: Words and Ways of the Saltwater Fishing Life, Sycamore Island Books (Boulder, CO), 2000.

(Coeditor, with Christian Weisser) *Ecocomposition: Theoretical and Pedagogical Approaches,* State University of New York Press (Albany, NY), 2001.

(With Christian Weisser) *Natural Discourse: Toward Ecocomposition,* State University of New York Press (Albany, NY), 2002.

Also former field editor and columnist for *Fisherman* magazine. Articles published in *Sportfishing Report, Yale Angler's Journal, JAC: A Journal of Composition Theory, College English, Composition Forum,* and *Dialogue: A Journal for Writing Specialists.* Former editor, *JAC.*

WORK IN PROGRESS: Writing Environments: Rhetoric, Texts, and The Construction of Nature, with Christopher J. Keller, for State University of New York Press; *Wild Things: Children's Literature, Ecocriticism, and Ecological Literacy,* with Kenneth Kidd, for Wayne State University Press; *A Closer Look: Twenty-one Essayists for the College Writer,* with Anis S. Bawarshi, for Mayfield Publishing Company; *Saving Place: An Ecoreader,* for Mayfield Publishing Company; editing *Protean Ground: Critical Ethnography in Composition Studies* with Stephen G. Brown for State University of New York Press.

*   *   *

DOE, Mimi 1958-

PERSONAL: Born December 11, 1958; daughter of Marsha Walch (a psychotherapist and author); married Thomas G. Doe; children: Whitney, Elizabeth. *Education:* Harvard University, Ed.M., 1984.

ADDRESSES: Office—P.O. Box 157, Concord, MA 01742. *E-mail*—mimi@spiritualparenting.com; MiDoe@aol.com.

CAREER: Writer, producer, professional speaker, and columnist. Founder of *Spiritual Parenting Web site.*

AWARDS, HONORS: Parents' Choice Seal of Approval, 1998, for *Ten Principles for Spiritual Parenting: Nurturing Your Child's Soul.*

WRITINGS:

(Editor, with Garland Waller) *Drawing Angels Near,* Pocket Books (New York, NY), 1995.
(Coauthor, with Marsha Walch) *Ten Principles for Spiritual Parenting: Nurturing Your Child's Soul,* HarperPerennial (New York, NY), 1998.
Busy but Balanced: Practical and Inspirational Ways to Create a Calmer, Closer Family, St. Martin's Griffin (New York, NY), 2001.

Author of weekly segment appearing on Hallmark Channel and ongoing column on *Beliefnet.com.*

SIDELIGHTS: An advocate for the fostering of spiritual traditions within the family unit, Mimi Doe received her master's degree in education from Harvard University. She often speaks before parenting groups, churches, and educational and professional groups, and has appeared on a number of television programs, including the *Oprah Winfrey Show.*

With Marsha Walch—a Mississippi psychotherapist who also happens to be Doe's mother—Doe wrote *Ten Principles for Spiritual Parenting: Nurturing Your Child's Soul.* These principles, each the subject of a chapter, include "Know That God Cares for You," "Listen to Your Child," "Add Magic to the Ordinary," and "Make Each Day a New Beginning." According to Doe and Walch, as quoted by Diego Ribadeneira in the *Boston Globe,* "Spirituality is the base from which grow self-esteem, values, morals, a sense of belonging." A reviewer for *Publishers Weekly* noted that "many of the ideas here are worth trying" but added that "the authors' approach is sentimental and oversimplified." Doe's *Busy but Balanced: Practical and Inspirational Ways to Create a Calmer, Closer Family* offers tips geared to particular seasons and months of the year.

BIOGRAPHICAL AND CRITICAL SOURCES:

PERIODICALS

Boston Globe, June 27, 1998, Diego Ribadeneira, review of *Ten Principles for Spiritual Parenting: Nurturing Your Child's Soul,* p. B2.

Publishers Weekly, June 29, 1998, review of *Ten Principles for Spiritual Parenting,* p. 46.
Today's Parent, October, 2000, review of *Busy but Balanced: Practical and Inspirational Ways to Create a Calmer, Closer Family,* p. 26.

ONLINE

Family Corner Web site, http://www.thefamilycorner. com/ (September 12, 2003), Kylie Ardill, review of *Ten Principles for Spiritual Parenting.*
Spiritual Parenting Web site, http://www. SpiritualParenting.com/ (September 8, 2003).
Spiritual Parenting with Mimi Doe, http://www. beliefnet.com/ (September 8, 2003).

*   *   *

DONSKIS, Leonidas 1962-

PERSONAL: Born August 13, 1962, in Klaip da, Lithuanian Soviet Socialist Republic (now Lithuania); son of Simas and Joana (Cukermanait) Donskis; married Jolanta Valuckait, 1986. *Education:* Lithuanian Academy of Arts, B.A., 1985; University of Vilnius, M.A., 1987, Ph.D., 1990; University of Helsinki, D.Soc.Sci., 1999. *Hobbies and other interests:* Music, literature, theater.

ADDRESSES: Office—Hill House, University of Montevallo, Station 6501, Montevallo, AL 35115-6000; fax 205-665-6523. *E-mail*—donskis@yahoo.com.

CAREER: University of Klaip da, Klaip da, Lithuania, teacher of philosophy and aesthetics, 1991-97, member of university senate, 1991-2001, department chair, 1991-97, director of Comparative Civilizations Center, 1995-97; Dickinson College, Carlisle, PA, international visiting scholar and visiting professor of philosophy, 1998-99; University of Montevallo, Montevallo, AL, Paschal P. Vacca Visiting Professor of Liberal Arts, 2001-02. Visiting lecturer at University of Vilnius and Vilnius Academy of Fine Arts, 1991-93; Karlskrona/ Ronneby University College (Sweden), visiting lecturer in East European studies, 1992; Estonian Institute of Humanities, visiting professor of philosophy and comparative civilizations, 1993, 1995, and 1998; Dickinson College, visiting fellow, 1993-94, teacher, 1994; Ohio University, visiting lecturer, 1994 and 1995; visiting lecturer at Hillsdale College and University of Michigan, 1995; Vilnius Technical University, visiting professor, 1996; University of Gothenburg, Swedish Institute guest researcher, 1997-98; University of Helsinki, visiting lecturer in East European studies, 1997, 2000, and 2001; University of Bradford, visiting research fellow, 1999-2000; University of Uppsala, guest professor, 2000; Gotland University College, visiting professor, 2000; Baltic Center for Writers and Translators, Visby, Sweden, scholar-in-residence, 2000; also lecturer at universities in the United States and elsewhere, including Shippensburg University, London School of Slavic and East European Studies, and University of Derby. Open Society College, Vilnius, director, 1996-97. Member of Lithuanian National Prize Committee for Culture and Art, 1992-94.

MEMBER: International Society for the Comparative Study of Civilizations, American Philosophical Association.

AWARDS, HONORS: Fellow of International Research and Exchanges Board, 1993-94; Fulbright scholar, 1994; fellow of Leverhulme Trust, 1999-2000.

WRITINGS:

An Outline of the Modern Philosophy of Culture (in Lithuanian), Science and Encyclopedia Press (Vilnius, Lithuania), 1993.

Modern Consciousness and Its Configurations: Culture between Myth and Discourse (in Lithuanian), Baltos lankos (Vilnius, Lithuania), 1994.

Between Imagination and Reality: Ideology and Utopia in Current Civilization Theory (in Lithuanian), Baltos lankos (Vilnius, Lithuania), 1996.

Between Carlisle, Pennsylvania and Klaip da: Essays in Social and Cultural Criticism (in Lithuanian), University of Klaip da Press (Klaip da, Lithuania), 1997.

The End of Ideology and Utopia? Moral Imagination and Cultural Criticism in the Twentieth Century, Peter Lang Publishing (New York, NY), 2000.

Identity and Freedom: Mapping Nationalism and Social Criticism in Twentieth-Century Lithuania, Routledge (New York, NY), 2001.

Editor of book series on Baltic studies, Rodopi International Publishers (Atlanta, GA), 2001—. Contributor to books, including *Ground Control:* *Technology and Utopia,* edited by Lolita Jablonskiene, Duncan McCorquodale, and Julian Stallabrass, Black Dog (London, England), 1997; *Between East and West: Cultural Encounters in East Central Europe,* edited by Karin Junefelt and Martin Peterson, FRN-Swedish Council for Planning and Coordination of Research (Stockholm, Sweden), 1998; *Ethnicity and Nationalism in Russia, the CIS, and the Baltic States,* edited by Christopher Williams and Thanasis D. Sfikas, Ashgate (Aldershot, England), 1999; and *New Ethics—New Society, or the Dawn of Justice,* edited by Timo Airaksinen and Olli Loukola, Philosophical Society of Finland (Helsinki, Finland), 2000. Contributor of articles and reviews to periodicals in the United States and abroad, including *Comparative Civilizations Review, East European Politics and Societies, Innovation: European Journal of Social Sciences, Soundings: Journal of Politics and Culture,* and *Journal of Interdisciplinary Studies.* Member of editorial board, *Liaudies kultura* (title means "Folk Culture"), 1992—, *Metmenys* (title means "Patterns"), 1993—, *Archiforma* (title means "Architectural Form"), 1996—, *Problemos* (title means "Philosophical Issues"), 1996—, and *Tiltai* (title means "Bridges"), 1997—.

WORK IN PROGRESS: Forms of Hatred.

SIDELIGHTS: Leonidas Donskis told *CA:* "As a nonfiction writer, I am foremost motivated by my academic and theoretical interests. Self-comprehension and interpretation of my multicultural background are also among the primary driving forces and concerns that motivate my research and writing.

"I have been greatly influenced by such eminent social scientists of the twentieth century as Lewis Mumford, Louis Dumont, Ernest Gellner, Isaiah Berlin, and Zygmunt Bauman. At the same time, I owe a great debt to such towering figures in literary scholarship as Lionel Trilling and Stephen Greenblatt. I consider Vytautas Kavolis (1930-1936), a great Lithuanian scholar who immigrated to the United States, as my mentor. Among my favorite philosophers I could list St. Augustine, David Hume, Immanuel Kant, and Oswald Spengler.

"My writing process absorbs me completely. I can prepare a manuscript very quickly, but then I have to spend much more time polishing it.

"My multicultural background and East European experience may be said to have been a major inspiration to write on the subjects I have chosen; namely, identity, freedom, tolerance, dialogue, inter-subjectivity, moral imagination, and exclusion."

*　　*　　*

DOWD, Gregory Evans 1956-

PERSONAL: Born 1956. *Education:* University of Connecticut, Storrs, B.A.; Princeton University, M.A., Ph.D.

ADDRESSES: Office—Dept. of History, University of Michigan, 435 South State St., Ann Arbor, MI 48109. *E-mail*—dowdg@umich.edu.

CAREER: Historian and educator. University of Notre Dame, Notre Dame, IN, Department of History, associate dean for undergraduate studies; University of Michigan, Ann Arbor, professor of history and American culture and director of Native American studies. Visiting professor at University of Connecticut, Storrs.

AWARDS, HONORS: Smithsonian fellow, 1990-91; Gustavus Myers Center Award, 1993, for *A Spirited Resistance: The North American Indian Struggle for Unity, 1745-1815;* Fulbright scholar, University of Witwatersrand, Johannesburg, South Africa, 1994; Arrell M. Gibson Award, Western History Association, 1997; Notre Dame teaching award, 1999; Lloyd-Lewis/National Endowment for the Humanities fellow, 1999-2000.

WRITINGS:

(With Peter T. Bartis and David S. Cohen) *Folklife Resources in New Jersey,* American Folklife Center (Washington, DC), 1985.
The Indians of New Jersey ("New Jersey History" series), New Jersey Historical Commission (Trenton, NJ), 1992.
A Spirited Resistance: The North American Indian Struggle for Unity, 1745-1815 ("Johns Hopkins University Studies in Historical and Political Science" series), Johns Hopkins University Press (Baltimore, MD), 1992.
War under Heaven: Pontiac, the Indian Nationals, and the British Empire, Johns Hopkins University Press (Baltimore, MD), 2002.

Work represented in books, including *Contact Points: American Frontiers from the Mohawk Valley to the Mississippi, 1750-1830,* edited by Fredrika Teute and Andrew R. L. Cayton, University of North Carolina Press (Chapel Hill, NC), 1998; *A Companion to American Indian History,* edited by Philip J. Deloria and Neal Salisbury, Blackwell (Malden, MA), 2002; and *Handbook of the North American Indians: Southeast,* edited by William Sturtevant, Smithsonian Institution (Washington, DC).

SIDELIGHTS: Historian Gregory Evans Dowd's research interests are reflected in his books, including *A Spirited Resistance: The North American Indian Struggle for Unity, 1745-1815.* In this volume Dowd examines the quest for unity of four tribes from different geographical regions—the Delaware, Shawnee, Cherokee, and Creek—in resisting Anglo expansion.

Dowd's observations of the native population from the colonial period until the end of the War of 1812 focus on some of the most well-known figures in the history of the conflict, including Pontiac, Tenskwatawa, Tecumseh, Osceola, and the Creek prophets and followers known as Red Sticks. Eric Hinderaker wrote in *American Indian Quarterly* that "while much of the ground Dowd covers has been plowed before in biographies, military narratives, and histories defined by tribal or territorial units, no one has attempted where Dowd succeeds: He discovers a unifying pattern that helps us make better and more comprehensive sense of the period."

Dowd argues that the political and prophetic movements of the period cannot be separated. Hinderaker noted that "historians have artificially separated movements for political autonomy from those seeking spiritual renewal. Religious prophets, in Dowd's view, gave shape and meaning to the political struggles of the period."

Historians have, for the most part, held that intertribal Native unity was impossible and one of the reasons Natives were unable to protect themselves from European conquest. Dowd argues that they could and did recognize their common goals, drawing on both religious and political ideals. *Historian*'s Robert A. Trennert felt that "this solid study is based on an overwhelming research effort. Dowd has gone over old territory with a fine-tooth comb, tracing down every possible confirmation of his thesis."

War under Heaven: Pontiac, the Indian Nations, and the British Empire was called an "elegantly written ethnohistorical study" by *Library Journal*'s John

Burch. It is Dowd's study of the period of bloody wars following the 1763 Treaty of Paris and France's relinquishing of most of the lands east of the Mississippi River to the British. The Great Lakes Indians and the French had maintained an alliance of convenience, but when the British replaced the French, they did so in a spirit of superiority. They refused to offer tokens to the tribes or in any way maintain the spirit of coexistence the Indians had enjoyed with the French. The resulting conflicts arose not out of any issues over land or trade, but out of British arrogance and lack of respect for Native sovereignty.

Ottawa chief Pontiac was a prominent leader in the bloody wars waged on the British from 1763 to 1767. The first assault was on the post of Detroit, and conflict soon spread to all Indian lands east of the Mississippi River, west of the Appalachian Mountains, and north of the Ohio River. The wars also held a clue to the future of the country as the prize of the Revolutionary War.

Dowd explores the roles religion and culture played on both sides of the conflict, including how the British military's attitudes toward the Indians were formed. The Delaware prophet Neolin announced that he had a vision from the Master of Life, in which he was told that if his people followed tribal ceremony and led moral lives, the oppressors would be overcome. Pontiac and other leaders were inspired by this vision, and so began what was, in part, a holy war.

Washington Times reviewer Elliott West wrote that Dowd "is especially original in his analysis of the war's legacy. Its prime lesson, its ambiguity, was part of a larger crisis of empire. As with the conflict with the colonies that followed immediately, England simply was unable to establish a mastery it felt was its due, and the result was a muddy, confused contradictory policy toward both Indians and colonists—the approach toward the western tribes treating them now as independent actors, now as dependent children. After the Revolution, Mr. Dowd says, the republic inherited this muddled and conflicted Indian policy." West concluded by calling *War under Heaven* a "tightly written and engaging history."

BIOGRAPHICAL AND CRITICAL SOURCES:

PERIODICALS

American Indian Quarterly, summer, 1993, Eric Hinderaker, review of *A Spirited Resistance: The North American Indian Struggle for Unity, 1745-1815,* p. 436.

Choice, September, 1992, R. L. Haan, review of *A Spirited Resistance,* pp. 204-205.
Historian, spring, 1993, Robert A. Trennert, review of *A Spirited Resistance,* p. 575.
Journal of American History, September, 1993, R. David Edmunds, review of *A Spirited Resistance,* p. 641.
Library Journal, November 1, 2002, John Burch, review of *War under Heaven: Pontiac, the Indian Nations, and the British Empire,* p. 104.
Michigan Historical Review, spring, 2003, Robert M. Owens, review of *War under Heaven,* p. 139.
Washington Times, December 1, 2002, Elliott West, review of *War under Heaven.**

*   *   *

DRUETT, Joan 1939-
(Jo Friday)

PERSONAL: Born April 11, 1939, in Nelson, New Zealand; daughter of Ralph Totten Griffin and Colleen de la Hunt Butcher; married Ronald John Druett (a maritime artist), February 11, 1966; children: Lindsay John, Alastair Ronald. *Education:* Victoria University of Wellington, B.A., 1960.

ADDRESSES: Home—70 Calcutta Street, Khandallah, Wellington, New Zealand. *Agent*—Laura J. Langlie, 275 President St., No. 3, Brooklyn, NY 11231.

CAREER: Teacher of biology and English literature until 1983; writer, 1983—.

MEMBER: Authors Guild, Martha's Vineyard Historical Society (Edgartown, MA), Mystic Seaport Museum, New Bedford Whaling Museum, Wellington Museum of City & Sea, Friends of the Turnbull Library (New Zealand), Friends of Te Papa (National Museum of New Zealand), Friends of the International Arts Festival (New Zealand), Friends of the New Zealand Symphony Orchestra.

AWARDS, HONORS: Best first prose book, International PEN, 1984, for *Exotic Intruders: The Introduction of Plants and Animals to New Zealand;* Fulbright Writer's Cultural Award, 1986; John Lyman Award for best book of American maritime history, 1992, for *"She Was a Sister Sailor": The Whaling Journals of Mary Brewster, 1845-1851;* Oysterponds Historical

Joan Druett

Society Scholar-in-residence Award, 1993; New York Public Library Award, 1998, for *Hen Frigates: Wives of Merchant Captains under Sail;* L. Byrne Waterman Award for outstanding contributions to history and women's history, 1999; John David Stout Research Fellowship Award, University of Wellington, 2001.

WRITINGS:

Exotic Intruders: The Introduction of Plants and Animals to New Zealand, Heinemann (Auckland, New Zealand), 1983.

Fulbright in New Zealand, New Zealand-U.S. Educational Foundation (Wellington, New Zealand), 1988.

Abigail (novel), Random House (New York, NY), 1988.

A Promise of Gold (novel), Bantam (New York, NY), 1990.

Petticoat Whalers: Whaling Wives at Sea, 1820-1920, illustrated by husband, Ron Druett, HarperCollins (Auckland, New Zealand), 1991, HarperCollins (New York, NY), 1992.

(Editor) *"She Was a Sister Sailor": The Whaling Journals of Mary Brewster, 1845-1851,* Mystic Seaport Museum (Mystic, CT), 1991.

Murder at the Brian Boru (novel), HarperCollins (Auckland, New Zealand), 1992.

(With Mary Anne Wallace) *The Sailing Circle: Nineteenth-Century Seafaring Women from New York,* introduction by Lisa Norling, Three Village Historical Society (East Setauket, NY)/Cold Spring Harbor Whaling Museum (Cold Spring Harbor, NY), 1995.

Hen Frigates: Wives of Merchant Captains under Sail, Simon & Schuster (New York, NY), 1998.

Rough Medicine: Surgeons at Sea in the Age of Sail, Routledge (New York, NY), 2000.

She Captains: Heroines and Hellions of the Sea, Simon & Schuster (New York, NY), 2000.

In The Wake of Madness: The Murderous Voyage of the Whaleship Sharon, Algonquin Books (Chapel Hill, NC), 2003.

Also author of *Captain's Daughter, Coasterman's Wife: Carrie Hubbard Davis of Orient,* 1994. Contributor to periodicals, including *Log of Mystic Seaport, Newport History, Sea History, Dukes County Intelligencer, Mains'l Haul,* and *No Quarter Given.* Author of science-fiction stories published under pseudonym Jo Friday in magazine *Worlds If.*

WORK IN PROGRESS: Perseverance Harbour, an account of the American sealing schooner in Lyttelton, New Zealand, in December of 1883.

SIDELIGHTS: Joan Druett is a former teacher whose interest in maritime history prompted her to conduct extensive research that has taken her across several continents and resulted in a collection of books about seafaring women. Among Druett's titles are *The Sailing Circle: Nineteenth-Century Seafaring Women from New York, Hen Frigates: Wives of Merchant Captains under Sail,* and *In the Wake of Madness: The Murderous Voyage of the Whaleship Sharon.*

Druett was born in 1939 in Nelson, New Zealand. She studied at Victoria University of Wellington and went on to become a teacher of both biology and English literature. In 1983, however, she decided to concentrate on a writing career. That year she published her first book, *Exotic Intruders: The Introduction of Plants and Animals to New Zealand,* which won an award from International PEN. Five years later, Druett completed two more projects, *Fulbright in New Zealand* and the novel *Abigail,* and in 1990 she issued *A Promise of Gold.*

Petticoat Whalers: Whaling Wives at Sea, 1820-1920, Druett's first nonfiction book about maritime history, was inspired by her discovery of a buried headstone. "My engrossing interest in the history of women in whaling began in May, 1984, when I came across a young Maori scraping at a patch of waste ground on the tiny South Pacific island of Rarotonga," she once explained to *CA.* "I was told that he had a dream in which an ancestor came to him and told him to clear the land because it was a lost graveyard. Three days later the young man had gone, so I investigated the heaps of weeds and broken stones and ended up falling into a hole where a great tree had been uprooted during a recent storm. At the bottom of that hole, I found a coral rock grave with a headstone set into it like a door. The inscription was a memorial to a twenty-four-year-old American girl, Mary Ann Sherman, the wife of the captain of the American whaling ship *Harrison,* who had died January 5, 1850. A girl on a whaling ship? It seemed impossible! How had she lived . . . and died? This was the beginning of my quest." The book is illustrated with paintings by Druett's husband, maritime artist Ron Druett.

After producing *Petticoat Whalers,* Druett served as editor of *"She Was a Sister Sailor": The Whaling Journals of Mary Brewster, 1845-1851,* which provides what a *Publishers Weekly* reviewer described as "detail concerning shipboard life and the whaling industry, as well as a portrait of missionary life on the island of Maui." She then published *Murder at the Brian Boru* and—three years later—*Captain's Daughter, Coasterman's Wife: Carrie Hubbard Davis of Orient,* released in 1994. In addition, she collaborated with Mary Anne Wallace in writing *The Sailing Circle: Nineteenth-Century Seafaring Women from New York.*

In 1998, Druett published *Hen Frigates: Wives of Merchant Captains under Sail,* which relates the experiences of women on shipping expeditions. Among the notable women in this volume is a teenager who replaced her dead father as commander and subsequently repelled a sexually aggressive sailor, quashed a mutiny, and even convinced her crew to dump the ship's alcohol overboard. Other women in Druett's study bear children, combat illnesses such as malaria and plague, and endure dangerous storms.

Hen Frigates won praise for its exploration of a little-known topic. An *Atlantic* critic said the book "casts light on an odd corner of nineteenth-century life," and *Library Journal* reviewer Roseanne Castellino called

it "informative and entertaining reading." Another reviewer, Margaret Flanagan, declared in *Booklist* that Druett's volume constituted "an intimate glimpse" back in time and concluded that *Hen Frigates* "provides the reader with an intriguing entrée into an exotic lifestyle." Holly Morris, meanwhile, wrote in the *New York Times Book Review* that Druett's work serves as "a valuable collective portrait of intrepid seafaring women."

Druett's other books include *Rough Medicine: Surgeons at Sea in the Age of Sail* and *She Captains: Heroines and Hellions of the Sea.* In *Rough Medicine* Druett describes the adventures of English physicians who put to sea in the early nineteenth century in the wake of John Woodall, considered "the father of sea surgery." Based on primary documents, Druett notes that the doctors were driven to dangerous positions on shipboard mainly for the sake of adventure. The latter volume relates the exploits of seafaring women from the time of Ancient Egypt to the twentieth century. Among the various figures in the book are Tomyris, a Massegetae queen who triumphed in battle against Persian forces, and Lucy Brewer, who posed as a man and obtained assignment as a sailor aboard the U.S.S. *Constitution.*

Upon its publication in 2000, *She Captains* received recognition as a provocative chronicle. *Booklist* reviewer Donna Seaman wrote, "Maritime lore has always been rich in romance and suffering; Druett's revelations increase its fascination tenfold." A *Publishers Weekly* reviewer was likewise impressed, describing *She Captains* as an "entertaining work . . . filled with fascinating characters." *Library Journal's* Roseanne Castellino remarked, "The stories are lively, the characters vivid and eccentric," while Louise Jarvis noted in the *New York Times Book Review* that *She Captains* presents "wild tales of women's bravery and bloodlust from antiquity to the twentieth century. . . . Druett descends on the gory tidbits and operatic tableaus with a cheeky tone that seems to acknowledge our own perverse fascination—delight even—with atrocities and hardships that would make Melville's or Hemingway's sea dogs buckle."

Having exhausted research documentation on seafaring women in her previous books, Druett's next work, *In the Wake of Madness: The Murderous Voyage of the Whaleship Sharon,* concentrated on a specific incident in maritime lore. In 1841 the whaler *Sharon,* led by Captain Howes Norris, "a seagoing psychopath of the classic mold," according to Peter Nichols of the *New York Times Book Review*, left Fairhaven, Massachusetts, for the South Pacific. When the ship returned three years later, only four of the original twenty-nine crew members were aboard, and Captain Norris was not among them. He had been murdered in the South Pacific by Kanaka tribesmen taken aboard as crew members. Based on the journals of Benjamin Clough, the third mate who recaptured the ship from the Pacific islanders who killed Norris, and Andrew White, the ship's cooper, Druett's book is the account to analyze Norris's behavior and show it to have been instrumental in his demise.

According to the records Druett uncovered, Norris was a racist and a drunkard who repeatedly beat and tortured his crew members and eventually killed his steward. In return, many men deserted the ship, which forced Norris to hire locals to flesh out the crew during the long voyage. The Kanaka tribesmen had no reason to remain loyal to the captain, so when the rest of the crew was offboard searching for whales, three of them hacked Norris in half with a sharp spade used for cutting whale blubber. For the remainder of their days, the surviving crew members largely skirted the truth about what happened during the voyage. Druett asserts they were ashamed by their lack of courage in standing up to a captain who did not have a firm grip on reality.

Many critics liked the book. A reviewer for *Publishers Weekly* called *In the Wake of Madness* "a terrific account of an unusually eventful voyage. . . . [that] manages a perfect balance between telling the story in an unfussy yet dramatic manner and honoring its complexity." *Library Journal* reviewer Robert C. Jones characterized the book as "a murder investigation mixed with equal parts whaling lore, mystery, retribution, and history" that is "informative and vividly recreated." Nichols wrote that Druett "draws a fine picture of the floating community of whalers and deserters scattered across the Pacific." Other critics also appreciated Druett's ability to evoke a detailed portrait of a bygone era. *In the Wake of Madness* provides an "excellent insight into the whaling life and human nature," wrote *Kliatt* reviewer Sunnie Grant, and a writer for *Kirkus Reviews* called the book a "swift, absorbing sage of the sea [that] invokes malice, mayhem, murder, and, hovering over it all, Herman Melville."

AUTOBIOGRAPHICAL ESSAY:

Druett contributed the following autobiographical essay to *CA:*

On a calm winter morning not so very long ago, I was driving along a country road to my home in Wellington, New Zealand. Then I drew over for safety's sake—not because of the traffic, but because of the stunning view. Ahead of me the snowcapped peaks of the Tararua mountain range stood out clearly against the pale sky, and the steeply descending slopes were an amazing blend of blues, purples, and indigo. The effect was so breathtaking I was not safe to drive until I had looked my fill—and yet this was not one of the so-called "scenic" parts of New Zealand. Now, because of the films that have been made here—*The Lord of the Rings* series being a very good example—people all around the globe are aware that New Zealand scenery is gorgeous. But did it make a difference for me to grow up in the biggest film-set in the world? What effect did being a citizen of "Middle Earth" have to do with my development as a writer? The short answer has to be, a great deal—and yet I write about American history, and my audience is American. So, why do I feel this empathy with America? What draws me to the American past?

Being very young at the time, I have no memories at all of "the War," which is the way New Zealanders still refer to the conflict between Germany, Italy, and Japan, on one side, and Great Britain, the Commonwealth, and the United States, on the other. When Japan entered the war, Kiwi troops were fighting on the other side of the world, and so American forces arrived here in the nick of time to save New Zealand from occupation—well, that was what I was told, and no doubt it was true. However, I don't remember the Americans who marched our roads or strolled along our sidewalks; what I do recollect is a huge carton arriving at our house, packed with good things from America like Cannon sheets and candy. Apparently my father, when working alongside U.S. servicemen in the Solomon Islands—he built airfields, latrines, useful things like that—had told interested listeners about rationing and shortages back home in New Zealand. No doubt he embroidered his yarns; my father was notorious as a gifted and imaginative raconteur. One of his listeners had written home, and his wife had collected up a box of goodies for this little family in New Zealand. As it happened, we were never short of the necessities of life, but because of the kindness of this unknown woman, I learned very early about the unquestioning generosity of ordinary American folk.

Another effect of this war was embodied in a couple of photographs in a big Victorian kitchen at the back of an ancient (by New Zealand standards) village apothecary shop. On wet or wintry Sunday afternoons, it was a custom for my father to drive us through the Manawatu Gorge to pay a call on his aunt and uncle. It was a winding, precipitous road—spectacular, of course!—and my brother and I used to amuse ourselves watching for the train dashing in and out of tunnels across the other side of the ravine. Then we would arrive in the village, and draw to a stop outside this little old pharmacy store which had had a "Closed Down" sign in its window for ever, as far as we could tell. My great-aunt and great-uncle lived in the back part of the house, and kept an eye on the shop in the front. They were very kind, if quiet, people, who had very little in the way of money or possessions, but their table positively groaned with cake and other good things ready for us to eat. The photographs were the reason they were quiet. They were of their two handsome sons, one in the uniform of the Royal Air Force, and the other in that of a captain in the British army. The first had been killed in the Battle of Britain, and the other had lost his life in Crete, on the first anniversary of his older brother's death. Their two good-looking sons had given their lives to the cause of the "mother" country, on the far side of the world. It was part of the reason, I vaguely understood, that the Americans had come to our rescue in the Pacific.

After we had drunk our cups of milky sweet tea and eaten all we could manage, my brother and I were sent to play in the apothecary store. In there, it was rather like the mysteriously abandoned ship *Marie Celeste,* because the shop was still furnished with counters, shelves of curvaceous bottles with beautifully scripted, meaningless labels, and cupboards of dusty books called "pharmocopaeia" and pamphlets with strong warnings about something mysterious called "self-abuse," all seemingly set to go if someone took down the "Closed Down" sign and opened the door. I was an avid reader, even if I hardly understood a word and was running the risk of going blind, and I am sure that this is where my fascination with pharmacology started, and where the book *Rough Medicine,* written many years later, was born. But there was something even more amazing stored in this place—a stack of huge oil paintings of old Maori chiefs! I studied them so closely that their proud, disdainful, tattooed faces were as familiar as those of my family. Where they had come from, I do not have a notion, but I can bring them vividly back to mind right now. The reason I saw them so clearly was that my brother and I played with the portraits, tipping

The author with husband Ron in Rarotonga, 1984

them against each other to make teepees. I shudder to think of the cultural blunder we were so innocently committing.

In New Zealand schools at the time, very little New Zealand history was taught, and no American history at all. Instead, we learned about English kings and queens, and English social life before and after the Industrial Revolution. All we knew about Maori—the Polynesians who discovered New Zealand about the same time that Europeans discovered America—was the story of the great voyager Kupe, who was the Maori Christopher Columbus. We had Maori playmates, of course, but we knew almost nothing about their heritage. By contrast, a little bit of American history was quite familiar—because we played Indians and cowboys, which was the reason we liked building teepees. We were Indians always, because one had to be rich to be a cowboy—a cowboy had to have a pistol, and, ideally, chaps, boots, and a leather vest as well. Bows and arrows were free, being easily made out of twigs and string—we turned into such good shots that it was a miracle that no one lost an eye— and there was this neat sound one could make by clapping a palm over one's hooting mouth.

However, I suspect that we would have been Indians even if we could afford the cowboy accoutrements, because we were thoroughgoing Kiwis, and Kiwis tend to side with the underdog. We never thought of playing Maori warriors versus English settlers, because no one had taught us about the Maori rebel wars of the eighteen-sixties, but if we had, we would have been Maori, despite the fact that we sprang from sturdy colonial stock. Not only were the tattooed and stalwart warriors so much more magnificent than musket-wielding Englishmen, but we were used to hero-worshipping great Maori players on the rugby field, rugby football being New Zealand's national obsession. I guess that is why I portray life under sail from the point of view of the harassed wives and underdog seamen, and from the perspective of the Pacific people, too—the islanders the American whalemen called "Kanakas," who sailed on American ships for the adventure.

And then there were American films. Westerns were tremendously popular, even if the cowboys always won. When I was at high school I used to make my pocket money by ushering people to their seats at a local movie theater which specialized in Westerns, and that is where I got early practice in creating dialogue. The other usherettes and I would sit in the back during the first showing, playing a game where we second-guessed what the characters were going to say next. It was surprising how often we could anticipate death-less lines like "This town ain't big enough for the two of us," before the film stars got them out. Occasionally, the game became hilarious—such as the time the film commenced with the hero (the "goodie") rushing down a hotel corridor. This is how it went:

> Halfway down the corridor he opened a door at random. Inside was a bedroom, complete with a lovely young woman who sprang up in bed. "Squeak!" she went, gripping the sheet to her chin. "Save me! The Nasties are after me," he entreated. "Get into bed," she instructed—displaying an admirable grasp of the situation, we thought, especially considering she was mysteriously in bed in the afternoon. (That was a line we did *not* anticipate!) "But I've got my spurs on," he cried, but this collected young lass merely hissed at him to hurry. Into bed beside her he popped, and she pulled the blankets over his head. Slam!—and the door opened to reveal the Nasties. Up she sat, and

again went, "Squeak!" Gentlemen despite their reputation, the gang retreated with bumbling apologies, the door shut, and the goodie sat up. "What do I do now?" he wondered. And with one voice we usherettes advised, "Take your ruddy spurs off!"

Needless to say, that was another line of dialogue we did not get right. However, we enjoyed the laugh. As well as having a boisterous sense of fun, my fellow usherettes were very interesting people, many of them being wives of sideshow men. They had an arrangement with the theater that they would work as usherettes every time the circus was in town, and so it seemed to us townies that they were always heralded with bands and elephants. We called them "carnies," or carnival folk, and their stories were as colorful as they were. About the same time, I discovered John Steinbeck, and recognized them instantly in his pages. I have been a tremendous fan of Steinbeck ever since. It is probably because of Steinbeck (though the apothecary shop must have been a factor) that I decided to be a biologist as well as a writer. Because of him, I knew that the two were not incompatible.

*

I was always going to be a writer. I wrote my first book at age four, after finding out that children were supposed to give their mothers presents at Christmas; a homemade book was the only present that came to mind. During the War a grade-school teacher lived next door, and she and my mother taught me how to read and write. I still have that book, and am mostly impressed by the perfect spelling; it has been downhill ever since. I won my first writing prize at the age of sixteen, in a satisfying combination of biology and literature. The competition was organized by a local farmers' club, and, while all the other entrants wrote poetic descriptions of sunlit meadows, I submitted a discussion of spontaneous abortion in cows, because I was pretty sure it was the kind of thing that farmers liked to read. The winning essay looked rather odd when published in the local paper, and my mother and her friends were rendered speechless, but I got a ten-pound book voucher, which was a lot of money in those days. The voucher went toward university text books—biology books, which seemed appropriate. Best of all was that I had proved to myself that it is always advisable to keep your market in mind—an excellent start for professional writing.

However, my career as a professional writer was fated to be stalled. In order to get a grant to go to university, I signed an agreement to teach school for three years after graduation. Was it because of those old Maori portraits that I opted to spend those three years in Maori schools? I'd like to think so. Whatever the motivation, it was tremendously rewarding. I learned the formal protocol of the *marae,* and, more importantly, the special qualities of the best of those people—their pride, their warmth and humanity, their unstinting hospitality, their capacity for sharing, and the infectious Polynesian sense of humor, which is creatively mocking but seldom malicious, and often self-deprecating. And their stories! I wrote a lot of them down, and sold them, under a pen name, to a Maori journal called *Te Ao Hou.* Then I blended some to make a novel, and sent it to the biggest editor of the biggest publishing house in New Zealand. And it was rejected! Even more crushing was the long, carefully considered letter from the editor, who advised me to stop writing, and experience life instead. I would know when I was ready to start writing again, he said. Everyone who hears this exclaims that it was a terrible piece of advice—which is probably true. At the time, however, it was strangely liberating. I finished my teaching obligation, packed my bags, and left New Zealand.

Over the last two or three generations it has become customary for young New Zealanders to travel overseas for several years. We call it "the big OE," which is short for "overseas experience," and is a reaction to our national consciousness that we are a long, long way from the rest of the world. Some people call this "the tyranny of distance." When the first settlers undertook the four-to six-month voyage to New Zealand, they knew that they were saying good-bye to the homeland forever. The shipping lines and the jumbo jet changed all that, but still there is a craving to go and see what the old world is like. Usually, this involves a return to Britain. By contrast, I was focused on North America, for several reasons. First, I am a fifth generation New Zealander on all sides of the family—I like to point out that if I were American, I would qualify for the Daughters of the Revolution. This means that for me there was no nostalgic link to Britain, because I had never known a family member who had memories of the country many Kiwis still insisted on calling "home." The games of Cowboys and Indians, along with all the Westerns I had seen, must have played a part in my decision, too, along with childhood memories that carton of goodies from America. I applied for a work permit in the United States—and was rejected. So I migrated to Canada.

I fell in love with cosmopolitan cities, falling snow, and the North American way of life. A wonderful job as a "printer's devil" in the old printery of Victoria University, Toronto—which involved trooping about in mini-skirts and heels lugging great trays of lead type—inspired a life-long addiction to the smell of printer's ink. In the university library, I discovered a special collection devoted to Pacific studies, and spent absorbed hours learning even more about the ocean peoples I had left behind. Reading about those magnificent Polynesian navigators must have made me restless, because for no real reason I left Toronto, and headed across the Atlantic. A year in London followed, still devoted to various branches of publishing—I wrote copy for *Popular Mechanics,* among other publications, and learned how to use a computer, which was room-sized in those days. Then I ran out of money and returned to New Zealand, lugging along my souvenir, Ron, the Englishman I married.

Ron is a maritime artist. He introduced me to sailing ships. Like all New Zealanders, I had spent countless childhood hours in boats and the water, but now I learned to appreciate the beauty of pyramids of canvas—not only because they were so splendid to look at, but because they were such amazing machines, driven by just the wind and the muscle power of men. But still, I did not write. Instead, I raised my own children, and taught the children of others, and enjoyed both jobs immensely. A letter came out of the blue, requesting permission to republish one of my Maori stories in an anthology (an amazing feat of detection on the part of the editor, considering it had been written under a pen name), but still I left my pen alone. Then, our children grew old enough for us to satisfy our urge to travel, and I found that writing stories for travel magazines was an excellent method of paying my way to exotic destinations. We went to America, Europe, Indonesia, and the Pacific Islands, and the trickle of articles became quite a stream. I was fast turning into a journalist-cum-teacher when one of the biggest editors of one of the biggest publishing houses in New Zealand came knocking at my door.

She was carrying a bottle of wine, and she had a proposition—that I should write a book about how exotic plants and animals came to be established in New Zealand. The combination of biologist and writer

Druett at Mary Ann Sherman's gravestone in Rarotonga

was perfect, she argued. Only reluctantly persuaded, I set to and wrote an outline and sample chapter, and sent it off. And it was rejected! Till then, I had not been all that entranced with the task, but now I had my dander up, and was determined to get that book published. I sent the proposal to another publisher, and it was accepted the same day. The book, *Exotic Intruders,* won the PEN and Hubert Church Awards, and I left teaching to write full time, flushed with confidence. Misplaced confidence, I soon found, as book proposals I churned out were rejected. However, I was still selling travel articles, and in May 1984 Ron and I went to Rarotonga, a favorite South Pacific island, in search of more material.

*

We had been to "Raro" many times, because we love it there. It is exactly as beautiful as any tropical island

poster, and the people are terrific. However, if the truth be known, tropical islands are boring. The locals work a great deal harder than most folk believe, and there is not much time left over for frivolity. So, tourists are left very much to their own devices—which, for us, meant cycling round the island. At noon on the first day we arrived at a place on the coast called Ngatangiia. I remember how beautiful it was, the sun glittering on the turquoise lagoon and the sapphire sea beyond the gray bulwark of the reef. The light was hot and bright on the stretch of coral rubble between the road and the beach, and the trunk of a great fallen tree lying over the white sand was shadow-black, its roots standing out starkly against the pale sky. Despite the heat, a young Maori man was working away in the rubble, clearing away the weeds—a thankless task, as little of use would ever grow there. When we got into town we asked why he was doing it and were told he had had a dream in which an ancestor ghost had instructed him to clear the ground—because it was a graveyard.

This was rather hard to credit, because burying grounds are very well looked after in Rarotonga. The locals believe that the ancestors never leave, Rarotonga being heaven, and so they make sure to tend their graves. There was more to the explanation, however. A long time ago, at about the beginning of the nineteenth century, an American ship had called at the island with a dead sailor on board, and the captain had asked the current queen—*pa ariki*—for permission to bury the lad. She had refused, as only Rarotongans were allowed to be interred there, but he had pleaded and her heart had been touched, and she had set aside this piece of ground as a graveyard for foreigners. Then, the sailing ships had stopped calling, and because there were no descendants around the graveyard had been neglected, until the young man had his dream.

Of course, Ron and I were fascinated. The day the young man was gone, his ghost-imposed task finished, we laid down our bicycles and fossicked for the headstones we thought we would find. But we found nothing. Over the decades, any headstones that had been there had been worn away to indecipherable bits of rubble. It was very hot, so I trudged over to where the dead tree's roots cast a patch of shade—and stumbled into the ivy-wreathed hole where those roots had grown. And there I found a grave that had been exposed to the light for the first time in more than one hundred fifty years, with a big, upright headstone where the words were as clear as the day they had been carved. And they read:

"To the Memory of Mary-Ann, the beloved Wife of Captn. A.D. Sherman of the American Whale Ship Harrison, Who departed this life January 5: 1850, Aged 24 Years."

This strange discovery had a thunderbolt-like impact. As I said, life on a tropical island is mostly uneventful, and I suppose that the find had all the greater effect because there was nothing going on to distract me. When I returned to my busy life in New Zealand, though, the questions raised still constantly raged. Had Mary-Ann Sherman been a rebel—some kind of adventuress? Or had she simply been dragged along by her husband to make his life more comfortable? What had she thought of the Pacific and its peoples? How had she died, and what had her life on board ship been like? I scavenged library catalogues, trying to find a book that would reveal the answers, but with total lack of success. I was forced to the conclusion that if the mystery of Mary Ann Sherman was ever to be solved, I had to research it myself.

I started by writing lots of letters. One was to Harry Morton, the author of *In the Whale's Wake* and *The Wind Commands*. The only address I had for Professor Morton was the History Department at Otago University in the far south of New Zealand. I had given up hope of getting a reply when the phone rang, and a gruff voice informed me in a Canadian accent that he had retired, and now lived in Blenheim. Then he instructed me to pack a bag, come to town, stay in the family sleep-out, and "go through what I have." Blenheim, now world-famous for the award-winning sauvignon blanc produced in vineyards of the area, is in the Marlborough Sounds at the northern tip of the South Island, and so I had to take a ferry across Cook Strait to get there, which seemed very apt at the time. I remember watching dolphins glide and leap, and talking with enthusiastic young Americans who had come to New Zealand to do their own "OE." Most of all, however, I remember the wealth of information and expertise that Harry bequeathed me. Not only did he let me free with boxes of notes taken from years of studying whaling logs and journals, but he showed me how to collate information, create databases, and write index cards, to create a foundation for history.

After I got home, two important letters arrived. One was from a whaling researcher who is famous for his

The author near the Charles W. Morgan, at the Mystic Seaport Museum, Connecticut, 1988

databases of shipping material, Rhys Richards. He had received my query while on tour in Australia, and his long reply had been handwritten in a series of hotels and motels, jotted down whenever he had a spare moment. Like Harry, he told me about the Pacific Manuscripts Bureau microfilming project, which resulted in an eleven-mile-long collection of American whaling logs and journals, a copy of which is in the Alexander Turnbull Library of the National Library of New Zealand—"*You can do no better* than exhaust these sources from *within* New Zealand first," he wrote. Then he advised me to get to New England: "Go first to Mystic Seaport Museum, a recreated *working* port that includes the *Charles W. Morgan* that visited NZ in 1842 and 1884. Then visit New Bedford, the real home of US whaling for volume, and then visit its origins on Nantucket." He added, "I really loved the entrée whaling gave me to a side of USA I could never have penetrated otherwise."

Excellent advice, which I could not wait to follow—but, while researching at the Turnbull Library was easy, getting to New England was a hurdle. However, it was solved by the second important letter. The smartly headed page informed me that I had been awarded a Fulbright fellowship to research in the great maritime museums and libraries of New England and Hawaii. It was a miracle. Three years later, when the US-NZ Educational Foundation contracted me to write a history of the first forty years of the Fulbright program in New Zealand, I was delighted. Not only did the job involve interviews with many fascinating and formidable scholars, but it was a chance to record the debt Kiwis like myself owe to the inspiration and support that this wonderful program provides.

I took up the fellowship in May, 1986, two years to the day after the discovery of the grave. The intervening months had been crammed with endless hours of reading microfilms at the library, and reading interloaned books about whaling at home. Librarians are magical people. The trick is to tell them about your mission, and they will perform amazing feats to help, something that the staffs of the Alexander Turnbull Library and the library of Victoria University at Wellington do to this very day. Through their auspices, I worked through hundreds of logbooks and journals on microfilm, and many dozens of books about sailing and whaling. Certain logbooks stand out in my memory, though, especially the first microfilmed log I ever read. It was kept by Captain Nelson Waldron on the ship *Bowditch* from 1849 to 1854, and was stuffed full of strange terminology. Puzzling out the topsails, buntlines, and parrel straps was immensely rewarding, however. Not only did I have a whole new vocabulary, but I learned to understand the ways of a whaleship at sea.

Captain Nelson Waldron made no mention of women at all, which I did not find surprising, because every book I read testified that a whaleship was an acutely macho environment, rough, tough, and intensely male. Then, to my surprise, I found a logbook that mentioned a whaling wife—not Mary Ann Sherman, but someone by the name of Mrs. George Raynor. The ship was the *Reindeer*, and my reason for reading the log was that the *Reindeer* had called at Rarotonga, and I thought it might mention Mary Ann's grave. Instead, it was a carping complaint about the captain and his "famaly." The logkeeper, the first mate, was annoyed that the captain and his wife and child were on shore "haveing a good time," while the ship and crew were hanging about waiting for them, instead of being off about their proper business of hunting whales.

The realization that Mary Ann Sherman was not just one lone adventuress—or victim of her husband—came as quite a surprise. It was also a hint that the sailors might not have been thrilled about the presence of the captain's wife on a voyage. Had other women sailed on the *Reindeer*? I hunted down the journals written on other *Reindeer* voyages, and lo, I found that not only had another woman, Adra Ashley, sailed on that ship, in 1856, but she had kept a diary! And what a gossipy account it was—full of chatter about other wives and what they got up to in the Hawaiian Islands. These whaling wives, it seemed, were not adventuresses or victims, but sturdy New England women. How had they coped with the strange seaborne existence—and what did people think of these redoubtable ladies? Intrigued, I turned to the papers.

"LADY WHALERS," blazoned a headline in the New Bedford *Whalemen's Shipping List* for February 1, 1853, going on to remark, "The *Honolulu Friend* says that there have been at one time enumerated in Honolulu the wives of twenty-five sea captains, and supposed that one in six of all whaling captains is accompanied by his wife." One in six! The American whaling fleet in the Pacific numbered over five hundred at the time, which meant that there were about ninety of these women sailing at that time—ninety! "Whether this estimate is correct or not, the number is very large," the editor assured me. "The enterprising ladies not only preserve unbroken the ties of domestic life that otherwise would be sundered," he rhapsodized; "not only cheer by their presence the monotony and discomforts of long and perilous voyages, not only exercise a good influence in the discipline of the ship, but they make capital correspondents, and through the female love of letter-writing, keep us well posted up in the catch and prospects of the season."

The editor's motives for writing this were pretty blatant, I thought; obviously, he was tired of captains who blithely sailed over the horizon and forgot to send back reports for the paper to print. And he was right, Victorian women were great writers—of journals as well as letters, which I thought extremely promising. Was there a great fund of female letters and journals hidden somewhere in New England? I was more anxious than ever to get there—and in May 1986 Ron and I, accompanied by our younger son, Alastair, flew to Boston and took the bus to New Bedford. I will never forget the moment of arrival. It was late afternoon, and the town lay spread out in the low light, all its silhouettes familiar because of the reading I had done. The spires of Fairhaven were sketched in the mild spring sky across the Acushnet River, and the cupolas and "widows' walks" of the mansions of County and Orchard Streets glinted near at hand. Because we were making a lengthy stay, we boarded with a family in the historic district; that, added to the fact that the librarians at the Old Dartmouth Historical Society Library at the New Bedford Whaling Museum knew all about my project already, having been deluged with correspondence, made us feel at home right away. I was so much at home, in fact, that when some tourists asked me for directions, I was able to direct them unerringly, because I had studied maps of old New Bedford until I knew them by heart.

Other moments stand out. I remember arriving at the Nicholson Whaling Room at the Providence (Rhode Island) Public Library, and holding the original log-book of the *Bowditch,* the first log I ever read on microfilm—and my astonishment when Paul Cyr, the genealogist in the Melville Room at the New Bedford Public Library, produced yet another microfilm, of a journal written on *the very same voyage* by the captain's wife. Her husband had recorded the ship's activities every day for more than five years, without a single mention of Elizabeth, or his two little daughters, not even when one of them was born! And then there was the moment that Paul Cyr informed me that Mary Ann Sherman had probably been illegitimate—and the shock when I found her grave in Padanarum cemetery, because it recorded her death year as 1845, the year she sailed, and not 1850, the date on the stone in Rarotonga. Had she committed such a sin by going off to sea that her adoptive family declared her dead and put up a gravestone to prove it? Probably so, I concluded—because of the first entry in the journal kept at sea by another seafaring Mary, Mary Brewster, which I read at Mystic Seaport Museum.

"With much opposition I left my native land," this other Mary had written; "few had to say one encouraging word—She who has extended a mother's love and watchfulness over me said her consent would never be given in no way would she assist me and if I left her she thought me very ungrateful and lastly though not least Her house would never be a home for me again." It was lucky Mary Brewster's adoptive mother did not go as far as announcing her death, because Mary survived that voyage and at least one more after that— which would have proved quite an embarrassment if a false gravestone had been erected. However, she stuck to her threat, and never again was Mary welcome in her childhood home. Young Mrs. Brewster was a resilient character, however, going on sturdily, "Well thank heaven it is all past and I am on board of the good ship *Tiger* and with my dear Husband." And from then on she recorded her experiences day by day, describing what it was like trying to create a home in that most undomestic place, a whaling ship at sea.

*

By the time I arrived back home in New Zealand, I had read and made abstracts of seventy-seven whaling accounts written by women like Mary Brewster. Some were letter collections, some were detailed journals, some were brief diaries, and others were reminiscent accounts. It was a goldmine of material, sufficient for dozens of articles and several books. The first book to be written was a novel, *Abigail,* which paid homage to the link between New Zealand and the New England I now knew and loved. The story was inspired by Captain William Mayhew of Edgartown, who, with his wife Caroline, came to New Zealand to settle in the eighteen-thirties, before the British had annexed the country. He helped found the first bank, acted as the Vice Consul for the United States, and owned a lot of property, including a half-share in an island. Ruined by the British takeover in February 1840, he returned to Martha's Vineyard. There are lots of stories, too, about his redoubtable wife, Caroline, a doctor's daughter, who was famous for leading a wallaby (a small kangaroo species) about on a string. The one I used in the novel was the story about her saving most of the crew of his ship when it was ravaged by an outbreak of typhoid. In reality she lived to sail another day, but in my story she passed away, leaving a small daughter for William to raise on his own. I called the little girl Abigail, and gave her the surname "Sherman" in honor of Mary Ann Sherman's grave. Her father acted differently from the real William Mayhew, too, fighting for his property instead of giving up and going back to New England. Because of the danger to both her life and her education, Abigail was sent to New Bedford to live with unwelcoming relatives. Rebellious and broken-hearted, she surprised herself by falling in love with the city—just as I did—but after learning that her father had been murdered she determined to get back to New Zealand to claim her inheritance, and after many adventures she managed it.

"The books mount up . . .", 1992

In many ways, Abigail was the adventuress I once imagined Mary Ann Sherman to be. By now, I had learned that there were no real whaling wives like that; their bravado was different, being the grit and stamina necessary to survive the dangers and discomfort of years-long voyages in far off, badly charted oceans. However, editors in New York, London, and Auckland loved my flamboyant heroine. *Abigail* was followed by another novel, *A Promise of Gold,* which had its own sequel, *Murder at the Brian Boru.* This last book was a very rare bird—a commissioned whodunit. HarperCollins wanted me to write a mystery set in a real mystery weekend hotel, which triggered the strangest research project I have ever carried out, because Ron and I experienced every facet of the business. Over many weekends he and I tended bar, washed dishes, accompanied busloads of tourists, waited at tables, looked after the hotel office, and took part in melodramatic murder mysteries.

There was a set routine. On the Friday evening we arrived at the hotel, in the historic gold-mining district of Thames, and the paying guests were assembled in a firelit Victorian parlor. There, over a lavish supper, they were informed that they would get up early and be taken on an adventure tour of the Coromandel—a spectacular trip that wound through forest-covered ravines to a picture-postcard beach, and involved white-water rafting as well as a freshly caught seafood lunch. Then, after a visit to a goldmine and a stamping mill, their instructions were to disguise themselves in fancy dress, ready for a banquet—and at some time in the midst of the festivities, one of the party would be murdered. The murderer would be one of the staff, or one of the guests—an actor who would have been dropping clues to his or her identity throughout the long day. Ron and I lost count of the times we were either murdered or the murderer—and it is quite a feat to kill off someone at the same time as tending bar! However, everyone enjoyed it immensely, especially the dressing-up part. The proprietress of the hotel provided the costumes, which ranged from priests' habits to pirate gear, and a great deal of eating and drinking and tomfoolery was involved. And hereby hangs another tale.

Drinks being expensive in the hotel, it was quite common for the guests to call into a local wine store for their own supplies. One Friday night I dropped into the store myself, to find that there was a new proprietress, a talkative middle-aged Englishwoman with an upper-crust accent. She asked me if I was staying in town or traveling through, and I told her that I was staying at the Brian Boru—at which she reared back, clapped a hand to her bosom, and exclaimed, "You mustn't! Strange things happen at the Brian Boru," she went on in hushed tones. "They do?" said I, my tone rather strangled. "Indeed!" she cried. "Last Saturday night a *priest* came in to buy wine, and, without a word of a lie, he was drunk! When he lifted his habit to reach his wallet, he was forced to *cling* to me to retain his balance. When he had gone, positively *reeling* down the street, I said to my husband that never would I have believed that I would ever see a man of the *cloth* under the influence of liquor, and he said to me, 'It's something to do with that Brian Boru, because strange things *happen* at the Brian Boru.'"

Despite all the books that were mounting up, and these weekends of frivolity, I still clung to my ambition to write a nonfiction account of the experiences of the whaling wives, *Petticoat Whalers.* Meanwhile, though, a letter arrived from Mystic Seaport Museum, proposing that I transcribe and edit the journals of Mary

Brewster, an opportunity I could not possibly resist. I had been fascinated by her ever since the tall book with its marbled covers and blue, lined pages had been put in front of me. Kept on the whaleship *Tiger* of Stonington, Connecticut, her whaling journals were probably the most candid and self-revealing of all the manuscripts I had read. Previous researchers had been put off by the fact that she was pious and constantly questioned the state of her conscience in a way that is foreign to us now, but I had the experience to know that she was merely typical of her setting and era, and so I had persisted to the end, and enjoyed her dry humor immensely. Devastatingly candid in her opinions, Mary was at her best when describing the posturing of missionaries, and the strange foibles of her husband's brother whaling skippers.

And she could tell a joke against herself, too. A good instance is the time that the *Tiger* was anchored in a bay off lower California, in company with a number of ships, including a couple where the captains had "season wives"—mistresses—on board. These men were neighbors at home, and their lawful wives were her friends, so Mary was predictably disgusted. When one of the dissolute skippers came on board to pay a call, she decided to take a strong stand (as they used to say in those days), despite the fact she was just starting on a favorite treat, a dish of oysters that were freshly shucked. She stood up—"so prim"—and marched out of the cabin, with a toss of her head. But did the erring captain feel ashamed, did he blush and stammer? Not on your tintype! He grinned; he rubbed his hands together—and sat down and ate her oysters.

Naturally, I accepted the offer of editing her journals like a shot. For the next four years Mary Brewster ruled our household while I looked up books and checked microfilms and wrote footnotes. Another trip to New England was necessary, and this time we lived in the shipyard of the museum. The many thousands who have visited Mystic Seaport will understand at once that this was an out-of-this-world experience, because the museum is a recreated Connecticut village port, complete with tall ships, including the whaler *Charles W. Morgan,* the full-rigged ship *Joseph Conrad,* the schooner *Brilliant,* and the fishing schooner *L. A. Dunton.* At night when the wind blew and the snow drifted down and the old ships creaked at their moorings while hanging signs in the little streets squeaked back and forth, the nineteenth century engulfed us. In the very early mornings, as the mist rose up from the

river, we would be woken by the cheerful singing out of the shipyard workers as they arrived with their toolboxes and their dinner pails. It was then that I would go to the whaler *Charles W. Morgan,* walk up the gangplank, duck under the "no admittance" rope, and sit where the captains' wives who had sailed on that ship—Lydia Landers, Charlotte Church, and New Zealander Honor Earle—had sat, and feel what it had been like to be Mary Brewster. At nine o'clock, I would unclip the rope to allow the first tourists of the day on board, and it was like time travel in reverse, back to the present century.

*

While this book was in production, *Petticoat Whalers* was published in New Zealand by HarperCollins. It was even better than I dreamed it would be, beautifully designed, enhanced with Ron's sketches and paintings as well as many images of the whaling wives themselves. Then, just as *Petticoat Whalers* was released in New York, an equally handsome volume, *'She Was a Sister Sailor': The Whaling Journals of Mary Brewster* came out—and won the John Lyman Best Book of American Maritime History award. A book tour followed, with the unexpected result that I was approached by two Long Island institutions, the Three Village Historical Society of East Setauket, and the Whaling Museum at Cold Spring Harbor, with the proposition that I be the writer-historian for a big museum exhibit on seafaring wives under sail. Normally, I would have been forced to decline, there being no way we could afford to rent a house on Long Island for the time involved, but again fate intervened. Ron, whose beautiful maritime paintings were beginning to be recognized internationally, and who by this time was a gallery artist with the Mystic Seaport Gallery, was invited by the William Steeple Davis Trust to apply for an artist-in-residence award.

William Steeple Davis (1884-1961) was a self-taught artist who spent his entire life in the little hamlet of Orient, at the tip of the North Fork of Long Island. Having found his own artistic inspiration in the ethereal, ever-changing local scenery, he endowed his small cottage and large barn studio for the use of landscape and maritime artists. It was never going to be easy—there was no stipend, and living in a largely unimproved mid-nineteenth century cottage promised to be quite a challenge. However, we took the plunge, and lived and worked there for the next thirty months.

We would not have survived without the unstinting encouragement and support of the local people, but it was one of the most satisfying experiences of our lives. The museum exhibit won funding from the National Endowment for the Humanities, and for many months, while Ron painted, I scoured Long Island for manuscripts and memories of Long Island wives who sailed under canvas in small coasters, great deep-sea merchant ships, and whalers.

The project was originally inspired by an oil painting that had been presented to the Three Village Historical Society, that in size and solemnity took me back to the great portraits of Maori chiefs of my childhood. This one, however, was of a woman—a woman who had gone with her husband to sea. It was no surprise to me to find that the subject was yet another Mary—Mary Swift Jones—because the painting is so evocative of the same stalwart Yankee femininity. Dressed plainly in black, her dress relieved only by white lace collar and cuffs and the small posy of flowers she holds in one hand, she is composed, formal, and elegant. In 1858, Mary Swift Jones had boarded the China-trade bark *Mary & Louisa,* and over the next three years had come to know the port of Yokohama as well as her village at home. Though she did not know it, her husband had stowed a coffin in the hold, because she was not expected to survive the voyage. As it happened, Mary Swift Jones did not die until a few days after they had arrived back in New York, and in the meantime she had written long, descriptive letters home. The Society also had access to the eloquent, down-to-earth journals kept by yet another Mary— Mary Rowland, who over a thirty-five-year seagoing existence sailed first on small merchantmen and then on larger ocean-going barks. She was a delight to read, being both forthright and poetic, her descriptions of childbirth, child-rearing, shiphandling, and getting along with the husband she adored unrivaled in their descriptive powers and their honesty. Years later, I had the privilege of submitting a selection of Mary's writing to the magnificent Library of America anthology, *American Sea-Writing,* and her pithy descriptions of life at sea sit very comfortably alongside extracts from such writers as Jack London and Emerson

Search as I would, though, it seemed impossible to find any record of the hundreds of women who had plied Long Island Sound on little sloops and schooners. In the nineteenth century there were thousands of these humble craft, carrying everything imaginable from horse manure to railroad tracks between New York and Connecticut; they were the trucks of the era. It was only logical that wives and daughters sailed along to cook and clean, sell and buy groceries, and keep accounts, but it seemed as if I would never prove it. Then, one afternoon I was sitting in the William Steeple Davis house idly leafing through the diary, dated 1878, that had been kept by his mother, Carrie Hubbard Davis. I was reading it only because I was living in her house, and felt a natural interest in her daily routine. Then, to my amazement, I read, "I started with Charlie and pa on a Trip in the vessel." Not only had Carrie sailed regularly, but the schooner, named *Jacob S. Ellis,* was owned by her mother, Jane Culver Hubbard. The revelation was like a magical gift. I had found the evidence I so badly needed of a woman's coasting—right in the house where I lived!

That the exhibit would now be such a well-rounded one was very satisfying, but of course I had a book about the general experiences of seafaring wives taking form in my head, already named *Hen Frigates.* It was now that living in New York yielded another treasure—literary agent Laura Langlie, who adopted my idea as enthusiastically as she took me on as a client. Just a couple of weeks after I sent her the proposal, Ron and I were carrying out some research at the Penobscot Marine Museum in Searsport, Maine, when I got the message that I was needed urgently on the phone. Laura had sold the proposal to Simon & Schuster, and she was even more excited about it than Ron and I were.

Hen Frigates, included by the New York Public Library in its list of Books to Remember for 1998, led to a kind of sequel, *She Captains: Heroines and Hellions of the Sea.* In reality it is a kind of anthology, being my mostly lighthearted tribute to the maritime adventuresses I had pictured back in May 1984, after the discovery of the grave in Rarotonga. The stories range over several thousand years, and cover all kinds of maritime women, from female captains and petticoat pirates to lady shipbuilders and cross-dressed marines. If I were asked to name a favorite in this line-up of resourceful females, I would probably choose Mistress Agnes Cowtie of sixteenth-century Dundee, who owned a fleet of little ships that carried wool to Europe and returned with timber, iron, and wine. In 1582, her ship *Grace of God* was seized and sacked by English pirates. Two rogues, Clynton and Purser, killed her two sons, and then horribly tortured

The author's husband, Ron Druett, an internationally recognized maritime artist

her "especial mariners" to extract the information of where the ship's box of bullion was stored. After the survivors, barefooted, blind, and crippled, arrived back in Dundee, Mistress Cowtie took her passionate protest to the baillies—the town magistrates. However, though they were sympathetic, they could do nothing more than petition Lord Walsingham. So Agnes wrote to King James VI of Scotland—and he sent a letter to his cousin, Elizabeth of England. Forthwith, Queen Elizabeth instructed a Judge of the Admiralty, Sir Julius Caesar, to capture the men who had seized the *Grace of God.* Not only did he succeed in that, but he cleared the English seas of pirates—and all because of an obstinate and angry female shipowner in Scotland.

The publication of *She Captains* marked a kind of closure to my full-length studies of women and the sea. As a project, this little-known aspect of women's history had proved immensely rewarding. Still today, I get many written and e-mailed queries about the wives' experiences on board ship, and descendants, who are proud of the sea-letters and diaries they hold, write to tell me about them. Some even photocopy these materials, and send the copy as a much appreciated gift. Usually, I ask permission to lodge the manuscript in some appropriate library or museum, so that other researchers can have the reward and pleasure of reading it, and more often than not the owners are glad for me to do so.

My books have also been surprisingly controversial. Feminist historians tend to disapprove of the pictures I draw of women who were proud to have a swept cabin floor and a saloon table loaded with good things to eat. I suspect they would be happier with women who rebelled against the demands of their society—and their menfolk. Obviously, most modern women would behave very differently if time travel whisked them back in time, to a windjammer at work, but I firmly believe that historical characters should be considered in the context of their own time and setting. The question I always ask myself after I have described one of these women is, would she recognize herself in these pages? If I believe the answer would be yes, then I am happy—and, to do my readers and critics justice, most of them are happy, too.

*

Apart from annual visits to New York and New England on research trips and author tours, Ron and I are now firmly settled in New Zealand. Despite the fact that most of my focus has been on America, the New Zealand creative community has been very supportive—and in 2001 I had the particular honor of being designated the John David Stout Fellow at Victoria University, Wellington, a position I held for the full academic year. The Fellowship is within the Stout Research Centre for New Zealand Studies, incorporating the Treaty of Waitangi Research Unit, which is devoted to the study of our culture and our past, both European and Maori. This is another harking-back to those great portraits of Maori chiefs that were such an unconventional prop in our childhood games, and those three years I spent in Maori schools; it reminds me, too, of the Pacific collection in the university library that I delved through during my spell as a printer's devil in Toronto. Now, because I am surrounded by New Zealand researchers and historians, and listen to their lively discussions, I link New Zealand and New England differently. Instead of looking at the Pacific from the point of view of the Americans who sailed here, I view those American mariners from the Pacific perspective, measuring the impact that they had on the communities of Oceania.

The first book that resulted from this new perspective was *In the Wake of Madness,* which Algonquin published in May 2003. It is a retelling of a notorious mutiny on board the whaleship *Sharon* in 1842. In this once-famous but now forgotten incident, three Pacific

Islanders assassinated Captain Howes Norris while the rest of the crew were off in the boats whaling. Then, they tried to flee with the ship. The attempt was foiled by the gallant third mate, Benjamin Clough, who swam on board in the dark of the night and single-handedly recaptured the vessel. The rousing story has been retold many times in books and papers, because Clough's undeniable heroism is such a sure seller. I looked at it differently, however—from my new Pacific perspective. *Why* had the natives slaughtered Norris? No one had asked that question properly before, because it had been assumed that savages, being "savage," did not need a reason. But I was certain not only that the three islanders had some motive for the crime, but that it was an overwhelmingly compelling one. They were seven hundred miles from the nearest inhabited land, and three men could not have sailed such a large ship so far on their own, so the murder must have been both unpremeditated and sudden. Something devastating had sparked the attack—but what?

Two of the three natives were killed during the recapture of the ship. The third was found cowering in the hold next day, but his only excuse was that "the captain was cross." What did that mean? At home in Martha's Vineyard, Norris was respected as a lucky and conscientious whaling master; he had the reputation of a good husband and kind parent. Did he behave differently at sea? Did he have a savage temper, for instance? I hunted down every record available, and found the last key to the secret when a descendant allowed me access to the journal kept by the heroic third mate himself, which is still in family hands. What I read gave me nightmares. For eight months, Captain Norris had tortured one of his black seamen, and then, in a frenzied rage, he had beaten him to death. In the weeks leading up to his murder, he was "beating and pounding the Kanakas"—the native seamen he had picked up when the ship called at various Pacific islands. So, when the three islanders attacked him, were they literally afraid for their lives?

This awful unfolding story was something I felt driven to write. It had special New Zealand significance, too. After Norris was murdered, the ship called at the Bay of Islands, and there the true account was whispered about the grogshops. As I have said before, Kiwis are traditionally on the side of the underdog, and these stories of sadism on the quarterdeck—and Norris was by no means the only brutal shipmaster—meant guaranteed public support for any beleaguered Yankee seaman with a complaint about his boss. In fact, ships

taken over by disaffected seamen deliberately steered for New Zealand. In 1884 the U.S. consul, Gilderoy Wells Griffin, complained in a letter to the State Department that his job was much harder in New Zealand than elsewhere, because "there is a general opinion throughout the Colony that American shipmasters are proverbially cruel and brutal to their sailors."

This led to the very strange affair of the Connecticut sealing schooner *Sarah W. Hunt*—a different story from the dark tale of the *Sharon,* but equally intriguing. In December 1883 the schooner arrived in Port Lyttelton in the South Island of New Zealand flying a flag of distress, with only the captain and the steward on board. By themselves, they had sailed the 116-ton vessel five hundred miles through the most storm-wracked, tempestuous seas in the world. It was an amazing accomplishment—but what, the locals asked, had happened to the other men? They had been lost off Campbell Island in the sub-Antarctic, said Captain Miner; he had given up all hope for their survival.

Because of the poor record of Yankee captains, the members the Christchurch Chamber of Commerce chose not to believe him. They petitioned the government for a search party to be sent to Campbell Island, but time went by and they lost patience, handed round the hat, and raised money to hire the government steamer *Stella* for the search—and the steamer arrived back in Port Chalmers, Otago, with six crippled, frostbitten survivors on board, the castaways of Campbell Island. The other six men, they said, had been lost. All hell broke loose as the headlines hit papers around the nation. Consul Griffin, a very competent and honorable U.S. representative, was forced to travel to Christchurch to supervise what rapidly turned into an international incident.

There is a book in this, of course, already named *Perseverance Harbour* in my mind—Perseverance Harbour being the anchorage at Campbell Island where the schooner originally dropped her anchor, and where the six castaways landed with the expectation that the captain would be waiting there, and glad to see them. It is also apt because they endured a shocking elevenday ordeal in a small open boat to get there. "Perseverance" also describes the diplomatic efforts of United States Consul Gilderoy Wells Griffin—a most able man, who was every bit as colorful as his predecessors in the surprisingly difficult job of representing the United States in New Zealand—to mediate between the public, the press, the survivors, the U.S. State Department, and the New Zealand Government.

Druett with agent Laura Langlie, New York City, 1997

Apart from this book, where will my new direction lead me? A mystery novel beckons—staged on the U.S. exploring expedition which sailed to the Pacific in 1838. A young Maori chief is with the fleet as the captain's translator. What would his shipmates look like, from his Polynesian point of view . . . and how would he set about solving a murder?

BIOGRAPHICAL AND CRITICAL SOURCES:

PERIODICALS

American History Illustrated, July-August, 1993, review of *"She Was a Sister Sailor": The Whaling Journals of Mary Brewster,* p. 17.

Atlantic, August 1, 1998, review of *Hen Frigates: Wives of Merchant Captains under Sail,* p. 104.

Booklist, May 15, 1998, Margaret Flanagan, review of *Hen Frigates: Wives of Merchant Captains under Sail,* p. 1570; February 15, 2000, Donna Seaman, review of *She Captains: Heroines and Hellions of the Sea;* September 15, 2000, William Beatty, review of *Rough Medicine: Surgeons at Sea in the Age of Sail,* p. 197.

Choice, April, 2001, review of *Rough Medicine: Surgeons at Sea in the Age of Sail.*

Journal of the American Medical Association, April 11, 2000, Hans A. Brings, "Nautical Medicine," p. 1894.

Journal of the Early Republic, winter, 1993, Mary Zwiep, review of *"She Was a Sister Sailor": The Whaling Journals of Mary Brewster,* p. 582.

Kirkus Reviews, March 1, 2003, review of *In the Wake of Madness: The Murderous Voyage of the Whaleship Sharon,* p. 359.

Kliatt, September, 2003, Sunnie Grant, review of *In the Wake of Madness: The Murderous Voyage of the Whaleship Sharon,* p. 60.

Library Journal, July, 1998, Roseanne Castellino, review of *Hen Frigates: Wives of Merchant Captains under Sail,* p. 108; March 15, 2000, Roseanne Castellino, review of *She Captains: Heroines and Hellions of the Sea,* p. 104; March 15, 2003, Robert C. Jones, review of *In the Wake of Madness: The Murderous Voyage of the Whaleship Sharon,* p. 96.

New York Times Book Review, July 26, 1998, "First Helpmates"; March 26, 2000, Louise Jarvis, "Dames at Sea," p. 15; May 4, 2003, Peter Nichols, "Psycho at Sea," p. 16.

Publishers Weekly, November 16, 1992, review of *"She Was a Sister Sailor": The Whaling Journals of Mary Brewster, 1845-1851,* p. 55; January 31, 2000, review of *She Captains: Heroines and Hellions of the Sea;* December 18, 2000, review of *Rough Medicine: Surgeons at Sea in the Age of Sail,* p. 70; April 28, 2003, review of *In the Wake of Madness: The Murderous Voyage of the Whaleship Sharon,* p. 61.

ONLINE

Joan Druett Web site, http://members.authorsguild.net/druettjo (November 17, 2003).

*   *   *

DRUFFEL, Ann 1926-

PERSONAL: Born 1926, in Riverside, CA; daughter of William (a municipal automotive worker) and Aileen (a schoolteacher; maiden name, Walsh) McElroy; married Charles K. Druffel, January 24, 1953; children: Ellen R. M., Diana Lee Druffel Mauldin, Carolyn Jean

Henry, Charlotte Bridget Druffel Bressler, Allis Ann. *Ethnicity:* "Celtic." *Education:* Immaculate Heart College, B.A.; graduate study at Catholic University of America. *Politics:* "Conservative/environmentalist." *Religion:* Roman Catholic. *Hobbies and other interests:* Scientifically related UFO research, psychic phenomena.

ADDRESSES: Home—257 Sycamore Glen, Pasadena, CA 91105. *Agent*—John White, 60 Pound Ridge Rd., Cheshire, CT 06410. *E-mail*—anndruffel@aol.com.

CAREER: Social caseworker and therapist in Los Angeles, CA, for five years; freelance writer and researcher, 1957—. Mobius Society, researcher and consultant, 1985-92.

MEMBER: Mutual UFO Network (member of Los Angeles board of directors; investigator, 1980—), National Rifle Association, Numbers USA, California Rifle and Pistol Association.

WRITINGS:

The Tujunga Canyon Contacts, Prentice-Hall, 1980, revised edition, New American Library (New York, NY), 1988.

(With Armand Marcotte) *Past Lives: Future Growth,* ACS Publications (San Francisco, CA), 1984.

(With Armand Marcotte) *The Psychic and the Detective,* ACS Publications (San Francisco, CA), 1985.

How to Defend Yourself against Alien Abduction, Crown (New York, NY), 1998.

Firestorm: Dr. James E. McDonald's Fight for UFO Science, Wild Flower Press (Columbus, NC), 2003.

Author of "California Report" and "Skynet Log," regular columns in *MUFON UFO Journal.* Contributor of nearly 200 articles to periodicals, including *Fate, Magnolia, Flying Saucer Review, International UFO Reporter, Skylook, Canadian UFO Report, Let's Live,* and *Journal of Scientific Exploration.* Associate editor, *MUFON UFO Journal.*

WORK IN PROGRESS: Research to locate the lost grave of Irish patriot Robert Emmet.

SIDELIGHTS: Ann Druffel told *CA:* "I write because I am impelled to write, and because there are so many fascinating earth mysteries about which the human race needs and desires more information. I write because I have researched earth mysteries—UFOs, sacred sites, psychic phenomena—since 1957 and feel the need to share with others what I have been able to learn—my hypotheses and evidence.

"I write whenever the thoughts come to me—in the middle of the night, in the daytime, whenever I get the chance or an inspiration. I have written five books, two columns, nearly 200 articles, five monographs, and I am working on a sixth book.

"As a schoolgirl in 1945 I viewed an inexplicable object, possibly in orbit, which released numerous smaller objects that took varying paths out from the main object. It appeared about two weeks before the Hiroshima bombing, and its appearance coincided rather closely with the first experimental A-bomb exploded in New Mexico. This event triggered my lifelong interest in the UFO phenomenon, which began my writing career. Because of apparent relationships of UFO events with other earth mysteries—psychic functioning, ley lines, sacred sites, et cetera—I branched out into these fields. Because of my Irish background, I have also used psychic archaeology as a scientific process in searching for the lost grave of patriot Robert Emmet."

*   *   *

DURHAM, Jennifer L. 1972-

PERSONAL: Born May 29, 1972, in Raleigh, NC; daughter of James F. (an employee of the U.S. Environmental Protection Agency) and Judith Althea (Hansley) Durham. *Ethnicity:* "Caucasian." *Education:* University of North Carolina—Chapel Hill, B.A., 1994. *Religion:* "I believe the Bible but am not into organized religion."

ADDRESSES: Home and office—Raleigh, NC. *Agent*—c/o American Bibliographical Center-Clio Press, 130 Cremona Dr., Santa Barbara, CA 93117. *E-mail*—jld44@earthlink.net.

CAREER: Advanced Concepts/Advacon/Glaxo Smith Kline, Research Triangle Park, NC, technical writer, 1999—.

WRITINGS:

Crime in America, American Bibliographical Center-Clio Press (Santa Barbara, CA), 1996.

Benjamin Franklin: A Biographical Companion, American Bibliographical Center-Clio Press (Santa Barbara, CA), 1997.

World Cultural Leaders of the Twentieth Century, American Bibliographical Center-Clio Press (Santa Barbara, CA), 2000.

WORK IN PROGRESS: A "semi-autobiographical novel about a young person trying to find his way through this world."

SIDELIGHTS: Jennifer L. Durham told *CA:* "Writing has always been the primary way I've expressed thoughts. There is no greater inspiration to write than simple observation of people, past and present. History has always fascinated me, and of my published work I enjoyed writing the biography of Benjamin Franklin the most. It's hard to pinpoint what inspires me to write on certain subjects—they are just things that interest me at particular points in life's journey."

*   *   *

DYKSTRA, Monique 1964-

PERSONAL: Born August 11, 1964, in Toronto, Ontario, Canada; daughter of Peter (a lawyer) and Gail (a teacher, secretary, and writer) Dykstra; married Saeb Hachem (a mathematician).

ADDRESSES: Home—4595 St. Kevin, Apt. 7, Montreal, Quebec, Canada H3T 1J1. *Office*—Box 1304, Place du Parc, Montreal, Quebec, Canada H2X 4A7. *E-mail*—monique@studioiris.ca.

CAREER: Montreal Gazette, Montreal, Quebec, Canada, columnist, 1992-98; freelance writer and photographer, 1998—. Dawson College, professor.

WRITINGS:

(And photographer) *My Heart on the Yukon River: Portraits from Alaska and the Yukon,* Washington State University Press (Pullman, WA), 1997.

(And photographer) *Alone in the Appalachians: A City Girl's Trek from Maine to the Gaspé,* Raincoast Book (Vancouver, British Columbia, Canada), 2002, published as *Alone in the Appalachians: A City Girl's Journey from Maine to the Gaspé,* Raincoast Books (San Diego, CA), 2002.

BIOGRAPHICAL AND CRITICAL SOURCES:

PERIODICALS

Canadian Geographic, July-August, 1998, Stephen Smith, review of *My Heart on the Yukon River: Portraits from Alaska and the Yukon,* p. 74; July-August, 2002, Alex Ross, review of *Alone in the Appalachians: A City Girl's Trek from Maine to the Gaspé,* p. 97.

E

EBSEN, Buddy
    See EBSEN, Christian (Rudolf, Jr.)

* * *

EBSEN, Christian (Rudolf, Jr.) 1908-2003
    (Buddy Ebsen)

OBITUARY NOTICE—See index for *CA* sketch: Born April 2, 1908, in Belleville, IL; died July 6, 2003, in Torrance, CA. Actor and author. Ebsen is best remembered for his leading roles in the television series *The Beverly Hillbillies* and *Barnaby Jones*. Ebsen, who was given the nickname Buddy by one of his aunts, started off in show business as a dancer in New York City. He first learned to dance from his father, who taught ballet at a dance studio, although Ebsen considered the skill an unmasculine pursuit when he was a child. Instead, he first aspired to be a doctor after seeing one of his sisters suffer from epilepsy. Toward that end, he attended pre-med courses at the University of Florida, but with insufficient funds to complete his education decided to try show business. He moved to New York City, appearing in the chorus of the successful musical comedy *Whoopee* during the late 1920s. He also formed a vaudeville dance act with his sister Vilma, with Ebsen playing the comical figure. His tall, lanky form was ideal for goofy dance moves, and when the two young dancers were spotted by columnist Walter Winchell as they were performing a dance to the tune "Ain't Misbehavin'," Winchell's glowing review became Ebsen's ticket to success. Vaudeville reviews such as *Broadway Stars of Tomorrow* followed, and in the 1930s Buddy and Vilma ap-

peared as feature dancers in Metro-Goldwyn-Mayer productions of *Flying Colors, Ziegfeld Follies of 1934,* and *Broadway Melody of 1936.* The pair were eventually separated by the studio, and Ebsen next performed in a number of musical movies, such as 1936's *Captain January,* in which he danced with Shirley Temple. He was also offered the role of the tin woodsman in *The Wizard of Oz,* but during the early stages of shooting the film had a reaction to the aluminum in his makeup; hospitalized for several weeks, he lost the part to Jack Haley. Still, Ebsen was in demand, but when the studio offered him a seven-year contract he turned it down because of the condition that the studio control his career. For this reason, he found himself blackballed. Finding it hard to get acting roles in Hollywood, Ebsen returned to Broadway until World War II interrupted career worries. Ebsen served in the U.S. Coast Guard as a lieutenant junior grade, working on a patrol frigate that searched for German U-boats. Returning to civilian life, he won a role in the 1946 stage production of *Show Boat,* but this was followed by a period of struggle during which he appeared in several B-movie Westerns. Ebsen's luck turned around when he was given the role of Davy Crockett's friend Georgie Russel in a series of television programs and movies produced by Walt Disney in the 1950s. This was followed by a regular role as Sergeant Hunk Marriner in the NBC television series *Northwest Passage* from 1958-59. His film career picked up somewhat, too, and he had a supporting role in *Breakfast at Tiffany's* (1961). The next year he was hired to star as Jed Clampett in the comedy series *The Beverly Hillbillies,* which ran from 1962-71. Then followed Ebson's title role in *Barnaby Jones* (1973-80), a television series about a private investigator. With the exception of a supporting part in the short-lived series *Matt Houston* (1984-85), and a cameo appearance as Barnaby Jones in the

1993 spinoff movie *The Beverly Hillbillies,* Ebsen eased out of acting after *Barnaby Jones.* In retirement, he engaged in many activities to occupy his time, including skippering his catamaran to several boat-race wins; he also owned a company that built catamarans. Ebsen was also a writer, and authored a number of plays—including *Honest John* (1948) and *Champagne General* (1964)—songs—including tunes that appeared on a *Beverly Hillbillies* album in 1965—and books—including his autobiography *The Other Side of Oz* (1993) and the novel *Kelly's Quest* (2001).

OBITUARIES AND OTHER SOURCES:

BOOKS

Contemporary Theater, Film, and Television, Volume 3, Gale (Detroit, MI), 1986.

PERIODICALS

Chicago Tribune, July 8, 2003, section 1, p. 4.
Los Angeles Times, July 8, 2003, p. B12.
New York Times, July 8, 2003, p. A25.
Times (London, England), July 18, 2003.
Washington Post, July 8, 2003, p. B7.

*　　*　　*

ENDERLE, Dotti 1954-

PERSONAL: Born January 11, 1954, in Killeen, TX; daughter of George (a moving company manager) and Doris (Wade) Varley; married Lenny Enderle (an estimator), March 31, 1984; children: Dori, Adrienne. *Hobbies and other interests:* Reading.

ADDRESSES: Home—P.O. Box 999, Richmond, TX 77406-0999. *Agent*—Erin Murphy Literary Agency, P.O. Box 2519, Flagstaff, AZ 86003-2519. *E-mail*—enderle@io.com.

CAREER: Author and storyteller. Worked as a banker teller and bookkeeper in Houston, TX, 1972-84, and an enrichment teacher and library assistant in Sugar Land, TX, 1993-99.

MEMBER: Society of Children's Book Writers and Illustrators, Writers League of Texas, Women Writing the West.

AWARDS, HONORS: Second place, Houston Storytellers Guild Annual Liar's Contest, 1994, 1997; honorable mention for children's nonfiction, *Writers Digest* Writing Competition, 1998; first place, CNW/FFWA Writing Competition, 2002; finalist, *Foreword Magazine* Book of the Year Award, 2002.

WRITINGS:

"FORTUNE TELLERS CLUB" SERIES

The Lost Girl, Llewellyn Publications (St. Paul, MN), 2002.
Playing with Fire, Llewellyn Publications (St. Paul, MN), 2003.
Magic Shades, Llewellyn Publications (St. Paul, MN), 2004.
Secrets of the Lost Arrow, Llewellyn Publications (St. Paul, MN), 2004.
Hand of Fate, Llewellyn Publications (St. Paul, MN), 2004.

"STORYTIME DISCOVERIES" SERIES

Physical Science, Teaching & Learning (Carthage, IL), 2003.
Earth Science, Teaching & Learning (Carthage, IL), 2003.
Biological Science, Teaching & Learning (Carthage, IL), 2003.

OTHER

Making Cents (electronic book), Kudlicka Publishing, 2002.
Aesop's Opposites—Interactive Aesop Fables, Teaching & Learning (Carthage, IL), 2004.

Contributor of poems and stories to children's magazines, including *Children's Playmate, Ladybug, Babybug, Nature Friend, Our Little Friend,* and *Lollipops.*

WORK IN PROGRESS: Fractured Reflections and *No Fortune Telling Allowed,* both for the "Fortune Tellers Club" series.

SIDELIGHTS: Starting as a school enrichment teacher and professional storyteller who specializes in interactive storytelling, Texas native Dotti Enderle has visited numerous schools, libraries, museums, and festivals over the years. In 1994 she decided that many of her original stories had passed the listening test, so she submitted them for publication in children's magazines. Since her debut in print, she has published dozens of stories and poems in many well-known magazines for children, including *Ladybug, Babybug, Turtle,* and *Children's Playmate.* "Every time I get something published in a major children's magazine, it feels like my first big break!" Enderle confided to an online interviewer at *Book Review Cafe.*

Enderle's writing reflects her own childhood memories. Growing up in Texas as the youngest of seven children, she once explained that her family's frequent moves from town to town adversely affected her confidence. Yet these new locations and the new experiences they brought fed her imagination. Her "Fortune Tellers Club" series mirrors her own obsessions as a teenager, wanting to know what the future would bring. "Young girls are curious about the future," she noted. "They want to know if they'll marry someone rich, or if they'll be famous or travel." Although Enderle and her friends never solved mysteries with a Ouija board, there was no reason her characters could not, the author said. Thus in this series, twelve-year-old friends Juniper, Anne, and Gena call themselves the Fortune Tellers Club and use various supernatural and natural means to solve mysteries. The first volume, *The Lost Girl,* which Elaine Baran Black of *School Library Journal* called a "breezy read," revolves around the trio's efforts to locate a missing child. In the early 2000s, Enderle turned out a steady stream of "Fortune Tellers Club" books, including *Playing with Fire* about Anne's crush on a cute football player and mysterious fires lighting up the school, and *Magic Shades,* about a pair of glasses that provides a new look at life.

BIOGRAPHICAL AND CRITICAL SOURCES:

PERIODICALS

School Library Journal, November, 2002, Elaine Baran Black, review of *The Lost Girl,* pp. 162-163.

ONLINE

Book Review Cafe, http://www.bookreviewcafe.com/ (June 19, 2003), "Interview with Dotti Enderle."
Dotti Enderle Home Page, http://www.dottienderle. com (June 19, 2003).

*   *   *

ENGLANDER, Nathan 1970-

PERSONAL: Born 1970, in New York, NY. *Education:* Binghamton University, B.A.; University of Iowa, M.F.A.; attended Hebrew University, Jerusalem, Israel.

ADDRESSES: Home—Jerusalem, Israel and New York, NY. *Agent*—c/o Author Mail, Random House, 1745 Broadway, New York, NY 10019.

CAREER: Writer. Worked as manager of a commercial photography studio.

AWARDS, HONORS: Bard Fiction Prize, Bard College, 2001; Pushcart Prize.

WRITINGS:

For the Relief of Unbearable Urges, Alfred A. Knopf (New York, NY), 1999.

Contributor of fiction to periodicals, including *New Yorker, Story, Atlantic,* and *American Short Fiction.* Contributor to anthologies, including *The Art of the Story* and *Neurotica.*

WORK IN PROGRESS: A novel, set in Argentina.

SIDELIGHTS: Nathan Englander's well-reviewed book *For the Relief of Unbearable Urges* is a collection of nine short stories, "a remarkable collection for a newcomer still in his twenties to produce," wrote Nicholas Clee in *New Statesman.* A balance of "comedy and tragedy, surrealism, and pathos" from the Jewish storytelling traditions of writers such as

Bernard Malamud and Isaac Bashevis Singer, the book demonstrates "poise and effectiveness" and reveals Englander to be "a writer of distinctive gifts," Clee remarked.

Born in New York City in 1970, Englander grew up on Long Island in "an Orthodox home in New York, where I had a right-wing, xenophobic, anti-intellectual, fire-and-brimstone, free-thought free, shtetl-mentality, substandard education," he said in an interview on the *Bold Type* Web site. He studied at a yeshiva throughout his youth and high school days, where he started writing when he was "discovered and rescued by that one teacher that fate inevitably puts in these parochial schools," Englander said in an *Atlantic Online* interview. His sincere theological questions were disdained, he said, "so when my English teacher got me started reading books, she opened the world to me. Writing became my lifeline."

Throughout his youth and young adulthood, Englander maintained strict observance of Jewish religious rules and traditions. Instead of continuing his Orthodox education, he enrolled at the State University of New York at Binghamton. Although he considered college to be "unbelievably eye-opening, coming from where I did," he continued to observe the rules of his religion, he said in the *Bold Type* interview. In his junior year, he traveled to Israel, a life-changing trip that found him abandoning his religion and delving deep into his work and identity as a writer.

Englander returned from Israel and graduated from college, then enrolled at the Iowa Writer's Workshop at the urging of the mother of a friend who saw an early draft of the short story "The Twenty-seventh Man," wrote Paul Zakrzewski on the *GenerationJ* Web site. He successfully completed the prestigious Iowa program and earned his M.F.A. in creative writing.

For the Relief of Unbearable Urges is "a superb short story collection that reveals the tension between the sacred and the profane for Orthodox Jews," wrote Frank Caso in *Booklist*. In the title story, Dov Binyamin, a Jewish man whose wife has undertaken self-imposed celibacy, seeks special permission from his rabbi to visit a prostitute. After his experiences with the prostitute, and the resulting case of venereal disease, Binyamin becomes less and less interested in his wife, even when her sexual appetite re-emerges. In "The Twenty-seventh Man," twenty-six of the most prominent Jewish authors under the Stalinist regime are rounded up, tortured, and executed. But the twenty-seventh man, Pinchas Pelovits, is there by mistake; he has never published a single word. While imprisoned, Pelovits composes and recites a story to his doomed comrades, and it is a masterpiece. The story "is a radiant little fable of acceptance and loss," Clee wrote.

The characters in "The Tumblers" are a group of Jews destined for the concentration camps, but who board the wrong train and find themselves with a group of entertainers. They devise an acrobatic act to save themselves, even though they are not acrobats and their performance is farcical, prompting one audience member to declare, ironically, that "They are as clumsy as Jews." But their determination saves them from a gruesome end. In "The Gilgul of Park Avenue" a gentile Protestant realizes, quite abruptly in the back of a Manhattan taxi cab, that he is Jewish. "Reb Kringle" depicts a New York rabbi who, every year, takes the job of a department store Santa Claus.

D. Mesher, writing in *Judaism*, called the collection "wonderful" and observed that the author "shows an impressive command of both art and artifice" in his writing. A *Publishers Weekly* reviewer called Englander "A wise and mature new voice," while another reviewer noted the "pathos and hilarity that is the signature key of these nine graceful and remarkably self-assured stories." The book's "memorable characters and equally memorable circumstances of their struggles make all nine stories a pleasure to read and contemplate," Caso concluded in *Booklist*.

BIOGRAPHICAL AND CRITICAL SOURCES:

PERIODICALS

Booklist, March 1, 1999, Frank Caso, review of *For the Relief of Unbearable Urges,* p. 1150; October 1, 1999, Ray Olson and Gilbert Taylor, review of *For the Relief of Unbearable Urges,* p. 322.
Judaism, winter, 2000, D. Mesher, review of *For the Relief of Unbearable Urges,* p. 120.
New Statesman June 28, 1999, Nicholas Clee, review of *For the Relief of Unbearable Urges,* p. 50.
Publishers Weekly, February 1, 1999, review of *For the Relief of Unbearable Urges,* p. 74; November 1, 1999, review of *For the Relief of Unbearable Urges,* p. 46.

ONLINE

Atlantic Unbound, http:/www.theatlantic.com/ (March 3, 1999), interview with Englander.

GenerationJ.com, http://www.generationj.com/ (September 16, 2002), Paul Zakrzewski, profile of Englander.

New York State Writers Institute Web site, http://www.albany.edu/writers-inst/ (March 28, 2000), profile of Englander.

Random House Web site http://www.randomhouse.com/ (September 16, 2002), interview with Englander.

Seattle Arts & Lectures Web site, http://www.lectures.org/ (April 12, 2000), biography of Englander.*

* * *

EUROPICUS
See COSER, Lewis A(lfred)

F

FADERMAN, Lillian 1940-

PERSONAL: Born July 18, 1940, in Bronx, NY; daughter of Mary Lifton; partner of Phyllis Irwin; children: Avrom. *Education:* University of California, Berkeley, A.B., 1962; University of California, Los Angeles, M.A., 1964, Ph.D., 1967.

ADDRESSES: Office—Department of English, California State University, Fresno, CA 93740. *E-mail—* lillian_faderman@csufresno.edu.

CAREER: California State University, Fresno, member of faculty beginning 1967, associate professor, 1971-72, professor of English, 1973—, chair of English department, 1971-72, dean of School of Humanities, 1972-73, assistant vice president of academic affairs, 1973-76. Visiting professor, University of California, Los Angeles, 1989-91.

AWARDS, HONORS: Best Lesbian/Gay Book Award, American Library Association, 1982, for *Surpassing the Love of Men: Romantic Friendship between Women from the Renaissance to the Present,* and 1992, for *Odd Girls and Twilight Lovers: A History of Lesbian life in Twentieth-Century America;* Lambda Literary Awards, 1992, for *Odd Girls and Twilight Lovers,* 1995, for *Chloe plus Olivia: Lesbian Literature from the Seventeenth Century to the Present,* and 2000, for *To Believe in Women: What Lesbians Have Done for America;* Monette/Horwitz Award for distinguished contributions to lesbian/gay scholarship, 1999; James Brudner Award for exemplary lesbian/gay scholarship, Yale University, 2001; distinguished senior scholar award, American Association of University Women, 2002.

Lillian Faderman

WRITINGS:

(With Barbara Bradshaw) *Speaking for Ourselves: American Ethnic Writing,* Scott, Foresman (Glenview, IL), 1969, 2nd edition, 1975.
(Editor with Luis Omar Salinas) *From the Barrio: A Chicano Anthology,* Canfield Press (San Francisco, CA), 1973.

(Editor and translator with Brigitte Eriksson) *Lesbian-Feminism in Turn-of-the-Century Germany,* Naiad Press (Tallahassee, FL), 1980, published as *Lesbians in Germany,* 1990.

Surpassing the Love of Men: Romantic Friendship and Love between Women from the Renaissance to the Present, Morrow (New York, NY), 1981.

Scotch Verdict: Miss Pirie and Miss Woods v. Dame Cumming Gordon, Morrow (New York, NY), 1983.

Odd Girls and Twilight Lovers: A History of Lesbian Life in Twentieth-Century America, Columbia University Press (New York, NY), 1991.

(Editor) *Chloe plus Olivia: An Anthology of Lesbian Literature from the Seventeenth Century to the Present,* Viking (New York, NY), 1994.

(With Ghia Xiong) *I Begin My Life All Over: The Hmong and the American Immigrant Experience,* Beacon Press (Boston, MA), 1998.

To Believe in Women: What Lesbians Have Done for America—A History, Houghton (Boston, MA), 1999.

Naked in the Promised Land: A Memoir, Houghton Mifflin (Boston, MA), 2003.

Contributor of articles to journals, including *Massachusetts Review, New England Quarterly, Journal of Popular Culture, Conditions, Signs, Journal of Homosexuality,* and *Journal of the History of Sexuality.* Contributor to periodicals, including *Advocate.*

SIDELIGHTS: Lillian Faderman's *Surpassing the Love of Men: Romantic Friendship and Love between Women from the Renaissance to the Present* "is a comprehensive and illuminating study of women's struggles to live and love as they please," Phyllis Grosskurth wrote in the *New York Review of Books.* Three historical periods—the sixteenth through the eighteenth centuries, the nineteenth century, and the twentieth century—are examined from both a literary and a cultural perspective in the book, summarized Benjamin DeMott in *Atlantic,* noting Faderman's focus on sexual as well as nonsexual woman-to-woman relationships.

According to Carolyn G. Heilbrun in the *New York Times Book Review, Surpassing the Love of Men* demonstrates that, "except when women preempted male power or tried to pass as men, they were usually, until quite recently, left free to love one another." Faderman's "quite thorough scholarship," noted *Washington Post Book World's* Joanna Russ, indicates that

"the Lesbian did not even exist in Europe until the 1880s and in the United States until 1910." She added, "Love between women, which did exist, was unlike Lesbianism in being socially honored, not secretive, and extremely common." Keith Walker wrote in the *Times Literary Supplement* that Faderman "stumbled over this not startlingly original version of events when she was reading Emily Dickinson's love poems and letters to Sue Gilbert," the woman who later became her sister-in-law, "and noticed that Dickinson showed no guilt and moreover that her niece, editing the letters early in this century, felt obliged to bowdlerize them."

Many critics have found *Surpassing the Love of Men* praiseworthy. Heilbrun described the book as "a welcome and needed history" and stated that "its account of women loving women before the twentieth century is invaluable." Walker, however, objected to "the cosy glow engendered by the belief that lesbian relationships are finer, more enduring, and more satisfying than heterosexual ones." Grosskurth, similarly, believes that probably "many such relationships exist, but by investing them all with a romantic coloration, [Faderman] never considers the tensions, irritations, or jealousy engendered by most close relationships." According to Russ, "At times she seems to say that sexism and the segregation of the sexes causes love between women, a confusingly negative view that contradicts her assertion of the normality (statistical and other) of such behavior."

"Despite my deep unease at some of these implicit assumptions," Grosskurth wrote, "I think this is an important book; certainly one of the most significant contributions yet made to feminist literature." DeMott concluded that *Surpassing the Love of Men* remains "a work of genuine interest and value. Its pages are filled with vivid portraits of heroes and heroines struggling to lead their contemporaries out of delusion on sex and gender matter, and with astonishingly fresh disclosures about details of sexist feeling from age to age."

Faderman's other studies of woman-to-woman love include *To Believe in Women: What Lesbians Have Done for America—A History.* Faderman asserts that many women who have been important in social reform movements can be considered lesbian, including suffragists Susan B. Anthony and Carrie Chapman Catt, first lady Eleanor Roosevelt, settlement house founder and peace activist Jane Addams, and medical doctors Marie Zakrzewska, Mary Walker, and Emily Blackwell. In this work, Faderman expands her definition of lesbianism beyond romantic love between women to "intense woman-to-woman relating and commitment." *New York Times Book Review* commentator Karla Jay called this a "generous definition," allowing that some will consider Faderman's "tendentious claims . . . a welcome corrective to biographies that erased lesbian existence." *Advocate* contributor Ricardo Ortiz noted that "whether or not they would have called themselves lesbian, each [of the women profiled] was able to effect change thanks partly to the support of a loving, long-term female life partner." Jay found it problematic, though, that Faderman puts such emphasis on the contribution of lesbian relationships to these women's activism. "Sexual orientation was probably less of a factor for these reformers than the financial wherewithal that freed them from the tedious demands of earning a living," Jay remarked. Also, Faderman holds up these relationships as models for both same-sex and mixed-sex couples to emulate in balancing personal life and career, but these female couples, Jay pointed out, sometimes had a very traditional division of labor, with one partner handling domestic matters so the other could work for her cherished causes. "Faderman may inadvertently be broadcasting a discouraging message about the prospects for combining family life with a profession or social activism," Jay concluded. Despite these reservations, she pronounced the book "a decent starting point for learning about these pioneers and their contributions to American life" and recommends it "for those who need a dose of pride and a slice of history."

Odd Girls and Twilight Lovers is a scholarly examination of the transition of women's close relationships of the nineteenth century to the rise of lesbianism in the 1920s, a societal change made possible by women's growing economic independence. However, once women's relationships were capable of supplanting heterosexual marriage, public acceptance of them fell by the wayside. Women's once-innocuous "romantic friendships" became something more sinister as norms continued to shift throughout the century.

Odd Girls was well received as a close examination of a previously overlooked topic, and in time the book became a standard text in many women's studies courses. One of Faderman's assertions in the book is that in the nineteenth and early twentieth century, before female same-sex relationships became widely suspect as 'abnormal,' women were able to express

their affections for other women, and even to live in female domestic partnerships, without suffering the opprobrium they would during the more restrictive decades of the mid-twentieth century. Patricia Sarles in *Library Journal* called the book "a necessity for women's studies collections." Jane Mills, reviewing the book for *New Statesman & Society,* remarked that Faderman illustrates that "even during the worst period of persecution, gay and lesbian subculture grew and defined itself more clearly than ever before." Noting that the contemporary idea of homosexuality didn't exist much more than a hundred years ago, *New York Times Book Review* writer Jeffrey Escoffier complimented Faderman's "grand narrative synthesis of the cultural, social and political history of lesbian life since the late nineteenth century."

Faderman's life story takes center stage in *Naked in the Promised Land,* in which she examines her roots as the daughter of a poor, single immigrant traumatized by the death of her parents at the hands of the Nazis. From the sweatshops of Brooklyn, the young Lillian saw her mother and aunt struggle. When the threesome moved to Hollywood in search of a better life, Lillian was determined to save her histrionic mother by becoming a movie star. Years of acting lessons and one nose job later, Lillian was inclined to drop out of school and use her body as a nude model and stripper while she came to grips with her sexual orientation. A vigilant career counselor steered her toward college, but the sex work continued, along with her twisted relationship with her psychologically fragile mother. During her senior year of high school, Lillian entered into a sham marriage with a gay Jewish psychologist—an ill-fated move that pleased her mother immensely. Lillian later put herself through college by posing nude and dancing under the name Mink Frost in San Francisco's Tenderloin district, a double life in the straight-laced 1950s if ever there was one.

After obtaining her Ph.D., Faderman was astounded to discover that the sexism she faced in academia, where all the tenured teaching positions went to her male classmates, mirrored the ostensibly harsher street life she thought she had left behind. Despite her academic standing, Faderman was offered only a low-prestige job at Fresno State. She took it, and as the years passed, rose through the ranks in academia, becoming a leading scholar at her university and helping to pioneer the field of women's studies. Having ended her marriage years earlier, she embarked on a life-long relationship with a colleague, Phyllis Irwin, and together they raised Faderman's son, who was conceived through artificial insemination.

Naked in the Promised Land garnered good reviews. Writing in *Publishers Weekly,* Michael Bronski noted that though Faderman's previous books "caused considerable alarm in conservative academic circles . . . uncovering the threads of past Sapphic desire was nothing compared to confessing to being a stripper decades ago." A writer for *Publishers Weekly* called the memoir "exceedingly honest, endearing and profound." Focusing largely on how Faderman's "identities as working-class, Jewish, female, lesbian, sex worker and student did not neatly mesh," wrote Susan Freeman in the *Miami Herald,* the story is a "tale of a life stretched long, encompassing the ghosts of Nazi Germany and hope for the future, the possibility not only embodied by the child but also by an extraordinary woman whose struggles and chutzpah merit our attention." Carolyn See, noting the similarities between Faderman's life and her own as a woman breaking new ground in the 1960s, wrote in the *Washington Post* that "Faderman is strong in her belief that all voiceless humans deserve voices, and a respectable place in our American history."

Other critics thought the memoir could have been more introspective. "Faderman's achievements are nothing short of awe-inspiring," wrote Kera Bolonik in the *San Francisco Chronicle,* but "a life as daring and rich as hers warrants a more psychologically probing memoir: Had Faderman showed less metaphoric flesh, then *Naked in the Promised Land* just may have bared a bit more soul." Similarly, Barbara Sjoholm of the *Seattle Times* called the book "fascinating," but concluded that "Faderman leaves us convinced of her success—yet still wondering, a little, who she is." But as Faderman told Bronski in an interview for *Publishers Weekly,* her previous books are about "giving public voice to people who had been silenced. This memoir is really about giving so many private parts of myself a public voice." Aside from herself, Faderman told Bronski, the book is about her mother. "From earliest childhood, I understood how difficult my mother's life was. And if fueled my desire to save her. It was my love for her—even when we fought so terribly—that allowed me to open myself up to the love of other women."

AUTOBIOGRAPHICAL ESSAY:

My childhood and young adulthood were unusual for someone who would one day become a scholar, but I think the unconventionality of my experiences helped me to envision the iconoclastic books I eventually published. Perhaps if I'd had a more usual youth I would have had some reluctance to undertake subjects that were generally considered inappropriate or odd at the time I began writing about them. From my first book publication in 1969 (*Speaking for Ourselves: American Ethnic Writing*) to my 1999 book, *To Believe in Women: What Lesbians Have Done for America—A History,* my research and writing was for me a form of activism that stemmed from a desire to help bring about social change in areas where I had personally observed the need for change. The books and articles that I published during those years focused primarily on the history and literature of minority groups, whether ethnic or sexual. My primary goals were not only to educate the general reader but also to help provide a voice for those who had been voiceless and to record a history for those who had been denied their history.

My mother, Gitta Mara Luft, was the oldest child in a poor family of tailors in Prael (sometimes spelled Preil), a little shtetl in Latvia. She came to America alone, in 1914, when she was eighteen years old and changed her name to Mary Lifton because she thought it sounded more American. My mother knew very little English when she arrived, and she was only semi-literate in the language at her death in 1979, though she did read and write Yiddish. Like many young immigrants of those years, she hoped somehow to earn enough money (or to marry a man who earned enough money) to enable her to bring the rest of the family to America.

As soon as my mother came to this country, she found work as a draper in the garment trade, an industry that was at the time largely unregulated by maximum hour/minimum wage laws and was subject to seasonal layoffs without even the protection of unemployment benefits. With subsistence wages, she could afford to live only in a furnished room and occasionally to send a few dollars back to her family. Finally, in 1923, she did succeed in bringing her sister Rivka to America. My mother did not marry until 1955, when I, her only child, was almost fifteen years old. By then the rest of her family—a brother, two sisters, and the sisters' families—were dead, killed by the Nazis in 1941, along with all of the other Jews of Prael. My mother's survivor guilt and shock brought on mental illness, manifested in her as obsessive-compulsive disorder but diagnosed in those days as "nervousness," which I witnessed throughout my childhood.

I was born in Bronx, New York, on July 18, 1940. For the eight years prior to my birth, my mother had had a relationship with Morris Federman, who did not wish to marry her even after she became pregnant. My mother sued "Moishe," as she called him, for child support when urged to do so by a caseworker, but he denied paternity in court and the judge declared in his favor. Despite his denials, my mother had him listed as my father on my birth certificate and school records.

For my first years my mother and I lived with my aunt, Rivka, whom I called My Rae. Like my mother, My Rae made her living in the garment trade, but she was sometimes able to do piece work at home; thus she could care for me when, after six months of county "relief," as welfare was called at the time, my mother had to take a job in a garment factory again. Both my mother and My Rae spoke to me mostly in Yiddish, and that became my main language. But once I went to nursery school and started speaking English, my tongue seemed to twist and stumble around Yiddish; and though My Rae and my mother continued to speak to me in that language, I answered them always in English. Soon (to my great regret later) I lost my speaking knowledge of Yiddish.

When my mother learned after the War that all the relatives in Latvia had been slaughtered in the Holocaust, her relationship with my aunt became tumultuous, as she blamed her for not having helped enough in her attempts to bring their siblings to America. My Rae left the Bronx under a hail of my mother's curses and imprecations, and she went to California; I went to day care until I entered Public School 62 in 1946. When the registrar asked my mother how to spell my last name, my mother replied, "Just like it sounds—F A. . . ." Thus my name was listed on the school records as "Faderman." That became the name I learned to spell, and I have kept it ever since.

My mother continued her relationship with Moishe as long as we remained in New York. On the one occasion that she took me to see him, she urged me to "say hello to your father." When I greeted him thus he announced to me, "I am not your father." Although I've always believed my mother's version of the story, and

The author's mother (right) and aunt, "My Rae"

the blood tests the court ordered taken showed that he could be my father, there was, of course, no indisputable evidence of paternity in those pre-DNA testing days.

On the Saturdays and Sundays when my mother was not with Moishe, we would often go to the movies together, and I was fascinated by the world that Hollywood opened to me, so different from my immediate surroundings. Through the movies I lost whatever vestiges of a Yiddish accent I had; I learned about lives that I could hardly imagine in the Bronx (and later in East Los Angeles); I formulated notions of the American dream that stuck with me well into adulthood. I longed desperately to become a movie actress, not only because I was enchanted by the glamour of the silver screen, but also because my mother encouraged it, and I came to see it as a means toward a noble mission: Coming home from the sweatshop, exhausted by her grueling labors, she would cry, "Rescue me from the shop, Lily!" And when I asked "How, Mommy, what should I do?" she answered, "Become a movie actress." Those words gave me direction for years: I would become a movie actress and rescue my mother from the shop.

In 1948 my aunt returned to New York in order to urge my mother to move to Los Angeles, where we would all be together again; and to my great joy, my mother acquiesced. To me, the move meant that we would be far away from Moishe, whom I despised now because it seemed to me that my mother's love for him increased her suffering. The move also meant we would be closer to My Rae, whom I loved passionately. And it meant too that I would be near Hollywood, where the movies were made. Through much of our train trip across the country, I did Al Jolson imitations—soft-shoe dancing up and down the aisles, singing "Mammy" and "California, Here I Come,"—longing to be discovered. My mother had told me that sometimes movie producers found their future stars in unexpected places, such as drug store soda fountains. Surely on our train there must be at least one movie producer on his way to Hollywood who was on the lookout for new talent.

We rented a furnished room in East Los Angeles, and my mother and aunt found jobs in garment factories while I went to Evergreen Avenue Elementary School and continued to dream of becoming a movie actress and rescuing my mother from her hard work. When the relationship between my mother and My Rae became stormy again, my aunt left us to marry Emanuel Bergman, a widower in his sixties. He was a gentle and generous man who was loving to me, but I felt the loss of My Rae deeply. I also felt more urgently than ever a need to succeed for the sake of my mother, to fulfill the Hollywood dreams which she shared with me, to make up for all the desertions and terrible losses she'd experienced in her life. I think my dreams centered on Hollywood because, like many children of poor immigrants at that time, movie stardom was the only example of significant success I'd had the opportunity to observe in my environment. How else did one escape from poverty? How else did one make a better life? There were certainly no doctors or lawyers or professors or even secretaries or bookkeepers in my ken that might inspire me to more realistic ambitions; nor did life in a furnished room permit me to distinguish between middle class comfort and fantastic wealth: There were rich people and poor people, and my mother and I were poor people.

Thus when a school of music and dramatic arts opened in East Los Angeles in 1952, I was delirious with excitement. I was able to convince the woman who directed the school to let me work in the office on weekends, answering the phone and writing receipts, in order to pay for all my lessons. Her husband, the acting coach, wrote dramatic monologues for me, generally about waifs, such as refugee children who had been separated from their mothers in concentration camps and were reunited in the course of the scene. With my mother's tragic tales of lost relatives in my head and my own worries about her, I had no trouble imagining the requisite emotions of displaced and anxious waifs, so I became the star of the children's acting classes. And when the director of the school signed me to an exclusive management contract after a year, it seemed that at last I was on my way to realizing my Hollywood dreams. Soon I was the mistress of ceremonies and a monologist in a children's amateur entertaining troupe she directed, and I traveled with the group to do shows almost weekly—to old age homes, children's hospitals, Hadassah groups, supermarket openings.

Though my Hollywood dreams never were realized, my childhood experiences as a would-be actress were invaluable because I learned fine work habits that stood me in good stead for the rest of my life—how to focus all my concentration on a piece; how to keep doing it over and over, sparing no efforts, until I got it right. I wonder now if my work-intensive research books would have been possible if I hadn't learned to labor so devotedly on my monologues as a twelve year old.

I also learned other things of value during the three years I took lessons at the East Los Angeles music and drama school. I found the school's director as beautiful, as cultured and sophisticated, as the actresses I admired most in the movies. She was my first flesh-and-blood role model, and I strove to imitate her walk, her gestures, her well-modulated voice. I formed my liberal political ideas out of hers. I was convinced of the importance of reading because she valued books.

The director became my first crush. My infatuation with her was an experience replete with all the intense joys and fears that adolescent crushes generally bring

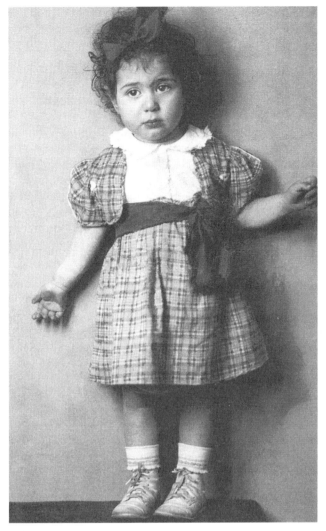

Lillian at age two

to introspective kids. Puzzled about the meaning of such powerful feelings for a woman, I haunted the neighborhood library, trying to find an explanation in books for those emotions that ostensibly no one else in the world had experienced; and I was temporarily relieved when I finally found a couple of volumes that assured me that adolescent crushes were "normal."

*

In the 1930s and 1940s East Los Angeles had been primarily a lower-middle-class, Jewish community, but by the 1950s, when I entered Hollenbeck Junior High School, most of the Jewish families, who were often second- or third-generation Americans, had bettered their economic status sufficiently to be able to move to the more affluent neighborhoods of the West side. Most

of the students at Hollenbeck when I attended the school were from economically disadvantaged Mexican or Japanese families. I became aware of ethnicities and cultures other than my own and of the multiple manifestations and effects of class in America. I felt alienated, too, aware that despite the poverty and minority status we shared, I was different from the other students—my fatherless state, my mother's terrible obsessive-compulsive episodes, the shabby furnished room in which we lived, my Jewishness, my crush on a woman that I could tell no one about. Reading and my work with the children's amateur entertaining troupe and junior high school drama competitions became my only escape from feelings of alienation.

In 1955 my mother, now fifty-eight years old, married a man several years her junior, Albert Gordin, who worked in a janitorial capacity in a hospital pathology laboratory. The marriage was not a love match, but rather one of mutual convenience, as was probably common among middle-aged immigrants in those years. Finally, she was able to leave her sweat-shop labors. I was relieved that my mother could quit the work she had always complained of so bitterly, though I was also sad that it had not been my success that made her escape possible, and I was shocked to have a stranger in our lives. For the next years, until I became an adult and grew to love Albert as a simple, decent man, I distanced myself not only from him as an uncomfortable, unaccustomed presence, but also from her.

Several months after the marriage I graduated from Hollenbeck Junior High School. Though I no longer had to worry about success for the sake of my mother, striving had become a habit of mind for me, and I now wished success for my own sake. My crush on the director of the East Los Angeles school of music and drama had not abated in the least, but I understood by now that I would need to attend a more professional acting school if I wanted to further my career. I enrolled in Geller Theater and School of Dramatic Arts in West Los Angeles. I was not yet fifteen years old, but I presented myself as eighteen in order to get an evening job in the theater office to pay for my lessons. My mother convinced Albert that we must move from East Los Angeles so I would not have to make a nightly across-town bus trip, and we rented an apartment in the Beverly-Fairfax area of Los Angeles, where the Jewish population had migrated years earlier.

I continued at Geller's in the evenings and on weekends even after I started Fairfax High School in the fall of 1955. Because the Geller acting classes and rehearsals kept me up late, I stayed home from high school frequently, and when I did attend I sat in the back row of my classes and read plays or memorized lines. I was visited a few times by a truant officer, who probably didn't pursue me more seriously because I was earning Ds and Fs in my classes and wasting the taxpayers' money when I did go to school. My mother, who had no formal education herself, was passive about my hooky playing—or perhaps she simply realized that she had no control over me. In any case, I continued to skip classes throughout my freshman year. Though I'd been a good student in junior high school I was untroubled by my failing grades now because I intended to quit school at age sixteen and work on my acting career full time.

What did trouble me was the realization that my face looked very little like the even-featured faces of the popular actresses of the 1950s, and I was convinced that plastic surgery on my nose would improve my chances for success. Unbeknownst to my mother or any of my associates, I worked as a pin-up and figure model in order to earn money for the surgery I had the summer I turned sixteen. But not even plastic surgery led to Hollywood offers.

That same summer I encountered again an acquaintance from East Los Angeles with whom I'd worked in the children's entertaining troupe. Now he told me he was gay, and, providing me with a fake ID, he introduced me to the Los Angeles gay bar scene. My visit to the Open Door, a lesbian bar, brought me a virtual epiphany, clarifying the probable meaning of my long crush, showing me the possibility of a sexual identity with which I felt comfortable. Because I was a literary young person, I again went to the library and sought information in books about what it means if a woman is attracted to other women. But the only books I could find on the topic were depressing and frightening. There were serious tomes by medical doctors and sexologists that depicted love between women as pathology; and there were novels, mostly of the pulp-fiction variety, in which lesbians generally met with horrifying fates—committing suicide, going crazy, drowning in wells of loneliness. Almost all the books about same-sex love were terrifying by design: they would probably not have escaped the censors of the era had they not had "redeeming social content,"

which meant that the lesbians had to end badly in order to affirm society's "moral standards."

I found the outlaw butch/femme life of the 1950s bar culture to be depressing and frightening as well. The vice squad often raided homosexual bars, and the patrons were carted off in Black Mariahs, their names published in the newspapers for the world to see. Just going to and from a lesbian bar was dangerous: the women were frequently harassed by toughs and even ran the risk of being beaten up. My lesbian relationship with Jan, whom I met at the Open Door, seemed to me even seamier than the terrible pulp novels I'd read: she proposed that I go off with her to New Orleans and support us by prostitution. When I left Jan at the end of that summer I was in despair and confusion and felt utterly without direction. What would I do with the rest of my life? Though I was only sixteen, my mother and Albert had no control over me. The law couldn't keep me in school any longer. But if I couldn't be an actress and wouldn't run off to New Orleans with Jan, what could I be? Where should I go?

Shortly before the school year started, I was fortunate to meet a social worker, Maury Colwell, who convinced me that I must not drop out of school—that if I thought I was a lesbian and would not be marrying, it was especially important to graduate from high school, go to college, and get a good job that would enable me to support myself. When Albert announced that we were moving to another area, I was happy because that meant I might go to a new school and start all over. That fall I became a student at Hollywood High School, where I was active in drama and speech, won several state speech tournaments, and with Maury Colwell's skillful urging, took my studies seriously enough to replace all my former Ds and Fs with As and a few Bs.

Though I stayed away from the Open Door, I continued to have gay friends, and through one of them I met a bisexual man, Mark Letson, seventeen years my senior, with whom I formed a friendship. Mark was a psychologist. I was awed by his learning and culture, and delighted that he was willing to teach me—about literature, music, politics, foreign travel. Several months before my high school graduation, I married him in what began as a "front" marriage that would enable him to pass as heterosexual in his office and would enable me to leave home. Soon, however, our relationship became intimate; and after graduation I went with him to Mexico, where he had been offered a visiting professorship in psychology. At the end of that summer, though, realizing that I could not be a wife any more than Mark could be a husband, I left him in Mexico and returned to Los Angeles. I had already been accepted at the University of California, Los Angeles, and now I remembered Maury Colwell's good advice: I needed to continue my education since I did not want to be married and would have to support myself. I would go to college.

I'd been given a small scholarship to cover books and tuition at UCLA, but I had no money for other expenses. If I went back to work for a few hours a week as a pinup and figure model, I decided, I could still have ample time to take classes and to study. I returned to the modeling agency where I'd worked a few years earlier, and now I did photo shoots on the weekends. Under the name "Gigi Frost" I appeared often in 1959 and 1960 pinup magazines, though no one during the course of my college career ever made the connection between Gigi and Lillian. The energy and focus I'd once poured into play acting I transferred now to studying for my UCLA classes.

At the end of my freshman year, in the summer of 1959, I met a woman from San Francisco who asked me to come live with her. Believing myself in love, I went with her to San Francisco and enrolled at University of California at Berkeley. Her father had supported her all her life because she was ill and could not work, but shortly after I met her, he died. I would have to find a job in the Bay Area in which I could make enough money for two and still would have sufficient time to take classes and study. For a while I had a minimum-wage job filing books in a library, but working twenty hours a week, I could not make enough money to pay our rent. I needed to stay in school and do well, and I needed to support myself and my partner. How could I do both? I found a weekend job as a waitress and the "Bubble Bath Girl" at Big Al's Hotsy Totsy Club in San Francisco. Then, a few months later, I took a better-paying job as an exotic dancer at the President Follies, one of the few remaining burlesque houses in America. That job would allow me to sit in the dressing room and study in between my brief stage appearances. It was the early 1960s. If my employment had been discovered by the dean of women at Berkeley, undoubtedly I would have been asked to leave school, but it was not discovered. I made the Dean's List almost every semester.

Though I began at Berkeley as a psychology major, still fascinated with the career I'd seen up close through Mark, I found that the courses that interested me the most were in the humanities. In my junior year I changed my major to English. I was especially excited by literature of social protest and writers that used fiction and poetry to bring about social change. I was very aware of the burgeoning student movements at Berkeley, but because I had to leave campus immediately after class each day to get to work, I could not participate. Yet I was passionately interested in social change, since the status quo seemed so unfavorable to the worlds I'd experienced—to people who were ethnically and sexually different from the main mass of Americans. I kept hoping that writers I read in my classes might sometimes reflect those differences, but in the early sixties, when the literary canon was still very narrowly defined, those hopes were seldom realized. I received a B.A. in June 1962 and entered UCLA as a graduate student in English that fall, wanting still to discover authors who had not been represented in my undergraduate classes at Berkeley and who wrote about diversity.

The course of study at UCLA in the early 1960s included perhaps six or seven women writers—Jane Austen, Charlotte and Emily Brontë, George Eliot, Emily Dickinson, Virginia Woolf, sometimes Willa Cather—and several hundred men writers. Richard Wright, James Baldwin, and Ralph Ellison were the only writers of color mentioned in classes—and were not necessarily read. The biographical details professors sometimes included in their lectures presented all writers as being either heterosexual or asexual. Any suggestion of homosexuality in a literary text was either glossed over in lectures or interpreted to mean something quite different. I realized quickly that if I wanted to read more women writers or writers who dealt with ethnic and racial experiences different from the mainstream of America, or if I wanted to know more about homosexual writers or the treatment of homosexuality in literature, I would have to make discoveries on my own. The proliferating movements for the rights of underrepresented groups—blacks, women, Chicanos—made me even more determined to discover such voices in literature, which continued to be ignored in English graduate studies.

At my advisor's urging, however, I put aside my interest in minority voices in literature and wrote my dissertation on a minor Victorian author whose complete

The author as a UCLA graduate, 1967

(voluminous) works had recently been acquired by the UCLA library. But while I was writing my dissertation on B. L. Farjeon, I met a high school teacher, Barbara Bradshaw, who shared my passion for underrepresented literary voices. We began gathering material for a book we would call *Speaking for Ourselves: American Ethnic Writing*. In addition to literature by writers from underrepresented European-American groups (e.g., Poles) and black writers who were just beginning to be included in school curricula, we wanted to find good fiction, poetry, and drama by Hispanic Americans, Asian Americans, and American Indians (as Native Americans were still called). Such material was not easy to find in the mid-1960s, but we felt sure there must be strong, though neglected, literary voices among writers of those groups. We did massive research in literary journals of other eras; we put out a call for writing that reflected American diversity. And finally we did get a mass of good material that enabled us to put together a proposal for a unique college textbook of multiethnic literature. Just as I was finishing my dissertation, in spring 1967, Barbara and I received a contract from Scott, Foresman to publish the book.

Though the preponderance of graduate students in English at UCLA was female during the years I was a student, there were only two women on the English faculty. The women students in the department were not ostensibly discriminated against; I, along with most of them, had a four-year teaching assistantship at UCLA and the same perks and training that were given to the male students. But upon graduation there was a significant difference between the employment offered to men and women. UCLA male graduates went on to teach at major universities. Woman graduates were seldom hired by research universities, and most of them took part-time teaching jobs, taught at junior colleges, or were offered lecturer positions with no hope of tenure. I felt lucky to get a tenure-track position at Fresno State College, which later became California State University, Fresno.

*

When I arrived on the Fresno campus in fall, 1967 there were a number of women teaching in areas such as nursing, home economics, and women's physical education, but I was the only woman on the English faculty, and one of the few women in an academic department. In addition to teaching the Victorian literature survey and composition courses during my first year, I also taught a seminar in multi-ethnic literature, in which I used the materials Barbara and I discovered. Though the student body was almost entirely white in 1967, the students in my seminar seemed as passionately interested as I in the literature that permitted them intimate glimpses of the experiences behind the proliferating movements of identity politics in the 1960s. Their interest was an inspiration for me to continue my work on *Speaking for Ourselves*. Barbara had taken a leave from her high school teaching job and had come with me to Fresno, where we finished the book in 1968. It was published the following year.

A few months later, in June 1969, I read about gay protests over a police raid in a bar in New York called The Stonewall, but, remembering all too well the repeated police raids of the gay bars in the fifties, the fearful secrecy we felt compelled to maintain about our personal lives, and the internalized homophobia that many of us harbored, I could not imagine that those protests might really be the start of a gay revolution. I did, however, become increasingly caught up in the feminist movement around that time, and was determined to help alter the literary canon by bringing women writers into my classes. In 1970 I offered a course that brought together literature and the women's movement that I called Women's Liberation in Literature, and the following semester I presented the class as a fifteen-week television series on a local TV station. In fall 1971, together with Phyllis Irwin, a music professor who had just been named assistant academic vice president at the college, I proposed and helped found the women's studies program, one of the first such programs in the country.

The nationwide agitation for women's equality had already had some effect on my campus, and more women were being hired in academic departments. I was elected chair of the English department in spring 1971, a position I held for only one year because, when the dean of the school of humanities resigned, I was named acting dean—the first woman academic dean on campus. The following year I was made an assistant academic vice president, in charge of innovative programs and the Experimental College, where, in addition to administering other new courses and methods of instruction, I arranged to have several gay studies courses offered in 1973-74. These too were some of the first such courses in America.

My interest in ethnic studies continued during this time, and in 1971 I began working with Chicano poet Luis Omar Salinas on an anthology of Chicano writers that we titled *From the Barrio.* At the time we signed the contract there had been no literary collection devoted to the fiction and poetry of Mexican Americans, which Omar and I knew to be worthy of a readership from the unpublished material we'd been gathering. Our book was published by Harper and Row in 1973. Barbara Bradshaw had gone back to Los Angeles, but she and I also continued working on a second edition of *Speaking for Ourselves,* which Scott, Foresman brought out in 1975.

Phyllis Irwin and I had by then become domestic partners, as we are to this day. When I told her before we lived together of my growing desire to have a child, she encouraged me. I'd wanted a baby primarily because I knew I had the capacity to love a child and to raise it well. But I'd wanted a child too to help make up for all of my mother's family that was killed in the Holocaust. My Rae had no children, I was my mother's only child, and no one else from the family had survived. If I did not have a child I would be the

end of their line; and because I loved my mother and aunt so deeply I could not bear to see that happen. But it had seemed to me that it would be extremely difficult to raise a child as a single parent with professional responsibilities. Phyllis assured me that I would not be a single parent, that she would be the child's mother too, and she has kept her word.

I conceived our son, Avrom Irwin Faderman, through donor insemination when I was thirty-three years old. He was born on January 27, 1975. His relationship with my mother until her death in 1979 and with My Rae until her death in 1984 was a great joy to all of us. Avrom received his Ph.D. in philosophy from Stanford University in 1998, at the age of twenty-three. He was engaged to be married in 2004.

After the birth of our son, I decided that, rather than continue a career in academic administration, I would prefer to go back to the classroom, not only because teaching would permit me to spend more hours at home with Avrom and because I missed my students, but also because I wanted to do serious scholarship in the area of lesbian studies. Though I'd never done such scholarship, I knew from having worked on my dissertation that I enjoyed research, and I hoped that my experience in bringing the two ethnic studies books to publication was evidence that I could design and execute a large project. I was intrigued with the theories of lesbian-feminism that were current in the early and mid-1970s, and I wanted to explore whether it was possible to analyze female same-sex relationships of earlier eras through the lens of those theories that rejected essentialist explanations of homosexuality in favor of existential and political explanations.

The deeper I got in my research, the more I felt that I wanted to help create a recorded lesbian history, such as had not yet been created and whose lack I had felt so sorely during that difficult period of my youth, when I came out into lesbian culture. It seemed to me that lesbian and gay people had been denied knowledge of their historical past; that such knowledge was vital in helping to define and legitimize a minority; and that without such knowledge those who are different are isolated and alienated, and their victimization (such as I had witnessed in the 1950s) is more easily effected. With Phyllis's encouragement, I got to work on my research in lesbian history early in 1975.

Between 1977-79 I published eight articles, most of them in refereed scholarly journals, on subjects such as the nineteenth-century sexologists' pathologizing of love between women which had earlier been seen as romantic friendship, twentieth-century censorship of lesbian history, and the encoding of lesbian subject matter by early twentieth-century writers. With the help of a German translator, Brigitte Eriksson, I also edited a collection of essays, poetry, and fiction, *Lesbian Feminism in Turn-of-the-Century Germany,* which was published in 1980 by Naiad Press. Most of the pieces selected for the collection were written during a relatively liberal era, in late-nineteenth and early-twentieth-century Germany, when both feminists and lesbians felt free to articulate their positions and to argue for their rights. Many of those authors suggested that lesbians were protofeminists or that the feminist critique of society was often identical to the lesbian critique. I wanted to show through these selections the large extent to which the ideas of lesbian-feminism had clear historical roots.

The research I did during the mid- and late-1970s was incorporated finally into my book, *Surpassing the Love of Men: Romantic Friendship and Love between Women from the Renaissance to the Present,* which was published by William Morrow in 1981. I considered a variety of sources from America, England, France, and Germany—trial records, love letters, pornography, canonized fiction and poetry, popular magazine literature, proclamations by the medical establishment—in order to trace the patterns and changing status of female same-sex love relationships over five centuries. I wanted to show the ways in which romantic friendship between women had been widely idealized in earlier eras, and also to make the point that if neither woman in a relationship was found to use "illicit inventions . . . to supplement the shortcomings of her sex," as Montaigne wrote in 1580, female same-sex intimacy was seldom punished as it had been in the twentieth century, when homophobia reached a height. Perhaps passion between women was not taken seriously in earlier era because it was assumed before the successes of the first wave of feminism (which gave women access to education and decent paying jobs) that a woman would have to marry regardless of her feelings for another woman, for economic reasons if for no other. Thus love between women was thought by many to be, as Henry Wadsworth Longfellow characterized it in his 1849 novel *Kavanagh,* "a rehearsal in girlhood of the great drama of woman's life." Female same-sex love came to be socially threatening in Europe and America, I found, when middle-class women started claiming those freedoms that had been reserved for men and, simulta-

neously, sexologists such as Richard von Krafft-Ebing and Havelock Ellis pathologized what had earlier been idealized or trivialized as "romantic friendship."

I was truly astonished when *Surpassing the Love of Men* was widely reviewed in the mainstream press, because I remembered so well those days of the 1950s when homosexuality was considered "the love that dared not speak its name" (and if its name sometimes was uttered in the mainstream press it was only to connect it to sickness or evil). But now, in 1981, the *Washington Post Book World* said that the book was "an important achievement in the process of demystifying social institution" (May 3, 1981). *The New York Review of Books* dubbed it "one of the most significant contributions yet made to feminist literature" (May 28, 1981). Caroline Heilbrun, writing for the *New York Times,* said that *Surpassing the Love of Men* was "a welcome and needed history" (April 5, 1981), and Benjamin DeMott, writing for the *Atlantic,* called *Surpassing the Love of Men* "instructive and humane . . . a work of genuine interest and value . . . a powerful summons to conscience" (March, 1981).

I must admit to some nervousness when the chair of my department circulated the *Atlantic* review on campus. Though Phyllis and I had never gone out of our way to hide our lesbian identities from our colleagues and students, over the last years I had heard about several women professors around the country who believed they were denied tenure because their scholarship was about lesbians. I'd been tenured in 1971 and made a full professor in 1974, but, still, I couldn't help feeling some vague twinges of trepidation now. How would people in Fresno, an agricultural community hundreds of miles away from an urban center, react to my having received national attention for writing a lesbian book?

My department threw a big party for me, and when I was named the Outstanding Professor by an all-university committee the following year, the mayor of Fresno officially proclaimed May 1, 1982 "Lillian Faderman Day." Clearly at least some of America had come a long way since I first set foot in the Open Door twenty-five years earlier.

During my research for *Surpassing the Love of Men* I discovered that Lillian Hellman had based her play, *The Children's Hour,* on a brief account that she'd read of a Scottish trial, which had appeared in *Bad Companions,* a book by Scottish law historian William Roughead. I'd been familiar with *The Children's Hour* since I played the evil girl, Mary, in an acting class when I was twelve years old; and as a young adult I was very disturbed by the play and the movie based on it, in which one of the main characters commits suicide after recognizing that she is a lesbian. Roughead's account intrigued me in the ways it differed from Hellman's play. The incidents that led to the trial actually occurred in Edinburgh in the early 1800s rather than in a little town in America in the 1930s, where Hellman sets her scene; but the most interesting differences were that in Roughead's account the two women who were accused of having a lesbian relationship won their lawsuit when they sued their accuser for libel, and Roughead mentions nothing about suicide.

I decided to analyze the trial transcripts and to try to find all the additional information I could about the principals involved because it seemed to me that this case had real bearing on my theories about the social views concerning love between women in other eras. How did the judges treat the accusation that Jane Pirie and Marianne Woods had a sexual relationship of which the students in the girls' school they ran were aware? How was such an accusation articulated in 1811? What evidence could I find about how the two women regarded their relationship? What would the materials reveal about the various social and sexual pressures that shaped early nineteenth-century women's lives?

Phyllis and I and our seven-year-old son headed to Edinburgh the next summer, and there I set to work—in the National Library of Scotland, the Central Library of Edinburgh, the Signet Library of the Parliament House of Scotland, the Scottish Registry Office, the Georgian House of Edinburgh, and the House of Lords Record Office—trying to recreate the events and the atmosphere of the time, as well as the characters of the women, their accusers and defenders, and the judges. When a friend volunteered to entertain Avrom from time to time, Phyllis worked by my side. Our joint efforts on the research inspired the form that *Scotch Verdict* eventually took: I present an unnamed twentieth-century American narrator and "Ollie," her partner (loosely based on myself and Phyllis), who go to Edinburgh in order to study the nineteenth-century trial and the lives of those who were its principals. I

reveal not only what happened in the case, but also the various possible meanings of what happened, by having the narrator and Ollie analyze the events and the individuals involved and argue over interpretations. The narrator and Ollie are presented as a literary device also to make a historical point that seemed to me worth articulating: They are to some extent twentieth-century versions of Marianne Woods and Jane Pirie—middle-class women, teachers, partners, in love with one another; but the differing eras in which the two couples lived, I wanted to show, made all the difference in their self-conception and how they were perceived by others.

*

In 1989 I was invited to become a visiting professor of English at UCLA and teach courses in gay and lesbian literature. Phyllis encouraged me to take this position at the university where I began as a freshman and then returned as a graduate student. Avrom was fourteen years old now. He had completed a high school equivalency exam at the age of twelve and had spent the last two years as a student at California State University in Fresno. Now he came with me and enrolled at UCLA. I was happy when my visiting professorship was renewed for a second year and I did not have to leave him, now only fifteen years old, alone at UCLA. Phyllis, who had become chair of the music department at CSUF, spent almost every weekend with us in Los Angeles during those two years.

The changes with regard to the treatment of lesbians and gays that I now saw at UCLA were as astonishing to me as my mainstream press reviews had been. I could not forget that when I first entered UCLA all freshmen had to take a battery of psychological tests that were intended, among other things, to identify "sexually deviant" students, and as UCLA's dean of students Milton Hahn and assistant dean Byron Atkinson wrote in the journal *School and Society* in 1955, to rout them out of college if they were unwilling to undergo psychiatric treatment to change their sexual orientation. Now, thanks to social progress, I was returning to UCLA to teach both homosexual and heterosexual students about what could not even be uttered aloud a few decades earlier.

I had begun researching a book on lesbian life in twentieth-century America shortly after the publication of *Scotch Verdict.* During my first year as a visiting professor at UCLA I used material that I had gathered for the book in my classes and I also finished the writing. *Odd Girls and Twilight Lovers* was published by Columbia University Press at the end of my second year, in 1991. I wanted this book to be a comprehensive history of the various evolutions of lesbian subcultures and identities in America, and to that end I examined sources that covered the century, including popular magazines and newspapers, unpublished manuscripts, song lyrics, medical and legal literature, fiction and poetry. I also wanted to bring living voices into the book, and so I interviewed close to two hundred self-identified lesbians between the ages of seventeen and eighty-six. I made sure to speak not only to white women, but also to those who were of Asian, African-American, Latina, and Native-American descent. I sought class diversity among my narrators, who included a woman who milked cows for a living in central California, another who was the primary heir of her grandfather, one of the richest oilmen in Texas, and those who in terms of socio-economics fell everywhere in between these extremes. I interviewed women in big cities as well as small towns, in New York, Massachusetts, Pennsylvania, Nebraska, Missouri, Texas, and California.

Odd Girls and Twilight Lovers is, to some extent, a sequel to *Surpassing the Love of Men.* In the 1991 book I show how once the nineteenth-century sexologists promulgated the concept that women who love other women are different from the rest of womankind—are "lesbians" (or "sexual inverts," as the sexologists sometimes called them)—then women who accepted the label went about creating cultural identities and ideologies. Widespread, diverse lesbian cultures could emerge in the twentieth century for a number of reasons, including the proliferation of jobs for women that allowed them economic independence; the sexual freedom of the 1920s and the 1960s; the social freedom that was a byproduct of World War II, as well as the increase in urbanization that provided a critical mass which made creation of lesbian social communities possible; the civil rights movement; the women's movement; and the radical women's movement.

As I wrote this book, I looked back over my personal experiences and was impressed by how the lesbian communities I had known over a period of thirty-plus years had shape-shifted and metamorphosed. What my research and interviews corroborated for me once

again was that self-conception is very dependent on what is going on in the rest of the society. I found, for instance, that lesbians such as those who had frequented the Open Door in the restrictive 1950s, and who had lived in fear and secrecy and saw themselves as outlaws because that's how they were defined by the world outside, had virtually disappeared in the more open society of the late 1980s. Similarly, the separatist lesbian-feminists of the 1970s, who were influenced by the radical women's movement and black separatism, had also virtually disappeared in the calmer, cooler decade. The only constant with regard to "the lesbian," I found, is that affectionally and/or erotically, she prefers women.

Odd Girls and Twilight Lovers received major attention from the mainstream press as well as from the lesbian and gay press. The *Washington Post Book World* praised it for having "the depth and evenhandedness of a scholarly classic" (June 23, 1991). The *San Francisco Chronicle* called it "an important and challenging work for lesbians and heterosexuals alike" (May 30, 1991). It was named one of the *New York Times* Notable Books of the year, and was given several awards, including the Lambda Literary Award and an American Library Association award. It had broad distribution when it was issued in paperback in 1992 by Viking-Penguin.

After my stint at UCLA, I returned to California State University, Fresno to resume my position as professor of English. Avrom, who was now sixteen and had taken a double major in math and philosophy, stayed on at UCLA to finish the work for his bachelor's degree. In addition to my teaching, I had an active lecturing career at universities across the country. I also accepted an appointment as co-editor, along with Larry Gross, of a Columbia University Press series, "Between Men/Between Women," which had published the hardcover edition of *Odd Girls and Twilight Lovers.* The series is devoted to books of serious scholarship dealing with gay and lesbian subjects in the social sciences and humanities. Through the series, Columbia University Press hoped to contribute to an increased understanding of lesbians and gay men and to provide through that understanding a wider comprehension of culture in general. The "Between Men/ Between Women" series was unique when it was established, since most academic presses were still refusing to accept gay and lesbian studies as a serious area of inquiry. Soon, however, several university presses established similar gay/lesbian book series. By the beginning of the twentieth-first century, such special series were less necessary than they had been in the early 1990s because lesbian/gay subject matter was now widely recognized as a legitimate focus for academic study. I believe that the series' considerable successes, as well as the changing times, contributed to the legitimization and proliferation of lesbian/gay scholarship.

My teaching of lesbian and gay studies at UCLA and my editorship of the "Between Men/Between Women" series made me aware of the kind of scholarship that still needed to be done in the area. Though many wonderful texts were already available, I felt that a well-designed anthology of lesbian literature that placed the works in a clear historical context would be a vital addition to the field. Thus, soon after *Odd Girls and Twilight Lovers* was published, I began collecting work from the seventeenth century to the 1990s that I could include in such a volume, which I would call *Chloe plus Olivia,* a title that refers to Virginia Woolf's *A Room of One's Own:* "Chloe liked Olivia," Woolf says, and then admonishes the reader, "Do not start. Do not blush. Let us admit in the privacy of our own society that these things sometimes happen. Sometimes women do like women." In *Chloe plus Olivia* I wanted to present lesser-known writers that might be unfamiliar to the reader and also writers whose literary importance had been widely acknowledged but who had seldom been read in a lesbian context. Therefore, I included work by poets and fiction writers such as Emily Dickinson, Christina Rossetti, Sarah Orne Jewett, Willa Cather, Amy Lowell, Katherine Mansfield, Virginia Woolf, and Carson McCullers.

In the introduction to *Chloe plus Olivia,* which was published in 1994, I examine the various attempts to define lesbian literature, and I postulate that none of the existing definitions were complete: *some* works (though certainly not all) showed the lesbian as an outsider; *some* depicted her as challenging gender roles; *some* lesbian literature followed the mother-daughter model or the Amazonian model; *some* depicted either a narrative of damnation or a narrative of enabling escape. But not one of those definitions could incorporate the diversity of lesbian literature. I attempt to categorize that diversity and then to select the very best examples of the various categories, including the literature of romantic friendship, sexual inversion, lesbian exoticism, encoded lesbian literature,

the literature of lesbian-feminism, and recent experimentations in lesbian writing. I was fortunate to be able to test the materials and theories I eventually incorporated into the book on my own classes in lesbian/gay literature that I now taught at California State University, Fresno.

*

In 1996 I was asked to write a regular column for the *Advocate,* the nation's largest gay/lesbian magazine, which combines national news pertinent to gays and lesbians with articles on gay/lesbian culture and opinion pieces. I accepted because I thought it would be an interesting challenge to write for the popular press. My columns were on topics such as the relationship between gays and lesbians or lesbian parenting or my observations of the lesbian/gay scene in St. Petersburg, Russia, where Phyllis, Avrom, and I had visited on our way to discover what I could about my mother's shtetl in Latvia. I continued the column, called "The Last Word," for over a year with some pleasure, though I found that it was not easy to write in the requisite breezy style and to put aside a more serious voice, in which I was continuing to write for academic periodicals such as the *Journal of the History of Sexuality,* essay collections such as *Professions of Desire,* published by the Modern Language Association, and a new book of lesbian history on which I had started working the previous year.

Late in 1996 I paused in my work on the lesbian history book because I found myself very involved in a different kind of project, one that would take me back to the area of ethnic studies, in which I had not published for many years. I undertook this new work for the same reason I undertook any of my projects: I felt strongly urged to do so because of personal experiences and personal observations. When I began teaching in Fresno, in 1967, almost all of my students were white and middle class, but by the 1970s, the college student population was changing all over the country. Because of various social movements, higher education came to be seen as the virtual right of all who were smart enough to complete a college curriculum, regardless of their race or the class into which they born. These changes were reflected especially in the state university system, which was more affordable than private colleges. Soon, I had many students who were the first in their families to go to college. Many of them came from homes in which little English was spoken. I felt a particular bond with these students, whose struggles and problems of adjustment to a culture so different from their parent culture made me recall some of my own battles in youth.

I was especially moved by a new population of students that came to my campus in the early 1990s: Hmong people, refugees from Laos who had to leave Southeast Asia because their parents had assisted America in the "secret war" we conducted in Laos during the Vietnam conflict. Almost all of my Hmong students had come to America as children in the 1980s and learned English as a second language in American schools. Their writing was often grammatically imperfect, but I found myself deeply moved by many of their essays. They wrote about the horrors of losing family members through the violence of the war, their difficult escapes from their little Laotian villages, their hard lives in Thai relocation camps as they waited for their families to get refugee status that would allow them into the United States. They wrote about their parents' difficulties moving from a society without plumbing and electricity into a confusingly technological world, their own sadness that they were forgetting their mother-tongue as they were learning English, their painful intergenerational conflicts due to becoming Hmong-American or even American while their parents remained Hmong. I imagine I was so stirred by their stories not only because they were moving in themselves but also because they reminded me of my mother's story and my own.

In one of my composition classes I had a student in his early twenties, Ghia Xiong, who had come to America at the age of ten. He was bright, articulate, well-respected among the other Hmong students, and seemed to be a natural leader. His essays about his life in Laos and Thailand were vivid and remarkable. I was right in thinking he would be an ideal assistant in a project of research and writing about the Hmong. Ghia introduced me to over fifty people in the Hmong community and helped me gather their oral histories. I sought people with diverse backgrounds—those who had grown up in Laos and fought in the war, those who escaped when they were young, those who were born in America and were fully Americanized. Through their narratives I wanted to tell the story of their group's experiences, which were different from and yet similar to those of many of the immigrants that came to America before them. In the introductions I wrote to the various sections of the book, I compared

the Hmong's story—coming to America from little villages in Southeast Asia, to my mother's story—coming from an Eastern European shtetl (strong in traditions but technologically undeveloped, as the Hmong villages had been), and I showed the similarities in their experiences of culture shock. I also made comparisons between my life as the child of an immigrant to the lives of the younger people who told me their stories. This book was published by Beacon Press in 1998 as *"I Begin My Life All Over": The Hmong and the American Immigrant Experience.*

After I finished *I Begin My Life All Over* I was anxious to return to the lesbian history project, on which I'd gotten a good start earlier and that I now called *To Believe in Women.* It was important to finish it, I believed, because it could be precisely the kind of book that would have made a huge difference to me when I first assumed a lesbian identity and perhaps it would make a huge difference to young people now. *To Believe in Women* is a historical study, but it was inspired by the insights I'd garnered from sharing my life with another woman for the preceding twenty-five years as we both worked in professional-level careers. My focus was on women of the late nineteenth and early twentieth centuries who were social pioneers and also shared their lives with a same-sex partner. In many instances both of the women in the relationship had been at the forefront of the battles that helped secure the privileges and rights that Americans enjoy today. I recognized that these women couples of earlier eras were different from myself and Phyllis because of their times: for instance, most of them probably did not even know the then-seldom-used word "lesbian," and if they did, they certainly would not have applied that term, which had such negative connotations at the time, to themselves. Nevertheless, in some important ways they were similar to us: They lived together in long-term, intimate relationships; they conducted careers that required great commitment; their domestic arrangements—their encouragement of one another, the balance and stability they created as a dyad— helped to make their pioneering professional lives possible. I was interested in showing in this book, as the various section titles indicated, "How American Women Got Enfranchised," "How America Got a Social Conscience," "How American Women Got Educated," and "How American Women Got Into the Professions." The book's title, *To Believe in Women,* came from an early twentieth-century letter by a former student at Bryn Mawr, then a women's college, to M. Carey Thomas, the pioneering president of the college, who had lived her entire adult life in intimate same-sex domestic arrangements. "I have forgotten everything I learned at Bryn Mawr," the woman wrote, "but I still see you standing in chapel and telling us to believe in women." Phyllis traveled with me to archives all over the country, assisting me in my research, encouraging me in word and deed toward the completion of the book, which was published in 1999 by Houghton Mifflin.

To Believe in Women was, I think, my major research effort and felt to me like the culmination of all my work in lesbian history. I received for it my third Lambda Literary Award, and I believe that book was partly responsible for other awards I received about that time, including the Monette/Horwitz award (1999), funded by the estate of Paul Monette and his partner, and Yale University's James Brudner Award (2001), both lifetime achievement awards in lesbian/gay studies, as well as the American Association of University Women's national award as Distinguished Senior Scholar (2002). I felt very gratified that others had found meaning in what to me had been a labor of love. I was especially flattered when the *Lambda Book Report* named my 1981 book, *Surpassing the Love of Men,* among the 100 best lesbian/gay books of the twentieth century, putting my work beside writers who had been so crucial to me all my adult life, such as James Baldwin and Virginia Woolf.

My writing about lesbian literature and history has come always out of my commitment to telling the stories that could not have been told when I entered the lesbian culture. I have written the kinds of books that I myself had longed to read. I believe I'm not unique among writers in that the passion I had for writing all my books—lesbian history as well as ethnic studies—is rooted in my deepest experiences and needs. But as a writer associated with the academy, I have had to look primarily outward rather than inward in my writing. Perhaps it was turning sixty that made me decide to move on to a different kind of work that would permit me to look inward. I became fascinated by the genre of creative nonfiction, which is so different from most of the academic writing in which I'd been engaged, and soon I was teaching creative nonfiction courses in my university's M.F.A. program and writing the memoir *Naked in the Promised Land* in the creative nonfiction style. Creative nonfiction demands that the writer tell a factual story using the literary devices of fiction: characterization, plot, dialogue,

Phyllis, Avrom, and Lillian, about 1979

vivid scene setting, and literary language such as image and metaphor. The *facts* may never be made up, but the writer of creative nonfiction must develop the imaginative talents of the novelist, and that became for me an exciting challenge.

I wanted to show in *Naked in the Promised Land,* which was published by Houghton Mifflin in 2003, how I became the person that I am. I wanted to look at all the seemingly contradictory parts of my life and see how they fit together, to make sense of them for myself as well as for my readers. I like to quip with my friends that writing this book was as good as ten years of psychoanalysis. And I think that I did learn a great deal about how my drives and dreams were formed and realized, from my childhood to 1979, the year of my mother's death, when the book ends.

But mere self-exploration is mere self-indulgence for a writer. I hope that I was successful in making *Naked in the Promised Land* transcend that pitfall, and that the book explains how a girl who had been a pin-up model and a stripper could become a university professor, how a daughter born to an unwed immigrant woman who could barely read and write could get a Ph.D. and become an author, and how my story is not just a personal one but also a story about how America gives us freedom to create and recreate ourselves.

BIOGRAPHICAL AND CRITICAL SOURCES:

BOOKS

Feminist Writers, St. James Press (Detroit, MI), 1995, pp. 167-168.

Gay and Lesbian Biography, St. James Press (Detroit, MI), 1997, pp. 160-163.

PERIODICALS

Advocate, June 22, 1999, Ricardo Ortiz, review of *To Believe in Women,* p. 127.

Atlantic, March, 1981.

Chronicle of Higher Education, June 11, 1999, p. 14.

Library Journal, August, 1991, Patricia Sarles, review of *Odd Girls and Twilight Lovers,* p. 128; March 15, 1998, review of *I Begin My Life All Over: The Hmong and the American Immigrant Experience,* p. 81.

Miami Herald, March 9, 2003, Susan Freeman, "Nazi Ghosts Shape a Life of Courage Resilience."

New Statesman, July 17, 1992, p. 48.

New York Review of Books, May 28, 1981.

New York Times Book Review, April 5, 1981; June 28, 1992, Jeffrey Escoffier, "Out of the Closet and Into History," pp. 1, 24; October 3, 1999, Karla Jay, review of *To Believe in Women,* p. 23.

Publishers Weekly, May 16, 1994, review of *Chloe Plus Olivia: An Anthology of Lesbian Literature from the Seventeenth Century to the Present,* p. 48; February 23, 1998, review of *I Begin My Life All Over: The Hmong and the American Immigrant Experience,* p. 59; November 18, 2002, review of *Naked in the Promised Land: A Memoir,* p. 49; February 24, 2003, Michael Bronski, "Memoir and Mystery," p. 48.

San Francisco Chronicle, March 2, 2003, Kera Bolonik, "A Scholar Laid Bare."

Seattle Times, June 29, 2003, Barbara Sjoholm, "Memoir Reveals Too Little of Inner Self."

Times Literary Supplement, September 4, 1981; September 23, 1983.

Washington Post Book World, May 3, 1981; February 21, 2003, Carolyn See, "Pleased to Meet Me," p. C4.

Women's Review of Books, December, 1999, Nan Alamilla Boyd, review of *To Believe in Women: What Lesbians Have Done for America—A History,* p. 6.

*   *   *

FAY, Laurel E.

PERSONAL: Female. *Education:* Cornell University, Ph.D. (musicology).

ADDRESSES: Agent—c/o Oxford University Press, 198 Madison Ave., New York, NY 10016.

CAREER: Musicologist. Has taught at Ohio State University, Wellesley College, and New York University; consultant specializing in Russian music for publisher G. Schirmer.

AWARDS, HONORS: Otto Kinkeldey Award, American Musicological Society, 2001, for *Shostakovich: A Life.*

WRITINGS:

Shostakovich: A Life, Oxford University Press (New York, NY), 2000.

Fay's articles have appeared in the *New York Times, Musical American, Opera News, Stagebill,* and *Keynote,* as well as various scholarly publications.

SIDELIGHTS: In the late 1970s, when Laurel E. Fay was still a graduate student in musicology at Cornell University, she became intrigued by rumors of the impending publication of a book purported to be the memoirs of Russian composer Dmitri Shostakovich, as told to writer Solomon Volkov. Fay, who was writing a dissertation on Shostakovich's string quartets, wrote Volkov to ask if she could provide any help to him, and also to ask whether he had any unpublished biographical material about the composer.

When Volkov's book came out, Fay was puzzled by it. She noticed that much of the material in it seemed familiar, as if she had read it before. In November 1979 another scholar noted that two substantial sections in Volkov's book were identical to passages in published interviews with the composer. "Then it all began to click for me," Fay told Paul Mitchinson in *Lingua Franca.* "And it didn't take me very long then to find another five passages." In April 1980 she presented her findings at a meeting of the Midwest chapter of the American Musicological Society. She then published her research in the academic journal *Russian Review.* Her article "Shostakovich versus Volkov: Whose Testimony?" presented damning evidence that Volkov had plagiarized much of his book from other sources. Volkov denied the charges, and his supporters launched into vitriolic attacks on Fay, largely because they opposed her view that Shostakovich was not, as Volkov had written, a dissident against the Soviet dictatorship. Fay, however, rarely mentions her attackers in print. As Mitchinson noted, "Fay coolly presents verifiable details about her subject."

In 2000 Fay published her own biography of the composer, *Shostakovich: A Life*. While researching the book, she spent three years in Russia, gleaning material from Russian archives. In an interview with Tamara Bernstein of the *National Post*, Fay said "I wanted [*Shostakovich*] to be a quiet book. I wanted it to be useful—so that when people want to know the background to a piece of music, for instance, they can go to something that will be accurate." Praising Fay's efforts, Jeremy Eichler wrote in the *Nation* that the book "is a remarkably straightforward, nonsensationalized treatment of the composer's life and work. As such, it is a sorely needed contribution to a field that has been overheated with controversy, the flames of which have been stoked by the very paucity of reliable facts about the composer's life." He added that Fay's adherence to only verifiable facts resulted in a relatively "flat" presentation. However, in *Notes*, Marina Frolova-Walker found this flatness to be desirable. She commented that although most biographies emphasize narrative and a certain injection of personal opinion on the part of the author, Fay avoids this in her biography of the composer, with favorable results: "Fay's dryness and her reluctance to exercise personal judgment has resulted . . . in a far more valuable contribution to Shostakovich studies." A *Publishers Weekly* reviewer called the book a "careful and detailed study." Simon Morrison, writing in the *Journal of the American Musicological Society*, praised Fay's "meticulous attention to detail," her avoidance of the ideological controversies surrounding Shostakovich, and her use of "the highest scholarly standards" to produce a "multifaceted portrait" of her subject. The critic also wrote, "Her documentary work is of value precisely because questions of intention will probably continue to inform audience experiences of the composer's music, and because of the troubling and perplexing nature of his career."

BIOGRAPHICAL AND CRITICAL SOURCES:

PERIODICALS

Booklist, November 1, 1999, Alan Hirsch, review of *Shostakovich: A Life*, p. 497.

Denver Post, February 21, 2001, Kyle MacMillan, review of *Shostakovich*, p. F1.
Journal of the American Musicological Society, summer, 2000, Simon Morrison, review of *Shostakovich*, p. 426.
Library Journal, November 1, 1999, Bonnie Jo Depp, review of *Shostakovich*, p. 83.
Lingua Franca, May-June, 2000, Paul Mitchinson, "The Shostakovich Variations."
Los Angeles Times, November 29, 1998, Chris Pasles, review of *Shostakovich*, p. 7.
Nation, February 14, 2000, Jeremy Eichler, review of *Shostakovich*, p. 25.
National Post, March 14, 2000, Tamara Bernstein, review of *Shostakovich*.
New York Times, April 6, 2003, review of *Shostakovich*, p. B25.
New York Times Book Review, January 2, 2000, Harlow Robinson, review of *Shostakovich*, p. 21.
Notes, December, 2000, Marina Frolova-Walker, review of *Shostakovich*, p. 347.
Opera News, May, 2000, Russell Platt, review of *Shostakovich*, p. 105.
Publishers Weekly, October 25, 1999, review of *Shostakovich*, p. 65.
Washington Post, November 28, 1999, Sudip Bose, review of *Shostakovich*, p. X03.

ONLINE

Seattle Symphony Web site, http://www.seattlesymphony.org/ (November 12, 2003), profile of Fay.*

*   *   *

FELDMAN, Lawrence H. 1942-

PERSONAL: Born November 27, 1942, in New York, NY; son of Jack (in business) and Ruth (a homemaker; maiden name, Menzer) Feldman. *Education:* San Diego State University, B.A., 1964; University of California—Los Angeles, M.A., 1966; Pennsylvania State University, Ph.D., 1971; Catholic University of America, M.L.S., 1992. *Politics:* Democrat. *Religion:* Jewish. *Hobbies and other interests:* Reading and writing science fiction and fantasy.

ADDRESSES: Home—P.O. Box 2493, Wheaton, MD 20915. *E-mail*—lawrence846@aol.com.

CAREER: Historian and author of nonfiction. Gettysburg College, Gettysburg, PA, instructor, 1971-72; University of Missouri—Columbia, curator, 1973-84; independent researcher and writer, 1984—. Also works as indexer.

AWARDS, HONORS: Fulbright fellow, 1987; Mellon fellow, 1998.

WRITINGS:

Indian Payment in Kind: The Sixteenth-Century Encomiendas of Guatemala, Labyrinthos (Culver City, CA), 1992.

Mountains of Fire, Lands That Shake: Earthquakes and Volcanic Eruptions in the Historic Past of Central America, 1505-1899, Labyrinthos (Culver City, Ca), 1993.

The Last Days of British Saint Augustine, 1784-1785: A Spanish Census of the English Colony of East Florida, Clearfield (Baltimore, MD), 1998.

Lost Shores, Forgotten Peoples: Spanish Explorations of the South East Maya Lowlands, Duke University Press (Durham, NC), 2000.

Author of several other books and monographs. Contributor to history journals.

WORK IN PROGRESS: Research for *Escape through Spain.*

SIDELIGHTS: Lawrence H. Feldman told *CA:* "My aim is to write on my scholarly activities. My next project is the Jews in Spain—how they escaped from Spain in 1492 and through Spain during World War II."

*   *   *

FERNGREN, Gary B(urt) 1942-

PERSONAL: Born April 14, 1942, in Bellingham, Washington; son of Al B. and Wilma (Edberg) Ferngren; married Agnes Loewen, March 26, 1970; children: Suzanne, Annie-Marie, Heather. *Education:* Western Washington University, B.A., 1964; University of British Columbia, M.A., 1967, Ph.D., 1973.

ADDRESSES: Home—2040 Northwest 23rd St., Corvallis, OR 97330-1202. *Office*—Oregon State University, Department of History, 304 Milam Hall, Corvallis, OR 97331. *E-mail*—GFerngren@orst.edu.

CAREER: Oregon State University, instructor, 1970-72, assistant professor, 1972-78, associate professor, 1978-84, professor of Greek and Roman history, 1984—.

MEMBER: International Society of the History of Medicine (vice president, 1996-97; U.S. delegate, councilor, 1997—; associate general secretary, 2000—), American Association for the History of Medicine, American Osler Society, History of Science Society.

AWARDS, HONORS: College Physicians of Philadelphia fellow, 1981; National Endowment for the Humanities fellow, 1990, 1991; Oregon Commission for the Humanities fellow, 1985, 1989, 1995; Canada Council fellow, three times; Joseph J. Malone fellow (Egypt); Templeton Foundation grant to develop and teach course on science and religion; teaching awards, including Oregon State University Elizabeth Ritchie Award for Outstanding Teaching.

WRITINGS:

(Editor, with Samuel Kottek and others) *From Athens to Jerusalem: Medicine in Hellenized Jewish Lore and Early Christian Literature,* Erasmus (Rotterdam, Netherlands), 2000.

(Editor) *Science and Religion: A Historical Introduction,* Johns Hopkins University Press (Baltimore, MD), 2002.

General editor, with others, *The History of Science and Religion in the Western Tradition: An Encyclopedia,* Garland (New York, NY), 2000. Contributor of articles to professional journals and of chapters to books.

SIDELIGHTS: Award-winning history professor Gary B. Ferngren's special research interests include the social history of ancient medicine, the relationship between science and religion throughout history, and religion and ancient medicine. He teaches ancient

Greek and Roman history at Oregon State University and has served as editor of two volumes on science and religion in history.

The first is *The History of Science and Religion in the Western Tradition: An Encyclopedia,* for which he was general editor. The volume contains 103 essays, written by seventy-six notable experts in their field and organized into ten categories: "Intellectual Foundations and Philosophical Backgrounds," "The Relationship of Science and Religion," "Biographical Studies," "Astronomy and Cosmology," "The Physical Sciences," "Earth Sciences," "The Biological Sciences," "Specific Religious Traditions and Chronological Periods," "Medicine and Psychology," and "The Occult Sciences." Periods covered are from the beginning of the era of Christianity up to the late 1990s, and topics include evangelicalism, fundamentalism, gender studies, environmentalism, and postmodernism.

R. J. Havlik, in a review for *Choice,* called the articles "insightful" and described the book as "valuable" to all those "struggling with this ever-present relationship." Dan Burton, in a review for *Science Books & Films,* praised *The History of Science and Religion in the Western Tradition* as "meaty" and concluded, "Teachers and professionals in both science and history will find it a superb resource and may be tempted to read it cover to cover." In an interview with Mark Floyd posted on the *Oregon State University Web site,* Ferngren said, "Since the late 19th century, the prevailing thought has been that religion in general and Christianity in particular had a long history of opposing scientific progress in the interest of preserving dogmatic theology. But scholarship of the past 20 years or so has challenged that thesis. . . . People can choose to look at the conflicts, and they can choose to pit creationism against evolution. But there are a growing number of people who believe there is room for both."

In a review for *Isis,* Aileen Fyfe pointed out that *The History of Science and Religion in the Western Tradition* perhaps overemphasizes Christianity, especially Protestantism, since there are only ten pages on Islam and eight on Judaism in the section on Western religions. Fyfe said she enjoyed the section on the history and philosophy of science and religion, saying it has the largest variety of viewpoints. However, she observed, some beginning students might be confused by the opposing viewpoints and even develop a one-sided view of issues if they do not read other articles on the same subject. Yet, she found, "It will be an excellent starting point for those just beginning to investigate science and religion." William P. Collins, of *Library Journal,* said the encyclopedia is "filled with respect for the roles and methodologies of both religion and science." However, he thought there should have been more biographical essays and that the book should have covered the Baha'i religion because it is the only Western faith that scripturally proclaims the relationship between religion and science.

Ferngren has also edited *Science and Religion: A Historical Introduction,* which consists of thirty definitive articles from *The History of Science and Religion in the Western Tradition,* designed to give readers who do not have the lengthy volume a good overview of what is covered there. Augustine J. Curley, of *Library Journal,* called the book "an essential purchase" for libraries without the original volume.

BIOGRAPHICAL AND CRITICAL SOURCES:

PERIODICALS

Choice, December, 2000, R. J. Havlik, review of *The History of Science and Religion in the Western Tradition: An Encyclopedia,* p. 685.

Isis, September, 2002, Aileen Fyfe, review of *The History of Science and Religion in the Western Tradition,* p. 547.

Library Journal, August, 2000, William P. Collins, review of *The History of Science and Religion in the Western Tradition,* p. 90; October 15, 2002, Augustine J. Curley, review of *Science and Religion: A Historical Introduction,* p. 78.

Science Books & Films, September, 2001, Dan Burton, review of *The History of Science and Religion in the Western Tradition,* p. 200.

ONLINE

Oregon State University Web site, http://oregonstate. edu/April 1, 2003), "Gary Ferngren."

*   *   *

FIELDS, Ronald J.

PERSONAL: Married; wife's name, Pamela; children: Chelsea, Alexander.

ADDRESSES: Agent—c/o Prentice Hall, One Lake St., Upper Saddle River, NJ 07458.

CAREER: Writer and producer. National Broadcasting Company, Inc. (NBC), staff writer for comedy *Marblehead Manor;* American Movie Classics (cable channel), head writer; vice president of development, Hollywood on Air.

AWARDS, HONORS: Emmy Award for outstanding informational special, 1986, for *W. C. Fields Straight Up.*

WRITINGS:

NONFICTION

W. C. Fields by Himself: His Intended Autobiography, Prentice-Hall (Englewood Cliffs, NJ), 1973.
W. C. Fields: A Life on Film, St. Martin's Press (New York, NY), 1984.
(With Shaun O'L. Higgins) *Never Give a Sucker an Even Break: W. C. Fields on Business,* Prentice Hall Press (Paramus, NJ), 2000.

OTHER

(And producer) *W. C. Fields Straight Up* (teleplay), Public Broadcasting Service (PBS), 1986.

Also author of screenplays *Run Buddy Run, Vietnam Visions,* and *Petals of the Chrysanthemum.*

SIDELIGHTS: Television writer Ronald J. Fields, grandson of actor W. C. Fields, found he had become his family's unofficial archivist and historian. As such, he became a valuable resource when the PBS network decided to produce a special on W. C. Fields's life and work. The network contacted Fields, who was able to provide them with vintage photographs, memorabilia, home movies, audio recordings, correspondence, and family memories of the actor. The show, *W. C. Fields Straight Up,* was originally broadcast in March 1986 and won an Emmy for outstanding informational special.

Interestingly, although Fields was intimately involved in the production of the film, he never met his famous grandfather, and for many years he was unaware that he was related to the actor. There were no photos of the actor in his family's home, and when he visited his grandmother, she did not have any belongings that would have indicated to whom she had been married. According to Andrew Miller in *City Paper,* Fields recalled watching an old W. C. Fields movie on television with his sister and laughing at the actor's antics. "That W. C. Fields is the funniest man who ever lived!," he told his sister. She replied, "You don't get it, do you? That's our grandfather."

Fields decided to find out all he could about his well-known grandfather and his career. This interest led to his involvement in the film as well as a biography, *W. C. Fields by Himself: His Intended Autobiography,* and a filmography, *W. C. Fields: A Life on Film.* Of this last work, John Nangle wrote in *Films in Review* that it "is surely the definitive book about the work of that great, bulbous-nosed misanthrope." A *Publishers Weekly* reviewer called the book "by far the best reference" on W. C. Fields.

Fields also cowrote *Never Give a Sucker an Even Break: W. C. Fields on Business.* The book features quotes on finance and business from the films of the famously verbose, cynical, and financially savvy actor, such as "Start every day with a smile and get it over with," and "You can't cheat an honest man." A *Publishers Weekly* reviewer commented that at times, this hunt for quotations seems a bit stretched, but wrote that although the book is not a wellspring of management wisdom, the quotes are amusing, and "as a source of Fields's one-liners and filmography . . . the book is helpful."

BIOGRAPHICAL AND CRITICAL SOURCES:

PERIODICALS

Booklist, January 1, 2000, David Rouse, review of *Never Give a Sucker an Even Break: W. C. Fields on Business,* p. 843; July, 2002, Candace Smith, review of *W. C. Fields Straight Up,* p. 1864.
Chicago Sun-Times, September 8, 1986, review of *W. C. Fields Straight Up,* p. 51.

Film Quarterly, summer, 1985, review of *W. C. Fields: A Life on Film,* p. 38.

Films in Review, February, 1985, John Nangle, review of *W. C. Fields: A Life on Film,* p. 118.

Los Angeles Times, March 7, 1986, Lee Margulies, review of *W. C. Fields Straight Up,* p. 29.

Publishers Weekly, September 28, 1984, Genevieve Stuttaford, review of *W. C. Fields: A Life on Film,* p. 110.

USA Today, March, 1990, review of *W. C. Fields Straight Up,* p. 97.

ONLINE

City Paper Web site, http://citypaper.net/ (February 3-10, 2000), Andrew Milner, review of *Never Give a Sucker an Even Break.**

*   *   *

FLEISCHMAN, John 1948-

PERSONAL: Born November 29, 1948, in New York, NY; married. *Education:* Antioch College, B.A. (English), 1970.

ADDRESSES: Home—Cincinnati, OH. *Office*—c/o American Society for Cell Biology, 8120 Woodmont Ave., Suite 750, Bethesda, MD 20814. *E-mail*—jfleischman@ascb.org.

CAREER: Worked for various newspapers and magazines (including *Yankee* and *Ohio*), and for a public radio station. Science writer for Harvard Medical School and American Society for Cell Biology. Freelance science writer, 1995—.

MEMBER: National Association of Science Writers.

AWARDS, HONORS: Orbis Pictus Honor Award for Outstanding Nonfiction, National Council of Teachers of English, James Madison Honor Book, Notable Children's Book selection, American Library Association (ALA), and Best Book for Young Adults selection, ALA, all 2003, all for *Phineas Gage: A Gruesome but True Story about Brain Science;* fellowships

from Alicia Patterson Foundation, Macy Foundation for Science Broadcast Journalism, and Marine Biological Laboratory.

WRITINGS:

The Ohio Lands (adult nonfiction), photographs by Ian Adams, BrownTrout Publishers (San Francisco, CA), 1995.

Phineas Gage: A Gruesome but True Story about Brain Science (juvenile nonfiction), Houghton Mifflin (Boston, MA), 2002.

Free and Public: One Hundred and Fifty Years at the Public Library of Cincinnati and Hamilton County, 1853-2003 (adult nonfiction), Orange Frazer Press (Cincinnati, OH), 2003.

Contributor of science articles to magazines, including *Discover, Muse,* and *Air & Space Smithsonian.*

WORK IN PROGRESS: A nonfiction science book for older children about the discovery of DNA.

SIDELIGHTS: While working as a journalist for newspapers and magazines, John Fleischman found himself reporting more and more often on scientific topics. Although he was interested in many areas of science, he eventually specialized in medical topics, going so far as to take a special laboratory course for journalists who wanted to write about cell biology. On assignment in the fall of 1998, he visited the town of Cavendish, Vermont, where residents were honoring the 150th anniversary of an accident famous in the annals of medical history. The accident happened to a man named Phineas Gage, who had a metal rod shot through his frontal cortex during an explosion and miraculously survived. At the time, scientists knew little about germs, let alone much about the brain, but Gage's doctor fortuitously washed his hands before bandaging Gage. Young, strong, and lucky, Gage recovered, but observers noticed significant changes in his behavior and personality. Eventually, scientists discovered that the part of the brain harmed in the blast controlled higher order functions that have much to do with personality.

After writing a magazine article for adults about this case, Fleischman thought children might be interested. "It took me another year, working on and off, to figure out what else kids would need to know about Phineas and then to write the book," Fleischman wrote at the *Scholastic* Web site. He had to provide historical background on the state of science, on how the accident could have taken place, and on the aftermath, which included the eleven years Gage lived following the injury. He also had to research photographs and other illustrations that might be used. In writing the text, Fleischman drew heavily on published writings by Gage's physician that had been collected and republished by a doctor in 1999. And he was inspired by the fact that Gage's actual skull was preserved at the Harvard Medical School, where Fleischman was working at the time as a science writer.

In 2002 *Phineas Gage: A Gruesome but True Story about Brain Science* rolled off the presses to good reviews. Among the work's enthusiasts was Lolly Robinson of *Horn Book,* who praised Fleischman's "bold present-tense writing," adding that while the author sometimes addresses the reader directly, "the serious subject and the author's skill keep the writing from becoming jejune." Steven Engelfried, writing for *School Library Journal,* also praised Fleischman's ability to avoid sensationalizing "the fascinating story" and to "[bring] a scientific viewpoint" to the story. *Booklist*'s Randy Meyer found the text "vivid" but predicted that readers only looking for the "gruesome story" of the title will "get bogged down in heavier sections." Other reviewers commented on the variety of scientific subjects Fleischman treats in the course of the narrative. For example, Deborah Stevenson remarked in the *Bulletin of the Center for Children's Books* that, with his "crisp" and "lucid" text, Fleischman "deftly introduces readers to a diverse range of relevant scientific history." In 2003, this "grisly but enlightening story," to quote *Science News* writer Cait Goldberg, won an Orbis Pictus Honor Award for Outstanding Nonfiction for Children.

BIOGRAPHICAL AND CRITICAL SOURCES:

PERIODICALS

Booklist, March 1, 2002, Randy Meyer, review of *Phineas Gage: A Gruesome but True Story about Brain Science,* p. 1101.
Book Report, November-December, 2002, Edna Boardman, review of *Phineas Gage,* p. 66.

Bulletin of the Center for Children's Books, May 1, 2002, Deborah Stevenson, review of *Phineas Gage,* p. 321.
Discover, June, 2002, Deborah Hudson, review of *Phineas Gage,* p. 79.
Horn Book, May-June, 2002, Lolly Robinson, review of *Phineas Gage,* pp. 343-344.
Kirkus Reviews, February 15, 2002, review of *Phineas Gage,* p. 254.
Publishers Weekly, April 15, 2002, review of *Phineas Gage,* p. 66.
School Library Journal, March, 2002, Steven Engelfried, review of *Phineas Gage,* pp. 247-248; May, 2003, John Peters, review of *Phineas Gage,* p. 102.
Science News, March 23, 2002, Cait Goldberg, review of *Phineas Gage,* p. 191.

ONLINE

Scholastic Web site, http://www2.scholastic.com/ (June 24, 2003), "John Fleischman's Interview Transcript."

*   *   *

FLOWERS, R(onald) Barri

PERSONAL: Born in Detroit, MI; married H. Loraine Flowers (a crime researcher and author). *Education:* Michigan State University, B.A., M.S. (criminal justice).

ADDRESSES: Home—Beaverton, OR. *Office*—c/o Charles C. Thomas, Publisher Ltd., 2600 South First St., Springfield, IL 62704. *E-mail*—barriborn2write@cs.com.

CAREER: Writer.

MEMBER: American Crime Writers League, Black Writers Alliance, Mystery Writers of America, Romance Writers of America, Good Book Club.

WRITINGS:

NONFICTION

Criminal Jurisdiction Allocation in Indian Country, Associated Faculty Press (Port Washington, NY), 1983.

Children and Criminality: The Child as Victim and Perpetrator, Greenwood Press (New York, NY), 1986.

Women and Criminality: The Woman as Victim, Offender, and Practitioner, Greenwood Press (New York, NY), 1987.

Minorities and Criminality, Greenwood Press (New York, NY), 1988.

Demographics and Criminality: The Characteristics of Crime in America, Greenwood Press (New York, NY), 1989.

The Adolescent Criminal: An Examination of Today's Juvenile Offender, McFarland (Jefferson, NC), 1990.

The Victimization and Exploitation of Women and Children: A Study of Physical, Mental, and Sexual Maltreatment in the United States, McFarland (Jefferson, NC), 1994.

Female Crime, Criminals, and Cellmates: An Exploration of Female Criminality and Delinquency, McFarland (Jefferson, NC), 1995.

The Sex Slave Murders, J. Flores (Miami, FL), 1995.

The Prostitution of Women and Girls, McFarland (Jefferson, NC), 1998.

Drugs, Alcohol, and Criminality in American Society, McFarland (Jefferson, NC), 1999.

Domestic Crimes, Family Violence and Child Abuse: A Study of Contemporary American Society, McFarland (Jefferson, NC), 2000.

(With wife, H. Loraine Flowers) *Murders in the United States: Crimes, Killers and Victims of the Twentieth Century,* McFarland (Jefferson, NC), 2001.

Runaway Kids and Teenage Prostitution: America's Lost, Abandoned, and Sexually Exploited Children, Greenwood Press (Westport, CT), 2001.

Sex Crimes, Predators, Perpetrators, Prostitutes, and Victims: An Examination of Sexual Criminality and Victimization, Charles C. Thomas (Springfield, IL), 2001.

Kids Who Commit Adult Crimes: Serious Criminality by Juvenile Offenders, Haworth Press (New York, NY), 2002.

Murder, at the End of the Day and Night: A Study of Criminal Homicide Offenders, Victims, and Circumstances, Charles C. Thomas (Springfield, IL), 2002.

Male Crime and Deviance: Exploring Its Causes, Dynamics, and Nature, Charles C. Thomas (Springfield, IL), 2003.

To Defend the Constitution: Religion, Conscientious Objection, Naturalization, and the Supreme Court, Scarecrow Press (Lanham, MD), 2003.

MYSTERY NOVELS

Deadly Secrets in the Motor City, Writers Club Press (Lincoln, NE), 2000.

Damning Evidence, iUniverse.com (Lincoln, NE), 2000.

Murder in the Rose City, iUniverse.com (Lincoln, NE), 2000.

When Night Falls, Xlibris (Philadelphia, PA), 2000.

Positive I.D., iUniverse.com (Lincoln, NE), 2001.

In the Dark of Night, iUniverse.com (Lincoln, NE), 2001.

Scheme of Things, Sadorian Publications (Durham, NC), 2002.

ROMANCE NOVELS

All for a Good Cause, Writers Club Press (Lincoln, NE), 2000.

For Old Times' Sake, Writers Club Press (Lincoln, NE), 2000.

The Loves of His Life, iUniverse.com (Lincoln, NE), 2000.

Contributor to periodicals, including *Mystery Readers Journal.*

SIDELIGHTS: Raised as one of five children in Detroit and educated in criminal justice at Michigan State University, R. Barri Flowers had devoted the bulk of his published work to crime and criminology. In some cases, his focus has been on actions deemed criminal, though not necessarily judged immoral in the view of modern society. Such is the case, for instance, with *To Defend the Constitution: Religion, Conscientious Objection, Naturalization, and the Supreme Court.* More often, he has focused his attention on persons who, while deemed criminal by authorities, may in turn have been victims themselves—for example, *The Adolescent Criminal: An Examination of Today's Juvenile Offender,* or the sex workers discussed in books such as *The Prostitution of Women and Girls.* Flowers has also examined victims and victimology from a number of angles.

Flowers has written not only about the causes of crime in males, females, minorities, and children, but also about some of the most hardened criminal minds of the modern age. In *Murders in the United States: Crimes, Killers, and Victims of the Twentieth Century*—written with his wife, H. Loraine Flowers—he discusses fifty-three major crimes. These range from the assassinations of presidents William McKinley in 1901 and John F. Kennedy in 1963 to the Manson Family murders of 1969, and from the Columbine school shooting in 1999 to the World Trade Center bombing of 1993.

In addition to Part One, "A Century of Murders," *Murders in the United States* includes a discussion of perpetrators in Part Two, "A Century of Murderers." These are organized by demographic categories—male, female, juvenile—as well as types or motivations: serial killers, hate-crime killers, caretaker killers, and killers of celebrities. Part Three, "A Century of Victims," looks at well-known victims such as Kennedy and his brother Bobby—killed by assassin Sirhan Sirhan in 1968—as well as singer Marvin Gaye, who was shot by his father in 1983. Subdivided into sections listing adult and child victims, this final third of the book examines both those victims who were known before their killing—for example, Charles A. Lindbergh III, whose father's fame made his 1932 kidnap and murder a national tragedy—as well as those who only became famous after their deaths—for example, six-year-old JonBenet Ramsey, who was killed in her Colorado home in 1996. Seven pages of bibliographic information, including Web resources, round out the volume.

"Despite its subject matter," wrote Mary Ellen Quinn in *Booklist*, *Murders in the United States* "generally manages to avoid sensationalism." "All in all," according to David Harrison in *Reference Reviews*, "*Murders in the United States* is a useful contribution to the popular literature of crime in the U.S.A."

Many of Flowers's works have dealt with sex crimes, as well as unlawful activity associated with sex, such as prostitution. *The Prostitution of Women and Girls*, written on the heels of a World Health Organization report that noted enormous increases in sex-trade activity in all countries studied, examines numerous subjects related to the principal topic. Among these are the roles of the pimp and the john (the steady male customer); juvenile prostitution and the incidence of runaways becoming involved in prostitution; male prostitution, virtually all of which is geared toward the male homosexual trade; the prevalence of childhood

abuse in the background of prostitutes; drugs and substance abuse; AIDS and other sexually transmitted diseases; and the relationship between prostitution and pornography, as well as that between prostitution and the burgeoning global market in "sex tourism."

The Prostitution of Women and Girls, noted Heather Lee Miller in the *Journal of Women's History*, "enumerat[es] and discuss[es] both quantitative and qualitative information about sex work and sexploitation." Mary Jane Brustman in *Library Journal* called it "a very readable study, intelligently presented and well supported with an extensive bibliography."

In *Sex Crimes, Predators, Perpetrators, Prostitutes, and Victims: An Examination of Sexual Criminality and Victimization* Flowers targets a particularly poignant topic within the larger subject of the sex industry. Of the 2001 book, Carlton W. Parks wrote in the *Archives of Sexual Behavior* that "This volume will satisfy [the] curiosity and thirst for information about sexual criminality and victimization in a manner that easily captures the attention of the intelligent layperson."

BIOGRAPHICAL AND CRITICAL SOURCES:

PERIODICALS

Archives of Sexual Behavior, December, 2002, Carlton W. Parks, review of *Sex Crimes, Predators, Perpetrators, Prostitutes, and Victims: An Examination of Sexual Criminality and Victimization*, p. 553.

Booklist, March 15, 2002, Mary Ellen Quinn, review of *Murders in the United States: Crimes, Killers, and Victims of the Twentieth Century*, p. 1277.

Journal of Women's History, summer, 2000, Heather Lee Miller, review of *The Prostitution of Women and Girls*, p. 222.

Library Journal, August, 1998, Mary Jane Brustman, review of *The Prostitution of Women and Girls*, p. 113.

Twentieth-Century Reference Reviews, Volume 16, issue 2, 2002, David Harrison, review of *Murders in the United States: Crimes, Killers, and Victims of the Twentieth Century*, pp. 18-19.

ONLINE

R. Barri Flowers Home Page, http://barribythebook. homestead.com (September 18, 2003).*

FORD, Arielle

PERSONAL: Born December 29, year unknown, in Miami, FL; daughter of Harvey Ford (an attorney and judge) and Sheila Fuerst (an entrepreneur); married Brian Hilliard (a business manager) June 22, 1998. *Education:* University of Florida, B.S., 1974.

ADDRESSES: Office—The Ford Group/Dharma Dreams LLC, 1250 Prospect St., Ste O-5, La Jolla, CA 92037. *E-mail*—fordgroup@aol.com.

CAREER: Publicist, editor, and author. The Ford Group (public relations firm), La Jolla, CA, founder, 1987—.

WRITINGS:

Hot Chocolate for the Mystical Soul: 101 True Stories of Angels, Miracles, and Healings, Plume Books (New York, NY), 1997.
More Hot Chocolate for the Mystical Soul: 101 True Stories of Angels, Miracles, and Healings, Plume Books (New York, NY), 1999.
Hot Chocolate for the Mystical Teenage Soul: 101 True Stories of Angels, Miracles, and Healings, Plume Books (New York, NY), 2000.
Hot Chocolate for the Mystical Lover: 101 True Stories of Soul Mates Brought Together by Divine Intervention, Plume Books (New York, NY), 2001.
Magical Souvenirs: True Spiritual Adventures from around the World, Plume Books (New York, NY), 2002.
(With Beth Goodman) *Owner's Manual,* Jodere Group (San Diego, CA), 2002.

SIDELIGHTS: Arielle Ford has been an influential figure in the New Age publishing world since 1987, when she founded the Ford Group. A public relations firm serving authors writing on alternative medicine, spirituality, mysticism, and other New Age topics, the Ford Group boasts a client list with famous names including Deepak Chopra, Marianne Williamson, Dr. Dean Ornish, and Kenny Loggins. After ten years publicizing the works of others, Ford began her own series of successful books. *Hot Chocolate for the Mystical Soul: 101 True Stories of Angels, Miracles, and Healings,* described by *Booklist* reviewer Ilene

Cooper as "a box of spiritual bonbons," soon led to the sequel *More Hot Chocolate for the Mystical Soul: 101 True Stories of Angels, Miracles, and Healings,* as well as the more specialized books *Hot Chocolate for the Mystical Teenage Soul: 101 True Stories of Angels, Miracles, and Healings* and *Hot Chocolate for the Mystical Lover: 101 True Stories of Angels, Miracles, and Healings.* "Even the cynical will find evidence of the divine" in Ford's second book, write a contributor to *Publishers Weekly.* Describing *Hot Chocolate for the Mystical Lover,* a writer for *Publishers Weekly* noted the book's appealing "warmth and frothy sweetness."

The collection *Magical Souvenirs: True Mystical Travel Stories from around the World* is in the same vein, though it does not bear the "Hot Chocolate" title. *Magical Souvenirs* compiles stories of chance meetings, strange coincidences, and prophetic dreams inspired by travel. In an interview with Revered Laurie Sue Brockway for the online magazine *Soulful Living,* Ford said that the stories in her books are often events that happen to most people. "A lot of people are having mystical experiences every day and they just don't see it as that. They just call it coincidence. Or Chance." Ford is also the author, with Beth Goodman, of *Owner's Manual,* a fill-in-the-blanks journal for romantic partners, addressing topics as diverse as pets, health, favorite foods, and sexual fantasies.

BIOGRAPHICAL AND CRITICAL SOURCES:

PERIODICALS

Booklist, February 1, 1998, Ilene Cooper, review of *Hot Chocolate for the Mystical Soul: 101 True Stories of Angels, Miracles, and Healings,* p. 880.
Publishers Weekly, September 20, 1999, "Wisdom From Home and Hearth," p. 68; November 20, 2000, review of *Hot Chocolate for the Mystical Lover,* p. 58.

ONLINE

Ford Sisters Web site, http://www.fordsisters.com/ (June 12, 2002).
Soulful Living, http://www.soulfulliving.com/ (June 12, 2002), interview with Ford by Rev. Laurie Sue Brockway.*

FORD, Catherine 1961-

PERSONAL: Born 1961, in Geelong, Victoria, Australia; married Jean-Jacques Portail; children: Louis, Nina. *Education:* Attended Presbyterian Ladies College, 1977-79; attended La Trobe University, 1980-82.

ADDRESSES: Home—Melbourne, Australia; France. *Agent*—The Text Publishing Company, 171 La Trobe St., Melbourne, Victoria 3000, Australia.

CAREER: Fitzroy Legal Services, assistant, 1985-87; Radio National, researcher, 1988-92; freelance journalist.

AWARDS, HONORS: Steele Rudd Australian Short Fiction Award, 1997, for *Dirt and Other Stories.*

WRITINGS:

Dirt and Other Stories, Text Publishing Company (Melbourne, Australia), 1996.
NYC (novel), Text Publishing Company (Melbourne, Australia), 2000.

SIDELIGHTS: Australian writer Catherine Ford has made a name for herself as the author of the award-winning *Dirt and Other Stories* as well as *NYC,* a novel. *Dirt and Other Stories,* a collection of ten pieces, launched Ford's career in 1996. It garnered praise from critics and won the prestigious Steele Rudd Australian Fiction Award the following year. Writing in *Time International,* Michael Fitzgerald commented on how Ford finds poetry in the mundane in her "striking and mysterious debut." In her appraisal for *Australian Book Review,* Katharine England also commented favorably, noting the "solid, earthy feel which is suggested by the title and borne out by the stories themselves. These are stories of earth, of the body weighed by its mortality, stories of no great lustre but of solid craftsmanship and shrewd understanding." England cited "The Remover of Obstacles" as the most memorable of the collection's stories and wrote that "in the main, *Dirt* impresses as a powerful and mature collection from an interesting new voice."

An off-shoot of one of the stories in *Dirt,* "July Four," became the novel *NYC,* the tale of an adopted Australian woman, Astrid, in search of her American

biological mother and father. The plot deals with Astrid's meeting with her mother in New York City, a locale with which Ford was familiar after having studied acting there. Ford explained to Jason Steger in *The Age* online, "The kernel of both stories ['July Four' and *NYC*] was about a decision to have children or not to have children, about how does one make such a decision. And how do you make a leap from being a single person into someone who's responsible for another." She continued, "The idea I had was a girl on the verge of womanhood who is quite privileged, good parents who care for her and love her but she's not actually theirs. And I suppose I just wanted to write about what happens when you know in every other aspect of her life she's a happy loved girl but at some critical fundamental level she feels that she has been abandoned." This theme has been explored by a number of Australian writers; Jan McKemmish, writing at the *Vicnet Web site,* asserted that "Ford's *NYC* is part of this literary movement."

Reviewers gave the novel qualified praise. "Ford writes as well as ever, and her feeling for regret and solitude has a salutary combination of depth and equanimity," wrote Owen Richardson in *The Age.* "But *NYC* isn't, I think, a successful novel, though it is full of fine things." Richardson cited Ford's portrayal of Astrid's estrangement; yet he wished that the characters, Astrid included, were more vividly portrayed. Astrid "is intentionally underarticulated, but she's not blocked in enough for her absence, as a literary theorist might say, to have enough presence." Likewise, McKemmish found strong points and weaknesses. "The novel is an exposition of what it is like to be in shock," the reviewer remarked, adding, "The writing and the story are perfect fits; they are spare, almost sub-realist." Even so, in McKemmish's view, the plot is a "little predictable and uncertain, meandering" yet "clever at times and measured" and takes "a while to hit its stride." Despite any perceived weakness, Fitzgerald found the work to be successful over all. "Ford's literary journey is as courageous as Astrid's," Fitzgerald concluded, "and her ability to find surprising flecks of realism and humor keeps cliché at bay. . . . *NYC* marks Ford as a novelist of distinction."

BIOGRAPHICAL AND CRITICAL SOURCES:

PERIODICALS

Australian Book Review, April, 1996, Katharine England, review of *Dirt and Other Stories,* p. 30.

Time International, May 15, 2000, Michael Fitzgerald, review of *NYC,* p. 66.

ONLINE

Age, http://theage.com.au/ (May 5, 2000), Jason Steger, "Manhattan Revelations" (interview); (May 15, 2000) Owen Richardson, review of *NYC.*
Vicnet, http://home.vicnet.net.au/ (December 19, 2001), Jan McKemmish, review of *NYC.**

*   *   *

FOX, Michael J. 1961-

PERSONAL: Born Michael Andrew Fox, June 9, 1961, in Edmonton, Alberta, Canada; son of Bill (a career officer in the Canadian Army and police officer) and Phyllis Fox; married Tracy Pollan (an actress), July 16, 1988; children: Sam Michael, Aquinnah Kathleen, Schuyler Frances, Esme Annabelle.

ADDRESSES: Office—Michael J. Fox Foundation for Parkinson's Research, Grand Central Station, P.O. Box 4777, New York, NY 10163. *Agent*—c/o Nanci Ryder, Baker Winokur Ryder, 9100 Wilshire Blvd., 6th Floor West, Beverly Hills, CA 90212.

CAREER:

Actor, author, director, and producer. Founder of the Michael J. Fox Foundation for Parkinson's Research. Television appearances include episodes of *Leo and Me,* Canadian Broadcasting Corporation (CBC), 1976-77; *Lou Grant,* Columbia Broadcasting System (CBS), 1979; *Trapper John, M.D. ,* CBS, 1979; *Family,* American Broadcasting Company (ABC), 1980; *Teachers Only,* National Broadcasting Company (NBC), 1982; *The Love Boat,* ABC, 1983; *Night Court,* NBC, 1984; *Tales from the Crypt,* Home Box Office (HBO), 1991; and various specials. Television series appearances include *Palmerstown, U.S.A.,* CBS, 1980; *Family Ties,* NBC, 1982-89; and *Spin City,* ABC, 1996-2000. Television movies include *Letters from Frank,* CBS, 1979; *High School U.S.A.,* King Features, 1983; *Family Ties Vacation,* NBC, 1985; and *Don't Drink the Water,* Buena Vista Home Video, 1994.

Film appearances include *Midnight Madness,* Anchor Bay, 1980; *Class of 1984,* Vestron, 1982; *Back to the Future,* Universal, 1985; *Teen Wolf,* Metro-Goldwyn-Mayer/United Artists, 1985; *The Secret of My Success,* Universal, 1987; *Light of Day,* Columbia TriStar, 1987; *Bright Lights, Big City,* United Artists, 1988; *The Return of Bruno,* HBO Home Video 1988; *Casualties of War,* Columbia, 1989; *Back to the Future Part II,* Universal, 1989; *Back to the Future Part III,* Universal, 1990; *The Hard Way,* Universal, 1991; *Doc Hollywood,* Warner Bros., 1991; *Where the Rivers Flow North,* Caledonia, 1993; *Life with Mikey,* Touchstone, 1993; (voice only) *Homeward Bound: The Incredible Journey,* Buena Vista, 1993; *For Love or Money,* Universal, 1993; *Coldblooded,* Polygram, 1995; *Blue in the Face,* Miramax, 1995; *The American President,* Columbia, 1995; (voice only) *Homeward Bound II: Lost in San Francisco,* Buena Vista, 1996; *The Frighteners,* Universal, 1996; *Mars Attacks!,* Warner Bros., 1996; (voice only) *Stuart Little,* Columbia, 1999; (voice only) *Atlantis: The Lost Empire,* Buena Vista, 2001; and (voice only) *Stuart Little 2,* Columbia, 2002.

Director of episode "The Trap," *Tales from the Crypt,* 1991. Producer of television series, including *Spin City,* ABC, 1996-2002, *Anna Says,* DreamWorks, 1999, and *Otherwise Engaged,* Lifetime, 2002. Producer of film *Coldblooded,* Polygram, 1995.

AWARDS, HONORS: Emmy Awards for best actor in a comedy series, Academy of Television Arts and Sciences, 1986, 1987, and 1988, and Golden Globe award for best actor in a television musical or comedy series, Hollywood Foreign Press Association, 1989, both for *Family Ties;* People's Choice Award for favorite male performer in a new television series, 1997, Golden Globe award for best actor in a television musical or comedy series, 1998, 1999, 2000, Screen Actors Guild Award for outstanding male actor in a comedy series, 1999, 2000, and Emmy Award for best actor in a comedy series, 2000, all for *Spin City.*

WRITINGS:

Lucky Man: A Memoir, Hyperion Press (New York, NY), 2002.

Writer of television series *Hench at Home,* ABC, 2003.

SIDELIGHTS: Beloved to audiences for his roles in the television series *Family Ties* and *Spin City,* as well as his performances in films that include *Back to the*

Future and many others, Michael J. Fox was reluctant to inform the public that he had been diagnosed with Parkinson's disease. The condition, caused by a malfunction in the brain that results in reduced production of the chemical messenger dopamine, manifests itself in outward signs that include tremors and slurred speech. Diagnosed in 1991, Fox shared the secret only with his closest loved ones until 1998, when he went public in an interview with Barbara Walters. The public response surprised him, he recalled in *Lucky Man: A Memoir:* instead of being put off by his illness, fans almost universally wished him well. "Even better," he went on, "much of the follow-up coverage centered less on me than on Parkinson's disease itself."

Though it bills itself as a memoir, *Lucky Man* is as much about Parkinson's disease, and one man's struggle with it, as it is about the actor's life and career. Fox is not the only well-known figure with Parkinson's; other victims have included Pope John Paul II, Billy Graham, Muhammad Ali, and Janet Reno. Yet he is particularly notable for his activism on behalf of sufferers, work that has included his establishment of, and fundraising for, the Michael J. Fox Foundation for Parkinson's Research.

Of his illness, Fox asks in the book, "Why me?" and then answers "Well, why not me?" Elsewhere he writes, "If you were to rush into this room right now and announce that you had struck a deal with God, Allah, Buddha, Christ, Krishna, Bill Gates, whoever—in which the ten years since my diagnosis could be taken away, traded in for ten more years as the person I was before, I would, without a moment's hesitation, tell you to take a hike." Yet most people would have readily traded places with the person Fox was before the diagnosis: a promising young actor with a winning personality, a beautiful wife and family, and numerous hits under his belt.

Born Michael Andrew Fox—he adopted the "J" in honor of legendary character actor Michael J. Pollard—Fox was the child of a sergeant in the Canadian Army Signal Corps. He and his parents and four siblings moved throughout the country until settling in Burnaby, British Columbia, when he was ten years old. As a child, he dreamed of playing professional hockey, and later took an interest in the guitar, as well as art and creative writing, before discovering his talent as an actor. At age fifteen, Fox made his professional debut in the Canadian Broadcasting Corporation

situation comedy *Leo and Me,* but after three years he left to seek the greater opportunities that awaited in Hollywood.

After a promising start on the critically acclaimed but short-lived Norman Lear/Alex Haley TV series *Palmerstown, U.S.A.,* Fox found himself struggling to survive. He lived on macaroni and cheese and seemed destined for the obscurity that awaits all but a very few of Hollywood's young hopefuls. Then, he did a second audition for the part of Alex P. Keaton on *Family Ties,* and his life changed forever. Thanks to Fox's boyish charm, the lovable conservative Alex almost instantly became an icon of the Reagan era, and by the mid-1980s, Fox had begun to branch out into film. By far his most notable role on the big screen was as Marty McFly in *Back to the Future,* which had two sequels later in the decade, and by the early 1990s he had accumulated some two dozen credits in a variety of films. He also married actress Tracy Pollan, whom he met on the set of *Family Ties,* in 1988, and they had four children. As a father, Fox sought roles in children's movies, providing the voice of Chance the dog in Disney's *Homeward Bound* movies, as well as voicing roles in the "Stuart Little" films.

But Fox had a secret problem—indeed, more than one—and when he first became aware of what turned out to be Parkinson's, he attributed it to a condition of which he (but not his fans) was well aware: his excessive drinking. Awakening one morning in 1990 while filming *Doc Hollywood* he looked down and saw that a single finger was shaking. Wrote Fox in *Lucky Man,* "I'd put away a lot of beers in my time, but had never woken up with the shakes: maybe this was what they called delirium tremens? I was pretty sure they would manifest themselves in a more impressive way—I mean, who gets the d.t.'s in one finger?" Within a few months, his wife told him, "The left side of your body is barely moving. Your arm isn't swinging at all." In the meantime, Fox realized that he was an alcoholic and he stopped drinking, but after a physician diagnosed him with Parkinson's, he went into a severe depression, only recovering with the help of an analyst.

Yet as the title of his memoir indicates, Fox, who retired from acting in 2000, considers himself fortunate—not only because of his fortune and fame, but for all his challenges and blessings. Lynn Andriani of *Publishers Weekly* called *Lucky Man* a "bravely honest autobiography," and Alex J. Wilner in the *Journal of* the American Medical Association wrote that "Lucky Man is an excellent read. Fox is intelligent, articulate, humorous, and passionate, and has a fascinating story to tell."

BIOGRAPHICAL AND CRITICAL SOURCES:

PERIODICALS

Calgary Sun, January 19, 2000, p. 36.
Cosmopolitan, April 1991, p. 170.
Current Science, September 27, 2002, "Fox Hunt," p. 4.
Entertainment Weekly, September 5, 1997, p. 32; February 4, 2000, p. 18; April 12, 2002, Bruce Fretts, review of Lucky Man, p. 68; September 12, 2003, Gillian Flynn, interview with Michael J. Fox, p. 160.
Esquire, February 1988, p. 104.
Gentleman's Quarterly, November 1989, p. 266.
Interview, January 5, 1988, p. 26; August 1996, p. 52.
Journal of the American Medical Association, November 13, 2002, Andrew N. Wilner, review of Lucky Man: A Memoir, p. 2337.
Ladies Home Journal, July 1993, p. 48.
Maclean's, December 7, 1998, p. 60; April 29, 2002, Brian D. Johnson, "Michael Then and Now," p 36.
Newsweek, May 11, 1987, p. 76; May 22, 2000, p. 62.
New York Times, January 10, 1988.
O, March, 2002, interview with Fox and Tracy Pollan, p. 142.
People, August 12, 1985, p. 82; December 23, 1985, p. 86; April 20, 1987, p. 86; December 4, 1989, p. 142; September 22, 1997, p. 164; December 7, 1998, p. 126; December 28, 1998, p. 85; December 25, 2000, p. 54.
Premiere, October 20, 1989, p. 84.
Publishers Weekly, July 31, 2000, p. 18; June 3, 2002, Lynn Andriani, review of Lucky Man: A Memoir, p. 32.
Reader's Digest, July, 2002, review of Lucky Man: A Memoir, p. 142.
Redbook, September 20, 1996, p. 106; May 2000, p. 112.
Rolling Stone, January 15, 1987, p. 25; March 12, 1987, p. 30.
San Francisco Chronicle, July 24, 2002, C. W. Nevius, review of Lucky Man: A Memoir, p. D1.
Saturday Evening Post, September, 2000, Patrick Perry, interview with Fox, p. 38.

Seventeen, July 1986, p. 90.
South Florida Sun-Sentinel, June 19, 2002, Oline H. Cogdill, review of Lucky Man: A Memoir, p. K6912.
Teen, March 1984, p. 51; August 1985, p. 57.
TV Guide, May 13, 2000, Steven Reddicliffe, "A Graceful Goodbye," p. 22.
Us, August 21, 1989, p. 21; January 8, 2001, Todd Gold, "Celebrity of the Year," p. 52.
Washington Post, April 9, 1987, p. C1.

ONLINE

Michael J. Fox Foundation for Parkinson's Research Web site, http://www.michaeljfox.org/ (September 10, 2003).*

*   *   *

FREEDMAN, Bryn

PERSONAL: Married Christopher Curry (an actor; marriage ended); married William Knoedelseder (a journalist). Education: Ithaca College, 1979.

ADDRESSES: Agent—c/o Faber and Faber, 19 Union Square West, New York, NY 10003.

CAREER: Journalist and writer. Columbia Broadcasting System, Inc., WRGB-TV, Albany, NY, news reporter; Fox Broadcasting Company, WTXF-TV, Philadelphia, PA, news reporter, 1994-97; USA Broadcasting, Los Angeles, CA, managing editor.

WRITINGS:

(With husband, William Knoedelseder) Family Value, Faber and Faber (Boston, MA), 1998, published as In Eddie's Name: One Family's Triumph over Tragedy, 1999.

SIDELIGHTS: Carolyn Kubisz, a reviewer for Booklist, wrote that In Eddie's Name: One Family's Triumph over Tragedy is "heartbreaking, moving, and inspirational." The book, written by journalist Bryn Freedman and her husband, journalist William

Knoedelseder, tells the story of a senseless murder and one family's struggle to survive in the wake of tragedy. In 1994 Eddie Polec, a sixteen year old from outside of Philadelphia, was found on the steps of his church after having been severely beaten by a gang of teenagers from another suburb. The attack on Polec was an attempt to avenge an earlier incident involving a drink being thrown on a friend of the gang; however, Polec was chosen as a random target, he had not been involved in the initial episode. On the night in question, dozens of calls to the 911 emergency system regarding the attack on Polec were ignored for as long as forty minutes, time that might have saved his life. A *Publishers Weekly* reviewer noted that the book "illuminate[s] the issue of victim's rights."

In Eddie's Name explores the effect of this brutal murder on Polec's family, noting that Polec might have lived if the emergency response system had worked as it was designed to. *Denver Post* writer Carol Kreck noted that the book "goes far beyond recounting true crime to offering a way to look at the world in the face of horrific tragedy." There is a thorough description of the long court battle to bring the attackers to justice, as well as the fight Polec's father waged to get the 911 emergency system changed so that it could effectively help people in danger. In addition, the authors discuss the foundation that seemed to hold the Polec family together after their tragedy, stressing that the emphasis Polec's parents placed on the importance of personal responsibility and accountability seemed to motivate them all.

Freedman told Debra Auspitz in *City Paper,* "The Polecs show how to raise a family," and added that what made her want to write about their story is "the extreme dignity of the family, a family so unmotivated by greed. . . . The Polecs had a slam-dunk, multimillion-dollar lawsuit, and the city was ready to sign the check, but for the Polecs it was never about the money." Bill Wallace wrote in the *San Francisco Chronicle,* "Freedman and Knoedelseder have written a story that is both inspiring and deeply moving. What happened to the Polecs could have happened to any family. The way this particular family responded is nothing less than heroic." *Library Journal* reviewer Tim Delaney wrote that *In Eddie's Name* is "An excellent book; highly recommended."

BIOGRAPHICAL AND CRITICAL SOURCES:

PERIODICALS

Booklist, November 15, 1999, Carolyn Kubisz, review of *In Eddie's Name: One Family's Triumph over Tragedy,* p. 583.

Denver Post, February 27, 2000, Carol Kreck, review of *In Eddie's Name,* p. I4.
Library Journal, November 15, 1999, Tim Delaney, review of *In Eddie's Name,* p. 83.
New York Times, December 26, 1999, review of *In Eddie's Name,* p. 14.
Publishers Weekly, October 11, 1999, review of *In Eddie's Name,* p. 64.
San Francisco Chronicle, May 14, 2000, Bill Wallace, review of *In Eddie's Name,* p. REV12.

ONLINE

City Paper, http://www/citypaper.net/ (August 26, 1999), Debra Auspitz, review of *In Eddie's Name.**

*   *   *

FREELING, Nicolas 1927-2003

OBITUARY NOTICE—See index for *CA* sketch: Born March 3, 1927, in London, England; died of cancer July 20, 2003, in Mutzig, France. Author. Freeling was an award-winning mystery novelist best known for his books featuring Dutch police inspector Piet van der Valk and Detective Henri Catang. Though born in England, he spent his early childhood in Brittany and spoke French first; his parents then moved the family to Southampton, and then to Ireland because of his mother's support of the Irish Free State. Freeling served in the Royal Air Force from 1947 to 1949, then attended the University of Dublin for two years before dropping out to move to France. While in France, he discovered he had a talent for cooking, and his first professional career was that of sous chef for a number of hotels in France, England, and the Netherlands. It was while working in Amsterdam that his career took an unexpected turn: He was arrested for stealing meat from the restaurant where he worked, and was even sent to prison for a short time. While there, he met a Dutch policeman who fascinated him, and he was also intrigued by police interrogation methods. After he was freed, he wrote his first novel, *Love in Amsterdam* (1961). Although Freeling meant the book to be a love story, it included crime elements and for that reason was marketed as crime fiction. The debut was a hit, and Freeling decided to try a career as an author. The police officer he had met in Amsterdam became the basis for his character van der Valk, who went on to appear in thirteen novels. Van der Valk also inspired two popular television series that aired on British television from 1972 to 1992, and so when Freeling killed his character off there was a general outcry among his fans. Despite such outrage, he determined not to bring van der Valk back, instead beginning a new series of novels featuring Henri Catang that became just as popular and critically acclaimed as his earlier work. Winning such awards as the Grand Prix de Roman Policier and the Edgar Allan Poe Award, Freeling was influenced by the novels of Georges Simenon. Sometimes compared to novelist John le Carré, he often emphasized the characters and relationships in his books as much or more than the murders themselves. During his career, Freeling published over three dozen books, including *Gun before Butler* (1963), *The King of the Rainy Country* (1966), *The Night Lords* (1978), *A Dwarf Kingdom* (1996), *One More River* (1997), and *Some Day Tomorrow* (2000). He was also the author of *The Kitchen: A Delicious Account of the Author's Years as a Grand Hotel Cook* (1970; also published as *The Kitchen Book: The Cook Book*). His last publications were *Village Book: A Memoir* (2001) and *The Janeites* (2002). Two movies, *Because of the Cats* and *The Amsterdam Affair*, were based on Freeling's books.

OBITUARIES AND OTHER SOURCES:

PERIODICALS

Los Angeles Times, July 24, 2003, p. B12.
New York Times, July 23, 2003, p. A17.
Times (London, England), July 23, 2003.
Washington Post, July 26, 2003, p. B7.

*   *   *

FREYMANN-WEYR, (Rhoda) Garret (Michaela) 1965-

PERSONAL: Born 1965, in New York, NY; daughter of Tom and Rhoda Weyr; married Jeffrey Freymann, 1997. *Education:* University of North Carolina, B.A.; New York University, M.F.A. (film)

ADDRESSES: Home—Baltimore, MD. *Agent*—Robin Rue, Writers House, 21 West 26th St., New York, NY 10010. *E-mail*—rhodagarret@mindspring.com.

CAREER: Writer. Worked in children's publishing.

AWARDS, HONORS: Best Book of the Year designations from *School Library Journal* and *Publishers Weekly,* and *Booklist* Editor's Choice designation, all 2002, Best Books for Young Adults selection, Young Adult Library Services Association, and Michael L. Printz Honor Book, American Library Association, both 2003, all for *My Heartbeat.*

WRITINGS:

(As Garret Weyr) *Pretty Girls,* Crown (New York, NY), 1988.
When I Was Older, Houghton Mifflin (Boston, MA), 2000.
My Heartbeat, Houghton Mifflin (Boston, MA), 2002.
The Kings Are Already Here, Houghton Mifflin (Boston, MA), 2003.

SIDELIGHTS: The author of the 2003 Michael L. Printz Honor Book *My Heartbeat,* Garret Freymann-Weyr writes about "how and why people make choices." As Freymann-Weyr once said, "The choices made early are usually made with more care and self-awareness than the ones made later on." The highly acclaimed author of three young adult novels—*When I Was Older* and *The Kings Are Already Here,* in addition to *Heartbeat*—Freymann-Weyr has also written an adult novel titled *Pretty Girls.* However, the world of young-adult fiction particularly interests her. "I write books where, so far, the main characters are fourteen to seventeen. There are some things about that age which are appealing to any writer. A fifteen-year-old girl is able and likely to sound like she's nine and then fifteen and then thirty and then eleven and finally nine again all in the space of an hour. I like the challenge of trying to capture that range."

Born Rhoda Garret Michaela Weyr in 1965, the author was brought up in New York City with three sisters. After attending the University of North Carolina in Chapel Hill and earning a master of fine arts in film at New York University, Freymann-Weyr published her first novel, *Pretty Girls,* in 1988. Taking the advice of most writing books to heart, she wrote about what she knew, setting her novel at the University of North Carolina and building the story around her three best friends during their sophomore semester. Dealing with themes of loyalty, friendship, and coming to terms with one's own worth, the novel is "post-feminist," according to *People*'s Joanne Kaufman. Best friends Alexandria—known as Alex since she was assaulted—

Caroline—whose thoughts range from her brother who was killed in Vietnam to the boyfriend from her freshman year—and Penelope—who is trying to get her busy and important father to notice her, even to the point of getting pregnant—are members of the Amazon Club. Nonstandard "pretty girls," the three learn, over the course of this one semester, about becoming young women. "One of the strengths of this novel is how well it captures the relentlessness of change in the lives of twenty year olds," wrote Linsey Abrams in a *Los Angeles Times* review of *Pretty Girls*. Freymann-Weyr's novel "charts a journey from innocence to experience," Abrams further commented.

A dozen years passed, during which time the author worked in children's publishing and married, before Freymann-Weyr published her next novel. While her first book deals with young women on the brink of adulthood, her second, *When I Was Older*, is consciously directed at a young-adult audience. Its themes, however, are no less sophisticated and demanding. A dead brother also figures prominently in this novel of "transition, love, and loss," as Angela J. Reynolds described the book in her review for *School Library Journal*. Fifteen-year-old Sophie Merdinger is a top student and a committed competitor in swimming, but her life is nonetheless still in a shambles, thrown upside-down with the death of her younger brother Erhart from leukemia three years earlier. That death not only affected Sophie, but also brought her parents' marriage to an end. Sophie can not yet forgive her father for having an affair during Erhart's final illness; she still has trouble relating to males on any level. All but Henry, that is, a brilliant chess player who is her classmate. Neither can she share her emotional state with her gorgeous older sister, Freddie. Dating is anathema to her, for she is afraid she will lose her own personality in such a relationship. Then her mother begins to go out with a history professor who has an interesting seventeen-year-old son. Francis lost his mother nine years before and can relate to Sophie's pain and confusion. He is more open than Sophie about his loss, bearing a teardrop tattoo under his left eye, and he helps her become more open as well. Sophie slowly learns to trust again as she builds a relationship with Francis, visiting the coffee shops and museum of Manhattan in the process.

Framed by a school essay written by Sophie, the plot of *When I Was Older* is "fairly standard," according to *Booklist* contributor Debbie Carton, although the philosophical issues covered by Freymann-Weyr provide the novel with "depth and meaning." For *Horn Book* reviewer Anita L. Burkam, the strong points of *When I Was Older* "lie in the concrete New York City setting and in Sophie's voice, a blunt, declarative sensibility that the author invests with ingenuous humor." Carton also had praise for Sophie's narrative voice, calling it a "delight," full of the black humor and biting wit of a teenager in transition. Reynolds felt that Freymann-Weyr tells "a fine story" in *When I Was Older*, while a reviewer for *Publishers Weekly* applauded the author's use of "humor and angst" in this tale of teen issues, and further noted that Sophie, "full of vinegar and sass, . . . carr[ies] the tale." Burkam concluded that Freymann-Weyr had written an "affecting" novel.

More life lessons are served up in Freymann-Weyr's 2002 award-winning novel, *My Heartbeat*. Susan Geye, writing in a *School Library Journal* review, called the author's third book a "tightly constructed novel about love, family, and the ambiguities of sexual identity." The author again sets her novel in contemporary Manhattan and tells of fourteen-year-old Ellen, who loves and idolizes her older brother, Link—a track star and math whiz—and his best buddy, James, both seniors. For James, with his long eyelashes and subtle smile, she has a particular affection, one she knows she will not outgrow, despite the older boy's teasing. Ellen hangs out with the older boys at every opportunity, even going to foreign films with them. A freshman, she enters their private Manhattan high school and begins to hear rumors of her brother's friendship. A popular classmate notes that Link and James actually seem like a couple. Ellen begins to wrestle with the question of whether they could actually be a couple, but is open-minded; if her brother and James are gay it is not a problem for her. A simple but curious question sets things off; Link denies that he and James are lovers, ends the friendship, begins dating a girl, and turns from math to music. This saddens and confuses Ellen, but also leaves the field open for her with James. After much discussion and much time spent together, she has her first sexual experience with James, which turns out to be James's first sexual experience with a female. Meanwhile, Ellen also attempts to understand her brother and make her overachieving parents accept both her and her relationship with James.

Highly acclaimed by reviewers, *My Heartbeat* earned starred reviews in several publications. A reviewer for *Publishers Weekly* called the novel a "sophisticated but gentle" story as well as a "thoughtful approach" to budding sexuality. Geye applauded Freymann-Weyr's "profound insights" on her characters' motivations and choices, while a critic for *Kirkus Reviews* dubbed the book "lovely and passionate," as well as "breathtaking in the purity of its emotion." Writing in *Horn Book*, Burkam felt that the author "sets up a riveting love triangle around Link's sexual ambiguity and Ellen's love for James and her brother," and *Booklist*'s Hazel Rochman found the novel "beautiful," a "frank, upbeat story of teen bisexual love in all its uncertainty."

My Heartbeat became a 2003 Michael L. Printz Honor Book and was highly praised for helping to fill the void within YA literature for such topics as teen sexuality. Freymann-Weyr, however, did not "set out to write something that could fill a void—it was just a story," as she told Whitney Matheson of *USA Today Online*.. "I was really interested in family loyalty and what you know about someone that you love and difficult siblings. And I was interested in an older man" for Ellen.

With her success, Freymann-Weyr has not rested on her laurels. Her third young-adult novel and fourth book, *The Kings Are Already Here,* appeared in 2003. Once again a precocious young woman is at the center of Freymann-Weyr's tale. Fifteen-year-old Phebe Knight is training to become a ballerina and is fixated on the goal of joining a dance company by the time she is sixteen. Then, suddenly, she begins to lose her focus and hopes that a summer spent with her father in Switzerland will help her regain it. In Switzerland, she meets sixteen-year-old Nikolai Kotalev, a chess champion who has become friends with her father. Unlike Phebe, Nikolai does not lose his focus. He is trying to train with the legendary chess champion Stas Vlajnik and thereby become a legend himself. Phebe aids him in his search across Europe for Stas, traveling with Phebe's father and his girlfriend; meanwhile she and Nikolai begin to examine the obsessions that drive their lives. A reviewer for *Horn Book* had high praise for Freymann-Weyr's "clarity of thought" and "remarkably lucid exposition," noting that the author has developed a new lexicon to describe "the pangs of coming of age." In *School Library Journal,* Sharon

Morrison called *The Kings Are Already Here* "beautifully written" and praised the author's portrayal of the "spiritual odyssey that both characters undertake," while in her *Voice of Youth Advocates* review, Diane Masla noted that Freymann-Weyr's protagonists, both "sophisticated beyond their years," build a "tentative friendship [that] reveals to each other the beauty both of other disciplines and of human relationships."

Often described as a writer whose primary focus in on family relationships and connections between friends and lovers, Freymann-Weyr rejects the idea of such theme-driven writing. "It would be really misguided to have a goal in writing," she once remarked. "Or to think about your audience while working. Or to want to reach them in any way. I write to satisfy my own standards. I sit down every day knowing that I am going to fail in some way. There's always a massive gap between what is in my head and what gets on the page. No one in their right mind would go through this for an audience. It's a private task which every now and then finds outside readers."

BIOGRAPHICAL AND CRITICAL SOURCES:

PERIODICALS

Atlanta Journal-Constitution, June 9, 2002, Julia Bookman, review of *My Heartbeat,* p. F3.
Booklist, November 1, 2000, Debbie Carton, review of *When I Was Older,* p. 524; June 1, 2002, Hazel Rochman, review of *My Heartbeat,* p. 1708.
Book Report, May-June, 2001, Deb I. Den Herder, review of *When I Was Older,* p. 58.
Bulletin of the Center for Children's Books, May, 2002, review of *My Heartbeat.*
Horn Book, January-February, 2001, Anita L. Burkam, review of *When I Was Older,* p. 90; May-June, 2002, Anita L. Burkam, review of *My Heartbeat,* p. 329; March-April, 2003, review of *The Kings Are Already Here.*
Kirkus Reviews, April 1, 2002, review of *My Heartbeat,* p. 491.
Los Angeles Times, March 20, 1988, Linsey Abrams, review of *Pretty Girls,* p. 9.
New York, May 27, 2002, Susan Avery, "When We Were Young and Gay," p. 84.

New York Times Book Review, April 10, 1988, Constance Decker Kennedy, review of *Pretty Girls,* p. 32.

People, May 2, 1988, Joanne Kaufman, review of *Pretty Girls,* pp. 25-26.

Philadelphia Inquirer, May 13, 2002, review of *My Heartbeat.*

Publishers Weekly, December 18, 1988, Sybil Steinberg, review of *Pretty Girls,* p. 54; November 6, 2000, review of *When I Was Older,* p. 91; March 18, 2002, review of *My Heartbeat,* p. 105.

Riverbank Review, fall, 2002, review of *My Heartbeat.*

School Library Journal, October, 2000, Angela J. Reynolds, review of *When I Was Older,* p. 160; April, 2002, Susan Geye, review of *My Heartbeat,* p. 148; April 2003, Sharon Morrison, review of *The Kings Are Already Here,* p. 158.

Voice of Youth Advocates, April, 2003, Diane Masla, review of *The Kings Are Already Here,* p. 48.

ONLINE

Freymann-Weyr Web site, http://www.mindspring.com/~rhodagarret/freymannweyr (February 13, 2003).

Houghton Mifflin Web Site, http://www.houghtonmifflinbooks.com/ (February 13, 2002), "Garret Freymann-Weyr."

USA Today Online, http://www.usatoday.com/ (May 16, 2002), Whitney Matheson, "Weyr's 'Heartbeat' Thumps with Passion."*

*   *   *

FRIDAY, Jo
See DRUETT, Joan

G

GALLENBERGER, Joseph (M.) 1950-

PERSONAL: Born March 20, 1950, in Menasha, WI; son of Michael (a printing company executive) and Leone (a homemaker; maiden name, Landig) Gallenberger; married Charleene Nicely (divorced); married Elena Hammond (a real estate agent), June 9, 2001; children: Sara Beth; (stepchildren) Kendra Hammond, Alexandra Hammond. *Education:* Catholic University of American, B.A. (psychology), 1972; Memphis State University, M.S., 1976, Ph.D. (clinical psychology), 1979. *Hobbies and other interests:* Gardening, hiking, piano.

ADDRESSES: Office—Rainbow Ventures, 1529 Greenville, Hwy., Hendersonville, NC 28739. *E-mail*—gammajo@bellsouth.net.

CAREER: Clinical psychologist and author. Trend Mental Health Center, Hendersonville, NC, psychological services director, 1979-81; clinical psychologist in private practice, 1981—. Monroe Institute, residential trainer; workshop presenter, mediator, and seminar leader.

MEMBER: American Psychological Association, North Carolina Psychological Association.

WRITINGS:

Brother Forever: An Unexpected Journey beyond Death, Hampton Roads (Charlotteville, VA), 1997.

Contributor to periodicals, including *Monroe Institute Focus* and *Journal of Hemi-Sync.*

WORK IN PROGRESS: A novel, *The Steam;* the poetry collection *Pillow Poems: Celebrating Love and Lust; Vegas Adventures,* a book on how to manifest what you desire; researching psychokinesis for use in energy healing, and Las Vegas gaming.

SIDELIGHTS: Joseph M. Gallenberger told *CA:* "I write to clarify my own experince to myself, to share and to teach. I write about areas of life that are often not fully discussed and have strong impact on our emotions and sense of meaning. My book, *Brothers Forever,* came about as I reached for enlightened grieving after my brother's suicide. I write from the heart and yet aim for clear and wise insight into my topic."

BIOGRAPHICAL AND CRITICAL SOURCES:

ONLINE

Rainbow Ventures: Joseph Gallenberger, http://www.raibowventures.net (November 16, 2003).

*   *   *

GOETZ, Ruth G(oodman) 1912-2001

PERSONAL: Born January 11, 1912, in Philadelphia, PA; died October 12, 2001, in Englewood, NJ; daughter of Philip Goodman (a theater producer) and Lily Cartun Goodman; married Augustus Goetz (a writer), 1931 (died 1957); children: Judy Goetz Sanger. *Education:* Miss Marshall's School, New York, NY and Paris, France.

CAREER: Story editor, costume designer, and playwright.

MEMBER: Dramatists' Guild.

AWARDS, HONORS: Academy Award (with Augustus Goetz), 1949, for best screenplay adaptation, for *The Heiress.*

WRITINGS:

(With Augustus Goetz) *One-Man Show* (play; first produced on Broadway, 1945), New York, NY, 1945.
(With Augustus Goetz) *The Heiress* (play; first produced on Broadway, 1947; based on the novel *Washington Square* by Henry James), Dramatists Play Service (New York, NY), 1948.
(With Augustus Goetz) *The Immoralist: A Drama in Three Acts* (play; first produced on Broadway, 1954; based on the novel by André Gide), Dramatists Play Service (New York, NY), 1954.
(With Augustus Goetz) *The Hidden River* (play; first produced on Broadway, 1957); based on the novel by Storm Jameson), Dramatists Play Service (New York, NY), 1957.
Sweet Love Remember'd, 1959.
(With Augustus Goetz) *The Heiress* (screenplay; based on their play), 1949.
(With Augustus Goetz) *Carrie* (screenplay), 1952.
(With Augustus Goetz) *Rhapsody* (screenplay) 1954.
(With Augustus Goetz) *Trapeze* (screenplay), 1956.
(With Augustus Goetz) *Stage Struck* (screenplay) 1957.
(With Bart Howard) *Play on Love,* produced in London, England, 1970.

Author, with Augustus Goetz and Arthury Sheekman, of produced play *Franklin Street;* author of *Madly in Love.* Works published in anthologies, including *Best Plays of 1947-1948,* John Chapman, editor, Dodd, Mead (New York, NY), 1948; and *Best Plays of 1953-1954,* Louis Kronenberger, editor, Dodd, Mead (New York, NY), 1954.

ADAPTATIONS: The Heiress was produced as an audiocassette recording, L.A. Theatre Works (Venice, CA), 1998.

SIDELIGHTS: Playwright Ruth Goodman Goetz was born in Philadelphia and grew up in New York City, where her father, Philip Goodman, produced plays. Goetz worked as a story editor and costume designer in the 1920s, but her career turned toward writing when she married aspiring author Augustus Goetz in 1931 and the two began a lifelong collaboration writing plays and screenplays.

The play *Franklin Street,* cowritten with Arthur Sheekman, was the Goetz's first team effort. Borrowing from Goodman's biography, the short-lived production drew lukewarm critical reaction.

Next, the couple penned *One-Man Show.* Published in 1945, the play had a brief run on Broadway that year. Set in the world of art dealers, the play's story emphasizes the emotional relationship between a father and daughter.

As the literary duo began to brainstorm their next script effort, Ruth Goetz suggested they adapt the Henry James novel *Washington Square.* The story of an overbearing, psychologically abusive father, his melancholy daughter, and the good-looking golddigger who woos her and betrays her was an international success. But *Washington Square* does not provide a neatly packaged happy ending, and one producer didn't like it. This producer, upon reading the couple's finished draft, talked the writers into changing the ending to an upbeat one in which the daughter reconciles with her worthless suitor.

This drastic change meant critical failure in Boston, but the couple learned a helpful lesson. They restored the somber ending, renamed it *The Heiress,* brought on Jed Harris to direct the Broadway production, and cast popular Basil Rathbone and Wendy Hiller in lead roles. Adam Bernstein, writing Goetz's obituary for the *Washington Post,* said, "The Goetzes reattached their original searing ending and the show was a sensation." A reviewer for the old *New York Daily Mirror* called the play "a bitter, relentless, absorbing character study."

The production lasted 410 performances; a successful film version, written by the Goetzes and directed by William Wyler, starred Ralph Richardson, Olivia de Havilland, and Montgomery Clift in 1949, and brought an Oscar win for the Goetzes and for de Havilland; among other revivals, in 1974, the play was produced as an opera, and in 1995, *The Heiress* won an Antoinette Perry—"Tony"—award for best revival (actress Cherry Jones also received a Tony for her performance). Mel Gussow, in his *New York Times* obituary, said Goetz felt she and her husband had added one important ingredient in adapting the classic Henry James' novel: the daughter's self-discovery through tragedy. (They also compressed the time span of the book.) Judith Flanders, reviewing the 1995 revival for the *Times Literary Supplement,* remarked, "This reduced time span produces a more dramatic but less interesting denouement."

Stefan Kanfer wrote in *New Leader,* "What one cannot imagine is James writing a play so tightly constructed or shrewdly cast as the Lincoln Center Theater production of *The Heiress.* . . . In essence, the story is a triangle with only two lovers: the shy, unprepossessing Catherine Sloper . . . and the handsome, unscrupulous Morris Townsend. . . . The third party is Catherine's father. . . Dr. Austin Sloper."

The Goetzes produced adaptations after 1954. *The Immoralist: A Drama in Three Acts* is an adaptation of the novel by André Gide, and the story of a gay man. Brooks Atkinson wrote in *New York Times* after it opened on Broadway, "Magnificently acted by a company led by Geraldine Page and Louis Jourdan, *The Immoralist* . . . retains the integrity of Gide and does credit to the taste of the Goetzes."

Several more film adaptations followed. The pair adapted Theodore Dreiser's novel *Sister Carrie* in a script version titled *Carrie;* they also wrote the screenplay adaptations *Rhapsody,* starring Elizabeth Taylor, *Trapeze,* and *Stage Struck,* the last directed by Sidney Lumet. Before Augustus Goetz died in 1957, the husband-and-wife writing partners completed a stage version of Storm Jamison's postwar suspense novel *The Hidden River.*

In 1957 Goetz wrote *Sweet Love Remember'd,* a story based on her husband. The play was produced in 1959 but experienced a short run due to the suicide death of lead actress Margaret Sullavan during the production's tryout phase.

In the following years, Goetz wrote the play *Madly in Love,* an adaptation of *L'amour fou* by André Roussin. Collaborating with Bart Howard, she also wrote *Play on Love,* produced in London.

Gussow said, "Speaking about the art of playwriting, Mrs. Goetz said, 'Dramatization is imagination made palpable, or visible, or understandable—instantly.'"

BIOGRAPHICAL AND CRITICAL SOURCES:

BOOKS

Coven, Brenda, *American Women Dramatists of the Twentieth Century,* Scarecrow Press (Metuchen, NJ), 1982.
Notable Names in the American Theatre, James T. White (Clifton, NJ), 1976.

PERIODICALS

America, April 29, 1995, James S. Torrens, review of *The Heiress,* p. 26.
Back Stage, November 27, 1981, Jennie Schulman, review of *The Heiress,* p. 83; March 24, 1995, David Sheward, review of *The Heiress,* p. 52.
Back Stage West, November 20, 1997, Kerry Reid, review of *The Heiress,* p. 9.
Booklist, May 25, 1999, Barbara Baskin, review of *The Heiress,* p. 1714.
Christian Science Monitor, Frank Scheck, review of *The Heiress,* March 17, 1995, p. 13.
New Leader, March 13, 1995, Stefan Kramer, review of *The Heiress,* pp. 22-23.
New Yorker, March 20, 1995, Nancy Franklin, review of *The Heiress,* pp. 108-109.
New York Times, October 4, 1980, Richard Eder, article, "After 33 years, 'Heiress' is an opera," p. 10; July 7, 1985, Howard Thompson, review of *The Heiress,* p. 20; June 16, 1989, Mel Gussow, review of *The Heiress,* p. B3; March 5, 1995, William Harris, "The Story behind an American Drama of Passion," p. H7; March 10, 1995, Vincent Canby, review of *The Heiress,* p. B1; March 19, 1995, Margo Jefferson, review of *The Heiress,* p. H33.
Times Literary Supplement, June 23, 2000, Judith Flanders, review of *The Heiress,* p. 22.
Variety, March 13, 1995, Greg Evans, review of *The Heiress,* p. 61.
Wall Street Journal, March 10, 1995, Donald Lyons, review of *The Heiress,* p. A12.

OBITUARIES:

PERIODICALS

American Theatre, December 2001, by Judith Ruther-
    ford James, pp. 14-15.
Back Stage, October 26, 2001, p. 47.
Independent, November 3, 2001, by Tom Vallance, p.
    WR6.
Washington Post, October 17, 2001, by Adam Bern-
    stein, p. B07.*

*   *   *

GOH, Chan Hon 1969-

PERSONAL: Born February 1, 1969, in Beijing,
China; immigrated to Canada, 1977; daughter of Choo
Chiat (founder of Goh Ballet Academy) and Lin Yee
(principal of Goh Ballet Academy) Goh; married Chun
Che (a dance instructor), August 29, 1997. *Ethnicity:*
"Chinese." *Education:* Trained in ballet by her father
at Goh Ballet Academy.

ADDRESSES: Home—26 Rowanwood Ave., Toronto,
Ontario M4W 1Y7, Canada.

CAREER: Dancer. National Ballet of Canada, Toronto,
Ontario, Canada, member of corps de ballet, 1988,
promoted to second soloist, 1990, promoted to first
soloist, 1992, promoted to principal dancer, 1994—;
Suzanne Farrell Ballet, guest dancer. With husband,
designer and owner of Principal Shoes. Served on
advisory panel, Metro Toronto Arts Council, 1991-93,
and as cultural advisor to the Chinese Cultural Centre
of Greater Toronto.

AWARDS, HONORS: Solo Seal Award, Royal Academy of Dancing; Lausanne Prize, International
Competition of Dance (Lausanne, Switzerland), 1986;
silver medal, Adeline Genee Competition (London,
England), 1988; named among Women of Achievement, *Chatelaine* magazine, 1988.

WRITINGS:

(With Cary Fagan) *Beyond the Dance: A Ballerina's
    Life,* Tundra Books (Toronto, Ontario, Canada),
    2002.

SIDELIGHTS: With the aid of Cary Fagan, prima ballerina Chan Hon Goh tells her personal story in *Beyond
the Dance,* which Allan Ulrich dubbed an "illuminating quasi-memoir," in a *Dance* review. Although both
of Goh's parents were professional ballet dancers in
China, after they immigrated to Canada when their
daughter Chan was only eight years old, they did not
encourage her to dance. Instead, they promoted other
creative activities, like playing the piano and singing,
allowing Chan to take a dance lesson at her father's
academy in Vancouver only once a week. Nevertheless, as Goh later recounted, in the same way she
determinedly learned English and excelled in her studies, she finally convinced her parents to allow her to
dance with a serious intent. "Dancing has almost been,
since the minute I was born, in my blood," Goh told
Joanna Slater of the *Far Eastern Economic Review.*

During the mid-1980s, Goh attracted considerable attention, winning international ballet competitions, and
in 1988, she was asked to join the National Ballet of
Canada, based in Toronto. There she quickly rose from
the corps to become a principal dancer and has appeared in numerous coveted classical roles as well as
world premieres of contemporary works. Knowing
that a dancer's professional life is short, she and
husband Chun Che founded the firm Principal Shoes,
that designs and sells a line of pointe and slipper ballet shoes for men and women. Another part of Goh's
life involves sharing her secrets of success. "I wrote
my autobiography to inspire hope," Goh once explained, "determination, and perseverance in today's
young adults infused in our multi-cultural (multi-
racial) society. With my Chinese-immigrant background and being the first Chinese-Canadian to hold
the position of principal dancer at the National Ballet
of Canada, I am proof that dreams can be realized."

In *Beyond the Dance,* Goh details her childhood in
China, the family's immigration to Canada and the
challenges they faced as immigrants, and Goh's rise to
prominence in ballet. She also gives a close look at
what a career in dance involves. "At present, I am a
mature artist at the height of my career," she once
noted, "and I want my readers to have the opportunity
to see me dance on stage as well as to read my story. I
also want to offer my readers more insight on the road
to becoming a professional (ballerina) dancer."

Considering such aspects as writing style, choice of
photographs, and reader appeal, reviewers found much
to like about this autobiography. In her *School Library*

Journal review, Cheri Estes called the work "highly readable" and "overwhelmingly positive" in tone. Indeed, Goh believes that hard work led to her success, as she recalled at the *Canadian Living* Web site: "My family's experience taught me not to be afraid of the hard work, and to persevere. Overcoming difficulty was a natural way of life." Eva Wilson of *Resource Links* found the language "somewhat stilted," yet asserted that the interesting subject matter overcomes this stylistic defect. Janice Linton of *Canadian Materials* suggested that while the narrative misses visceral appeal and "lacks drama," the simple language and the success story of an immigrant family would make this title a good choice for students learning English as a second language.

BIOGRAPHICAL AND CRITICAL SOURCES:

PERIODICALS

Canadian Materials, January, 2003, Janice Linton, review of *Beyond the Dance.*
Chinatown News, March 18, 1994, Max Wyman, "Chan Hon Goh: Canadian National Ballet's Principal Dancer," p. 14.
Dance, August, 1994, Deidre Kelly, "The Actress," p. 64; April, 2003, Paula Citron, "Ballerina as Entrepreneur," pp. 22-23; June, 2003, Allan Ulrich, review of *Beyond the Dance,* p. 70.
Far Eastern Economic Review, February 19, 1998, Joanna Slater, "On Her Toes," p. 70.
Resource Links, February, 2003, Eva Wilson, review of *Beyond the Dance,* pp. 49-50.
School Library Journal, Cheri Estes, review of *Beyond the Dance,* p. 182.

ONLINE

Canadian Living, http://www.canadianliving.com/ (June 24, 2003), Karen Brown and Nancy Eskin, "Chan Hon Goh."
National Ballet of Canada, http://www.national.ballet. ca/ (June 24, 2003), "Chan Hon Goh."
Perspectives, http://perspectives.ubc.ca/ (February, 2003), review of *Beyond the Dance.*
SEE Magazine, http://greatwest.ca/ (March 21, 2002), Salena McDougall, "World of Dance: A Gala Performance."*

GOOD, David L. 1942-

PERSONAL: Born June 29, 1942, in Detroit, MI; son of Raymond E. (a school principal) and Marcelle Good; married Janet R. Lohela, November 27, 1971; children: Christopher L., Leslie S., Marcelle J. *Education:* University of Michigan, B.A., 1964, M.A., 1966.

ADDRESSES: Home—710 North Waverley, Dearborn, MI 48128.

CAREER: Detroit News, Detroit, MI, reporter and editor, 1966-2000.

WRITINGS:

Orvie, the Dictator of Dearborn, Wayne State University Press (Detroit, MI), 1989.

Author of screenplay *Company Town.*

WORK IN PROGRESS: The Detroits, a screenplay; *Julia!,* a libretto for a play.

*   *   *

GORDON, Jay 1948-

PERSONAL: Born 1948; married; children: one daughter.

ADDRESSES: Office—901 Montana Ave., Santa Monica, CA 90403. *E-mail*—Jay@drjaygordon.com.

CAREER: Pediatrician, author, lecturer, and consultant. University of California Medical School, Los Angeles, teaching attending faculty member; Cedars-Sinai Medical Center, Los Angeles, teaching attending faculty member. Consultant for film and television programs; medical consultant for children's programming for CBS-TV; medical correspondent for *Home Show.* Member, La Leche League professional advisory board.

AWARDS, HONORS: Sloan-Kettering Institute senior fellowship.

WRITINGS:

Good Food Today, Great Kids Tomorrow: Fifty Things You Can Do for Healthy, Happy Children, Michael Wiese Productions (Studio City, CA), 1994.
(With Brenda Adderly) *Brighter Baby,* LifeLine Press (Washington, DC), 1999.
(With Maria Goodavage) *Good Nights: The Happy Parents' Guide to the Family Bed, and a Peaceful Night's Sleep!,* St. Martin's Griffin (New York, NY), 2002.
Listening to Your Baby: A New Approach to Parenting Your Newborn, Perigree (New York, NY), 2002.

Contributor to parenting Web sites and magazines; columnist for *Fit Pregnancy.* Consulting physician for *Natural Home Remedies,* Future Medicine Publishing (Puyallup, WA), 1994.

SIDELIGHTS: Jay Gordon is a pediatrician in private practice in Santa Monica, California, and the author of several books on parenting. He is a frequent contributor to parenting and pregnancy periodicals and Web sites, and has also worked as a television script consultant on medical matters. Gordon's patients include the children of Hollywood's top celebrities, a fact that has earned him a reputation as "Tinseltown's top kids' doctor."

Gordon developed an interest in nutrition and alternative medicine during his medical training and accepted a senior fellowship in pediatric nutrition at the Sloan-Kettering Institute in New York City. He completed his residency at Children's Hospital, Los Angeles, before becoming a teaching and attending faculty member at the University of California—Los Angeles Medical School. Gordon's first book, *Good Food Today, Great Kids Tomorrow: Fifty Things You Can Do for Healthy, Happy Children,* covers the role of nutrition in childhood illnesses and also discusses juvenile weight problems and ways to discuss nutrition with young children. Interestingly, Gordon advocates a vegetarian diet; as Nathaniel Mead commented in *Natural Health,* "What's lacking from Gordon's discussion . . . is a clear statement of the possible dangers of vitamin B-12 deficiency in children

on strict vegetarian diets." However, Mead concluded, over all, Gordon's "commonsense advice should appeal to diet-conscious parents from all walks of life." In his second book, *Brighter Baby,* Gordon offers parents advice for increasing their child's intelligence through massage, nutrition, and mental exercises.

In *Good Nights: The Happy Parents' Guide to the Family Bed, and a Peaceful Night's Sleep!* Gordon and coauthor Maria Goodavage weigh in on the issue of whether children should share a bed with their parents, arguing in favor of the practice. He offers advice on safety, maintaining a healthy sex life, and handling outside criticism. *Library Journal* contributor Annette V. Janes noted that while many people are skeptical of the practice, "the authors conducted impressive research and present it convincingly." Janes concluded that while the book is "not for everyone," it "provides a good alternative" to dealing with difficult bedtimes. In *Listening to Your Baby: A New Approach to Parenting Your Newborn* Gordon covers topics of concern to new parents, such as child development, breastfeeding, and sleep patterns, and advocates an instinctual approach to parenting.

BIOGRAPHICAL AND CRITICAL SOURCES:

PERIODICALS

Express on Sunday (London, England), June 2, 2002, Elaine Lipworth, "Doctor to the Stars," p. 60.
Library Journal, August, 2002, Annette V. Janes, review of *Good Nights: The Happy Parents' Guide to the Family Bed, and a Peaceful Night's Sleep!,* p. 132.
Natural Health, May-June, 1995, Nathaniel Mead, review of *Good Food Today, Great Kids Tomorrow: Fifty Things You Can Do for Healthy, Happy Children,* p. 168.

ONLINE

Dr. Jay Gordon, http://www.drjaygordon.com (June 19, 2003).*

*   *   *

GORE-BOOTH, Eva (Selena) 1870-1926

PERSONAL: Born May 22, 1870, in Lissadell, County Sligo, Ireland; died June 30, 1926, in London, England; daughter of Sir Henry and Georgina (Hill) Gore-Booth.

CAREER: Poet, playwright, and political activist.

WRITINGS:

Poems, Longmans, Green (London, England), 1898.

The One and the Many, Longmans, Green (London, England), 1904.

Unseen Kings, Longmans, Green (London, England), 1904.

Women Workers and Parliamentary Representation, Lancashire and Cheshire Women Textile and Other Workers' Representation Committee (Manchester, England), 1904.

The Three Resurrections and The Triumph of Maeve, Longmans, Green (London, England), 1905.

The Egyptian Pillar, Maunsel (Dublin, Ireland), 1907.

The Sorrowful Princess, Longmans, Green (London, England), 1907.

Women's Right to Work, Women's Trade and Labour Council (Manchester and Salford, England), 1908.

The Agate Lamp, Longmans, Green (London, England), 1912.

The Perilous Light, Macdonald (London, England), 1915.

Religious Aspects of Non-Resistance, League for Peace and Freedom (London, England), 1915.

Broken Glory, Maunsel (Dublin, Ireland), 1918.

The Sword of Justice, Headley (London, England), 1918.

Select Passages Illustrating Florentine Life in the Thirteenth and Fourteenth Centuries, Society for Promotion of Christian Knowledge (London, England), 1920.

A Psychological and Poetic Approach to the Study of Christ in the Fourth Gospel, Longmans, Green (London, England), 1923.

The Shepherd of Eternity, Longmans, Green (London, England), 1925.

The House of Three Windows, Longmans, Green (London, England), 1926.

The Inner Kingdom, Longmans, Green (London, England), 1926.

The World's Pilgrim, Longmans, Green (London, England), 1927.

Poems of Eva Gore-Booth, Longmans, Green (London, England), 1929.

The Buried Life of Deirdre, Longmans, Green (London, England), 1930.

Prison Letters of Countess Markievicz, Longmans, Green (London, England), 1934.

The Plays of Eva Gore-Booth, , edited by Frederick S. Lapisardi, Mellen (San Francisco, CA), 1991.

SIDELIGHTS: Largely associated with the Celtic revival that swept over her homeland at the turn of the twentieth century, Irish author Eva Gore-Booth was the author of nine books of poetry, seven plays, and several collections of spiritual essays and studies of the Gospels. Just as important to her legacy, however, are the many pamphlets and essays she published while living in England that deal with the political issues of her day, including the fight for equal rights for women. In addition to being a writer, Gore-Booth was also a political activist, and one of the first female suffragists to advocate extending the vote to both female property owners and women in the working class. "Sex is an accident," Gore-Booth once wrote, summing up her motivation to fight for equal rights. Gore-Booth's equally strong belief in pacifism was evident in many of her works, including the protest play The Buried Life of Deirdre (1930).

From an aristocratic background, Gore-Booth began writing poetry in the early 1890s, and her talent was immediately noticed by some well-known Irish literary figures, including the great poet William Butler Yeats. Recognizing that despite her talent Gore-Booth was still an undisciplined writer, Yeats gave her several books to read in an effort to help polish her craft. "I'm always ransacking Ireland for people to set at writing Irish things," Yeats wrote in an 1895 letter. "She does not know that she is the last victim—but is deep in some books of Irish legends I sent her and might take fire." Indeed, in spite of the fact that Gore-Booth lived most of her adult life away from Ireland, many critics have maintained that her work is a good representation of Irish literature of the period.

Gore-Booth's poetry, especially such later works as The One and the Many and The Egyptian Pillar, include themes of social change and sexual liberation. For example, the latter collection makes numerous references to strong and independent women from ancient times, including Sheba and Cleopatra. Two of her poetry collections, The Perilous Light and Broken Glory, published during World War I, express pacifist themes. Despite the praise she received from many contemporary critics, modern readers have largely neglected Gore-Booth's work. Some scholars believe that her writings should not be forgotten, however, because they offer a unique perspective on some of the most important issues of her time. "Gore-Booth deserves a far more prominent place in the canon of British literature of the early twentieth century," wrote John C. Hawley in the *Dictionary of Literary Biography.*

The daughter of Anglo-Irish landowners, Gore-Booth was born in 1870 into a life of privilege. The private education she received helped spawn her independent thinking and creative self-expression. The death of her grandmother, Lady Hill, when Gore-Booth was nine years old was a shaping force throughout her life. In the years following Lady Hill's death, Gore-Booth felt the constant presence of her grandmother's spirit. Some critics have noted that such a belief led to Gore-Booth's lifelong interest in mysticism and theosophy, which she explores in many of her writings. In fact, spirituality is a central concern of her final two books of poetry, *The Shepherd of Eternity* and *The House of Three Windows.*

In 1896, while on a trip to Italy, Gore-Booth met Esther Roper, a leading suffragist and activist. The two women became lifelong partners, although there is no evidence that they were lovers. Under Roper's tutelage, Gore-Booth became a leading voice in the suffragist movement, especially after they moved to the English industrial city of Manchester. There the two women helped female factory workers organize and fight for better working conditions. In 1900 Gore-Booth became a leading figure of the Manchester Trade Union Council, which was enormously influential in the formation of dozens of other female unions.

Political activities never prevented Gore-Booth from writing, and she continued to publish regularly right up to the time of her death. Having suffered poor health throughout much of her adult life, Gore-Booth died of intestinal cancer on June 30, 1926, in London, where she had moved just a few years earlier. Shortly before she died, she privately published a magazine called *Urania,* which circulated around London. In it Gore-Booth made a prophetic statement that symbolizes much of what she believed. "There is a vista before us of a Spiritual progress which far transcends all political matters," she declared. "It is the abolition of the 'manly' and the 'womanly.' Will you not help to sweep them into the museum of antiques?"

BIOGRAPHICAL AND CRITICAL SOURCES:

BOOKS

Dictionary of Literary Biography, Volume 240: *Late Nineteenth- and Early Twentieth-Century British Women Poets,* Gale (Detroit, MI), 2001.*

*   *   *

GRACE, Carol
See MATTHAU, Carol (Grace Marcus)

*   *   *

GRACE, Susan Andrews 1949-

PERSONAL: Born February 26, 1949, in Tisdale, Saskatchewan, Canada; daughter of Thomas Joseph and Mary Elizabeth (Cavanagh) Grace; married Gordon Andrews, August 29, 1970; children: Katherine Mary, Thomas Gordon, Patrick Daniel. *Education:* University of Saskatchewan, B.A., 1998; University of Nevada, Las Vegas, M.A.

ADDRESSES: Office—c/o Nelson Fine Art Centre, 625 Front St., Suite 301, Nelson, BC, V1L 4B6, Canada. *E-mail*—nfac@netidea.com

CAREER: Poet and textile artist. Volunteer in Saskatchewan arts community, 1974-97; former administrator of fine arts center; publisher of *Hag Papers;* Nelson Fine Art Centre writing program, Nelson, British Columbia, Canada, member of faculty. *Exhibitions:* Solo exhibitions include *Inside/Out,* 1991; *100Unknown Fibre,* 1994; and *Cov(r)n,* 2000. Co-designer and coordinator for community project for *Peace Quilt,* 1987; and various group exhibitions.

MEMBER: League of Canadian Poets (chair of Feminist caucus, 1991-93).

AWARDS, HONORS: Canada Council Explorations grant, 1987; Peace Messenger Award, United Nations, 1987, for *Peace Quilt* community project; Philosophy Prize, St. Thomas More College, University of

Saskatchewan, 1998; Saskatchewan Book of the Year Award, 1998, for *Ferry Woman's History of the World;* several Saskatchewan Arts Board grants.

WRITINGS:

Wearing My Father (chapbook), Underwhich Editions, 1990.
Water Is the First World, Coteau Books (Regina, Saskatchewan, Canada), 1991.
Ferry Woman's History of the World, Coteau Books (Regina, Saskatchewan, Canada), 1998.

Contributor to numerous literary journals and anthologies, including *Women and Words: The Anthology,* Harbour Publishing, 1984; *Cracked Wheat,* Coteau Books, 1985; *Heading Out: The New Saskatchewan Poets,* Coteau Books, 1986; *A Labour of Love: An Anthology of Poetry on Pregnancy and Childbirth,* Polestar Press, 1989; and *Our Fathers,* Rowan Books, 1995.

SIDELIGHTS: Poet and textile artist Susan Andrews Grace has been active in the Canadian arts world for a quarter of a century. She has published three books of poetry and has contributed to numerous literary journals and anthologies. Having earned a master's degree in creative writing, she is on the writing faculty at the Nelson, British Columbia, Fine Art Centre.

Grace's most recent book of poetry, *Ferry Woman's History of the World,* has its roots in the poet's own exploration of her family's history back to its noble Norman ancestor, Raymond le Gros. *Ferry Woman* has been called an "alternative prayerbook," according to Pauline Ferrie, in a review for *Bookview Ireland.*

The book is organized into three sections: "The Book of Gilliosa," where the central narrator discovers the Ferry Woman, a crone who takes her to meet matriarchs Mary and Nesta and to explore the many aspects of a woman's life; "Ferry Woman: A Book of Authority," in which they continue on their watery and spiritual journey; and "The Book of Fitzgerald," in which Gilliosa researches her ancestry and explores religious beliefs.

The book is described as both novel and long poem, although it is written mostly in verse. Beryl Baigent, writing in the *Canadian Book Review Annual,* pointed out that its three sections could also warrant its classification as "a Celtic triad of short stories." But, she noted, it is really none of these, as Grace "is offering the reader the wholeness of chaos, from which one must find one's own yin and yang." In an afterword, Grace tells the reader of her own experiences with "the Ferry Woman." Baigent thought it might have provided more access to *Ferry Woman's Critical History of the World* as a foreword, but she concluded, "presumably, though, access is not the point."

BIOGRAPHICAL AND CRITICAL SOURCES:

PERIODICALS

Canadian Book Review Annual, 1998, Beryl Baigent, review of *Ferry Woman's History of the World,* p. 225-226.

ONLINE

Bookview Ireland, http://www.bookviewireland.ie/ (February, 1999), Pauline Ferrie, review of *Ferry Woman's History of the World.*
League of Canadian Poets, http://www.poets.ca/ (April 1, 2003), "Susan Andrews Grace."
Nelson Fine Art Centre, http://www.nfac.ca/ (April 1, 2003), "Susan Andrews Grace."*

*   *   *

GRAHAM, Winston (Mawdsley) 1910-2003

OBITUARY NOTICE—See index for *CA* sketch: Born June 30, 1910, in Manchester, England; died July 10, 2003, in Buxted, East Sussex, England. Author. Graham was a popular British novelist best known for his "Poldark" historical series. A sickly youth, he was educated at home by his mother, who encouraged his literary efforts when he began to write and supported Graham financially when he started to produce novels for a living. His first publication successes were short stories for periodicals such as *Windsor* magazine, and genre novels for London publisher Ward, Lock, which paid him very little for these early books. During the London blitz many of Graham's early novels were destroyed, but he was not overly upset because, as he later admitted, they were not very good. One of his first bestsellers was the thriller *Night without Stars* (1950), which won him a contract with Hodder & Stoughton that was much more lucrative than his Ward, Lock arrangement. By then, Graham was already becoming popular for his various genre books, which now included thrillers, crime novels, gothic romances, and, most famously, his historical novels featuring the Poldark family and beginning with *Ross Poldark: A Novel of Cornwall, 1783-1787* (1945). Over the course of his career, Graham would follow the Poldark family and their rivals, the Warleggans, in twelve books, concluding with *Bella Poldark: A Novel of Cornwall, 1818-1820* (2002). These books are beloved for their detailed portrayal of historical Cornwall, where the author lived for thirty years, and their colorful characters, who occupied themselves in various intrigues. The "Poldark" series was adapted for two television series, one airing during the 1970s and 1980s, and the other debuting in 1993. Graham also found success outside of the "Poldark" books; a number of his novels were turned into movies, most notably the 1964 Alfred Hitchcock film *Marnie* and the movie *The Walking Stick* (1969), based on his 1967 story. Despite selling many books, Graham remained a private man and avoided fame. Some of his other notable books include *The Little Walls* (1956), which won a Crime Writers Association award; *Angell, Pearl, and Little God* (1970); and his autobiography *Memoirs of a Private Man* (2003). For his memorable contributions to literature, Graham was honored as a fellow of the Royal Society of Literature in 1968 and named to the Order of the British Empire in 1983.

OBITUARIES AND OTHER SOURCES:

BOOKS

Contemporary Novelists, seventh edition, St. James Press (Detroit, MI), 2001.
Writers Directory, 18th edition, St. James Press (Detroit, MI), 2003.

PERIODICALS

Independent (London, England), July 11, 2003, p. 16.
Los Angeles Times, July 11, 2003, p. B13.
New York Times, July 12, 2003, p. A21.
Washington Post, July 15, 2003, p. B7.

GRAY, Paul 1918-2002

PERSONAL: Born 1918, in Chicago, IL; died of congestive heart failure July 26, 2002, in Washington, DC; married; wife's name, Virginia (divorced); married; second wife's name, Gerda; children: (first marriage) Lorraine, Steven. *Education:* University of Chicago, B.A., M.D., 1942; Baltimore-Washington Psychoanalytic Institute, graduated 1951.

CAREER: Psychoanalyst and educator. Psychoanalyst in private practice, Washington, DC, beginning 1950s; Washington-Baltimore Psychoanalytic Institute, Washington, DC, on staff, 1953-2002, training and supervising analyst, 1956-86, training analyst emeritus, 1986-2002. Affiliated with Center for Advanced Psychoanalytic Studies, Princeton, NJ. *Military service:* U.S. Navy, 1944-46..

WRITINGS:

The Ego and Analysis of Defense, Jason Aronson (Northvale, NJ), 1994.

Contributor to medical journals.

SIDELIGHTS: Psychoanalyst Paul Gray was born in Chicago, Illinois but grew up in Aberdeen, South Dakota. He was the son of hardy pioneer stock, and his father rose from working on the railroad to become president of the union. During his lifetime, Gray saw significant changes in his discipline, and his experience caused others in the field to seek his opinion. As a training and supervising analyst, he taught candidates and graduates, as well as social workers and psychiatric residents.

Gray's *The Ego and Analysis of Defense* is a response to a theory developed by Sigmund Freud and published in 1923, after Freud dismissed hypnosis as a cure. Hartvig Dahl wrote in *Contemporary Psychology* that "the new theory explicitly recognized that patients' defenses against unconscious wishes are themselves often unconscious and resistant to change." Therefore, treatment was structured to help patients recall not only their unconscious wishes, but also their defenses as a mechanism to changing the latter. Dahl said that in the book, "Gray's thesis is that, in their attempts to overcome the inevitable resistances that arise from unconscious defenses, psychoanalysts have too often lagged behind a central implication of the theory, that is, the need to analyze such defenses."

Mardi J. Horowitz noted in the *American Journal of Psychiatry* that "Gray's use of examples gives the book clinical utility and freshness. The result is a modern emphasis on collaboration and interaction, not just on neutral, authoritarian, and theory-dictated interpretations. Gray shows how to give the patient new tools for understanding personal fantasies and intentions throughout his or her future life."

Marianne Goldberger, who dedicated her *Danger and Defense: The Technique of Close Process Attention* to Gray on the occasion of his seventy-fifth birthday, conducted an interview with Gray, the transcript of which is available on the Web site of Gray's publisher, Jason Aronson. Goldberger asked Gray how his ideas about analytic technique evolved.

Gray explained to Goldberger that, "at some point in my analytic training, I became aware of what seemed to me a puzzling discrepancy: In teaching, analysts emphasized the importance of following the events in the patient's mind; but in clinical conferences, continuing case presentations, and supervision, they frequently showed interest in the patient's behavior outside the analytic situation, an interest I had come to associate with psychotherapy. . . . I believe that focusing attention consistently on what happens 'inside' the analytic hour helps patients become aware of the many unconscious activities they use to resolve conflict at the time they're using them." Gray felt that this demonstrates to patients that their defenses present themselves in many forms, including those of memory.

Until the time of his death, Gray continued to teach and consult at his office at the Baltimore-Washington Psychoanalytic Institute. Richard Pearson of the *Washington Post* wrote his obituary, saying that Gray, "who gained a reputation as a creative and gifted teacher, was a master at finding exactly the right word, whether communicating with students or patients."

BIOGRAPHICAL AND CRITICAL SOURCES:

BOOKS

Goldberger, Marianne, *Danger and Defense: The Technique of Close Process Attention* (festschrift), Jason Aronson (Northvale, NJ), 1996.

PERIODICALS

American Journal of Psychiatry, April, 1996, Mardi J. Horowitz, review of *The Ego and Analysis of Defense,* p. 571.
Contemporary Psychology, October, 1995, Hartvig Dahl, review of *The Ego and Analysis of Defense,* p. 992.

ONLINE

Jason Aronson, http://www.aronson.com/ (March 29, 2003), Marianne Goldberger, interview with Gray.

OBITUARIES:

PERIODICALS

Washington Post, July 26, 2002, Richard Pearson, p. C6.*

*   *   *

GRIFFIN, Rod L. 1966-

PERSONAL: Born April 26, 1966, in Austin, TX. *Hobbies and other interests:* Golf, martial arts, reading, biking.

ADDRESSES: Office—$olvency International Inc., 1550-F3 McMullen Booth Rd., No. 187, Clearwater, FL. 33759. *Agent*—Jeremy Fosterfell, Arthur Arthur—Theatrical, 6542 U.S. Hwy 41 N., Suite 205-A, Apollo Beach, FL 33572. *E-mail*—si@peoplepc.com.

CAREER: Author, entrepreneur, and real estate counselor. Former martial arts instructor.

WRITINGS:

How to Finance Your Way to Wealth, $olvency International (Clearwater, FL), 1996.
The Profit Formula, $olvency International (Clearwater, FL), 1997.

How to Make Fast Cash in Real Estate with No-Money-down Deals, International Wealth Success (Merrick, NY), 1999.

The Love of My Life (romance), $olvency International (Clearwater, FL), 2002.

The Way of the Cosmic Fist: A Beginners' Guide into the Art of Tai-Ch'uan-Tao, $olvency International (Clearwater, FL), 2002.

How to Buy and Flip Real Estate for a Profit!, International Wealth Success (Merrick, NY), 2002.

A Lost Innocence (novel), $olvency International (Clearwater, FL), 2002.

SIDELIGHTS: Roy L. Griffin told *CA:* "By age fourteen, I had earned a black belt in kung fu, and by age fifteen I was teaching in my own martial arts school. I later became a five-time Florida state sport karate champion. At age seventeen I dropped out of school and obtained my GED. I began investing in real estate at age twenty-seven, and still serve as a real estate consultant. The pursuit of my dreams—acting, and a passion for arts and the theater—is what has led me to writing fiction. My writings in nonfiction include real-estate investing and martial arts. Through my writing, I have worked to instill good moral values in our children and in people across the country. Ever the hopeless romantic, I love to write poetry and romance."

*   *   *

GROSS, Nancy Lammers 1956-

PERSONAL: Born February 20, 1956, in St. Louis, MO; daughter of John V. and Elnor R. Lammers; married John R. Gross, September 5, 1987; children: Anna Catherine, Abigail Louise. *Ethnicity:* "Caucasian." *Education:* Willamette University, B.S., 1978; Princeton Theological Seminary, M.Div., 1981, Ph.D., 1992; studied vocal pedagogy and performance privately, 1998-99.

ADDRESSES: Home—34 Prospect Ave., Plainsboro, NJ 08536. *Office*—Princeton Theological Seminary, P.O. Box 821, Princeton, NJ 08542-0803; fax: 609-497-7870. *E-mail*—nancy.gross@ptsem.edu.

CAREER: Ordained Presbyterian minister, 1981; associate pastor of Presbyterian church, Burlingame, CA, 1981-85; Eastern Baptist Theological Seminary,

assistant professor, 1991-98, associate professor of homiletics, 1998-2001; Princeton Theological Seminary, Princeton, NJ, associate professor of speech communication in ministry, 2001—. Princeton Theological Seminary, visiting lecturer, 1991-92 and 1994-2001. Member of New Brunswick Presbytery of the Presbyterian Church; substitute or guest pastor at Presbyterian churches throughout New Jersey and western Pennsylvania, beginning 1986; Lutheran Seminary, Philadelphia, PA, member of governing council, Academy of Preachers, 1993-96.

MEMBER: National Communication Association, Religious Communication Association, Academy of Homiletics.

AWARDS, HONORS: Grant from Wabash Center for Teaching and Learning, 2000.

WRITINGS:

If You Cannot Preach like Paul . . . , William B. Eerdmans Publishing (Grand Rapids, MI), 2002.

Contributor to books, including *Word and Witness,* edited by Paul Scott Wilson, 1998; and *Abingdon Women's Preaching Annual, Volume 2, Year A,* edited by Nora Tubbs Tisdale. Contributor of articles and reviews to periodicals, including *Academy Accents, in-Ministry: Eastern Baptist Theological Seminary,* and *KOINONIA.*

*   *   *

GUSS, Jeffrey R. 1953-

PERSONAL: Born October 3, 1953, in Louisville, KY; son of Donald and Gloria Joyce (Goldsmith) Guss. *Education:* Northwestern University, B.A.; University of Louisville, M.D. *Hobbies and other interests:* Music, theater, art.

ADDRESSES: Home—10 Park Ave., No. 24D, New York, NY 10016. *Office*—77 Park Ave., Suite 1C, New York, NY 10016; fax: 212-213-1374. *E-mail*—Jeffrey.Guss@verizon.net.

CAREER: Educator and author. University of Michigan Affiliated Hospitals, Ann Arbor, MI, resident; New York University, New York, NY, clinical assistant professor of psychiatry at School of Medicine, 1993—.

MEMBER: International Association of Relational Psychoanalytic Programs, American Psychiatric Association, American Academy of Psychoanalysis, American Academy of Addiction Psychiatry.

WRITINGS:

(Editor with Jack Drescher) *Addictions in the Gay and Lesbian Community,* Haworth Medical Press (New York, NY), 2000.

Also contributor to *Journal of Gay and Lesbian Psychotherapy.*

H

HALABY, Najeeb E(lias) 1915-2003

OBITUARY NOTICE—See index for *CA* sketch: Born December 19, 1915, in Dallas, TX; died July 2, 2003, in McLean, VA. Businessman, attorney, and author. Halaby was a former airline executive at Pan American World Airways who was more famously known as the father of Queen Noor of Jordan. The son of a Lebanese-Syrian man who married an American citizen, Halaby became Americanized and forgot the little Arabic he learned after his father died when he was young. He attended Stanford University, where he earned his A.B. in 1937, followed by law school at the University of Michigan and Yale University, where he graduated with an L.L.B. in 1940. Training as a pilot while a teenager, he worked for the Lockheed Aircraft Corp. for a year before joining the U.S. Navy during World War II as a test pilot of such planes as the Messerschmitt Me262, Focke-Wulf FW190, and Bell XP59 jet. After the war he worked as an advisory to the U.S. Secretary of Defense and then as deputy assistant for international security for the U.S. State Department. During the 1950s Halaby also worked for L. S. Rockefeller & Bros. from 1953 to 1956, and was secretary-treasurer and counsel for Aerospace Corp. and president of American Technology Corp. After practicing as a private attorney for two years, in 1961 Halaby was appointed by President John F. Kennedy as head of the Federal Aviation Agency (FAA), making him the highest-ranking Arab American in government at the time. Some of his accomplishments while with the FAA including creating closer ties with the Civil Aeronautics Board and establishing the U.S. Flight Academy in Oklahoma City. In 1968 he was hired as president of Pan American Airlines, becoming chairman and chief executive officer the next year. While with Pan Am, Halaby encouraged the use jumbo jets, which he correctly predicted would become a popular means of transportation, though he incorrectly predicted that supersonic jets would become the rage in later years. Halaby also pressed for better treatment of minorities within Pan Am and worked to increase security in light of the growing risks of hijackings during the 1960s. When Pan Am found itself in financial trouble, however, Halaby became the scapegoat and was fired in 1972. He went on to found Halaby International Corp. in 1973, and DartRail in 1980. His interest in railway systems also led to his chairmanship of Dulles Access Rapid Transit, Inc., from 1985 until 1998. Halaby spent his final years doing charity work as chair of the Save the Children Foundation from 1992 to 1998. Despite his accomplishments in the transportation field, he perhaps gained his greatest fame as the father of Lisa Halaby, who became Jordan's Queen Noor in 1978, thus making Halaby King Hussein I's father-in-law. Halaby was the author of *Crosswinds: An Airman's Memoir* (1978).

OBITUARIES AND OTHER SOURCES:

PERIODICALS

Chicago Tribune, July 6, 2003, section 4, p. 9.
New York Times, July 3, 2003, p. A22.
Times (London, England), August 12, 2003.
Washington Post, July 3, 2003, p. B7.

*   *   *

HARDEMAN, Martin J. 1946-

PERSONAL: Born February 14, 1946, in Chicago, IL; son of Killious and Julia Alberta (Martin) Hardeman; married Clare Louise McCulla, June 25, 1997. *Ethnicity:* "Black." *Education:* University of Chicago, Ph.D.

Politics:"Occasionally."*Religion:*"Sometimes."*Hobbies and other interests:* Chess, movies, military miniatures.

ADDRESSES: Office—Department of History, 3522 Coleman Hall, Eastern Illinois University, Charleston, IL 61920. *E-mail*—cfmjh@eiu.edu.

CAREER: Educator and author. Eastern Illinois University, Charleston, professor of history, c. 1992—.

WRITINGS:

The Structure of Time: Pike County, Mississippi, 1816-1912, Peter Lang Publishing (New York, NY), 1999.

*   *   *

HARRISS, Clarinda 1939-
(Clarinda Harriss Lott)

PERSONAL: Born March 9, 1939, in Baltimore, MD; daughter of Robert P. (a writer) and Margery (an educator; maiden name, Willis) Harriss; married Hubert E. Lott (divorced); children: Lisa, Andrew Tyler. *Education:* Goucher College, B.A., 1960; Johns Hopkins University, M. A., 1962. *Politics:* Democrat. *Religion:* Episcopalian, Friends. *Hobbies and other interests:* Grandmothering, dancing, gardening, cooking.

ADDRESSES: Home—541 Piccadilly Rd., Towson, MD 21204. *Office*—Towson University, 8000 York Rd., Towson, MD 21286. *E-mail*—charriss@towson.edu.

CAREER: Educator, administrator, and poet. Towson University, Towson, MD, professor and chair, English, 1971—; BrickHouse Books, Inc., Baltimore, MD, editor/director, 1973—. Member, mayor's advisory council on art and culture, 1980-89; Arttscape, 1980-98; Writers Club, Maryland House of Correction for Men, 1979—.

MEMBER: American Civil Liberties Union, American Association of University Professors, American Association of University Women, Edgar Allan Poe Society.

AWARDS, HONORS: First Place, Cooper House Chapbook Competition, 1994, for *License Renewal for the Blind; Story* short fiction competition honors, 1997, for "Elements of Structure," and short-short fiction honors, 1998, for "Sick Man Tie"; Donn Goodwin Poetry First-Place Award, Milwaukee Irish Fest, 2001, for "Aerlingus."

WRITINGS:

The Bone Tree (poetry), NPS, 1971.
(As Clarinda Harriss Lott, with Sara deFord) *Forms of Verse: British and American* (college text), Appleton-Century-Croft (New York, NY), 1971.
(As Clarinda Harriss Lott) *The Night Parrot* (poetry), Salmon Publishing (Galway, Ireland), 1988.
License Renewal for the Blind (poetry), Cooper House, 1994.

Columnist and reviewer, *Baltimore Sun,* 1980—. Contributor of over three hundred poems to journals and periodicals.

WORK IN PROGRESS: Editor and collaborator, *Velmarine's Page,* a book-length memoir by woman incarcerated in a Texas prison; contributor to *When Divas Dance* (women's poetry); research on writers in prison, especially female.

SIDELIGHTS: Clarinda Harriss told *CA:* "My motivation and main work tool is obsession. This is what keeps me doing my own writing while chairing a very large English department, teaching numerous courses, and running an off-campus small press."

*   *   *

HARTINGER, Brent 1964-

PERSONAL: Born 1964, in Olympia, WA; son of Harold (an attorney) and Mary Anne (a homemaker) Hartinger; partner of Michael Jensen (a writer). *Ethnicity:* "Caucasian." *Education:* Gonzaga University, B.S., 1986. *Politics:* Democrat. *Hobbies and other interests:* Reading, playing computer games, traveling, attending movies and plays.

ADDRESSES: Agent—Jennifer DeChiara Literary Agency, 254 Park Ave. S., Suite 2L, New York, NY 10010. *E-mail*—brenthartinger@earthlink.net.

CAREER: Freelance writer. Guest columnist, *News Tribune* (Tacoma, WA). Cofounder of Oasis (support group for gay and lesbian young people). South Sound Playwriting Festival, vice president.

MEMBER: Society of Children's Book Writers and Illustrators, Dramatists' Guild.

AWARDS, HONORS: Audience Award, Dayton Playhouse Futurefest Festival of New Plays, and runner-up, Festival of Emerging American Theatre Award, both for *The Starfish Scream;* Fort Lauderdale Film Festival Screenwriting-in-the-Sun Award; Judy Blume grant for best young-adult novel, Society of Children's Book Writers and Illustrators; Seattle Arts Commission Tacoma Artists Initiative grant and Development of a New Work grant; University of Southwestern Louisiana Young-Adult Fiction Prize.

WRITINGS:

Geography Club, HarperTempest (New York, NY), 2003.
The Last Chance Texaco, HarperTempest (New York, NY), 2004.

Contributor of over four hundred essays, articles, cartoons, and stories to periodicals, including *Omni, Boy's Life, Plays, Emmy, Seattle Weekly, Genre, San Francisco Bay Guardian, Noise,* and *Advocate.* Also author of plays, including *The Starfish Scream* (for young adults, produced at Dayton Playhouse Futurefest Festival of New Plays; other plays produced at Heartland Theatre Company, Tacoma Little Theatre, Milwaukee Repertory, and Wings Theatre, New York, NY.

WORK IN PROGRESS: The novels *Grand and Humble,* publication expected 2005, and *The Order of the Poison Oak* (a sequel to *Geography Club*), publication expected 2006, both for HarperCollins (New York, NY); several middle-grade fantasy projects; an adaptation of *Geography Club* for the stage in both young-adult and commercial theater versions.

SIDELIGHTS: Although for over a decade Brent Hartinger had been successfully writing articles, plays, and screenplays, it was not until he had wracked up

eight unpublished novels, nine thousand query letters, and seventeen rejections of his then-current manuscript that his young-adult novel *Geography Club* found a home at HarperCollins in 2001. In this novel, Hartinger tells the story of high school student Russel Middlebrook, who is convinced that he is the only homosexual person in his high school. When Russel discovers differently, he and his friends form the Geography Club, a secret support group. Unlike other publishers, HarperCollins decided to take a gamble on a book with possibly limited appeal, and the gamble paid off. "At the time, everyone claimed there was no market for a gay teen novel," Hartinger recalled in a press release posted on his Web site. "Of course, now that the book has gotten all these great reviews and is selling strongly, all these editors are coming to my agent and saying she didn't send the manuscript to them!"

Hartinger based his first-person novel on many of his personal experiences, and many of the characters also reflect his friends and acquaintances. The novel "gave me a chance to rewrite my teenage years but give it a little more of a happy ending," he wrote at his Web site. Another influence was ancient mythology. "I always saw Russel's journey as epic," he continued. "I think of him as a classic hero who, like Odysseus and so many other Greek and Norse champions, must experience being both prince and outcast before he can claim his rightful 'crown' of true belonging." Despite the serious subject matter—acceptance—Hartinger wanted to use a light touch, as he told Amanda Laughtland of the Tacoma *News Tribune:* "I wanted my book to be fun and funny—a fast read. Not broccoli, but dessert."

When it appeared in 2003, *Geography Club* attracted a readership among teens and adults alike, earning good reviews from a number of critics, despite what some people might find objectionable. For his part, Hartinger told *Publishers Weekly Online* interviewer Kevin Howell, "Tempest is known for edgier teen fiction. I was never encouraged to tone anything down. It's not for younger readers but there's not anything that teenagers today would find too threatening."

Several reviewers commented on the work's verisimilitude, among them *Horn Book*'s Roger Sutton, who ranked the work highly among books portraying gay characters and noted that Russel's "agonies of ostracism (and first love) are truly conveyed." A *Publishers Weekly* contributor also commented that *Geography*

Club "does a fine job of presenting many of the complex realities of gay teen life." Writing in the *School Library Journal,* Robert Gray praised the characterizations, calling them "excellent," and predicting that teens of all sexual preferences would "find this novel intriguing." Several critics were a little less generous in their appraisals, such as *Booklist*'s Hazel Rochman and a *Kirkus Reviews* contributor. Both reviewers thought the plot flawed, with Rochman finding the plot strands "settled a little too neatly in the end." Even so she considered the first-person narrative voice, dialogue, and portrayal of prejudice accurate. Despite imperfections in the plot, the *Kirkus Reviews* writer found the book "provocative, insightful, and . . . comforting." As Hartinger noted on his Web site, "Many gay men like to read these books to relive their teenage years."

The editors at HarperCollins were so pleased with the success of *Geography Club* that they signed Hartinger on for three more titles, including *The Order of the Poison Oak,* a sequel to *Geography Club.* In 2003, Hartinger was also busy adapting *Geography Club* for the stage, with versions for both professional and amateur performers. He is gratified about the success of the novel; when asked about the best aspects of being a writer, Hartinger wrote on his Web site: "Having people say they liked or were somehow touched by your work. It just never gets old."

On his Web site, Hartinger answers many readers' questions about *Geography Club* and offers advice about writing. Becoming a writer means being an avid reader, he explained: "I read constantly—hundreds of books a year, and several newspapers a day. And when I'm not reading, I go to movies and plays, and play computer games," all activities that involve a creative activity. Along with reading widely, Hartinger recommends that writers outline their works-to-be. "I know that while character and beautiful language are important, story is what keeps readers turning the pages. But story is all about structure, and structure almost never just 'happens.'"

"Finally," Hartinger wrote, "don't get discouraged. Because good writing is personal, it's hard not to take rejections personally. But being a sane writer means having an ego of granite with a Teflon coating. And being a successful writer means being very, very, very, very persistent."

BIOGRAPHICAL AND CRITICAL SOURCES:

PERIODICALS

Booklist, April 1, 2003, Hazel Rochman, review of *Geography Club,* p. 1387.

Horn Book, March-April, 2003, Roger Sutton, review of *Geography Club,* pp. 209-211.

Kirkus Reviews, December 15, 2002, review of *Geography Club,* p. 1850.

Publishers Weekly, February 3, 2003, review of *Geography Club,* pp. 76-77.

School Library Journal, February, 2003, Robert Gray, review of *Geography Club,* pp. 141-142.

ONLINE

Brent's Brain: The Brent Hartinger Home Page, http://www.brenthartinger.com (June 25, 2003).

News Tribune Online (Tacoma, WA), http://www.Tribnet.com/ (March 2, 2003), Amanda Laughtland, "Gay Teen Novel Fills a Void."

Publishers Weekly Online, http://www.publishersweekly.com/ (March 21, 2003), Kevin Howell, "Gay YA Novel, *Geography Club,* Goes to the Head of the Class."

*   *   *

HARTKE, Vance (Rupert) 1919-2003

OBITUARY NOTICE—See index for *CA* sketch: Born May 31, 1919, in Stendal, IN; died of a heart attack July 27, 2003, in Fairfax, VA. Politician, attorney, and author. Hartke was a former U.S. senator from Indiana who gained national attention for his opposition to the Vietnam War and support of civil liberties. A graduate of the University of Evansville in 1941, he joined the U.S. Coast Guard and the Navy, rising from seaman to lieutenant during World War II. He then returned to college, completing a law degree at Indiana University in 1948. For the next two years he ran a private law practice, and was appointed deputy prosecutor for the city of Evansville, Illinois, in 1950. In 1955 he was elected mayor of Evansville, and in 1958 he won the U.S. Senate seat. While in the senate Hartke served on the commerce and finance committees and was also chair of the U.S. Senate Committee on Veterans' Affairs; he fought for the 1964 Civil Rights Act, the 1965 Voting Rights Act, and for Medicare and Medicaid legislation. He also opposed the Vietnam War as early as 1965, and when he ran for the office of president in 1972 his platform included the promise to withdraw all U.S. troops from Indochina. Although he lost the presidential election, Hartke served one more term as senator before losing his seat in 1976. He then set up the law firm of Hartke & Hartke. Hartke's writings include *The American Crisis in Vietnam* (1968) and *You and Your Senator* (1970).

OBITUARIES AND OTHER SOURCES:

BOOKS

Tucker, Spencer C., editor, *Encyclopedia of the Vietnam War: A Political and Military History,* American Bibliographic Center-Clio (Santa Barbara, CA), 1998.

PERIODICALS

Chicago Tribune, July 29, 2003, section 1, p. 11.
Los Angeles Times, July 29, 2003, p. B13.
New York Times, July 29, 2003, p. A23.
Times (London, England), August 11, 2003.
Washington Post, July 29, 2003, p. B6.

*   *   *

HARTMAN, James D. 1949-

PERSONAL: Born March 2, 1949, in Pittsburgh, PA; son of Sanford (in business) and Henrietta (a homemaker; maiden name, Lavar) Hartman; married Evelyn Berger (a psychologist), June 10, 1984; children: Jacob, Alisa, Benjamin. *Education:* Graduate Center of the City University of New York, Ph.D., 1996.

ADDRESSES: Home—3333 Henry Hudson Parkway, No. 3E, Bronx, NY 10463. *Office*—De Vry Institute, 3020 Thomson Ave., Long Island City, NY 11101. *E-mail*—jhartman@ny.devry.edu.

CAREER: De Vry Institute of Technology, Long Island City, NY, associate professor of English, c. 1999—.

WRITINGS:

Providence Tales and the Birth of American Literature, Johns Hopkins University Press (Baltimore, MD), 1999.

WORK IN PROGRESS: Books on the Little League and Zionism

*   *   *

HEAGLE, John L.

PERSONAL: Male. *Education:* Catholic University of America, M.A.; Pontifical Lateran University (Rome, Italy), licentiate in canon law.

ADDRESSES: Office—Therapy and Renewal Associates, 1037 South 102nd St., Seattle, WA 98168; fax: 206-763-7566.

CAREER: Roman Catholic priest and psychotherapist. Ordained 1965; served as a pastor, college teacher, and campus minister; cofounder and codirector of Therapy and Renewal Associates, Seattle, WA; Seattle University, Seattle, adjunct faculty member at the School of Theology and Ministry, 1985—.

WRITINGS:

Life to the Full, Thomas More Press (Chicago, IL), 1976.
Our Journey toward God, Thomas More Press (Chicago, IL), 1977.
On the Way, photographs by Todd Brennan, Thomas More Press (Chicago, IL), 1981.
Suffering and Evil, Thomas More Press (Chicago, IL), 1987.
(With Fran Ferder) *Partnership: Women and Men in Ministry,* Ave Marie Press (Notre Dame, IN), 1989.
(With Fran Ferder) *Your Sexual Self: Pathway to Authentic Intimacy,* Ave Maria Press (Notre Dame, IN), 1992.
Jesus: Divine and Human, Fortress Press (Minneapolis, MN), 1995.

(With Fran Ferder) *Tender Fires: The Spiritual Promise of Sexuality,* Crossroad Press (New York, NY), 2002.

SIDELIGHTS: Roman Catholic priest John L. Heagle has written a number of books, including several with Fran Ferder, a Franciscan sister who, like Heagle, was originally with a La Crosse, Wisconsin diocese. They worked together for decades, holding retreats and conducting workshops, and they founded Therapy and Renewal Associates (TARA) in Seattle, Washington, where they also co-teach a graduate course in Christian sexuality at Seattle University. They primarily work with couples, married and unmarried, straight and gay, advising them to spend more time communicating and really listening to each other. Heagle told Gerry Mc-Carthy in an interview for *Social Edge* online that "it's a real challenge in our information-based culture where we tend to be more 'human doings' than human beings. We get so stressed out that we don't value the need for emotional and physical nourishment that comes from closeness."

Heagle and Ferder's *Tender Fires: The Spiritual Promise of Sexuality* was reviewed in *National Catholic Reporter* by Joan H. Timmerman, who noted that the authors begin chapters with quotes from such diverse sources as the Beatles, scripture, *The Velveteen Rabbit,* Miguel de Unamuno, and Teilhard de Chardin.

In the *Tender Fires'* foreword, the authors address why the opinions of two celibates can be significant for a broader audience. In fact, they write from their experiences as therapists, rather than from a solely religious perspective. They say that "like our clients, our students, and our brothers and sisters everywhere, we have been compelled by our sexuality and challenged by its demands. We have been energized by it, struggled with it, and cried about it. In the end, we have come to recognize that human sexuality embraces everyone in its sacred mysteries. It is a love story that belongs to all of us."

In an interview published in *National Catholic Reporter,* Heagle said that "celibacy doesn't just mean not having sex; it's a different way of loving. It's not a higher level of loving, just a different one. Celibacy is something that one can devote one's life to for the sake of service, relationships, and community. Or one can be celibate for a time and then move on. On the other hand, the church needs to finally recognize the profound sacredness of marriage and covenantal partnerships."

Timmerman commented that Heagle and Ferder "want to make accessible 'a spiritual vision that guides our approach to relationships.' When they capture something like this connection between sexuality and fire, it can be exhilarating, a reminder of the best workshops one has ever taken (or given): 'When human persons love one another they are stepping into the energy field where little universes of fire are ignited, where chemistry occurs, where something within them will be set aflame. . . . In so doing they are truly communicating with the divine.'"

BIOGRAPHICAL AND CRITICAL SOURCES:

PERIODICALS

Best Sellers, July, 1976, Stephen J. Casey, review of *Life to the Full,* p. 132.
Library Journal, October 1, 2002, Graham Christian, review of *Tender Fires: The Spiritual Promise of Sexuality,* p. 104.
National Catholic Reporter, August 30, 2002, Joan H. Timmerman, review of *Tender Fires* and "Energies of Attraction and Connection" (interview), p. 17.

ONLINE

Social Edge, http://www.thesocialedge.com/ (December, 2002), Gerry McCarthy, "The *Social Edge* Interview: Fran Ferder and John Heagle Speak about the Spiritual Promise of Sexuality."*

*   *   *

HEDGES, Chris(topher Lynn)

PERSONAL: Male. *Education:* Colgate University, B.A.; Harvard University, master of divinity.

ADDRESSES: Agent—c/o Author Mail, PublicAffairs Books, 250 West 57th St., Suite 1321, New York, NY 10107.

CAREER: Journalist. Interim minister, Boston, MA; National Public Radio, Washington, DC, correspondent; *Christian Science Monitor,* Boston, MA, El Salvador correspondent; *Dallas Morning News,* Dallas, TX, Central America bureau chief, Middle East bureau chief; *New York Times,* New York, NY, reporter, Middle East bureau chief, Balkan bureau chief. Columbia University Graduate School of Journalism, New York, NY, part-time faculty member, spring, 2003; Princeton University Council of the Humanities, Princeton, NJ, faculty member, fall, 2003.

AWARDS, HONORS: Inter-American Press Association award for spot news reporting, 1986, and for continuing attention to inter-American affairs, 1987; Scripps-Howard Ernie Pyle Award for feature writing, 1991; *New York Times* publishers award for foreign reporting from Bosnia, 1996, Serbia, 1997, and Kosovo, 1998; Prix Bayeux des Correspondents de Guerre, 1998; Nieman fellowship, 1998-99; Francis Frost Wood Courage in Journalism Award, 1999; Amnesty International global award for human-rights journalism, 2002. Member of *New York Times* team awarded Pulitzer Prize for explanatory journalism, 2002.

WRITINGS:

War Is a Force That Gives Us Meaning, PublicAffairs Books (New York, NY), 2002.
What Every Person Should Know about War, Free Press (New York, NY), 2003.

Contributor to newspapers and magazines, including *Washington Post, Globe and Mail* (Toronto, Ontario, Canada), *Harper's,* and *Foreign Affairs.*

WORK IN PROGRESS: Decalogue, dealing with the role of the Ten Commandments in modern life.

SIDELIGHTS: Chris Hedges's career as a war correspondent, which began in the early 1980s when he was a recent divinity school graduate interested in the conflicts in Central America, has taken him to battlefields in that part of the world plus the Middle East and Eastern Europe. Having produced prize-winning coverage for the *New York Times* and other media outlets, Hedges used his experience of war and his study of others' experiences in writing his first book, *War Is a Force That Gives Us Meaning.*

In this book, Hedges examines why people engage in war and how they justify it to themselves. War, he argues, can give a nation's citizens a common bond and a sense of purpose; they convince themselves they are working together for a noble cause and that their adversary is fighting for an evil one. These, he argues, are the myths of war, as addictive as the most potent drug and the cause of incalculable suffering over the centuries—suffering he describes in graphic detail. Although he concludes that war is sometimes necessary—he writes, "There are times when the force wielded by one immoral faction must be countered by a faction that, while never moral, is perhaps less immoral"—he calls on humanity to develop a mind-set that will help avoid armed conflict, "some new way given to speak that lays bare the myth as fantasy and the cause as bankrupt."

Hedges has written "a brilliant, thoughtful, timely and unsettling book whose greatest merit is that it will rattle jingoists, pacifists, moralists, nihilists, politicians and professional soldiers equally," commented Abraham Verghese in the *New York Times Book Review.* Hedges, Verghese continued, has made a case that "we are all culpable" in the making of war. As *Nation* contributor Joseph Nevins explained, "All wars, even those waged by sides . . . [Hedges] supports, are based on national myths, most of which are, at their core, racist, he contends. They are racist in that they assert the inherent goodness of 'us' over the evil of 'them.' This black-and-white thinking allows us to kill the enemy without conscience, while celebrating our success in slaying without mercy those who oppose us. . . . We all have the capacity for great evil, a capacity that war helps to realize." Hedges believes that Americans' faith in the myths of war lessened greatly just after the war in Vietnam, but he sees this faith as having risen again since the 1980s and likely to gather more strength in the wake of the terrorist attacks of September 11, 2001.

Those who oppose their country's leaders in wartime are also sometimes guilty of buying into myths, according to Hedges. He deals with the fact that "the political left in the United States and Europe, for example, has disposed at times of its moral precepts and critical faculties in supporting anti-status quo forces," Nevins related. But, Nevins remarked, there sometimes are genuine moral differences between opposing parties, and partisans of one or the other are not necessarily fooling themselves; in his skepticism about opposition movements, Hedges displays an "occasional tendency to generalize about entire groups of people unflatteringly," the reviewer observed.

Unlike some people in these movements, Hedges does not identify as a pacifist. "Despite detesting war," noted George Jaeger in the *New Leader,* "he argues that where the industrial nations can save lives . . . they have a responsibility to take quick and effective action." *National Catholic Reporter* reviewer Tom Roberts commented, though, that "while Hedges accepts that some wars must be fought, his critique of war is so total that it is difficult to see how any might be legitimate." This critique, Roberts added, includes "personal witness" to "an indescribable amount of grotesque death and human suffering," and these accounts make the book "more than just another treatise on the futility of war."

Nevins pointed out that "this book does not offer any concrete prescription for those struggling for a better world, one without the horrors of war its author so compellingly describes," but Hedges does urge compassion for all, including wartime adversaries, and recognition of their common humanity. "In this sense," Nevins wrote, "Chris Hedges ultimately does put forth a radical utopian vision—or at least the beginnings of one—especially if we understand, and thus contest, mass violence in all its roots and manifestations." Similarly, *New York Times* contributor Robert Mann observed that Hedges's book "is a persuasive call for humility and realism in the pursuit of national goals by force of arms." To Hedges, Jaeger added, "the only antidotes to war's inhumanity and self-destruction are humility, compassion and brave acts of love. These qualities may not always triumph or avert massive damage, but they can at least help expose the myths and keep us human, as the author's most moving stories demonstrate." Verghese concluded that Hedges's "ultimate aim" is for readers, particularly Americans, "to recognize war for what it is, so that 'we, who wield such massive force across the globe, see within ourselves the seeds of our own obliteration.'"

BIOGRAPHICAL AND CRITICAL SOURCES:

PERIODICALS

Nation, November 18, 2002, Joseph Nevins, "Letting out the (War) Dogs," p. 50.

National Catholic Reporter, November 29, 2002, Tom Roberts, "Seeing through the Lie That Is War: From the Nightmare of the Battlefield, a Warning against National Self-Worship," p. 11.
Naval War College Review, summer, 2003, Jon Czarnecki, "Such Is War's Effect," p. 157.
New Leader, September-October, 2002, George Jaeger, "The Danger of Good Intentions," p. 22.
New York Times, October 22, 2002, Robert Mann, "A Reporter Scrutinizes War and Its Myths," p. E5.
New York Times Book Review, September 29, 2002, Abraham Verghese, "Wars Are Made, Not Born," p. 21; July 6, 2003, Robert Pinsky, "How War Is," p. 9.
Sojourners, January-February, 2003, Molly Marsh, "An Enticing Elixir," p. 48.*

*   *   *

HEDRICK, Floyd D(udley) 1927-2003

OBITUARY NOTICE—See index for *CA* sketch: Born January 19, 1927, in Lynchburg, VA; died of renal cancer July 9, 2003, in Annandale, VA. Businessman and author. Hedrick specialized in purchasing management and was a former purchaser for the Library of Congress. A graduate of Virginia Commercial College, where he received a B.S. in 1948, he eventually earned a doctorate in business administration from the University of California at Davis. After serving in the U.S. Navy during World War II, his first job as a purchasing manager was with Trailways, Inc., where he worked from 1948 to 1966, and he was also employed by the J. B. Kendall Steel Co. These early years were interrupted by the Korean War, when Hedrick was recalled to active duty; he remained in the Naval Reserve until 1972, retiring as a commander. Hedrick became vice president of the food service company Macke Co. in 1966, as well as being vice president, and then president, of Atlantic Supply Co., a Macke subsidiary. In 1973 he was hired by the Library of Congress to be its chief of procurement and contracting, and retired in 1993. Hedrick wrote several books focusing on the field of business purchasing, including *Purchasing Management in the Smaller Company* (1971) and *Purchasing for Owners of Small Plants* (1976). He was also editor of the American Management Association's *Management Handbook,* and was elected to that organization's Wall of Fame in 1982.

OBITUARIES AND OTHER SOURCES:

PERIODICALS

Washington Post, July 11, 2003, p. B6.

* * *

HEISKELL, Andrew 1915-2003

OBITUARY NOTICE—See index for *CA* sketch: Born September 13, 1915, in Naples, Italy; died July 6, 2003, in Darien, CT. Businessman, philanthropist, and author. Heiskill was the former head of Time, Inc., and became a major philanthropist in New York City after his retirement. Born to expatriate Americans living in Italy, Heiskell was only six years old when his parents divorced, and he spent his youth living in various countries in Europe as he traveled with his peripatetic mother. He did not start receiving a formal education until he was ten years old, attending school in Lausanne, Switzerland; he later attended the École du Montcel in France, where he passed his baccalaureate. Heiskell briefly taught math and geology at Montcel and also worked as a bartender. When he moved to the United States in 1935, he thus considered himself more European than American. Applying to Harvard University, he bypassed undergraduate school to attend the university's business school for a year, but dropped out because he did not enjoy the courses. He next got a job, briefly, writing for the *New York Herald Tribune* before joining the staff of Time, Inc., to work on science and medical stories for *Life* magazine. By 1946 Heiskell had, remarkably, worked his way up to the position of publisher of *Life,* and in 1949 he became vice president of Time, Inc. This was followed by promotions to chairman in 1960 and chief executive office in 1969. While at Time, Heiskell oversaw such profitable efforts as the creation of Time-Life Books and the founding of *People* magazine, while other ventures proved disappointing, such as the eventual cessation of *Life,* and the unsuccessful effort to publish foreign magazines. Still, when he retired from Time in 1980, Heiskell could say he had left behind a profitable company. Unfortunately, he was saddened by the company's later merger with Warner Communications and then AOL. But Heiskell moved on to other activities in which he found great satisfaction. As director,

and then chairman, of the New York City Public Library, he campaigned to raise funds for the crumbling system, including the rehabilitation of the landmark main branch. He was also responsible for the revival of Bryant Park into a beautiful and safe public recreation area, and he worked diligently to raise funds for public housing projects. For all these initiatives, the city of New York gained considerably from Heiskell's tireless efforts. Heiskell related much of his personal story in his autobiography, *Outsider, Insider: An Unlikely Success Story* (1998).

OBITUARIES AND OTHER SOURCES:

PERIODICALS

Los Angeles Times, July 9, 2003, p. B10.
New York Times, July 7, 2003, p. A15.
Washington Post, July 8, 2003, p. B8.

* * *

HEMINGWAY, Amanda
    See ASKEW, Amanda Jane

* * *

HIGHAM, John 1920-2003

OBITUARY NOTICE—See index for *CA* sketch: Born October 26, 1920, in Jamaica, NY; died of a cerebral aneurysm July 26, 2003, in Baltimore, MD. Historian, educator, and author. Higham was a cultural historian who was interested in the concept of the United States as a melting pot of various ethnic and racial groups. He received his B.A. from Johns Hopkins University in 1941 and his M.A. from the University of Wisconsin the next year, before joining the U.S. Army Air Corps during World War II. He spent the war years in Italy working in the history section, returning home after the war to complete his Ph.D. at Wisconsin in 1949. While working on his doctorate, he was an editorial assistant for the *American Mercury* for a year; after graduation he started his academic career at the University of California, Los Angeles, during the early 1950s. From 1954 to 1960 he was on the faculty at Rutgers University, and this was followed by thirteen years at the University of Michigan in Ann Arbor. Higham next moved to Johns Hopkins University, where he taught history from 1973 until his retirement as professor emeritus in 1989. While other historians focused more and more on individual minority groups in their publications, Higham usually preferred to look at how native and immigrant Americans came together to share national traits and values. However, his first book, the John H. Dunning Prize-winning *Strangers in the Land: Patterns of American Nativism* (1955; second edition, 1988), actually analyzed anti-immigrant feelings among native peoples for Europeans. Higham followed this with other works on immigration and changing American culture, including *From Boundlessness to Consolidation: The Transformation of American Culture, 1848-1860* (1969), *Send These to Me: Jews and Other Immigrants in Urban America* (1975; revised edition, 1984), and his last book, *Hanging Together: Unity and Diversity in American Culture* (2002). Other works by Higham include *History: Humanistic Scholarship in America* (1965; revised edition, 1989), *Writing American History: Essays on Modern Scholarship* (1970), and a number of edited history books and contributions to scholarly works and journals.

OBITUARIES AND OTHER SOURCES:

PERIODICALS

Los Angeles Times, August 20, 2003, p. B8.
New York Times, August 18, 2003, p. A17.

*　　*　　*

HOFFMAN, Elizabeth P(arkinson) 1921-2003

OBITUARY NOTICE—See index for *CA* sketch: Born March 23, 1921, in Pittsburgh, PA; died of a neurological disease July 16, 2003. Librarian, educator, and author. Hoffman was a librarian whose interest in ghosts led to her writing several books for children and young adults. Finishing her undergraduate degree at Dickinson College in 1942 and her library-science degree at Drexel University in 1961, Hoffman actually started out as an elementary-school teacher in Pennsylvania during the late 1950s and early 1960s. She was then hired as coordinator of the division of school

libraries for the Pennsylvania Department of Education in 1966. In 1975 she joined the faculty at Villanova University as an associate professor of library science and chair of the department until 1978, and the next year she became director of the Havertown Township Free Library in Pennsylvania until her retirement in 1991. During the 1970s Hoffman began publishing books for young readers, several of which were inspired by the house she lived in, which house was supposedly haunted. Her works include *This House Is Haunted* (1977), *Here a Ghost, There a Ghost* (1978), and *In Search of Ghosts: Haunted Places in the Delaware Valley* (1992), as well as the somewhat less spooky *Palm Reading Made Easy* (1971) and *Palm Reading* (1977).

OBITUARIES AND OTHER SOURCES:

PERIODICALS

Library Hotline, August 11, 2003, p. 6.

*　　*　　*

HOPE, Bob 1903-2003

OBITUARY NOTICE—See index for *CA* sketch: Born Leslie Townes Hope, May 29, 1903, in Eltham, England; died of pneumonia July 27, 2003, in Toluca Lake, CA. Comedian, actor, and author. Over the course of eight decades, Hope became a legendary entertainer of stage, radio, and screen, and was a cherished icon of American culture. Though it might come as a surprise to some that Hope was actually born in England, his parents brought him to the United States when he was only four, and he was a thoroughly Americanized citizen by 1920. After studying dance briefly, Hope's first foray into a career was as an amateur boxer under the name Packy East. He quickly gave up the sport in favor of entertaining, however. This began when he started doing dance routines with friend Mildred Rosequist in a vaudeville act. Not long after, he was hired by film star Fatty Arbuckle to be in his vaudeville act; Hope did a dance routine with Lloyd Durbin and later, George Byrne, and he would also ad lib jokes. By 1930 he was performing solo acts and began focusing more on his joke routine; soon, he was appearing on Broadway with such performers as Fred MacMurray,

Eve Arden, Fannie Brice, Jimmy Durante, and Ethel Merman. His movie career also began in the 1930s, first in short films such as his movie debut *Paree, Paree* (1934), *Watch the Birdie* (1935), and *Don't Look Now* (1938), then on to feature-length films like *Thanks for the Memory* (1938), in which he sang the title song that became his theme music for the rest of his life, and *The Cat and the Canary* (1939). During this time, Hope, who also frequently appeared on radio shows, developed his trademark character: a brash, greedy egomaniac who, whenever the going gets tough, becomes a wisecracking coward. Hope's on-screen persona struck audiences as supremely human and humorous, and it gained its full force especially in the many "Road to..." films in which Hope starred with friends Bing Crosby and Dorothy Lamour. In these movies, Hope and Crosby played a couple of hucksters who inevitably run into outrageous trouble and fight over the beautiful Lamour. One unique characteristic of these movies was the actors' willingness to stop in the middle of the action to speak directly to the audience, thus breaking the "willing suspension of disbelief." There were seven road films in all, beginning with *The Road to Singapore* (1940) and ending with *The Road to Hong Kong* (1961). Hope also starred solo in a number of successful films during this time, including *Monsieur Beaucaire* (1946), *The Paleface* (1948), *Fancy Pants* (1950), *The Seven Little Foys* (1955), *Call Me Bwana* (1963), and *I'll Take Sweden* (1967). At the same time, though, Hope was becoming renowned for his work entertaining American troops all over the world. He first started giving performances with the U.S.O. in 1941, during World War II, and continued actively touring during both war- and peacetime until his last show in Saudi Arabia in 1990. Hope often traveled to dangerous locations at great risk to his personally welfare, and this tremendous contribution to the morale of U.S. troops did not go unrecognized. He received numerous honors from the U.S. government, including the Presidential Medal of Freedom, the Medal of Merit, the Presidential Gold Medal, and the Distinguished Service Medal, as well as being named a Knight Commander of the Order of the British Empire by the British government. On the other hand, Hope often joked for decades that the Oscar remained elusive to him. However, to compensate, he was presented with five special Oscars by the Academy of Motion Picture Arts and Sciences, including the Jean Hersholt Award. As a performer, Hope seemed to be indefatigable. He continued to appear in motion pictures into the 1990s, although later mostly playing himself in such films as *Spies like Us* (1985), *Entertaining the Troops* (1989), and *Off the Menu: The*

Last Days of Chasen's (1998). He also appeared in numerous television specials throughout his career, which ran from 1950 to 1996, and was the author of eleven books, including *I Never Left Home* (1944), *I Owe Russia $1,200* (1963), *The Road to Hollywood: My Forty-Year Love Affair with the Movies* (1977), written with Bob Thomas, and *Dear Prez, I Wanna Tell Ya!: Bob Hope's A Presidential Jokebook* (1996). When he was not performing, Hope was an avid golfer, often teaming up on the links with celebrities and other actors, and he organized his own professional tournament, the Bob Hope Desert Classic, in Palm Springs, California. Becoming wealthy through smart investments and by insisting on maintaining ownership of a percentage of his films, Hope was also a philanthropist who gave away much of his money through the Bob and Dolores Hope Foundation.

OBITUARIES AND OTHER SOURCES:

BOOKS

Contemporary Theater, Film, and Television, Volume 42, Gale (Detroit, MI), 2002.
Encyclopedia of World Biography, second edition, Gale (Detroit, MI), 1998.
St. James Encyclopedia of Popular Culture, St. James Press (Detroit, MI), 2000.
Writers Directory, 18th edition, St. James Press (Detroit, MI), 2003.

PERIODICALS

Chicago Tribune, July 29, 2002, section 1, pp. 1, 16.
Los Angeles Times, July 29, 2003, p. A1.
New York Times, July 29, 2003, pp. A21, A22.
Times (London, England), July 29, 2003.
Washington Post, July 29, 2003, pp. A1, A7.

*   *   *

HUSTON, Perdita (Constance) 1936-2001

PERSONAL: Born May 2, 1936, in Portland, ME; died December 4, 2001, in Silver Spring, MD; daughter of Thomas Augustus and Marion Althea (Brooks) Huston; married Yves Champey, January 2, 1958 (divorced); married Marcel Diennet, September 1,

1972 (divorced); children: (first marriage) Francoise Maude, Jeanne-Marie, (second marriage) Pierre-Marc. *Education:* University of Colorado, 1954-55; University Grenoble (France), certificate, 1956; Ecoles Supierieure de Journalisme, (Paris, France), 1958, journalism degree.

CAREER: English-language assistant to Tunisian minister, Tunis, 1956-60; French Army, social worker in Ain Mokra, Algeria, 1960-61; *Life,* Paris, France, assistant to chief, 1961-63, reporter, 1966-67; *New Yorker,* research assistant, 1963; United Nations, Algiers, consular FAO, 1963-66; Time, Inc., Paris, France, corporate public affairs director, 1969-71; American Revolution Bicentennial Administration, Washington, DC, director of women's programs, 1971-74; Festival U.S.A. and Horizons '76 programs, director, 1974-76; freelance writer, 1963-66, 1976-78. Polio Village Camps Foundation, Inc., Memorial National Women's Political Caucus, Federally Employed Women, secretary-treasurer; Peace Corps, regional director, for North Africa, Near East, Asia and Pacific, 1978-81; scholar-in-residence at Wheaton College, MA; public affairs director for World Conservation Union, Switzerland, and International Planned Parenthood Federation, London, 1985-90; Peace Corps, country director in Mali and Bulgaria, 1997-2000.

WRITINGS:

Message from the Village, Epoch B Foundation (New York, NY), 1978.
Third World Women Speak Out: Interviews in Six Countries, Praeger (New York, NY), 1979.
Motherhood by Choice: Pioneers in Women's Health, Feminist Press at the City University of York (New York, NY), 1992.
The Right to Choose: Pioneers in Women's Health & Planning, Earthscan Publications (London, England), 1992.
Families As We Are: Conversations from Around the World, Feminist Press at the City University of York (New York, NY), 2001.

SIDELIGHTS: Perdita Huston had quite a lifetime of accomplishments before her untimely death to ovarian cancer in 2001 at the age of sixty-five. Huston was an advocate for impoverished women, bringing life to their voices. Huston is probably best known for her

groundbreaking work on issues of family throughout the world. She did not get caught up in the scientific aspects of research, but rather on the human condition. She championed the right of the illiterate in Third-World countries to be heard, believing that they had a lot of wisdom to share. She was incensed by the planners who would come into these third world conditions with lofty ideas of how things needed to be changed without once giving pause to what the people living there had to say about it. She believed that although these people did not have the resources necessary to make change, they did have the knowledge of what needed to be done.

"*Third World Women Speak Out* is aimed at informing those delivering aid to the Third World about the problems and aspirations of women in these countries," explained a critic in the *Harvard Educational Review.* For this book, Huston sought out women of a variety of social statures in six impoverished countries and spoke with them regarding their societies and lifestyles, as well as their hopes and dreams. Dan Chekki in *Sociology* explained, "Despite differences in their socioeconomic, political, and cultural settings the women have similar problems." Chekki noted that Huston uses common terminology to speak to a general audience and "this volume stands out in its approach, method and content." Chekki surmised that although Huston "seems to over-generalize her ideas to make them apply to all women and men" the book "offers valuable insights for social scientists and planners. . . . and it should be of interest to all those involved in the process of development and change." A critic for the *Harvard Educational Review* also voiced concern for Huston's somewhat overpowering tone in the book, which may lead to a misinterpretation of what some of the women said. *Library Journal*'s Beverly Miller "Highly recommended" the book, stating that "the rich and varied stories of twelve previously uncelebrated family planning pioneers from both Western and Third World nations. . . . are fascinating." Susan G. Allison continued with the praise for Huston's work, revealing that *Third World Women Speak Out* "is both a story and a tribute to past efforts in the field . . . it is a 'call to arms' for women's leadership in the social issues of our times." The *Harvard Educational Review* critic summed it up best by observing that Huston "does not pretend to offer scientific data, but rather to present voices which are not usually heard or heeded in the drive toward development."

In *The Right to Choose: Pioneers in Women's Health and Family Planning* Huston discusses the various catalysts leading to the lack of family planning programs throughout the world. She relates how religious and communistic strongholds have created a barrier to talking about the issue of family planning in many parts of the world. According to Maggie Jones in *New Scientist,* Huston's view is that "women—poor as well as rich—had the right to choose if and when to have children." Jones continued, "for many of the pioneers, dedication to the cause of family planning came about through their own suffering." It is this passion that pushed these women to fight for their cause, but according to Huston, it seems it was a losing battle. These women were unable to break through the steel barriers created by government and the cultures where the women lived. Jones' final assessment of the book was that Huston "draws some interesting lessons from the experience of the past and the reality faced by many women in today's world for whom the right to control their fertility remains a distant dream."

Huston's final book, *Families as We Are,* chronicles the lives of several generations of families in various countries. It is a look at "how individuals are coping with changes in concepts of human rights and with economic transformations brought about by increased technology," stated Vanessa Bush in *Booklist.* These changes not only make a difference individually, they also impact the family as a whole. Huston interviews "ordinary people, who so seldom have our attention," wrote Sharon Dirlam of *Peace Corps Writers.* Dirlam went on to say that governments need to look at this book, "that at least some might see the need to support families of all kinds through these troubled times." Dirlam relayed that Huston not only writes about biological families, but also writes of families of circumstance thrown together by "a common bond" but who clamor together for the love and support they receive. She stated that "Huston recognizes the family as a constant force, although it takes a variety of forms." *Library Journal*'s Paula Dempsey called the book "an important contribution to collections on the family, multiculturalism, internal policy, and sociology." The chapters of *Families* are "arranged by topics," commented Dirlam, that "focus on the elderly, women's changing roles, men's changing roles, ways in which childhood is changing, environmental issues, health and politics, disintegrating families, and finally, public policies." Dirlam wrapped up her praise of the book, stating, "The inclusion of family photographs enriches the book. These priceless pictures capture the essence of their subjects, their love for each other, and their pride in being chosen."

Huston was passionate about her ideas of how to make change to bridge "the gap between the developed and the developing world," according to Rushworth M. Kidder in the *Christian Science Monitor.* In the same interview Kidder relayed that Huston "points to three qualities most needed to close the gap: a willingness to listen, a rethinking of male-female relationships, and what she calls 'nature literacy'. . . . respect for both human equality and for natural environment." "How on earth . . . can you expect to live in peace and security in a world where two thirds of the population is in dire straits?" she questioned in a round table discussion for *Ms.* In her lifetime she made every attempt to answer that question.

BIOGRAPHICAL AND CRITICAL SOURCES:

PERIODICALS

Booklist, July 2001, Vanessa Bush, review of *Families as We Are,* p.1957.

Christian Science Monitor, July 12, 1989, Rushworth M. Kidder, "Listen to the Developing World," p. 12.

Harvard Educational Review, November 1979, review of *Third World Women Speak Out,* p. 557.

Kliatt Young Adult Paperback Book Guide, May 1993, Susan G. Allison, review of *Motherhood by Choice,* p. 24.

Library Journal, November 1, 1992, Beverly Miller, review of *Motherhood by Choice,* pp. 108-110; August 2001, Paula R. Dempsey, review of *Families as We Are,* p142.

Ms., March 1985, "If Women Had a Foreign Policy," p.41.

New Scientist, June 27, 1992, Maggie Jones,"Planning for the Future," p. 44.

Sociology, January-February 1980, Dan A. Chekki, review of *Third World Women Speak Out,* p. 34.

ONLINE

Families as We Are, http://www.familiesasweare.com/ (April 10, 2002).

Peace Corps Writers, http://peacecorpswriters.org/ (April 10, 2002), Sharon Dirlam, review of *Families as We Are.*

OBITUARIES:

PERIODICALS

Washington Post, December 9, 2001, p. C8.*

I-J

IMRICH, Jozef 1958-

PERSONAL: Born June 5, 1958, in Kezmarok, Spis, Czechoslovakia; son of Jozef (a carpenter) and Maria (a chef; maiden name, Pecharcikova) Imrich; married February 10, 1984; wife's name Lauren (a business analyst); children: Alexandra, Gabriella. *Education:* Sydney Technological College, diploma (library science), 1983; Deakin University, B.A. (politics), 1991; Flinders University, diploma (business management), 1996. *Politics:* "Victory over want." *Religion:* Christian.

ADDRESSES: Home—Box 139, Grange 4051, Queensland, Australia. *Office*—Queensland Writers Centre, Metro Art, Brisbane 4000, Queensland, Australia. *E-mail*—jozefimrich@authorsden.com.

CAREER: Researcher, clerk, and memoirist. Technomat, Poprad, Czechoslovakia, buying agent, 1979-80; New South Wales Legislature, Sydney, Australia, reference officer and clerk to committees. *Military service:* Czech Army, 1977-79.

MEMBER: Victory over Want, Amnesty International, Toastmasters International, Queensland Writing Centre.

WRITINGS:

Cold River: A Survivor's Story (memoir; e-book), Double Dragon (Markham, Ontario, Canada), 2002, revised, 2003.

Contributor of essays to periodicals.

WORK IN PROGRESS: Stranger in the House, for Double Dragon, 2004.

SIDELIGHTS: Jozef Imrich considers his greatest achievement to have escaped through the Iron Curtain from Czechoslovakia to Austria in July of 1980, a trip during which two of his best friends drowned. Imrich told *CA:* "As a survivor living in an exile, mothered by necessity, my stories reflect a search for identity that is inspired by the memory of my drowned friends, ghosts of my communist upbringing, and the cold reality of homelessness. I realized some time ago that I am not the most talented wrier. But I have the determination needed to succeed. In the region of my heart I somehow feel that I needed to endure my own suffering in order to make people believe in a struggle of freedom. My work provides a voice for all those like myself, who are lost in the sea of ironic macroisms of human life, and who need to learn how to express their hidden emotions. I create a reflection of my experience that is also a reflection of experiences of thousands and thousands of Eastern and Central Europeans.

"What currently fascinates me is the duality of views on migration, our ability to be imbued with such goodness and yet have a capacity for such evil. For one generaton of boat people to have the heart to drown the next generation of boat people."

BIOGRAPHICAL AND CRITICAL SOURCES:

ONLINE

AuthorsDen.com, http://www.authorsden.com/ (November 16, 2003), interview with Imrich.

Double Dragon Publishing, http://www.double-dragon-e-books.com/ (November 16, 2003).

* * *

IVERSON, Carol (L.) 1941-

PERSONAL: Born November 29, 1941, in Minneapolis, MN; daughter of Wallace R. Walters (a house builder) and Lorraine V. Walters Swenson; married Arthur C. Iverson (a guidance counselor and special-education teacher), May 20, 1961; children: Terri Jean O'Connell, Arthur C. III, Lynn Myung Iverson-Eyestone. *Religion:* Lutheran. *Hobbies and other interests:* Reading, walking, movies, games.

ADDRESSES: Home—1158 Highland Ave., Northfield, MN 55057. *E-mail*—cliverson@charter.net.

CAREER: Writer.

MEMBER: Society of Children's Book Writers and Illustrators, Minnesota Christian Writers Guild, Minnesota Writers for Children.

WRITINGS:

"I BET YOU DIDN'T KNOW THAT" SERIES

Fish Sleep with Their Eyes Open and Other Facts and Curiosities, illustrated by Jack Lindstrom, Lerner Publications (Minneapolis, MN), 1990.
Hummingbirds Can Fly Backwards and Other Facts and Curiosities, illustrated by Jack Lindstrom, Lerner Publications (Minneapolis, MN), 1990.
There Are Golf Balls on the Moon and Other Facts and Curiosities, illustrated by Jack Lindstrom, Lerner Publications (Minneapolis, MN), 1990.
You Can't Sink in the Dead Sea and Other Facts and Curiosities, illustrated by Jack Lindstrom, Lerner Publications (Minneapolis, MN), 1990.

OTHER

The Mystery of the Doll in the Window, DiskUs Publishing (Albany, IN), 2001.

Houses, Creative Education (Mankato, MN), 2002.

Also contributor of articles and short stories to periodicals, including *Highlights for Children, U*S* Kids, Girls' Life,* and *Writer.*

WORK IN PROGRESS: Distant Shores, about a fifth-grade adopted Korean girl; *Holly and the Carousel Horse,* about an eleven-year-old girl who travels back in time on a carousel horse; and *Luke, Me, and the Storm of the Century,* about a twelve-year-old girl and her six-year-old brother "who fight against the elements of a snowstorm."

SIDELIGHTS: Carol Iverson first published a series of humorous trivia books loosely organized by subject. Thus, *Fish Sleep with Their Eyes Open and Other Facts and Curiosities* contains thirty-two pages of surprising facts about birds, fish, and insects, while *Hummingbirds Can Fly Backwards and Other Facts and Curiosities* reveals amusing trivia about plants and animals. *There Are Golf Balls on the Moon and Other Facts and Curiosities* focuses on arts and entertainment trivia, while *You Can't Sink in the Dead Sea and Other Facts and Curiosities* relays short curious facts about human societies throughout history. Jan L. McConnell of *Wilson Library Bulletin* predicted that the books would be enjoyed by fans of the *Guinness Book of World Records* series, encouraging readers to "Fool your friends, stump your teachers." While pointing out that Iverson doesn't cite resources for her facts, a reviewer for *Appraisal* remarked, "this series is in the trivia book genre for entertainment and will not disappoint if considered for that purpose," and Eva Elisabeth Von Ancken of *School Library Journal* recommended the books for reluctant readers.

"I started writing after I married and had children," Iverson explained to *CA.* "I wrote for ten years off and on before I had anything published. So my advice to any aspiring writer would be to hang in there and not give up—if writing is what you really want to do.

"I am currently working on a children's novel with my Korean daughter and an adult novel with my older daughter, and having fun doing both."

BIOGRAPHICAL AND CRITICAL SOURCES:

PERIODICALS

Appraisal, winter, 1991, review of "I Bet You Didn't Know That" series, pp. 68-69.

School Library Journal, February, 1991, Eva Elisabeth Von Ancken, review of "I Bet You Didn't Know That" series, p. 89.

Wilson Library Bulletin, March, 1991, Jan L. McConnell, review of "I Bet You Didn't Know That" series, p. 8.

*   *   *

JACKOWSKI, Edward J.

PERSONAL: Male. *Education:* Baruch College, City University of New York, B.B.A.; International University for Graduate Studies, Ph.D. (behavioral management).

ADDRESSES: Office—c/o Exude, Inc., 16 East 52nd St., New York, NY 10022. *E-mail*—lee@exude.com.

CAREER: Writer, fitness adviser, public speaker, certified personal trainer, and instructor of aerobic conditioning. Founder of Exude, Inc. (fitness center), New York, NY. Founder and chief executive officer of Escape Your Shape (developer, producer, and marketer of fitness products). Board member of Hereditary Neuropathy Foundation.

MEMBER: American College of Sports Medicine, International Dance and Exercise Association.

WRITINGS:

America You're Exercising Wrong: One Hundred Fallacies, Facts, and Tips, Exude (New York, NY), 1993, published as *Hold It! You're Exercising Wrong!,* Simon and Schuster (New York, NY), 1995.

Escape Your Shape: How to Work out Smarter, Not Harder, Simon and Schuster (New York, NY), 2001.

Escape Your Weight: How to Win at Weight-Loss, St. Martin's Press/Thomas Dunne Books (New York, NY), 2004.

Contributor to newspapers, including *USA Today.* Author of sports and fitness column in *New York Daily News;* columnist for *Modern Maturity,* 1998.

SIDELIGHTS: Founder of Exude, Inc., a New York City-based personal training center, Edward J. Jackowski is one of the nation's leaders in one-on-one motivational fitness training. While still an undergraduate studying business management (he eventually earned a Ph.D. in behavioral management), Jackowski began to develop a vision of an entrepreneurial enterprise based in fitness, and started his business with a $400 loan from a fellow student.

The result was Exude, the principles behind which he delineates in the books *Hold It! You're Exercising Wrong!; Escape Your Shape: How to Work out Smarter, Not Harder;* and *Escape Your Weight: How to Win at Weight-Loss.* Jackowski also founded and serves as chief executive officer of Escape Your Shape, which develops and markets fitness products.

Central to Jackowski's philosophy is the concept that no single exercise regimen fits all persons—or, more properly, all body types. He has identified four basic body types, concepts he has copyrighted: the Hourglass, whose body weight is evenly distributed top and bottom; the Spoon, who tends to be skinnier above the waist and heavier below; the Cone, who is the opposite of the spoon (i.e., top-heavy rather than bottom-heavy); and the Ruler, who is straight up and down. Half of all males tend to be Rulers, while approximately forty percent of all females are Hourglasses.

Each body type requires a particular exercise program which combines aerobic exercise such as running or jumping rope—a Jackowski favorite—as well as anaerobic strength-training activities such as lifting weights or doing pull-ups. For example, most exercises benefit Rulers, whereas Hourglasses should avoid exercising on an incline or lifting heavy weights. Likewise a Cone, because he or she likely has an upper body that is already well-developed in proportion to the lower, should eschew heavy weights for the upper body in favor of exercises that develop the quadriceps, hamstrings, and other muscles below the waist. A ski machine set on high resistance for the upper body can help a Spoon, who can also benefit from upper-body strength training.

Hold It! You're Exercising Wrong!, which first presented Jackowski's ideas to a national audience under the title *America You're Exercising Wrong,* received relatively wide reviews for a self-published, direct-marketed book. Clarence Petersen in the *Chicago Tribune* described it as "full of surprises," noting that, for example, stair-climbing machines could actually *increase* lower-body bulk for some body types. He also noted one of the key ideas promoted by Jackowski: that "an eleven-dollar jump rope is one of the most important pieces of exercise equipment in which you can invest."

Wendy Schmid of *Vogue,* who went to Jackowski for one-on-one training, soon found herself with a jump rope—what she called "Jackowski's secret weapon in the war on fat"—in her hand. She went on to note that "This simple two-handled rope is the crux of the Exude philosophy. Beneficial for all body types, the jump rope, according to Jackowski, will burn fat, define muscles, and—the coup de grace of fitness—even get rid of cellulite."

Schmid went to see Jackowski after hearing how, at the request of noted developer and celebrity Donald Trump, he helped former Miss Universe Alicia Machado lose twenty pounds. Her own goals were modest: a basically fit Hourglass, she wanted to "fine-tune my particular shape," which was getting overly muscular in some areas. "You've been working out this way," Jackowski told her, moving his arms "air-traffic controller like." Instead, she needed to be moving from side to side.

At the end of eight weeks, Schmid had lost only five pounds, but had reduced a total of five and a half inches from her body measurements. Though Jackowski also had her work with a nutritionist, she managed this feat without major change to her diet.

Though he has noted that proper diet is of course important to overall fitness and health, Jackowski observed in a *USA Today* article that "A great exercise program can make up for a poor diet, but a great diet can never make up for a lack of exercise." For weight loss, he prescribes what described thus: "alternating two-and three-minute intervals of aerobic exercise, such as jumping rope, with two or three minutes of anaerobic work, such as strength training, with as many as fifty repetitions for each triceps kickback, biceps curl, military press, or [other] exercise."

Not all authorities agree with Jackowski's program. "I don't think your should choose a specific aerobic exercise based on your body shape," John Porcari,

commented in the Arlington, Illinois, *Daily Herald* that, "No matter what their shape, people need to choose an aerobic exercise that they like and that they'll stick with. Same with resistance training." At the same time, many people have benefited from Jackowski's principles, which he has laid out for readers in an easy-to-understand format. Sue-Ellen Beauregard in *Booklist* called *Hold It! You're Exercising Wrong!* a "sensible basic fitness guide" whose key information, presented in boldface type, makes for ready comprehension.

BIOGRAPHICAL AND CRITICAL SOURCES:

PERIODICALS

Booklist, January 1, 1995, Sue-Ellen Beauregard, review of *Hold It! You're Exercising Wrong!,* p. 789.
Chicago Tribune, March 14, 1993, Clarence Petersen, review of *America You're Exercising Wrong,* p. 148.
Daily Herald (Arlington, IL), July 30, 2001, Hilary Shenfeld, "Triumph over Your Body Type," p. 1.
Houston Chronicle, April 11, 1993, "Take Notice," p. 2.
USA Today, March, 2003, Edward Jackowski, "Don't Fool Yourself about Getting in Shape," p. 60.
Vogue, August, 1997, Wendy Schmid, "Roped In," p. 142.

ONLINE

Escape Your Shape, http://www.escapeyourshape.com/ (September 16, 2003).
Exude, http://www.exude.com/ (September 16, 2003).*

* * *

JACKSON, Brenda Streater 195(?)-

PERSONAL: Born February 2, 195(?) in Jacksonville, FL; married; children: two sons. *Education:* Jacksonville University, B.S. (business administration).

ADDRESSES: Home—Jacksonville, FL. *Home and office*—P.O. Box 28267, Jacksonville, FL 32226. *E-mail*—gjbj@aol.com.

CAREER: Insurance manager and romance novelist. State Farm (insurance company), manager.

MEMBER: Romance Writers of America (First coast chapter), Women Writers of Color (founding member).

AWARDS, HONORS: Emma Award for favorite book of the year, 2000, for *Secret Love,* 2001, for *Surrender;* Romance in Color Award, best contemporary romantic fiction of the year, and readers' choice award for favorite book of year, both 2001, both for *A Family Reunion.*

WRITINGS:

Tonight and Forever, Pinnacle (Chicago, IL), 1995.
One Special Moment, BET Arabesque (Washington, DC), 1998.
Fire and Desire, BET Arabesque (Washington, DC), 1999.
Whispered Promises, BET Arabesque (Washington, DC), 1999.
Secret Love, BET Arabesque (Washington, DC), 2000.
True Love, BET Arabesque (Washington, DC), 2000.
A Family Reunion, St. Martin's (New York, NY), 2001.
Surrender, BET Arabesque (Washington, DC), 2001.
Delaney's Desert Sheikh, Silhouette (New York, NY), 2002.
Perfect Timing, Dafina (New York, NY), 2002.
Ties That Bind, St. Martin's (New York, NY), 2002.
Perfect Fit, Kensington (New York, NY), 2003.

Contribor to several romance anthologies.

SIDELIGHTS: Brenda Streater Jackson is a prolific writer of romance stories prominently featuring African-American characters. Gwendolyn Osborne, online reviewer for *Romance Reader,* explained that Jackson "doesn't merely write novels," she "organizes reunions that reconnect her readers with the solid, multifaceted characters they have come to know and to care about." This aspect of her writing has gained Jackson's work a large following.

Among the recurring characters who feature in many of her stories are the Madaris brothers, Justin, Dex, and Clayton, as well as other assorted family members. Doctor Justin Madaris was the first to appear in

Jackson's debut 1995 novel, *Tonight and Forever.* The author's Web site even includes a Madaris family tree and family trivia. Among the characters whose lives intersect with the Madaris' are Hollywood superstars Diamond McSwain and Sterling Hamilton. The Madaris clan possesses its share of glamour, wealth, and romance, but also plenty of hardships. Commenting on *Secret Love,* the story of the secret marriage of tycoon Jake Madaris and movie star, Diamond, reviewer Osborne stated that Jackson "is an excellent storyteller who has created wonderful connecting stories about strong African-American families." Also reviewing *Secret Love,* a contributor to *Publishers Weekly* praised Jackson's "talent for character development." While some readers enjoy the extended family scenario in the books, others, such as Andrea Pool, in an online review for *All about Romance,* cautioned that "she found endlessly irritating . . . the sheer number of people who showed up" in *Surrender,* one of the many books featuring the Madaris family.

Jackson features a different cast of characters in *Perfect Timing,* in which a class reunion cruise reunites childhood friends Mya Rivers and Maxine Chandler who parted ways after high school. The reunion comes at a perfect juncture in their lives when the two friends are struggling with emotionally difficult situations. Mya fears her husband is being unfaithful, and Maxine, who lost her fiancé just before their wedding, is now facing a hysterectomy. *Booklist*'s Lillian Lewis remarked that "the result is a warm reading experience."

Ties That Bind follows the entanglement of a group of Howard University students over the course of thirty years. While at college in the 1960s Angela drugged Randolph in order to get him to sleep with her. Angela became pregnant and Randolph married her even though he was in love with Jenna. Twelve years later, Jenna is widowed and Randolph and Angela are separated; the two old flames are able to rekindle their relationship. A host of other college friends figure in the story, and their lives become more entwined as their children date and marry. In her review for *Booklist,* critic Lewis remarked that the "novel is a wonderful, wholesome story about love, life, friendship, and family." Robyn Glazer, reviewing *Ties That Bind* online for *Romantic Times,* labeled it a "powerful book."

BIOGRAPHICAL AND CRITICAL SOURCES:

PERIODICALS

Black Issues Book Review, July-August, 2002, review of *Perfect Timing,* p. 39.

Booklist, April 1, 2002, Lillian Lewis, review of *Perfect Timing,* p.1306; October 15, 2002, review of *Ties That Bind,* p. 386.

Library Journal, November 1, 2002, Ann Burns, review of *Ties That Bind,* p. 111.

Publishers Weekly, June 21, 1999, review of *Fire and Desire,* p. 65; December 13, 1999, review of *Secret Love,* p. 69; August 21, 2000, review of *True Love,* p. 55.

ONLINE

All about Romance, http://www.likesbooks.com/ (May 15, 2003).

Brenda Jackson Home Page, http://www.brendajackson.net (May 15, 2003).

Romance in Color, http://www.romanceincolor.com/ (June 5, 2003).

Romance Reader, http://www.theromancereader.com/ (May 15, 2003), Gwendolyn Osborne, review of *One Special Moment* and *Secret Love.*

Romantic Times, http://www.romantictimes.com/ (May 15, 2003), Robyn Glazer, review of *Ties That Bind.**

*   *   *

JACKSON, Richard L. 1937-

PERSONAL: Born 1937.

ADDRESSES: Agent—c/o Author correspondence, Howard University Press, 2225 Georgia Ave. N.W., Suite 720, Washington, DC 20059.

CAREER: Carleton University, Ottawa, Canada, professor emeritus.

WRITINGS:

The Black Image in Latin-American Literature, University of New Mexico Press (Albuquerque, NM), 1976.

Black Writers in Latin America, University of New Mexico Press (Albuquerque, NM), 1979.

The Afro-Spanish American Author: An Annotated Bibliography of Criticism, Garland Publishing (New York, NY), 1980.

Black Literature and Humanism in Latin America, University of Georgia Press (Athens, GA), 1988.

The Afro-Spanish American Author II: The 1980s: An Annotated Bibliography of Recent Criticism, Locust Hill Press (West Cornwall, CT), 1989.

Black Writers and the Hispanic Canon, Twayne Publishers (New York, NY), 1997.

Black Writers and Latin America: Cross-Cultural Affinities, Howard University Press (Washington, DC), 1998.

SIDELIGHTS: Richard L. Jackson has contributed to a body of scholarly work on Afro-Latin American authors and their thematic concerns. From early studies on depiction of black characters in white Latin American literature, Jackson moved to considerations of African-descended Latin-American novelists and poets, with emphasis on their sense of humanism and cultural authenticity. In *Hispania,* Clementine C. Rabassa noted that Jackson's work "may be regarded as a comprehensive reflection of the trajectory and scope that defines the relatively new area of literary criticism dealing with prose fiction and poetry by or about Spanish-speaking black writers."

In a *Choice* review of *Black Writers and Latin America: Cross-Cultural Affinities,* M. S. Arrington, Jr. concluded that Jackson's book "lays the groundwork for much future research on this expansive topic." Richard K. Barksdale in *World Literature Today* commented that Jackson's "historical and critical assessment of Latin America's major black writers is an excellent contribution to the field of Afro-Hispanic Studies."

BIOGRAPHICAL AND CRITICAL SOURCES:

PERIODICALS

Choice, December, 1989, L. Hallewell, review of *The Afro-Spanish American Author II: The 1980s: An Annotated Bibliography of Recent Criticism,* p. 612; November, 1999, M. S. Arrington, Jr., review of *Black Writers and Latin America: Cross-Cultural Affinities,* p. 530.

Hispania, September, 1981, Clementine C. Rabassa, review of *The Afro-Spanish American Author: An Annotated Bibliography of Criticism,* pp. 480-481.

Modern Fiction Studies, winter, 1978, Patricia M. Pacifico, review of *The Black Image in Latin-American Literature,* pp. 699-703; summer, 1981, Gerald Guinness, review of *Black Writers in Latin America,* pp. 419-423; summer, 1989, Edna L. Steeves, review of *Black Literature and Humanism in Latin America,* pp. 310-312.

World Literature Today, autumn, 1977, Charles M. Tatum, review of *The Black Image in Latin-American Literature,* pp. 598-599; winter, 1981, Richard K. Barksdale, review of *Black Writers in Latin America,* pp. 72-73.*

*   *   *

JACKSON, William 1958-

PERSONAL: Born April 28, 1958, in Chester, PA; son of William, Sr. (an instrument technician) and Elizabeth (a homemaker; maiden name, Mielnyczuk) Jackson. *Education:* California State University, B.A. (comparative literature); Barnes Foundation, certificate (art).

ADDRESSES: Home—92 Hersey Dr., Pottstown, PA 19465-8137. *E-mail*—billyfey@netzero.net.

CAREER: Fiction writer.

MEMBER: Dramatists Guild.

WRITINGS:

The First Step (short fiction), Neshui Press (St. Louis, MO), 1999.

BIOGRAPHICAL AND CRITICAL SOURCES:

ONLINE

Neshui Press Web site, http://homepage.mac.com/bbrigitte/neshui/ (November 20, 2003).

JACOBSEN, Josephine (Winder) 1908-2003

OBITUARY NOTICE—See index for *CA* sketch: Born August 19, 1908, in Cobourg, Ontario, Canada; died of kidney failure July 9, 2003, in Cockeysville, MD. Author. Jacobsen was a poet and short-story author who once served as consultant to the Library of Congress, which was the equivalent of the current post of U.S. poet laureate. Although she did not attend college, she became a prolific author of fiction, verse, and literary criticism, winning critical acclaim for all these efforts. However, she gained the most attention for her poetry, which ranges from traditional forms to free verse. Her staunch Catholicism imbues much of her poetry, which is often concerned with the mysteries of being human and the relationships between the physical and spiritual worlds. She wrote in her spare time when not busy raising her family, and did not have any type of formal job until she became the Library of Congress poetry consultant from 1971 to 1973 and honorary consultant in American letters from 1973 to 1979. Honored with two *Prairie Schooner* awards for fiction, a National Book Award nomination for *The Shade-Seller: New and Selected Poems* (1974), several honorary degrees, and other awards, Jacobsen completed eleven poetry collections, including *The Human Climate: New Poems* (1953), *Adios, Mr. Moxley* (1986), and *In the Crevice of Time: New and Collected Poems* (1995). She also wrote such short story collections as *A Walk with Raschid and Other Stories* (1978) and *What Goes without Saying: Collected Stories of Josephine Jacobsen* (1996), as well as several critical works and contributions to anthologies.

OBITUARIES AND OTHER SOURCES:

BOOKS

Contemporary Literary Criticism, Volume 102, Gale (Detroit, MI), 1998.

Contemporary Poets, seventh edition, St. James Press (Detroit, MI), 2001.

Dictionary of Literary Biography, Volume 244: *American Short-Story Writers since World War II,* Gale (Detroit, MI), 2001.

PERIODICALS

Chicago Tribune, July 12, 2003, section 2, p. 11.
Los Angeles Times, July 12, 2003, p. B20.

New York Times, July 12, 2003, p. A21.
Washington Post, July 12, 2003, p. B6.

*   *   *

JANTZEN, Grace M. 1948-

PERSONAL: Born 1948, in Saskatoon, Saskatchewan, Canada; daughter of a farming couple. *Education:* University of Saskatchewan, B.A., M.A. (philosophy); University of Calgary, Ph.D. (philosophy); Oxford University, D.Phil. (theology). *Religion:* Society of Friends (Quakers). *Hobbies and other interests:* Playing the cello.

ADDRESSES: Office—Centre for Religion, Culture, and Gender, Department of Religions and Theology, University of Manchester, Oxford Road, Manchester M13 9PL, England. *E-mail*—grace.jantzen@man.ac.uk.

CAREER: University of Manchester, Manchester, England, research professor of religion, culture, and gender and associate director of Centre for Religion, Culture and Gender.

WRITINGS:

God's World, God's Body, Westminster Press (Philadelphia, PA), 1984.
Julian of Norwich: Mystic and Theologian, Paulist Press (New York, NY), 1988, 2nd editon, 2000.
Power, Gender, and Christian Mysticism, Cambridge University Press (New York, NY), 1995.
Becoming Divine: Toward a Feminist Philosophy of Religion, Indiana University Press (Bloomington, IN), 1999.

Editor of book series on religion, culture, and gender for Manchester University Press. Contributor to scholarly periodicals.

WORK IN PROGRESS: The multi-volume promect "Death and the Displacement of Beauty"; studying the sedimentation of violence in Western culture and peaceful alternatives.

SIDELIGHTS: Grace M. Jantzen is a philosopher of religion whose interests include medieval Christian mysticism, feminist constructs in religion, and systems of thought that counter Western preoccupations with violence and death. Jantzen's body of work on these and other topics has found an audience on both sides of the Atlantic. To quote David A. Pailin in *Religious Studies,* she has provided "a welcome contribution to current theological understanding and . . . creative insights that deserve serious consideration."

Julian of Norwich: Mystic and Theologian presents not only the writings of the medieval female mystic but also illuminates details of her life and the political/religious climate in which she found herself. Jantzen makes the important distinction between a self-centered mysticism and one like Julian's that was founded in her relationship with Christ and her understanding of His teachings. As Ellen L. Babinsky put it in *Church History,* Jantzen's book "participates in the discussion regarding the validity of religious experience and is a helpful contribution to the secondary literature analyzing the thought of Julian of Norwich." In her *Journal of Religion* review of the same title, Caroline Walker Bynum suggested that Jantzen "has written a sensitive explication of the theology of Julian of Norwich."

Power, Gender, and Christian Mysticism is a philosophical exploration of the role gender plays in Christian mystical experiences, their interpretations, and their contribution to religious empowerment. Jantzen explores the history of women's Christian mysticism, demonstrating that it sometimes brought faithful Christians under suspicion in a patriarchal society. Jantzen also suggests that female mysticism is more socially acceptable now because mysticism in general has been marginalized. In the *Times Literary Supplement,* Monica Furlong observed: "Jantzen's comments on mysticism are part of a feminist intention, which is to show how remorselessly through the centuries women were excluded from important areas of religious debate." In *Commonweal,* Lawrence S. Cunningham noted that Jantzen "makes a sustained argument that one must not only understand Christian mysticism in terms of historical context but, and this is the burden of her work, a serious investigation of gender will greatly change how one views mystical experience."

BIOGRAPHICAL AND CRITICAL SOURCES:

PERIODICALS

Choice, September, 1996, C. MacCormick, review of *Power, Gender, and Christian Mysticism,* p. 144; November, 1999, E. O. Springsted, review of *Becoming Divine: Toward a Feminist Philosophy of Religion,* pp. 556-557.

Church History, March, 1990, Ellen L. Babinsky, review of *Julian of Norwich: Mystic and Theologian,* pp. 81-82.

Commonweal, November 22, 1996, Lawrence S. Cunningham, review of *Power, Gender, and Christian Mysticism,* p. 29.

Journal of Religion, April, 1990, Caroline Walker Bynum, review of *Julian of Norwich,* pp. 310-311.

Religious Studies, December, 1984, David A. Pailin, review of *God's World, God's Body,* pp. 688-692; September, 1989, Ann Loades, review of *Julian of Norwich,* pp. 403-405.

Scottish Journal of Religious Studies, spring, 1998, "Necrophilia and Natality: What Does It Mean to Be Religious?"

Times Literary Supplement, March 22, 1996, Monica Furlong, "What the Beguines Began," p. 10.

ONLINE

University of Manchester, Department of Religions and Theology, http://www.art.man.ac.uk/RELTHEOL/(November 4, 2003), "Professor Grace Jantzen."

JOHNSON, Bernard 1933-2003

OBITUARY NOTICE—See index for *CA* sketch: Born November 5, 1933, in Lutterworth, Leicestershire, England; died June 8, 2003. Educator and author. Johnson gained appreciation from the academic community for his translations of Serbo-Croat literature into English. After serving in the Royal Air Force from 1952 to 1954, and being trained by the military as a Russian interpreter, he studied at the University of Nottingham, where he earned his doctorate in 1960. Johnson taught Slavonic languages and literature at his alma mater for the next five years before joining the faculty at the University of London's School of Economics and Political Science. He became head of the university's language center, and remained in London until his retirement in 1999. Johnson was the editor of *New Writing in Yugoslavia* (1970), which is still considered one of the most important collections of Yugoslavian literature in English translation available today.

OBITUARIES AND OTHER SOURCES:

PERIODICALS

Times (London, England), August 22, 2003, p. 35.

*   *   *

JOYCE, Judith
   See SCHWARTZ, Ruth L.

K

KAILBOURN, Thomas R.

PERSONAL: Male.

ADDRESSES: Home—Wellsville, NY. *Agent*—c/o Author Mail, Stanford University Press, Stanford, CA 94305-2235.

CAREER: Writer, editor, and house painter. Associate editor, *Daguerreian Annual.*

MEMBER: Daguerreian Society.

AWARDS, HONORS: Caroline Bancroft History Prize, Denver Public Library, 2001, for *Pioneer Photographers of the Far West: A Biographical Dictionary, 1840-1865.*

WRITINGS:

(With Peter E. Palmquist) *Pioneer Photographers of the Far West: A Biographical Dictionary, 1840-1865,* Stanford University Press (Stanford, CA), 2000.

WORK IN PROGRESS: Pioneer Photographers from the Mississippi River to the Rocky Mountains, the second volume of the "Pioneer Photographers" series, with Peter E. Palmquist.

SIDELIGHTS: Thomas R. Kailbourn is the coauthor of *Pioneer Photographers of the Far West: A Biographical Dictionary, 1840-1865,* a 2000 reference book—written with Peter E. Palmquist—that contains approximately 1,500 entries. The publication includes photographs of some of the subjects, and it also features works by some of them. An entry on Ellison I. Crawford, for example, includes Crawford's photograph of a fern. Benjamin Markovits, in his review for the *Times Literary Supplement,* declared that "browsing through the dictionary itself feels slightly like walking through a military cemetery," and he added that "the entries themselves resemble a kind of elaborate headstone, rich in dates and places." For Kailbourn, *Pioneer Photographers of the Far West* "has the fascination of a graveyard." Another reviewer, Jonathan Kirsch, affirmed in the *Los Angeles Times* that *Pioneer Photographers of the Far West* constitutes "an authoritative reference work," and he expressed particular praise for the entry on Edweard James Muybridge, which includes a photograph in which the celebrated figure sports a hat that resembles a box camera. Kirsch acknowledged the publication as a "well-written . . . dictionary," and he added that "it's possible to open the book at random and find something fascinating, illuminating or funny, and sometimes all of them at once."

BIOGRAPHICAL AND CRITICAL SOURCES:

PERIODICALS

Los Angeles Times, August 8, 2001, Jonathan Kirsch, "Turning Curious Eyes on a Rough-edged Frontier," pp. E1, E3.
Times Literary Supplement, February 8, 2002, Benjamin Markovits, "How the West Was Shot," p. 7.*

KASTNER, Laura 1953-

PERSONAL: Born October 27, 1953, in Rockville Centre, NY; daughter of Rexford and Joan Allen Kastner; married Philip Mease, August 11, 1984; children: Cameron, Lindley Allen. *Education:* University of Virginia, Ph.D. (psychology), 1979; University of Washington, post-doctoral internship (clinical psychology), 1980.

ADDRESSES: Home—Seattle, WA. *Office*—University of Washington, Department of Psychiatry and Behavioral Sciences, Box 359300, Seattle, WA 98195. *E-mail*—kastner@u.washington.edu.

CAREER: Professor, psychiatrist, and author. University of Washington Children's Hospital, supervisor in consult and liaison division of child psychiatry, staff psychologist in adolescent clinic, and lecturer in teaching programs of psychiatry and behavioral science, child psychiatry, social work, and adolescent medicine and practices, 1980—; psychiatrist in private practice, 1982—.

MEMBER: American Psychological Association, Washington State Psychological Association.

WRITINGS:

(With Jennifer Wyatt) *The Seven-Year Stretch: How the Family Works Together to Grow through Adolescence,* Houghton Mifflin (Boston, MA), 1997.
(With Jennifer Wyatt) *The Launching Years: Strategies for Parenting from Senior Year to College Life,* Three River's Press (New York), 2002.

Contributor to *The Inside Story on Teenage Girls,* American Psychological Association; contributor to academic journals.

SIDELIGHTS: Laura Kastner is a clinical associate professor of psychiatry and specializes in work and research regarding adolescents. Her two books, both co-written with Jennifer Wyatt, give parents insights and strategies for dealing with their young teenagers.

The Seven-Year Stretch: How Families Work Together to Grow through Adolescence, examines the growth of a young person within the framework of a family.

Kastner considers such topics as self-esteem, freedom, risk-taking, and social skills through a series of vignettes involving families struggling with these issues. A *Publishers Weekly* reviewer commented that "the authors' conversational, anecdotal, and holistic approach has something to offer nearly all parents of teens." Kay L. Brodie of *Library Journal* called this book a "valuable resource."

In *The Launching Years: Strategies for Parenting from Senior Year to College Life* Kastner offers parents various approaches to help cope with the stress of "launching" their teen from the safe haven of home, out into the world. Topics include the college application process, graduation, leaving siblings behind, and parenting from far away. Highlighted in the book is the fact that these days, parenting lasts longer than it used to. Many kids still need someone to help keep them on track with studies, give advice about social situations, and even help with the job search after college. Stephanie Dunnewind in the *Seattle Times* quoted Kastner as saying, "People don't get married until twenty-five and twenty-seven. . . . It takes longer to develop the emotional, social, and coping skills to live in a more complex society." Norman Goldman noted in *Blether Book Review* online that "a great strength of the book is the down to earth advice and easy-to-read format. To enliven the material, authors effectively use sidebars . . . summarizing the major principles they advocate." Vanessa Bush of *Booklist* explained that "this book aims to help parents and adolescents negotiate new rules in their relationships."

BIOGRAPHICAL AND CRITICAL SOURCES:

PERIODICALS

Booklist, August, 2002, Vanessa Bush, review of *The Launching Years: Strategies for Parenting from Senior Year to College Life,* p. 1897.
Library Journal, May 1, 1997, Kay L. Brodie, review of *The Seven-Year Stretch: How the Family Works Together to Grow through Adolescence,* p. 134.
Publishers Weekly, February 17, 1997, review of *The Seven-Year Stretch,* p. 215.

ONLINE

Blether Book Review, http://blether.com/ (December 9, 2002), Norman Goldman, review of *The Launching Years.*

IDS News, http://idsnews.com/ (December 9, 2002),
Molly Wolfe, "Sadness Is the Norm When Junior
Is at the Dorm."

Launching Years, http://www.launchingyears.com/
(December 9, 2002), interview with Kastner and
Wyatt.

Seattle Times Online, http://seattletimes.nwsource.com/
(December 9, 2002), Stephanie Dunnewind,
"Launching a Ten: Getting a High School Senior
off to College."

USA Today Online, http://www.usatoday.com
(December 9, 2002), Patty Rhule, "Leaving Can
Ruffle the Nest."

* * *

KEMBLE, E(dward) W(indsor) 1861-1933

PERSONAL: Born January 18, 1861, in Sacramento,
CA; died September 19, 1933 in Ridgefield, CT; son
of Col. Edward Cleveland Kemble (a newspaper
publisher) and Cecilia Amanda Windsor; married Sarah
Briggs, 1885; children: Edward Brewster, Beth Elsie,
Schuyler, Frances Gail. *Education:* Attended Art
Students' League, 1880.

CAREER: Cartoonist and illustrator. Contributed illustrations to *Harper's Bazaar; Daily Graphic,* staff
cartoonist from 1881, book illustrator from 1885; *Century,* illustrator from 1885, advertising illustrator from
1891; illustrator for *New York World* and *New York
Journal* from late 1890s. *Military service:* Seventh
Regular New York National Guard.

MEMBER: Manhattan Athletic Club; Lambs Club;
Salmagundi Club.

WRITINGS:

*Kemble's Coons: Drawings of Colored Children and
Southern Scenes,* Russell (New York, NY), 1896.
The Blackberries and Their Adventures, Russell (New
York, NY), 1897.
A Coon Alphabet, Russell (New York, NY), 1898.
Comical Coons, Russell (New York, NY), 1898.
The Billy Goat and Other Comicalities, Scribners
(New York, NY), 1898.

Coontown's Four Hundred, Life Publishing (New
York, NY), 1899.
Kemble's Sketch Book, Russell (New York, NY), 1899.
Kemble's Pickaninnies, Russell (New York, NY), 1901.

SELECTED BOOKS; ILLUSTRATOR

Mark Twain (pseudonym of Samuel Clemens), *Adven-
tures of Huckleberry Finn,* Webster (New York,
NY), 1884.
Mark Twain, *Mark Twain's Library of Humor,* Webster
(New York, NY), 1888.
Thomas Nelson Page, *Two Little Confederates,* Scrib-
ners (New York, NY), 1888.
Harry Stillwell Edwards, *Two Runaways and Other
Stories,* Century (New York, NY), 1889.
Louis Beauregard Pendleton, *King Tom and the Run-
aways,* Appleton (New York, NY), 1890.
Francis Hopkinson Smith, *Colonel Carter of Carters-
ville,* Houghton, Mifflin (Boston, MA), 1891.
Harriet Beecher Stowe, *Uncle Tom at Home in Ken-
tucky,* 2 volumes, Houghton, Mifflin (Boston,
MA), 1892.
Joel Chandler Harris, *On the Plantation,* Appleton
(New York, NY), 1892.
James Whitcomb Riley, *Poems Here at Home,* Century
(New York, NY), 1893.
Washington Irving, *Knickerbocker's History of New
York,* Putnam (New York, NY), 1894.
Mary Mapes Dodge, *The Land of Puck,* Century (New
York, NY), 1894.
W. W. Jacobs, *Many Cargoes,* Stokes (New York, NY),
1895.
Joel Chandler Harris, *Daddy Jake* [and] *The Runaway,*
Century (New York, NY), 1896.
Ruth McEnery Stuart, *Solomon Crows Christmas
Pockets and Other Tales,* Harper (New York, NY),
1896.
Frank R. Stockton, *A Story-Tellers Pack,* Scribners
(New York, NY), 1897.
Ruth McEnery Stuart, *Moriah's Mourning,* Harper
(New York, NY), 1898.
Thomas Nelson Page, *Two Prisoners,* Russell (New
York, NY), 1898.
Paul Laurence Dunbar, *Folks from Dixie,* Dodd, Mead
(New York, NY), 1898.
Mark Twain, *Pudd'nhead Wilson and Those Extraordi-
nary Twins,* Harper (New York, NY), 1899.
Paul Laurence Dunbar, *The Strength of Gideon, and
Other Stories,* Dodd, Mead (New York, NY), c.
1900.

John Phoenix (pseudonym of Gorge Horation Derby), *Phoenixianna; or, Sketches and Burlesques,* Appleton (New York, NY), 1903.

Paul Laurence Dunbar, *The Heart of Happy Hollow,* Dodd, Mead (New York, NY), 1904.

Joel Chandler Harris, *The Tar-Baby. And Other Rhymes of Uncle Remus,* Appleton (New York, NY), 1904.

Wallace Irving, *At the Sign of the Dollar,* Duffield (New York, NY), 1905.

Don Marquis, *Danny's Own Story,* Doubleday (Garden City, NY), 1912.

Ruth McEnery Stuart, *Plantation Songs and Other Verses,* Appleton (New York, NY), 1916.

Irwin Russell, *Christmas Night in the Quarters. And Other Poems,* Century (New York, NY), 1917.

Joel Chandler Harris, *Uncle Remus: His Songs and His Sayings,* Appleton (New York, NY), 1920.

Kenneth Brown, *Putter Perkins,* Houghton Mifflin (New York, NY), 1923.

John C. McNeill, *Lyrics from Cotton Land,* Stone & Barringer (Charlotte, NC), 1927.

Joseph Lincoln, *Cape Cod Ballads, and Other Verses,* Albert Brandt (Trenton, NJ), 1929.

Contributed to periodicals, including *Harper's Bazar, Harper's Young People, Harper's Weekly, Life, St. Nicholas, Century, Harper's Monthly, Youth's Companion, Ladies' Home Journal, Cosmopolitan, Harper's Round Table, Leslie's Weekly, Collier's, Good Housekeeping* and *Judge.*

SIDELIGHTS: E. W. Kemble is best known for his guffawing, pen-and-ink drawings from the late nineteenth century. Known primarily as a book and magazine illustrator, he published a few collections of his caricatures as children's books—many of them his trademark "black comicalities." As Francis Martin, Jr. wrote in the *Dictionary of Literary Biography:* "Kemble is so identified with these comicalities that there is often the erroneous impression that he worked exclusively with this theme." Moreover, those drawings have become important to more recent scholars; Kemble's references to disturbing issues prove a valuable reflection of public sentiment at the turn of the twentieth century.

Edward Windsor Kemble's parents were affluent people from established New York families; Kemble's father was a descendant of William Whipple, who signed the Declaration of Independence. Kemble was encouraged in his artwork from an early age—perhaps because his father, a publisher, recognized the value of a controlled pen. By 1880, Kemble showed his comic drawings to Charles Parsons, the art editor of Harper and Brothers Publishers. Parsons purchased the teenager's drawings for seventy dollars in gold; Kemble became a working artist on the spot.

In New York, Kemble soon found a steady income as a staff artist at the *Daily Graphic,* where he was encouraged to pump out drawings quickly. One sketch impressed writer Samuel Clemens Mark Twain so much that he hired Kemble to illustrate his *Adventures of Huckleberry Finn,* published under Clemens' pseudonym Mark Twain. Kemble composed 175 pen-and-ink drawings, each rendering Clemens's world visually. Martin noted: "The illustrations were a critical success and are in many ways the perfect visual counterpart to Twain's great novel, and they certainly made Kemble's reputation as one of the most recognized illustrators of his day." Kemble's work, however, ultimately wore on Clemens, who called it "blackboard outlines and charcoal sketches." The humorist also complained of Kemble's lack of imagination; in an 1884 letter to his publisher, Clemens sighed: "If Kemble's illustrations for my last book were handed me today, I would understand how tiresome to me the sameness would get to be, when distributed through a whole book, and I would put them promptly in the fire."

During the 1880s Kemble was nonetheless called upon increasingly to sketch scenes of "southern life" for *Century,* a new magazine. In its pages, Kemble drew illustrations for stories by writers such as Richard Malcolm Johnston, Frank R. Stockton, Joel Chandler Harris, Maurice Thompson, Thomas Nelson Page, and James Whitcomb Riley. During this period, Kemble also married Sarah Briggs, with whom he raised four children. The Kembles lived in northern Manhattan, New Rochelle, New York, and finally in Ridgefield, Connecticut. In his spare time, Kemble, a member of the Manhattan Athletic Club, would often perform there with the Lambs Star Minstrel on weekends.

In 1890 Kemble traveled south, wanting even more to depict rural life. During the 1890s he illustrated several significant books, including Harriet Beecher Stowe's *Uncle Tom at Home in Kentucky,* Riley's *Poems Here at Home,* Washington Irving's *Knickerbocker History of New York,* Harris's *Daddy Jake. The Runaway,* Twain's *Pudd'nhead Wilson and Those Extraordinary Twins* and Paul Laurence Dunbar's *Folks from Dixie,*

For *Folks from Dixie,* a collection of poems by a prominent black author that was published in 1898, Kemble and Dunbar were both criticized for creating "comical" and undignified stereotypes of black people. Martin suggested: "They (the cartoons) were meant to entertain in a period when racial themes formed a large part of the humor found in many of the leading magazines and newspapers; however, Kemble drew them with more sympathy and understanding than many artists." Nevertheless, Kemble's collections of drawings in this vein—collections with titles such as *Kemble's Coons: Drawings of Colored Children and Southern Scenes,* and *Kemble's Pickaninnies*—would soon seem repugnant to readers.

Not surprisingly, then, Kemble's work fell out of favor in his later years. Though he kept publishing political cartoons for magazines such as *Collier's* and *Harper's Weekly* into the 1910s, his eyesight and reputation declined sharply. Moreover, much of Kemble's original artwork was destroyed in a house fire. Kemble's work is also remembered for reminding viewers of stereotypes of the late nineteenth century. Kemble died in his home after completing one final "comical" drawing.

BIOGRAPHICAL AND CRITICAL SOURCES:

BOOKS

Dictionary of Literary Biography, Volume 188: *American Book and Magazine Illustrators to 1920,* Gale (Detroit, MI), 1998.*

*   *   *

KINDLEBERGER, Charles P(oor) II 1910-2003

OBITUARY NOTICE—See index for *CA* sketch: Born October 12, 1910, in New York, NY; died July 7, 2003, in Cambridge, MA. Economist, educator, and author. Kindleberger was a prominent economist who was renowned for his theories that government intervention is necessary to prevent economic crises, as well as for his key role in developing the Marshall Plan following World War II. Educated at the University of Pennsylvania, where he earned his undergraduate degree in 1932, and Columbia University, where he completed his Ph.D. in 1937, Kindleberger went on to gain practical experience in his field by working for the government. At the time, the Great Depression was still in progress, and his focus was on international trade and finance for the Federal Reserve Bank in New York City, and then for the Bank for International Settlements in Basle, Switzerland. From 1940 to 1942 he was in Washington, D.C., working as a research economist for the Federal Reserve, and for a year he was American secretary for the Joint Economic Committee of the United States and Canada. With the onset of World War II, Kindleberger joined the Office of Strategic Services—the precursor of the Central Intelligence Agency—and received a Bronze Star for helping select targets for bombings in Europe. With the war over, he returned to Washington, D.C., this time as chief of German and Austrian Economic Affairs and adviser on European economic recovery. As such, he was instrumental in helping to devise the economic recovery of Europe, which became known as the Marshall Plan after then secretary of state George C. Marshall. In 1948, Kindleberger left government work behind for academia. He joined the Massachusetts Institute of Technology as an associate professor, becoming a full professor of economics in 1951 and Ford International Professor of Economics emeritus in 1976. During his career, he wrote or edited forty books, including several influential textbooks and 1991's *The Life of an Economist: An Autobiography.* Other books by Kindleberger include *Foreign Trade and the National Economy* (1962), *The World in Depression, 1929-1939* (1973; revised edition, 1986), *Manias, Panics, and Crises* (1978), *A Financial History of Western Europe* (1984; revised edition, 1993), *Marshall Plan Days* (1987), *Historical Economics: Art or Science?* (1990), and *Comparative Political Economy: A Retrospective* (2000).

OBITUARIES AND OTHER SOURCES:

PERIODICALS

Los Angeles Times, July 11, 2003, p. B12.
New York Times, July 9, 2003, p. C13.
Times (London, England), July 17, 2003.
Washington Post, July 10, 2003, p. B6.

KIRCHWEY, Karl 1956-

PERSONAL: Born February 25, 1956, in Boston, MA; son of George Washington and Ellen-Douglas (Allen) Kirchwey; married Tamzen Flanders, 1988; children: Tobias Elinor. *Education:* Yale University, B.A., 1979; Columbia University, M.A., 1981.

ADDRESSES: Office—English House, Bryn Mawr College, 101 North Merion Ave., Bryn Mawr, PA 19010-2899. *E-mail*—kkirchwe@brynmawr.edu.

CAREER: Columbia University, New York, NY, instructor in English composition, 1980-81; American School in Switzerland (Tasis), Lugano, instructor, 1981-82; Elizabeth Irwin High School, New York, NY, instructor, 1982-84; Unterberg Poetry Center, 92nd Street YM-YWHA, New York, NY, assistant director, 1984-87, director, 1987-2000; Bryn Mawr College, Bryn Mawr, PA, director of creative writing, 2000—. Also instructor at Smith College, Northampton, MA (Grace Hazard Conkling writer-in-residence, 1995-97), Yale University, New Haven, CT, Wesleyan University, Middletown, CT, and the writing division, Columbia University, New York, NY.

AWARDS, HONORS: Norma Farber First book award from the Poetry Society of America, for *A Wandering Island,* 1991; Ingram Merrill Foundation fellowship, 1993; Guggenheim fellowship, 1994; Rome Prize in Literature, Academy of Arts and Letters, 1994-95; Paris Review Prize for Poetic Drama, 1997, for *Airedales and Cipher;* National Endowment for the Arts literature fellowship (poetry), 1996; honorary membership in Phi Beta Kappa (Alpha of Connecticut), 2000; Rosalyn R. Szhwartz teaching award, Bryn Mawr College, 2003.

WRITINGS:

POETRY

A Wandering Island, Princeton University Press (Princeton, NJ), 1990.
Those I Guard, Harcourt (San Diego, CA), 1993.
The Engrafted Word, Holt (New York, NY), 1998.
At the Palace of Jove, Putnam (New York, NY), 2002.

Also author of play in verse, *Airedales and Cipher,* based on Euripides' *Alcestis,* presented in public readings at 92nd Street YM-YWHA and at Appalachian Summer Festival, Boone, NC. Contributor of poems to periodicals, including *Nation, New Yorker, Paris Review, New Republic, New York Review of Books, Poetry,* and *Yale Review.* Poems and translations represented in anthologies, including *The Best of the Best American Poetry, 1987-1998, Penguin Book of the Sonnet,* and *After Ovid: New Metamorphoses.*

SIDELIGHTS: Karl Kirchwey's poems frequently invoke the classical era, finding inspiration in ancient societies. Kirchwey is often seen "mapping the ghostly presences conjured by travel and the historical imagination," related a *Publishers Weekly* contributor in a review of *The Engrafted Word.* Kirchwey compares modern catastrophes to the events of Greek tragedies, composes elegies for vanished cultures, and scrutinizes tourists viewing millennia-old ruins. He also makes references to more recent history, discussing, say, Mozart or nineteenth-century U.S. statesman Carl Schurz. And sometimes he deals with highly personal subjects, such as his loved ones. Kirchwey's poems are "spare" and "lucid," observed the *Publishers Weekly* critic, and are marked by careful word choice.

The Engrafted Word, Kirchwey's third collection, includes numerous poems that meditate on his travels through the former Roman Empire and the relevance of the past to the present. Also featured are family-related poems such as "Zoo Story" and "In Transit," remembrances of his parents, and "He Considers the Birds of the Air," in which he reflects on his young son. "Sharply etched and richly worked as Kirchwey's classical travelogue is, it would feel a bit stuffy if unrelieved by such personal lyrics," commented Bill Christopherson in *Poetry. Library Journal's* Steven R. Ellis, meanwhile, praised Kirchwey for creating "an art where no word is out of place." And Mary Jo Salter, writing for the *New York Times Book Review,* said: "To Read *The Engrafted Word* is to experience the fusion of a living soul with those who came before us. It's a task Karl Kirchwey performs with skill and unwavering integrity."

In *At the Palace of Jove,* Kirchwey remains "concerned with memory and ways of processing pasts personal and historical," noted a *Publishers Weekly* contributor.

Kate Bolick, writing in the *New York Times Book Review,* found that although some poems fail to spring to life, the collection is full of "confident, witty, and often surprising ruminations." "He has mined mythology and history to create poems that enable us to expand our understanding of life," exclaimed Michael Peich of the *Philadelphia Inquirer.*

Kirchwey told *CA:* "Beginning with a poem such as 'The Geographer's Line' in my first book, *A Wandering Island,* I have been interested in the relationship between geographical place and a feeling of being at home. My family moved around a great deal while I was growing up; what I lost in domestic stability I gained, perhaps, in having seen many different places and people. While I consider myself an American poet, the fact that I lived in England and Switzerland for a number of years places the cultural balance point for me somewhere between Europe and the United States. The Second World War, which marked my parents' generation, I have felt as a legacy stronger than that of the war in Vietnam, which was the defining historical event for my older siblings. Several journeys through Greece with my family when I was a teenager started my preoccupation with the Greco-Roman past, which I read as if it were present. Frost said, 'A poem is best read in the light of all the other poems ever written,' and it is my belief that a poem is best *written* in this light as well."

BIOGRAPHICAL AND CRITICAL SOURCES:

PERIODICALS

Library Journal, April 15, 1998, Steven R. Ellis, review of *The Engrafted Word,* p. 83.

New Criterion, June, 1998, William Logan, "Soiled Desires," p. 61.

New York Times Book Review, August 9, 1998, Mary Jo Salter, review of *The Engrafted Word;* January 12, 2002, Kate Bolick, review of *At the Palace of Jove,* p. 19.

Philadelphia Inquirer, December 22, 2002, Michael Peich, review of *At the Palace of Jove,* p. H18.

Poetry, September, 1999, Bill Christopherson, review of *The Engrafted Word,* p. 345.

Publishers Weekly, February 23, 1998, review of *The Engrafted Word,* p. 68; November 4, 2002, review of *At the Palace of Jove,* p. 77.

KLEIN, Étienne 1958-

PERSONAL: Born 1958. *Education:* Earned degree of docteur en philosophie des sciences.

ADDRESSES: Office—Commissariat à l'Énergie Atomique, 31/33 rue de la Fédération, 75752 Paris, Cedex 15, France.

CAREER: Physicist. Commissariat à l'énergie atomique, Paris, France, assistant director of material science; École Centrale de Paris, professor of quantum and particle physics and of the philosophy of science.

AWARDS, HONORS: Prix Jean Perrin, Société Française de Physique, 1997.

WRITINGS:

Conversations avec le sphinx, Albin Michel (Paris, France), 1991, translation by David Le Vay published as *Conversations with the Sphinx: Paradoxes in Physics,* Souvenir Press (London, England), 1996.

(With Bernard d'Espagnat) *Regards sur la matière: des quanta et des choses,* Fayard (Paris, France), 1993.

(Editor, with Michel Spiro) *Le temps et sa flèche,* Editions Frontières (Luisant, France), 1994.

(With Marc Lachièze-Rey) *La quête de lunité: l'aventure de la physique,* Albin Michel (Paris, France), 1996, translation by Axel Reisinger published as *The Quest for Unity: The Adventure of Physics,* Oxford University Press (New York, NY), 1999.

(With Marie de Solemne, André Comte-Sponville, and Jean-Yves Leloup) *Aimer désespérément,* Dervy (Paris, France), 1998.

L'atome au pied du mur, Pommier (Paris, France), 2000.

L'unité de la physique, Presses Universitaires de France (Paris, France), 2000.

(With Bernard Bonin and Jean-Marc Cavedon) *Moi, U 235, atome radioactif,* Flammarion (Paris, France), 2001.

Les tactiques de chronos, Flammarion (Paris, France), 2003.

Columnist for magazine *La Recherche* (France).

SIDELIGHTS: French physicist Étienne Klein has written numerous books about his specialties, particle and quantum physics, but only a few of them have been translated into English. The most notable of his works available to English readers are *Conversations with the Sphinx: Paradoxes in Physics* and *The Quest for Unity: The Adventure of Physics.*

Mark Buchanan, who reviewed *Conversations with the Sphinx* for *Nature,* stated that it begins with a "well-written, carefully conceived essay" that argues that the discovery of paradoxes is a crucial means by which scientific discovery moves forward. This essay, which draws on theories introduced by philosophers such as nineteenth-century European theorists Friedrich Nietzsche and Søren Kierkegaard, is suffused with "a rich sense of philosophy and literature," noted *School Library Journal* reviewer Ted R. Spickler. The second half of the book consists of brief summaries of seven paradoxes present in modern physics, including the wave-particle duality. "Both lay and professional readers will gain valuable insights from" *Conversations with the Sphinx,* A. M. Saperstein commented in *Choice.*

The Quest for Unity expresses the desire present in scientists to find a single, coherent set of rules or equations to explain all of the phenomena that occurs in the universe. The areas in which modern physics has managed to find unity, including classical and quantum mechanics and relativity theory, are "expertly surveyed" by Klein and his coauthor, Marc Lachièze-Rey, T. Eastman declared in *Choice.*

BIOGRAPHICAL AND CRITICAL SOURCES:

PERIODICALS

Choice, September, 1997, A. M. Saperstein, review of *Conversations with the Sphinx: Paradoxes in Physics,* p. 170; November, 1999, T. Eastman, review of *The Quest for Unity: The Adventure of Physics,* p. 562.

Nature, November 28, 1996, Mark Buchanan, review of *Conversations with the Sphinx,* p. 325.

Publishers Weekly, April 19, 1999, review of *The Quest for Unity,* p. 52.

School Library Journal, September, 1997, Ted R. Spickler, review of *Conversations with the Sphinx,* p. 168.

ONLINE

Oxford University Press, http://www.mnemosyne.oup-usa.org/ (February 9, 2000), summary of *The Quest for Unity.*

Salon-Livre-Presse-Jeunesse, http://www.ldj.tm.fr/ (October 27, 2003), "Étienne Klein."

Société d'astronomie de Nantes Web site, http://www.san-fr.com/ (October 24, 2003), "Étienne Klein."*

*   *   *

KLEMPERER, Paul (David) 1956-

PERSONAL: Born August 15, 1956; son of Hugh G. and Ruth M. M. (Jordan) Klemperer; married Margaret Meyer, 1989; children: two sons, one daughter. *Education:* Peterhouse College, Cambridge, B.A. (with first class honors), 1978; Stanford University, M.B.A., 1982, Ph.D. (economics), 1986.

ADDRESSES: Office—Nuffield College, Oxford University, Oxford OX1 1NF, England; fax: +44-1865-278557. *E-mail*—paul.klemperer@economics.ox.ac.uk.

CAREER: Educator and author. Arthur Andersen and Co., senior consultant, 1978-80; Oxford University, Oxford, England, lecturer in operations research and mathematical economics, 1985-90, reader, 1990-95, Edgeworth Professor of Economics and fellow of Nuffield College, 1995—, John Thomson fellow and tutor at St. Catherine's College, 1985-95. Visiting professor at Massachusetts Institute of Technology, 1987, University of California, Berkeley, 1991 and 1993, Stanford University, 1991 and 1993, Yale University, 1994, and Princeton University, 1998. Consultant to U.S. Federal Trade Commission, Office of Fair Trading, British National Audit Office, and to private firms.

MEMBER: British Academy (fellow), Econometric Society (fellow).

AWARDS, HONORS: Harkness fellow, Commonwealth Fund, 1980-82.

WRITINGS:

The Economic Theory of Auctions, Edward Elgar Publishing (Northampton, MA), 2000.

Auctions: Theory and Practice (Toulouse Lecture in Economics), Princeton University Press (Princeton, NJ), 2003.

Editor, *RAND Journal of Economics,* 1993-99; member of editorial staff, *Review of Economic Studies,* 1989-97, *Journal of Industrial Economics,* 1989-96, *Oxford Economic Papers,* 1986-2000, *International Journal of Industrial Organization,* 1993—, *European Economic Review,* 1997—, *Review of Economic Design,* 1997-2000, *Economic Policy,* 1998-99, *Economic Journal,* 2000—, *Frontiers in Economics,* 2000—, and *B. E. Journal of Economic Analysis and Policy,* 2001—.

* * *

KNAUSS, Sibylle 1944-

PERSONAL: Born 1944.

ADDRESSES: Agent—c/o Author Mail, Random House, 1745 Broadway, New York, NY 10019.

CAREER: Novelist.

WRITINGS:

NOVELS

Ach Elise, oder, Lieben ist ein Einsames Geschäft, Hoffmann und Campe (Hamburg, Germany), 1981.
Das Herrenzimmer, Hoffmann und Campe (Hamburg, Germany), 1983.
Erlkönigs Töchter, Hoffmann und Campe (Hamburg, Germany), 1985.
Charlotte Corday, Hoffmann und Campe (Hamburg, Germany), 1988.
Ungebetene Gäste, Hoffmann und Campe (Hamburg, Germany), 1991.
Die Nacht mit Paul, Hoffmann und Campe (Hamburg, Germany), 1994.
Die Missionarin, Hoffmann und Campe (Hamburg, Germany), 1997.
Evas Cousine, Claassen (Munich, Germany), 2000, translationd by Anthea Bell published as *Eva's Cousin,* Ballantine Books (New York, NY), 2002.
Füsse im Feuer, Claassen (Munich, Germany), 2003.

SIDELIGHTS: A German novelist, Sibylle Knauss has written well-received novels that focus on the lives of German missionaries in the East Indies and French Revolutionaries. To English-speaking readers she is primarily known as the author of *Eva's Cousin.* Based on Eva Braun's real-life cousin, Gertrude Weisker, who was interviewed by the author after fifty years of silence, the novel tells the story of Marlene, a young woman summoned to the Berghof, Hitler's mountain retreat, to entertain a bored and lonely Eva while Hitler is away in Berlin. For a while the two lead a fairly idyllic life, cut off from the horrors of the war and the Nazi monstrosities at home, though Eva continues to pine for her absent lover. Eventually Eva leaves to join Hitler, and Marlene finds herself torn between love for an S.S. officer and her desire to protect a Ukrainian refugee from a slave camp who has found his way to her cabin retreat. At last, the world intrudes, and Marlene finds herself fleeing the burning grounds of the Berghof as the war closes in; Eva herself commits suicide alongside Hitler in Berlin.

Library Journal contributor Barbara Conaty wrote that Knauss "has transformed the banal facts of a light friendship between two cousins into a novel 'for readers who know and respect the mystery of fiction.'" "The result is a strange, moving and disturbing book. . . . But it is impossible to know where the fiction starts," noted *New York Times Book Review* contributor Alan Riding. Whether fiction or biography, the story struck a chord with many reviewers. "When Knauss implies that Marlene's experience can explain mass support for the Nazi regime, the moral center of the book falters, but her sparely poetic and intense portrait of a young girl caught between her own ethical code and the promise of power is unrelentingly powerful," concluded a *Publishers Weekly* contributor.

BIOGRAPHICAL AND CRITICAL SOURCES:

PERIODICALS

Library Journal, September 15, 2002, Barbara Conaty, review of *Eva's Cousin,* p. 92.
New York Times Book Review, September 1, 2002, Alan Riding, "The Marriage of Eva Braun: The Prequel," p. 5.
Publishers Weekly, July 1, 2002, review of *Eva's Cousin,* p. 51.

ONLINE

Romantic Times, http://www.romantictimes.com/ (October 28, 2003), Sheri Melnick, review of *Eva's Cousin.**

*   *   *

KNODE, Helen 1957-

PERSONAL: Born 1957, in Calgary, Alberta, Canada; immigrated to United States; married James Ellroy (a novelist).

ADDRESSES: Home—Northern California. *Office*—c/o Author Correspondence, Harcourt, Inc., 15 East 26th St., New York, NY 10003-4793.

CAREER: Journalist and novelist. *L.A. Weekly,* Los Angeles, CA, film critic, 1985-91. Lecturer on film criticism at colleges.

WRITINGS:

The Ticket Out, Harcourt (New York, NY), 2003.

SIDELIGHTS: Helen Knode brings her experience as a film critic to bear on her debut novel, *The Ticket Out.* Knode's heroine, Ann Whitehead, is a jaded critic who balks at her editor's suggestions that she pander to the industry. When a young, aspiring screenwriter is found stabbed to death in Ann's bathtub, Ann sees the murder as a way to branch out into investigative journalism. *The Ticket Out* describes Ann's explorations of not one but several murders in the seedy underbelly of Hollywood, where powerful executives take advantage of ambitious women who want entrée into the business.

A *Kirkus Reviews* critic noted that the milieu Knode creates in her novel is "a violent and soiled Hollywood that Raymond Chandler would appreciate." The same critic felt that the book reveals "a promising start" for Knode as a novelist. In *Book,* Stephanie Foote praised *The Ticket Out* as "part noir lament, part witty liberal rant." A *Publishers Weekly* reviewer found

the work "a juicy portrait of contemporary L.A." in which "Knode's clever, sophisticated plotting packs a punch." Joanne Wilkinson in *Booklist* concluded that *The Ticket Out* is a "very entertaining novel with a busy plot and attitude to spare."

In an interview on the *Harcourt Books Web site,* Knode said she was happy working as a journalist until her husband, author James Ellroy, encouraged her to write a novel. She said that Ellroy "runs around telling everybody that they should write novels if they want to. He says writing novels is a blast, and everything that goes on the page is absolutely yours. That was the first time it occurred to me to write a novel. Now I hope I never do anything else."

BIOGRAPHICAL AND CRITICAL SOURCES:

PERIODICALS

Book, January-February, 2003, Stephanie Foote, review of *The Ticket Out,* p. 77.
Booklist, December 1, 2002, Joanne Wilkinson, review of *The Ticket Out,* p. 649.
Charlotte Observer, January 16, 2003, Salem Macknee, "Knode's 'The Ticket Out' Quickly Hooks Readers with Its Fresh Style."
Entertainment Weekly, February 14, 2003, Rebecca Ascher-Walsh, review of *The Ticket Out,* p. 76.
Kirkus Reviews, October 15, 2002, review of *The Ticket Out,* p. 1497.
Library Journal, November 15, 2002, Susan Clifford Braun, review of *The Ticket Out,* p. 101.
Publishers Weekly, December 16, 2002, review of *The Ticket Out,* p. 45.

ONLINE

Harcourt Books, http://www.harcourtbooks.com/ (May 19, 2003), interview with Knode.**

*   *   *

KOPÁCSI, Sandor 1922-2001

PERSONAL: Born March 5, 1922, in Miskolc, Hungary; died March 2, 2001, in Toronto, Canada; immigrated to Canada, 1975; son of Joseph and Ilona (Simon) Kopácsi; married Ibolya (a clerk; December 28, 1944; children: Judy Kopácsi Gelberger. *Educa-*

tion: University of Budapest, graduated; University in Political Science and Law, Ph.D. (cum laude), 1969. *Religion:* Presbyterian. *Hobbies and other interests:* Swimming, cross-country skiing, photography, and travel.

CAREER: Writer and journalist. Lathe operator and draftsman, Diosjyor, Hungary, 1940-45; police officer, Miskolc-Budapest, Hungary, 1945-56; imprisoned in Hungary, 1956-63; safety officer, Solymar, Hungary, 1963-75; janitor, Toronto, Canada, 1975-87.

MEMBER: International P.E.N. Club Center for Writers in Exile, American branch.

WRITINGS:

Au nom de la classe ouvriere kes mémoires du pret de police de Budapest en 1956, R. Laffont (Paris, France), 1979, translation by Daniel and Judy Stoffman published as *In the Name of the Working Class: The Inside Story of the Hungarian Revolution,* Grove Press (New York, NY), 1986.
Die Ungarische Tragödie, Deutsche Verlags-Anstalt (Stuttgart, Germany), 1979.
Az 1956-os magyar forradalom &eaucute;s a Nagy Imre per (title means "The Hungarian Revolution and the Imre Nagy Trial"), Magyar Öregdi´k Szövetség (New Brunswick, NJ), 1979.
Wegry 1956: 13 dni nadziei, Wydawnicza (Warsaw, Poland), 1982.
1984 Kalendarz entuzjastow, Wydawnicza (Warsaw, Poland), 1984.
(With Tibor Tardos) *Életfogytiglan,* Biblioteka (Budapest, Hungary), 1989.

SIDELIGHTS: Writer and journalist Sándor Kopácsi was born in Miskolc, Hungary in 1922. He worked as a lathe operator and draftsman and then as a police officer until the mid-1950s. From 1956 until 1963, he was imprisoned. After his release, he worked as a safety officer in Solymar, Hungary until he immigrated to Canada in 1975. He worked as a janitor in Toronto from 1975 until 1987.

A member of the International P.E.N. Club Center for Writers in Exile, Kopácsi has written a number of books concerning the Hungarian Revolution. *In the*

Name of the Working Class: The Inside Story of the Hungarian Revolution is one such book. Charles Gati, a reviewer for the *New York Times Book Review,* called the book "eminently readable." As the only survivor of the Imre Nagy political group living in the West, Kopácsi, Gati noted, "offer[s] . . . new information about the secret trial of the Nagy group in 1958." *In the Name of the Working Class* "recounts Mr. Kopácsi's experiences within the party and the role he played in the events of 1956." Gati called the book "a timely and disturbing reminder of the events" it covers. Carlo Gebler, a reviewer in *Books,* called the book "fascinating." A contributor to *Foreign Affairs* noted the book's "swiftly moving narrative studded with vivid encounters." Ferenc Feher, in a review for the *Los Angeles Times Book Review,* stated that "Kopácsi's memoirs alone remain a singularly important document of modern political history."

BIOGRAPHICAL AND CRITICAL SOURCES:

PERIODICALS

Books, August, 1989, Carlo Gebler, "Retelling Hungary's Pain," p. 16.
Foreign Affairs, spring, 1988, review of *In the Name of the Working Class: The Inside Story of the Hungarian Revolution,* p. 885.
Los Angeles Times Book Review, October 25, 1987, Ferenc Feher, "Imre Nagy: Heroism behind Closed Doors," p. 2.
New Statesman & Society, July 7, 1989, Norman Stone, "Nagy's Rehabilitation," pp. 40-41.
New York Times Book Review, January 10, 1988, Charles Gati, "Saved by His Proletarianism," p. 12.*

*   *   *

KUO, Pao Kun 1939-

PERSONAL: Born June 27, 1939, in Hebei Province, China; immigrated to Singapore, 1949; married Goh Lay Kuan (a dancer and choreographer). *Education:* Graduated from National Institute of Dramatic Art, Sydney, Australia, 1964; advanced coursework, 1971.

ADDRESSES: Office—31 International Business Park, No. 01-05 Creative Resource, Singapore 609921.

CAREER: Playwright and artistic director. Worked at radio stations in Singapore and Australia; Practice Performing Arts School, Singapore, cofounder and artistic director, 1965—, codirector of theatre training and research program, 2001—; The Theatre Practice, Singapore, founding artistic director, 1986—; The Substation (arts center), founding artistic director, 1990-95. National Institute of Education, Nanyang Technological University, lecturer in drama and performance, beginning 1994.

AWARDS, HONORS: Singapore National Cultural Medallion, 1989; Japanese Chamber of Commerce and Industry culture award, 1992, ASEAN performing arts award, 1993; Chevalier des Arts et des Lettres, French government, 1997; Asian Leadership fellow, 1997.

WRITINGS:

PLAYS

(Adapter) Bertolt Brecht, *Caucasian Chalk Circle,* produced, 1967.
(Adapter) Lorraine Hansberry, *A Raisin in the Sun,* produced, 1968.
Hey, Wake Up! produced, 1968.
The Struggle, produced, 1969.
The Spark of Youth, produced, 1970.
Growth, produced, 1974.
(Adapter) Kala Dewata, *Atop Roof, Tile Roof,* produced 1981.
The Little White Sailing Boat, produced 1982.
(Adapter) Athol Fugard, *The Island,* produced, 1985.
(Adapter) Arfin C. Noer, *Kapai Kapai,* produced, 1986.
The Coffin Is Too Big for the Hole (produced in Hong Kong, 1986), published in *The Coffin Is Too Big for the Hole, and Other Plays,* Times Book International (Singapore, China), 1990.
No Parking on Odd Days (produced in Hong Kong, 1986), published in *The Coffin Is Too Big for the Hole, and Other Plays,* Times Books International (Singapore, China), 1990.
Kopitiam, produced, 1986.
(Adapter) Max Frisch, *The Fire Teasers,* produced, 1987.
The Silly Little Girl and the Funny Old Tree (produced in Hong Kong, 1987), published in *The Coffin Is Too Big for the Hole, and Other Plays,* Times Books International (Singapore, China), 1990.

Day I Met the Prince (produced, 1988), published in *The Coffin Is Too Big for the Hole, and Other Plays,* Times Books International (Singapore, China), 1990.
Mama Looking for Her Cat (produced, 1988), published in *The Coffin Is Too Big for the Hole, and Other Plays,* Times Books International (Singapore, China), 1990.
The Coffin Is Too Big for the Hole, and Other Plays, Times Books International (Singapore, China), 1990.
The Eagle and the Cat, produced, 1990.
Lao Jiu, produced, 1990.
OZeroO1, produced, 1991.
The Evening Climb, produced, 1992.
Descendants of the Eunuch Admiral, produced, 1997.
(And director) *Grandpa's Meat-Bone Tea* (television play), produced by Television Corporation of Singapore, 1997.
The Spirits Play, produced, 1998.
Images at the Margins (collection of plays written in Chinese), Times Books International (Singapore), 2000.

Contributor to journals, including *TDR.*

Author's plays have been translated into Tamil, German, Malay, Arabic, and Japanese.

SIDELIGHTS: Kuo Pau Kun is a Singaporean playwright whose body of work "reflects the profound political, economic, and social shifts that have taken place in [his country] . . . during the postindependence era," according to essayist William Peterson in *Contemporary Dramatists.* His role in the Singapore arts community has been a pivotal one; in founding The Substation in 1990 he created one of the region's leading arts organizations, and his work as an educator and artistic director has influenced several generations of Singaporean actors. In October of 2000 Kuo saw three of his major plays performed in trilingual editions at Tokyo's Asian Arts Festival. The Chinese-born playwright and director was praised by *AsiaWeek.com* contributors Jim Erickson and Santha Oorjitham as "the kind of man who likes to bridge divides—between generations, cultures and attitudes."

Kuo began his career by founding, together with his wife, Goh Lay Kuan, the Practice Performance Arts School in 1965, and saw his first play, an adaptation of Bertolt Brecht's *Caucasian Chalk Circle* produced two years later. His first original work, the overtly political *Hey, Wake Up!*, made it to the Singapore stage two years later, According to Peterson, Kuo's early work was altered due to the playwright's incarceration during the government's crackdown on subversive leftist activists. Arrested and imprisoned without trial in 1976 under Singapore's Internal Security Act, he was released in 1980. After this point he viewed his responsibilities as playwright differently: as Kuo noted in an essay published in *TDR*, "Forced by circumstances and the innate need to take stock of two decades of artistic pursuit, I turned the imprisonment years into a fertile period of reflection." Rather than as a forum for political criticism, Kuo advocated for creative diversity. He also began drawing on native rather than Western influences, and while writing in English or Mandarin began to include local dialects, Malay, and Tamil in his texts. As Peterson explained: "the political and social criticism imbedded in Kuo's work since the early 1980s [became] . . . metaphoric, indirect and laced with humor and Singaporean colloquialisms." Kuo's most notable play, *The Coffin Is Too Big for the Hole*, first produced in 1985, comes out of this period, while 1988's *Mama Looking for Her Cat* was cited by Peterson as "one of Singapore's most aggressively multilingual plays" with its interweaving of Malay, Mandarin and English.

During the 1990s, according to Peterson, Kuo "directly or indirectly dealt with aspects of Singaporean identity . . . lost as the country join[ed] . . . the race to make it to the top of the economic heap in an age dominated by Western culture and mediated by the values of global capitalism." Working under government censorship, the playwright couched his social and political commentary within multicultural plots. Kuo's 1995 play, *Descendants of the Eunuch Admiral*, which touches upon the interplay between sex and power, reads on one level as a historical drama set within the fifteenth century; yet, according to Peterson, the play "provides piquant social criticism . . . in a manner that is artfully indirect." Into 2000 the playwright responded to continued shifts in Singapore's social demography. As he noted in *TDR*, "I have been trying to make plays comprised of characters of different ethnicities, each using their own language/dialect." Influences from India and Indonesia, as well as the aesthetic of the increasingly affluent, Chinese-educated populace that makes up much of his audience, has also prompted a change in directorial style to what Kuo calls "more creative theatre." As he

explained: "Rooting its expressive power almost entirely in the performers acting in an empty space, gestures alone create the entire universe. . . . this influence from Chinese traditional theatre [taking] . . . me further and further away from . . . stage realism." Continuing his role as innovator, Kuo also became increasingly active in the medium of television, telling *AsiaWeek.com* contributors Erickson and Oorjitham "My chief interest is in the expansion of television drama. I want to open it to theater and film, to a healthy flow of people, ideas and ways of work."

Discussing the role of art in a society increasingly focused on material things, Kuo explained to *Business Times—Asia* interviewer Jaime Ee: "Art is work like any other profession. Like any other profession, it involves discipline, training and frustrations. Art is the most personal of occupations. It requires the individual to be responsible for conceptualising, planning and executing a piece of art. He controls the concept and process, and is solely responsible for its result. What better way to nurture confidence, independence, imagination, intellectual and creative power."

BIOGRAPHICAL AND CRITICAL SOURCES:

BOOKS

Contemporary Dramatists, St. James Press (Detroit, MI), 1999, pp. 375-377.

PERIODICALS

Australasian Drama Studies, October, 1993, Jacqueline Lo, "Theatre in Singapore" (interview), pp. 135-146.
Business Times—Asia, February 27, 1993, Jaime Ee, "The State of the Arts" (interview).
New Straits Times, May 19, 2000, Janadas Devan, interview with Kuo; March 5, 2001, "Delightful Dig at Big Brother."
TDR, summer, 1994, Kuo Pao Kun, "Time/Space with a Simple Gesture," p. 59.

ONLINE

AsiaWeek.com, http://www.asiaweek.com/ (2001), Jim Erickson and Santha Oorjitham, "Call It a Soap Substitute."
Chinese High School, http://www.chs.sg/ (June 26, 2002), "Kuo Pao Kun: The Man and His Works."*

KUPFERBERG, Audrey E. 1949-

PERSONAL: Born June 25, 1949, in Amsterdam, NY; daughter of Samuel Leib (a dry goods store proprietor) and Rae (dry goods store proprietor; maiden name, Abramson) Kupferberg; married Rob Edelman (a writer and educator), April 30, 1987. *Ethnicity:* "Eastern-European American Jew." *Education:* State University of New York, Albany, B.A., 1971; New York University, M.A., 1976; International Federation of Film Archives Summer School, Berlin, West Germany, graduate, 1978. *Politics:* Democrat. *Religion:* Jewish. *Hobbies and other interests:* Racquetball, golf, watching minor league baseball, shopping for clothes.

ADDRESSES: Home and office—378 Division Street, Amsterdam, NY 12010.

CAREER: American Film Institute, Washington, DC, *The American Film Institute Catalog,* researcher and writer, 1972-74, motion picture and video archivist, 1976-83; American Film Institute, Los Angeles, CA, assistant director of National Center for Film and Video Preservation and project director of *American Film Institute Catalog,* 1983-84; Yale University, New Haven, CT, director of Film Study Center, 1987-90; consultant, archivist, and researcher for various film collections, museums, libraries, and universities, 1990—. State University of New York at Albany, lecturer in film history, 1998—.

MEMBER: Association of Moving Image Archivists.

WRITINGS:

(With husband, Rob Edelman) *Angela Lansbury: A Life on Stage and Screen,* Carol Publishing Group (Secaucus, NJ), 1996.
(With Rob Edelman) *The John Travolta Scrapbook,* Carol Publishing Group (Secaucus, NJ), 1997.
(With Rob Edelman) *Meet the Mertzes: The Life Stories of I Love Lucy's Other Couple,* Renaissance Books (Los Angeles, CA), 1999.
(With Rob Edelman) *Matthau: A Life,* Taylor Trade Publishing (Lanham, MD), 2002.
World War II ("People at the Center of" series), Blackbirch Press (San Diego, CA), 2002.

American Decades, Volume 2: *1910-1919,* Volume 3: *1920-1929,* Gale (Detroit, MI), 2003.

WORK IN PROGRESS: A biographical memoir about Ida Lupino by her daughter, Bridget Duff, to be cowritten by Audrey Kupferberg and Rob Edelman, possibly for 2005.

SIDELIGHTS: Audrey Kupferberg told *CA:* "I am a film historian and moving image archivist. My favorite period of film history is the 1910s through 1946. I love getting my hands dirty going through nitrate films to discover the unique or best-surviving treasures of our film heritage.

"My favorite authors are women. I particularly appreciate Dorothy Parker, Edna St. Vincent Millay, Edith Wharton, Fannie Hurst, and Maya Angelou. These authors not only tell stories, but delve into the female experience. The first three often do so with wit, and the last two show down-to-earth emotion.

"Because I love early twentieth-century film and theater, I am drawn to writing about entertainers from this period. Since I find life to be an interesting puzzle, biography is my favorite type of writing. Someday I plan to write a novel about my mother's childhood in Bialystok, Poland, before World War I. It will be partly historical, but mainly fantasized."

BIOGRAPHICAL AND CRITICAL SOURCES:

PERIODICALS

Los Angeles Times, June 20, 1983, Judith Michaelson, "Push is on to Preserve Film History," section VI, p. 1; September 16, 1983, Dale Pollock, "Collectors: Film Heroes or Villains?" p. 1.
Publishers Weekly, September 23, 2002, review of *Matthau: A Life,* p. 61.

*   *   *

KUTCHINS, Herb

PERSONAL: Male. *Education:* University of Chicago, A.B.; University of California, Berkeley, M.S.W. and D.S.W.

ADDRESSES: Office—Business Administration Building 3124, College of Health & Human Services, California State University, Sacramento, Solano Hall No. 5002, 6000 J Street, Sacramento, CA 95819. *E-mail*—kutchins@csus.edu.

CAREER: California State University, Sacramento, professor of social work.

AWARDS, HONORS: Book of the year award, Mind, 2000, for *Making Us Crazy: DSM; The Psychiatric Bible and the Creation of Mental Disorders.*

WRITINGS:

(With Stuart A. Kirk) *The Selling of DSM: The Rhetoric of Science in Psychiatry,* A. de Gruyter (New York, NY), 1992.

(With Stuart A. Kirk) *Making Us Crazy: DSM; The Psychiatric Bible and the Creation of Mental Disorders,* Free Press (New York, NY), 1997.

WORK IN PROGRESS: A book titled *Where the Buck Stops: Charitable Foundations and the American Way of Giving.*

SIDELIGHTS: Herb Kutchins, a professor of social work, and his collaborator Stuart A. Kirk, a professor of social welfare, have written two books that critique the methods by which the psychiatric establishment determines and defines mental illness. These two books, *The Selling of DSM: The Rhetoric of Science in Psychiatry* and *Making Us Crazy: DSM; The Psychiatric Bible and the Creation of Mental Disorders,* attempt to expose the methodological foundation of the *Diagnostic and Statistical Manual of Mental Disorders*—commonly known as the *DSM*—and, by extension, the *DSM*'s creator, the American Psychiatric Association (APA).

In *Making Us Crazy,* which *Health and Social Work* contributor Carlton E. Munson described as "a meticulously researched analysis," Kutchins and Kirk trace the history of revisions to the *DSM* since its inception in 1952. The authors debate whether the diagnosis of mental illness is a purely scientific process that aims to ensure human interest and health, or whether there are political and monetary issues that

are underlying. Among the evolving diagnoses that Kutchins and Kirk examine is homosexuality, which was originally defined as moral weakness, then as a personality disorder, was later changed to a "sexual orientation disorder," only to finally be removed from the 1987 edition of the *DSM* after the APA voted that homosexuality could not be considered an illness. The politicization of what is often assumed to be a rigorously scientific field "is one of the book's most disturbing revelations," Ken Livingston commented in a *Public Interest* review of *Making Us Crazy.*

BIOGRAPHICAL AND CRITICAL SOURCES:

PERIODICALS

Community Mental Health, April, 2000, Kevin Corcoran, review of *Making Us Crazy,* pp. 217-219.
Health and Social Work, February, 2000, Carlton E. Munson, review of *Making Us Crazy,* p. 75.
Journal of the American Medical Association, October 13, 1993, Steven S. Sharfstein, review of *The Selling of DSM: The Rhetoric of Science in Psychiatry,* pp. 1749-1750.
Lancet, March 14, 1998, Eve Leeman, review of *Making Us Crazy,* pp. 842-843.
Library Journal, November 15, 1997, Mary Ann Hughes, review of *Making Us Crazy,* p. 67.
Nature, October 23, 1997, review of *Making Us Crazy,* p. 805.
New England Journal of Medicine, April 15, 1993, Richard C. Shelton, review of *The Selling of DSM,* pp. 1132-1133.
New York Times Book Review, November 23, 1997, Mim Udovitch, review of *Making Us Crazy,* p. 22.
Public Interest, winter, 1999, Ken Livingston, review of *Making Us Crazy,* pp. 105-109.
Times (London, England), November 27, 1997, Tunku Varadarajan, review of *Making Us Crazy,* p. 15.
Times Literary Supplement, October 29, 1999, Carol Tavris, review of *Making Us Crazy,* p. 6.
Washington Monthly, January-February, 1998, E. Fuller, Torrey, review of *Making Us Crazy,* pp. 54-55.

ONLINE

College of Health and Human Services, University of California, Sacramento, Web site, http://www.hhs.csus.edu/ (October 24, 2003), "Herb Kutchins."*

L

LABRIOLA, Jerry

PERSONAL: Born in CT; married. *Education:* Thomas Jefferson University, Jefferson Medical College, 1957. *Politics:* Republican.

ADDRESSES: Agent—c/o Author Mail, Strong Books, P.O. Box 715, Avon, CT 06001. *E-mail*—Jerry@JerryLabriola.com.

CAREER: Physician, politician, and author. Practiced medicine for thirty-five years; Waterbury Hospital, Waterbury, CT, former chief of staff; University of Connecticut Medical School, assistant professor. Elected Republican Connecticut state senator, 1994; ran for Connecticut state governor and for U.S. Senate. *Military service:* U.S. Navy.

MEMBER: Goshen Writer's Group, Mystery Writers of America, International Association of Crime Writers, Connecticut Authors and Publishers Association (past president).

WRITINGS:

Murders at Hollings General, Strong Books (Avon, CT), 1999.
(With Henry Lee) *Famous Crimes Revisited: From Sacco-Vanzetti to O. J. Simpson: Including Lindbergh Kidnapping, Sam Sheppard, John F. Kennedy, Vincent Foster, JonBenet Ramsey,* Strong Books (Avon, CT), 2001.

Murders at Brent Institute: A Dr. David Brooks Medical Murder Mystery, Strong Books (Avon, CT), 2002.

WORK IN PROGRESS: The Maltese Murders (tentative title).

SIDELIGHTS: Born and raised in Connecticut, Jerry Labriola, a retired physician, former politician, and author, has enjoyed writing all his life. As quoted by a reviewer for the *Green Bay Press-Gazette* he said: "I have short stories scattered all over the house, none with the intention of publishing. It's difficult in tiny, short stories to make them in the mystery genre. I decided when I retired I would write mysteries." Labriola retired after thirty-five years of practicing medicine in his hometown of Naugatuk, Connecticut. He now writes full time, does book tours, and hosts writers' conferences.

When Labriola coauthored *Famous Crimes Revisited: From Sacco-Vanzetti to O. J. Simpson: Including Lindbergh Kidnapping, Sam Sheppard, John F. Kennedy, Vincent Foster, JonBenet Ramsey,* with renowned forensic scientist, Dr. Henry Lee, he was able to draw on his own background in forensic medicine, a field he entered while serving in the U.S. Navy. For this book, the authors researched seven of the most famous crimes of the twentieth century: the Sacco-Vanzetti case, the Lindbergh baby kidnapping, the Nicole Brown Simpson murder, the John F. Kennedy assassination, the JonBenet Ramsey murder, the Sam "the Fugitive" Sheppard case, and the Vincent Foster suicide. R. Saferstein reviewed the book for *Choice,* and commented that it "does an excellent job of providing readers with detailed overviews."

Labriola, who has studied creative writing at Wesleyan University, New York University, New School University, and Simmons College, has written two novels. *Murders at Hollings General* centers around Dr. David Brooks—a charming physician who sports a floppy mustache, floppy bow ties, and an attache case nicknamed "Friday"—who sleuths a string of murders committed by an impostor surgeon at a famous New England teaching hospital. He is encouraged by his police detective fiancee to investigate the murders. Unlikely victims, professional rivalries, power struggles, foreign drug cartels, and a subplot involving the physician-sleuth and his fiancée, make for a power-packed plot.

The follow-up murder mystery, *Murders at Brent Institute: A Dr. David Brooks Medical Murder Mystery,* finds Brooks preferring guns to practicing medicine. After solving five murders in two weeks, his new client, head of a genome research institute, is murdered. Activity at the institute is suspect; medical, biological, and technical research is underway and provides ample material for the plot, while genetic engineering, stem cell research, and bioterrorism become major threats to society. Rex E. Klett commented in *Library Journal* that the book is "short on subtlety and transition but long on action and adventure."

A reviewer for the *Green Bay Press-Gazette* commented: "Labriola is a master at plotting a complex, yet fast-paced mystery," and wrote that, in this book, Labriola's goal was to create not just a "whodunit," but to keep the motive a mystery until the very end. Labriola also said he never makes up the facts. He has his protagonist explain embryonic stem cells, cloning, and DNA while answering questions from his detective fiancée. According to the *Press-Gazette* reviewer, Labriola said: "I feel it is important not only to tell a story and entertain, but also to share some of the knowledge I've garnered over the years."

BIOGRAPHICAL AND CRITICAL SOURCES:

PERIODICALS

Choice, October, 2001, R. Saferstein, review of *Murders at Brent Institute: A Dr. David Brooks Medical Murder Mystery,* p. 329.
Green Bay Press-Gazette, September 29, 2002, review of *Murders at Brent Institute,* p. 5.

Library Journal, November 1, 2002, Rex E. Klett, review of *Murders at Brent Institute,* p. 132.

ONLINE

Jerry Labriola Home Page, http://www.jerrylabriola.com (May 6, 2003).*

*   *   *

LATOW, (Muriel) Roberta 1931-2003

OBITUARY NOTICE—See index for *CA* sketch: Born September 27, 1931, in Springfield, MA; died of cancer February 4, 2003, in Oxford, England. Art dealer, interior designer, and author. Latow had an early interest in art, and left her conservative, small-town life in Massachusetts to study interior design at the Parsons School of Design in New York City. She then worked as an interior designer in Manhattan and became friends with many prominent abstract and pop artists of the time, including Mark Rothko and Andy Warhol; many, in fact, credit her with giving Warhol the idea to paint his famous soup cans. Encouraged by her friends, she opened an art gallery in 1960 but had to close it in 1966 because of competition from more established galleries. She then found employment with the Brooklyn Museum, which sent her on art-hunting expeditions in the Middle East, Africa, and Europe. She enjoyed this work and international travel until she retired from it in 1981 to write erotic romance novels and continue her work as an interior designer. Latow's novels became popular for their descriptive details of far-off places with which the author was very familiar, as well as for their erotic interludes; the stories were often drawn from her personal experiences and then embellished. Over a period of about two decades she completed twenty-two novels, including *Three Rivers* (1981), *Cheyney Fox* (1991), *Love Chooses* (1993), *Hungry Heart* (1994), *Forbidden* (1995), *Objects of Desire* (1995), *Embrace Me* (1999), and *Take Me Higher* (c. 2000).

OBITUARIES AND OTHER SOURCES:

PERIODICALS

Times (London, England), February 21, 2003, p. 39.

LAWRENCE, Cynthia Miller

PERSONAL: Female. *Education:* University of Chicago, Ph.D., 1978.

ADDRESSES: Office—Temple University, Department of Art History, Ritter Hall Annex, 8th Floor, Philadelphia, PA 19122. *E-mail*—CML6@ix.netcom.com.

CAREER: Temple University, Philadelphia, PA, professor of art history.

WRITINGS:

Flemish Baroque Commemorative Monuments, 1566-1725, Garland Publishing (New York, NY), 1981.
Gerrit Adriaensz. Berckheyde (1638-1698): Haarlem Cityscape Painter, Davaco (Doornspijk, Netherlands), 1991.
(Editor) *Women and Art in Early Modern Europe: Patrons, Collectors, and Connoisseurs,* Pennsylvania State University Press (University Park, PA), 1997.

Contributor of articles to *Art Bulletin 80,* June 1999; *Nederlands Kunsthistorisch Jaarboek 45,* 1994; and *Crossways 3,* December 1994.

SIDELIGHTS: Cynthia Miller Lawrence, art historian, and professor of early modern art in the Low Countries at Temple University's department of art history, specializes in post-Tridentine art and architecture, the work of Rubens, and northern baroque sculpture. *Women and Art in Early Modern Europe: Patrons, Collectors, and Connoisseurs,* edited and with an introduction by Lawrence, was designed to reflect the role women played in developing the aesthetic culture of the late medieval period through the early modern period.

In *Renaissance Quarterly,* Fredrika H. Jacobs began her review of *Women and Art in Early Modern Europe* by repeating the question posed by Joan Kelly-Gadol in her seminal essay in the 1970s: "Did women have a Renaissance?" This question sparked an explosion of interest among scholars—hotly debated even decades later—as to women's roles in early modern Europe. Lawrence's anthology is her effort to reveal the influ-

ence women exerted in that era by specifically addressing their involvement in the arts. "This focused concentration . . . has a broad chronological span, covering roughly 1350-1750. Lawrence's introduction provides a lucid over-view of the issues that define the collection as a whole: shared iconographies, gendered misperceptions, shared motives, and the effects of conjugal relationships," wrote Jacobs.

Alice E. Sanger wrote in her review for *Burlington* that "An important strength of this anthology must be its broad chronological and geographical range" and added that it "offers an opportunity to consider the diverse projects of figures such as Jeanne d'Evreux, Queen of France, Eleonora da Toledo, Duchess of Florence, and Hogarth's patron Mary Edwards."

While a reviewer for *Virginia Quarterly Review* felt that the essay selection in *Women and Art in Early Modern Europe* is "largely uninspired," the reviewer was also encouraged by the fact that the essays' subject matter is of considerable importance in expanding the knowledge and understanding of women's roles in the arts during the period under consideration. Julia A. De Lancey of Truman State University also reviewed the book in *Sixteenth Century Journal.* She wrote: "As Cynthia Lawrence promises in her introductory essay, *Women and Art in Early Modern Europe* presents important contributions in two growing areas in art historical scholarship: the history of the involvement of women in the arts, and the history of patronage and collecting."

In the anthology, born from a symposium held at Temple University in April 1990 titled "Matronage: Women as Patrons and Collectors of Art, 1300-1800," the author of each essay focuses on women in these roles rather than as actual artist. Contributing essayists are Carla Lord, Alexandra Carpino, Clifford Brown, Carolyn Smyth, Sheila Ffolliott, Alice T. Friedman, Geraldine A. Johnson, Marilyn Dunn, Kathleen Szpila, Magdalena Kasman, Elena Ciletti, Nadia Tscherny, and, of course, Lawrence. The volume includes a comprehensive bibliography and black-and-white illustrations.

Sanger noted in her review that by patronizing art and artists, including architects, women could "negotiate political and dynastic imperatives" and thus establish for themselves and their families "both devotional and secular spaces for these purposes."

De Lancey wrote: "Finally, the volume not only underscores the highly respected status of women patrons in the art world, but also provides insight into critical subjects such as new home designs, the collecting of antiquities, the creation of memorial monuments, and the amassing and care of important collections in which women played a recognized, leading, and defining role."

BIOGRAPHICAL AND CRITICAL SOURCES:

PERIODICALS

Burlington, October, 1998, Alice E. Sanger, review of *Women and Art in Early Modern Europe: Patrons, Collectors, and Connoisseurs,* p. 702.
Renaissance Quarterly, summer, 1999, review of *Women and Art in Early Modern Europe,* p. 525.
Sixteenth Century Journal, summer, 1998, Julia A. De Lancey, review of *Women and Art in Early Modern Europe,* p. 591.
Virginia Quarterly Review, summer, 1997, review of *Women and Art in Early Modern Europe,* p. 92.

ONLINE

PennState, Our Books, http://www.psupress.org/ (May 6, 2003), brief description of *Women and Art in Early Modern Europe.*
Temple University, http://www.temple.edu/ (May 6, 2003), short biography of Cynthia Lawrence.*

*   *   *

LAWTON, Clive A. 1951-

PERSONAL: Born July 14, 1951, in London, England; son of Reginald Samuel Clifford and Regina (Attias) Lawton; married Sara Joy Leviten, April 1, 1984 (divorced December 31, 1992); children: Anna Meriam, Evie Penina. *Ethnicity:* "White/Jewish." *Education:* University of York, B.A. (English and education), 1973, postgraduate education certification, 1974; Polytechnic of North London, M.A. (theatre studies), 1984; University of Liverpool, M.Ed. (religious studies), 1991; University of East London, M.Sc. (educational management), 1998; Institute of

Education, study toward Ph.D. *Politics:* Labour. *Religion:* Jewish. *Hobbies and other interests:* "DIY, theatre going, travel, photography."

ADDRESSES: Home—363 Alexandra Rd., Muswell Hill, London N10 2ET, England. *E-mail*—clive@ calawton.freeserve.co.uk.

CAREER: Teacher of English and drama, 1974-79; Board of Deputies, London, England, executive director of education and community relations departments, 1979-84; King David High School, Liverpool, England, headmaster, 1984-91; Liverpool City Local Education Authority, Liverpool, deputy director and head of Planning, Development and Equal Opportunities Service, 1991-94; Jewish Continuity, chief executive, 1993-96; Limmud, executive director, 1997—. Visiting lecturer at various institutions, including Chichester College, European Center for Leadership Development and Training, and Florence Melton Adult Mini-School; fellow at London School of Jewish Studies. Chair of North Middlesex University Hospital NHS Trust, and magistrate on Haringey Bench, 1999—; African Child Association, director, 2000—. Freelance writer, broadcaster, lecturer, and teacher trainer. Member, management board of NHS London Board Leadership programme; advisor to Home Secretary's Race Equality advisory panel. Member, Shap Working Party on World Religions in Education; board member, Commonwealth Jewish Council. Creator of *The Jewish Year Game* (board game), 1982.

MEMBER: Jewish Action for a Just World.

WRITINGS:

The Jewish People: Some Questions Answered, Board of Deputies (London, England), 1982.
A Jewish Family Event: Barmitzvah (educational filmstrip), Board of Deputies (London, England), 1982.
A Synagogue Tour (educational filmstrip), Board of Deputies (London, England), 1983.
The Calendar of World Religions' Festivals, Commission for Racial Equality (London, England), 1983-1994.
The Seder Handbook, Board of Deputies (London, England), 1984.

Matza and Bitter Herbs, Hamish Hamilton (London, England), 1984.

I Am a Jew, photographs by Chris Fairclough, Franklin Watts (New York, NY), 1984.

Pesakh: The Festival of Passover (video), Inner London Educational Authority TV (London, England), 1986.

Passport to Israel, Franklin Watts (New York, NY), 1987.

Religion through Festivals: Judaism, Longman (London, England), 1989.

(With Clive Erricker) *Themes in Religions: Judaism,* Longman (London, England), 1992.

(With Peggy Morgan) *Ethical Issues in Six Religious Traditions* (for adults), Edinburgh University Press (Edinburgh, Scotland), 1996.

Celebrating Islam, Young Library (Corsham, Wiltshire, England), 1996.

Celebrating Jewry, Young Library (Corsham, Wiltshire, England), 1996.

Which Planet Are You On? Does Religion Ever Come down to Earth?, Church of England National Society (London, England), 1997.

The Story of the Holocaust, Franklin Watts (London, England), 1999, Scholastic (New York, NY), 2000.

Auschwitz: The Story of a Nazi Death Camp, Candlewick Press (Cambridge, MA), 2002.

Hiroshima, Franklin Watts (New York, NY), 2003.

Columnist for *London Jewish News,* 1996—; member of editorial board of Oxford University *Journal of Holocaust Studies* and *Jewish Renaissance.* Contributor of articles to periodicals, including, *Times Educational Supplement, British Journal for Religious Education, Shap Journal, World Religions in Education, Tablet, Oxford Junior Encyclopedia, Resource, Religious Education in the Primary School, Assembly File, Dictionary of Religious Education, Jewish Chronicle, Jewish Quarterly, Avar Ve'atid, British Journal for Multicultural Education, Le'eylah, Westminster Journal of Religions, Testing the Global Ethic, International Journal of Children's Spirituality, International School, Freedom and Authority in Religions,* and *Religious Education.*

SIDELIGHTS: From picture books about life in an Orthodox Jewish household to an introduction to the Holocaust and an examination of the Auschwitz concentration camp, British educator Clive A. Lawton has clearly demonstrated his desire to explore the Jewish religion, culture, and history for young readers.

His early works, which include books, filmstrips, and videotapes, deal with Jewish religious customs and practices, as well as the middle-grade title *Passport to Israel,* described in *Booklist* as "clear, succinct, and fact filled." Over the decades, Lawton has held numerous positions in educational and humanitarian organizations that strive for the betterment of Jewish life and society in general.

"In the 1980s, I was heavily involved in introducing education about the Holocaust to school-aged children in what I hope was a responsible way," Lawton told *CA.* "My concern was to ensure that this did not become a defining story about the Jews, but about humanity. The lesson to be learned was how to avoid becoming a perpetrator in the future, not a victim. That may not be in our hands." In this effort, Lawton created the television program *Problems and Dilemmas in Teaching the Holocaust,* which aired on Inner London Educational Authority TV in 1984. Nearly twenty years later, Lawton continued to educate about this dark time in human history in several books: *The Story of the Holocaust* and *Auschwitz: The Story of a Nazi Death Camp.* Although adults have argued about the appropriateness of teaching grade-school children about this horrific event, Lawton has long believed that children need to know in order to deal with anti-Semitic imagery that they may encounter. Using carefully chosen photographs and words, Lawton presents the facts about this attempted genocide in *The Story of the Holocaust.* "I want the book to be factual," he told Tom Deveson of the *Times Educational Supplement,* "which is not the same as dispassionate. I don't want to point a facile moral lesson. I want readers to make up their own minds." Lawton also briefly discusses post-World War II attempts at genocide in Cambodia, Rwanda, and Serbia, bringing home the necessity of discussing such an onerous topic. "This book can only do good, by making children think as well as feel and, above all, by making them ask disturbing but necessary questions," concluded Deveson.

In the 2002 title *Auschwitz,* Lawton focuses on the death camp in Nazi-occupied Poland in which over 1.5 million men, women, and children perished. As with *The Story of the Holocaust,* he uses a many-faceted perspective and carefully chosen photographs and text to educate readers about Nazi anti-Semitism, the operation of the camp, prisoner transportation, medical experiments carried out upon prisoners, slave labor, and finally the liberation of the prisoners by Allied forces. The work elicited praise from reviewers, among them *Booklist*'s Hazel Rochman, who called it "stirring," and Linda R. Silver, who described it as an "excellent account" in her *School Library Journal* review. A *Kirkus Reviews* contributor wrote, "Scrupulously documented, this is short but packs a lot of information."

Also beginning in the 1980s, Lawton "became more and more involved in the attempts to broaden British Religious Education—compulsory in all State[-run] schools—from purely Christian to a well-informed exploration and discovery of world religions, including an intelligent education about Christianity," as he told *CA*. Therefore, over the next twenty years he wrote such educational titles as *Religion through Festivals: Judaism, Celebrating Jewry, Celebrating Islam,* and *Which Planet Are You On? Does Religion Ever Come down to Earth?* for the Church of England. Lawton also teamed up with Peggy Morgan to write *Ethical Issues in Six Religious Traditions* for adults. "I sincerely believe that a child/adult is not well educated if they've not thought intelligently and maturely about the issues religions address," he told *CA*.

BIOGRAPHICAL AND CRITICAL SOURCES:

PERIODICALS

Booklist, May, 1988, review of *Passport to Israel,* p. 1609; July, 2000, Gillian Engberg, review of *The Story of the Holocaust,* p. 2024; August, 2002, Hazel Rochman, review of *Auschwitz: The Story of a Nazi Death Camp,* p. 1943.
Books, fall, 1999, review of *The Story of the Holocaust,* p. 22.
Junior Bookshelf, December, 1984, review of *I Am a Jew,* p. 256.
Kirkus Reviews, July 1, 2002, review of *Auschwitz,* p. 957.
Reading Teacher, March, 1986, review of *I Am a Jew,* p. 720.
School Library Journal, April, 1986, Kathy Piehl, review of *I Am a Jew,* p. 82; August, 1988, Sue A. Norkeliunas, review of *Passport to Israel,* p. 103; September, 2002, Linda R. Silver, review of *Auschwitz,* pp. 246-247.
Times Educational Supplement, November 16, 1984, Mary Jane Drummond, "Noble Failures," review of *I Am a Jew,* p. 24; December 3, 1992, Andrew Scott, "Living Faiths," p. 36; September 24, 1999, Tom Deveson, review of *The Story of the Holocaust,* p. 63.

LEAL MASSEY, Cynthia 1956-

PERSONAL: Born March 14, 1956, in San Antonio, TX; daughter of Ernesto (in the U.S. Air Force) and Irma (a homemaker; maiden name, Castillo) Leal; married David Massey (in government), June 28, 1986; children: Michael, Meghan. *Education:* St. Mary's University, B.A. (English, communication arts), 1978, M.A. (English), 1983. *Politics:* Independent. *Religion:* Roman Catholic. *Hobbies and other interests:* Reading, gardening, decorating.

ADDRESSES: Home—P.O. Box 294, Helotes, TX 78023. *Office*—San Antonio College, 1300 San Pedro Ave., San Antonio, TX 78212. *E-mail*—CMass22@ aol.com.

CAREER: Journalist, educator, and fiction writer. Southwest Research Institute, San Antonio, TX, editor, 1979-89; *San Antonio Light* (newspaper), San Antonio, correspondent, 1989-91; San Antonio College, San Antonio, adjunct English instructor, 1991—. Helotes Cub Scout Pack 401, treasurer, 1997-99; Friends of the San Antonio Library, program chair, 1997-99.

MEMBER: Women Writing on the West (president, 2001—).

AWARDS, HONORS: Third-place award for Best Historical or Western Novel, Southwest Writers Workshop, 1998, and Eppie finalist for Best Historical Novel, and *Writer's Digest* International Self-published Books Award honorable mention, both 2002, both for *Fire Lilies.*

WRITINGS:

Fire Lilies (e-book), Rocking M Press, 2001, revised edition, Booksurge.com, 2002.
The Caballeros of Ruby, Texas, Panther Creek Press (Spring, TX), 2002.

Contributor to *New Texas 2000 Anthology of Texas Authors,* 2001; contributor to periodicals, including *Cricket* and *Scene in San Antonio.*

WORK IN PROGRESS: A middle-grade mystery; a short-story collection.

SIDELIGHTS: Cynthia Leal Massey told *CA:* "Several years ago, my late great-aunt told me stories about her life as a member of an upper-class Mexican family, and how the Mexican Revolution changed the course of her life. Today more than twenty-five million Americans of Mexican ancestry live in the United States, many of them descendants of the half-million immigrants who sought a new home here because of the Mexican Revolution of 1910. It is for the descendants of these immigrants, as much as for myself, that I write stories about our heritage. I am particularly interested in breaking stereotypes about Mexicans."

BIOGRAPHICAL AND CRITICAL SOURCES:

ONLINE

Cynthia Leal Massey Web site, http://www.cynthia lealmassey.com (November 20, 2003).

*   *   *

LeBOX, Annette 1943-

PERSONAL: Born April 21, 1943, in England; married Edward Bates, 1970 (divorced); common-law wife of Michael Sather; children: (first marriage) Christian Bates, Sara Bates. *Education:* Simon Frasier University, bachelor of education, 1984; University of British Columbia, M.F.A. (creative writing), 1996. *Hobbies and other interests:* Conservation.

ADDRESSES: Home and office—21837 Laurie Ave., Maple Ridge, British Columbia V2X 7V9, Canada.

CAREER: Novelist and author of children's books.

MEMBER: Writers Union of Canada, British Columbia Federation of Writers, British Columbia Teachers' Federation, Pitt Polder Preservation Society, Burns Bog Conservation Society, International Crane Foundation.

AWARDS, HONORS: First prize, Maple Ridge Poetry Contest, 1995, for "i steal flowers"; Environmental Excellence Award (education), Burns Bog Conserva-

tion Society, 2003; Skipping Stones Book Award (nature and ecology), 2003, for *Salmon Creek;* Christie Harris Illustrated Children's Literature Prize, 2003.

WRITINGS:

Miss Rafferty's Rainbow Socks (picture book), illustrated by Heather Holbrook, HarperCollins (Toronto, Ontario, Canada), 1996.
The Princess Who Danced with Cranes (picture book), illustrated by Kasia Charko, Second Story Press (Toronto, Ontario, Canada), 1997.
Miracle at Willowcreek (young adult novel), Second Story Press (Toronto, Ontario, Canada), 1998.
Wild Bog Tea (picture book), illustrated by Harvey Chan, Groundwood Books (Toronto, Ontario, Canada), 2001.
Salmon Creek (picture book), illustrated by Karen Reczuch, Groundwood Books (Toronto, Ontario, Canada), 2002.

Also author of poem "i steal flowers." Contributor of poetry to numerous literary magazines, including *Dry Crik Review, Prairie Journal, Whetstone, Canadian Writer's Journal,* and *Poetry Canada;* contributor of short stories to *Grain* and *Fiddlehead.* Short story "Man Watching His Sarongs Dry" included in *Vintage '93, The League of Canadian Poets National Poetry Contest Anthology.*

WORK IN PROGRESS: Mei-li's Journey, "a young-adult novel about a young Chinese girl who travels across the sea on a smuggler's ship and ends up working as a seamstress in a New York sweatshop. Magic realism and facts are blended into a tale of adventure and search for a family."

SIDELIGHTS: Environmental activist and author Annette LeBox has combined her interests in several of her books for children and teens. Her second picture book, *The Princess Who Danced with Cranes,* is the story of a nature-loving princess who is slow to realize what she has lost when her father drains the local marsh to create larger playing fields for Gullywhupper, a sport played with a ball and mallet. When Princess Vivian realizes that the cranes that once lived in the marsh are nearly gone, she begins to tear down the dam that blocks water from entering the marsh, even though she too loves to play Gullywhupper. In

The Princess Who Danced with Cranes, LeBox's "smooth prose, with hints of poetry and humor, delivers a clear ecological message without becoming preachy," Christine Linge wrote in *Canadian Book Review Annual.* Similarly, *Quill & Quire* reviewer Barbara Greenwood found that the author's use of "a strong central image" and "a story form built around archetypal characters" allows her to "deliver a message without seeming didactic."

LeBox's next picture book, *Wild Bog Tea,* "demands more of the reader" than *The Princess Who Danced with Cranes,* Wendy A. Lewis commented in *Quill & Quire,* "but it's worth it." In *Wild Bog Tea,* LeBox illustrates the life cycle of a wetland as it evolves from marsh to peat bog to forest, parallel to the life cycle of a boy who enjoys visiting the area with his grandfather. After the boy has become an adult and a parent himself, he looks back on the time that the two spent walking together among the wetland's plants and animals, eating cranberries and plucking sprigs of Labrador tea to make the wild bog tea of the title. The story is "an interesting look at a unique habitat as well as a sensitive intergenerational tale," noted *School Library Journal* reviewer Judith Constantinides.

In *Salmon Creek,* LeBox for the first time tells an environmental story from the point of view of an animal rather than a human. The tale's hero is Sumi, a female coho salmon whom the reader first encounters as a freshly laid egg. Sumi hatches, is carried downstream past the predators who would make a meal out of the baby salmon, grows to adulthood, and then returns to the stream three years later to lay her own eggs. Told in rhythmic language that shifts between rhyme and free verse, *Salmon Creek* is a "stellar picture-book combination of fiction, science, and ecology," Ellen Mandel wrote in a review for *Booklist.*

LeBox's first picture book, *Miss Rafferty's Rainbow Socks,* is unique among her works in not having an environmental theme. The title character, Miss Aldona Rafferty, receives a magical pair of rainbow-colored socks for her seventh birthday. Every time she puts the socks on, she wants to dance, and since the socks keep getting bigger as she does, she never outgrows them. When Miss Rafferty is an old woman, she becomes friends with the little girl next door, Winnie Latham, and turns her rainbow socks into a marvelous doll for the child. As Bridget Donald wrote in a review of *Miss Rafferty's Rainbow Socks* for *Quill & Quire,* "The

prose is delightfully rhythmic: flowing and elaborate in some places, sharp and tapping in others."

LeBox is also the author of the young-adult novel *Miracle at Willowcreek,* "a real treat for nature lovers," claimed *Quill & Quire* critic Hadley Dyer. Tess De Boer is an outsider in rural British Columbia. She grew up in the big eastern city of Toronto and only visited her grandfather's farm at Willowcreek in the summers. But after her grandfather dies, Tess and her mother move to the farm with her Uncle Randall. Tess's mother does not like being outdoors, and her uncle is hoping to sell the land to developers who want to build an amusement park there. Despite this, Tess makes friends with some locals who are trying to prevent a local flock of sandhill cranes from dying out, a project that conflicts directly with her uncle's plans. At the center of the plot is a baby crane named Miracle that Tess and her friends strive to raise and re-release into the wild. "Details about cranes and other aspects of nature are meticulously researched and threaded seamlessly into the text," providing an environmental education in addition to the book's "impressive . . . portrayal of the affinity that can exist between humans and animals," commented *Canadian Book Review Annual* contributor Sheree Haughian.

LeBox told *CA:* "I have come to writing late, only ten years ago. Once I discovered writing, I wanted to learn the craft as quickly as possible so I went back to school and earned my master's of creative writing at the University of British Columbia. I like my books to inspire as well as inform, which means that I spend a great deal of time doing research to ensure my books are accurate.

"I live near a beautiful wetland called the Pitt Polder that is home to an abundance of plants and wildlife. The Polder is a place that nourishes my spirit and inspires my writing. My second book, *The Princess Who Danced with Cranes,* is an allegory about the choices we make when we drain wetlands to build golf courses. When a housing development threatened the Polder in 1996, the issue sparked a fierce debate in our community. A small flock of greater sandhill cranes, only ten in total, were in danger of dying out if they lost their habitat. In an effort to prevent the rezoning by the municipality of Pitt Meadows, we formed an organization called the Pitt Polder Preservation Society. Against all odds, our society took the municipality to the Supreme Court of Canada and won our case. This experience inspired me to write the young adult novel *Miracle at Willowcreek.*

"In 1998 our group fought to protect Blaney Bog, the inspiration for my picture book *Wild Bog Tea.* Two years later, the bog was set aside as a regional park. For the past two years, we have been working to protect Blaney Creek, a salmon-bearing creek running through the Codd Island Wetlands. This fish habitat will be destroyed by a cranberry operation if it is not set aside as a conservation area. My latest book, *Salmon Creek,* is a plea to protect special places and the salmon that inhabit them. Sometimes fighting for a place I care for becomes overwhelming, and my art suffers. Yet for me, art and activism seem so closely intertwined that it is sometimes difficult to see where one ends and the other begins. My challenge is to strike a balance between the two."

BIOGRAPHICAL AND CRITICAL SOURCES:

PERIODICALS

Booklist, December 15, 2001, GraceAnne A. DeCandido, review of *Wild Bog Tea,* p. 740; January 1, 2003, Ellen Mandel, review of *Salmon Creek,* p. 881.

Canadian Book Review Annual, 1996, Ted McGee, review of *Miss Rafferty's Rainbow Socks,* p. 6055; 1997, Christine Linge, review of *The Princess Who Danced with Cranes,* pp. 479-480; 1998, Sheree Haughian, review of *Miracle at Willowcreek,* p. 512.

Canadian Materials, November 29, 2002, Valerie Nielsen, review of *Salmon Creek.*

Quill & Quire, June, 1996, Bridget Donald, review of *Miss Rafferty's Rainbow Socks,* p. 54; May, 1997, Barbara Greenwood, review of *The Princess Who Danced with Cranes,* p. 42; June, 1998, Annette Goldsmith, review of *Miracle at Willowcreek,* p. 61; June, 2001, Wendy A. Lewis, review of *Wild Bog Tea,* p. 51.

Resource Links, October, 2001, Gillian Richardson, review of *Wild Bog Tea,* p. 4; December, 2002, Jennifer Batycky, review of *Salmon Creek,* pp. 25-26.

St. Catharines Standard (St. Catharines, Ontario, Canada), November 14, 2001, Lian Goodall, "The 2001 Governor's General Award for Illustration."

School Library Journal, September, 2001, Judith Constantinides, review of *Wild Bog Tea,* p. 193.

ONLINE

Groundwood Books Web site, http://www.groundwoodbooks.com/ (May 29, 2003).

Pitt Polder Preservation Web site, http://www.pittpolder.com/ (December 4, 2003).

Writers' Union of Canada Web site, http://www.writersunion.ca/ (May 29, 2003), "Annette LeBox."

*   *   *

LEE, Linda Francis

PERSONAL: Born in Texas; married; husband's name, Michael. *Education:* Graduated from Texas Tech University.

ADDRESSES: Home—New York, NY. *Office*—c/o Ballantine Publishing Group/Ivy Books, 1540 Broadway, New York, NY 10036. *E-mail*—LFranLee@aol.com.

CAREER: Novelist. Former teacher of mathematic probability and statistics.

AWARDS, HONORS: Nomination for best historical romance of the year, *Romantic Times,* 1996, for *Blue Waltz;* RITA award, romance Writers of America, nomination, 2000, for *Dove's Way,* and finalist, 2001, for *Nightingale's Gate.*

WRITINGS:

ROMANCE NOVELS

The Ways of Grace, Ivy Books (New York, NY), 2002.
Looking for Lacey, Ivy Books (New York, NY), 2003.
The Wedding Diaries, Ivy Books (New York, NY), 2003.

"VICTORIAN NEW YORK" TRILOGY

Blue Waltz, Jove Publishing (New York, NY), 1996.
Emerald Rain, Jove Publishing (New York, NY), 1996.

Crimson Lace, Jove Publishing (New York, NY), 1997.

"VICTORIAN BOSTON" TRILOGY

Dove's Way, Ivy Books (New York, NY), 2000.
Swan's Grace, Ivy Books (New York, NY), 2000.
Nightingale's Gate, Ivy Books (New York, NY), 2001.

SIDELIGHTS: Born and raised in Texas, Linda Francis Lee has, thanks to her husband Michael's career, lived in a number of locations throughout the United States. While suffering through a particularly cold winter in Boston in 1994—"I was never meant for the cold," she wrote in an autobiographical sketch at her Web site—she began writing what became *Blue Waltz,* her first published novel.

Blue Waltz begins a trilogy that includes *Emerald Rain* and *Crimson Lace,* all historical romances featuring ladies of the evening in nineteenth-century Manhattan. In *Crimson Lace,* Lily Blakemore, forced into her profession by hard times, has to return to Manhattan—which she left in disgrace a decade earlier—to care for her deceased brother's children. With a gubernatorial candidate rumored to be among Lily's clients, investigative reporter Morgan Elliott poses as a household employee in order to garner salacious details of the affair. According to a review in *Publishers Weekly,* "the intensity of feeling once the first layer of secrets is stripped off will have readers falling in love right along with Lily and Morgan."

Another trilogy, set in nineteenth-century Boston, begins with *Dove's Way,* in which Finnea Winslet returns from Africa to marry the embittered Matthew Hawthorne. *Swan's Grace,* set in 1892, takes its name from the ancestral home of heroine Sophie Wentworth, whose father has sold the home place in order to support the demands of his greedy second wife. As Sophie learns, to her chagrin, he has also given her hand in marriage to the wealthy Grayson Hawthorne, who, like his brother Matthew, has been hardened by his hurts. Sophie, however, remembers Grayson as he was when they first met at a much younger age, and as his betrothed, she seeks to bring out that gentler side. *Nightingale's Cove* crosses paths with the world of the *Blue Waltz* trilogy as another Hawthorne, Lucas, finds himself on trial for murdering a prostitute. In a move highly unusual for the 1890s, he hires a female at-

torney, Alice Kendall. According to a reviewer in *Booklist,* "this romance can certainly stand on its own, although readers will be overcome by the urge to find the earlier titles once the last page is turned."

Grace Colebrook, the title character in *The Ways of Grace,* discovers her fiancé having sex with another woman on their wedding day. Disconsolate, she sits—still in her wedding dress—on a bench across the street from her apartment. The night is cold, and when Jack Berenger looks out his window and sees her sitting there, he brings her a coat. Irresistibly drawn to one another, they wind up on her kitchen table, making love. Grace already knew who Jack was, but he had never seen her before, and in the morning, she is horrified that she had sex with a virtual stranger. Things get worse when she loses her job after an assistant steals one of her ideas. *The Ways of Grace,* wrote Jill M. Smith in *Romantic Times,* "provides a moving look into the hearts of lovers." According to Maria Hatton in *Booklist,* "As Lee expertly reveals the personal issues that make Jack and Grace kindred spirits, she creates two of the most lovable and convincing characters in recent romances."

Whereas Grace's life was falling apart, the title character in *Looking for Lacey* suffers from an opposite problem: one of being too controlled. A single mother, Lacey Wright is meticulous in her ways, which makes her ideally suited to run the sports bar for which she has been hired as business manager. But she has lied on her resume, and she fears discovery by the owner, Bobby McIntyre. A retired football quarterback, Bobby is easygoing, and the contrast between them breeds an inevitable attraction. A secondary plot involving Lacey's sixteen-year-old daughter rounds out the story. "Adept at Victorian historicals," wrote Mary K. Chelton in *Booklist,* "Lee also excels in this contemporary."

BIOGRAPHICAL AND CRITICAL SOURCES:

PERIODICALS

Booklist, September 15, 2001, review of *Dove's Way,* p. 212; May 1, 2002, Maria Hatton, review of *Nightingale's Gate,* p. 1671; August, 2002, Maria Hatton, review of *The Ways of Grace,* p. 1935; February 15, 2003, Mary K. Chelton, review of *Looking for Lacey,* p. 1057.

Publishers Weekly, November 17, 1997, review of *Crimson Lace,* p. 59; August 28, 2000, review of *Swan's Grace,* p. 61; August 26, 2002, review of *The Ways of Grace,* p. 50.

ONLINE

Linda Francis Lee Home Page, http://www.lindafrancislee.com (September 16, 2003).
Romantic Times Web Site, http://www.romantictimes.com/ (September 16, 2003), Jill M. Smith, review of *The Ways of Grace.**

*   *   *

LEITH, Prudence (Margaret) 1940- (Prue Leith)

PERSONAL: Born 1940, in England; married Rayne Kruger (a writer and businessman), 1974; children: Daniel, Li-Da. *Education:* Attended Cape Town University.

ADDRESSES: Home—Oxfordshire, England. *Office*—94 Kensington Park Rd., London W11 2PN, England.

CAREER: Leith's Restaurants, owner; Leith's School of Food and Wine, founder and lecturer; author; *Take Six Cooks* and *Tricks of the Trade* television programs, producer. Whitbread, board member; Halifax Building Society, director; Argyll Group, director; Ramblers' Association, vice president; Women in Finance and Banking, vice-patron; British Railways Board, member; Department of the Environment's National Training Task Force, member; Safeway, food advisor; Kinghurst Centre for Tomorrow's Company Enterprises, chair.

MEMBER: Royal Society of Arts (president), Restaurateurs' Association of Great Britain (chair).

AWARDS, HONORS: Honored with Order of the British Empire, 1989; named Veuve Clicquot Businesswoman of the Year, 1991; six honorary degrees and fellowships from British universities.

WRITINGS:

(As editor) *Parkinson's Pie: Recipes of the Stars,* Quartet Books/World Wildlife Fund (London, England), 1974.
Prue Leith's Cook, Part 2, HarperCollins (London, England), 1982.
Prue Leith's Dinner Parties, Pan MacMillan (London, England), 1987.
The Cook's Handbook, A & W Publishers (New York, NY), 1981.
(With Polly Tyrer) *Entertaining with Style,* W. Morrow (New York, NY), 1985.
The Sunday Times Slim Plan, Headline Publishers (London, England), 1992.
(With Caroline Waldegrave and Fiona Burrell) *Leith's Complete Christmas,* Bloomsbury (London, England), 1992.
(With Caroline Waldegrave) *Leith's Book of Baking,* Bloomsbury (London, England), 1993
Leith's Step-by-Step Cookery Recipes and Techniques, Bloomsbury (London, England), 1993.
Leith's Vegetarian Cookery Book, Bloomsbury (London, England), 1993.
Leith's Guide to Wine, Bloomsbury (London, England), 1995.
(With Caroline Waldegrave) *Leith's Cookery Bible,* Trafalgar Square (London, England), 2000.
Leaving Patrick (fiction), Thomas Dunne Books/St. Martin's Press (New York, NY), 2001.
Sisters (fiction), Thomas Dunne Books/St. Martin's Press (New York, NY), 2001.

Has also written food columns for London newspapers.

SIDELIGHTS: Prue—short for Prudence—Leith has spent most of her life absorbed in the creation of meals. She has also established a restaurant and catering dynasty, founded a cooking school, written numerous cookbooks, authored various newspaper food columns, and advised supermarket giant Safeway on food. She has also been involved with two television shows about food: *Take Six Cooks* and *Tricks of the Trade.* When she is not thinking about food, she is serving on the boards of several business and community organizations. More recently, however, she has decided to explore another aspect of her creativity and has published two books of fiction, which, as a side feature, incorporate the topic of food.

Leith has built a great reputation in Great Britain as a food expert, according to Rachel Kelly in the London *Times:* "Anything that she doesn't know about food could be written on the back of a button mushroom." But Leith was not always so well known. She started on a very small scale, first opening a catering business in 1960, which served only lunches to actors. To manage this, she had to bribe doormen in order to carry her trays of sandwiches backstage. The name of this first catering business was Matinee Collations, and it closed down after the cost of bribing the doormen cut too deeply into her profits.

Leith did not give up on catering, however, and nine years later not only did she have a successful business, but she was doing so well that she opened Leith's Restaurant. This quickly pushed her into the limelight, as the restaurant gained prestige and popularity. Then in 1975, she decided that Great Britain needed a place to teach future chefs not only how to cook, but how to best serve the expanding tourism industry. So she opened a culinary school called Prue Leith College of Food and Wine. The school is built on the philosophy that students need experience in the kitchen, but also need to immediately apply that experience to the general public. A public restaurant is attached to her school where patrons can eat and then provide direct feedback to student chefs. It is upon the success of her restaurant and school that Leith has been able to build a multi-million-dollar empire. Along the way her growing celebrity has helped to spur the selling of her many cookbooks.

Leith has written about various aspects of food preparation for over three decades, sometimes, as in her *Cookery Bible,* concentrating on general techniques and recipes, and at other times focusing on specific topics, such as in *Prue Leith's Dinner Parties* and *Leith's Vegetarian Cookery Book.* In her cookbooks, she provides recipes and also tips on how to present meals, how to save time in their preparation, and even how to organize the kitchen. Writing these books flowed naturally from her trade. However, after selling her catering business to a French company and then turning over her restaurant business to her business partner, Carline Waldegrave, Leith decided to write something purely creative.

She completed her first book of fiction, *Leaving Patrick,* then sweated out the response. This "hugely efficient woman," as Emma Brockes described Leith in the London *Guardian,* "is not known for the frailty of her nerves." And yet Leith has been concerned about trying to carve out a new career for herself as a fiction writer. "I would be skeptical of a novelist who suddenly decided to open a restaurant," she told Brockes. Although she would have, in the end, supported the right of the novelist-turned-restaurateur to change careers midstream, she told Brockes that while she waited for the critical response to her first novel she "braced for a bad reaction." She need not have worried as her first work of fiction proved to be very well received.

In *Leaving Patrick,* protagonist Jane, a high-powered and well-paid London maritime attorney, decides to leave her husband, Patrick, who is in the restaurant business. The couple drifts apart, and in an attempt to find something more refreshing about life, Jane drops everything and runs away to India, where she falls in love with her tour guide. Meanwhile, back in London, Patrick falls for a female food critic. Both affairs end disastrously, prompting Jane and Patrick to reassess their relationship.

Kathy Ingels Helmond, in the *Library Journal,* pointed out that the overall thesis of *Leaving Patrick* is based on the adage: "Be careful what you wish for." Although a *Publishers Weekly* reviewer found the plot "fairly standard," the critic added that Leith is able to maintain "a credible tension until the final page." The same reviewer also praised Leith's "insider's view of the food service business," which helps enliven the story.

Leith spent much of her childhood in South Africa, the same place where the protagonists of her second novel *Sisters* were raised. Poppy and Carrie reflect somewhat opposite natures, in lifestyle and in appearance. Poppy is a successful actress who has grown a bit plump in her happy marriage and motherhood. Carrie, on the other hand, a London caterer, retains a sleek beauty but has turned to alcohol to settle her nerves and coat her disappointments in the many failed relationships she has suffered through. Although it appears that the two sisters have maintained a good relationship into their adult years, Carrie grows increasingly jealous of Poppy's seeming contentment with life. In an attempt to unsettle her sister, Carrie flirts with Poppy's husband, Eduardo, and eventually succeeds in seducing him. The rest of the story, according to a *Publishers Weekly* reviewer, "is devoted to cleaning up the mess."

Although *Sister* was not quite as popular with readers as Leith's first book, Mark Knoblauch wrote in *Booklist* Leith is able "to move a story forward compellingly" and *Sisters* has the potential of being turned into a screenplay. Despite the betrayals and frustrations woven into this tale, a *Kirkus Reviews* writer, referring to the food motif in the story, summed the novel up as "a meal with a sweet ending."

BIOGRAPHICAL AND CRITICAL SOURCES:

PERIODICALS

Booklist, March 1, 1986, review of *Entertaining with Style,* p. 935; December 1, 2002, Mark Knoblauch, review of *Sisters,* p. 646.
Choice, June, 1982, review of *The Cook's Handbook,* p. 1374.
Guardian (London, England), August 3, 1999, Emma Brockes, review of *Leaving Patrick,* pp. T4-T5.
Independent, July 8, 1996, Paul Vallely, "If Anyone Can Do It, Prue Can Do It," pp. S2-S3.
Kirkus Reviews, September 15, 2001, review of *Leaving Patrick,* p. 1317; August 15, 2002, review of *Sisters,* p. 1166.
Library Journal, October 15, 2001, Kathy Ingels Helmond, review of *Leaving Patrick,* p. 108; October 1, 2002, Kathy Ingels Helmond, review of *Sisters,* p. 128.
New York Review of Books, February 18, 1982, Diane Johnson, review of *The Cook's Handbook,* pp. 18-20.
Observer (London, England), January 19, 1997, William Leith, review of *Leith's Cookery Bible,* p. 18.
Publishers Weekly, September 18, 1981, Sybil S. Steinberg, review of *The Cook's Handbook,* p. 147; October 8, 2001, review of *Leaving Patrick,* p. 42; October 14, 2002, review of *Sisters,* p. 64.
Punch, December 5, 1984, review of *Prue Leith's Dinner Parties,* p. 85.
Spectator, Jennifer Paterson, review of *Leith's Complete Christmas,* p. 51.
Times (London, England), September 6, 1995, Rachel Kelly, "'I'm Bossy and an Egoist. I'd Love to be Lady Leith'; Prue Leith," p. 15; February 11, 2000, Ann Treneman, "Art, Farce, Politics, and Pigeons," pp. 37-38.

Virginia Quarterly Review, autumn, 1986, Walker and Claudine Cowen, review of *Entertaining with Style,* p. 142.*

*   *   *

LEITH, Prue
See LEITH, Prudence

*   *   *

LE MOINE, James MacPherson 1825-1912

PERSONAL: Born January 24, 1825 in Québec City, Québec, Canada; died February 5, 1912; son of Benjamin and Julia Ann (MacPherson) Le Moine; married Harriet Atkinson, 1856. *Education:* Attended Petit Séminaire, Québec, Canada. *Hobbies and other interests:* Ornithology (study of birds).

CAREER: Lawyer, romance novelist, travel writer, and historian. Institute Canadien, cofouncer, 1847; practiced law, 1850-69; inspector of inland revenue for District of Quebec, 1869-99.

MEMBER: Royal Society of Canada (founding member; president of French section; president, 1894-95), various Canadian, American, and European historical and cultural societies.

AWARDS, HONORS: Knighted, 1897, for literary services.

WRITINGS:

Ornithologie du Canada, 2 volumes, Fréchette (Québec City, Québec, Canada), 1860, 1861.
The Legendary Lore of the Lower St. Lawrence (poems), Mercury (Québec City, Québec, Canada), 1862.
Maple Leaves: A Budget of Legendary, Historical, Critical, and Sporting Intelligence, 7 volumes, Hunter, Rose. (Québec City, Québec, Canada), 1863-1906.
Les pêcheries du Canada, Atelier (Québec City, Québec, Canada), 1863.

Album canadien; histoire, archeologie-ornithologie, Press Mecaniques (Québec City, Québec, Canada), 1870.

L'album du touriste, Côté (Québec City, Québec, Canada), 1872.

Québec, Past and Present, Côté (Québec City, Québec, Canada), 1876.

The Chronicles of the St. Lawrence, Lovell (New York, NY), 1878.

Origin of the Festival of Saint-Jean-Baptiste. Québec, Its Gates and Environs, Morning Chronicle (Québec City, Québec, Canada), 1880.

Picturesque Québec: A Sequel to Québec, Past and Present, Dawson (Montréal, Québec, Canada), 1882.

Monographies et esquisses, Gingras (Québec City, Québec, Canada), 1885.

Chasse et pêche au Canada, Hardy (Québec City, Québec, Canada), 1887.

Historical Notes on Québec and Its Environs, Darveau (Québec City, Québec, Canada), 1887, enlarged, 1890.

The Explorations of Jonathan Oldbuck, Demers (Québec City, Québec, Canada), 1889.

The Legends of the St. Lawrence, Holiwell (Québec City, Québec, Canada), 1898.

The Port of Québec, Chronicle (Québec City, Québec, Canada), 1901.

SIDELIGHTS: James MacPherson Le Moine, a Canadian literary pioneer of a diverse and literary background, paid homage to his native Québec in many of his works.

Le Moine had an English-Canadian mother and a French-Canadian father. His father's family was among the few of nobility to settle in Québec, then called New France. Le Moine's father died when his son was just three years old, and maternal grandfather Daniel MacPherson adopted the young child. MacPherson, a United Empire loyalist, eventually moved with his grandson to one of Québec's aristocratic estates. Young James had access to elite schools, and despite his grandfather's English background, was instructed in French at the village school. Le Moine progressed to the Petit Séminaire of Québec. As a young man in his twenties, he apprenticed with a prominent Québec lawyer, and in 1847 assisted in founding the Institut Canadien.

In 1850 Le Moine began his own law practice, which lasted for the next nineteen years. However, struck by

the majesty of the Canadian countryside, his boyhood interest in bird life and the little-documented history of his beloved homeland, Le Moine spent much of the 1850s indulging his personal passions. He then published two volumes on Canadian bird life, titled *Ornithologie du Canada.* Le Moine lived at Spencer Grange, a large, rural estate outside Québec City, where he established a private museum, meticulously gathering appropriate specimens, artifacts and natural and historical writings relating to bird study and naturalist fields.

The Legendary Lore of the Lower St. Lawrence, a collection of poems, signified Le Moine's shift from birds to history, and he went on to produce other chronicles reflecting his love of Québec. He followed with the first installment in a seven-volume series, *Maple Leaves: A Budget of Legendary, Historical, Critical, and Sporting Intelligence.* The volumes, which spanned forty-three years, contain various anecdotes, sketches, musings, travel guides and folklore. The volumes feature a wide range of information and entertainment, including tales surrounding the St. Lawrence seaway for travelers and natives and recollections of the heroes and founders of Canada's eastern region.

Le Moine exposed the romanticism of French Canada to an English-speaking audience. In 1865, for example, author William Kirby bought one of Le Moine's volumes while on an excursion from his home in Niagara, New York, to Québec City. According to Carole Gerson in the *Dictionary of Literary Biography,* Le Moine's "book of sketches and essays" inspired the author's "ponderous historical romance," *The Chien d'Or.* Kirby, apparently, was "excited by Le Moine's chapters on Chateau Bigot, The Golden Dog, and La Corriveau," and *The Chien d'Or,* published in 1877, was ultimately "praised in nineteenth-century Canada as the finest Canadian novel."

After Le Moine abandoned his law practice to accept an appointment as inspector of inland revenue for the district of Québec, novelist Gilbert Parker approached him. According to Gerson, Parker "was searching for a suitably romantic subject for a historical novel on Québec. Le Moine directed Parker to the fourth volume of *Maple Leaves,* which contained a sketch of the adventures of Maj. Robert Stobo." Inspired by Le Moine's book, Parker published *The Seats of the Mighty* in 1896, which became a best seller. One year later, after cultivating a friendship with American Francis Parkman, Le Moine was knighted.

Le Moine retired as inspector of inland revenue in 1899, but remained busy. Some critics have dismissed Le Moine's works as sporadic and inexact; others even accused him of plagiarizing the works of other historical and travel writers. However, most have recognized the significance of his contributions.

BIOGRAPHICAL AND CRITICAL SOURCES:

BOOKS

Dictionary of Literary Biography, Volume 99: *Canadian Writers before 1890,* Gale (Detroit, MI), 1990.

PERIODICALS

Canadian Magazine, April, 1913.*

*   *   *

LEONG, Albert 1935-2002

PERSONAL: Born December 10, 1935, in Portland, OR; died of pancreatic cancer August 31, 2002. *Education:* University of Texas, Austin, 1953-54; University of Chicago, A.B. (with honors), 1961; attended Moscow State University and Leningrad State University, 1964-65; University of Chicago, A.M., 1966, Ph. D., 1970.

CAREER: Sichuan Institute of Foreign Languages, Chongqing, China, visiting lecturer in comparative Russian literature and culture, 1984; University of Oregon, Portland, director, Russian and East European Studies Center, 1985-91, head of department of Russian, 1985-91, 1998, professor of Slavic languages, 1991-2002.

AWARDS, HONORS: University of Chicago, fellowship, 1961-62; fellowships at University of Chicago, 1961-62, 1962-63, 1963-64, 1965-66; Inter-University

Committee on Travel grants/Fulbright-Hays fellowship to USSR, 1964-65; Summer Faculty Research Award, University of Oregon, 1971.

WRITINGS:

(Editor) Ernst Neizvestny, *Space, Time, and Synthesis in Art: Essays on Art, Literature and Philosophy,* Mosaic Press (Oakville, NY), 1990.
(Editor) *Oregon Studies in Chinese and Russian Culture,* Peter Lang (New York, NY), 1990.
(Editor) *The Millennium: Christianity and Russia, 988-1988,* St. Vladimir's Seminary Press (Crestwood, NY), 1990.
Centaur: The Life and Art of Ernst Neizvestny, Rowman & Littlefield (Lanham, MD), 2002.

SIDELIGHTS: Albert Leong taught for many years at the University of Oregon, presiding over the Russian and East European Studies Center and heading the Russian department, ultimately serving as professor of Slavic languages. In this capacity, he became an expert on the history and culture of Russia, and one of the foremost experts on Ernst Neizvestny, a leading Soviet-era sculptor and theorist who defied Soviet restrictions on artistic expression. In 1990, Leong published a collection of Neizvestny's essays setting forth the artist's views on a wide variety of artistic movements and personalities and tying his own work to these predecessors, often in rather argumentative terms. "However much this brash, confrontational style shows spirit and provides a welcome respite from cautious, scholarly argument, the connections he makes as he integrates himself into group after group of prominent names can be taken with a pinch or two of salt," concluded reviewer Jeremy Howard in the *Slavonic and East European Review.*

That same year, Leong published *Oregon Studies in Chinese and Russian Culture,* a wide-ranging series of essays on various aspects of art from "Man as a Visual Sign" to one of Leong's own essays, "Creative Uses of Technology in Teaching Language and Culture." "The primary focus, however, is on literary criticism, and the standard is consistently high," explained reviewer Geoffrey Smith in the *Slavonic and East European Review.* "And," Smith added, "as translation is itself a subject considered . . . it is fitting to conclude with praise for the six translations included here. I cannot be sure if Albert Leong's translations are periphrastic, lexical, or literal, but they have unfailingly come out as clear and eminently readable English."

In *The Millennium: Christianity and Russia, 988-1988,* another series of essays edited and sometimes translated by Leong, the authors confront one of the most important cultural influences in Russian history. Essays cover the original conversion of the Kievan Rus', its relation to Byzantine diplomacy, the influence of two remarkable princesses, Olga and Anna, and the influence of the church of a thousand years, and its anomalous position in the officially atheist Soviet Union. "The preface by Albert Leong explores Christianity and Russia, giving the lay reader a wonderful tour of the humanities and letters in Kievan Rus' and Russia. . . . Its brief argument on the distinctive phenomenon of *dvoeverie,* or 'double faith,' the two streams of culture which run through Russian society, one sponsored by the State, and the other a strong underground current, unofficial, yet powerful and deeply rooted in the life of the community, is intriguing," noted *Canadian Slavonic Papers* contributor David J. Goa.

Leong's final book, *Centaur: The Life and Art of Ernst Neizvestny,* is the first full-length biography of the Russian monumental sculptor. Drawing on years of study and a long personal relationship with Neizvestny himself, as well as on interviews with friends and family and numerous archival materials, Leong covers all the aspects of this combative artist. Neizvestny was willing to go toe to toe with Soviet Premier Nikita Khruschev himself to defend the right of the artist against the rigid control of the state, although it meant ten years of artistic obscurity. Indeed, much of the book concerns Neizvestny's complex relationship with Khruschev. After the fallen premier's death, Neizvestny constructed a graveside monument that included jagged pieces of white marble and black granite to illustrate the mix of idealism and repression in Khruschev's character. The book "excels at placing Neizvestny in the context of Soviet political and cultural history, and examining how he was misunderstood initially in the United States because of cold war stereotypes," wrote *New York Times Book Review* contributor Harlow Robinson. Robinson did fault Leong for sometimes providing too much documentation and too little insight, and for sometimes intruding too much on Neizvestny's story with his own travel

experiences. Still, Robinson concluded, "These weaknesses aside, 'Centaur' is a serious and worthy consideration of the vexing moral and philosophical issues underlying the career of a courageous artist who . . . confronted the evil of the Soviet system *mano a mano.*"

BIOGRAPHICAL AND CRITICAL SOURCES:

PERIODICALS

Canadian Slavonic Papers, March-June, 1992, David J. Goa, review of *The Millennium: Christianity and Russia, 988-1988,* pp. 169-171.
New York Times Book Review, August 25, 2002, Harlow Robinson, "The View from Khruschev's Head" p. 10.
Slavonic and East European Review, January, 1992, Geoffrey Smith, review of *Oregon Studies in Chinese and Russian Culture,* pp. 149-150; April, 1992, Jeremy Howard, review of *Space, Time, and Synthesis in Art,* pp. 341-342.*

* * *

LERNER, Lisa 1960-

PERSONAL: Born 1960. *Education:* Cornell University, B.A., 1981.

ADDRESSES: Home—New York, NY. *Agent*—Jane Gelfman, Gelfman Schneider Literary Agents, 250 West 57th St., Suite 2515, New York, NY 10107. *E-mail*—info@justlikebeauty.com.

CAREER: Writer and performance artist. Previously worked as writing teacher, textbook writer, and editor.

AWARDS, HONORS: Franklin Furnace Performance Art Award; MacDowell Artist's Colony fellowship.

WRITINGS:

Snakes Reach You Faster (play), produced in New York, NY, 1990.
Just like Beauty, Farrar, Straus, and Giroux (New York, NY), 2002.

Contributor of nonfiction, short fiction, and essays to journals, including *Bust* and *Self.*

WORK IN PROGRESS: A novel that follows young characters living in the future as they struggle with issues of violence, cults, and environmental deterioration.

SIDELIGHTS: Lisa Lerner spent years as a New York City performance artist working under the name Cowboy Girl, and it was during this period that she came up with the idea that eventually became her debut novel, *Just like Beauty.* The concept began as an idea for a one-woman show. One year later, Lerner realized the story worked better in novel form, and she started writing. After five years of writing and rewriting, her manuscript was accepted by a publisher in 2000.

Just like Beauty took five years to write because the first draft met its demise in the fireplace. "I finished the book, and I hated it. I was absolutely bored by it," Lerner told Jessica Yerega in *Writer's Digest.* After tossing it on the flames, she acknowledged the need to tell her story, and accepted the fact that she would have to begin from scratch. She buckled down, disciplined herself, and started to enjoy writing.

The result of those seasons of dedicated writing is the futuristic, dark coming-of-age story of fourteen-year-old Edie Stein, a girl determined to make her mother happy by participating in the town's local beauty pageant. The Feminine Woman of Conscience event is no ordinary pageant, however, and Edie and her fellow participants face seemingly insurmountable obstacles, including events in which they must sacrifice their pet rabbits, simulate sex with the Electric Polyrubber Man, and display their knowledge of chemical substances. The list of ridiculous expectations never ends, and neither do the challenges Edie must face.

Despite years of tutelage and pageantry preparation at the hands of her pill-popping mother, Edie remains ambivalent about the contest; she is more concerned with the usual woes of adolescence and puberty, which include a first crush on next-door neighbor Lana Grimaldi. Rebellious Lana is everything Edie is not, and Edie dreams of the next time she will kiss Lana's cigar-wielding lips. Aside from her budding lesbianism, Edie struggles to contend with her estranged parents as well as with manacing thugs known as the Blow Torchers. This brutal gang thrives on torturing and disfiguring pageant contestants, and their efforts rarely fail.

Just like Beauty is a satiric social commentary on the values and priorities of materialistic culture. Specifically, Lerner uses the novel to analyze and criticize society's expectations of its female citizens. The older Edie grows, the more twisted and tangled her life becomes. Womanhood seems like a goal to be reached, and the journey is rife with humiliation and submission, degradation and seduction.

Deansville, Edie's fictional hometown, is Lerner's warning to her readers. In Deansville, people eat "Just Like" foods—Just like Meat, Just like Bread—foods produced by the Just like That food and chemicals conglomerate. This company has a monopoly on the town; it even sponsors the Feminine Woman of Conscience Pageant. Deansville is also home to giant mutant grasshoppers the size of crows that thrive on the poison set out for them on neighborhood lawns.

Edie Stein is Lerner's Everywoman, and critics have noted that Lerner successfully mixes science fiction with the bildungsroman to give readers a heroine with the strength and courage to embrace her individuality against all odds. According to Emily White in the *New York Times,* "In a lesser writer's hands, such an exaggerated view of womanhood might have seemed silly or unbelievable. But Lerner has the gifts to make it all work."

BIOGRAPHICAL AND CRITICAL SOURCES:

PERIODICALS

Booklist, December 1, 2001, Joanne Wilkinson, review of *Just like Beauty,* p. 628.

Courier-Mail (Brisbane, Australia), January 26, 2002, Emily White, review of *Just like Beauty,* p. M06.

Kirkus Reviews, October 1, 2001, review of *Just like Beauty,* p. 1386.

Knight-Ridder/Tribune News Service, February 6, 2002, Evelyn Mcdonnell, review of *Just like Beauty,* p. K1863.

Lambda Book Report, October 1, 2001, Eleanor J. Bader, review of *Just like Beauty,* p. 141.

Library Journal, June-July 2002, Christopher Hennessy, review of *Just like Beauty,* p. 20.

New York Times, January 6, 2002, Emily White, review of *Just like Beauty,* p. 22; January 23, 2002, Richard Eder, review of *Just Like Beauty,* p. E10.

People Weekly, March 18, 2002, Michelle Vellucci, review of *Just like Beauty,* p. 43.
Publishers Weekly, December 3, 2001, review of *Just like Beauty,* pp. 40-41.
Writer's Digest, January, 2002, Jessica Yerega, "First Success: Lisa Lerner's *Just like Beauty.*"

ONLINE

Bookpeople, http://www.bookpeople.net/ (January 13, 2002), Mary Abshire, review of *Just like Beauty.*
Cornell Alumni Magazine, http://www.cornell-magazine.cornell.edu/ (January-February, 2002), review of *Just like Beauty.**

*   *   *

LEWIS, Norman 1908-2003

OBITUARY NOTICE—See index for *CA* sketch: Born June 28, 1908, in London, England; died July 22, 2003, in Saffron Walden, Essex, England. Author. Lewis was best known as a travel writer, although he also wrote novels and was a photographer and journalist. Enduring an unhappy childhood with a father who invented a bogus medicine and then became a spiritual medium aided by his wife, Lewis was largely raised by aunts living in Wales. When he was older, he worked for his father for a time, then separated from his family to become a wedding photographer. His love of motorcycles fueled his adventuresome nature, and he soon began writing about his travels, publishing *Spanish Adventure* (1935) and *Sand and Sea in Arabia* (1938) before World War II. Lewis was also adept at languages, and during the war he served in British Army Intelligence in Algeria, Tunisia, and Italy, where he was a liaison officer. He later wrote about his wartime experiences in Italy in *Naples '44: An Intelligence Officer in the Italian Labyrinth* (1974). After the war Lewis continued to travel and write about his journeys in such works as *A Dragon Apparent: Travels in Indo-China* (1951), *The Changing Sky: Travels of a Novelist* (1959), and *A Goddess in the Stones: Travels in India* (1991). He was also a productive author of suspense novels, producing *The Sicilian Specialist* (1974), *Cuban Passage* (1982), and *The Man in the Middle* (1984), among others. Though he never won a major literary prize, Lewis was considered by his peers—including

the likes of Graham Greene and V. S. Pritchett—to be a talented author who brought remote regions of the planet vividly to life. Unlike most travel writers, he did not dwell on descriptions of beautiful landscapes; instead, he honestly portrayed the often harsh lives of native peoples surviving under difficult circumstances. He also lamented the demise of traditional customs and cultures at the hands of modern industrialization, and as a journalist for newspapers and magazines he reported on examples of political oppression, such as the killing of Amazonian natives by the Brazilian government. The story of Lewis's own life is set down in his *Jackdaw Cake: An Autobiography* (1985), which was revised in 1994 as *I Came, I Saw,* and *The World, the World* (1996). Lewis's final book, *A Tomb in Seville,* was scheduled to be published posthumously.

OBITUARIES AND OTHER SOURCES:

PERIODICALS

Los Angeles Times, July 28, 2003, p. B9.
New York Times, July 25, 2003, p. A19.
Times (London, England), July 23, 2003.

*   *   *

LISTOWEL, Judith (de Marffy-Mantuano) 1904-2003

OBITUARY NOTICE—See index for *CA* sketch: Born July 12, 1904, in Kaposvar, Hungary; died July 15, 2003. Journalist and author. Listowel was an ardent anti-communist, conservative journalist who spent over seven decades reporting on events in eastern Europe and Africa. The daughter of a Hungarian diplomat, she studied economics in Budapest and history at the London School of Economics, where she earned a B.Sc. in 1929. She then embarked on a career as a freelance journalist, writing for Hungarian newspapers while living in England. In 1933 she became the countess of Listowel after marrying the fifth earl of Listowel, but the marriage broke up a few years later. Listowel never remarried, instead devoting herself to reporting on the rise of Nazism and lecturing in England and the United States. These activities quickly put her on the Nazi black list, which meant she would have faced execution if the Germans had conquered

England. When World War II started she worked as a civilian lecturer for the British Armed Forces and also trained as a nurse and worked in a hospital to help support herself. With the defeat of the Nazis, Listowel's next concern became the spread of Communism within the Eastern Bloc. Beginning in 1944, she edited and published the weekly journal *East Europe,* which was later renamed *East Europe and Soviet Russia,* and then *Soviet Orbit.* The journal remained in publication for about ten years and had subscribers in over forty countries. Banned from entering her native country because of her reportage, Listowel attempted to smuggle herself in to Hungary during that country's 1956 revolution; she succeeded briefly, but left when it became clear she would be executed if caught by Russian authorities. In the 1960s, as more and more African nations won independence from European imperialists, she became hopeful of a new beginning for Africa. However, as she witnessed the corruption of the petty military dictators who gained power in that continent, Listowel became dismayed and reported against their power-hungry activities. She was sued by Ugandan President Idi Amin for her book *Amin* (1973), which portrays the ruler in a very negative light, and because her reports could not be substantiated because witnesses were too terrified to testify against Amin, she lost the lawsuit. Despairing of the future of Africa, Listowel gained new hope for eastern Europe in the 1980s after the collapse of the USSR; she returned to her reportage of events there, especially in Hungary and Poland, continuing her work as a journalist into her nineties. In addition to her journalism, she published nine books during her career, including *Crusaders in the Secret War* (1952), *The Making of Tanganyika* (1966), *Dusk and the Danube* (1969), and *A Hapsburg Tragedy: Crown Prince Rudolf* (1978).

OBITUARIES AND OTHER SOURCES:

PERIODICALS

Daily Telegraph (London, England), July 22, 2003, p. 1.
Herald (Glasgow, Scotland), August 2, 2003, p. 18.
Times (London, England), July 30, 2003, p. 27.

LOTT, Clarinda Harriss
  See HARRISS, Clarinda

*   *   *

LOUÇÃ, Francisco 1956-

PERSONAL: Born November 12, 1956, in Lisbon, Portugal; son of António (a naval officer) and Noémia Louçá. *Education:* Technical University of Lisbon, Ph.D. *Politics:* Socialist.

ADDRESSES: Office—Instituto Superior de Economic e Gestão, Universidade Técnica de Lisboa, Rua do Quelhas 6, 1200 Lisbon, Portugal. *E-mail*—flouc@iseg.utl.pt.

CAREER: Economist, educator, and author. Technical University of Lisbon, Lisbon, Portugal, professor of economics, 1996—. Also member of Portuguese parliament.

WRITINGS:

A maldição de Midas: a cultura do capitalismo tardio, Cotovia (Lisbon, Portugal), 1994, translated by the author as *Turbulence in Economics: An Evolutionary Appraisal of Cycles and Complexity in Historica Processes,* Edward Elgar Publishing (Lyme, NH), 1997.
(Editor with Jan Reijnders) *The Foundations of Long-Wave Theory: Models and Methodology,* Edward Elgar Publishing (Northampton, MA), 1999.
(Editor with Mark Perlman) *Is Economics an Evolutionary Science? The Legacy of Thorstein Veblen,* Edward Elgar Publishing (Northampton, MA), 2000.
(With Chris Freeman) *As Time Goes By: From the Industrial Revolutions to the Information Revolution,* Oxford University Press (New York, NY), 2001.

*   *   *

LYON, Winston
  See WOOLFOLK, William

M

MacEOIN, Gary 1909-2003

OBITUARY NOTICE—See index for *CA* sketch: Born June 12, 1909, in Curry, County Sligo, Ireland; died of a heart attack July 9, 2003, in Leesburg, VA. Journalist and author. MacEoin focused his writing primarily on the Roman Catholic Church and the social and political conditions in Latin America. A Catholic himself, he studied for the priesthood, but dropped out of the seminary one week before ordination. Instead, he completed an undergraduate degree at the University of London in 1941, followed by a master's degree from the National University of Ireland in 1942 and a Ph.D. in modern languages in 1951. A man of many talents, MacEoin spoke nine languages and was admitted to the Irish Bar in 1943. His journalism career began in 1933 as a reporter, feature writer, and critic for newspapers in Dublin and London. In 1944 he moved to Trinidad to become editor of the *Port-of-Spain Gazette*. After a brief stint as information officer for the Caribbean Commission, he moved to New York City to edit Spanish-language publications during the 1950s and became a freelance writer in 1963. Noticing while in New York how the U.S. media largely ignored Latin-American affairs, he traveled throughout that ignored region and published several books on the subject, among them *Latin America: The Eleventh Hour* (1962), *Columbia, Venezuela, the Guianas* (1965), and *Revolution Next Door: Latin America in the 1970s* (1971). Being familiar with the Catholic Church because of his position as a former seminarian, MacEoin also frequently wrote about the Church and its followers in books such as *Father Moreau: Founder of Holy Cross* (1962), *New Challenges to American Catholics* (1965), and *What Happened in Rome?* (1966). In the 1970s MacEoin turned increasingly to academia, teaching at Fordham University as an adjunct professor during the early 1970s, and at Fairleigh Dickinson University for a year; he also lectured at numerous other universities. His more recent writings include *Central America's Options: Death or Life?* (1988), *Unlikely Allies: The Christian-Socialist Convergence* (1990), and *The People's Church: Bishop Samuel Ruiz of Mexico and Why He Matters* (1996); he was also the author of the memoirs *Nothing Is Quite Enough* (1953) and *Memoirs and Memories* (1986).

OBITUARIES AND OTHER SOURCES:

BOOKS

Writers Directory, 18th edition, St. James Press (Detroit, MI), 2003.

PERIODICALS

New York Times, July 20, 2003, p. A25.
Washington Post, July 13, 2003, p. C11.

*   *   *

MALLORY, Tess

PERSONAL: Female; married, three children. *Hobbies and other interests:* "Writing songs, plays, and musicals, painting furniture."

ADDRESSES: Home—Texas hill country. *Office*—Dorchester Publishing Company, 200 Madison Ave, Suite 2000, New York, NY 10016. *E-mail*—tessmallory@yahoo.com.

CAREER: Novelist. Former journalist, radio disc jockey, theater costume designer, clown, and professional storyteller. Conducts workshops for writers in Texas.

MEMBER: Romance Writers of America, North Texas Writers Guild, San Antonio Romance Authors, Golden Triangle Writers Guild.

WRITINGS:

Jewels of Time, Dorchester Publishing Company (New York, NY), 1994.
To Touch the Stars, Dorchester Publishing Company (New York, NY), 1998.
Highland Dream, Dorchester Publishing Company (New York, NY), 2001.
Highland Fling, Dorchester Publishing Company (New York, NY), 2003.
Circles in Time, Dorchester Publishing Company (New York, NY), 2003.

Contributor to books, including *Midsummer Night's Magic,* Dorchester Publishing Company (New York, NY), 1997. Contributor to periodicals, including *Highlights for Children.*

SIDELIGHTS: Tess Mallory specializes in novels that include elements of time travel, romance, science fiction, and fantasy. A former journalist, Mallory was inspired to write her first novel, *Jewels of Time,* in the early 1990s, and has since established a career as a romance novelist specializing in Celtic themes.

Highland Fling, the sequel to Mallory's *Highland Dream,* revolves around heroic highlander Griffin Campbell, who hails from seventeenth-century Scotland, and modern-day wallflower physicist Chelsea Brown. The two are taken from their own time and transported together to the Old West of the nineteenth century, as well as to twenty-first-century Scotland and modern-day Texas. Both characters are unlucky in romance, but have instant chemistry with each other.

The experience of living in the Old West, which features mean outlaws and a meaner sheriff, helps Chelsea come out of her shell, and she even rescues Griffin at one point in the action-packed novel. In *Library Journal,* Kristin Ramsdell wrote that "although the Wild West segment is a bit much, the appealing, complementary protagonists and the appearance of several characters from [*Highland Dream*] . . . will definitely please series fans."

Mallory told *CA:* "I believe that my interest in writing came about primarily because of my father's influence. This taught me that it was possible to create my own worlds, my own stories, and as I grew up he always encouraged me to 'write it down.' I've found that my writing process is one of being inspired by something—it could be almost anything—which then turns into an idea for a book, which sits in my head and jells for an indeterminate length of time until it finally starts clamoring for attention and making so much noise that I have to write it down! At that point I write a proposal which consists of three chapters and a synopsis—a short one for the editor and a long one for myself, which hopefully, I send to my agent and then begin the long process of waiting for an editorial response from the publisher.

"The most surprising thing I've learned as a writer is that selling a book doesn't nave so much to do with your talent as a writer as it does in finding an editor who LIKES your style of writing. This is the real challenge in becoming a published author, and also in finding an agent. Just as people have their favorite authors they like to read, editors and agents have theirs. It sounds simple but it really was a surprise to me. I assumed editors and agents would like any well-written story, but it has to fit their criteria. That's why when you ask an editor what kind of writing they like, they will invariably say 'I'll know it when I read it.'

"My favorite book is actually the novella I wrote for the Leisure/Lovespell anthology, *Midsummer Night's Magic.* My novella was 'The Fairy Bride' and I loved it because it is pure fairy tale with a really fun hero and a lot of humor. I set it in Ireland, my favorite spot in the world, and named the characters after my daughters, my son, and my son-in-law. The premise that the king of Fairyland has to find and marry a mortal woman was so much fun to work with, and the fantasy adventure surrounding it made it a lark to write! I still want to write a full-length book based on the characters I created for *The Fairy Bride.*

"There have been times in my life when a favorite author's books have cheered me and encouraged me and taught me a little more about my own strength. I hope this is how my books effect my readers. I also hope my books make them laugh and make them cry; I hope they won't be able to put my books down and when they get through reading them, they feel extremely happy with the stories and with themselves for reading them. There is nothing worse to me as a reader than feeling I have wasted my time reading a boring or badly written book. I hope when a reader finishes one of my books, they smile and say, 'Now, that was a good book.'"

BIOGRAPHICAL AND CRITICAL SOURCES:

PERIODICALS

Booklist, February 15, 2003, Shelley Mosley, review of *Highland Fling,* p. 1057.
Library Journal, February 15, 2003, Kristin Ramsdell, review of *Highland Fling,* p. 122.

ONLINE

Leisure Books Web site, http://www.dorchesterpub. com/ (June 14, 2003).
Romantic Times, http://www.romantictimes.com/ (June 14, 2003), "Tess Mallory."
Tess Mallory Web site, http://www.sff.net/people/ tessmallory (June 14, 2003).
Visit Wimberley, http://www.visitwimberley.com/ (June 14, 2003), Marcia Bennett, interview with Mallory.*

* * *

MARCUS, Morton 1936-

PERSONAL: Born September 10, 1936, in New York, NY; son of Max Pincus (a garment manufacturer) and Rachel (a dress shop owner; maiden name, Babchek) Marcus; married Wilma Kantrowich, 1958 (divorced, 1971); married Donna Mekis, 1986; children: Jana Lin, Valerie Anna. *Education:* Attended Washington University, St. Louis, MO, 1956-58; State University of Iowa, B.A., 1961; Stanford University, M.A., 1968.

Morton Marcus

ADDRESSES: Home—1325 Laurel Street, Santa Cruz, CA 95060.

CAREER: Elementary school teacher, Point Arena, CA, 1962-63; high school English and history teacher, San Francisco, CA, 1965-68, high school basketball coach, 1965-66; Cabrillo College, Aptos, CA, instructor in English and film, 1968-98. Director of county poetry-in-the-schools program, Monterey and Santa Cruz, CA, 1972-75; poet-in-residence at State University of New York at Buffalo, 1974, State University of New York at Alfred, 1976, University of Arkansas Graduate Writing Program, 1997, Providence College, 1998, and Fullerton College, 2001. Foothill Writers Conference, organizer, 1986—. Co-host of *Poetry Show* (radio show), KUSP, and *CinemaScene* (televsision show), KRUZ; also created sixteen-part television series *Movie Milestones. Military service:* U.S. Air Force, 1954-58.

MEMBER: Poets and Writers, King Fisher Flats Foundation (president).

AWARDS, HONORS: Woodrow Wilson fellowship, 1961-62; MacDowell Colony fellow, 1975; Santa Cruz County Artist of the Year, 1999.

WRITINGS:

Origins (poetry), Kayak (San Francisco, CA), 1969, 3rd edition, 1974.

The Santa Cruz Mountain Poems, Capra (Santa Barbara, CA), 1972.

Where the Oceans Cover Us (poetry), Capra (Santa Barbara, CA), 1972.

The Armies Encamped in the Fields beyond the Unfinished Avenues: Prose Poems, Jazz Press (Los Angeles, CA), 1977.

Big Winds, Glass Mornings, Shadows Cast by Stars: Poems, 1972-1980, Jazz Press (Los Angeles, CA), 1980.

The Brezhnev Memo (novel), Dell (New York, NY), 1981.

Pages from a Scrapbook of Immigrants: A Journey in Poems, Coffee House Press (Minneapolis, MN), 1988.

When People Could Fly, Hanging Loose Press (Brooklyn, NY), 1997.

Moments without Names: New & Selected Prose Poems, White Pine Press (Buffalo, NY), 2002.

Shouting Down the Silence: Line Poems, 1988-2001, Creative Arts (Berkeley, CA), 2002.

Author of play *The Eight Ecstasies of Yaeko Iwasake: A Legend in Poetry, Dance, and Music,* produced in California, 1984. Work represented in more than eighty anthologies, including *California Poets: A Centennial Anthology,* 1976; *Best Poems of 1975: Borestone Mountain Awards,* 1976; *A Geography of Poets,* Bantam (New York, NY), 1979; *Remembering Ray,* Capra (Santa Barbara, CA), 1993; *The Geography of Home: California's Poetry of Place,* Heyday (Berkeley, CA), 1999; *The Body Electric,* Holt (New York, NY), 2002; and *No Boundaries: Prose Poems by Twenty-four American Poets,* Tupelo Press (Dorset, VT), 2003. Contributing editor, *Prose Poem: An International Journal.* Contributor of over 400 poems to more than 600 literary journals, including *Poetry Northwest, Nation, Chicago Review, Ploughshares, Denver Quarterly, TriQuarterly,* and *Hanging Loose.*

WORK IN PROGRESS: Bear Prints: New and Collected Verse Poems, 1959-2002, and *The Woodhouse Conspiracy,* a novel.

SIDELIGHTS: Morton Marcus is a multifaceted poet whose work has been widely published in books, periodicals, and over eighty anthologies. He was a literature instructor for thirty years at Cabrillo College in California, where he also taught film history and criticism. Though he has concentrated on prose poetry since the 1990s, Marcus has also produced a considerable body of lined and narrative poems, written a stage play, and published an espionage novel titled *The Brezhnev Memo.* Long a supporter of the poetry community in California through his classes, workshops, readings, and radio shows, Marcus has sought to convey the vitality of contemporary prose poetry to the general public. Highly regarded by his peers, Marcus was named Santa Cruz County Artist of the Year in 1999, an honor shared previously by only two other poets, Adrienne Rich and William Everson. Summarizing Marcus's early work in the journal *Shock,* Andrei Codrescu described the writer as "the kind of priest-poet who . . . gets to the Light by tearing up the universe in ecstatic dance."

Marcus's poetry has shifted form considerably over the years. Originally working with traditional poetic structures, Marcus eventually gravitated toward free verse, which eliminated many constrictions of form, and then explored prose poetry, which has no line form at all. Marcus described this journey in an interview with Ray Gonzalez in the *Bloomsbury Review:* "When I gave up closed verse for free verse, I experienced a latitude, a freedom of choice, and found a more lively, vital voice. When I gave up the line, however, I experienced new ways of seeing and saying. It was a complete turnabout of traditional ways of doing things in poetry for me."

Marcus's *Moments without Names: New and Selected Prose Poems* contains five thematic sections of twenty-two poems each. Rather than order the works chronologically, he structured the book to mirror common watershed events in many peoples' lives: "Beginnings," "At Home," "On Streets and Roads," "Travels," and "Ends." Roughly half of the poems are new, and the rest are taken from his previous collections. In *Shouting down the Silence: Line Poems, 1988-2001* Marcus gives readers a new selection of lined poems, most of which were written at the same time he was writing prose poems, highlighting his versatility. Some may consider it unusual for a poet to immerse himself in two diverse forms simultaneously, but as Marcus explained to Gonzalez, "I let the form of each poem I write be dictated by the particular impulse that drives me to put those particular words on paper, a process that remains as mysterious to me now as it was the first day I found myself writing a poem."

Because some in the poetry community have yet to fully acknowledge the legitimacy of prose poems, Marcus admits he has been somewhat marginalized, mainly because so few journals will publish his prose work. Add to that the fact that much of his work highlights the comic foibles of human nature, rather than the more prevalent theme of solipsism, and his audience shrinks even further. "I've always been on the margins of the American poetry scene," he told Gonzalez. As for his fondness for humor, he said that he's "drawn to the holy fools, cosmic clowns, idiot savants, not just for their boisterous, fun-loving, and at times scathingly sardonic attitudes toward humanity and the bumbling ways of the universe, but because they upset our habitual ways of seeing the world." Despite this, his work is praised by critics as being accessible. "With their unaffected, journalistic plainspeak," said *Santa Cruz Sentinel* writer Wallace Blaine, "Marcus's prose poems read as breezily as a newspaper clipping or a storyteller's monologue."

Marcus told *CA:* "A successful poem should speak not only to the head and heart but to the reader's cells, where the seeds of the universe's purpose have been embedded since the beginning of time, as if our chromosomes have been laid down like paving stones, one after another, and provide a silent, sure direction for us beyond rational understanding. The successful poem, then, taps each cell with an instinctive kind of knowing that causes it to resonate like a gong, until the millions of cells in the reader's body for an instant become an orchestra that trembles and swells with the music of recognition, a symphony of cosmic plentitude and unity.

"What poets come to learn is that language is inadequate to express what they want to say, yet paradoxically they have chosen language as their medium. Maybe that's because they don't want to *say* anything. They want to evoke everything they can: a mood, an experience, even an idea. It is this realization that makes them start using language to express what cannot be said.

"The craft of poetry is such that poets must use words to convey the experience: they don't tell what the poem is about, nor do they preach—they show, allowing (or insisting) that the reader participate in the work at hand.

"The poets' language, besides being free of clichés and trite phrases, is grounded in the senses: poets look at the world through their bodies, for they have captured the vision spirit inside their skins. Therefore, they use language in bursts of sense impressions called images.

"The image should never be used for ornament. It must always contain vision, always be profound and direct the reader to the overall vision of the poem.

"I conceive of the poet as an entertainer in words. But he also plays a social and spiritual role in that while he entertains he simultaneously reminds us of what is important in our lives, in many cases what we've forgotten or lost in terms of cultural traditions and a sense of our place in the universe.

"In the poem, the poet allows us to rediscover our spiritual selves. His function is to put us in touch with our feelings, or, in a deeper sense, to reveal to us once again 'the primal vision'—the psychic and physical goals of both the human race and life itself, which are indelibly stained on our chromosomes. In a way, and I don't mean to be presumptuous, poets are like doctors. The poem is their medicine. In this metaphor, the readers' illness is that they do not know, or have forgotten why, they are in this world and where they are going. As doctors of the spirit, the poets in their poems *show* the answers to the readers' questions, and in doing so they allow the readers to experience the way in which they can once more psychically enter the harmony of the universe."

AUTOBIOGRAPHICAL ESSAY:

My grandmother's family was from Grodno, Lithuania, then part of Russia. They "dealt in oil and grain, and had a mill on the river." She married beneath her, a peasant originally from the Ukraine, a hard man, a blacksmith with restless energy and that sense of dreaming, no matter how material or self-serving it may be, that inspires humans to give up all they know either to seek a better life or just to see what's on the other side of the ocean.

My grandfather came to the United States in 1908, but he was so poor it took him six years of endless labor to earn enough money to bring his wife and five children to this country. The family settled first in the Brownsville section of Brooklyn and later in a house in East Flatbush where my grandfather owned a cow, a goat, chickens, and a horse; he sold eggs and milk in the neighborhood, and dabbled in real estate. His two youngest boys, my uncles Abe and Frankie, got into mischief early and soon were involved in the gang life of Brooklyn. Abe became a numbers runner for, and later a friend and advisor to, the notorious Abe Reles (aka "Kid Twist"), whom he may have known from his early years in Brownsville. When Reles joined Murder Incorporated, he supposedly "gave" my uncle control of Brownsville. Frankie, purported to have a tinder-box temper, was my uncle's enforcer.

Is this true, or is it family myth? The story goes that my uncle earned millions in the numbers racket, paid the cops and judges in the area, and had interests in several restaurants. The family insists he wasn't a gangster but a gambler, while others, taking the middle road, said he was a racketeer.

What is fact is that on September 24, 1941, he was found slumped in his car with two bullets in the back of his head, and his murder drew headlines in New York newspapers for a number of days afterwards. What is also fact is that my uncle's money was never found and Frankie, realizing a contract out on Abe had to have marked him as well, disappeared. The day before he left, someone called my mother and said if anyone investigated or tried or avenge Abe's murder, the whole family would be killed, "starting with the kids." The panic this caused made everyone vow to forget Abe and the murder.

It was the great family tragedy. Abe was loved by everyone and considered the head of the family after my grandfather's death, and the mention of his name would send my mother and Aunt Bertha, her older sister, into hysterical tears for years to come. But the newspaper headlines were also a public humiliation, and the family quietly changed its name from Bab-chek to Balzac a few weeks after the shooting.

While all this turmoil was going on, my mother had grown into a woman of movie-star beauty. Men and women would stop her in the street and ask for her autograph. She was a willful girl, determined to make it out of Brooklyn into the glamorous life of money and fast living across the river in Manhattan. Dropping out of school in the fourth grade, she learned early that her beauty could be the key to open all the

doors she wanted to walk through. She never liked men, really; they were to be used: merely a means to an end—money and a good address.

By the time Abe was killed, my mother was thirty-four years old and had been married five times—it's still unclear how many marriages she had—and had been separated from my father for two years. He was also a Russian Jewish immigrant, who had risen to be one of the top manufacturers in the garment industry, and had given my mother two of her dreams—the move from Brooklyn to Manhattan, and an apartment in an exclusive neighborhood.

My mother was not selfish about her good fortune. She provided for her mother in her last years, paid medical bills for her brothers and sisters and their children, and had her chauffeur drive her nephew and his friends in her cream-colored Cord to play baseball in Prospect Park.

I was born into this milieu in 1936. I hardly remember my father. Because of his addiction to gambling, his womanizing, and his jealousy of me, my mother said, she left him when I was three. Supposedly, he wanted to have her complete attention and to parade her in all her beauty in public. After the separation, my mother and I moved to Brooklyn for a time, and Abe, a bachelor, lived with us until his death.

My troubled youth, however, began years before my uncle was murdered. My beautiful mother had a life to live, a life that promised wealth and excitement, and a little boy was a barrier to such aspirations. Therefore, by 1940 I had already been sent to several boarding schools while we were on trips to Florida, and after Abe's death in 1941, I was a permanent resident at thirteen different boarding schools for neglected or emotionally troubled children. In fact, from the time I was three years old to the time I was twenty-one, I spent a total of three years at home—and in the summers, my mother sent me to camps.

The schools were similar to the ones immortalized by Charles Dickens in the nineteenth century, and when I first read *Oliver Twist* I seemed to recognize many of the places I'd spent my early years. Not that I needed to read great literature; such films as *Tom Brown's School Days* and *David Copperfield* showed me my life on film, so that I accepted my lot as being the normal course of every child's life.

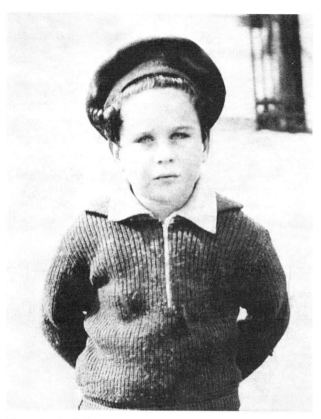

The author in 1940

I may have thought such a youth was normal, but that didn't keep me from rebelling against it. I was a boy without a father, as my schoolmates were quick to remind me, and my mother was not only a divorcee, a status regarded by most Americans at the time as close to whoredom, but, it seemed clear, she had abandoned me. I did not obey teachers or staff members, I refused to eat or learn my lessons, and was always fighting or moping in a corner somewhere. No wonder I was expelled from one school after another, and by the time I was nine I was running away from these institutions, which were not only in Brooklyn but in Westchester County, New York, and Connecticut.

Always the new boy at these schools, I was constantly beaten up by the bullies from the age of three. This situation of victimization continued until, at the age of six, I had an ingenious idea. Instead of letting the bullies beat me up, I would beat them up. I quickly discovered it was an idea that was easy to put into successful action. I would observe from the lead bully and his cohorts' words and approach when they were about to begin their ritual of intimidation or to attack. At such moments, I struck, and struck first, doing things no dull-brained bully would—not pushing or

wrestling (as one would suspect, I was always smaller than the ringleader) but punching, and not only to the stomach and the chin but to the throat. So ferocious was my attack that I was left alone afterwards, for after the leader recovered I was usually offered a place in his inner sanctum, an offer I refused.

It was in this role as bully-beater that I learned the first great lesson of my life. I never accepted the bullies' generous offer to become a member of their bands because I knew what the cowed and victimized felt like, and instead of joining the bullies, I'd warn them to leave the other kids alone or they'd have to deal with me again. I didn't know it at the time, but out of these empathetic feelings arose a sense of compassion. So pronounced was my identification with the lot of others when I was six that I believe the roots of my writing and social activism in later years originated with this early response to bullies.

These early years were seminal in many ways. I continued to be an inattentive, rebellious student, and I was continually sent from the classroom to stand in a corner of the hall and stare at a fire extinguisher or a broom, or I remained in the class, sitting in a corner, wearing a conical paper dunce cap. Left to myself in these ways, I was forced to construct with my imagination the simplest of explanations of how things worked. Again, this was not a conscious undertaking, just a child's natural curiosity to learn how things functioned.

By the time I was ten, I had a complex cosmology in place, composed of popular cultural assumptions, Old Testament Bible tales, radio programs, advertisements, and comic books that combined to create an eccentric if not absurd universe where everything from why the stars came out at night to how can openers worked took on serious, convoluted, and, in many cases, interconnected explanations. These explanations were accompanied by a variety of daily rituals it was my responsibility to perform in order to maintain the order of the universe.

For example, to make sure the sun would rise each morning, I would hold open my eyes to that blazing star the day before. If the day was cloudy, I would walk in circles a number of times or not touch the floor with my feet when I got out of bed in the morning, agilely sliding my toes into the mouths of my waiting shoes, which on behalf of the world carried my feet gently all day in their obedient jaws. These rituals were endless and most of the time performed on behalf of the planet, if not the universe, rather than for myself. They were childish superstitions, of course, and maybe inadvertent admissions of early delusions of grandeur, or incipient megalomania, but I like to think of them more as the honing of my imagination rather than the workings of a diseased mind. Out of them emerged a world of wonder and mystery, which has inspired my writing and my vision of life.

At the same time, and very much a part of these rituals, I began to play a strange game that was to have far-reaching consequences. I'm sure the game arose because I couldn't draw. Even in kindergarten art periods, I created the most wretched stick figures saluting the flag or, with hands joined, setting off on a smiling family outing.

This deficiency in my artistic abilities inspired me to paint word pictures of anything on which my eye might alight. I started playing this word game when I was seven years old. I was at the Hudson School in New Rochelle, New York, and my room was adjacent to the house mother's. A heavy-set woman who always wore a gray uniform, she would get up at around 5:30 each morning and turn on the radio, first listening to gospel music, then news of the war in Europe, and finally Arthur Godfrey. That was her ritual, and it took place an hour and a half before she woke the boys and girls in her "house." But the radio woke me, and soon I was looking forward to hearing the church music and opening my eyes in the pre-dawn dark to see the plane of light outlined at the bottom of the old woman's door.

By overhearing the news reports on the old woman's radio, my world was enlarged beyond the school grounds and New Rochelle. I became aware of world events and history. World War II was raging in Europe and the Pacific, and like litanies I murmured over and over again the strange names I heard: Guadalcanal, Bataan, Midway, Stalingrad, Leningrad, and the Urals. On one report accompanying news of the Russian front, there was a dramatization of Napoleon's march into Russia and his defeat by both the winter weather and the heroic Russians.

That program and other news reports of events at the Russian front led me to idealize Russia. After all, my family on both my mother and father's sides came from Russia. In Russia, I was convinced, I would not be an outsider. I would be a heroic fighter, loved by the world.

These were the kinds of notions that scampered through my brain each morning, as I lay undisturbed before the other students woke. And as I thought about the news reports, or the experiences of the previous day, or the longings for my mother who was in such faraway places as "Frisco" or Little Rock, Arkansas, I would create pictures of those events or places, pictures that were drawn with words I'd mouth, piles of words I would pick among like a scavenging bird, discarding some, choosing others, until I had words that best described what I was seeing in my head.

Soon I was playing this word game throughout the day, snatching the words that would capture how the wind moved in the trees across the road, what the cruel mathematics teacher looked like when he was angry, and what the sound resembled when all the hundred or more boys and girls were let loose after dinner on the athletic field.

Was this the beginning of my becoming a writer? I have no doubt it was. Did I know it at the time? Of course not. I was just a seven-year-old kid playing a lonely boy's game, a game, like the rituals, which gave him a sense of his place, if not his power, in the world, and allowed him to avoid thinking of how alone he was and why his mother, who would call him on the phone every week from one faraway place or another, wouldn't visit him—or take him home.

Another reason the games didn't immediately point to my future as a writer was that I wasn't able to read until I was almost ten years old, when the man who became my mother's sixth husband taught me to sound out the words on billboards as we drove through New York City or in the country. Even playing the word game didn't inspire me to master the function of reading, so I could bury my loneliness in books. I was a morose, angry, lonely child.

*

My life in the schools continued until I was ten years old, when my mother remarried. She and her new husband, a rich garment manufacturer, bought an estate in Westchester County, thirty miles north of the city. Finally I had a home, my mother, and a father. My miseries seemed to be over. But the idyllic family situation lasted less than a year, when my new father revealed homicidal tendencies. The ugly divorce proceedings were reported in all the New York tabloids, and their salacious articles were highlighted with endless photos of my beautiful mother.

My mother and I moved to an apartment in New York City after that, and she kept me home, sending me to a public junior high school, where I discovered my athletic prowess, developing into an excellent basketball and baseball player. I also discovered I had a sense of humor, which was sharpened by the street wit of the boys I hung around. I wasn't a loner anymore, and would play ball with my new friends in the schoolyard and in Central Park until all hours. But the guys I was mingling with also stole and dealt drugs, and in the spring of 1949, two uniformed cops paid my mother a visit and advised her to send me out of town for my own good. I hadn't done anything wrong yet, they said, but it was only a matter of time.

The result was that my mother sent me to boarding school again. But now there was a difference. Always aware of status, she managed to enroll me in a highly regarded Ivy League prep school, where the new headmaster wanted to break the school's anti-Semitic entrance policies. I had three fights the first week I was there, but my athletic abilities and street humor won my classmates over. I played varsity basketball and baseball, and the headmaster was so pleased with my accomplishments in race relations and sports that he awarded me an athletic scholarship for the following year.

But of all the events that befell me that first prep school year, the most important was my meeting Roger Maren. There is an old saw that each of us will meet the person who will change his life forever. For me, that person was Roger Maren.

Maren was the master of the freshman dormitory. He had been hired that year as the school's English teacher (the school only had 100 or so students), and he was a linguist, musician, translator, and writer. He was in his early twenties, and so thin that when he was sitting or standing his postures were those of a contortionist, as he bent his arms around his body or wrapped his legs around each other.

Marcus with his mother, Rae, 1943

At night before lights out, he would invite the students into his room, where he passed around a gallon jar of apple cider, played the guitar, sang folk songs in several languages, played 78-rpm records of Django Reinhardt, Louis Armstrong, Bessie Smith, and Ledbelly, and told us about their lives. Most of the other students thought Maren was "weird," but he fascinated me with his stories and songs. I learned his renditions of "Sam Hill" and "Barbara Allen" by heart as well as a dozen other English folk songs within a month, and I was mesmerized by the big sound of Ledbelly's twelve-string guitar and Django's unique picking style.

"Any time anyone wants to come in and talk, or wants to borrow a book, just knock," Maren said the first night he invited everyone into his room. I took him up on his offer in my inimitable New York street style. I knocked on his door a week later, told him I'd like to read a book, and when he asked what kind, I answered, "Something dirty."

Without hesitating, he took down James T. Farrell's "Studs Lonigan" trilogy. "I'll give you this and any book you would like to read, but on one condition: You've got to discuss it with me after you're finished and write down questions you may have while you're reading it."

And so I was introduced to the world of books with my personal tutor. Next came *Gulliver's Travels* and Rabelais, and the questions and discussions went deeper and deeper. My grades, even in English, remained deplorable, but I was reading everything I could get my hands on, transported by the word pictures in books to other places and other times and into the lives of other people, in many cases into lives similar to my own.

In mid-November, Maren gave me the key to the school's library, which stretched in glass cases down one side of the classroom hallway in the main building. I read almost all the books in Random House's "Modern Library" series—histories, novels, poetry—with Maren showing me the fine points or directing me to the significance of what I was reading. Soon, I was tackling everything from Richard Wright's *Native Son* and *Black Boy* to James Joyce's *Ulysses,* and Franz Kafka's *The Trial.*

By Christmas vacation, I'd begun to write, trying to put my own word pictures on paper. But my efforts were mostly science-fiction stories or satirical fantasies. Then, somewhere I heard that a poet's "sensitivity" made him "attractive" to the opposite sex, so I turned my literary endeavors to poetry—bad poetry, really bad poetry. The word pictures were somehow forgotten for a time and replaced by abstract protestations using a lot of "thy's," "o'er's," and "yee's."

As for Maren, his strange body movements and bohemian ways made him the subject of ridicule behind his back. I became his defender: first verbally, then physically; and let everyone know that if they bothered him they would have to cross me, and now that I was one of the school jocks, a part of the "in" crowd, only a belligerent few wanted to get on my bad side. Actually—and it occurred to me even then—I was once more defending someone I considered a victim of the bullies.

On the weekends when Maren had on-campus duties, he had visitors. One who came several times was the poet, fiction writer, and social theorist, Paul Goodman, whose book on the growing disaffiliation of youth in America, *Growing up Absurd,* would be an important contribution to the thinking of the 1960s. Maren introduced me to him, the first "real" writer I had ever

met, and he encouraged me to keep writing. His early book of short stories, *The Break-up of Our Camp,* had a profound influence on the direction of my work.

In the city on holidays or during the summer before I went to camp, I became a haunter of bookstores—the used book row below 14th Street and the Marboro Book Shops with their seemingly endless tables of remainder books. In addition, I joined the headmaster's ballet and opera clubs, and with them went to the city to attend performances of the New York City Ballet and the Metropolitan Opera.

That summer I honed my basketball and baseball skills at camp, sharing my passion for books as well as my tales of love with a wonderfully compassionate and athletic counselor called Whitey, who showed me that a man could be sensitive as well as manly, another lesson I was not to forget.

For the month after camp was over and before school began, I once more played basketball every day at the 81st Street courts in Central Park, but the guys I had hung around with the year before were no longer there, and I never saw them again. Now, however, I started playing early and leaving by two or three o'clock in the afternoon to sit or wander until closing time through the nearby Metropolitan Museum of Art, a sweaty kid in T-shirt and sneakers the guards at first eyed with concern, but after a while would smile at and nod to in greeting. I had changed. What my mother and the headmaster had intended was happening. My rough edges were being smoothed.

*

Although my thinking became a jumble of notions about death, Taoism, and existentialism over the next ten years, my writing didn't take a serious turn until I was in the Air Force. I enlisted in the fall of 1954 because I had flunked out of high school the previous spring and was at loose ends. My basketball career seemed over, and after living with my mother for three months I thought that even an experience that resembled boarding school life was preferable to remaining in the tiny apartment with her.

Two days after I enlisted I realized that by the time I was discharged I would have spent one fourth of my life in the military and eighteen of my twenty-one

The author in high school, 1954

years living in dormitories. Maybe that's why writing became more important to me than ever before: I needed to write for both solace and self-understanding. This need started during a pass from boot camp in November of 1954 and has continued unabated ever since. I bought three stapled booklets by Kenneth Patchen at a Syracuse bookstore while on the pass, and read them to pieces. At Scott Air Force Base in Illinois, where I was assigned after boot camp, I began studying and copying poetic techniques, especially closed forms and poems that demonstrated varied diction and different tones of voice. My models were Richard Wilbur, Karl Shapiro, Theodore Roethke, Elizabeth Bishop, Muriel Rukeyser, and the young Adrienne Rich. I found many of those poets in the Twayne *Mid-Century American Poets* anthology that I had also bought in Syracuse. I was especially intrigued with evoking spoken American through closed forms and marveled at how Robert Frost projected a New England voice through rhymed, metered quatrains and sonnets. I also learned a lifelong lesson, namely, that even the smallest and most innocent library *could,* and probably *did,* carry literary gems and oddities. At Scott's library I found David Ignatow's *The Gentle Weightlifter* in the poetry section and renewed it again and again. Ignatow's plain, spoken style intrigued me.

I also read and liked the work of T. S. Eliot, not for its endless allusions, but for the subtly nuanced speech rhythms he used in "Prufrock," "Gerontion," "Journey of the Magi," and other poems. And, of course, I was drawn to the poems of William Carlos, whose imagist background and concerns with American speech patterns were enormous influences.

At the same time, I discovered the main library in downtown St. Louis and began dating one of the librarians. She introduced me not only to her wholesome Midwest family, but also to the small St. Louis literary world, and had me send my poems to the library's annual contest in which I took third place. At the awards ceremony I wore my uniform and read my poem. I was an anomaly—a warrior poet. On the basis of the award, several fledgling poets my own age courted me, and the editors of local literary journals published my early poems.

I was also taking out books from the library on such subjects as history, literary criticism, and biography. Maurois' biography of George Sand, and her relationship with Balzac, fascinated me, since my family, wanting to avoid notoriety, had changed its name from Babchek to Balzac after my uncle's assassination.

The most instructive books were Brooks and Warren's *Understanding Fiction* and *Understanding Poetry.* I read them diligently and came away with many ideas.

All this literary activity was suspended during a six-month self-pitying drinking binge after which I began putting my life together. I had my mother ship me my text books, got my high school diploma, and decided to go to night school at Washington University in nearby St. Louis. I seemed to be blossoming with questions like a thorny rose bush. My first two years in the Air Force had made me hungry to learn because I had been directly exposed to war, politics, and military folderol. I wanted to know why certain things had happened in the past, how things worked, and why people acted as they did as a species and as individuals—and what the great thinkers had to say about those subjects, which, of course, were history, philosophy, the physical and social sciences, and literature.

I took a number of classes at Washington University, including a creative writing class taught by Jarvis Thurston, a wonderful short story writer and editor of the national literary quarterly *Perspective.* Thurston, who was in his late fifties, was married to the poet Mona Van Duyn, who co-edited *Perspective* with him. Both of them were very encouraging, and I found Thurston's excitement about literature infectious. He taught me that reading and writing were inseparable and that a reader should read as a writer wrote and intended—or that the act of reading was as creative in its way as was the act of writing. I attended the workshop for the year and a half left of my enlistment.

A few months before my discharge, friends told me about the Writers Workshop at the University of Iowa. I mentioned it to Jarvis after the next workshop meeting. He smiled and told me that he and Mona had taught there and he would be happy to send a letter of recommendation for me. Coincidences seemed to be pointing me in a definite direction, and I decided to let them carry me along. "Besides," Thurston said, "Mona and I have accepted one of your poems for *Perspective.* So you're now a nationally published writer, and Paul loves having published writers in the workshop."

And so he did. With Jarvis' letter in one hand and my high school and Washington University transcripts in the other, Paul Engle, the director of the Writers' Workshop, walked my admissions form through the registrar's office at the State University of Iowa and found me a place to live.

On a hot, humid August day in 1958, my discharge papers and college acceptance forms on the seat beside me, I drove my Volkswagen beetle north along the western shore of the Mississippi River to Iowa and the life of a bona fide writer.

*

My three years at Iowa was a period of great change, not only because of my studies, but because I was married the previous spring. I had met Wilma Kantrowich during the fall of my senior year of prep school. She was two years younger than I and an intelligent, aspiring dancer. She was intrigued by my knowledge of dance, music, books, and art in general. She had never met a boy who knew about art, particularly dance. We corresponded and began to date when I came home during the holidays, and we continued writing each other almost daily when I was in the Air

Force. Her intelligence, our mutual commitment to the arts, and our intimate rapport led to our marriage a few months before my discharge.

The apartment Engle had found us in Iowa City belonged to the poets Don Finkel and Constance Urdang, who were leaving town. I had read a number of Don's poems in literary journals and enthusiastically accepted his invitation to dinner and his advice as we sat around the table. Two things he said have allowed me to avoid many mental and emotional pitfalls in my writing life. First he warned me to beware of competition and second he urged me to continue writing without regard to whether I was a good writer. From what Don and Connie said I realized that writing was a solitary, individual undertaking in which one could not compete with another. In the same way, one didn't have to be a "good writer" since one could only write what one wrote and goodness or badness had nothing to do with a writer's undertakings—only the desire (or the need) to perform the act of writing was important, and performing it to the best of one's ability.

I entered Iowa as an undergraduate in English but was allowed to attend the graduate poetry workshop. In a way, it was like having the best of two worlds. But if my experiences in my undergraduate studies in Iowa were more than I had expected, the writers' workshop proved to be much less.

I had come to the Poetry Workshop thinking I would learn the secrets of writing I had not been able to discover on my own. What I found instead were several teachers and their acolytes rigidly promulgating assumptions about what constituted a successful poem. Iowa had become a bastion of what was termed at the time "academic poetry"—a poetry that was founded on closed forms and was almost entirely concerned with technique. Not only sonnets but such forms as sestinas and villanelles were held in high regard by the powers that be. Students experimenting with free forms were not only frowned upon but derided in class—if their poems were discussed at all.

Technique wasn't the only area of the workshop's concerns. There was an unspoken rule that subject matter and theme should be impersonal and non-controversial. Most of the poems, therefore, were about scenes, characters, or stories from Greek and Roman mythology, fairy tales, and the Bible, from which the poet would make ironic and/or insightful comments. Visionary poetry or ecstatic utterances were not fit subjects for discussion.

Although these guidelines would loosen somewhat in the early 1960s, when Anne Sexton, Robert Lowell, and W. D. Snodgrass published the first books of confessional poetry, I found the limited scope of the workshop depressing. I was relishing my new friends and all my other classes at Iowa except the one I had come to the university to attend. In the end, the situation in the workshop acted as a catalyst that made me confront my reasons for writing. Certainly I didn't want to write about the Greek gods or comment about Biblical tales. And witty irony was no more a part of my writing than it was of my personality.

By the end of my first two months at Iowa, I had decided to work in free verse, writing in an informal, conversational American idiom. My subject matter would be taken from common everyday life and I would elevate the ordinary to the marvelous, as if in my poetry I was uncovering a glittering diamond buried in a clump of mud. This thematic direction was pursued more than understood by me for years to come, but attendant with it was a grasping for the visionary over the insightful, the intuitive over the rational, and the resultant poems were rendered in a non-rational imagery that welled up from I knew not where in my psyche—an imagery that would be called by others surreal, subconscious, "deep," and heaven knows what else.

The best thing about any creative workshop is the people you meet there. They are usually your own age and as dedicated to writing as you are. Soon you and several classmates are meeting outside class, discussing writers and writing, trading manuscripts, and commenting on each other's work. The relationships are many times the most intense, long-lasting, and artistically satisfying you will ever have.

It was no different in Iowa. There were five of us who liked the direction and quality of each other's work. We got to talking individually or in groups and finally began to meet regularly in the student union cafeteria after Monday's class, where we would rehash what had just transpired in the workshop. After several cups of coffee, we would wander downtown to Kenny's Bar where we would meet with others and talk writing and

politics for the rest of the evening. Although I was the only undergraduate in the writers' workshop, most of us were Korean vets on the G.I. bill. We were not naïve kids but men in our early to mid-twenties, who were questioning everything about the tranquil, buttoned-down world of America in the 1950s.

*

Since I had a 4.0 average from my classes at Washington University, I was admitted to Iowa as an honor student, which, under a new policy, encouraged me to visit any professor in his office at any time for private conferences. It was this part of my stay at Iowa that far exceeded my expectations. I took philosophy classes from an as yet unknown Richard Popkin, and made an intensive study of Chinese civilization under Professor Mei Yi Pao, the world's foremost authority on Mo Tzu. I had gone to his office to inquire about a Chinese literature course and come away minoring in Chinese civilization.

As an undergraduate, I was expected to take a number of required courses. One of them, geology, was a revelation, and accounted for one of the most memorable and important experiences of my life. The head of the department, knowing my presence in the "famous" workshop and my position as honor student, asked me if I would like to take his field geology course in place of the second semester of introduction to geology. The second half his class, he said, would be spent outdoors, digging up fossils. I didn't hesitate to say yes.

The first day in the field was sunny, but a late winter chill was still in the air. We drove in a school bus to a farm outside Cedar Rapids. The rusted barbed wire fence on the gate proclaimed KEEP OUT—STATE PROPERTY, but the state had leased the land to a farmer.

The professor unlocked the gate and herded the fifteen of us onto a stony wagon path that hadn't been used in years. Sparse patches of grass had grown down the middle of the track, and we followed it for several hundred yards, when it curved downward, below the level of the ground, descending for a hundred feet or so into a quarry with a muddy green pond at the bottom.

We trudged down the path, leaving the sunlight and the upper world behind us. It was shadowy and chilly, and most of us had stopped talking before we reached the quarry floor. We were surrounded on all sides by a giant wall.

"Okay," said the professor. "I want you to line up against the wall, facing me." He waited until we did. "Now this is what we've been talking about in class that many of you doubted was true. Ready? I want you to turn around and look at the wall."

We did as he instructed. I actually gasped and heard the same reaction from several others. I was facing a gray wall of compacted bushes and sea creatures, and the pattern of animal remains and vegetation continued from the floor of the quarry for as far up as I could see.

As we watched transfixed, the professor continued to talk. "As I said in class, Iowa was once part of a tropical inland sea. What you are looking at—and standing in the middle of—is a reef 400 million years old that's crammed with fossils. A hundred years ago this was a limestone quarry that the owners had to abandon because of all these little buggers. It was a nuisance to them, but a goldmine to geologists. We'll be visiting five or six more quarries like this, but now, to work. I want you. . . ."

I was entranced, and the professor's words whirled away in the vortex of time. I recalled the naturalist Loren Eiseley descending a narrow cave on the Great Plains, each footstep down taking him thousands of years back in the earth's history. It was a mystical experience for Eiseley, and I realized that the descent into the quarry was a mystical experience for me. Suddenly time, that ungraspable dimension, was palpable. I felt claustrophobic, hemmed in by the immensity of the time trapped in the wall around me. One hundred feet of wall equaled hundreds of millions of years. In many ways, I was standing nose to nose with my ancestors, creatures who would eventually crawl onto land and stand erect in the thin air. I felt like a flyspeck, less than a blink of dust in the scheme of things. My ego deflated like a punctured balloon.

I worked for the next six hours in a daze, breaking open rocks and exposing the fossils of trilobites and other ancient sea animals.

That evening I brought eight of my cronies to the quarry, a half-drunk squadron of poets and fiction writers carrying several six-packs of beer. We scrambled over the barbed wire, ripping our clothes and hands, and made our way, stumbling and traipsing, arms cradling the six-packs, down the gravel road to the quarry. When we reached the bottom, I lined the motley crew up against the wall in the dimming light, and as the professor had done, told them to turn around. Again, as the class had earlier in the day, several of my friends gasped, but then all of them stood silently and marveled. Though covered in a darkening layer of shadow, the details of the reef were still visible. A few of my friends went up to the wall and ran their fingers along the edges of the fossils. Soon all of them were running their palms over the contours, caressing the wall as they would a woman.

Slowly the light drained from the quarry and soon we were all talking at once, opening the beers, and becoming more and more boisterous as darkness enveloped the quarry and our voices echoed across the black pond. It seemed as if we were trying to dispel the eerie atmosphere and the pervasive chilliness around us. Then someone said, "Hey, look up," and we turned our gazes skyward to see a scattering of stars above the quarry's small rounded opening. I shivered. I felt I was at the bottom of a well looking up at eternity spreading far beyond my gaze and the limitations of my vision. Several of the guys let out wild whoops, and one began a drunken stomping dance. All of us joined in, and I suddenly conceived of us as prehistoric men living in a primeval world, dancing in fear and celebration at the immensity of our ignorance in the cosmic scheme of things, which at the same time we felt an integral part of. . . .

What I learned that day, more immediately than any book could have told me, was the immense span of geologic time and humankind's infinitesimally small place in it. One could say that I came away with a view not of human but of cosmic history. This vision, if I may be so bold as to call it that, was to inform the themes of my writing and can be seen in both the selection and treatment of my subject matter and the very conception of my imagery and metaphors. It would become the foundation of my thinking. Although this notion can be seen continually surfacing throughout my work, it is most clearly stated in the poem "My Aloneness," which is the opening poem of my 2002 poetry collection, *Shouting down the Silence*.

*

By the spring semester of my third year at Iowa I was getting ready to graduate. My grades put me in the top ten percent of my class, I made Phi Beta Kappa, and the professors in the English department had nominated me for a Woodrow Wilson fellowship, which I easily won. Although I had planned to do graduate work at Iowa in Chinese studies, the terms of the Fellowship insisted I do my graduate studies at another college. Hoping to continue my Chinese studies at Columbia or the University of California at Berkeley, I almost offhandedly applied for admission to Stanford as well. Ironically, Stanford was the only one of the three that deigned to answer my inquiries. I had applied there for admission in English literature rather than Chinese studies, and this simple, absent-minded mistake determined the future course of my career.

A month later, Wilma and I packed our little Volkswagen with our few belongings and headed for California. Although we didn't know it, Wilma was pregnant with our first child, a girl we would name Jana.

After a year at Stanford, Wilma, the baby, and I lived in northern California and New York City before settling in San Francisco in 1965, when I was hired as English and history teacher and sometime basketball coach at Lick Wilmerding high school. I also set up regular visits to the school by local writers. But Lick didn't occupy all my time during the three years I taught there. I was writing steadily and publishing in journals throughout the country, and during the spring of 1966, I began to organize poetry readings with two other poets at the I-Thou Coffee Shop in the Haight Ashbury district of the city.

More important, I was one of the original group that founded the Artists Liberation Front, an organization that was attempting to stop both censorship and centralization of the arts in San Francisco. I became vice chair of the Neighborhoods Committee, which was headed by George Hitchcock, an actor, playwright, poet and activist who had started publishing *Kayak* magazine the year before. In time, he would publish not only my poems regularly but my first book as well.

Among the many things the committee did was put on art festivals around the city and seek out neighborhood arts groups and encourage them to organize. I

Teaching high school, 1967

was living in the largely Latino Mission district and found a group of painters, musicians, and poets at the community center, and helped them organize into a Latino arts group. At the same time I organized the first neighborhood performance of the Front, which consisted of bilingual readings by Latino and Anglo poets as well as jazz music and a recitation by a Gaucho poet from Argentina who was living in the Mission.

I met many members of the San Francisco arts community through my association with the Front, a number of whom I asked to read at the coffee shop as well as at Lick. One person was a Yugoslav professor of literature who was in the United States on a Fulbright fellowship. He asked if he could read translations he had made from the work of the Yugoslav poet Vasko Popa. I thought it would be a novel event, and I accepted. Would I look over the translations and "brush them up," the professor then asked? I shrugged a disinterested acceptance, but when I read the poems I underwent one of those moments archaeologists must experience when they unexpectedly discover a treasure-laden tomb or lost civilization. Even in their awkward English renditions, the originality of the poems struck a response in me that poems seldom do.

Popa wrote sequences of short, ten-to-sixteen-line poems that took their direction from riddles and, I discovered later, Serbian folk tales. Poems from one sequence in particular, "Games," set me off on a three-month explosion of writing, which turned out to be a sequence in itself, and, within the year, my first book, *Origins*. From that point on, half my work has been conceived of in sequences. Popa had entered my consciousness. Several years later, he would enter my life.

The coffee shop was jammed for every performance, and I was learning more about organizing and publicizing with each event I put on. I was also being invited to give readings of my own in other venues in the Haight and in different parts of the city, and I gave a number of readings at different city libraries.

The Artist Liberation Front meetings took place at the Fillmore Auditorium on Monday nights, when the rock and roll palace was closed. Bill Graham, its owner and entrepreneur, was on the steering committee. The meetings were tumultuous and more emotionally exhausting every week. Fewer and fewer people were in attendance from one meeting to the next, and the group dwindled from three hundred to less than fifty. Finally, I stopped going regularly, then did not go at all. In January 1967, I received a phone call inviting me to a goodbye party for the Front; the organization was disbanding. The party would be a "gathering of the tribes," the caller said, mostly the original members and a "few friends" of the organization.

When I arrived at the Polo Grounds in Golden Gate Park that afternoon of January 14, 1967, an unexpected sight greeted me. The "few friends" had turned out to be 20,000 people, painted, costumed, wearing garishly colored tie-dyed shirts and paisley-patterned blouses and trousers. Jefferson Airplane played, Allen Ginsberg and Lawrence Ferlinghetti read, and Jerry Rubin, Timothy Leary, and others spoke, as the crowd passed around food, drugs, and drink.

I stood on a slope overlooking the Polo Fields with several friends from the Front, and we stared speechless at the masses of people below, a crazy-quilt patchwork of colors. "Well, I guess we did it," one of us finally said. I nodded. What we had tried to do—ignite the minds and souls of the country to new political, social, and cultural possibilities—seemed to be rising like a phoenix out of the ashes of the Front's demise. The next day the newspapers described the gathering as a "be-in." It was the first one. Woodstock wouldn't happen until two years later.

The be-in at the polo fields signaled more than the end of the Artists Liberation Front. It was also the beginning of the end of the creative explosion known as the Haight Ashbury years, as well as my stay in San Francisco. The following year I moved to Santa Cruz, California, where I had been offered a job teaching English at Cabrillo College. There were four of us now, Wilma, Jana, me, and a new daughter, Valerie.

*

In 1968 Santa Cruz was still a small, rural county, hugging the California coast seventy miles south of San Francisco, and extending twenty miles inland through a landscape of mountains and redwood forests.

Most of Santa Cruz's population consisted of farmers, fishermen, shop workers, and retirees. The only industries were the food freezing and canning factories and apple storage barns in Watsonville and south county, and the Wrigley gum and Lipton tea factories on the outskirts of the town of Santa Cruz.

But cosmopolitan changes were already taking place by the time Wilma and I and our two daughters arrived. In 1965 the University of California had opened its ninth campus on the old Henry Cowell ranchero above the town of Santa Cruz, and, more important, the county had established a community college in 1961 whose administrators and teachers were actively changing the political, social, and cultural world of the county.

Wilma and I wanted to live by the sea, but we found an idyllic rental high in the Santa Cruz Mountains. It was well off the road, part of an undeveloped forty-acre parcel owned by an old couple who lived in a small house at the front of the property. Our house, set against a redwood grove, had been the main house when the owners were young and raising a family.

The rest of the property consisted of dirt roads and gravel paths that continued onto thousands of uninhabited acres of county water-table land and second-growth forest. There were no fences or boundary markers in the shadowy woods, and I was free to wander wherever I liked in the uphill-downhill landscape that occasionally opened on an upland meadow and led, in one direction, to an abandoned quarry that fell more than a thousand feet in three tiers and resembled, even with its rusty machinery, the ruins of an ancient civilization.

After tentatively exploring the edges of this world, I plunged deeper and deeper into it, spending whole days wandering through it alone or taking six-year-old Jana or Wilma with me for short walks. Soon I was taking long hikes alone, carrying a light backpack filled with sandwiches and bottles of water or wine, and after the first poems announced themselves in my head, I added a spiral notebook to my gear.

The word "announced" is carefully chosen here because I was not writing the poems, but hearing them—in many cases fully written—in my head. The whole process was very mysterious, and at times frightening. But I gave myself up to whatever was happening to me. At times I would sit on a lichen-covered tree trunk and watch the play of light and shadow or observe the animal life—birds and deer mostly—that would go about their business unconcerned after I had remained still for a while. At other times I would nap, jolting awake at voices that seemed to whisper from the wind or mutter from the mulch of leaves that carpeted the trails and hillsides around me. At such times I would grab the notebook and write what I "heard."

Am I being fanciful here or giving in to poetic delusion? Whatever the situation I was experiencing, that was the impetus that accounted for hundreds of short, Chinese- and haiku-like poems in the next three years, and, more important, put me intimately in touch with, I still like to think, a mysterious element in my surroundings. The novelist James D. Houston defined it as my discovery of nature, and I'm sure he's correct. As a city boy, even though I attended schools in the countryside outside Manhattan, I was living in a closeness with nature in Santa Cruz I had never experienced before.

In 1971 I chose the best of the poems I had been writing for the past three years and arranged them in a sequential order approximating a day-long walk through the mountains that simultaneously was a trip through a year, and I shaped the group into a manuscript I called *The Santa Cruz Mountain Poems.* There is no doubt that in the poems I was further purifying my notions of language that had occurred in the unpunctuated poems of *Origins,* and was employing Popa's practice of sequencing to a greater degree than in the earlier book, although those concerns were unconscious at the time and the final work was nothing I could have imagined when I began "recording" the forest voices.

My second year at Cabrillo I founded a poetry series that brought poets to campus who had published at least one book. George Hitchcock was the first poet I chose. He drove from the San Francisco, participated in a gathering of four English classes, and gave a reading. In the course of his meeting with classes, he was asked what writing meant to him. He said he wrote to achieve heightened consciousness for as many minutes or hours as he could each day. That statement reminded me of the beginning of a Richard Eberhart poem I repeated to myself over and over almost daily: "If I could only live at the pitch that is near madness." Hitchcock's quest for heightened consciousness struck me as the precise rendering of that line in two words, and I have used the phrase ever since to explain my pursuit of the creative life.

Through my contacts in the literary world, I soon had more poets requesting readings than I could handle. In addition to old friends from San Francisco, there were poets on tour from all over the country, such as Robert Bly, Charles Simic, Galway Kinnell, Allen Ginsberg, John Logan and a number of others whose names were a veritable roll call of the best American poets of the 1970s and 1980s.

In the spring of 1970, Vasko Popa came to America. I was his West Coast host for the State Department. Not only did he give a memorable reading at Cabrillo and spend a week with me, but I arranged for him to read at the University of California at Berkeley and meet Czeslaw Milosz, the Polish poet in-exile who would eventually win the Nobel Prize.

The following year, I began organizing readings in downtown Santa Cruz, after realizing how many first-rate writers and emerging young writers lived in the area. My idea was to have two local writers present their work one night each week in a local restaurant, one of them an established author, the other, a young writer just beginning to publish. All who read received a meal for two and all the wine or beer they could drink, a deal I worked out at the three restaurants where the readings were held over the next five years. Crowds packed the premises every week.

It was a time of extraordinary creative energy in Santa Cruz, with painting, theater and handicrafts thriving, as well as the literary arts. I made friends among all the groups and would give occasional readings at

The author in the early 1970s

potters' sheds while they worked, and regular readings at the Big Creek pottery school, at that time the biggest ceramics school in the world. I also experimented with presenting poetry and dance, although not with Wilma. She and I were divorced in 1971. Luckily, she remained in Santa Cruz and I was able to see my daughters every weekend. My experiments in dance culminated in an epic work for theater called *The Eight Ecstasies of Yaeko Iwasaki,* which had two successful runs on the West Coast in 1985.

In 1972 Noel Young at Capra Press published my second and third books, *Where The Oceans Cover Us,* a selection of published poems written before and after *Origins,* and *The Santa Cruz Mountain Poems,* lavishly illustrated with drawings on every page by Gary Brown who had done the illustrations for *Origins.*

Poetry wasn't all I was writing, however. Over the years I have enjoyed reading well-written mysteries and novels of intrigue. I think some of the best contemporary fiction is produced in those genres. In the spring of 1979, someone challenged me to write a thriller of my own. I think that's how it happened anyway. Whatever the impetus, I attacked the project with gusto. I had enough material from a five-month trip to Greece in 1975 to place the piece in an exotic setting. "What if?" I said to myself the first morning I sat down to write. "What if someone I knew from America approached me in Athens and . . . ?" It was an old ploy, but within fifteen minutes I had the entire plot of the novel sketched out. I knew that genre fiction was driven by plot, but at this point I set myself a problem I have never abandoned in writing fiction: namely, that although the story line may be the main concern of a genre novel, the work must seem as if the characters are causing the various events to happen because of their personalities, interests, or, more simply, their moral failings or strengths.

The writing was easier than I had imagined. Guided by a rule I had learned from poet and fellow classmate in Iowa, George Keithley, I made sure I wrote at least one page every day (George had pointed out that writing a novel seemed less daunting if one wrote at least a page a day, since that meant one would complete 365 pages in a year, and if one wrote two pages a day, 730 pages).

I followed the same regimen every morning, dressing, exercising, and eating at the same time, and reading the last one or two pages I had written the previous day before I began to work. I wasn't concerned with style, and strictly forbade myself any polishing or rewriting. I just concentrated on getting the material on paper. As a result, I finished the novel in six weeks, having rewritten it not once but three times during that period.

On a night out in San Francisco a week later, I told my friend Leonard Gardner, the author of *Fat City,* about the novel, and without looking at a word of it, he called a highly placed Hollywood agent, urging him to read it. Two weeks later, the agent sold the book, now titled *The Brezhnev Memo,* to a big New York publishing house for $20,000. With that money I took my daughters to Europe, letting them choose where they wanted to go. Valerie, then twelve, chose Germany; and Jana, sixteen, Italy. It was a memorable trip for the three of us, made just before both girls blossomed into young adulthood and became preoccupied with their own lives.

Writing fiction had taken me away from poetry for over a year. At the request of a small publisher, I collected the best of the verse I had written between 1972 and 1979, and he brought it out under the title *Big Winds, Glass Mornings, Shadows Cast by Stars* in 1981. The same publisher had brought out a small book of prose poem experiments in 1977. Other than that, I wrote no poetry between 1979 and 1981, and found I had gone longer without writing than at any time since high school. My creative impulses were further stifled by the burden of teaching new classes and correcting student papers—a predicament I had sworn years before I would not allow to happen.

To curb the situation, I set up another self-imposed, what I considered "artificial," writing regimen in the spring of 1981. I would rise at 6 A.M., eat a small breakfast, and write whatever came into my head from 6:30 to 8:30, when I would get ready for my 9 A.M. class. At the end of the second week, I realized I was writing about different aspects of my family's immigration to the United States and my growing up as a first-generation American. By the fall I had completed the rough draft of a book, *Pages from a Scrapbook of Immigrants.* Not surprisingly, the book turned out to be a sequence. Maybe less surprising in light of the fiction writing I had been doing since 1979, the poems were narrative in approach, although each one concentrated on the lyric moment within a narrative event.

I wrote and rewrote the poems for the next seven years, and Coffeehouse Press published the book in 1988. I was elated, and thought for a while that my entire writing career had been a training period that had prepared me to write my family's history in this way. So strong was this notion that I even considered that by writing the book I had fulfilled my purpose as a poet and I would never write a poem again.

*

In the course of the seven years leading to the publication *Pages from A Scrapbook of Immigrants,* I had remarried and, with Donna Mekis and her young son, Nick, I finally found a stability I had never known before. I have been absorbed into her family of six brothers and sisters and a long line of Croatian aunts and uncles in Watsonville as well as in the old country, which we've visited a handful of times, and she and

Marcus and wife Donna, 1984

Nick have become integral parts of my daughters' lives and my family's in New York. Nick and my daughters are like brother and sisters, and Donna is a confidante to both girls. Meanwhile, I became more and more involved in school politics and finally became president of the union.

During this time I also became a film historian and critic and wrote a television history of film in sixteen episodes, which has been shown on numerous cable TV channels and was for some years the main visual history of film at the Australian National Film School where I lectured several times while on a poetry reading tour of Australia in 1989.

That was not all. I had come to realize that all my actions over the years had been directed to community affairs, and that I had even conceived of my art as a communal undertaking, since I had almost unconsciously chosen a community of ordinary men and women as my readership. My work, I hoped, would enrich their lives by making them acutely aware of their neighbors, their surroundings and their place in the universal scheme of things.

I was only mildly interested in the prose poem when I published *The Armies Encamped in the Fields beyond the Unfinished Avenues* in 1977 The brilliant ink drawings by Futzi Nutzle, at that time a featured artist in *Rolling Stone,* enlivened what amounted to a chapbook of experiments. But when I was asked to write a long review of a collection of prose poems in 1992, everything changed. There is no doubt that my writing such a detailed piece forced me to look at ramifications of the prose poem I had been unwilling or too lazy to see before. Many of the things I said about the book I was reviewing, I discovered, allowed me to verbalize my own practices and concerns and to recognize directions in my work I had either half developed or hadn't pursued. Two of the most important realizations were that my work had veered toward the parable ever since I had first put pen to paper all those years ago in high school, but I had ignored that impulse to write in an accepted form of poetry. As I said in an interview several years later in the *Bloomsbury Review:*

> When I first immersed myself in the prose poem in the early 1990s, I discovered freedoms I had been unaware I could attain until then. Another way of putting this is that while writing prose poems I discovered restrictions in lined poetry I hadn't known existed. I had learned early on that the way poets of the past had solved the problems of getting from one line to another determined the way that I did. They had shown me the way(s), so to speak, in their poems. But I also found that the line in closed verse determined how I used language and how I conceived of developing the structure of a poem. When I gave up closed verse for free verse, I experienced a latitude, a freedom of choice, and found a livelier, vital voice. When I gave up the line, however, I experienced new ways of seeing and saying. It was a complete turnabout of traditional ways of doing things in poetry for me. What I came to realize was that the line had inhibited my thinking process, since my choice of words and sense of structure (in terms of word choice, syntax, and overall development of the poem) was determined as much by the line as by the way I conceived of moving from one thought, image, or metaphor to another, and how, in the end, I structured the entire poem. In other words, I found content was as much determined by my using or not using the line as free verse had been in releasing me from the tried and true ways of getting from one line to another in closed verse. Thus, in getting rid of the tyranny of the line, I had also gotten rid of the baggage I had not realized came with it. The scales fell away from my eyes all right, but at the same time—joyous

surprise!—the chains fell away from my imagination, and I decided to let that shape-shifting beast guide my words and determine the structure of the poem. Ultimately my greatest discovery in writing the prose poem was its ability to free the imagination, and this freeing has everything to do with my vision as a poet, since I seek the level below consciousness from which to speak. My world is composed of funhouse-mirror distortions of reality, dream visions rooted in metaphor and symbol, which for me evoke a more resonant picture of the world than everyday realism does. Looked at another way, my choice to abandon the line has allowed me to pursue an unshackled phrase as my basic unit of rhythm, which at times extends phrases to 13 and even 15 beats before a caesura—"a sweep of words," as I wrote in *The Prose Poem: An International Journal,* "that in its unfolding opens unexpected vistas of content by releasing my imagination from conventional modes of thought which the line and other poetic devices, it seems, unconsciously dictate." At the same time, I employ all the techniques of poetry, such as figurative language, assonance, consonance, and even internal as well as end-line rhyme to drive my rhythms and energize my poems.

The result of all this thinking and verbalizing was that, several months after I wrote the article, I experienced an eruption of writing even more explosive than during the period I created *Origins* or *Pages from a Scrapbook of Immigrants.*

The pieces seemed new, fresh, exploiting language, image, and idea, as I never had before. My imagination constantly surprised me. As usual at such times, I let my flights of fancy carry me along, not understanding what I was writing at first, but trusting the energy that was directing me. Many times I discovered that the fantastic situations and outlandish images I would put on paper were the beginning of extended metaphors, or parables that themselves, in the end, were metaphors.

While all these elements were surging to the fore of my work, humor, a constant in much of my poetry, gushed up more antic than ever, spreading in garish colors over the poems. As I said in the *Bloomsbury*

Review interview, "My predilections for the comic extend to my favorite authors: Rabelais, Cervantes, Stern, Swift, Aristophanes, Zhuang zi (Chuang Tzu), Rumi of the *Mathnawi,* and the folk hero Nasrudin. I'm drawn to the holy fools, the cosmic clowns and idiot savants, not just for their boisterous, fun-loving, and at times scathingly sardonic attitudes toward humanity and the bumbling ways of the universe, but because they upset our habitual ways of seeing the world, show us new perspectives by presenting us with the unexpected, and destroy our comfortable expectations and conventional values so we will once again encounter the world in fresh ways, renewed." It is interesting to note that most of the writers I listed in that quotation speak in parables and extended metaphors.

My prose poems took many forms. Some were outlandish satires of travel books, historical monographs, and saints' tales. I wrote on an enormous range of subjects, and literally, as the poet Jack Marshall said, "constructed a private universe."

I sent the new poems to Peter Johnson, who had just started *The Prose Poem: An International Journal.* Peter, a fine prose poet himself, so appreciated what I was doing that he included my new prose poems in every issue of the journal, asked me to do a long review of Russell Edson's selected prose poems, *The Tunnel,* and made me an contributing editor of the journal. He also invited me for a three-day visit to speak at Providence College, the university at which he taught.

In what seemed quick succession, Hanging Loose Press began accepting a number of the prose poems for their magazine and brought out an entire book of them in 1997 under the title *When People Could Fly.* New Rivers Press included two of the pieces in its definitive anthology of North American prose poetry, *The Party Train,* and asked to do a book of my selected poems two years later. That book, which came out with White Pine Press in 2002, was called *Moments without Names.* Later that year Creative Arts Book Company published *Shouting down the Silence,* a selection of verse poems written since the *Immigrants* book came out.

Long forgotten was my notion that I had written my last poem with the end of *Pages from a Scrapbook of Immigrants.* I felt more like a moth who rose from its

The author in Prague, 2003

cocoon to find it was a radiant butterfly. But all this didn't mean that I was abandoning the verse poem. On the contrary, I am writing both prose and lined poetry on a regular basis.

*

My mother came to live near me in 1995. For the first time we got to know each other. One of the turnabouts was that she had to depend on me in her last years, and was surprised to find someone she could both rely on and trust. Her sharpness of mind, charisma and sense of humor delighted everyone she met. She also got to know Donna, and loved her, I think, as she never had anyone else. The three of us spent many happy days together, and my mother and I were able to lay to rest the problems of the past.

I retired from Cabrillo in 1998, and the following year I was named Santa Cruz County Artist of the Year. Since then I have published three more books and am finishing another novel. I still host *The Poetry Show,* a radio program I've been doing since 1986, and since 1998 I have been the co-host of a movie-review television show that is broadcast in San Francisco, Santa Cruz, and most of the San Francisco Bay Area. My friends say I'm busier now than when I was teaching. I smile at that, knowing I'm just trying as much as I can each day "to live at the pitch that is near madness."

BIOGRAPHICAL AND CRITICAL SOURCES:

PERIODICALS

Bloomsbury Review, March-April, 2001, Ray Gonzalez, "In Praise of the Prose Poem: An Interview with Morton Marcus," pp. 3-4, 30.
Caesura, spring, 2000, Elliot Roberts, review of *When People Could Fly,* pp. 10-12.
Cream City Review, summer, 1988, Jerome Mazzaro, "Morton Marcus and the Ethical Lyric," pp. 30-42.
Dryad, no. 10, 1970, Gail Barnett, "Three Kayak Poets," pp. 62-66; no. 13 (Morton Marcus issue), 1975, Michael Hefernan, "The Poetry of Morton Marcus."
Kayak, summer, 1981.
Minnesota Review, winter, 1970, Vern Rutsala, review of *Origins,* pp. 262-265.
Poetry, October, 1969.
Red Wheelbarrow, spring, 2002, Ken Weisner, "An Interview with Morton Marcus."
Rolling Stone, January 18, 1973, James D. Houston, review of *The Santa Cruz Mountain Poems.*
Santa Cruz Sentinel, April 7, 2002, Wallace Blaine, "Morton Marcus Remains a Pro's Poet."
Shock, March, 1974, Andrei Codrescu, "The Mystic Twang," pp. 71-84.
Sun, November 17, 1988, Tom Maderos, "Morton Marcus's Family Portrait," p. 28.
West Coast Poetry Review, autumn-winter, 1972-73.

ONLINE

Morton Marcus Web site, http://mortonmarcus.jlmphotography.com (November 17, 2003).

*   *   *

MARIE, Rose 1923-

PERSONAL: Born Rose Marie Mazzetta, August 15, 1923, in New York, NY; married Bobby Guy (a musician), 1946 (died, 1966); children: a daughter, "Noop." *Hobbies and other interests:* Plate collector, animal rights.

ADDRESSES: Home—San Fernando Valley, CA. *Agent*—c/o Author Mail, University Press of Kentucky, 663 South Limestone St., Lexington, KY 40508-4008.

CAREER: Singer, actor, and entertainer. Actor, appearing in numerous television shows, most notably the *Dick Van Dyke Show,* 1961-66, and as a panelist on *Hollywood Squares,* 1966-81.

WRITINGS:

Hold the Roses, University Press of Kentucky (Lexington, KY), 2002.

Sound recordings include, *Top Banana,* 1993.

SIDELIGHTS: Best known for her role as Sally Rogers on the 1960s' *Dick Van Dyke Show* and as a panelist for fourteen years on *Hollywood Squares,* Rose Marie actually began her career in the 1920s at the age of three as Baby Rose Marie. Except for a brief retirement from show business during her teen years, she has worked steadily in show business, from radio and movies to theater and television. In 2002, Rose Marie's memoirs, *Hold the Roses,* was published, detailing her eight decades as a singer, actress, and comedian.

Rose Marie was born in 1923 as Rose Marie Mazzetta. At the age of three, she entered a talent contest at New York City's Mecca Theatre, in which she sang "What Can I Say Dear, After I Say I'm Sorry." Her powerful, grown-up voice impressed the judges and she won the contest. NBC radio signed the child to a contract and she became an instant radio star as "Baby Rose Marie the Child Wonder" in 1929. She also played the vaudeville circuit traveling throughout the United States. In the early 1930s she appeared as "Baby Rose Marie" in several musical shorts and films, most notably the feature film *International House* starring comedian W. C. Fields.

Unlike most child stars, who grow into puberty and find their careers are over, Baby Rose Marie simply changed her stage name to Miss Rose Marie and forged ahead with her career. During the 1940s she sang in clubs throughout the country, from New York

City's famous Copacabana and Latin Quarter clubs to Las Vegas, where she opened at the first luxury casino, the Flamingo, with co-headliners Jimmy Durante and Xavier Cugat. Her fame and popularity was so widespread that the famous Glenn Miller Orchestra played at her sixteenth birthday party while crooner Tony Martin serenaded her.

In the 1950s Rose Marie began to work as a character actor, primarily on stage. She costarred on Broadway with comedians Milton Berle in *Spring in Brazil* and Phil Silvers in *Top Banana*. She also appeared in the film version of *Top Banana* in 1954. The role led to subsequent film work in such movies as *Dead Heat on a Merry-Go-Round* and *Cheaper to Keep Her,* among others.

As television sitcoms began to make inroads into television, Rose Marie found a new niche in show business. In the 1950s she appeared in television shows such as *Gunsmoke* and the *Adventures of Jim Bowie* and then landed a recurring role as Bertha in the 1960 television series *My Sister Eileen.*

In 1961 Rose Marie landed the role of Sally Rogers on the classic comedy series the *Dick Van Dyke Show.* Her role as a wisecracking comedy writer for a television show who was always trying to land a man reestablished her as a household name in homes across America. The show premiered in 1961, and "Sally Rogers" was one of the first female characters on television who was a "working woman" in a decidedly "man's world."

After the show ended in 1966, Rose Marie signed on with the popular game show *Hollywood Squares,* where she spent the next fourteen years continuing to play herself in the same vein as the spinster Sally Rogers character, a wisecracking woman who was often asked age- or sex-related questions. For example, on one show she was asked, "During a tornado, are you safer in the bedroom or in the closet?" Rose Marie replied, "Unfortunately . . . I'm always safe in the bedroom."

In reality, Rose Marie led a conservative lifestyle and was happily married for twenty years to musician Bobby Guy until he died in 1966. she continued to work, appearing on many television shows and in mov-

ies, as well as touring for a time in the highly successful revue *4 Girls 4,* alongside Rosemary Clooney, Helen O'Connell, and Margaret Whiting.

In her memoir, *Stop the Roses,* Rose Marie recounts her lifelong career in show business and highlights the many working relationships and encounters she had with both the famous and the infamous. For example, she tells about playing in President Franklin D. Roosevelt's Oval Office as a child and how she once received a diamond ring from "Uncle" Al Capone, who said he would watch over her. She also knew gangster Bugsy Siegel from working in the early days of casinos in Las Vegas.

Despite her success at a young age, Rose Marie makes it clear in her book that her young life was far from perfect. Her father, a vaudeville performer who worked under the stage name of "Frank Curly," was cruel in managing her career and personal life. He routinely scared off boyfriends as she grew older for fear of losing out on his daughter's earning power. He ended up gambling away most of the money Rose Marie made as a minor.

Writing in *Publishers Weekly,* a contributor noted, "Though thin on personal commentary and insight, the book's fast pace and happy memories will please Rose Marie's fans." David Marshall James, writing in South Carolina's the *State,* noted, "With a veritable lifetime of show business credits, the author . . . has packed the pages of her memoir with unforgettable vignettes dating back to the Roaring Twenties."

In 2001 Rose Marie received a star on the Hollywood Walk of Fame. As reported by the New Jersey *Star-Ledger,* she commented, "I'm usually not speechless, but I am now."

BIOGRAPHICAL AND CRITICAL SOURCES:

BOOKS

Marie, Rose, *Hold the Roses,* University Press of Kentucky (Lexington, KY), 2002.

PERIODICALS

Publishers Weekly, October 28, 2002, review of *Hold the Roses,* p. 63.

Star Ledger (Newark, NJ), October 6, 2001, "Hollywood Tribute Leaves Rose Marie Speechless," p. O34.

ONLINE

Classic Hollywood Squares Web site, http://www.classicsquares.com/ (May 6, 2003), "Rose Marie."
Rosemary Clooney Palladium Web site, http://www.rosemaryclooney.com/ (May 6, 2003), "Rose Marie."
Rainbow Electronic Reviews, http://rainboreviews.com/ (May 6, 2003), review of *Stop the Roses.*
State online (University of South Carolina), http://www.thestate.com (January 26, 2003), David Marshall James, review of *Stop the Roses.**

*   *   *

MARIEN, Mary Warner

PERSONAL: Education: Syracuse University, Ph.D., 1978.

ADDRESSES: Office—Department of Fine Arts, Syracuse University, 308 Bowne Hall, Syracuse, NY 13244-1200. *E-mail*—mwmarien@mailbox.syr.edu.

CAREER: Historian and author. Syracuse University, Syracuse, NY, professor of history of photography and theory.

WRITINGS:

Photography and Its Critics: A Cultural History, 1839-1900, Cambridge University Press (New York, NY), 1997.
Photography: A Cultural History, Harry N. Abrams (New York, NY), 2002.

Contributor to periodicals, including the *Christian Science Monitor.*

WORK IN PROGRESS: An investigation of the women's movement in the late twentieth century and its relationship to feminist art and art theory.

SIDELIGHTS: Reviewing Mary Warner Marien's *Photography and Its Critics: A Cultural History, 1839-1900,* Paul S. MacDonald noted in the *British Journal of Aesthetics* that "She carefully distinguishes the writing of such an account from an historical survey of photography as an art form or a history of techniques." Rather, Marien's concern is the *idea* of photography itself, and in both *Photography and Its Critics* and *Photography: A Cultural History,* the author—a professor at Syracuse University in New York—addresses fundamental questions about the nature of photography itself.

As articulated by Helene E. Roberts in *Victorian Studies,* among the issues addressed in the first section of *Photography and Its Critics* are photography's "origin (was it a natural phenomenon or a human invention? if an invention, who deserved credit for it?), its nature (was it a product of science or art, technology or magic, genius or craft?), and its ability to copy (did it copy nature or human sight? was it a mirror or a window?)." Though the modern world takes photography for granted as an invention that helps record the world as people see it, the pioneers of photography had other ideas, according to MacDonald. Both Henry Fox Talbot and Jacques Daguerre, who developed the first successful photographic techniques, referred to their work as a discovery of a natural process rather than an invention. MacDonald went on to note that "One of the strong sections of Marien's book is devoted to a detailed investigation of the invention of photography's inventors."

In developing her exhaustive investigation, Marien necessarily draws on a number of related phenomena. For example, there is this passage from *Photography: A Cultural History,* quoted approvingly by Andy Grundberg in *Artforum:* "Surveys were often organized for a variety of purposes, including providing clean water to European settlers, transcribing the geology of an area, scouting routes for railroads, and recording archeological or architectural sites. Often the surveys were carried out by military engineers, who had already recognized the value of photography for determining artillery range and reproducing maps and sketches."

According to Grundberg, "While Marien is apt and to the point when discussing the nineteenth-century practices of photography, . . . the real strength of her history lies in her organized account of late-twentieth-century photography." Reviewing *Photography: A Cultural History* in *Library Journal*, Savannah Schroll maintained that Marien "winnows the abundant photography production of the mid-nineteenth to the late twentieth centuries to harvest a concise and essential chronology of the medium's technologies and aesthetics."

BIOGRAPHICAL AND CRITICAL SOURCES:

PERIODICALS

Artforum, summer, 2003, Andy Grundberg, "Camera Obscured," p. 26.
British Journal of Aesthetics, January, 1999, Paul S. MacDonald, review of *Photography and Its Critics: A Cultural History, 1839-1900*, pp. 90-92.
Choice, May, 2003, C. Stroh, review of *Photography: A Cultural History*, p. 1543.
Christian Science Monitor, July 23, 1997, Terry W. Hartle, "A Snapshot of Photography's Revolutionary Early Days," p. 13.
Library Journal, February 15, 2003, Savannah Schroll, review of *Photography: A Cultural History*, p. 134.
Victorian Studies, spring 1999-2000, Helene E. Roberts, review of *Photography and Its Critics: A Cultural History, 1839-1900*, pp. 565-567.

ONLINE

Syracuse University College of Arts and Sciences Web site, http://www-hl.syr.edu/ (September 17, 2003).

*   *   *

MARIENGOF, Anatoly Borisovich 1897-1962

PERSONAL: Born 1897, in Nizhny Novgorod (now Gorky), Russia; died 1962, in Leningrad, USSR.

CAREER: Poet, playwright, and author of criticism. Central Executive Committee publishing house, Moscow, Russia, member of staff, beginning 1918.

WRITINGS:

Magdalina, 1919.

Konditerskaya solnts (title means "Pastry Shop of the Suns"), 1919.
Bunyan-Ostrov (poetry; title means "Bunyan-Island"), 1920.
Stikhami chvanstvuyu (poetry; title means "I Show off My Poetry"), 1920.
Tuchelet (poetry; title means "Cloud Flight"), 1921.
Roman bez vran'ya (autobiography), 1927, [New York, NY], 1978, translated by José Alaniz as *A Novel without Lies*, Glas Publishers (Birmingham, England), 2000.
Tsiniki (novel; title means "Cynics"), 1928.
Brityi chelovek (title means "Shaven Man"), 1929.

Works translated and published in anthologies, including *Modern Russian Poetry*, edited by V. Markov and M. Sparks, 1967. Contributor to journals and almanacs. Editor of *Gostinitsa dlya puteshestvuyushchikh v prekrasnom*.

PLAYS

Zagovor durakov (title means "The Conspiracy of Fools"), 1922.
Dvunogie (title means "The Bipeds"), 1925.
Taras Bulba, 1940.
Malen'kie komedii (title means "Little Comedies"), 1957.
Rozhdenie poeta (title means "Birth of the Poet"), 1959.

SIDELIGHTS: Poet, playwright, and memoirist Anatoly Borisovich Mariengof was a member of the Russian Imagist school. A close friend of fellow poet and aesthete Sergei Esenin during the early part of the twentieth century led Mariengof into a bohemian lifestyle and renown as one of the foremost practitioners of imagist poetics. Known for the 1920 poetry collection *Buyan-ostrov* as well as for plays, novels, and the autobiography *Roman bez vrea'ya*, which details the author's life as a dandy, Mariengof also worked as a journalist and ended his career as a playwright in Leningrad. Describing the Russian writer as "a minor poet and dramatist, and an intriguing novelist with a style strongly influenced by early cinema," *Times Literary Supplement* contributor Lesley Chamberlain added of Mariengof that "His greatest achievement was to record in a prose saturated with memorable images (and free from ideological concerns) what it was like to be alive in the Soviet 1920s."

Banned when it was first published in 1927, *Roman bez vran'ya* was later translated into English as *A Novel without Lies,* and was described by *Library Journal* contributor Scott Hightower as "a loose collection of impressions of Mariengof's flamboyant friendship" with Esenin within the world of the "post-revolutionary Russian avant-garde."

Noting that as a poet Mariengof's "typical features are heteroaccentual rhyme and unusually long and intricate stanzas," a contributor to the *Handbook of Russian Literature* maintained that the poet focused on such themes as the Russian revolution, love, sex, urban society, and violence. Leaving poetry behind in 1928, the thirty-one-year-old writer moved to Leningrad, where he wrote for the Soviet cinema and authored such stage plays as *Taras Bulba* and *Rozhdenie poeta* prior to his death in 1962 at age sixty-five.

BIOGRAPHICAL AND CRITICAL SOURCES:

BOOKS

Terras, Victor, editor, *Handbook of Russian Literature,* Yale University Press (New Haven, CT), 1985, p. 274.

PERIODICALS

Library Journal, November 15, 2000, Scott Hightower, review of *A Novel without Lies,* p. 68.
London Review of Books, March 7, 2002, Tony Wood, "I'm with the Imagists," p. 19.
Times Literary Supplement, August 2, 2002, Lesley Chamberlain, "The Hooligan Years," p. 21.*

*   *   *

MARIE-VICTORIN, Frère 1885-1944

PERSONAL: Born Conrad Kirouac, April 3, 1885, in Kingsey Falls, Québec, Canada; died in an automobile accident July 15, 1944; son of Cyrille (a grain merchant) and Philomène (Luneau) Kirouac. *Education:* University of Montreal, Ph.D., 1922. *Religion:* Roman Catholic.

CAREER: Secondary school teacher, Mont-de-la-Salle de Maisonneuve seminary and elsewhere; College de Longueuil, 1905-44; University of Montreal, Montreal, Quebec, Canada, professor of botany, 1920-44. Member, Biological Board of Canada, 1927; Canadian representative, Congress of the Pacific, 1933, 1939; cofounder, Cercles des Jeunes Naturalistes, 1931, and L'Eveil (nature school for preschoolers), 1935; founder, Jardin Botanique de Montreal (Botanical Gardens of Montreal), 1939.

MEMBER: Association Catholique de la Jeunesse Canadienne, Association Canadienne pour l'Avancement des Sciences (cofounder, 1924), Société Canadienne d'Histoire Naturelle (cofounder, 1924), British Association for the Advancement of Sciences.

AWARDS, HONORS: Royal Society of Canada fellow, 1924; Societe Botanique de France fellow, 1932; Prix Coincy, French Academy of Sciences, 1935, for *Flore laurentienne.*

WRITINGS:

La flore du Témiscouata: mémoire: sur une nouvelle exploration botanigue de ce comté de la province de Québec, Laflamme (Montreal, Quebec, Canada), 1916.
Récits laurentiens, Frères des Écoles Chrétiennes (Montreal, Quebec Canada), 1919, translated by James Ferres as *The Chopping Bee and Other Laurentian Stories,* Musson (Toronto, Ontario, Canada), 1925.
Croquis laurentiens, Frères des Écoles Chrétiennes (Montreal, Quebec, Canada), 1920.
Les filicinees du Québec, Populaire (Montreal, Quebec, Canada), 1923.
Charles le Moyne; Drame canadien en trois actes, Frères des Écoles Chrétiennes (Montreal, Quebec, Canada), 1925.
Peuple sans histoire fantaisie; dramatigue en un acte et trois tableaux, Frères des Écoles Chrétiennes (Montreal, Quebec, Canada), 1925.
Flore laurentienne, Imprimerie de la Salle (Montreal, Quebec, Canada), 1935.
(With Frère Léon) *Itinéraires botaniques daps file de Cuba,* 3 volumes, Frères des Écoles Chrétiennes (Montreal, Quebec, Canada), 1942, 1944, 1956.
(With Frère Rolland-Germain) *Flore de l'Anticosti-Minganie,* Presses de l'Université de Montréal (Montreal, Quebec, Canada), 1969.

Pour l'amour du Québec, edited by Hernias Bastien, Éditions Paulines (Sherbrooke, Ontario, Canada),1971.

Confidence et combat: lettres, 1924-1944, edited by Gifies Beaudet, Lidec (Montreal, Quebec, Canada), 1969.

Marie-Victorin's scientific correspondence is held by the University of Montréal.

SIDELIGHTS: A French-Canadian botanist and literary figure, Frère Marie-Victorin helped to establish the place of science—formerly neglected in favor of the humanities—in French-Canadian higher education. His greatest work, *Flore laurentienne* (1935), classifies and names the botanical species of the St. Lawrence valley. He was also a tireless popularizer of science and founded several programs to encourage children's scientific curiosity, as well as establishing the city of Montreal's botanical gardens.

Born Conrad Kirouac to Cyrille and Phiomene Kirouac, Marie-Victorin and his family moved from Kingsey Falls in Québec to Québec City. He attended primary school in St.-Saveur and secondary school at the Academie Commercials de Québec, which was run by the Christian Brother at the time Catholic religious orders dominated education in French-speaking Canada.

Kirouac took the name Marie-Victorin when he joined the religious order of the Christian Brothers (Frères Chretiennes) in 1901 and entered the Mont-de-la-Salle de Maisonneuve seminary. Although he had not received a diploma, he began to teach at the Brothers' schools, and after several brief posts, he settled permanently in Longueuil, just across the St. Lawrence River from Montreal, in 1905. Marie-Victorin was diagnosed with tuberculosis in 1903, and his interest in botany began when he began to take walks around the St. Lawrence River, at the recommendation of his doctor. He took his students on field trips to study local vegetation and began to study botany with other interested members of his religious order. Through his walks and studies, he became well acquainted with local plants and with the principles of scientific methodology.

In 1908 Marie-Victorin began to publish as a botanist, and in the next dozen years published more than forty papers. During this period, he also published three books: his first book on botany, *La flore du Temiscouata: memoire sur une nouvelle exploration botanigue de ce comte de la province Québec* (1916). His short story collection, *Recits Laurentiens* (1919), translated as *The Chopping Bee and Other Laurentian Stories,* drew from childhood memories, and he also wrote a book of essays about natural sites in Québec titled *Croguis laurentiens* (1920). Each of these works, as Michel Gaulin pointed out in the *Dictionary of Literary Biography,* "evince a talent for the close observation and meticulous attention to detail which is the hallmark of the later Flore Laurentienne."

When the University of Montreal was founded, along with the first French-Canadian science faculty, Marie-Victorin secured a position as associate professor of botany. Because he did not have a university degree, he submitted as part of his application a study of the ferns of Québec as a doctoral thesis. Thus Marie-Victorin not only got a job, but he also received the first doctorate awarded by the university in 1922. He held the university's chair in botany until his death, and also directed its botanical institute.

Marie-Victorin built the botanical institute on the grounds that later became the municipal Jardin Botanique de Montreal in 1939. The Jardin Botanique serves as a public garden as well as a research and teaching facility, and is considered one of Marie-Victorin's greatest accomplishments. The Jardin Botanique brought the public into contact with a wide variety of plant species as the same time that it advanced professional knowledge.

Marie Victorin was a vital figure in establishing the field of science at the university level. He helped found the Association Canadienne pour l'Avancement des Sciences and the Societe Canadienne d'Histoire Naturelle in 1924, both of which offered French-Canadian scientists a forum for discussing ideas across disciplines. His reputation attained an international stature.

At the same time, he popularized science for both adults and children, and he took part in many naturalist organizations. One of his pet projects was to promote scouting for children. He believed that children need contact with nature as much as they require more conventional studies. He was, as affirmed by Gaulin, "sensitive to the drawbacks of a purely bookish knowledge" and believed that young people "should be awakened early to the beauty and poetry of nature." The Cercles des Jeunes Naturalists movement began in 1931, largely due to his efforts, and Eveil, a nature school for preschool age children, started in 1935. Marie-Victorin also developed summer field-training programs for teachers to enable them to integrate field trips into their schools' curricula.

In 1935 Marie-Victorin published his *Flore laurentienne,* a lavishly illustrated study of the flora of the St. Lawrence Valley, in which he describes, classifies, and provides French names to about two thousand species, featured in roughly 2,800 illustrations. Gaulin called it "his most enduring work, and one which strengthened the bonds French Canadians felt to the land settled by their forebears." The work updates Abbe Leon Provancher's *Flore canadienne* (1862). Demonstrating the same attention to detail as did his earlier writings, the book won him the French Academie des Sciences' Prix Coincy.

Marie-Victorin was on his way home from a botanical expedition when he died, at the age of fifty-nine, in a car accident. While his primary achievements were in the field of botany, his contributions to the discipline of science went beyond his specialty. A *Notable Twentieth-Century Scientists* contributor called him "the most visible scientist in French Canada" for the last twenty years of his life. As scholar, naturalist, and writer he shared his enthusiasm for botany and for his native region with children and adults, laypersons and professionals, Canadians and the world.

BIOGRAPHICAL AND CRITICAL SOURCES:

BOOKS

Dictionary of Literary Biography Volume 92: *Canadian Writers, 1890-1920,* Gale (Detroit, MI), 1990, pp. 228-231.
Notable Twentieth-Century Scientists Gale (Detroit, MI), 1995, pp. 1321-1322.*

*   *   *

MARKS, Walter 1934-

PERSONAL: Born January 15, 1934, in New York, NY. *Education:* Amherst College, B.A.; attended Columbia University.

ADDRESSES: Agent—c/o Carroll and Graf Publishers, 161 William St., 16th Floor, New York, NY 10038.

CAREER: Composer and author.

WRITINGS:

The Wild Party (screenplay), 1975.
Dangerous Behavior, Carroll and Graf (New York, NY), 2002.

Also composed music for several plays, including *Bajour,* 1964, *Golden Rainbow,* 1968, *The Butler Did It,* 1980, and *Body Shop,* 1995; composed score for film *The Wild Party,* 1975. Author of lyrics for songs, including "I've Gotta Be Me" and "I Enjoy Being a Girl."

SIDELIGHTS: For most of his career, Walter Marks has worked with music, composing scores for Broadway plays and writing lyrics for such artists as Ella Fitzgerald, Sammy Davis, Jr., Steve Lawrence, Liza Minnelli, and even the Muppets. He turned to the non-lyrical when, in the 1970s, he wrote the screenplay for James Ivory and Ismail Marchant's production of *The Wild Party,* starring Raquel Welch and James Coco, about a silent movie director and his mistress and an ill-fated party. More recently, Marks has written fiction, producing a mystery novel which a *Kirkus Reviews* critic referred to as a "promising debut."

That mystery novel is *Dangerous Behavior* a psychological thriller, whose protagonist, David Rothberg, a bright but inexperienced psychiatrist, must determine if an imprisoned killer deserves to be paroled. Victor Thomas Janko, known as the Baby Carriage Killer because he murdered a young mother while her child watched from a nearby carriage, has spent fifteen years of his prison term in solitary confinement. During that time, Janko has been a model prisoner and has become a somewhat celebrated prison artist, painting realist landscapes of beaches. Although he pleaded guilty to the crime when he was tried in court, Janko now claims to have no memory of the incident; and his longtime girlfriend swears Janko is innocent. Also in his favor is the fact that some of the evidence in his case points to another potential suspect.

But not everything points to Janko's innocence. Added to the conflicting evidence that Rothberg must sort through are the remarks of some of the prison guards, who tell Rothberg that they have heard Janko brag about the crime. Rothberg has also been warned that Janko is very gifted when it comes to persuading people of his lack of guilt.

It is up to Dr. Rothberg to decide whether the accused murderer goes free, a difficult decision for even a well-seasoned psychiatrist to make. In order to gather more information, Rothberg not only convinces his boss to allow him to carry out long interviews with the prisoner, he also dons the role of crime investigator as he searches for more definitive clues that might point to another suspect. But the deeper Rothberg probes, the more confused he becomes until he reaches the point where he wonders if he suffers from paranoia. Why are there so many contradictory stories? What are the motives behind the people he interviews? What interests could they have in lying to him? The more he tries to analyze the people around him, the more he must analyze himself. The challenge begins to engulf him and eventually threatens to destroy him.

The story is "tightly written" with "considerable suspense," wrote a critic for *Kirkus Reviews*. Michael Gannon for *Booklist* suggested that Marks's book "should be popular with crime novel buffs."

BIOGRAPHICAL AND CRITICAL SOURCES:

PERIODICALS

Booklist, November 1, 2002, Michael Gannon, review of *Dangerous Behavior,* p. 477.
Kirkus Reviews, September 1, 2002, review of *Dangerous Behavior,* p. 1269.
Publishers Weekly, October 7, 2002, review of *Dangerous Behavior,* pp. 51-52.*

*   *   *

MARTIN, Robert F. 1946-

PERSONAL: Born 1946. *Education:* Wofford College, B.A.; University of North Carolina, Chapel Hill, M.A. and Ph.D.

ADDRESSES: Office—Department of History, University of Northern Iowa, Seerley 308, Cedar Falls, IA 50614-0701. *E-mail*—Robert.Martin@uni.edu.

CAREER: Historian and educator. North Carolina State University, Raleigh, assistant professor of history; University of North Carolina, Chapel Hill, instructor in history; University of Northern Iowa, Cedar Falls, professor of history, 1981—.

AWARDS, HONORS: Iowa Regents' Award for Faculty Excellence.

WRITINGS:

Howard Kester and the Struggle for Social Justice in the South, 1904-1977, University Press of Virginia (Charlottesville, VA), 1991.
Hero of the Heartland: Billy Sunday and the Transformation of American Society, 1862-1935, Indiana University Press (Bloomington, IN), 2002.

Contributor of articles and essays to periodicals.

SIDELIGHTS: A professor of history at the University of Northern Iowa, Robert F. Martin has authored several book-length studies of individuals who strove to transform the American south during the early twentieth century. In *Howard Kester and the Struggle for Social Justice in the South* he profiles a little-known civil rights leader, while in *Hero of the Heartland: Billy Sunday and the Transformation of American Society, 1862-1935* a more well-known figure is brought to life.

A Congregationalist minister based in Virginia, Howard Kester worked to advance the lives of both blacks and the rural Southern poor during the years between World Wars I and II. An idealist and socialist who defended striking coal miners and investigated lynchings of blacks for the fledgling NAACP, Kester eventually flirted with the quasi-communist Fellowship of Southern Churchmen in the mid-1930s before admitting defeat. Noting Martin's focus on Kester's "attraction to radicalism but his inability to embrace it" due to his strong religious convictions, *Journal of Southern History* contributor Melissa Kirkpatrick praised *Howard Kester and the Struggle for Social Justice in the South* for adding to readers' "understanding of the intrawar South." John Salmond praised the work in the *Journal of American History* as "a fine study of . . . a decent man who campaigned for economic and social justice in the South" before such efforts gained national attention, while in *Choice*, R. D. Ward cited the book as "more a study of Kester's intellectual journey than an analysis of the milieu in which he lived." Martin's work helps to fill "major gaps in the study of southern social activism prior to the civil rights movement," added *Reviews in American History* contributor Stewart Burns, the critic going on to praise Martin for penning an "exquisite, stirring biography" that not only "illuminates the vital role of religious commitment in southern progressive reform, but [also] . . . examines the major paths of faith-based activism and how they were shaped by personal values, cultural legacies, and social conditions."

Beginning life as an orphan, Iowa-born William Ashley "Billy" Sunday was a baseball player for the Chicago White Stockings before discovering his evangelical talents. Touring the United States after 1896, he promoted the traditional values of a nation moving toward urbanization while gripped with a nostalgia for its rural frontier past. Weaving together Sunday's meteoric rise as a charismatic speaker to the growth of Progressivism and Protestantism, in *Hero of the Heartland* Martin "does an excellent job in portraying Billy Sunday as the forerunner of contemporary televangelists," according to *H-Net* reviewer David G. Vanderstel, who praised the author for linking the rhetorical and theatrical methods used by such men and women back to "God's original heroic and 'muscular' preacher." In *Library Journal*, contributor Theresa R. McDevitt praised *Hero of the Heartland* as a "beautifully written" and "concise scholarly study" of the man often referred to as the "entrepreneurial evangelist."

BIOGRAPHICAL AND CRITICAL SOURCES:

PERIODICALS

Choice, January, 1992, R. D. Ward, review of *Howard Kester and the Struggle for Social Justice in the South*, p. 805.
Journal of American History, June, 1992, John Salmond, review of *Howard Kester and the Struggle for Social Justice in the South*, pp. 329-330.
Journal of Southern History, November, 1992, Melissa Kirkpatrick, review of *Howard Kester and the Struggle for Social Justice in the South*, p. 738.

Library Journal, October 15, 2002, Theresa R. McDevitt, review of *Hero of the Heartland: Billy Sunday and the Transformation of American Society, 1862-1935*, p. 80.
Reviews in American History, June, 1993, Stewart Burns, review of *Howard Kester and the Struggle for Social Justice in the South*, pp. 291-296.

ONLINE

H-Net Reviews, http://www2.h-net.msu.edu (January, 2003), David G. Vanderstel, "God's Man for Urban America.*"

*   *   *

MATTHAU, Carol (Grace Marcus) 1932-2003
(Carol Grace)

OBITUARY NOTICE—See index for *CA* sketch: Born September 11, 1932, in New York, NY; died of a brain aneurysm July 20, 2003, in New York, NY. Actress and author. The former wife of both author William Saroyan and actor Walter Matthau, Matthau was a well-known socialite who wrote about her debutante lifestyle in her 1992 autobiography, *Among the Porcupines: A Memoir*. After a rough start in life—she never knew her biological father and ended up in foster care while her Russian-immigrant mother worked—Matthau's luck changed when her mother married a wealthy business executive. From that time on, her life was charmed: she lived in a fancy Fifth Avenue apartment, enjoyed the best things money could afford, and attended the best schools, where she met and became friends with the likes of Gloria Vanderbilt and Oona O'Neill. She quickly developed other friendships with celebrities and artists, among them Truman Capote, Henry Miller, Cary Grant, and Isak Dinesen. She met and fell in love with Pulitzer Prize-winning novelist Saroyan while still a teenager, and the couple married in 1943. Unfortunately, according to Matthau's autobiography, Saroyan was abusive to her and they divorced; though they reconciled and remarried in 1951, this second attempt lasted only half a year. After divorcing, Matthau earned her living by acting, and she also wrote a novel, *The Secret in the Daisy* (1955), under the name Carol Grace. She met actor Walter Matthau while working as an understudy for a play he was in. They married in 1959, and this time the marriage worked; the Matthaus remained together until her actor husband's death in 2000. Matthau's other claim to fame was that, according to her autobiography, she was the inspiration for Truman Capote's fictional character Holly Golightly in the novella *Breakfast at Tiffany's.*

OBITUARIES AND OTHER SOURCES:

BOOKS

Writers Directory, 18th edition, St. James Press (Detroit, MI), 2003.

PERIODICALS

Chicago Tribune, July 25, 2003, section 3, p. 12.
Los Angeles Times, July 25, 2003, p. B14.
New York Times, July 24, 2003, p. A21.
Times (London, England), July 29, 2003.

*   *   *

MAYS, David John 1896-1971

PERSONAL: Born November 22, 1896, in Richmond, VA; died February 17, 1971, in Richmond, VA; son of Harvey James and Helga (Nelson) Mays; married Ruth Reams, July 3, 1926. *Education:* Randolph-Macon College, attended 1914-16, 1999-20, Litt.D., 1955; University of Richmond, LL.B., 1924, LL.D., 1954,

CAREER: Attorney, educator, and historian. Admitted to the Bar of the State of Virginia, 1923; Tucker, Bronson & Mays (law firm), Richmond, VA, founding partner, 1928; Mays, Valentine, Davenport & Moore, Richmond, senior partner; Virginia Legislative Commission, counsel, 1955; State of Virginia, counsel, 1959. University of Richmond, law lecturer, 1926-42, member of advisory committee trustees, 1959-71; University of Virginia McGregor Library, advisor, 1955-70. Virginia Commission on Constitutional Government, chairman, 1958-71; Virginia Library Board, member, 1953-63, chairman 1954-57; member of Virginia Legislative Commission. *Military service:* U.S. Army; served in Mexican Border Service, 1916-17; served in France 1918-19; attained rank of first lieutenant.

MEMBER: American Bar Association, Virginia Bar Association (president, 1958-59), Richmond Bar Association (president, 1955), Virginia Historical Society (president, 1963-66), Bar Association of the City of New York, Fellows American Bar Foundation, Association of American Trial Lawyers, American Judicature Society, Institute for Early American History and Culture, American Historical Association, Historic Richmond, Phi Beta Kappa, Sigma Nu Phi.

AWARDS, HONORS: American Association of State and Local History Award of Merit, 1952; Institute for Early American History and Culture award, 1953; Pulitzer Prize for Biography, 1953, for *Edmund Pendleton, 1721-1803.*

WRITINGS:

Business Law, William Byrd (Richmond, VA), 1933.
Edmund Pendleton, 1721-1803: A Biography, two volumes, Harvard University Press (Cambridge, MA), 1952, reprinted, Virginia State Library (Richmond, VA), 1980.
(Editor) *The Letters and Papers of Edmund Pendleton, 1734-1803,* two volumes, Virginia Historical Society/University Press of Virginia (Charlottesville, VA), 1967.
The Pursuit of Excellence: A History of the University of Richmond Law School, University of Richmond (Richmond, VA), 1970.

Contributor to journals, including *Annual Reports of the Virginia State Bar Association.*

SIDELIGHTS: Virginia attorney David John Mays was a leading citizen of Richmond, an advocate of racial equality in state law, and a respected historian. He won the Pulitzer Prize for Biography in 1953 for his two-volume *Edmund Pendleton, 1721-1803,* a biography of the eighteenth-century attorney who, after actively participating in the American Revolution, became chief judge of the Virginia Commonwealth.

In a review of *Edmund Pendleton, 1721-1803* for the *New York Times,* Dumas Malone wrote that Mays "has not been content with recovering Pendleton in full likeness, but has also sought to re-create the society in which he lived. The author fears that the accounts of tobacco culture, of the country and general courts of pre-Revolutionary Virginia, and of the decline of the plantation system may be regarded as 'encumbrances'; but they are among the best things in his book."

In addition to writing the definitive biography of Pendleton, Mays also edited a collection of Pendleton's papers, which was published in 1967. In *The Letters and Papers of Edmund Pendleton, 1734-1803* Mays organizes speech transcripts, letters, and other papers by date, providing a view not only of Pendleton's life but also of the development of state and federal law as the newly formed nation made the transition from British law to a unique American system of justice.

In addition to his historical writing, Mays also published *Business Law* in 1933, and *Pursuit of Excellence,* a 1970 history of his alma mater, the University of Richmond Law School.

BIOGRAPHICAL AND CRITICAL SOURCES:

BOOKS

Hart, James D., editor, *Oxford Companion to American Literature,* fourth edition, Oxford University Press (New York, NY), 1965.

PERIODICALS

New York Times Book Review, September 7, 1952, Dumas Malone, review of *Edmund Pendleton, 1721-1803,* pp. 6, 26.

OBITUARIES:

PERIODICALS

New York Times, February 18, 1971.*

*   *   *

McDOUGAL, Susan 1954-

PERSONAL: Born 1954, in Camden, AR; married James McDougal (an investor and convicted felon; deceased).

ADDRESSES: Agent—c/o Carroll & Graf Publishers, 161 William Street, 16th Floor, New York, NY 10038.

CAREER: Author. Zubin and Nancy Mehta, bookkeeper and personal assistant.

WRITINGS:

(With Pat Harris) *The Woman Who Wouldn't Talk,* Carroll & Graf (New York, NY), 2003.

SIDELIGHTS: Susan McDougal made headlines in the mid-1990s when she refused to corroborate a statement made against then-President Bill Clinton. Kenneth Starr, the government's independent counsel, was searching for evidence that Clinton had been involved with McDougal and her husband, James, in an illegal investment that was referred to as the Whitewater scheme. Her silence caused her to serve a prison sentence for contempt of court. Her book *The Woman Who Wouldn't Talk* relates her experience.

McDougal was born in a small town in Arkansas, the middle child of seven. Her position in her family trained her to be a great diplomat, or as Beverly Lowry put it in the *New York Times,* McDougal learned early about appeasement and it became "the philosophy she would adhere to and depend on as the solution to any problem that arose, for the rest of her life."

After college McDougal met and married James McDougal, a man much older than she and one who suffered from depression and, at times, the mishandling of investments. James, along with James Hale, sought funds for the Whitewater real-estate development plan. Both men asked some of their friends, including the Clintons, to buy into Whitewater. The Clintons did, and although the investments were tainted with illegalities, Starr could not prove that the Clintons knew about them.

McDougal's husband, threatened with a long prison sentence, agreed to testify against the Clintons. His evidence, however, proved to be inconclusive. Hale, disappointed that the Clintons did not come to his defense, also provided the prosecutors with a story that incriminated the by-now president and first lady. But the attorneys wanted more, so they turned to Mc-

Dougal; she refused to verify the testimonies. McDougal states in her book that she was actually willing to answer Starr's questions, but that was not what Starr really wanted. As McDougal related in an online interview for *BuzzFlash,* "They told me that was not what the meeting was about. Even though they had never met me before, they said that they would trade global immunity for a proffer against the target of their investigation, Bill and Hillary Clinton." When she refused, they increased the pressure on her, threatening to prosecute her and send her to jail. McDougal states that when she refused again, the investigators began to threaten her three brothers, who had also worked with her husband. "I was not going to give them a lie," she told the *BuzzFlash* interviewer. "So I decided I would go to trial, and I'd be found innocent. I wasn't. I was found guilty."

Lowry, in her *New York Times* article, stated that the beginning of McDougal's autobiography would have sounded more authentic if she had sought the service of a good editor. The use of too much "wisecracking" and "offhand prose," made Lowry question the validity of McDougal's statements. However, in the second half of the book, McDougal relates her prison experience, and it is here that the "narrative voice shifts dramatically." It is in the latter part of the book that McDougal "resists the urge to entertain in order to fulfill a higher calling," Lowry commented.

McDougal spent almost two years in seven different high-security prisons, locked up with people who were convicted murderers or mentally ill. In one of the prisons she was put into a glass enclosure through which she could see other prisoners but could hear nothing. It was also lit twenty-four hours a day. A guard in a tower watched everything she did. "Most of the people on that block," McDougal stated to her *BuzzFlash* interviewer, "were there for being mentally ill. And the things that you could see were just unimaginable, unbelievable." Many of these prisoners were abused, McDougal relates, because they did not follow orders, which McDougal implies they could not do. One of the main reasons behind her book is to tell their story.

A *Publishers Weekly* reviewer pointed out that McDougal relates all the "horrific details" of her dealings with Starr "with righteous fury," but also offers readers tales of "positive experiences with fellow inmates and supportive friends." These experiences—both the

ordeal in court and the suffering in prison—made her "the poster girl for the excesses and overreaching of the Office of Independent Counsel," wrote Ilene Cooper for *Booklist.* It was the expression of her contempt for that counsel that a *Kirkus Reviews* writer found most powerful about McDougal's story. In addition, the reviewer thought that the "most forcefully presented" material also includes "her reasons for refusing to testify: the twisting of her words that could easily result in perjury" and her "overdue need to assert some control over her life."

BIOGRAPHICAL AND CRITICAL SOURCES:

PERIODICALS

America's Intelligence Wire, January 20, 2003, "Susan McDougal Explains Her Actions in Whitewater."
Booklist, December 1, 2002, Ilene Cooper, review of *The Woman Who Wouldn't Talk,* p. 627.
Kirkus Reviews, November 15, 2002, review of *The Woman Who Wouldn't Talk,* pp. 1678-1679.
Library Journal, December, 2002, Karl Helicher, review of *The Woman Who Wouldn't Talk,* pp. 155-156.
National Review, February 19, 2001, Byron York, "The McDougal Pardon: If You Knew Susan like He Knows Susan."
New York Times, January 26, 2003, Beverly Lowry, review of *The Woman Who Wouldn't Talk,* p. 14.
Publishers Weekly, December 9, 2002, review of *The Woman Who Wouldn't Talk,* p. 74.
U.S. News & World Report, April 16, 2002, Paul Bedard, Suzi Parker, Richard J. Newman, and Ulrich Boser, "It's Not Senator McDougal—Yet!," p. 8.

ONLINE

American Politics Journal online, http://www.americanpolitics.com/ (February 11, 2003), review of *The Woman Who Wouldn't Talk.*
BuzzFlash, http://www.buzzflash.com/ (February 14, 2003), "'The Woman Who Wouldn't Talk,' Susan McDougal, Talks with BuzzFlash.com."
Mothers in Prison Web site, http://www.aetn.org/mip/ (October 31, 2003), interview with Susan McDougal.*

McDOWELL, L(ee) R(ussell) 1941-

PERSONAL: Born April 11, 1941, in Lyons, NY; son of Russell Gale (a farmer) and Ida (a homemaker; maiden name, Lee) McDowell; married Lorraine Worden, June, 1965; children: Suzannah McDowell Huttengs, Joanna, Teresa McDowell Ingly. *Ethnicity:* "English-Scots, Irish, German." *Education:* Alfred Agricultural and Technical School, A.A.S., 1961; University of Georgia, B.A., M.S., 1965. *Politics:* "Conservative." *Religion:* Methodist. *Hobbies and other interests:* History of nutrition.

ADDRESSES: Home—5805 Southwest 177th St., Archer, FL 32618. *Office*—Department of Animal Sciences, University of Florida, P.O. Box 110910, Gainesville, FL 32611-0910; fax: 352-392-7652. *E-mail*—mcdowell@animal.ufl.edu.

CAREER: Educator and author. University of Florida, Gainesville, professor of animal nutrition, 1971—. Consultant to Hoffman-LaRoche and International Minerals.

MEMBER: American Society of Animal Science (fellow), American Society of Dairy Science.

AWARDS, HONORS: International awards from American Society of Animal Science, 1988, and American Society of Dairy Science.

WRITINGS:

Nutrition of Grazing Ruminants in Warm Climates, Academic Press (San Diego, CA), 1985.
Vitamins in Animal Nutrition: Comparative Aspects to Human Nutrition, Academic Press (San Diego, CA), 1989, second edition published as *Vitamins in Animal and Human Nutrition,* University of Iowa Press (Iowa City, IA), 2000.
Minerals in Animal and Human Nutrition, Academic Press (San Diego, CA), 1992.

BIOGRAPHICAL AND CRITICAL SOURCES:

PERIODICALS

BioScience, October, 1990, Margie Lee Gallagher, review of *Vitamins in Animal Nutrition: Comparative Aspects to Human Nutrition,* p. 693.

MCGLINCHEY, Charles 1861-1954

PERSONAL: Born December 21, 1861, in Meentiagh Glen, Clonmany, Inishowen Peninsula, Ireland; died 1954; son of Niall (a weaver and tailor) and Sile (Harkin) McGlinchey.

CAREER: Weaver, tailor, and storyteller.

WRITINGS:

The Last of the Name, edited by Brian Friel, Blackstaff Press (Belfast, Ireland), 1986, J. S. Sanders (Nashville, TN), 1999.

SIDELIGHTS: Although Irishman Charles McGlinchey rarely left the small town of his birth, he managed to weave grand tales of Irish culture and history, relying on the observations he made of his friends and neighbors, as well as on the stories handed down to him by previous generations. One of six children born to a weaver and his wife, McGlinchey was never formally educated, and followed in his father's footsteps by becoming a weaver and tailor. His family spoke only Gaelic, but as he grew older, he learned to speak English, and later taught himself to read both English and Gaelic.

McGlinchey never married; as a young man he had no property or money that could be offered as the dowry necessary in order to take a bride. As an adult, McGlinchey became increasingly isolated after family members emigrated to the United States or died. Eventually he was left to live alone on his family's farm, but rather than withdrawing into seclusion, the ever-sociable and optimistic man became an important fixture in his local community. He was known for his ability to recall ancient legends and events of past eras as well as for his storytelling ability. In the late 1940s and early 1950s he became friends with a local schoolmaster, Patrick Kavanagh, who realized that McGlinchey's tales were an important historical and cultural link to Ireland's increasingly forgotten heritage. Kavanagh spent long hours with McGlinchey, listening to his stories and transcribing them longhand.

These manuscripts remained in the Kavanagh family until the mid-1980s, when Patrick Kavanagh's son gave them to playwright Brian Friel, who edited them into a book, *The Last of the Name.* The book preserves McGlinchey's stream-of-consciousness narrative style and is divided into eighteen chapters dealing with subjects such as the Irish Potato Famine, emigration from Ireland, poets, Irish whiskey, pubs, and religious pilgrimages.

The book is notable for its emphasis on local events in McGlinchey's remote village; as George O'Brien noted in the *Washington Post,* although McGlinchey occasionally traveled to Dublin and even into England, he spends only a line or two on these events, preferring to discuss events in Clonmany in great detail. Friel commented in his introduction to the book, "Nothing but life in the Glen was important to him." O'Brien remarked that McGlinchey did not focus on himself, however; he is "less interested in drawing attention to his own experiences than in mulling over his immediate milieu. . . . [Earlier] generations have such a prominent presence in *The Last of the Name* that they amount to a virtual, or parallel, community." Stories handed down from these generations give the book a vast historic range, reaching as far back as the Napoleonic wars and occasionally farther. In *British Book News,* D. W. Harkness described the book as "a pleasure to read," and Carol Peace Robbins, writing in the *New York Times Book Review,* praised McGlinchey's "wonderfully appealing" voice.

In Clonmany a summer school has been named after McGlinchey. The author of a profile of McGlinchey on the town of Clonmany's Web site noted, "McGlinchey lives on in the hearts and minds of the people of Clonmany as he has given them a gift that no money can buy—the gift of their past."

BIOGRAPHICAL AND CRITICAL SOURCES:

BOOKS

McGlinchey, Charles, *The Last of the Name,* edited by Brian Friel, Blackstaff Press (Belfast, Ireland), 1986.

PERIODICALS

British Book News, November, 1986, D. W. Harkness, review of *The Last of the Name,* p. 668.

Library Journal, September 15, 1999, Pam Kingsbury, review of *The Last of the Name,* p. 91.
New York Times Book Review, Carol Peace Robbins, review of *The Last of the Name,* October 17, 1999, p. 23.
Washington Post, September 26, 1999, George O'Brien, review of *The Last of the Name,* p. X04.

ONLINE

Clonmany Web site, http://www.clonmany.com/ (November 24, 2003), profile of McGlinchey.*

*　　♦　　*

McKENNA, Kevin (E.) 1950-

PERSONAL: Born March 12, 1950, in Rochester, NY; son of John W. (a mail carrier) and Helen (Lavell) McKenna. *Ethnicity:* "White Anglo." *Education:* St. John Fisher College, B.A., 1972; St. Bernard's Seminary, M.Div., 1976, M.A., 1981; Gregorian Pontifical University, Rome, J.C.L., 1984; St. Paul's University, Ottawa, J.C.D., 1990; University of Ottawa, Ph.D., 1990. *Politics:* Independent. *Hobbies and other interests:* Sports, especially baseball.

ADDRESSES: Office—St. Cecilia Church, 2732 Culver Rd., Rochester, NY 14622; fax: 716-544-8889. *E-mail*—mckenna@dor.org.

CAREER: Diocese of Rochester, Rochester, NY, ordained Roman Catholic priest, 1977, priest intern, 1977-79, associate pastor, 1979-82, vice chancellor, 1984-88, canonical consultant to bishop and judge in marriage tribunal, both 1990-2001, director of legal services, 1991-2001, chancellor, 1992-2001, pastor of St. Cecilia Parish, Irondequoit, 2000—, also member of diocesan conciliation board. Catholic University of America, instructor, 1998; St. Bernard's Institute, adjunct associate professor of pastoral studies; Roberts Wesleyan College, guest lecturer; workshop presenter. Member of board of directors, St. Bernard's Institute, bishop's advisory board for clergy misconduct, and Becket Hall House of Formation; Catholic Charities, member of corporate board.

MEMBER: Canon Law Society of America (member of board of governors, 1997-99; vice president, 2000—), Canadian Canon Law Society.

WRITINGS:

The Ministry of Law in the Church Today, University of Notre Dame Press (Notre Dame, IN), 1999.

(Chief editor) *The Church Finance Handbook,* Canon Law Society of America (Washington, DC), 2000.

A Concise Guide to Canon Law: A Practical Handbook for Pastoral Ministers, Ave Maria Press (Notre Dame, IN), 2000.

Contributor to periodicals, including *America, Pastoral Life, Priest, Review for Religious, Studia Canonica, Human Development, ParishWorks,* and *Today's Parish.* Editor, *Legal Update;* past member of editorial board, *Catholic Courier.*

WORK IN PROGRESS: A Concise Guide to Catholic Social Teaching.

BIOGRAPHICAL AND CRITICAL SOURCES:

PERIODICALS

Library Journal, November 1, 1998, Anna M. Donnelly, review of *The Ministry of Law in the Church Today,* p. 90.

*   *   *

McKINLEY, Catherine E(lizabeth) 1967-

PERSONAL: Born April 25, 1967, in Boston, MA; daughter of Donald Sellers and Elizabeth (Wilson) McKinley. *Education:* Attended University of West Indies, 1987-88; Sarah Lawrence College, B.A., 1989; attended Cornell University (African studies), 1989-91.

ADDRESSES: Home—P.O. Box 277, Cooper Square Station, New York, NY 10276. *Agent*—c/o Author Mail, Tanya Mckinnon, Mary Evans, Inc. 242 East Fifth St., New York, NY 10003.

CAREER: Writer, editor, and educator. Feminist Press of the City University of New York, editorial assistant, 1991-92; Marie Brown Associates Literary Services,

New York, NY, associate, 1992-94; Eugene Lange College, New School University, New York, NY, writing instructor, 1995; PEN writers fund coordinator and open book committee, 1996-97; City College of New York, teacher of creative writing and associate director of publishing certificate program, 1997—.

AWARDS, HONORS: Audre Lorde Award, New York Foundation for the Arts; MacDowell Colony for the Arts residency; Fulbright scholar in Ghana, West Africa, 1999-2000.

WRITINGS:

(Editor with L. Joyce DeLaney) *Afrekete: An Anthology of Black Lesbian Writing,* Anchor Books (New York, NY), 1995.

The Book of Sarahs: A Family in Parts (memoir), Counterpoint (Washington, DC), 2002.

SIDELIGHTS: Catherine E. McKinley coedited a first with L. Joyce Delaney—*Afrekete: An Anthology of Black Lesbian Writing.* The volume's title comes from the name of a lover in "Tar Beach," an essay excerpted from Audre Lorde's autobiography *Zami: A New Spelling of My Name* and included in the collection.

In reviewing *Afrekete* for the *Lambda Book Report,* Karen Shoffner noted that in her essay, coeditor Linda Villarosa "details the condemnations of homosexuality sometimes cloaked as concern for her soul she endured and the education she gave herself in biblical scripture. Finally feeling intellectually equipped, she searched for a spiritual home. Villarosa's experiences are heartening, and the clarity of her writing immensely satisfying."

The volume contains essays, stories, and poetry, and begins and ends with Lorde, the last piece being "Today is Not the Day," written shortly before Lorde's death. "It is moving not only because of her death," said Shoffner, "but also because of her magic with words and the strength she had in facing mortality which is apparent behind her words."

Advocate writer Nikki Baker wrote that "as are most anthologies, *Afrekete* is uneven. Some pieces are better than others, but all are provocative."

In addition to the well-known writings of Lorde, Michelle Cliff, and Pat Parker, the editors have included young writers whose work has never before been read. Among the younger contributors are Michelle Parkerson, Jocelyn Maria Taylor, and Jamika Ajalon. *Women's Review of Books* contributor Adrian T. Oktenberg "was disappointed" by the contributions made by these three, and particularly commented on filmmaker Taylor's essay on exhibitionism and sex work. "Their pieces all include highly interesting information on the theme of what it means to be a young Black Lesbian now," said Oktenberg, "but the editors could have helped the writers by cutting and shaping their pieces to better effect. Ajalon in particular is highly talented. Her autobiographical and aptly named fiction 'Kaleidoscope,' though it is too long and focuses on nearly everything . . . nevertheless shines through with energy and narrative drive."

Oktenberg noted as an example of the "wonderful writing" to be found in *Afrekete* Carolivia Herron's story "The Old Lady," wherein the narrator recalls the loves of her younger self. "Written in an incantatory, rhythmic prose that shines and shimmers and moves with light, this story is gorgeous, powerful writing," said Oktenberg, who addded that Michelle Cliff's "Screen Memory," from her collection *Bodies of Water,* is "similarly powerful, and as exact and richly atmospheric." Oktenberg noted that the editors have not tried to cover all there is to say about black lesbianism, but noted that what they have done "is a great deal to accomplish in a single book. One can only say, it's about time, and welcome."

McKinley grew up the biracial adopted child of a politically progressive family in a small, predominantly white, working-class town in Massachusetts. As an adult, she researched her birth history, made difficult by the fact that hers had been a closed adoption for which the records were sealed. She had always assumed, and wanted to believe, that her natural parents were black, but what she eventually learned was that her mother was a white Jewish woman, and that it was her father who was black and part Native American. The book in which McKinley reveals the complexities of her search, *The Book of Sarahs: A Memoir of Race and Identity* is so titled because her mother named three of her daughters Sarah: the author, an older sister who was also given up for adoption, and a half-sister. McKinley also met seven of her father's eleven other children.

A *Kirkus Reviews* contributor noted that "McKinley's eight-year search for family did not bring her what she expected or wanted to find, but instead a big crazy quilt from which she had to construct a pattern and stitch her own self-image." A *Publishers Weekly* reviewer said that "McKinley writes beautifully in this debut memoir, never resorting to sentimentality or easy emotions within this tangled web of emotional and family secrets." "In the end, the treasure McKinley seems to have discovered is her own independent self," wrote Ellen D. Gilbert in *Library Journal.*

McKinley told *CA:* "I started writing *The Book of Sarahs* in a period of intense mourning that followed a year of overwhelming revelations: in 1997, after seven years of searching for my birth family, I reunited with my biological parents and several of a dozen siblings, including two sisters who shared my original name, Sarah. The story of the Sarahs revealed my birthparents' choices and huge inabilities (partly stemming from my birthmother's struggle with mental illness). At the same time, I began integrating my Jewish birthmother and African-American and Choctaw father's heritage into my heretofore unspecified (because my adoption records were legally closed) 'bi-racial' black life. All of this new knowledge forced me to reckon with perhaps the most uncomfortable truth: the extent of the protective skein of fantasies and the lies I'd told on myself since early childhood.

"I am a fiction writer, and my creative wrestlings with transracial adoption originally came to me as fiction, but very soon, the real narrative of my birth history eclipsed my imagination. A writer I admire, Philip Gourevitch, has remarked: 'This is what fascinates me most in existence: the peculiar necessity of imagining what is in fact real.' He is writing about genocide in Rwanda. It's a wonderful quote, perhaps inappropriately applied here to individual tragi-comedy. Yet I am a child of a once-projected genocide. I grew up as one of just a few thousand black and bi-racial children adopted into white homes in the 1960s-1970s, when black social workers were calling up the specter of the mass destruction of black children as they organized to end such adoptions. I spent most of my young life in the realm of imagination—imagining, re-imagining and re-making myself a thousand times into the black woman I thought I would be if I had grown up with my biological family, bucking my adoptive parents' largely socially isolated life of wilderness-seeking. At the same time, I was being handed a heritage, and a connection to other black lives through literature. I had trouble talking; I was alone most of the time. Writing became a way to communicate, and to place myself comfortably within community. By the time I began my search, I knew that I wanted to try to write, in an exacting way, about the inside of transracial adoption, and a facet of post-1960s transracially adopted 'mulatted' social experience. Everyone was projecting the tragic—I wanted to expose the pain and reach for the comic, the unsentimental.

"Now, if, even at the end of searching, my biological family—and what I once hoped would be a pass to easy, 'legitimate' membership in a race, a family, is still lost to me, I do have the community of the word, and the power as a writer to insert trans-bi girls into the literary imagination."

BIOGRAPHICAL AND CRITICAL SOURCES:

BOOKS

McKinley, Catherine E., *The Book of Sarahs: A Memoir of Race and Identity,* Counterpoint (Washington, DC), 2002.

PERIODICALS

Advocate, May 16, 1995, Nikki Baker, review of *Afrekete: An Anthology of Black Lesbian Writing,* p. 64.
Booklist, October 1, 2002, Vanessa Bush, review of *The Book of Sarahs: A Memoir of Race and Identity,* p. 299.
Kirkus Reviews, July 1, 2002, review of *The Book of Sarahs,* p. 935.
Lambda Book Report, July-August, 1995, Karen Shoffner, review of *Afrekete,* p. 27.
Library Journal, June 1, 1995, Lisa Nussbaum, review of *Afrekete,* p. 114; July, 2002, Ellen D. Gilbert, review of *The Book of Sarahs,* p. 106.
Ms., May-June, 1995, Mattie Richardson, review of *Afrekete,* p. 74.
Publishers Weekly, April 24, 1995, review of *Afrekete,* p. 68; July 1, 2002, review of *The Book of Sarahs,* p. 65.
Women's Review of Books, July, 1995, Adrian T. Oktenberg, review of *Afrekete,* p. 30.

ONLINE

Zami.org, http://www.zami.org/ (October 19, 2002), review of *The Book of Sarahs.*

* * *

McKINNEY, Joseph A. 1943-

PERSONAL: Born May 21, 1943, in Marion, NC; son of Henry Clay (a grocer) and Mary (a teacher; maiden name, Greene) McKinney; married Nancy Petersen (a nurse), 1966; children: Laura McKinney Joseph, David John Michael. *Ethnicity:* "Caucasian." *Education:* Berea College, B.A., 1965; Michigan State University, M.A., 1967, Ph.D., 1970. *Politics:* Republican. *Religion:* Baptist. *Hobbies and other interests:* Travel, studying Christian theology.

ADDRESSES: Home—9515 Stony Point, Waco, TX 76712. *Office*—Department of Economics, Hankamer School of Business, Box 98003, Baylor University, Waco, TX 76798-8003; fax: 254-710-1092. *E-mail*—Joe_McKinney@baylor.edu.

CAREER: U.S. Department of State, research assistant, 1967; Michigan State University, East Lansing, instructor in economics, 1969-70; University of Virginia, Charlottesville, assistant professor of economics, 1970-76; Baylor University, Waco, TX, faculty member, 1976—, currently Ben H. Williams Professor of International Economics. Seinan Gakuin University, exchange professor, 1977-78; University of Caen, visiting professor at Institut d'Administration des Enterprises, 1996; Middlesex University, Fulbright professor at Center for the Study of International Affairs, 1996; guest lecturer at other institutions, including University of Paris, Upper Business School of Grenoble, University of Montpellier, Friedrich Schiller University, University of Ghent, Texas A & M University, and University of Houston. Testified before U.S. Trade Deficit Review Commission, U.S. International Trade Commission, and other government agencies.

MEMBER: International Trade and Finance Association, European Community Studies Association, American Economic Association, Association of

Christian Economists (founding member), Association of Japanese Business Studies (founding member), Association for Canadian Studies in the United States.

AWARDS, HONORS: Woodrow Wilson fellow; designated outstanding university professor, Baylor University, 1985; grants from Embassy of Canada, 1988, 1991, 1994, 1997, U.S. Congress Joint Economic Committee, 1990, and Max Kade Foundation, 1992; best paper award, international education division, American Marketing Association, 1994, for "Is the Japanese Marketing System Changing? An Empirical Investigation of the Experiences of U.S. Firms Operating in Japan"; grants from International Research and Exchanges Board and Government of Canada, both 2000.

WRITINGS:

(Editor with Keith A. Rowley) *Readings in International Economic Relations,* Stipes Publishing, 1989.
(Editor with Glen E. Lich) *Region North America: Canada, the United States, and Mexico,* Program in Regional Studies, Baylor University (Waco, TX), 1990.
(Editor with Rebecca M. Sharpless) *Implications of a North American Free Trade Region: Multidisciplinary Perspectives,* Program in Regional Studies, Baylor University (Waco, TX), 1992.
(Editor with Melissa Essary, and contributor) *Free Trade Area for the Americas: Issues in Economics, Trade Policy, and Law,* Baylor University (Waco, TX), 1995.
Created from NAFTA: The Structure, Function, and Significance of the Treaty's Related Institutions, M. E. Sharpe (Armonk, NY), 2000.

Contributor to books, including *Biblical Principles and Economics: The Foundations,* edited by Richard C. Chewning, Navpress, 1989; *North America without Borders?,* edited by Stephen J. Randall, University of Calgary Press (Calgary, Alberta, Canada), 1992; *The Challenge of NAFTA: North America, Australia, New Zealand, and the World Trade Regime,* edited by Robert G. Cushing and others, Lyndon B. Johnson School of Public Affairs, University of Texas—Austin (Austin, TX), 1993; *The North American Free Trade Agreement,* edited by Khosrow Fatemi, St. Martin's

Press (New York, NY), 1993; and *The Future of the Atlantic Community: Expansion, Integration, Security, and Trade,* edited by Douglas Eden, St. Martin's Press (New York, NY), 2000. Contributor of articles and reviews to professional journals, including *Journal of Business Ethics, International Business Review, International Journal, Journal of World Trade, Business Horizons, Venture Japan, Organizational Dynamics, Atlantic Economic Journal, Business Economics,* and *Applied Economics.*

WORK IN PROGRESS: Research on dispute settlement under the side accords of the North American Free Trade Agreement; research on the dispute settlement experience of less-developed countries at the World Trade Organization.

BIOGRAPHICAL AND CRITICAL SOURCES:

PERIODICALS

Hispanic American Historical Review, May, 1995, Jose Cuello, review of *Implications of a North American Free Trade Region: Multidisciplinary Perspectives,* p. 317.
Latin American Research Review, summer, 1994, Manuel Pastor, Jr., review of *Implications of a North American Free Trade Region,* p. 154.

*   *   *

MCKINNON, Karen

PERSONAL: Married Rick Zurita, 1994. *Education:* Received M.A. degree (psychology) and M.A. (liberal studies and twentieth-century literature).

ADDRESSES: Home—New York, NY. *Office*—Washington Heights Community Service of New York State Psychiatric Institute, 1051 Riverside Drive, New York, NY 10032. *E-mail*—Kmm49@columbia.edu.

CAREER: Psychologist and writer. Washington Heights Community Service of New York State Psychiatric Institute, coordinator of training and research. Before graduate school worked at Sony Ridge Winery, 1982; first job as research scientist, started 1987.

AWARDS, HONORS: New Voice Fiction Award, Francine Prose.

WRITINGS:

Narcissus Ascending, Picador USA (New York, NY), 2002.

First short story published in 2000.

SIDELIGHTS: A psychiatrist who specializes in the study of HIV and severe mental illness, Karen McKinnon has also published short fiction and the novel *Narcissus Ascending.* The novel, which was inspired by *The Culture of Narcissism* by Christopher Lasch, is about a group of friends who met in college and have reunited in New York's East Village. The four are in their twenties and share the experience of having been hurt by a once-mutual friend, Callie. The narrator, Becky, is an artist who is about to have her first big exhibition of photo collage self-portraits. Her best friend is Dalhia, a dancer. The occasion has brought Hugh, who was once Callie's boyfriend, and Max, who has dated all three women, back into their lives. All still feel used by the beautiful and manipulative Callie, which convinces Dahlia that Becky's show is the perfect opportunity for revenge. She wants to show Callie how happy they are without her. When Becky is finally persuaded to go along with the plan, it results in a dramatic collision between her and Callie. These events are described by Becky in a kind of colloquial shorthand that uses short sentences and no quotation marks.

McKinnon's unconventional narration in *Narcissus Ascending* is one of the novel's strongest elements, according to reviewers. A *Publishers Weekly* writer noted that the "fast-paced story" features writing that is "exquisitely economical"; the book's ending was described as its weakness, as the story is said to drop into "adolescent melodrama." Similarly, *Los Angeles Times* critic Mark Rozzo felt that the "promising" exploration of Callie's—and then Becky's—emerging narcissism does not reach its full potential. In the *New York Times Book Review* Sarah Haight called the story "an occasionally moving examination of the torturous dynamic" between friends. Haight also commended McKinnon's writing, calling it "raw and knowing."

Even stronger praise came from a *Kirkus Reviews* critic, who described *Narcissus Ascending* as having "the breathtaking, self-important, urgency of youth"

and classed it as "a gripping, revealing, entertaining debut." In a review for *Curled up with a Good Book,* Kristi Bowen said that the "stream-of-consciousness narrative and dialogue . . . give the novel a swiftness and immediacy which works with its subject." She assessed it as "an exciting read." *Booklist*'s Kristine Huntley called the novel "taut and fast-paced" and commented that it "offers both insight into an artist's mind and an insightful portrait of the dynamics of a group of friends." In the *Philadelphia Inquirer,* Carlin Romano credited the author with drafting "a sly face-off between art world ethics and aesthetics." He enjoyed the book as "an ambitious pentathlon," in which "much of the pleasure . . . emerges from Becky's casual psychologizing."

BIOGRAPHICAL AND CRITICAL SOURCES:

PERIODICALS

Booklist, June 1, 2002, Kristine Huntley, review of *Narcissus Ascending,* p. 1687.
Kirkus Reviews, April 1, 2002, review of *Narcissus Ascending,* p. 466.
Los Angeles Times, June 9, 2002, Mark Rozzo, review of *Narcissus Ascending,* p. 14.
New York Times Book Review, July 14, 2002, Sarah Haight, review of *Narcissus Ascending,* p. 20.
Publishers Weekly, June 3, 2002, review of *Narcissus Ascending,* p. 62.

ONLINE

Curled up with a Good Book Web site, http://curledup.com/ (2002), Kristi Bowen, review of *Narcissus Ascending.*
Philadelphia Inquirer online http://philly.com/ (June 30, 2002), Carlin Romano, review of *Narcissus Ascending.*

*   *   *

McKINZIE, Clinton 1969-

PERSONAL: Born June 7, 1969, in Los Angeles, CA; son of Carl Wayne (an attorney) and Rena (a teacher; maiden name, Williams) McKinzie; married Justine Kaufman, September 21, 1997; children: Colin Williams. *Education:* Attended Santa Monica College,

1989-91; Millsaps College, B.A., 1993; University of Wyoming, J.D., 1997. *Hobbies and other interests:* Rock climbing.

ADDRESSES: *Home*—Denver, CO. *Agent*—John Talbot, John Talbot Agency, 540 West Boston Post Rd., P.M.B. 266, Mamaroneck, NY 10534-3437. *E-mail*—cmkn2@earthink.net.

CAREER: Attorney and novelist. Eighteenth Judicial District, Englewood, CA, deputy district attorney for Arapahoe and Douglas counties, 1997-2000; attorney in private practice and writer, 2000—.

WRITINGS:

FICTION

The Edge of Justice, Delacorte Press (New York, NY), 2002.
Point of Law, Delacorte Press (New York, NY), 2003.
Trial by Ice and Fire, Delacorte Press (New York, NY), 2003.
Crossing the Line, Delacorte Press (New York, NY), 2004.

SIDELIGHTS: Clinton McKinzie told *CA:* "My primary motivation for writing is pleasure. I love daydreaming my way through scenes, characters, and plots. It allows me to live multiple lives, and in more than one world.

"I draw on my experience as a deputy district attorney and passionate rock climber to try and provide the reader with a vicarious thrill. It's my goal to make readers feel like they're on the rock with 1,000 feet of air beneath their heels, or as if they're in the courtroom awaiting a crucial verdict. James Ellroy, Michael Connolly, and Jon Krakauer are among my contemporary literary heroes.

"I write at all hours of the day and night. When an idea grips me I have no choice. I work on a portable laptop computer, on legal pads, and on torn scraps of napkins—anything at all I can put words on. Between writing sessions I do the business stuff or, preferably, go climbing.

"I write about the two greatest adrenaline kicks I have known: alpine climbing and prosecuting criminals. Both are topics I'm passionate about, and years spent in both pursuits have provided me with a wealth of stories to tell."

BIOGRAPHICAL AND CRITICAL SOURCES:

PERIODICALS

Kirkus Reviews, April 1, 2002, review of *The Edge of Justice,* p. 447.
Library Journal, May 1, 2002, Joel W. Tscherne, review of *The Edge of Justice,* p. 134.
Publishers Weekly, March 18, 2002, review of *The Edge of Justice,* p. 73.

*   *   *

McLEAN, Maria Coletta 1946-

PERSONAL: Born May 25, 1946, in Toronto, Ontario, Canada; son of Loreto (a truck driver) and Josephine (a homemaker; maiden name, Giorgio) Coletta; married Robert McLean (in business), August 22, 1964; children: Rob, Ken, Carole McLean Garvin, Paula, Kathryn, Christopher. *Ethnicity:* "Italian-Canadian." *Education:* York University, B.A. (with honors), 1995. *Politics:* Liberal. *Religion:* Roman Catholic.

ADDRESSES: *Home*—R.R.1, Bradford, Ontario, Canada L3Z 2A4; fax 416-745-4560. *Agent*—Carolyn Swayze, WRPS, Box 29588, White Rock, British Columbia, Canada V4A 9P3. *E-mail*—coletta@interlog.com.

CAREER: Writer, 1993—. Columbia Coffee and Tea Co., Toronto, Ontario, Canada, vice president, 1995—, currently president.

AWARDS, HONORS: Queen's Golden Jubilee Medal (Canada), 2002, for service to community and nation.

WRITINGS:

My Father Came from Italy (memoir), Raincoast Book Distribution (Vancouver, British Columbia, Canada), 2000.

WORK IN PROGRESS: A novel, *The Woman Who Ran Away.*

SIDELIGHTS: Maria Coletta McLean told *CA:* "In my first book *My Father Came from Italy* I wanted to take the reader on a journey to my father's village in Italy, to share the sights, sounds, and smells. Since I wrote the stories strictly from the heart, the reader is able to laugh and cry along with us. Readers tell me they feel they were walking the cobblestone streets of Supino with me. They say they read more slowly as they reached the last few pages because they didn't want the story to end. They say they want to go to Italy, and they say thank you."

BIOGRAPHICAL AND CRITICAL SOURCES:

ONLINE

Maria Coletta Web site, http://www.mariacoletta.com/ (November 18, 2003).

*   *   *

McMORRIS, Jenny 1946-2002

PERSONAL: Born 1946; died of a brain tumor November 5, 2002.

CAREER: Oxford English Dictionary, Oxford, England, archivist, 1985-2002.

WRITINGS:

The Warden of English: The Life of H. W. Fowler, Oxford University Press (New York, NY), 2002.

SIDELIGHTS: As an archivist at the *Oxford English Dictionary* (*OED*), Jenny McMorris had ample access to the letters and papers of Henry Watson Fowler, whose *Dictionary of Modern English Usage* has been continually in print since its first publication in 1926. Known simply as "Fowler's," this work has been an influential guide for English writers and journalists for most of a century, alternately embraced and condemned, but always consulted due to its author's

determination to steer between sloppy writing and a rigid attachment to archaic forms and rules. McMorris published *The Warden of English: The Life of H. W. Fowler,* the first full-length biography of the famed grammarian, to coincide with the seventy-fifth anniversary of Fowler's best-known work.

"Do the life and times of this curious individual provide for an interesting book? By and large they do," concluded *Report Newsmagazine* contributor Virginia Byfield. Not that the life was terribly dramatic. After seventeen years as a somewhat gloomy and pedantic schoolmaster in Yorkshire, he retired to Guernsey to write and grow tomatoes with his brother Frank. The two produced a translation of the works of Lucian that impressed the editors at Oxford University Press, and they were tapped to produce "concise" and "pocket" preludes for the massive *Oxford English Dictionary.* Sensing that the public longed for an equally definitive guide to grammar and style, Fowler produced the work that now goes simply by his name. In addition to noting Fowler's dedication to work and family, McMorris chronicles his eccentricities, in particular his odd attitude toward money. He often insisted on taking less than Oxford offered for his pieces, objected to the practice of Christmas bonuses, and refused to ever write again for the *Spectator* after they paid him for an essay they decided not to publish. She also covers his decision, at age fifty-six, to join the British army in 1915. (He briefly saw action on the frontlines.) "While shy on bells and whistles, this is a thorough biography," wrote *Library Journal* contributor Scott Hightower. For *Harper's* contributor Guy Davenport, McMorris's book "is an affectionate, hero-worshiping book that convincingly pictures the Great Grammarian, who swam and ran a mile every morning of the year, lost an eye to lexicography, and didn't think you went to hell for splitting the infinitive, as quite a lovable old cooter."

Sadly, McMorris died of a brain tumor shortly after publication of her biography. In a tribute to her long and productive work as an archivist, Elizabeth Knowles noted on the *Oxford English Dictionary Newsletter* online: "Any future historian of the *OED* will owe a tremendous debt to Jenny for her ordering and indexing of the *OED* Archives. Those of us who knew her will remember also her ability to communicate the interest and excitement she found in her work."

BIOGRAPHICAL AND CRITICAL SOURCES:

PERIODICALS

Harper's, November, 2001, Guy Davenport, review of *The Warden of English,* p. 73.
Library Journal, September 1, 2001, Scott Hightower, review of *The Warden of English,* p. 179.
Library Quarterly, July, 2003, William A. McHugh, review of *The Warden of English,* p. 361.
London Review of Books, June 27, 2002, Alex Oliver, review of *The Warden of English,* p. 36.
Report Newsmagazine, January 21, 2002, Virginia Byfield, "Mentor to the Wordsmiths."

ONLINE

Oxford English Dictionary Newsletter online, http:// dictionary.oed.com/newsletters/ (December, 2002), Elizabeth Knowles, "Jenny McMorris."*

*　　*　　*

McNAIRN, Jeffrey L. 1967-

PERSONAL: Born December 15, 1967, in Ontario, Canada. *Education:* Wilfrid Laurier University, B.A., 1989; Oxford University, M.Phil., 1991; University of Toronto, Ph.D., 1997.

ADDRESSES: Home—Toronto, Ontario, Canada. *Agent*—c/o Author Mail, University of Toronto Press, 10 St. Mary St., Suite 700, Toronto, Ontario, Canada M4Y 2W8. *E-mail*—jeffreym@unipissing.ca.

CAREER: Educator and author. Nipissing University, North Bay, Ontario, Canada, assistant professor of history, 2000—.

AWARDS, HONORS: John Bullen Prize, Canadian Historical Association, 1998.

WRITINGS:

The Capacity to Judge: Public Opinion and Deliberative Democracy in Upper Canada, 1791-1854, University of Toronto Press (Buffalo, NY), 2000.

Contributor to periodicals, including *Canadian Historical Review.*

WORK IN PROGRESS: (Re)Inventing Capitalism: Studies in Economic Ideas and Culture in Birthing North America, c. 1750-1870.

*　　*　　*

McNAMARA, Robert (James) 1950-

PERSONAL: Born March 28, 1950, in New York, NY; son of James and Doris (a homemaker; maiden name, Maier) McNamara; married Judith Lightfoot (a writer), September 21, 1993; children: Caitlin C. *Education:* Amherst College, B.A., 1971; Colorado State University, M.A., 1975; University of Washington, Ph.D. (English), 1985.

ADDRESSES: Office—Department of English, Box 354330, University of Washington, Seattle, WA 98195-4330. *E-mail*—rmcnamar@u.washington.edu.

CAREER: University of Washington, Seattle, senior lecturer, 1988.

MEMBER: Academy of American Poetry.

AWARDS, HONORS: National Endowment for the Arts creative-writing fellowship, 1987; Fulbright fellowship, 1993.

WRITINGS:

Second Messengers, Wesleyan University Press (Middletown, CT), 1990.
(Translator from the Bengali) Sarat Kumar Mukhopadhyay, *Birajmohan and Other Poems,* Cambridge India (India), 1998.

Poetry published in periodicals, including *Agni Review, Antioch Review, Field, Gettysburg Review, Massachusetts Review, Missouri Review, Notre Dame Review, Northwest Review, Ohio Review, Poet Lore, Poetry Northwest, Quarterly West,* and *Seattle Review.*

SIDELIGHTS: Robert McNamara told *CA:* "When I ask myself why I write poetry, the answer that comes to me is, 'Because it's what I do.' It's a way of getting on in the world—not of getting ahead, but getting from one day to the next by making things. Some of what I make is very satisfying, and some of it is just part of the job. Being a writer means I write.

"Over my thirty years of writing poetry, I've acquired the habit, anyway. For several hours a day I want to be in the kind of space—emotional, intellectual, physical—from which I can produce poems, or writing that will grow into poems. Spending the hours in that space is sometimes more important than the actual pages I get out of them. The time has a certain meditative quality, and I feel deprived if I have to do without it.

"Over time I've gotten used to working from small project to small project and not insisting on having a sense of how they may add up. They get inspired by different things. A couple of years ago I did a lot of reading in American history and philosophy and ended up writing many poems on American themes the following year. Then I stopped that and did something else. Recently I was thinking about sacred places and wrote four or five poems that started from places that feel sacred to me in some way. A series of poems I call 'Inlets' came from a conscious decision to write a poem every day while staying on a friend's boat. Somewhere behind it all there's a kind of coherence. I've gotten used to not being hugely surprised when I attempt to put together a book manuscript and find a kind of unity. Maybe some coherence comes from the voice I try to create. I try to speak with a voice I would want to listen to. This means resisting the temptation to create a lyrically seductive voice or to let sound run away with sense into mere oratory.

"Lately what's helped in this discipline is a renewed attraction to form. Free verse (of which I've written a lot) can be too easy, and poems stop being interesting to me when they lack inner resistance. So I seek out material and language that will push back. I try to choose something to write about that will be difficult, and say something through the form that can't be said in any other way."

*   *   *

MEMMOTT, Roger Ladd 1944-

PERSONAL: Born June 21, 1944, in Salt Lake City, UT; son of Orion (a Union Pacific railroad engineer) and Nelda (a school teacher; maiden name, Petersen) Memmott); married Sharon Benton, July 28, 1966

(divorced); married Marrianne Wood (a retailer), July 1, 1989; children: Christian Aaron. *Education:* University of California—Irvine, M.F.A., 1970; Brigham Young University, B.B., 1967. *Politics:* Republican. *Religion:* Church of Jesus Christ of Latter-day Saints (Mormon). *Hobbies and other interests:* Folk guitar, banjo, dulcimer.

ADDRESSES: Office—WhiteLight Motion Pictures, Inc., 130 North Butte Street, Suite A, Willows, CA 95988. *Agent*—Meredith Bernstein, Meredith Bernstein Literary Agency, 2112 Broadway, Suite 503-A, New York, NY 10023. *E-mail*—rlmstory@aol.com.

CAREER: Fiction writer, poet, editor, and educator. University of Cincinnati, Cincinnati, OH, assistant professor, 1970-80; University of Connecticut—Stamford, adjunct professor, 1981-85; WhiteLight Motion Pictures, Inc., Willows, CA, vice president of marketing, 1986—.

AWARDS, HONORS: Ohio Arts Council editorial grant; Coordinating Council of Literary Magazines editorial grant; William H. Taft creative writing fellowship; Charles Phelps Taft creative writing grant; First place, Brass Ring Award, IAAPA, 1996, for writing and design; honorable mention, *Flyway* magazine, 1998, for short story; first place, *Fiction 59* Award, 2000, for short fiction; *Writer's Digest* National Book Award for Poetry.

WRITINGS:

Catharsis (novella), Millennium Press, 1985.
Gardening without Gloves (short stories), Gemstone Books/XLibris (Philadelphia, PA), 2001.
The Gypsy Lover (novel), Gemstone Books/XLibris (Philadelphia, PA), 2001.
Sweet Sally Ann (novel), Gemstone Books/XLibris (Philadelphia, PA), 2002.

Contributor of short fiction and poetry to periodicals, including *Cou-wester, Confrontation,* and *New Millennium Writings.* Former editor, *Eureka Review.*

*   *   *

MISCIONE, Lisa 1970-

PERSONAL: Born April 26, 1970 in Hartford, CT; married 2000; husband's name Jeffrey. *Education:* Graduate of Eugene Lang College, New School University. *Hobbies and other interests:* Kung Fu, sea kayaking, boating, swimming, biking, SCUBA diving.

ADDRESSES: Home—Florida. *Agent*—Elaine Markson, Elaine Markson Literary Agency, 44 Greenwich Ave., New York, NY 10011. *E-mail*—lmiscion@ tampabay.rr.com.

CAREER: Novelist.

MEMBER: Mystery Writers of America, Sisters in Crime.

WRITINGS:

Angel Fire, St. Martin's Minotaur (New York, NY), 2002.
The Darkness Gathers, St. Martin's Minotaur (New York, NY), 2003.
Twice, St. Martin's Minotaur (New York, NY), 2004.

SIDELIGHTS: A former associate director of publicity for New York-based publisher Penguin Putnam, Lisa Miscione was inspired to write her first book while visiting a small church in the New Mexico desert. As she told an interviewer for *Bookreview Cafe* online, "I knew I would write about the church. It was a couple of years later . . . that I was sitting in my then-boyfriend's car . . . that I pulled a napkin out of the glove compartment and started writing." Miscione continued the habit, writing on napkins and hotel stationery, whenever and wherever she had time. Her first novel, *Angel Fire,* was the result.

Lydia Strong, the heroine of *Angel Fire,* is a crime writer with a sixth sense that helps her when she consults on criminal cases. Unfortunately, Strong's experience with crime is too personal. When she was fifteen, she found her mother's murdered body. The novel takes place in New Mexico, where Strong is on the trail of a serial killer. With police chief Simon Morrow and former FBI agent—and love interest—Jeffrey Mark, she delves into a world of gruesome murders surrounding a mysterious church, its priest, and the priest's mystic nephew. A reviewer for *Publishers Weekly* commented of *Angel Fire* that the book "isn't for readers with weak stomachs, but it remains gripping and terrifying right through the carnage of its final scene."

In Miscione's *The Darkness Gathers,* the 2003 sequel to *Angel Fire,* Strong and Mark follow their intuition to Miami, Florida, after receiving a disturbing taped message from a missing girl named Tatiana Quinn. They meet with the police detective assigned to the case as well as with the girl's Albanian mother Jenna and wealthy stepfather Nathan. The case becomes more complex than a kidnapping, as Jenna's involvement with her Albanian mafia boyfriend and Nathan's shady dealings surface. The plot further thickens with the addition of numerous murders, a trip to Eastern Europe, sexual slavery, and the activities of the FBI and the Miami police force. Jenny McLarin praised the novel in her *Booklist* review as being "an exciting story enriched by a glamourous writer-heroine who carries a Glock and knows how to use it."

Miscione told *CA:* "I guess I've always been fascinated by the dark side, the underbelly. I want to know what's happening behind the locked door, who the dark form is in the window, what that noise is under the stairs. I also like the way the mystery thriller genre allows you to push the edges of reality a bit. Obviously, as a writer, research is important to me and I try to be as accurate as possible with the 'facts' in my fiction. But occassionally I like to allow the lines to go a bit gray, allow my characters to be just a little bit tougher, a little bit cooler, a little bit more mysterious than the rest of us.

"To me, writing is its own reward and I think that success is really measured by knowing that you are doing the best you can. However, I'm always so unspeakably touched and pleased when a reader takes the time out of his or her day to write me. It means more to me than anything because it's so real. My favorite comment from my readers is: 'I'm so tired today because your book kept me up all night.' Every time someone tells me that I'm thrilled.

"As a child I grew up in Connecticut, Holland, England, and New Jersey. Reading became a part of my life early on, largely because my parents were avid readers, but also because moving around a lot led me to be pretty independent and somewhat solitary. Reading was a major source of entertainment for me, and I literaly don't remember a time in my life when I was not writing. It has always been the place where I most naturally express myself, the place where I am most truly me.

"As far as writing habits go, I work at home on my laptop, but the wheel is always turning, so I also find myself writing in notepads, on napkins, whatever is handy at the moment. In terms of a schedule, I like to approach it like any other business. In other words, I get up in the morning and start to write. I have a goal of ten good pages each day. Of course, some days are more productive or inspired than others. In terms of outlining and plot development, I have a general idea of where I'm going, what themes are brewing, and where the story is set. But then I just sit down and write. I don't plot much before I begin the book. I like the narrative to take me where it wants to go. I write for the same reason that I read: because I want to know what's going to happen."

BIOGRAPHICAL AND CRITICAL SOURCES:

PERIODICALS

Booklist, February 15, 2003, Jenny McLarin, review of *The Darkness Gathers,* p. 1055.
Kirkus Reviews, November 15, 2001, review of *Angel Fire,* p. 1584; February 1, 2003, review of *The Darkness Gathers,* p. 191.
Library Journal, January, 2002, Rex Klett, review of *Angel Fire,* p. 156; March 1, 2003, Rex Klett, review of *The Darkness Gathers,* p. 122.
Publishers Weekly, January 7, 2002, review of *Angel Fire,* p. 49; February 17, 2003, review of *The Darkness Gathers,* p. 60.

ONLINE

Book Review Cafe, http://www.bookreviewcafe.com/ (June 14, 2003), interview with Miscione.
Lisa Miscione Web site, http://www.lisamiscione.com (May 9, 2003).

*   *   *

MITCHELL, Marianne 1947-
(Marianne Olson)

PERSONAL: Born June 7, 1947, in Phoenix, AZ; married James C. Mitchell (a journalist and writer). *Education:* University of Redlands, B.A., 1968; University of Louisville, M.A., 1988.

ADDRESSES: Home—P.O. Box 65618, Tucson, AZ 85728. *E-mail*—mariannemitchell@earthlink.net.

CAREER: Bilingual elementary education teacher, Peoria, AZ, 1978-82; University of Louisville, Louisville, KY, lecturer in Spanish, 1985-90.

MEMBER: Society of Children's Book Writers and Illustrators, International Reading Association, National League of American PEN Women, Sisters in Crime.

AWARDS, HONORS: Highlights for Children fiction contest, first place, 1998; Storyteller World Award, 2002, for *Joe Cinders; Joe Cinders* and *Gullywasher Gulch* named Southwest Books of the Year, Tuscon-Pima Library, 2002; Bank Street College Best Books of the Year citation, and Storytelling World Award Honor Book, both 2003, both for *Joe Cinders.*

WRITINGS:

Maya Moon/Doña Luna, illustrated by John Martinez Z., Sundance Publishing (Littleton, MA), 1995.
Say It in Spanish!: Language and Activities for the Elementary Classroom (for adults), Teacher Ideas Press (Portsmouth, NH), 1997.
Coo, Coo, Caroo, illustrated by Marilyn Henry, Richard C. Owen (Katonah, NY), 1997.
(As Marianne Olson) *Over the Waves,* Rafter Five Press (Tucson, AZ), 1999.
Gullywasher Gulch, illustrated by Normand Chartier, Boyds Mills Press (Honesdale, PA), 2002.
Joe Cinders, illustrated by Bryan Langdo, Henry Holt (New York, NY), 2002.
Finding Zola, Boyds Mills Press (Honesdale, PA), 2003.

Contributor of articles to magazines, including *Guide, Jack and Jill, New Moon, Pockets,* and *Highlights for Children.* Several of her stories have been printed in anthologies, including *Stories from Highlights.* Translator of writings from Spanish to English.

WORK IN PROGRESS: Firebug, for Boyds Mills Press; research into an historical mystery set in Colorado in the late 1800s.

SIDELIGHTS: Marianne Mitchell's books express her heritage—both Western U.S. and European—and her desire to entertain children. Born and raised on a ranch in Phoenix, Arizona, Mitchell earned her teaching credentials in bilingual Spanish/English education. As she told *CA,* "Professional writing evolved out of my years as a teacher. Teachers are always making up activities, skits, and stories for their students. So one day I decided to turn those efforts into fiction writing for children." Her first story appeared in *Guide* magazine in 1992, and since then more than eighty of her short works have been published in children's magazines. She became a frequent contributor to *Highlights for Children* and author of that magazine's regular feature "The Bear Family." "I write all kinds of things for *Highlights,* from rebus stories for beginning readers to adventure stories for older readers," she told Julia Durango in a *By the Book* interview. Writing for magazines, Mitchell pointed out, might be easier due to the variety of pieces possible to sell. "However, just because a story is shorter than a book doesn't mean it's easy to write."

Mitchell's early book-length works, *Say It in Spanish!: Language and Activities for the Elementary Classroom* and the early reader *Coo, Coo, Caroo,* were also inspired by her teaching activities. She wrote the bilingual *Maya Moon/Doña Luna* because she wanted to make sure this Hispanic tale was not lost. Even after becoming published, Mitchell did not want to cloister herself at home. She enjoys visiting libraries and schools and makes talking with children a regular part of her routine. "My favorite part of being an author is going to schools to share my love of reading and writing with the students. It keeps me in touch with their interests and enthusiasm," she wrote at the *Boyds Mills Press* Web site.

Like many authors, Mitchell had a family story that she wanted to share with readers. Her grandmother immigrated from Sweden to the United States in 1880, and in 1914, when the woman decided to visit her homeland, she found it difficult and dangerous to return to America because of World War I. Although Mitchell's grandmother died when Mitchell was only four years old, as a girl she had heard this family story and wanted to know more. Conversations with her mother and other genealogical research resulted in the historical novel *Over the Waves,* based on the incident. When asked about the impetus to record the tale, Mitchell told Durango, "I think that it's really important to preserve family stories." When doing school visits and other talks, Mitchell encourages children "to seek out their own family stories and write them down."

Living in the American Southwest has also influenced Mitchell's writing, as she explained to Durango: "Growing up in Arizona has taught me the 'lingo' of the West, cowboy talk. This helped me a lot with word choice and voice when I wrote the stories." The author's Western-influenced works include the picture books "Joe Cinders," a Western retelling of the Cinderella story featuring a male protagonist, and *Gullywasher Gulch,* a tale that is also a nod to Mitchell's father, who, she added, "was always saving stuff for 'some rainy day.'" In *Gullywasher Gulch,* Eb Overall, who lives in a shack above the town of Dry Gulch, is a gold prospector and packrat who has for years buried things all around his home. Though the townsfolk often chide him for "saving things for a rainy day," in the end, when a sudden downpour washes out the town, they are thankful for Eb's eccentricities and generosity, for he donates lumber and a stash of gold nuggets to rebuild the town. Ruth Semrau of *School Library Journal* found *Gullywasher Gulch* to be a "facile story," while a *Kirkus Reviews* contributor described the tale as "swell" and Eb as a "shining example" of a generous soul.

Also published in 2002 was the award-winning *Joe Cinders,* in which the stepbrother Joe does all the work on the ranch while his three mean stepbrothers laze around calling him a step-skunk. When he and the brothers are invited to the fall fiesta at the ranch of the rich and beautiful Rosalinda, Joe is stuck watching over the herd of cattle. Much to his surprise, a mysterious stranger in a sombrero and serape arrives and changes the situation. In new clothes and red cowboy boots, Joe is on his way to the fiesta in a new red pickup truck. Soon he arrives just in time to rescue Rosalinda from a bull on the loose, and she falls in love with him. But true to form, Joe must leave before midnight and during the fireworks loses a red boot in a prairie dog hole. According to a *Kirkus Reviews* critic, readers will delight in these "marvelously funny details, Western words, and classic fairy tale base." Ruth Semrau also predicted in *School Library Journal* that "younger readers . . . will enjoy noting the similarities and differences" between this Westernized version and the fairy tale classic.

As a child, Mitchell was an avid mystery reader who "grew up on Nancy Drew, Agatha Christie, and Edgar Allan Poe," she told *CA.* As an adult, she learned to love the mysteries of Pete Hautman, Mary Logue, Tony Hillerman, and Wendelin Van Draanen, so it seemed natural for Mitchell to eventually write a mystery novel of her own, *Finding Zola.* Handicapped after an automobile accident that also killed her father, thirteen-year-old Crystal tries to come to grips with his death as well as with her own now-limited physical abilities. Crystal and her mother are staying at the home of Grandmother Emilia, who has recently passed away. Unexpectedly, Crystal's mother, an artist, is called away to an art exhibit in another town, and Crystal is left in the supervision of her grandmother's friend Zola. But when Zola goes missing, it is up to Crystal to find the answers to a host of baffling questions. For characters and plot, *Finding Zola* earned a good review from Debbie Stewart, who wrote in *School Library Journal* that Crystal's dreams and memories of the deceased are "well handled and evoke sympathy," and that the "pacing is fast enough to entertain reluctant readers." Although a *Kirkus Reviews* contributor called the novel "run-of-the-mill mystery writing for fans of the simple solution," the critic appreciated Mitchell's integration of the interior and exterior action. Writing in *Booklist,* critic Ellen Mandel found Crystal a sympathetic character, remarking that "her adventures will entertain as they heighten awareness of the physical and emotional challenges of the disabled."

Sharing her thoughts about writing with *CA,* Mitchell offered these words of wisdom: "My advice to aspiring writers, children and adults, is to read, read, read. How-to books are fine for nuts and bolts, but nothing beats reading how other authors handled descriptions, plot, dialogue, and characters."

BIOGRAPHICAL AND CRITICAL SOURCES:

PERIODICALS

Booklist, October 15, 2002, Connie Fletcher, review of *Joe Cinders,* p. 408; May 15, 2003, Ellen Mandel, review of *Finding Zola,* p. 1661.
Daily Times (Ottawa, IL), September 24, 2002, Julia Durango, "Hot Diggety Dog! Two New Books from Marianne Mitchell."
Horn Book Guide, spring, 2003, review of *Joe Cinders.*
Kirkus Reviews, September 1, 2002, review of *Joe Cinders,* p. 1315; September 15, 2002, review of *Gullywasher Gulch,* p. 1396; January 15, 2003, review of *Finding Zola,* p. 144.

School Library Journal, September, 2001, review of *Coo, Coo, Caroo,* p. S62; November, 2002, Ruth Semrau, review of *Gullywasher Gulch,* p. 132; December, 2002, Ruth Semrau, review of *Joe Cinders,* p. 102; February, 2003, Debbie Stewart, review of *Finding Zola,* p. 146.

ONLINE

Boyds Mills Press Web site, http://www. boydsmillspress.com/ (October 27, 2003), "Authors and Illustrators: Marianne Mitchell."
Marianne Mitchell Home Page, http://www. mariannemitchell.net/ (July 2, 2003).

*   *   *

MITCHELL, Syne 1970-

PERSONAL: Born 1970, in Jackson, MS; daughter of Robert David (a college professor) and Bryce Jeanne (a college professor and psychologist; maiden name Mahoney) Mitchell; married Eric Stephen Nylund, June 21, 1997; children: Kai Mitchell. *Education:* St. Leo's College, B.S. (business administration), 1985; Florida State University, M.S. (solid-state physics), 1992. *Hobbies and other interests:* Spinning, weaving, dyeing, kayaking, kung fu.

ADDRESSES: Home and office—P.O. Box 860, North Bend, WA 90845. *Agent*—Donald Maass Literary Agency, 160 West 95th St., Suite 1-B, New York, NY 10025. *E-mail*—syne@sff.net.

CAREER: Novelist and technical writer. Mulberry Senior High School, Clarion, WA, former physics teacher; Internet Gaming Zone, Web developer; Microsoft Corp., member of editorial staff, programmer-writer for Windows Software Development Kit, then Web Developer for .NET SDK team, until 2002.

MEMBER: Science Fiction and Fantasy Writers of America, Sisters in Crime.

AWARDS, HONORS: Baltimore Science-Fiction Society Compton Crook/Stephen Tall Memorial Award, 2002, for *Murphy's Gambit.*

WRITINGS:

Murphy's Gambit, Roc (New York, NY), 2000.
Technogenesis, Roc (New York, NY), 2002.
The Changeling Plague, Roc (New York, NY), 2003.

WORK IN PROGRESS: A novel, tentatively titled *End in Fire.*

SIDELIGHTS: Science-fiction novelist Syne Mitchell combines her love of science with her experiences growing up in the southern United States during the civil rights era. Raised in Mississippi and earning a master's degree in physics at Florida State University, Mitchell eventually got serious about her first love—writing—and enrolled in the Clarion West six-week writer's workshop in Seattle, Washington. Spurred by her experience at Clarion, Mitchell wrote her first novel, *Murphy's Gambit,* which was published by Roc in 2001 and won the Compton Crook/Stephen Tall Memorial Award of the Baltimore Science Fiction Society.

In *Murphy's Gambit,* readers met Thiadora Murphy, a military pilot on Earth. Accepting a test mission aboard a prototype spacecraft, Murphy soon realizes that the motives for her mission are not what she has been led to believe, and that the future of the planet is at stake. Reviewing the novel for *Library Journal,* Jackie Cassada noted that "Mitchell combines first-rate hard-sf storytelling with a strong female protagonist in a fast-paced space adventure."

In addition to writing, Mitchell was employed for several years as a computer writer and programmer, working for both Microsoft and the Internet Gaming Zone. Her interest in computer science inspired her second novel, 2002's *Technogenesis.* This thriller is set in the future where most people are interconnected by the worldwide net. Mitchell's protagonist, Jasmine Reese, discovers an intelligence called Gestalt, a self-aware entity generated from the collected consciousness of eight billion networked people that threatens to take control of the entire planet. Harriet Klausner wrote in an online review for *Books 'n' Bytes* that "Mitchell has written an absorbing and creative science fiction tale that is fine entertainment for those fans that like a futuristic drama."

In the spring of 2002 Mitchell retired from Microsoft to write full time, and her third novel, *The Changeling Plague* was published the following spring. In this book Mitchell used her knowledge of physics to create a medical thriller where an illegal genetic therapy goes awry, threatening a worldwide plague. Regina Schroeder, writing for *Booklist,* called *The Changeling Plague* "Cloaked in fast-paced entertainment," and added that "Mitchell's futurist medical thriller and cyberpunk meditation is at heart a very human story of the desire to become more than we are."

BIOGRAPHICAL AND CRITICAL SOURCES:

PERIODICALS

Booklist, February 15, 2003, Regina Schroeder, review of *The Changeling Plague,* p. 1060.
Library Journal, November 15, 2000, Jackie Cassada, review of *Murphy's Gambit,* p. 101.

ONLINE

Books 'n' Bytes, http://www.booksnbytes.com/ (July 9, 2003), Harriet Klausner, review of *Technogenesis.*
Science Fiction and Fantasy Writers of American Web site, http://www.sfwa.org/ (October 3, 2002), "Syne Mitchell."
SFF.net, http://www.sff.net/people/ (February 2, 2004).*

*   *   *

MITCHELL, Tony William 1949-

PERSONAL: Born 1949, in Palmerston North, New Zealand; son of William (a schoolteacher) and Moyra (a schoolteacher; maiden name, Ratcliff) Mitchell; married Diane Powell, December, 1994 (divorced). *Ethnicity:* Pakeha (NZ). *Education:* University of Auckland, M.A. (English), 1972; University of Bristol, Ph.D. (drama), 1976.

ADDRESSES: Home—31 Scarborough St., Bundeena, New South Wales, 2230, Australia. *Office*—University of Technology, Sydney, P.O.Box 123, Broadway, New South Wales, 2007, Australia. *E-mail*—Tony.Mitchell@ uts.edu.au.

CAREER: Educator, writer, and producer. University of New South Wales, Sydney, New South Wales, Australia, tutor, 1984-88; University of Technology, Sydney, senior lecturer, 1989-2002. Producer of radio programming.

MEMBER: International Association for the Study of Popular Music (chairperson, 1997-99).

WRITINGS:

(With Philip Hayward and Roy Shuker) *North Meets South: Popular Music in Aotearoa/ New Zealand,* John Libbey Publications (Sydney, Australia), 1994.

(With Andrew Jakubowicz and others) *Racism, Ethnicity, and the Media,* Allen & Unwin (Sydney, Australia), 1994.

High Art in a Foreign Tongue: Adelaide Ristori Tours, Australasian Drama Studies Association (Australia), 1996.

Popular Music and Local Identity: Rock, Pop, and Rap in Europe and Oceania, University of Leicester Press (New York, NY), 1996.

Dario Fo: People's Court Jester, Methuen (London, England), 1999.

(Editor) *Global Noise: Rap and Hip Hop outside the USA,* Wesleyan University Press (Middletown, CT) 2001.

Contributor to journals, including *Popular Music, Perfect Beat, Popular Music and Society,* and *Theatre Journal.* Contributor to books, including *Alter/Asians, Our Australian Theatre in the 1990s, Dario Fo: Stage, Text and Tradition,* and *Screen Scores.* Contributor to broadcast materials, including *Dario Fo and Franca Rame: Comics of the People,* ABC Radio National, 1985; *Pier Paolo Pasolini: Passion and Ideology,* Radio Helicon, ABC Radio National, 1987; *Anna Magnani: My Life and Films,* Radio Helicon, ABC Radio National, 1990; *Vaclav Havel: Playwright, Political Prisoner, President,* ABC Radio National Radio Helicon, 1991; and *Dacia Maraini: Stravaganza,* Radio Helicon, 1992.

WORK IN PROGRESS: Editing *Liminal Sounds and Images: Transnational Chinese Popular Music,* and researching Australasian hip hop and the films of Clara Law.

SIDELIGHTS: Tony Mitchell told CA: "I aim to write accessible critical academic commentaries on important figures in film, performance, and popular music who are critically neglected."

Mitchell's 1996 book *Popular Music and Local Identity: Rock, Pop, and Rap in Europe and Oceania* examines the global streams of contemporary music, providing case studies showing how local identity is articulated through a region's music. Mitchell considers such regions as the Czech Republic, Italy, Australia, and New Zealand, and provides information on "extra-musical aspects" as well. For example, as Karl Neuenfeldt explained in *Popular Music and Society,* "Mitchell's analysis of the interplay of pop and politics in the Czech Republic highlights the unpredictable post-'fall of the wall' trajectory of popular music in Eastern Europe." Neuenfeldt described the book as "eclectic, well-researched, and interesting."

Mitchell covers similar ground in the collection *Global Noise: Rap and Hip Hop outside the USA,* which he edited. The thirteen essays explore local hip hop and rap cultures in Asia, Australia, Canada, and Europe, and examine how this music is not a simple emulation of African-American music, but a way for each culture to define itself. Subjects covered include Islamic rap in Europe, German-language rappers who are grappling with the issue of immigration, and a Chinese singer who uses the music to ask some difficult political questions. David Valencia in *Library Journal* found *Global Noise* to be an "Excellent overview of the phenomenon of rap and hip hop."

BIOGRAPHICAL AND CRITICAL SOURCES:

PERIODICALS

Library Journal, January, 2002, David Valencia, review of *Global Noise: Rap and Hip Hop outside the USA,* p. 106.

Popular Music and Society, summer, 1998, Karl Neuenfeldt, review of *Popular Music and Local Identity: Rock, Pop, and Rap in Europe and Oceania,* p. 129.

Reference & Research Book News, August, 1997, review of *Popular Music and Local Identity,* p. 132.

Times Educational Supplement, August 16, 1985, Steve Grant, "Teacher and Clown," p. 23; June 2, 1989, "Writers' Files Exposed," p. B20.

ONLINE

University of Technology—Sydney Web site, http://www.uts.edu.au/ (August 10, 2002), review of *Global Noise.*

University Press of New England Web site, http://www.upne.com/ (August 10, 2002).

Village Voice online, http://www.villagevoice.com/ (August 10, 2002), Robert Christgau, review of *Global Noise.*

* * *

MIZE, B. Ray 1946-

PERSONAL: Born February 12, 1946, in Fort Worth, TX; son of Ray (a railroad brakeman) and Murial (a nurse; maiden name, Gallandar) Mize; married Deborah Beck, 1972 (divorced); married Sharon Cormack (an attorney), November 26, 1976. *Education:* University of North Texas, B.A., 1971. *Politics:* Republican. *Religion:* Baptist. *Hobbies and other interests:* Horseback riding, golfing, reading.

ADDRESSES: Home and office—809 Sessions Lane, Kenner, LA 70065. *Agent*—Joyce Domborian, 201 St. Charles Avenue, New Orleans, LA 70170. *E-mail*—braymize@att.net.

CAREER: Deloitte & Touche, Dallas, TX, senior auditor; B. Ray Mize, New Orleans, LA, oilfield investigator. Ocean Drilling & Exploration Co. (ODECO), New Orleans, LA, chief of audit and security, then president of ODECO credit union. *Military service:* U.S. Army, 1965-68, became sergeant.

MEMBER: American Institute of Certified Public Accountants, Association of Certified Fraud Examiners.

WRITINGS:

The Comancheria: A Kill Line (fiction), Bald Cypress Press (Kenner, LA), 2002.

WORK IN PROGRESS: A second "Comancheria" novel, titled *A Divisive Line,* for Bald Cypress Press.

* * *

MLYNOWSKI, Sarah 1977(?)-

PERSONAL: Born c. 1977, in Montreal, Quebec, Canada. *Education:* McGill University, B.A.

ADDRESSES: Home—New York, NY. *Agent*—c/o Author Mail, Harlequin Publishers, 225 Duncan Mill Road, 4th Floor, Don Mills, Ontario M3B 3K9, Canada.

CAREER: Writer. Previously worked in marketing at Harlequin Publishers in Toronto, Canada.

WRITINGS:

Milkrun, Red Dress Ink (Don Mills, Ontario, Canada), 2001.

Fishbowl, Red Dress Ink (Don Mills, Ontario, Canada), 2002.

As Seen on TV, Red Dress Ink (Don Mills, Ontario, Canada), 2003.

SIDELIGHTS: Sarah Mlynowski's debut novel, *Milkrun,* was the first book published by Red Dress Ink, a subsidiary of Harlequin Publishers that offers an alternative take on traditional romance novels. Aimed at twentysomethings, Mlynowski's first two books—both published while the author was herself in her early twenties—have been received as fresh and stylish romances for the younger generation. "I love exploring and satirizing the anxieties of today's twentysomething woman," Mlynowski told *Heartstrings'* Lori A. May.

Mlynowski was born and raised in Montreal, Canada. She attended a Jewish high school where she was taught Hebrew, Yiddish, French, and English. "A lot of my Hebrew I don't remember but I did speak Yiddish fluently at one point," she explained to Caroline Westbrook in an interview for *Jewish.co.uk.* After graduating with a degree in English from McGill University, where she served as fiction editor for the school's literary journal and also contributed a biweekly column to the newspaper, Mlynowski moved to Toronto to work for Harlequin's marketing department. After *Milkrun* started her off on a three-book contract with Red Dress Ink, she relocated to New York to write full-time.

Milkrun, Mlynowski's first book, was described by a reviewer for *Publishers Weekly* as an "entertaining debut" with "both humor and substance." The novel centers on the life of twenty-four-year-old Jackie, who has only just recently moved to Boston with her boyfriend when he tells her that he wants to go on a long trip to Thailand—without her. Jackie, a copyeditor for a romance publishing company, decides not to waste time being emotionally distraught about the breakup, but rather to get back out into the dating scene right away. She enlists the help of her friends, buys some sexy boots, and hangs out at a trendy singles bar called Orgasm; finding the right guy, though, turns out to be harder than she ever expected. "Mlynowski is acutely aware of the plight of the twentysomething single woman," the *Publishers Weekly* reviewer noted. Reviewers also admired Mlynowski's upbeat, offbeat style: "The author has made every word an effortless step toward the next. Her style of flirty dialogue and quick-wit narrative is both touching and humorous, hitting every beat dead on," May wrote in a review for *Heartstrings.*

Mlynowski drew on her friends' and her own dating experiences to create the character of Jackie and the other women that people the book, which *Mercury*'s Ellen Whinnett called "edgy" with "a nice collection of female characters." *Booklist*'s Kristine Huntley, who admittedly found Jackie to be "at times annoyingly neurotic," nonetheless described her as "a likable heroine." Some critics, though, found the tone and characterizations to be a bit too lightweight, such as *Daily Beacon Online*'s Leslie Wylie, who wrote of the "lackluster romantic misadventures" and "chatty" characters. However, Wylie concluded that "those seeking a perky take on how love does and doesn't happen may find *Milkrun* their cup of tea." Most reviewers felt that Mlynowski's playful style offers a fresh alternative to traditional romance novels. Linda Robertson wrote in the *Evening Times,* "It's definitely one which should be filed under 'chick lit,' but it stands head and sholders above the rest."

Mlynowski followed *Milkrun* with *Fishbowl* a year later. "*Fishbowl* takes three strangers and binds them

into a rental contract that harnesses their freedom and unleashes their undesirable traits," May summarized. In *Fishbowl* the rental contract is in Toronto, and the three strangers are Allie, a perky but naïve twenty-two year-old; Jodine, a perfectionistic law student; and Emma, a beautiful fashion editor's assistant with a tendency to party hard and sleep around. The narrative voice switches between all three women, and Mlynowski throws in a fourth omniscient narrator for good measure. "I thought this narrative technique would be the best way to capture the roommate experience," the author told May. "I wanted to show what all three roommates were thinking and how they interpreted and misinterpreted every event." Although some reviewers felt the characterization to be overdone—*Romantic Times*'s Samantha J. Gust, for example, wrote that the book is "plagued with unsympathetic characters"—critics for the most part responded positively. Huntley described the novel as having "fully dimensional characters and a terrific story."

As the three women are busy trying to reconcile their differences, disaster strikes—an accidental fire damages their kitchen, and, lacking insurance, they are forced to come up with the repair money on their own. In typical Mlynowski style, the women generate all sorts of schemes, including throwing parties at a local bar and presenting a "How to Pick Up Women" seminar, all the while learning unexpected things about each other and themselves. "Mlynowski delivers a solid if formulaic roommate caper," a *Publishers Weekly* reviewer commented, and a writer for *Scribes World* noted that "personality clashes, fight scenes and sex make this a perfect book for the MTV generation."

Mlynowski plans to continue writing for Red Dress Ink. She spoke to Westbrook about creating a heroine for the modern reader: "They don't necessarily need heroines who are perfect and gorgeous and fabulous and always classy—our heroines these days are a little more realistic, a little more likely to fall over, to lose something, to not be able to string a perfect sentence together."

BIOGRAPHICAL AND CRITICAL SOURCES:

PERIODICALS

Arizona Republic, November 23, 2002, Sally Mesarosh, "Novel Romance Team: Mother, Daughter Share Love of Writing," p. 1.

Booklist, December 15, 2001, Kristine Huntley, review of *Milkrun,* p. 708; October 1, 2002, Kristine Huntley, review of *Fishbowl,* p. 305; September 15, 2003, Kristine Huntley, review of *As Seen on TV,* p. 224.

Evening Times (Glasgow, Scotland), May 25, 2002, Linda Robertson, review of *Milkrun,* p. 39.

Mercury (Hobart, Australia), May 4, 2002, Ellen Whinnett, review of *Milkrun,* p. 39.

Publishers Weekly, October 29, 2001, review of *Milkrun,* p. 34; August 26, 2002, "One of the Most Successful Authors at Harlequin's 'Chick Lit' Imprint," p. 13; October 28, 2002, review of *Fishbowl,* pp. 52-53.

ONLINE

Best Reviews, http://www.thebestreviews.com/ (November 3, 2001), Harriet Klausner, review of *Milkrun;* (September 28, 2002) Harriet Klausner, review of *Fishbowl.*

Daily Beacon Online, http://dailybeacon.utk.edu/ (March 11, 2002), Leslie Wylie, review of *Milkrun.*

Heartstrings, http://romanticfiction.tripod.com/ (October 15, 2002), Lori A. May, review of *Milkrun* and interview with Mlynowski.

Jewish.co.uk, http://www.jewish.co.uk/ (April 24, 2002), Caroline Westbrook, interview with Mlynowski.

Red Dress Ink Web site, http://www.reddressink.com/ (May 31, 2003), interview with Mlynowski.

Romantic Times, http://www.romantictimes.com/ (May 31, 2003), Christine Chambers, review of *Milkrun;* Samantha J. Gust, review of *Fishbowl.*

Scribes World, http://www.scribesworld.com/ (May 31, 2003), review of *Fishbowl.**

* * *

MONAHAN, Jean 1959-

PERSONAL: Born September 2, 1959, in Salem, MA; daughter of John and Patricia Monahan; children: Lilah Violet. *Education:* Bates College, B.A., 1981; Columbia University, M.F.A., 1985. *Hobbies and other interests:* Eating.

ADDRESSES: Agent—c/o Anhinga Press, P.O. Box 10595, Tallahassee, FL 32302. *E-mail*—jehane@world.std.com.

CAREER: Poet and media producer. WGBH, Boston, MA, producer/writer, 1990-97; Agency.com, Boston, MA, creative director, beginning 1998. Formerly taught English in China.

AWARDS, HONORS: Grolier award, 1988, for poem; Anhinga Press prize, 1991, for *Hands;* Open Voice award, West Side YMCA, 1994, for poetry; *River Styx* award, 1998, for poetry.

WRITINGS:

Hands (poetry), Anhinga Press (Tallahassee, FL), 1992.
Believe It or Not (poetry), Orchises (Washington, DC), 1999.

Contributor of poetry to publications and journals including *Atlantic, Ploughshares, American Scholar, Heliotrope, Orion, Cortland Review, DoubleTake, Atlanta Review, MIT Oceanographic Institute Newsletter, Manhattan Review, Cider Press Review, Hubbub, American Scholar, Poetry International, New Republic, Seneca Review, River Styx, Button,* and *Webster Review.* Contributor to anthologies including *Orpheus & Company,* University Press of New England, 1999; and *Emily Dickinson Anthology,* Universities West Press, 1998.

SIDELIGHTS: Jean Monahan told *CA:* "What inspires me to write is often a sense of disbelief or rollicking good humor about the way the world works, most often based on something I have read or been told about. I write to keep some sense of order in soul. I am influenced by Bishop, Moore, Stevens, Lorca, Rilke, Hoagland—but mostly by nonfiction. My writing is becoming less ironic and sardonic and more, dare I say, benevolent (but still just this side of wacky)."

BIOGRAPHICAL AND CRITICAL SOURCES:

ONLINE

Anhinga Press Web site, http://www.anhinga.org/ (February 9, 2003), "Jean Monahan."

MONIN, Lydia

PERSONAL: Female.

ADDRESSES: Agent—c/o Trafalgar Square Books, P.O. Box 257, Howe Hill Road, North Pomfret, VT 05053.

CAREER: Author. Coproducer of four-part television documentary *The Devil's Gardens: A History of Landmines.*

WRITINGS:

(With Andrew Gallimore) *The Devil's Gardens: A History of Landmines,* Pimlico/Trafalgar Square (London, England), 2002.

SIDELIGHTS: Lydia Monin, together with Andrew Gallimore, produced the four-part television documentary and accompanying book *The Devil's Gardens: A History of Landmines* to further the cause of ridding the world of one of the most personally destructive weapons. Their work provides a history of the development and use of landmines and the weapon's catastrophic effects on people all over the world.

Landmines have been used in warfare since World War I. The original prototypes were not much more than tunnels filled with explosives. Later the portable anti-tank mine was created, followed by anti-personnel landmines, some small enough to fit in the palm of a hand. As Alex de Waal observed in a review of *The Devil's Gardens* for the *Times Literary Supplement,* landmine manufacturers have stated in their advertisements that the "explosive has been precisely calculated to have the blast effect and not the fragmentation effect to make the man disabled and incapacitate him permanently." In their book Monin and Gallimore emphasize the debilitating effects of these weapons, which, according to John Pearn in the *British Medical Journal,* are triggered and explode at a rate of two to three thousand times each month in countries around the world.

The more contemporary landmines are insidious weapons, which, as De Waal stated, are "designed to spring from the ground to the height of a metre before exploding, smashing their fragments into the victim's genitals, torso and face." By the early 2000s more than twenty-eight countries were planted with landmines, including several regions of Africa as well as Afghanisan, where it is feared that the land will not be cleared for another century. Landmines, according to Pearn, are ranked as one of the "top six preventable causes of child mortality in developing nations."

The Devil's Gardens also discusses the efforts of international movements to ban landmines and to clear existing minefields. Well-known figures such as Princess Diana and Paul McCartney helped to raise public awareness of the problem. The 1997 Ottawa Treaty, which prohibited the use of landmines, and the 1997 Nobel Peace Prize, which went to the International Campaign to Ban Landmines, has legitimized the movement and brought critically needed support. Some countries, such as Australia, have made a concerted effort to destroy stockpiles of the weapons. But other countries, in contrast, have actually increased their use. Groups such as Adopt-a-Minefield have since formed and helped to raise money for the clearing of landmines.

"Anyone trying to grasp the full dimensions of this deadly international problem," wrote Jim Doyle in his review of *The Devil's Gardens* for *Library Journal,* "should read this book."

BIOGRAPHICAL AND CRITICAL SOURCES:

PERIODICALS

British Medical Journal, June 29, 2002, John Pearn, review of *The Devil's Gardens: A History of Landmines,* p. 1589.
Contemporary Review, May 2002, review of *The Devil's Gardens,* p. 316.
Library Journal, November 1, 2002, Jim Doyle, review of *The Devil's Gardens,* p. 108.
New Scientist, February 9, 2002, review of *The Devil's Gardens,* p. 45.
Publishers Weekly, November 4, 2002, review of *The Devil's Gardens,* p. 74.
Times Literary Supplement, May 24, 2002, Alex De Waal, review of *The Devil's Gardens,* p. 28.*

MULLEN, Harryette (Romell) 1953-

PERSONAL: Born 1953, in Florence, AL; daughter of James Otis (a social worker and administrator) and Avis Ann Mullen. *Ethnicity:* African American. *Education:* University of Texas, Austin, B.A., 1975; University of California—Santa Cruz, M.A., 1987, Ph.D., 1990. *Religion:* Protestant. *Hobbies and other interests:* Yoga, tai-chi, music, art, travel, popular culture.

ADDRESSES: Office   Department of English, University of California, Los Angeles, Los Angeles, CA 90095-1530.

CAREER: Poet and educator. Cornell University, Ithaca, NY, professor of African-American and other ethnic literature; University of California, Los Angeles, professor of African-American literature and creative writing. Also worked in Artists-in-Schools program sponsored by Texas Commission on the Arts.

AWARDS, HONORS: Artist grant, Texas Institute of Letters; artist grant, Helene Wurlitzer Foundation of New Mexico; faculty fellowship, Cornell Society for the Humanities, 1991-92; Gertrude Stein Award in Innovative American Poetry, 1994-95; Rockefeller fellowship, 1994-95; First Prize, Katherine Newman Award for Best Essay, *MELUS,* 1996; invited artist, Virginia Center for Creative Arts, 1999; finalist for National Book Award for Poetry, National Book Critics Circle Award, and *Los Angeles Times* Book Award, all 2002, all for *Sleeping with the Dictionary.*

WRITINGS:

POETRY

Tree Tall Woman, Energy Earth (Galveston, TX), 1981.
Trimmings, Tender Buttons (New York, NY), 1991.
S*PeRM**K*T, Singing Horse (Philadelphia, PA), 1992.
Muse and Drudge, Singing Horse Press (Philadelphia, PA), 1995.
Blues Baby: Early Poems ("Bucknell Series in Contemporary Poetry"), Bucknell University Press (Lewisburg, PA), 2002.
Sleeping with the Dictionary, University of California Press (Berkeley, CA), 2002.

Contributor of essays to periodicals and journals, including *American Book Review, Callaloo, Chain, Diacritics, Light Work Annual, Antioch Review,* and *MELUS.* Fiction and poetry published in numerous journals, magazines, anthologies, and textbooks.

ADAPTATIONS: Verses from *Muse and Drudge* set to music by T. J. Anderson as *Seven Cabaret Songs,* 1995, and by Christine Baczewzka as *O Rose,* 1997.

SIDELIGHTS: Harryette Mullen is a poet and a professor of English at the University of California, Los Angeles, where she teaches creative writing and African-American literature. Her poetry has been hailed by critics as unique, powerful, and challenging. Elisabeth A. Frost wrote in *Contemporary Literature:* "Crossing the lines between often isolated aesthetic camps, Harryette Mullen has pioneered her own form of bluesy, disjunctive lyric poetry, combining a concern for the political issues raised by identity politics with a poststructualist emphasis on language."

Mullen was born in Alabama, but spent most of her childhood in Texas. "I've loved to write from childhood. I wrote to entertain my family, my friends, and myself," she told Emily Allen Williams in an interview for the *African American Review.* Mullen began writing poetry more seriously in high school, when she had her first poem published in a local newspaper. After receiving her undergraduate degree from the University of Texas, she went to the University of California at Santa Cruz, where she wrote her dissertation on slave narratives. Even when writing essays and fiction, though, poetry continued to be important to her. "I feel that I need to write in order to know what I think and what I believe," she told Williams. "It's a way of keeping in touch with the inner landscape, I guess. And it makes me more alert to the outer landscape."

A key aspect of Mullen's relationship to poetry developed when she began going to poetry readings. "It was through the poetry-[reading] circuit that I began to realize that poetry is not just something on the page, but a community of readers and writers," she told Williams. Mullen's poetry draws on oral tradition, music, and the spoken word. Mullen described her intention to Frost in an interview for *Contemporary Literature:* "I am writing for the eye and the ear at once, at that intersection of orality and literacy, wanting to make sure that there is a troubled, disturbing aspect to the work so that it is never just a 'speakerly' or a 'writerly' text."

Mullen's first book of poetry, *Tree Tall Woman,* was published before she went to graduate school; the poems from this first book are included, along with other early poetry, in the more recent publication *Blues Baby: Early Poems. Trimmings,* her second book, came ten years after *Tree Tall Woman. Partisan Review's* Stephen Yenser called it "an ebulliently feminist, black and bluesy, bebop, wicked, scatty, addictive sequence of mazy prose poems, ostensibly about wardrobe accessories and the ramifications thereof, and in fact about language and semiotics in general." Mullen's characteristic dense, meaning-packed style is in full play here; Yenser wrote of her poems, "Compact, sometimes no more than eight or ten words, they are as loaded as chocolate truffles and the finest Vegas dice." Drawing much inspiration from Gertrude Stein's *Tender Buttons,* Mullen is unafraid to delve into the racial subtext ignored by Stein; as Molly Bendall noted in *Antioch Review,* she "brings her own contemporary African-American female voice to these poems." In one particular section, for example, she examines the common representation of femininity as "pink" and "white," inquiring how a black female might interact with these poetic constructions. Frost wrote in *Women's Review of Books* that "these relationships among femininity, clothes and language are beautifully orchestrated in word-play that dramatizes complex issues about gender and culture without offering easy or predictable answers."

Mullen followed *Trimmings* with *S*PeRM**K*T,* published the next year. Like the previous book, it consists of short, fragmented prose poems, this time with the wordplay revolving around the supermarket—both the concept and, as in the title of the piece, the word itself. "Mullen speeds up and down the aisle-like margins of American life spying out those strangest interstices of commodity and racial culture," *MultiCultural Review's* Aldon L. Nielsen explained. Race, sex, gender, and consumer culture interact in thought-provoking ways as Mullen's poetry comments on the racial and erotic subtexts of our commodified society. "The intertwinings of the commercial and the erotic are the crucial subject of Mullen's slim book—itself 'packaged' in a saranwraplike wrap-around photo of a meat case of packaged beef and interlarded with other photos of stocked shelves," Yenser wrote in *Yale*

Review. Mullen explained to Williams some of the political ideas she explored while writing *S*PeRM**K*T:* "When I was writing this poem it made me very conscious of what I was doing in the supermarket—how we behave as consumers and define ourselves by the products we purchase. . . . We really are what we eat, what we consume. As a nation, as a culture, as a society, we consume way more than the rest of the world."

Mullen's fourth book of poetry, *Muse and Drudge,* examines gender, race, and art in an exploration of "the tension and creative possibilities between inspirational, existential, and mundane work," George Yancy wrote in *CLA Journal.* The title mentions two female roles common throughout the history of art: the idealized muse who inspires the artist, and the laboring drudge whose behind-the-scenes toil supports him (a "him" because of the male-oriented tradition to which Mullen is referring.) An exploration of race also plays a large role in these poems, which, as Yancy pointed out, are "hypertextually and intertextually linked to the lived experiences of being black in America and the religious and spiritual semiotic spaces of Africa and Afro-America." In fact, Mullen told Frost that the book "was written specifically to try to bring different audiences together;" after discovering that her two previous books reached a mostly white audience, Mullen wanted to her work to reach the black community as well. However, she understands that the dense wordplay and numerous references that contribute to her highly intertextual work require every person to read and understand the poem differently. She told Frost: "The reader is getting whatever the reader can get. . . . Black people get certain things particularly, and Spanish speakers get certain other things. There are people who recognize Sappho lines or Bessie Smith lines."

Muse and Drudge contrasts to her previous free verse and prose poems in that it is written in fairly regular quatrains; yet, as *American Book Review's* Mark Scroggins noted, she still "manages to keep her readers consistently off balance, surprised by a rhyme or disappointed at its absence." Mullen explained to Frost the meaning of this style: "It is very much a book of echoes. Some of the fragments rhyme and some don't, and that is basically the principle of the book—the recycling of fragments of language." At the same time, Scroggins noted, she "makes it all seem so easy: the language here dances, shakes, and splits itself into puns, allusions, and double-entendre, all the while maintaining a jaunty funkiness."

Mullen's wordplay becomes even more structurally avant-garde in her next book, *Sleeping with the Dictionary,* which was nominated for a National Book Award. Carol Muske-Dukes wrote in the *Los Angeles Times Book Review* that "poetic expression here springs from a formal device, a game, a premeditated romp: a little like the Muse playing Scrabble"; many of these devices, such as replacing nouns with ones found seven entries away in the dictionary, were developed by the international literary group OuLiPo. "More diverse" than her previous books, according to a *Publishers Weekly* reviewer, *Sleeping with the Dictionary* is filled with styles ranging from "exhaustive alphabetical language salads" to "strange rewrites of classics" (two poems that rework a famous Shakespeare sonnet). "Many of the poems' titles are careful twists on dead metaphors and other commonly used phrases," noted Hoke S. Glover II in *Black Issues Book Review;* "This is her art: to reconstruct, redefine and create out of splicing and stitching back together the pieces of meaning in language."

UCLA Today's Meg Sullivan felt that *Sleeping with the Dictionary* assumes "a more playful posture" than Mullen's previous works, but other critics felt the opposite, that the work is more serious. With Mullen's poetry these binaries of play and work, comedy and tragedy, coexist. "For me the comic is the other side of the coin of tragedy or oppression. They work together. I know people sometimes have a problem when the tone shifts abruptly. Some people find that disturbing, but for me it feels right," she told Frost. Mullen's poetry continually challenges the reader, and does so on many levels. As Yancy wrote, Mullen is "a word warrior. She preaches, poeticizes, and raps us, indeed, envelops us, into a tropological maze. She invites us to enjoy the logic of discursive possibilities, emotional entanglements, and the force of language."

Mullen told *CA:* "Writing became important to me when I was very young. It was the only way I could communicate with my father after my parents were divorced. My mother believed in educating 'the whole child.' She made sure my sister and I always had books to read, and she somehow found money to pay for music and dance lessons. She also encouraged us to draw and write. My sense of poetry was awakened by the formal and informal, written and oral rhymes and rhythms of family, church, and school.

"In all of my books, I try to find a balance between serious work and humorous play. At the moment, *Sleeping with the Dictionary* is my favorite because I enjoyed experimenting with different ways of creating poetry."

BIOGRAPHICAL AND CRITICAL SOURCES:

PERIODICALS

African American Review, winter, 2000, Emily Allen Williams, "The Queen of Hip Hyperbole" (interview), p. 701.
American Book Review, May, 1997, Mark Scroggins, review of *Muse and Drudge,* p. 17.
Antioch Review, winter, 1993, Molly Bendall, review of *Trimmings,* p. 154.
Black Issues Book Review, July-August, 2002, Hoke S. Glover III, review of *Sleeping with the Dictionary,* p. 63.
Callaloo, summer, 1996, Calvin Bedient, "The Solo Mysterioso Blues: An Interview with Harryette Mullen," pp. 651-669.
CLA Journal, June, 2001, George Yancy, review of *Muse and Drudge,* pp. 522-527.
Contemporary Literature, fall, 2000, Elisabeth A. Frost, "An Interview with Harryette Mullen," pp. 397-421.
Georgia Review, fall, 1996, Fred Chappell, review of *Muse and Drudge,* pp. 584-600.
Los Angeles Time Book Review, March 31, 2002, Carol Muske-Dukes, review of *Sleeping with the Dictionary,* p. 6.
MultiCultural Review, March, 1994, Aldon L. Nielsen, review of *S*PeRM*K*T,* pp. 72-73.
Partisan Review, Volume 61, 1994, Stephen Yenser, review of *Trimmings,* pp. 350-355.
Publishers Weekly, September 25, 1995, review of *Muse and Drudge,* pp. 51-52; December 17, 2001, review of *Sleeping with the Dictionary,* p. 85.
Sulfur, fall, 1992, Juliana Spahr, review of *Trimmings,* pp. 265-266.
Women's Review of Books, February, 1993, Elisabeth Frost, review of *Trimmings,* pp. 11-12.
Yale Review, April, 1994, Stephen Yenser, review of *S*PeRM*K*T,* pp. 161-181.

ONLINE

Academy of American Poets Web site, http://www.poets.org/ (August 1, 2001), biography of Mullen.

Arras, http://www.arras.net/ (May 30, 2003), review of *Sleeping with the Dictionary.*

Bucknell University Press Web site, http://www.departments.bucknell.edu/univ_Press/ (May 30, 2003).

Center for African American Studies at UCLA Web site, http://www.sscnet.ucla.edu/caas/ (May 30, 2003), biography of Mullen.

New York Times, http://www.nytimes.com/ (December 29, 2002), Mary Park, review of *Sleeping with the Dictionary.*

UCLA Today online, http://www.today.ucla.edu/ (May 30, 2003), Meg Sullivan, review of *Sleeping with the Dictionary.*

University of California Press Web site, http://www.ucpress.edu/ (May 30, 2003).

*   *   *

MUMMA, Howard E. 1909-

PERSONAL: Born June 27, 1909, in Springfield, OH. *Education:* Yale University, B.S. (with honors), 1936, B.D., 1939, M.S.T., 1944.

ADDRESSES: Agent—Paraclete Press, 365 Southern Eagle Cartway, Boston, MA 02631-1558.

CAREER: Ordained Methodist minister, 1940; pastor of Methodist churches in Columbus, OH, and Cuyahoga Falls, OH; United Methodist Church, district superintendent of Akron District, Northeast Ohio Conference, and chairperson of cabinet for bishop of Ohio. Guest preacher at churches throughout Europe. Mount Union College, past member of board of trustees. Formerly worked as social worker in "Hell's Kitchen" district, New York, NY; also worked at steel plants and with power company construction gangs.

AWARDS, HONORS: D.Div., Ohio Northern University, 1955; LL.D., Salem College (Salem, WV), 1965.

WRITINGS:

Take It to the People: New Ways in Soul Winning— Unconventional Evangelism, World Publishing (New York, NY), 1969.

Albert Camus and the Minister, Paraclete Press (Brewster, MA), 2000.

Contributor to periodicals, including *Pastor* and *Methodist Story.*

SIDELIGHTS: Howard E. Mumma told *CA:* "I have had a varied career. During two summers I was a social worker in 'Hell's Kitchen,' in New York City, working with typical 'dead-end kids.' I have worked in steel plants and on construction gangs for an Ohio power company. For two years I was a lecturer on effective speaking at a Midwestern university. Since becoming a pastor, I have served on mediation boards and, through my efforts, several labor disputes have been successfully concluded.

"I have made five extensive tours into eastern Europe. In 1948 I was interred for four days in Warsaw, Poland, by the Communist regime. I visited concentration camps in Poland, Czechoslovakia, East Germany, and Yugoslavia. In all of these countries I had the opportunity to study the plight of the common man. I sat in conference with high government officials in Prague, Warsaw, and Berlin. I was a guest in the home of Archbishop Joseph Beran, Roman Catholic prelate of Czechoslovakia, on the very day the archbishop was arrested by the Communists. I have visited Methodist churches and mission schools in thirty-four countries, including visits to Africa, India, and the Far East."

*   *   *

MUNROE, Jim 1972-

PERSONAL: Born 1972.

ADDRESSES: Agent—c/o Author Mail, Four Walls Eight Windows, 39 West 14th Street, No. 503, New York, NY 10011. *E-mail*—jim@nomediakings.org.

CAREER: Adbusters (magazine), former managing editor; author.

WRITINGS:

Flyboy Action Figure Comes with Gasmask, Harper-Collins (Toronto, Ontario, Canada), 1999.

Angry Young Spaceman, No Media Kings (Toronto, Ontario, Canada), 2000, Four Walls Eight Windows (New York, NY), 2001.

Everyone in Silico, Four Walls Eight Windows (New York, NY), 2002.

SIDELIGHTS: Canadian author Jim Munroe has lived in South Korea, Vancouver, and the Annex neighborhood in Toronto. He has made a name not just as a science-fiction writer but as an anticorporate activist who disengaged himself from a contractual agreement with HarperCollins for his second novel. Munroe is the former managing editor for *Adbusters* magazine, which cut at the culture of corporate consumption with slashing satirical articles. In keeping with his passionate stance against media consolidation, he created his own imprint—No Media Kings. His quirky Web site is designed to promote his work; advise authors on the pros, cons, and how-tos of self-publishing; and express his subversive viewpoints about media monopoly. In an interview with Jeffrey Yamaguchi of *Bookmouth.com,* Munroe noted that the publicity surrounding his rejection of Rupert Murdoch's huge conglomerate "was a good media hook, but it helped that I had a slick website, a marketing plan, and a political motivation."

When Munroe's first novel, *Flyboy Action Figure Comes with Gasmask,* hit the shelves, reviewers seemed to appreciate his fresh, humorous style. "Don't read this book on public transit, in a doctor's waiting room, or anywhere else where people will stare at you strangely if you start laughing out loud," wrote Heather Ganshorn for *Resource Links.* Peter Darbyshire commented in *Quill & Quire* that the book is a "genuinely hip, young, and urban tale. Forget about all the other fiction that poses as slick and cool, forget the stylish authors that promise to be the voice for the next generation and then fail to deliver. . . . Munroe will be the writer to watch."

The central character in *Flyboy,* Ryan, is a twenty-two-year-old, quirky but likable University of Toronto student who has the secret ability to turn himself into a fly. He meets Cassandra, a bisexual punk-rocker waitress who can make things disappear and who had an alien lover by whom she has a clairvoyant toddler daughter. The loners become lovers, discuss their deepest secrets, and decide to become superheroes. Donning costumes and calling themselves Flyboy and Ms.

Place, they fight the forces of social injustice—cigarette companies, conservative mainstream media, sexist cops, and laws against marijuana. Meanwhile, they must deal with the usual personal issues faced by young college students. A reviewer for *Publishers Weekly* commented: "For all their efforts, the Superheroes cannot save themselves from the excessive moralizing that makes this novel resemble a slightly less wholesome after-school special." However, one reviewer for *Booklist* described the novel as "witty and sensitive," while Roberta Johnson, also for *Booklist,* wrote: "This is a Gen-X novel to treasure."

Munroe's second book not only became his first self-published novel, it was also available as a free download from his Web site. The book's plot elicited excited reviews from the likes of Bonnie Schiedel, who wrote in *Quill & Quire:* "As an allegory, *Angry Young Spaceman* isn't particularly subtle, and as the title implies, it's not intended to be. . . . And when Munroe takes aim at the management and co-opting of subcultures, the satire is dead-on and more intriguing." This story is set in 2959 and its twenty-something hero, Sam Breen, is angry and disillusioned by the powerbrokering of Earth, which now has political control of the entire universe. The only way Sam can escape Earth's ultraconsumerism is to head for the far reaches of the galaxy. He ends up in the underwater world of Octavia to teach English as a foreign language to its eight-legged inhabitants. However, the catch for Sam is that Earth's push to assimilate the entire galaxy by enforcing English as the universal language, so he finds himself torn between his escape route and perpetuating Earth's control.

Adrian Baker wrote in the online *Danforth Review:* "The fact that *Angry Young Spaceman* is self-published may not seem to have anything to do with the actual content of the book. However, much of Sam's dislike for Earth is based on their need to control and license intellectual property." Becky Olshen commented in a review for *Bookreporter.com:* "The great thing about science fiction is how it turns a sledgehammer into a scalpel. . . . And if that novel is rich and well written enough to stand on its own, message or no message, that's even better. . . . Munroe so deftly weaves progressive politics into an engrossing story that you barely notice he's doing it."

In Munroe's self-published third book, *Everyone in Silico,* every aspect of life in 2036 Toronto has become corporatized. Lori Hahnel made note in the *Danforth*

Review about the "long tradition of novels whose ideals follow the high road, novels that comment on the nasty underbelly of the human condition in our society." She named Aldous Huxley's *Brave New World,* George Orwell's *1984,* and Anthony Burgess's *A Clockwork Orange* among them. Munroe's third novel is one such book, she commented, "in spirit if not in execution."

In *Everyone in Silico,* individuals in a post-scarcity, consumption-obsessed society can trade their messy, organic life on a polluted Earth for a digital existence where anything is available for a price. Self is the ultimate computer program into which the favored few can have their brains uploaded and to exist mentally in a gigantic utopian computerized space called Frisco. "Your experience of Frisco depends on what package you can afford," wrote a reviewer for *GoodReports. net,* "with lowly silvers and golds being subject to relentless advertising while platinum members get to surf banner-free. But people start wondering where their bodies are." A *Publishers Weekly* reviewer commented that "Munroe exuberantly studs the action with grotesque extrapolations of politics and advertising that most people accept unthinkingly." The reviewer for *GoodReports.net* contemplated the fact that Munroe not only expresses his disdain and dislike for the evils of consumerism, globalization, and corporate conglomerates, but, by self-publishing, is acting upon his philosophies. And, the reviewer asked, "Can big publishing produce books as original as this?"

BIOGRAPHICAL AND CRITICAL SOURCES:

PERIODICALS

Booklist, November 1, 1999, Roberta Johnson, review of *Flyboy Action Figure Comes with Gas Mask,* p. 513; January 1, 2000, p. 819.

Kirkus Reviews, August 15, 2002, review of *Everyone in Silico,* p. 1173.

Magazine of Fantasy and Science Fiction, July, 2000, Charles de Lint, review of *Angry Young Spaceman,* p. 29.

Publishers Weekly, October 4, 1999, review of *Flyboy Action Figure Comes with Gasmask,* p. 65; August 27, 2001, review of *Angry Young Spaceman,* p. 61; September 2, 2002, review of *Everyone in Silico,* p. 58.

Quill & Quire, February, 1999, Peter Darbyshire, review of *Flyboy Action Figure Comes with Gasmask,* p. 33; May, 2000, Bonnie Schiedel, review of *Angry Young Spaceman,* p. 30.

Resource Links, October, 2002, Heather Ganshorn, review of *Flyboy Action Figure Comes with Gasmask,* p. 54.

ONLINE

Bookmouth.com, http://www.bookmouth.com/ (April 7, 2003), Jeffrey Yamaguchi, "An Interview with Jim Munroe, Author and Publisher of *Angry Young Spaceman.*"

Bookreporter.com, http://www.bookreporter.com/ (April 7, 2003), Becky Olshen, review of *Angry Young Spaceman.*

Danforth Review online, http://www.danforthreview. com/ (April 7, 2003), Adrian Baker, review of *Angry Young Spaceman;* Lori Hahnel, review of *Everyone in Silico.*

Digital Web, http://www.digital-web.com/ (April 7, 2003), James McNally, review of *Everyone in Silico.*

GoodReports.net, http://www.goodreports.net/ (April 7, 2003), review of *Angry Young Spaceman* and *Everyone in Silico.*

Montreal Mirror online, http://www.montrealmirror. com/ (June 14, 2003), Juliet Waters, "Jim Munroe's Guide to Interplanetary Publishing Success."

No Media Kings Web site, http://www.nomediakings. org/ (April 7, 2003).

SciFi.com, http://www.scifi.com/ (April 7, 2003), Paul Di Filippo, review of *Angry Young Spaceman;* Donna McMahon, review of *Everyone in Silico.*

* * *

MURAV'EVA, Irina
See MURAVYOVA, Irina

* * *

MURAVYOVA, Irina 1952-

PERSONAL: Surname sometimes transliterated "Murav'eva"; born September 21, 1952, in Moscow, USSR (now Russia); immigrated to United States, 1985, naturalized U.S. citizen; daughter of Lazar (a writer) and Tamara (Pankzatova) Shtainmets; married

Victor Muravyov, July, 1974; children: Igor. *Ethnicity:* "Russian." *Education:* Attended Moscow State University; Brown University, Ph.D. *Religion:* Christian.

ADDRESSES: Home—Dover, MA. *Agent*—c/o Author Mail, Ivan R. Dee, 1332 North Halsted St., Chicago, IL 60622.

CAREER: Fiction writer.

WRITINGS:

Kudriavyi Leitenant: Rasskazy (title means "Curly-haired Lieutenant"), Hermitage Publishers (Tenafly, NJ), 1995.
Filemon i Bavkida: Povesti, Rasskazy, Vagrius (Moscow, Russia), 2000.
The Nomadic Soul (novella and short stories), translated by John Dewey, Ivan R. Dee (Chicago, IL), 2000.

BIOGRAPHICAL AND CRITICAL SOURCES:

PERIODICALS

Publishers Weekly, July 10, 2000, review of *The Nomadic Soul,* p. 45.
World Literature Today, autumn, 2000, Margaret Ziolkowski, review of *The Nomadic Soul,* p. 880.

*   *   *

MYERS, Minor, Jr. 1942-2003

OBITUARY NOTICE—See index for *CA* sketch: Born August 13, 1942, in Copley, OH; died of complications from lung cancer July 22, 2003, in Bloomington, IL. Educator, administrator, and author. Myers was the president of Illinois Wesleyan University. He was an alumnus of Carleton College, where he received his B.A. in 1964, and Princeton University, where he completed a Ph.D. in 1972. Myers then embarked on an academic career, beginning at Connecticut College, where he started as an instructor in 1968 and became professor of government in 1981. During the late 1980s he was provost, dean of faculty, and professor of political science at Hobart and William Smith Colleges, accepting the position as president of Illinois Wesleyan in 1989. A staunch advocate of liberal-arts education, he helped transform Illinois Wesleyan into an institution with a national reputation, adding academic programs, constructing library and science buildings, and expanding study-abroad programs. Despite his busy schedule, Myers also managed to also publish several books, including *Liberty without Anarchy: A History of the Society of the Cincinnati* (1984) and *Illinois Wesleyan University: Continuity and Change, 1850-2000* (2001).

OBITUARIES AND OTHER SOURCES:

BOOKS

Writers Directory, 18th edition, St. James Press (Detroit, MI), 2003.

PERIODICALS

Chicago Tribune, July 27, 2003, section 4, p. 7.
Plain Dealer (Cleveland, OH), July 28, 2003, p. B5.

N

NATION, Carry A(melia Moore) 1846-1911

PERSONAL: Born November 25, 1846, in Gerrard County, KY; died June 2, 1911, in Leavenworth, KS; daughter of George (a stock dealer and planter) and Mary (Campbell) Moore; married Charles Gloyd (a physician), November 21, 1867 (died); married David Nation (a lawyer, minister, and journalist), 1877 (divorced, 1901); children: (first marriage) Charlien.

CAREER: Activist and writer. Worked as a schoolteacher.

MEMBER: Women's Christian Temperance Union.

WRITINGS:

The Use and Need of the Life of Carry A. Nation, F. M. Steves & Sons (Topeka, KS), 1904.

Contributor to periodicals, including *Hatchet, Home Defender,* and *Smasher's Mail.*

SIDELIGHTS: Carry A. Nation is among the more colorful figures in American social activism. During her heyday in the 1890s and early 1900s, Nation became known throughout the country as an axe-wielding activist given to vehement rants, replete with Biblical references, and violent outbursts which sometimes involved the destruction of private property. "Today," wrote Robert Day in *Smithsonian,* "her notoriety and fame rest largely on the cartoon image she forged in the nation's press in the early 1900s." He described Nation's image as that of "a huge-headed woman with a hatchet in her right hand and what appear to be pool-table stanchions for legs under a plain black skirt."

Nation was born in 1846 in Gerrard County, Kentucky, and was raised in an atmosphere of religious fanaticism and insanity. After training as a teacher, she married an alcoholic physician, but after becoming pregnant, she left her spouse, who died soon afterward. While raising her child, who proved mentally and physically feeble, Nation worked as a school teacher. In 1877, she married David Nation, a lawyer who had also worked as a minister and journalist, and the couple eventually moved to Medicine Lodge, Kansas.

In 1889, after surviving a fierce fire in town, Nation grew increasingly convinced that she had been spared in order to promote Christianity or, more precisely, to oppose what she believed to be hedonism in society. She became active in urging the enforcement of prohibition legislation in Kansas, and in the ensuing years developed a formidable reputation as a temperance activist given to fits and the violent destruction of saloons. Nation's extreme behavior—evident in lectures and other stage appearances as well as her assaults on saloons—exerted considerable appeal to a certain portion of the American public, which pledged support and financed her campaigns through donations and the purchase of such souvenirs as plastic axes. Frances Grace Carver, writing in *Religion and American Culture,* attributed Nation's celebrity to her "genius at self-promotion and her remarkably media-genic personality."

However, if she proved effective in drawing public attention, Nation failed to entirely galvanize sympathizers, and she even alienated fellow members of the Women's Christian Temperance Union. In addition, she saw the end of her second marriage when her husband sued for divorce on grounds of desertion. Excursions to San Francisco and Washington, D.C., proved similarly frustrating for Nation, who saw herself increasingly perceived as deranged and violent. Another tour, in which she condemned Ivy League schools as demonic environments, likewise damaged her reputation, and a tour of Great Britain also failed to impress.

After returning from Great Britain, Nation withdrew to her farm in the Ozark Mountains of Arkansas. When she showed signs of dementia, she gained admittance to a hospital in Leavenworth, Kansas. She died there in 1911.

Nation's writings include an autobiography, *The Use and Need of the Life of Carry A. Nation,* which she published in 1904, and contributions to various publications advocating her causes. Day reported in *Smithsonian* that she wrote, "'I believe I have always failed in everything I undertook to do the first time, but I learned only by experience, paid dearly for it and valued it afterwards.'" Day added: "It would be reassuring if we could believe those are the words of a woman who grew wise with age. But it is hard to forget the outrageousness of her later years."

BIOGRAPHICAL AND CRITICAL SOURCES:

BOOKS

American Women Writers, St. James Press (Detroit, MI), 2000.
Grace, Fran, *Carry A. Nation: Retelling the Life,* Indiana University Press (Bloomington, IN), 2001.

PERIODICALS

Religion and American Culture, winter, 1999, Frances Grace Carver, "With Bible in One Hand and Battle-Axe in the Other," p. 31.
Smithsonian, April, 1989, Robert Day, "Carry from Kansas Became a Nation All unto Herself," pp. 147-164.*

NEENAN, Benedict 1949-

PERSONAL: Born January 3, 1949, in Kansas City, MO; son of James Patrick (in business) and Helen (a homemaker; maiden name, Dierks) Neenan. *Education:* Colorado State University, B.A. (history), 1971; Catholic University of America, S.T.B. (theology), 1988, Ph.D. (church history), 1996. *Religion:* Roman Catholic.

ADDRESSES: Home—Conception Abbey, P.O. Box 501, Conception, MO 64433. *Office*—Conception Seminary College, P.O. Box 502, Conception, MO 64433. *E-mail*—benedict@conception.edu.

CAREER: Conception Abbey, Conception, MO, prior, 1990-93; Conception Seminary College, president, rector, and instructor in church history, 1996—.

MEMBER: American Benedictine Academy.

WRITINGS:

Thomas Vernor Moore: Psychiatrist, Educator, and Monk (biography; based on Ph.D. dissertation), Paulist Press (Mahwah, NJ), 2000.

Contributor to *Annuarium Historiae Conciliorum.*

WORK IN PROGRESS: Research on nineteenth-century monastic history and a biography of Abbot Frowin Conrad, O.S.B.

BIOGRAPHICAL AND CRITICAL SOURCES:

ONLINE

Paulist Press Web site, http://www.paulistpress.com/ (November 20, 2003).

*   *   *

NELSON, Sioban 1943-

PERSONAL: Born 1943, in Cork, Ireland. *Education:* La Trobe University, B.A. (history), 1976; Royal Darwin Hospital, R.N., 1985; Griffith University, Ph.D. (ethics), 1996. *Hobbies and other interests:* Movies, music, "going bush," cooking and eating.

ADDRESSES: Office—School of Nursing, Faculty of Medicine, Dentistry, and Health Sciences, University of Melbourne, Level 1, 723 Swanston Street, Carlton, Victoria 3053, Australia. *E-mail*—siobanmn@unimelb. edu.au.

CAREER: Registered nurse, Northern Territory and Queensland, Australia; Queensland University of Technology, faculty member; University of Melbourne, Melbourne, Australia, associate professor at School of Postgraduate Nursing, deputy head of school, chair of research committee, adjunct fellow of Centre for the Study of Health and Society; *Nursing Inquiry,* editor; City University, London, England, visiting professor; Rosenstadt Visiting Professor, University of Toronto, 2001. Foundation director, Australian Nursing History Project.

AWARDS, HONORS: Faculty of Medicine, Dentistry, and Health Sciences postdoctoral fellowship awards, 1997.

WRITINGS:

(Editor with Michael Clinton) *Advanced Practice in Mental-Health Nursing,* Blackwell Science (Malden, MA), 1999.
A Genealogy of Care of the Sick, Nursing Praxis Press (Southsea, England), 2000.
Say Little, Do Much: Nurses, Nuns, and Hospitals in the Nineteenth Century, University of Pennsylvania Press (Philadelphia, PA), 2001.

Also author of numerous journal articles, book chapters, and reviews.

WORK IN PROGRESS: A general history of nursing and an examination of virtue ethics in medical professions.

SIDELIGHTS: Sioban Nelson, a registered nurse with a bachelor's degree in history and a doctorate in humanities, received a three-year postdoctoral fellowship in 1997, during which time she researched and wrote a history of nineteenth-century religious nurses in Australia, Britain, and North America. She was interested in the impact of these nuns on the professional formation of nursing. Previous scholarship on the history of nursing had largely ignored the contributions of these women, focusing instead on Florence Nightingale as the traditional founder of modern nursing. Nelson's study emphasizes the earlier efforts of women she refers to as "vowed women," a term that includes nuns, sisters, and deaconesses of various religions. Her work was published in 2001 as *Say Little, Do Much: Nurses, Nuns, and Hospitals in the Nineteenth Century.*

Nelson's wide-ranging book discusses the development of modern professional nursing and the many religion-based hospitals, as well as the male bias that these early nurses had to face from both physicians and religious clerics. The nuns faced many challenges in dealing with the sick and they learned very quickly, in the words of *Journal of the American Medical Association* reviewer Linda K. Strodtman, how to overstep the "gender boundaries to address the health care needs of poor immigrants, frontier settlers, soldiers, and victims of epidemics." These women came from many different religious denominations including the Roman Catholic, Anglican, Lutheran, and Methodist.

Nelson points out many interesting facts. One such detail is that in the United States, by 1900, Catholic nuns had founded almost 300 different hospitals. Seventeen years later, these Catholic hospitals represented half of the health care system in the States. "These nurses," wrote Strodtman, "were experts in their craft—clinically, politically, financially—and understood the value of these elements in furthering their work."

One of the reasons that these pre-Florence Nightingale nurses were not recognized, Nelson posits, is that religious orders discouraged egotism. The nuns worked as a unit, a community. As Bernadette McCauley put it in *New York Time,* Nelson argues "that together they were just as influential as Nightingale, models who made nursing an acceptable occupation for all women later on, not just for nuns." Although McCauley expressed disappointment that Nelson does not discuss the influence of religion on the nuns' works and lives, she concluded that *Say Little, Do Much* offers a "compelling" case for "some re-evaluation of the history of nursing."

Nelson is foundation director of the Australian Nursing History Project, an interdisciplinary multimedia project that aims to promote the study of nursing history, to assist in the preservation of historical material through the establishment of a register and database of nursing resources, and to provide Internet access to a database of historical resources in collaboration with the Australian Science and Technology Heritage Centre.

BIOGRAPHICAL AND CRITICAL SOURCES:

PERIODICALS

English Historical Review, November 2002, Anne Summers, review of *Say Little, Do Much: Nurses, Nuns, and Hospitals in the Nineteenth Century,* pp. 369-370.
Journal of the American Medical Association, August 28, 2002, Linda K. Strodtman, review of *Say Little, Do Much.*
New York Times, December 16, 2002, Bernadette Mc-Cauley, "Carry on, Nurse," p. 16.

OTHER

Irish Hour (radio transcript), SBS Radio, 1998.
The Scattering: The Irish Empire (five-part television series), SBS/BBC Television.

*   *   *

NETTLE, Daniel 1970-

PERSONAL: Born 1970, in London, England. *Education:* University of Oxford, B.S.; University College London, Ph.D., 1996.

ADDRESSES: Home—Newcastle upon Tyne, England. *Agent*—c/o Author Mail, Oxford University Press, Great Clarendon St., Oxford OX2 6DP, England. *E-mail*—d.nettle@open.ac.uk.

CAREER: London Guildhall University, lecturer; Merton College, Oxford, England, fellow, 1996-99; Open University, lecturer in biological psychology, 2001-03; University of Newcastle upon Tyne, lecturer in biology, 2003—.

MEMBER: Royal Anthropological Institute (council member), Human Behavior and Evolution Society.

AWARDS, HONORS: Wilde Prize for Philosophy, University of Oxford, 1993; British Association for Applied Linguistics Book Prize, 2001.

WRITINGS:

The Fyem Language of Northern Nigeria, Lincom Europa (Munich, Germany), 1998.
Linguistic Diversity, Oxford University Press (New York, NY), 1999.
(With Colin Renfrew) *Nostratic: Examining a Linguistic Macrofamily,* McDonald Institute for Archaeological Research (Cambridge, England), 1999.
(With Suzanne Romaine) *Vanishing Voices: The Extinction of the World's Languages,* Oxford University Press (New York, NY), 2000.
Strong Imagination: Madness, Creativity, and Human Nature, Oxford University Press (New York, NY), 2001.

Contributor of articles to journals, including *Brain and Cognition, Human Biology, Cognition, British Journal of Psychology, Human Nature,* and *Emotion, Evolution, and Rationality.*

WORK IN PROGRESS: Happiness: An Introduction to Hedonics.

SIDELIGHTS: In *Vanishing Voices: The Extinction of the World's Languages* Daniel Nettle, a lecturer in biological psychology at Open University, and coauthor Suzanne Romaine explain why half of the world's languages—which amount to some 5,000 to 6,700 languages—will be nonexistent by the year 2100. In *Vanishing Voices* Nettle and Romaine provide short biographies on the last-known persons to speak various languages. They also provide statistics for the different languages spoken throughout the world, and explain why it is important that these languages are passed on and stay alive. The authors discuss why and how languages disappear. Finally, they provide information on how the extinction of languages can be prevented. *Verbatim* contributor Steve Kleinedler praised the book, noting that "Nettle and Romaine provide a compelling look at the ways in which languages are rapidly disappearing from the face of the earth." "This is a powerfully written and carefully researched appeal to linguists, ethnographers, and the scientific community as a whole to wake up to the dramatic consequences of neglecting the issue of linguistic diversity," commented Jim Walker in a review for *Human Ecology.*

In *Strong Imagination: Madness, Creativity, and Human Nature* Nettle analyzes mental illnesses and their connection to creativity. He proposes that mental illnesses, such as schizophrenia and manic depression, are predisposed and are caused by the same genes that determine creativity. *Times Literary Supplement* contributor Ray Dolan called it "a very stimulating book."

Nettle told *CA:* "I am a scientist as well as a writer, but my chief passion is trying to understand how big ideas from science, from ecology, genetics, evolution, and psychology relate to our experience as human beings, and to the social issues that face our world today. I was inspired as a student by the works of Douglas Hofstadter, Richard Dawkins, and Jared Diamond, who wrote serious books about things that mattered but nonetheless spoke in a language people could understand. By trying to apply scientific ideas to the human condition, they had become the great humanist philosophers of our time. They made me want to study human evolution and to write books of my own. I have learned—paradoxically—that you often have to have a deeper understanding of something in order to communicate it to the public than you would in order to communicate to specialists."

BIOGRAPHICAL AND CRITICAL SOURCES:

PERIODICALS

Antiquity, December, 1999, N. James, review of *Linguistic Diversity,* p. 940.
British Medical Journal, July 7, 2001, Iain McClure, review of *Strong Imagination: Madness, Creativity, and Human Nature,* p. 55.
Human Ecology, March, 2002, Jim Walker, review of *Vanishing Voices: The Extinction of the World's Languages,* p. 145.
Journal of the Royal Anthropological Institute, December, 2000, Merritt Ruhlen, review of *Nostratic: Examining a Linguistic Macrofamily,* p. 738.
Library Journal, June 15, 2000, Marianne Orme, review of *Vanishing Voices,* p. 83.
M2 Best Books, October 2, 2002, review of *Vanishing Voices.*
Nature, January 18, 2001, Dylan Evans, "Not So Crazy after All," p. 284.
Times Higher Education Supplement, October 5, 2001, David Pilgrim, "A Polluted Puddle of Poetry and Psychosis," p. 32.
Times Literary Supplement, August 31, 2001, Ray Dolan, "Through Cells of Madness," p. 10.
USA Today, January, 2001, Steven G. Kellman, review of *Vanishing Voices,* p. 79.
Verbatim, winter, 2002, Steve Kleinedler, review of *Vanishing Voices,* p. 27.
Whole Earth, fall, 2000, review of *Vanishing Voices,* p. 102.

ONLINE

Open University Web site, http://www.open.ac.uk/ (May 9, 2003), "Daniel Nettle."
Oxford University Press Web site, http://www.oup-usa. org/ (April 17, 2002).
Red Herring, http://www.redherring.com/ (April 17, 2002), Peter Rojas, "Examining the Death of Language."

*   *   *

NEWMAN, Richard (Alan) 1930-2003

OBITUARY NOTICE—See index for *CA* sketch: Born March 30, 1930, in Watertown, NY; died of a brain tumor July 7, 2003, in Boston, MA. Educator, editor, minister, and author. Newman was an authority on African-American history and culture. Originally studying for the ministry, he completed a bachelor's degree at Maryville College in 1952 and earned his M.A. in divinity at Union Theological Seminary in 1955, the same year he was ordained in the Presbyterian Church. He began work as a minister for the Westminster Presbyterian Church in Syracuse, New York, during the late 1950s, followed by a position at Vassar College as an instructor in religion. A meeting with the Rev. Martin Luther King, Jr., when Newman was twenty-five years old shaped the remainder of his life; from that point on he vowed not only to work on behalf of civil rights but to do whatever he could to help blacks in everything from education to employment. Attending graduate school at Syracuse University and Harvard University, he became chair of the department of social sciences at Boston University from 1964 to 1973. He then embarked on an editing career, first at G. K. Hall from 1973 to 1979, then as executive editor at Garland Publishing from 1978 to 1981, and finally as manager of publications at the New York Public Library from 1981 to 1992. In 1992 he was appointed director of research at Harvard University's black studies program, where he also became managing editor of *The Harvard Guide to African-American History.* Newman was famous for his encyclopedic knowledge of all things African American, and gave generously of his time to advise students and colleagues on the subject. In response to those who asked why he, a white man, chose to study African Americans, he responded that he did not, for example, have to be a woman living in sixteenth-century England to study Queen Elizabeth I. Newman wrote extensively about his specialty in such books as *Black Power and Black Religion: Essays and Reviews* (1987), *Words like Freedom: Essays on African-American Culture and History* (1996), and *African-American Quotations* (1998), in addition to editing or contributing to numerous other publications.

OBITUARIES AND OTHER SOURCES:

PERIODICALS

Boston Globe, July 8, 2003, p. B8.

* * *

NICOLL, Ruaridh 1969-

PERSONAL: Born 1969, in Arbroath, Scotland; son of a mill operator and sheep farmer; married Alison Watt (a painter).

ADDRESSES: Home—Edinburgh, Scotland. *Agent*—Antony Harwood, 109 Riverbank House, 1 Putney Bridge Approach, London SW6 3JD, England.

CAREER: Writer and journalist. *Scotland on Sunday,* Edinburgh, Scotland, became environment and science correspondent, 1994; *Observer,* London, England,

became Washington, DC correspondent, 1995; *Guardian,* Manchester, England, southern Africa correspondent until 1998. Previously worked for Lloyds of London.

WRITINGS:

White Male Heart (novel), Doubleday (London, England), 2001, Justin, Charles (Boston, MA), 2003.
Wide Eyed (novel), Doubleday (London, England), 2003.

SIDELIGHTS: Though he comes from the Scottish highlands that provide the setting for his first novel, *White Male Heart,* Ruaridh Nicoll spent much of his young adulthood traveling far from his home. Recalling his childhood for an autobiographical sketch at the *Justin, Charles, and Company Books Web site,* he wrote, "There was no television at home[;] the signal could not penetrate the glen's high walls and so I spent the hours of darkness reading. If I devour fancy literature now, it's only because it sits contentedly on the plump belly of all the Desmond Bagley, Wilbur Smith, Sven Hassel, George Macdonald Fraser, Dick Francis, and Gerald Seymour novels I consumed as a boy."

In *White Male Heart* young protagonists Hugh MacIntyre and Aaron Harding fall under the spell of Mac Seruant, an embittered poacher whose sense of alienation from local society is only heightened by his black skin and African ancestry. When a docile whippet wins a dog race at a local festival, Mac's Jack Russell terrier attacks it. At the same festival, Hugh meets Becky, a young girl visiting from London. The violent Aaron soon begins to resent Becky, as well as the friend he regards as a traitor, and takes out his frustration on his own girlfriend, the gentle Alison.

"Hugh's passionate and giddy coming-of-age story blossoms under this poised menace," promised David Wright in *Library Journal,* while a reviewer in *Publishers Weekly* concluded that "With a breathtaking denouement, it's an auspicious debut." A commentator in *Kirkus Reviews* warned readers of "scenes of rape and murder that surpass Patricia Highsmith at her darkest." Wright also noted that "flashes of brutality . . . may prove too gamey for some readers, but those with strong stomachs will enjoy."

Nicoll's second novel, *Wide Eyed,* is set on the Scottish coast and begins after the sinking of a boat called the *Albatross.* Betsy Gillander, visiting from London with her unloving fiancée, becomes drawn into local events: she leaves the fiancée for James Rego, owner of the boat, and befriends Helen, whose lover was the captain.

BIOGRAPHICAL AND CRITICAL SOURCES:

PERIODICALS

Kirkus Reviews, February 1, 2003, review of *White Male Heart,* p. 171.
Library Journal, February 15, 2003, David Wright, review of *White Male Heart,* p. 170.
Publishers Weekly, April 7, 2003, review of *White Male Heart,* p. 48.

ONLINE

Justin, Charles, and Co. Books Web site, http://www.justincharlesbooks.com/ (September 16, 2003).*

*   *   *

NOLAN, Janet 1956-

PERSONAL: Born October 27, 1956, in Chicago, IL; daughter of Donald and Audrey (a travel agent) Gould; married Bill Nolan (a computer sales consultant), April 18, 1982; children: Tom, Megan. *Education:* Evergreen State College (Olympia, WA), B.A., 1979; University of Illinois—Chicago, M.U.P., 1986. *Hobbies and other interests:* Swimming, reading, "taking very long walks."

ADDRESSES: Agent—c/o Author Mail, Albert Whitman, 6340 Oakton St., Morton Grove, IL 60053-2723. *E-mail*—jignol@ameritech.net.

CAREER: Writer. Worked as a waste auditor for a recycling company; also worked as a professional meeting facilitator; volunteer at local schools. Member of West Cook County Solid Waste Commission and Oak Park Solid Waste Commission.

MEMBER: Society of Children's Book Writers and Illustrators, League of Women Voters.

WRITINGS:

The St. Patrick's Day Shillelagh, illustrated by Ben F. Stahl, Albert Whitman (Morton Grove, IL), 2002.

WORK IN PROGRESS: A Father's Day Thank You, for Albert Whitman (Morton Grove, IL), publication expected in 2005.

SIDELIGHTS: Janet Nolan told *CA:* "I still find it hard to believe the words I wrote at my dining room table have been edited, illustrated, and bound into an actual book. While I never would have checked 'yes' in the 'do you want to be a writer?' box, I think I've been on the path toward writing my entire life. Unfortunately, I never stopped to read the signs along the way.

"While every female emotion from early adolescence to the present has been recorded in diaries, journals, and spiral notebooks, I did not consider my personal reflections 'writing.' It was private. Because I did not share my words with anyone, they were just thoughts on paper.

"If not a writer, I have always been a reader. What I love about reading is getting lost. I believe getting lost in a story that has the power to take me to a different place, a different reality, or a different time is a gift. What I've recently discovered is that getting lost in writing is a gift as well.

"I had to take a rather odd detour through the garbage to figure that out. I was working as a waste auditor for a recycling company. It was a very cool job: clipboard, hard hat, and steel-toed boots. It's the kind of thing people with graduate degrees in urban planning and a desire to save the planet do. I analyzed the waste/recycling streams out of large downtown Chicago buildings. My writing was technical and academic. Somewhere along the way I was asked to write a brochure for children to explain a plastics recycling program. I wrote the brochure at work, and at home I wrote 'Patti Petunia's Pink Bubble Bath Bottle: An Adventure in Recycling.' While that story did not launch my career, it did wake up some sleeping brain cells. I wrote one terrible children's story after another. It didn't matter how horrible they were. They were private. I didn't show them to anyone; therefore I wasn't a writer. I considered my writing was the artistic equivalent of singing in the shower: harmless but fun. Then came a wonderful moment after a family wedding in Philadelphia.

"Everyone was walking down the street except for my cousin's three-year-old daughter. She was dancing, in a world of her own, in mismatched patent-leather 'tapping shoes' and a dress that spun when she twirled. The combination of family togetherness and one child's ability to be part of the family yet uniquely independent inspired me.

"Finally, I had something to write about: what I felt, not what I wanted to say. I did not set out to write a book chronicling the lives of an Irish-American family. I wanted to write a book that gave my niece a reason to dance. The first character I created was the grandfather, a man who walked with a cane and told wonderful stories of Ireland that my niece always wanted to hear. Over time—years actually—with the help of my wise critique group and patient editor, a story emerged. The grandfather's cane—the shillelagh—became the link that tied the generations of my niece's family together.

"The story begins with the Irish potato famine, a young lad named Fergus, and his favorite blackthorn tree. St. Patrick's Day became the holiday when the stories of my niece's ancestors and their shillelagh were told. *The St. Patrick's Day Shillelagh* ends as it originally began, when a little girl . . . begins to dance.

"I am also excited about my upcoming book, *A Father's Day Thank You.* The book puts a humorous twist on traditional Father's Day gift giving."

BIOGRAPHICAL AND CRITICAL SOURCES:

PERIODICALS

Booklist, January 1, 2003, Lauren Peterson, review of *The St. Patrick's Day Shillelagh,* p. 909.

School Library Journal, December, 2002, Piper L. Nyman, review of *The St. Patrick's Day Shillelagh,* p. 104.

*   *   *

NOLAN, Simon 1961-

PERSONAL: Born 1961. *Education:* Attended University of Sussex.

ADDRESSES: Agent—Caroline Davidson Literary Agency, 5 Queen Anne's Gardens, London W4 1TU, England.

CAREER: Former clerical officer; self-employed musician and teacher; writer.

WRITINGS:

As Good as It Gets (novel), Quartet Books (London, England), 1998.
The Vending Machine of Justice (novel), Quartet Books (London, England), 2001.

SIDELIGHTS: A self-employed musician and teacher, Simon Nolan burst onto London's literary scene in 2000 with *As Good as It Gets.* Not to be confused with the similarly titled U.S. feature film, Nolan's novel follows a quartet of twentysomethings from Brighton, England. Steve, Ward, Kelvin, and Marina share an apartment and struggle for money. Circumstances change, however, when a seedy friend, Ben, shows up for a visit only to disappear during the night and be murdered, leaving behind a backpack. Opening the backpack, the roommates are amazed to find five kilos of high-grade cocaine wrapped in plastic. Now they must decide what to do with their windfall: keep it for themselves, sell it, or just get rid of it. The foursome's options "are explored with both humor and suspense while Nolan's aimless, cynical characters keep busy in their own way," noted James Klise in a *Booklist* review. *Observer* critic Christina Patterson likewise cited the author's "sharp satirical gaze" that makes *As Good as It Gets* "a confident and genuinely comic contribution to the Brit Lit druggie genre."

Nolan followed his debut with a second novel, *The Vending Machine of Justice.* This tale, set in the author's home town of Hove, Sussex, finds protagonist Elsa called to jury duty, during which she is engulfed in a scenario involving carved pineapples, a Black & Decker cordless drill, and Malibu, California.

BIOGRAPHICAL AND CRITICAL SOURCES:

PERIODICALS

Booklist, November 15, 2000, James Klise, review of *As Good as It Gets,* p. 619.
Observer (London, England), July 26, 1998, review of *As Good as It Gets,* p. 15.*

*   *   *

NOLTE, David 1959-

PERSONAL: Born January 30, 1959. *Education:* Cornell University, B.A. (physics), 1981; University of California—Berkeley, Ph.D. (physics), 1988.

ADDRESSES: Office—Department of Physics, Purdue University, 4155 Eisenhower Rd., West Lafayette, IN 47905. *E-mail*—nolted@purdue.edu.

CAREER: Lawrence Berkeley Laboratory, Berkeley, CA, research assistant for Center for Advanced Materials, 1984-88; A.T.&T. Bell Labs, Murray Hill, NJ, postdoctoral member of technical staff, 1988-89; Purdue University, Purdue, IN, assistant professor, 1989-94, associate professor, 1994-99, professor of physics, 1999—. Holoscan, Ltd., member board of directors, 2000; Science for Peace Program, NATO consultant, 2000.

MEMBER: American Physical Society, Optical Society of America, Phi Beta Kappa.

AWARDS, HONORS: Young Author Best Paper Award, International Conference on the Physics of Semiconductors, 1990; research initiation award, National Science Foundation, 1990-93; research fellowship, Alfred P. Sloan, 1990-94; Presidential Young Investigator, National Science Foundation, 1991-96; fellowship,

Optical Society of America, 1997; Ruth and Joel Spira Award for Best Undergraduate Physics Teacher, Purdue University, 1997.

WRITINGS:

(With N. M. Haegel and K. W. Goossen) *Photo-induced Space-charge Effects in Semiconductors,* Materials Research Society (Pittsburgh, PA), 1992.
Photorefractive Effects and Materials, Kluwer Academic Publishers (Dordrecht, Netherlands), 1995.
The Intelligence of Light: From Visual Communication to Holographic Computers and the Optical Internet, Simon & Schuster (New York, NY), 2001.
Mind at Light Speed: A New Kind of Intelligence, Free Press (New York, NY), 2001.

Contributor to numerous science encyclopedias, trade journals, and magazine.

SIDELIGHTS: Physicist David Nolte has spent much of his career experimenting and developing computers that use light instead of electricity to compute, which is the subject of his book, *Mind at Light Speed: A New Kind of Intelligence.*

In what Elizabeth Corcoran in the *Boston Globe* called "a gentle tour through the highlights of modern physics," *Mind at Light Speed* describes the technological advances that may take place over the next century that will give birth to computers with incredible power. These computers will use crystals, lasers, and quantum properties to achieve intelligence that surpasses even human capabilities. Nolte describes this evolution in three stages, the first of which is the Internet using photonics. He notes that by 2020, holographic computers will be commonplace, and by 2050, computers will actually achieve artificial intelligence. Nolte also predicts the impact these computers may have on people and our way of life. A *Publishers Weekly* writer commended the book, saying that it "gives compelling insights into the nature of human thought and technology." Mark Williams of *Red Herring* maintained that *Mind at Light Speed* "explains it all as comprehensibly as you'll find anywhere, synthesizing explanations on converging fields, like holography, optical communications technology, and computational theory."

BIOGRAPHICAL AND CRITICAL SOURCES:

PERIODICALS

Publishers Weekly, November 5, 2001, review of *Mind at Light Speed: A New Kind of Intelligence,* p. 53.
Research and Development, February 20, 2002, review of *Mind at Light Speed,* p. 25.
Science News, March 23, 2002, review of *Mind at Light Speed,* p. 191.

ONLINE

Boston Globe online, http://www.boston.com/globe/ (August 12, 2002), Elizabeth Corcoran, "Harnessing the Speed—and Power—of Light."
OE Magazine online, http://oemagazine.com/ (August 12, 2002), "New Book Predicts Future of Optical Computing."
Purdue News online, http://news.uns.purdue.edu/ (August 12, 2002), Emil Venere, "World Will See Computers in Whole New Light."
Purdue University Physics Department Web site, http://www.physics.purdue.edu/ (March 17, 2002).
Red Herring, http://www.redherring.com/ (August 12, 2002), Mark Williams, "Photonic Computing Takes a Quantum Leap."*

*   *   *

NYEMBEZI, C(yril) L(incoln) S(ibusiso) 1919-2000

PERSONAL: Born December 6, 1919, in Babanango, Natal Province, South Africa; died June 25, 2000, in Pietermaritzburg, South Africa; son of a Methodist minister; married, c. 1950; wife's name, Muriel; children: four. *Education:* University of South Africa, B.A., 1946; University of the Witwatersrand, Johannesburg, South Africa, B.A. (with honors), 1947, M.A. 1954.

CAREER: Writer, editor, and teacher. University of the Witwatersrand, Johannesburg, South Africa, Department of Bantu Studies, lecturer, 1948-53; University of Fort Hare, 1955-59; Shuter & Shooter Pietermaritzburg, South Africa, editor.

AWARDS, HONORS: Named Outstanding citizen, Pietermaritzburg Transitional Local Council, 1997.

WRITINGS:

NOVELS

Ubododa abukhulelwa (title means "When Boys Were Men"), Shuter & Shooter (Pietermaritzburg, South Africa), 1953.
Mntanami! Mntanami! (title means "My Child! My Child!"), Lincroft Books (Pietermaritzburg, South Africa), 1950, published as *Ushicilelo lwesithathu,* 1965.
Inkinsela yaseMgungundlovu (title means "The Tycoon from Pietermaritzburg"), Shuter & Shooter (Pietermaritzburg, South Africa), 1961.

OTHER

Zulu Proverbs, Witwatersrand University Press (Johannesburg, South Africa), 1954, revised edition, 1963.
Uhelo lwesiZulu (Zulu language studies), Shuter & Shooter (Pietermaritzburg, South Africa), 1956.
Learn Zulu, Shuter & Shooter (Pietermaritzburg, South Africa), 1958.
Izibongo zamakhose, Shuter & Shooter (Pietermaritzburg, South Africa), 1958.
(Translator) Alan Paton, *Lafa elihle kakhulu* (translation of *Cry the Beloved Country*), Shuter & Shooter (Pietermaritzburg, South Africa), 1958.
(With O. E. H. Nxumalo) *Ingolobane Yesizwe* (title means "The Treasury of the Nation"), Shuter & Shooter (Pietermaritzburg, South Africa), 1966.
(Compiler, with G. R. Dent) *Scholar's Zulu Dictionary: English-Zulu, Zulu-English,* Shuter & Shooter (Pietermaritzburg, South Africa), 1969, reprinted, 1991.
Learn More Zulu, 2nd edition, Shuter & Shooter (Pietermaritzburg, South Africa), 1990.
Uhelo Iwesxizulu, 5th edition, Shuter & Shooter (Pietermaritzburg, South Africa), 1991.
AZ: Isichazimazwi sanamuhla nangomuso, Reach Out Publishers (Pietermaritzburg, South Africa), 1992.
Usizo enkingeni yokufunda nokubhala isingisi (title means "Aid to Reading and Writing English"), Reach Out Publishers (Pietermaritzburg, South Africa), 1993.

EDITOR

Imisebe yelanga (poetry), Afrikaanse Pers Boekhandel
  (Johannesburg, South Africa), 1959-61.
Imikhemezelo (poetry), Shuter & Shooter
  (Pietermaritzburg, South Africa), 1963.
Amahlunga aluhlaza (poetry), Shuter & Shooter
  (Pietermaritzburg, South Africa), 1963.
Izimpophoma zomphefumulo, Shuter & Shooter
  (Pietermaritzburg, South Africa), 1964.
Compact Zulu Dictionary: English-Zulu, Zulu-English,
  compiled by G. R. Dent, Shuter & Shooter
  (Pietermaritzburg, South Africa), 1964, 6th revised
  and enlarged edition, 1995.
Compact Setswana Dictionary: English-Setswana,
  Setswana-English, compiled by G. R. Dent,
  translated by F.T. Haasbroek and C.M. Haasbroek,
  Shuter & Shooter (Pietermaritzburg, South Africa),
  1994.

Also contributor to journals, including *Bantu Education Journal, African Studies,* and *Review of Zulu
Literature.*

ADAPTATIONS: Inkinsela yaseMgungundlovu was
adapted for television and radio.

SIDELIGHTS: A prominent writer in the Zulu language
and a dedicated proponent of African language and
culture, C. L. S. Nyembezi wrote three novels and
several children's readers. He also wrote, edited, or
compiled many books on the Zulu language, including
dictionaries, books of Zulu poetry, and a volume of
Zulu idioms and proverbs.

In his novels, Nyembezi tended to be didactic but also
kept a sense of humor as he dealt with important issues of the time. In his first novel, *When Boys Were
Men,* Nyembezi tells the story of a poor orphan who
overcomes life's obstacles and becomes a success
through the virtues of hard work. His second novel,
My Child! My Child!, is derivative of Alan Paton's
Cry, the Beloved Country, which Nyembezi translated
into Zulu. The novel tells the story of a young man
who winds up in jail in Johannesburg.

In a show of black African pride, Nyembezi resigned
from his teaching post at the University of Fort Hare
in 1959 when the government decided to enforce laws
saying that universities must be segregated. Although

Nyembezi did not lose his job, he resigned on principal
when several of his black colleagues were fired. After
his resignation, he worked as an editor at the publisher
Shuter & Shooter and wrote his third, and most successful, novel. *The Tycoon from Pietermaritzburg,*
published in 1961, is a satire about black Africans
becoming too enamored with Western culture and
values. In it, a despicable con artist exploits others on
his way to becoming a rich tycoon who dresses in
European clothes and adopts Western mannerisms.
The book was so popular that it became a series on
South African radio and a television show.

Because many Zulu-speaking people were illiterate,
Nyembezi's novels were not best sellers. Nevertheless,
their use in schools and universities provided him with
a good income. Nyembezi turned from writing novels
to nonfiction, but was known to be encouraging and
helpful to budding writers who asked him to read their
manuscripts. Having studied under noted African
languages scholar B. W. Vilakazi, he turned his energies to educating Zulus, especially the young. In addition to a series of eight Zulu readers for grade school,
he developed Zulu grammar books and a dictionary.
He also helped to increase the appreciation of Zulu
literature by editing several anthologies of Zulu writings, primarily poetry, and a book of traditional praise
songs for Zulu kings.

Nyembezi saw language as a tool to help foster a sense
of pride among black South Africans. "For Nyembezi,
language had an almost spiritual dimension," wrote
the author of an obituary in South Africa's *Sunday
Times.* "It bestowed identity, self-esteem, and a sense
of individual worth, in a world where it was only too
easy for blacks to succumb to the tidal wave of
'white'—American and European culture—and condemn themselves to a life of inferiority in the process."

A statement issued by Sbu Ndebele and posted on the
African National Congress Kwazulu Natal Web site,
noted that Nyembezi was "an inspiration to generations in the spirit of the African Renaissance. He was
able to use culture to instill hope when there was
hopelessness. He provided invaluable guidance to us
in our effort of making the African renaissance a
popular force in our rebirth as a people."

BIOGRAPHICAL AND CRITICAL SOURCES:

BOOKS

Hedrick, Donald E., editor, *African Authors: A
  Companion to Black African Writing, Volume 1:*

1300-1973, Black Orpheus Press (Washington, DC), 1973, pp. 306-307.

Nkabinde, A. C., editor, *Anthology of Articles on African Linguistics and Literature: A Festschrift to C. L. S. Nyembezi,* Lexicon Publishers (Johannesburg, South Africa), 1988.

OBITUARIES:

PERIODICALS

Sunday Times (South Africa), July 9, 2000, "Man Who Taught His Pupils the Value of Words."

ONLINE

African National Congress Kwazulu Natal Web site, http://www.anc.org.za/ (June 27, 2000), "Death of Pro Nyembezi."*

O

O'BRIEN, William V(incent) 1923-2003

OBITUARY NOTICE—See index for *CA* sketch: Born July 9, 1923, in Washington, DC; died of head injuries suffered from a fall July 8, 2003, in Washington, DC. Educator and author. O'Brien was a former professor of government at Georgetown University who specialized in international law and ethics. His life seemed to center around Georgetown University: He was born at Georgetown University hospital and spent his college years there, earning a Ph.D. in 1953. He spent his entire academic career there, too, beginning as an instructor in 1950, and retiring as professor emeritus in 1993. O'Brien's years at Georgetown were interrupted only by World War II, during which he served in the U.S. Army and saw action in the Pacific theater; after the war he remained in the Army Reserves and achieved the rank of lieutenant colonel. While teaching at Georgetown, O'Brien served as chair of the government department twice and also of the university's Institute of World Policy; he also helped to create the Goldman visiting Israeli professorship. His main interest as an academic involved the definition of the just war doctrine; he wrote extensively on this topic in books such as *Christian Ethics and Nuclear Warfare* (1961), coauthored with Ulrich S. Allers; *War and/or Survival* (1969); *The Conduct of Just and Limited War* (1981); and *Law and Morality in Israel's War with the PLO* (1991). O'Brien was also a former president of the Catholic Association of International Peace and former chair of the International Relations Committee at the Third-World Congress of the Law Apostolate. He was honored for his contributions in 1993 when Georgetown University established the William V. O'Brien Lecture in International Law and Morality.

OBITUARIES AND OTHER SOURCES:

PERIODICALS

Washington Post, July 19, 2003, p. B6.

ONLINE

Hoya, http://www.thehoya.com/ (August 29, 2003).

*   *   *

O'DONNELL, Roseann 1962-
(Rosie O'Donnell)

PERSONAL: Born March 21, 1962, in Commack, NY; daughter of Edward (an engineer) and Roseann (a homemaker) O'Donnell; partner of Kelli Carpenter; children: (adopted) Parker Jaren, Chelsea Belle, Blake Christopher; (born to partner, Kelli Carpenter) Vivienne Rose. *Education:* Attended Dickinson College and Boston University.

ADDRESSES: Agent—International Creative Management, 8899 Beverly Rd., Los Angeles, CA 90048.

CAREER: Comedienne, actress, and talk show host. *Rosie* (magazine), New York, NY, editorial director, 2001-02. Founder of For All Kids Foundation and Rosie's Readers (with eToys).

Actor in films, including (as Doris Murphy) *A League of Their Own*, Columbia, 1992; (as Gina Garrett) *Another Stakeout*, Buena Vista, 1993; (as Becky) *Sleepless in Seattle*, TriStar, 1993; *Fatal Instinct* (also known as *Triple Indemnity*), Metro-Goldwyn-Mayer, 1993; (as Lucille Toody) *Car 54, Where Are You?* Orion, 1994; (as Betty Rubble) *The Flintstones*, Universal, 1994; (as Sheila Kingston) *Exit to Eden*, Savoy, 1994; (as makeup person) *I'll Do Anything*, Columbia, 1994; (as Roberta Martin) *Now and Then* (also known as *The Gaslight Addition*), New Line Cinema, 1995; (as Gina Barrisano) *Beautiful Girls*, Miramax, 1996; (as Ole Golly) *Harriet the Spy*, Paramount, 1996; (as herself) *A Very Brady Sequel*, Paramount, 1996; (as Sister Terry) *Wide Awake*, Miramax, 1998; (as herself) *Get Bruce*, Miramax, 1999; and (as voice of Terkoz) *Tarzan* (animated), Buena Vista, 1999.

Actor in television series, including (as Maggie O'Brien) *Gimme a Break*, National Broadcasting Company (NBC), 1986-87; (as host and executive producer) *Stand-Up Spotlight*, VH1, 1989; (as Lorraine Popowski) *Stand by Your Man*, Fox, 1992; and (as host and executive producer) *The Rosie O'Donnell Show*, syndicated, 1996-2002.

Actor in television series episodes, including (as herself) "Destiny Rides Again," *Beverly Hills 90210*, Fox, 1992; (as Sheri) "There's No Ship like Kinship," *Living Single*, Fox, 1994; (as herself) "Breast Augmentation," *Night Stand*, syndicated, 1995; (as Peg) "I Am Not My Sister's Keeper," *Bless This House*, Columbia Broadcasting System (CBS), 1995; (as herself) "Eight," *The Larry Sanders Show*, Home Box Office (HBO), 1995; (as Cozette), *The Nanny*, CBS, 1995; (as taxi driver) "Where's the Pearls?," *The Nanny*, CBS, 1996; (as herself) "The Rosie Show," *The Nanny*, CBS, 1996; (as Naomi) *All My Children*, American Broadcasting Companies (ABC), 1996; (as herself) *Spin City*, ABC, 1996; (as herself) *Suddenly Susan*, (NBC), 1996; (as herself) "Ways and Means," *Suddenly Susan*, NBC, 1997; (as Ann Marie Delany, Secretary 92) "Man and Woman," *Murphy Brown*, CBS, 1997; and (as herself) "Blue's Birthday," *Blue's Clues*, Nickelodeon, 1998. Also appeared on *Star Search*, syndicated; *The Dennis Miller Show*, syndicated; *The Late Show with David Letterman*, CBS; (as voice of Head Barrette Beret Girl, "Eat My Cookies," *Ren and Stimpy Show* (animated), Nickelodeon; and (as host) *Saturday Night Live*, NBC.

Appearances in television specials, including *Showtime Comedy Club All-Stars*, Showtime, 1988; *A Pair of Jokers: Bill Engvall and Rosie O'Donnell*, Showtime, 1990; *Hurricane Relief*, Showtime, 1992; *Back to School '92* (also known as *Education First!*), CBS, 1992; *A Gala for the President at Ford's Theatre* (also known as *President's Night at Ford's Theatre*), ABC, 1993; *In a New Light '94*, ABC, 1994; *Good Hope Fairy, Sesame Street's All-Star Twenty-fifth Birthday: Stars and Street Forever!* ABC, 1994; *The Cindy Crawford Special*, Music Television (MTV), 1994; (as host) *The Flintstones: Best of Bedrock*, Fox, 1994; *Barbara Walters Presents the Ten Most Fascinating People of 1996*, 1996; (as host) *Catch a Rising Star Fiftieth Anniversary—Give or Take Twenty-six Years*, CBS, 1996; *Ladies' Home Journal's Most Fascinating Women of '96*, CBS, 1996; *The Good, the Bad, and the Beautiful* (also known as *Popcorn Venus*), Turner Broadcasting (TBS), 1996; *Vanessa Williams and Friends: Christmas in New York*, ABC, 1996; *Very Personal with Naomi Judd*, Family Channel, 1996; *Fifty Years of Television: A Celebration of the Academy of Television Arts and Sciences Golden Anniversary*, HBO, 1997; (as host) *Broadway '97: Launching the Tonys*, Public Broadcasting (PBS), 1997; *Farm Aid '97*, Turner Nashville Network (TNN), 1997; *Happy Birthday Elizabeth: A Celebration of Life*, ABC, 1997; *I Am Your Child* (also known as *From Zero to Three*), ABC, 1997; *Say It, Fight It, Cure It*, Lifetime, 1997; *Voices of Hope: Finding the Cures for Breast and Ovarian Cancer*, Lifetime, 1997; *Walt Disney World's Twenty-fifth Anniversary Party*, ABC, 1997; *Elmopalooza*, ABC, 1998; and *Take a Moment*, Disney Channel, 1998.

Television appearances at awards presentations, including *The Forty-fourth Annual Primetime Emmy Awards*, Fox, 1992; *The MTV Movie Awards*, MTV, 1993; *The Forty-eighth Annual Tony Awards*, 1994; *The Sixty-sixth Annual Academy Awards Presentations*, 1994; *The Eight Annual Kids' Choice Awards*, 1995; (as cohost) *The Ninth Annual Kids's Choice Awards*, 1996; *The Twenty-third Annual Daytime Emmy Awards*, 1996; (as host) *The Tenth Annual Kids' Choice Awards*, 1997; *The Twenty-fourth Annual Daytime Emmy Awards*, 1997; (as host) *The Fifty-first Annual Tony Awards*, 1997; (as host and coproducer) *The Eleventh Annual Kids' Choice Awards*, 1998; *The Twenty-fourth Annual People's Choice Awards*, 1998; *The Twenty-fifth Annual Daytime Emmy Awards*, 1998; and (as host and coproducer) *The Fifty-second Annual Tony Awards*, 1998.

Director of *We're Funny That Way* (film), 1998; appeared in (as Betty Rizzo) *Grease* (stage), Eugene O'Neill Theatre, New York, NY, 1994; (as Jackie) *The Twilight of the Gods* (television movie), Showtime, 1997, and *Cat in the Hat* (stage), Broadway, 2001.

AWARDS, HONORS: American Comedy Award nomination, best female performer in a television special, and CableAce Award nomination, best entertainment host, both 1994, both for *Stand-up Spotlight;* American Comedy Award nomination, best actress in a motion picture, 1994, for *Another Stakeout;* American Comedy Award nomination, best supporting female in a motion picture, 1994, for *Sleepless in Seattle;* Emmy nomination, outstanding guest actress in a comedy series, 1996, for "Eight," *The Larry Sanders Show;* named Woman of the Year, *Ms.,* 1996; Emmy (shared), Outstanding Variety, Music, or Comedy Special, 1999; Lucy Award, Women in Film, 2002; Montblanc Arts Patronage Award, 2002; Vito Russo Award, GLAAD, 2003; multiple Daytime Emmy awards as executive producer and as host of *The Rosie O'Donnell Show.*

WRITINGS:

Kids Are Punny: Jokes Sent by Kids to the Rosie O'Donnell Show, Warner Books (New York, NY), 1997.
Kids Are Punny 2: More Jokes Sent by Kids to the Rosie O'Donnell Show, Warner Books (New York, NY), 1998.
(With Deborah Axelrod and Tracy Chutorian Semler) *Bosom Buddies: Lessons and Laughter on Breast Health and Cancer,* Warner Books (New York, NY), 1999.
Find Me, Warner Books (New York, NY), 2002.

Contributor of foreword to *Portraits of Hope: Conquering Breast Cancer: Fifty-two Inspirational Stories of Strength,* by Marcia Stevens Sherrill, Wonderland Press (New York, NY), 1998, and *I'd Rather Laugh: How to Be Happy Even When Life Has Other Plans for You,* by Linda Richman, Warner Books (New York, NY), 2001; performer on sound recordings, including *A Rosie Christmas,* Columbia, 1999; *Another Rosie Christmas,* Sony Music, 2000; *No Wrapping Required,* Lyric Street, 2001; and *This Is the Moment,* Universal Classics, 2001.

ADAPTATIONS: Find Me was adapted for audio (three cassettes; unabridged), Time Warner AudioBooks, 2002.

SIDELIGHTS: Rosie O'Donnell's long and successful career as a star of stage, screen, and standup comedy took off with her appearances on VH1's *Stand-up Spotlight.* Over the decades that followed, she became a producer, as well as a performer, a publisher, and an advocate for children through her nonprofits and generous donations to charitable causes.

O'Donnell grew up in an Irish-Catholic family on Long Island, New York. Her mother died of cancer when O'Donnell was ten, and her father, an engineer who designed cameras for spy satellites, became withdrawn, leaving O'Donnell and her four siblings to look to each other for support. O'Donnell immersed herself in watching television. She inherited her love of comedy, music, dance, and theater from her mother, however, and idolized such notable women as Lucille Ball, Bette Midler, and Carol Burnett. She loved Barbra Streisand, because her mother had played her records while she cooked dinner, and the children had learned all of the songs. After her mother died, her father took the children to Ireland, and upon their return, everything of their mother's was gone—except for the record collection. Their father, who hoped to erase the pain by eliminating her possessions, had not known that the Streisand records were, in fact, the most poignant reminder of the children's mother. Years later, when Streisand walked onto the stage of *The Rosie O'Donnell Show* and O'Donnell faced her idol for the first time, she broke down and wept.

A popular high school student, O'Donnell was chosen prom queen, homecoming queen, class clown, and class president. She was athletic and played drums in a rock band. She also performed comedy on the high school stage and in local clubs. After graduation, she briefly attended college, but her calling was comedy. In 1984, she was a semifinalist on *Star Search,* and she used the prize money to move to Los Angeles. Two years later, she landed a small part on a sitcom and was then hired by VH1 to introduce music videos. When that gig ended, she convinced the network to let her produce and host *Stand-up Spotlight,* a showcase for comedic talent. O'Donnell continued getting small television parts, but in 1992, she was cast in her first major film role.

In the film *A League of Their Own* O'Donnell plays Doris Murphy, former bouncer and now third baseman on an all-female professional baseball team. She plays Madonna's pal, and in working together, the two women began an actual friendship. The one thing they did have in common was that they had both lost their mothers when they were young. O'Donnell's portrayal was widely praised, and she was cast to play Becky, an editor and best friend of Annie (Meg Ryan) in the film *Sleepless in Seattle.*

Writer and producer of the film, Nora Ephron, said in a *Redbook* article that as she was casting, she "thought it would probably take awhile to find the person who would have the qualities we needed for the part: someone funny, of course, and someone whom the women in the audience would immediately believe they, too could be best friends with. The first day of casting, Rosie came in to audition, and I never saw another actress." Ephron, who was interviewing O'Donnell nearly two decades after the release of *Sleepless,* said that women "all feel that Rosie is someone they could be friends with. But she serves other functions as well: She's conscientious, unafraid of taking political positions, and she's a philanthropist, donating millions of dollars to charity. In an era when politicians have to take lessons in being authentic, she has become successful without blunting her personality. At a time when people want to be famous in order to be famous, she wants to be famous almost entirely to do good things for others."

O'Donnell was cast in major roles in a number of other films, including as Betty Rubble in *The Flintstones.* She presented a new Rosie when she starred as a leather-clad dominatrix in *Exit to Eden,* a part that had been turned down by Sharon Stone. She acted in several more films and made her Broadway debut as Betty Rizzo in Tommy Tune's revival of *Grease.* She began hosting her own daytime television show in 1996, offering a comfortable and friendly talk format that contrasted sharply with some of the more volatile shows of the time. In 2001 O'Donnell launched a magazine, *Rosie,* which replaced *McCall's.* Both the magazine and the show folded in 2002.

O'Donnell has garnered many awards for her work and has hosted a long list of shows that have honored the work of others. Through the sale of two collections of jokes sent in by children, she has raised funds for her charity, the All Kids Foundation. In addition, she coauthored *Bosom Buddies: Lessons and Laughter on Breast Health and Cancer* with Deborah Axelrod, head of the breast cancer center at Manhattan's St. Vincent's Hospital, and health reporter Tracy Chuto-

rian Semler. Axelrod writes about risk factors, self-exams, and treatments, while O'Donnell's contributions are light-hearted quips that provide intermittent relief from the heavy reading. Well-known breast cancer survivors like Peggy Fleming and Diahann Carroll offer their own comments. A *People* reviewer wrote that *Bosom Buddies* "delivers the knowledge women need to take control of their own health" and concluded by saying that "laughter is indeed the best medicine."

O'Donnell is parent to her family of adopted children and the natural child of her partner, Kelli Carpenter. She continues to work for the welfare of children, particularly those who are neglected and abused.

In *Find Me* O'Donnell touches briefly on her own childhood abuse and her lesbianism, but the bulk of the novel-like memoir is a recounting of her relationship with a young woman with multiple personality disorder. The girl O'Donnell calls Stacy contacted the celebrity's adoption hotline, and O'Donnell returned her call because Stacy said she was a fourteen-year-old rape victim. O'Donnell, who admits to having a compulsive need to help others, was drawn into Stacy's life via frequent e-mails and calls by Stacy to O'Donnell's home at every hour of the day and night. Ultimately, O'Donnell had to face a number of truths about Stacy that were difficult to deal with.

O'Donnell completed the book without help. Jeff Guinn noted in a *Detroit Free Press* review that she "can certainly write well." Guinn called the book "part memoir, part self-psychoanalysis, part the sad story of someone sick reaching out to a celebrity. . . . But Stacy is essentially the canvas on which O'Donnell is painting a portrait of herself." A *BookPage* writer said that O'Donnell's "endearingly self-effacing style and frank portrayal of events will keep readers hooked."

BIOGRAPHICAL AND CRITICAL SOURCES:

BOOKS

Goodman, Gloria, *The Life and Humor of Rosie O'Donnell: A Biography,* William Morrow (New York, NY), 1998.

Mair, George, and Anna Green, *Rosie O'Donnell: Her True Story,* Carol Publishing Group (Secaucus, NJ), 1997.

Newsmakers, Gale (Detroit, MI), 1994.

O'Donnell, Rosie, *Find Me,* Warner Books (New York, NY), 2002.

Parish, James Robert, *Rosie: Rosie O'Donnell's Biography,* Carroll & Graf (New York, NY), 1997.

Prud'homme, Alex, *Rosie O'Donnell: Biography,* Time (New York, NY), 1999.

Spreng, Patrick, *Everything Rosie: The Ultimate Guide for Rosie O'Donnell Fans,* Carol Publishing Group (Secaucus, NJ), 1998.

PERIODICALS

BookPage, April, 2002, review of *Find Me,* p. 2.

Good Housekeeping, June, 1998, Joanna Powell, "Rosie's Devotion" (interview), p. 100.

Library Journal, October 15, 1999, BetteLee Fox, review of *Bosom Buddies: Lessons and Laughter on Breast Health and Cancer,* p. 96; February 15, 2003, Danna Bell-Russel, review of *Find Me* (audio), p. 183.

People, November 15, 1999, review of *Bosom Buddies,* p. 49.

Publishers Weekly, October 18, 1999, review of *Bosom Buddies,* p. 77; March 4, 2002, review of *Find Me,* p. 71.

Redbook, November, 1998, Deanna Kizis, "Rosie O'Donnell: What She Really Wants—and It's not Tom Cruise!" (interview), p. 122; February, 2000, Nora Ephron, "The Real Rosie (Really!)" (interview), p. 86.

ONLINE

Detroit Free Press online, http://www.freep.com/ (May 5, 2002), Jeff Guinn, review of *Find Me.**

*   *   *

O'DONNELL, Rosie
    See O'DONNELL, Roseann

*   *   *

OGG, Alex

PERSONAL: Born in Scunthorpe, Lincolnshire, England. *Education:* University degree in drama.

ADDRESSES: Agent—c/o Omnibus Press, 8/9 Frith St., London W1D 3JB, England.

CAREER: Journalist and author.

WRITINGS:

(With David Upshal) *The Hip Hop Years: A History of Rap* (includes CD), Channel 4 Books (London, England), 1999, Fromm International (New York, NY), 2001.

Radiohead: Standing on the Edge, Boxtree (London, England), 2000.

Top Ten: The Irreverent Guide to Music, Channel 4 Books (London, England), 2001.

The Def Jam Record Story, Omnibus Press (London, England), 2002.

Rebels without a Pause, Music Sales Limited (London, England), 2002.

Rap Lyrics: From the Sugarhill Gang to Eminem, Wise Publications/Omnibus Press (London, England), 2002.

Author of introduction, *The Guinness Who's Who of Indie and New Wave Music,* edited by Colin Larkin, Gullane Publishing (London, England), 1992; contributor to *The Rough Guide to Rock,* edited by Mark Ellingham and Jonathan Buckley, Rough Guides (London, England), 1999.

SIDELIGHTS: Alex Ogg is a journalist who has written or contributed to a number of books on popular culture, music, musicians and music history. Among these are *Radiohead: Standing on the Edge,* about the influential British band Radiohead, and *Top Ten: The Irreverent Guide to Music,* based on the popular British television program. With David Upshal, he cowrote *The Hip Hop Years: A History of Rap,* a guide to the development of hip hop in the United States up to the 1999 Grammy Awards. The book offers interviews of more than 100 rappers, DJs, music writers, and producers who found unprecedented success, or merely a fleeting moment of fame, in the genre that attacked the mainstream until it became mainstream.

The rap movement began in New York City in the 1970s when gang members turned to competing against each other, not in combat but with break dancing moves as each vied to put on the best show. At ten years old, Afrika Bambaataa was a Bronx DJ for parties that offered a safer environment for street kids he organized as the Zulu Nation. Grandmaster Flash (Joseph Sadler) was also a talented South Bronx DJ who trained others in mixing the sound for the rappers who were then known as MCs. At that time, the lyrics were happy and not violent or antisocial. Run-DMC, from Queens, took pride in the music that emanated from their neighborhood.

The themes changed in the 1980s, in part because rappers were looking for original and untested ways of getting noticed. The breakthrough came when Public Enemy began recording for Def Jam Records. The politicizing of rap lyrics took off with their second album, *It Takes a Nation of Millions to Hold Us Back,* released in 1988. Paula Friedman wrote in the *Los Angeles Times Book Review,* "From here on in *The Hip Hop Years,* Ogg and Upshal adopt an almost thriller-like approach in recounting the birth of gangster rap, and the toll it took on the lives of its practitioners."

West Coast rap, called by the authors "the poor relation to New York's hyper-creative hip hop expansion," began to be heard in the late 1980s, first with rapper Ice-T. The group N.W.A., featuring Ice Cube, Dr. Dre, and others, recorded songs filled with violence and obscenity, and achieved high sales numbers.

Friedman noted that "the notorious Southern California rival gangs the Bloods and the Crips made their way into rap primarily via the company Death Row Records, a group that allegedly employed members of the Bloods. Artists like Snoop Doggy Dog . . . and Tupac Shakur . . . helped forge the relationship between rap and real life violence." Some feel that the popularity of rap began to wane after the highly publicized murders of Shakur in 1996 and the Notorious B.I.G. the following year.

Library Journal's Richard Koss maintained that in this history, "the nurturing role of underground radio, the growing contributions of Latino rappers, and the influence of Five Percent Nation ideology are among several themes that are largely ignored." A *Publishers Weekly* reviewer who called this book "essential," wrote that the authors, "by detailing rap's lasting contribution to global culture . . . offer a corrective to the way rap is so often covered by the press."

BIOGRAPHICAL AND CRITICAL SOURCES:

PERIODICALS

Library Journal, April 15, 2001, Richard Koss, review of *The Hip Hop Years: A History of Rap,* p. 96.
Los Angeles Times Book Review, May 28, 2001, Paula Friedman, "A Music Genre and the Culture That Defines It," p. E1.
Publishers Weekly, April 16, 2001, review of *The Hip Hop Years,* p. 54.
Times (London, England), May 6, 2000, Mike Pattenden, review of *Radiohead: Standing on the Edge,* p. 22.*

*   *   *

OLIVER, Jamie 1975-

PERSONAL: Born May, 1975; married, wife's name Jools; children: Poppy, Daisy Boo. *Education:* Attended Westminster Catering College. *Hobbies and other interests:* Drumming.

ADDRESSES: Office—Fifteen Restaurant, 15 Westland Place, London N1 7LP, England.

CAREER: Chef, television personality, and author of cookbooks. Neal Street Restaurant, London, England, former head pastry chef; River Café, London, chef. Fifteen (restaurant), London, head chef. Host of television series *The Naked Chef* and *Jamie's Kitchen.*

AWARDS, HONORS: British Academy of Film and Television Arts Award for Best Feature, 2001, for *The Naked Chef* (television series).

WRITINGS:

The Naked Chef, Hyperion (New York, NY), 2000.
The Return of the Naked Chef, Michael Joseph (London, England), 2000.
The Naked Chef Takes Off, Hyperion (New York, NY), 2001.
Happy Days with the Naked Chef, Hyperion (New York, NY), 2002.

Jamie's Kitchen: A Complete Cooking Course, Hyperion (New York, NY), 2003.

Books have been translated into eleven languages.

SIDELIGHTS: Jamie Oliver stands out among the latest generation of celebrity chefs as young, hip, energetic, and accessible. In 2000 Oliver was named one of the sexiest men alive by *People* magazine, and, according to Judith Sutton in her *Library Journal* review of *The Naked Chef Takes Off,* "he's practically become a household name." Known as "the Naked Chef" to Food Network viewers, Oliver explained in his Web site biography that "the idea behind *The Naked Chef* was to strip food down to its bare essentials—to prove that you didn't need to dress up ingredients or buy a load of fancy gadgets to make something really tasty." He advocates adapting recipes to what one has in one's own cupboard, refrigerator, or garden.

Although Oliver worked his way into London's culinary upper echelon, his popularity has come in large part from his down-to-earth approach; a reviewer for *Publishers Weekly* in a review of *Happy Days with the Naked Chef* noted: "perhaps never has a personality cookbook ranged so far across high and not-so-high cuisine." Oliver writes in a breezy, colloquial tone that puts readers at ease, though his instructions may strike some novice cooks as too vague. With them in mind he includes, in *Happy Days with the Naked Chef,* a chapter of "quick fixes" that involve minimal preparation and cleanup. Reviewing *The Naked Chef,* a *Publishers Weekly* contributor concluded that "Oliver delivers a hip classic that will appeal to a new generation of modern epicureans who face the challenge of cooking within the confines of tiny urban kitchens on time-pressed schedules."

Oliver began his fascination with cooking while working summers and weekends in his parents' pub-restaurant, The Cricketers, in Clavering, Essex, England. He left school at age sixteen to attend Westminster Catering College, then spent time working in France; he returned to London to work as head pastry chef at the Neal Street Restaurant under Antonio Carlucci. It was at his next position, at the River Café, that Oliver was discovered. As the chef described on his Web site, "a documentary about the restaurant was being filmed and the editors decided to show a lot of this cheeky kid who was so into the cooking that he'd answer back to the crew—telling them to get out of the way, or whatever." The day after the documentary aired, five different producers contacted Oliver about a possible new television show. The series *The Naked Chef* eventually aired on the British Broadcasting Corporation and met with great success. Licensed to more than fifty countries, the show gained popularity in the United States on the Food Network.

In addition to his televised cooking series, Oliver has created *Jamie's Kitchen,* a multi-part television documentary that "follows Oliver as he fulfills his dream of opening his own restaurant, Fifteen, as he trains fifteen young, unemployed Londoners to be chefs in this nonprofit restaurant," according to Debra Johnson in *Variety.* In January of 2003, Fifteen was nominated for the Tio Pepe Carlton Ondon Restaurant Award. Oliver has hoped to make a lasting contribution by serving as a mentor to other young chefs, and he hoped to create several more restaurants on the Fifteen model.

Oliver's Web site, with 180,000 hits per month, is the most popular food Web site in the United Kingdom. In addition to recipes, it includes a diary that keeps fans up-to-date on Oliver's work, travels, and weekend plans.

BIOGRAPHICAL AND CRITICAL SOURCES:

PERIODICALS

Library Journal, August, 2000, Judith Sutton, review of *The Naked Chef,* p. 145; August, 2001, Judith Sutton, review of *The Naked Chef Takes Off,* p. 150; October 15, 2002, Judith Sutton, review of *Happy Days with the Naked Chef,* p. 90.

People, August 6, 2001, Max Alexander, review of *Happy Days with the Naked Chef,* p. 53.

Publishers Weekly, September 18, 2000, review of *The Naked Chef,* p. 145; October 7, 2002, review of *Happy Days with the Naked Chef,* p. 69.

Variety, February 3, 2003, Debra Johnson, *Naked Truth about Chef Oliver,* p. 28.

ONLINE

Jamie Oliver Web site, http://www.jamieoliver.com (November 14, 1999).*

OLSON, Marianne
See MITCHELL, Marianne

*   *   *

O'NEILL, Anthony 1964-

PERSONAL: Born 1964, in Melbourne, Australia; son of a policeman and a stenographer. *Education:* Attended Christian Brothers College (St. Kilda, Australia).

ADDRESSES: Home—Melbourne, Australia. *Agent*—c/o Author's Mail, Scribner, c/o Simon & Schuster, 1230 Avenue of the Americas, New York, NY 10020.

CAREER: Novelist. Worked variously as a bank clerk, storeman, warehouse supervisor, video store manager, and computer salesman.

WRITINGS:

Scheherazade: A Tale, Flamingo (New York, NY), 2001.
The Lamplighter: A Novel, Scribner (New York, NY), 2003.

O'Neill's work has been translated into several language, including French.

WORK IN PROGRESS: A mystery novel featuring Napoleon Bonaparte.

SIDELIGHTS: Australian author Anthony O'Neill wrote his first novel-length work of fiction when he was only twelve years old. Deciding against college, he took on jobs that allowed him enough time and energy to focus on writing. O'Neill's first published novel, *Scheherazade: A Tale,* was written using the technique of writing one page per day for at least 365 days. The book, which retells the story of Arabian queen Scheherazade, gained international acclaim and has been translated into several languages.

In 2003 O'Neill came out with his second book, *The Lamplighter: A Novel.* A murder mystery based on months of research on location in Edinburgh, Scotland,

the novel recalls tales of Jack the Ripper due to its dark plot and sinister undertones. A *Publishers Weekly* reviewer praised *The Lamplighter,* calling O'Neill "a masterful storyteller with a thorough knowledge of both the urban life and the literary tropes of late 19th-century Britain. . . . But readers won't pause too long to admire his erudition—the thrilling story will have them turning pages compulsively." *Library Journal* contributor Wilda Williams dubbed *The Lamplighter* "a treat for fans of traditional and contemporary Victorian thrillers," while Kate Mediatore noted in *Booklist* that "readers will enjoy the Victorian gothic setting and the characters, even though they will likely figure out who the murderer is long before the end."

In in interview for *Publishers Weekly,* O'Neill discussed his work on "A mystery-adventure that involves Napoleon. I've done 18 months of research, and I'm about to start the first draft—I plan it like a military invasion. I plot everything out in advance. Then I can't wait to get everything on the page."

BIOGRAPHICAL AND CRITICAL SOURCES:

PERIODICALS

Australian (Sydney, Australia), June 13, 2001, James Bradley, review of *Scheherazade,* p. 13B.
Booklist, March 1, 2003, review of *The Lamplighter,* p. 1149.
Boston Globe, April 20, 2003, Anna Mundow, "Death and Danger, on Sailing Ships, in Squalid Cities," p. D6.
Daily Telegraph (Sydney, Australia), March 15, 2003, Lucy Clark, "Escape into Horror," p. 38.
Evening News (Edinburgh, Scotland), May 27, 2003, Thom Dibdin, review of *The Lamplighter,* p. 23.
Globe and Mail, July 5, 2003, Margaret Cannon, review of *The Lamplighter.*
Guardian (London, England), June 14, 2003, Maxim Jakubowski, review of *The Lamplighter.*
Independent on Sunday (London, England), February, 5, 2002, Wendy Bardsley, review of *Scheherazade.*
Library Journal, February, 15, 2003, Wilda Williams, review of *The Lamplighter,* p. 170.
Publishers Weekly, March 10, 2003, interview and review of *The Lamplighter,* p. 53.
Sydney Morning Herald, April 17, 2003, Graham Williams, review of *The Lamplighter.*

Weekend Australian, April 28, 2001, Helen Elliott, "Romancing Madonna," p. R12; March 1, 2003, Kathy Hunt, review of *The Lamplighter,* p. B10.

ONLINE

All Reader.com, http://www.allreaders.com/ (July 12, 2003), Harriet Klausner, review of *The Lamplighter.*

January, http://www.janmag.com/ (March, 2003), Sarah Weinman, review of *The Lamplighter.*

Mostly Fiction, http://mostlyfiction.com/ (June 18, 2003), Mary Whipple, review of *The Lamplighter.**

*　　*　　*

OSBORN, Elinor 1939-

PERSONAL: Born 1939, in OH; married George Osborn (a musician), 1961. *Education:* University of Rochester, B.Mus., 1961, and M.Mus. *Hobbies and other interests:* Cross-country skiing.

ADDRESSES: Home—91 Coachman Dr., Penfield, NY 14526. *E-mail*—elinor@rochester.rr.com.

CAREER: Music teacher at public schools in Fairport, NY, for thirty years; photographer, with work exhibited in shows at Rochester Museum and Science Center, 1998, and elsewhere. Member of Penfield Conservation Board.

MEMBER: North American Butterfly Association, Audubon Society, National Wildlife Federation, Xerces Society, Dragonfly Society of the Americas, Nature Conservancy, Wilderness Society, Sierra Club, Rochester Area Children's Writers and Illustrators.

AWARDS, HONORS: Grand prize, Wetlands Photography Contest, U.S. Environmental Protection Agency, 2002.

WRITINGS:

(And photographer) *Project UltraSwan* (nonfiction), Houghton Mifflin (Boston, MA), 2002.

Contributor of photographs to various books. Contributor of articles and photographs to periodicals, including *Vermont Life* and *Cross Country Ski.*

WORK IN PROGRESS: Research on glacial geology.

BIOGRAPHICAL AND CRITICAL SOURCES:

PERIODICALS

Booklist, December 15, 2002, Karen Hutt, review of *Project UltraSwan,* p. 758.

Bulletin of the Center for Children's Books, December, 2002, Deborah Stevenson, review of *Project UltraSwan.*

Horn Book, January-February, 2003, review of *Project UltraSwan,* pp. 100-101.

Junior Library Guild, fall, 2002, review of *Project UltraSwan,* p. 4.

P

PAHLEN, Kurt 1907-2003

OBITUARY NOTICE—See index for *CA* sketch: Born May 26, 1907, in Vienna, Austria; died July 24, 2003, in Lenk, Switzerland. Conductor, composer, educator, and author. Pahlen worked throughout his life to make music, especially orchestral and operatic works, accessible to general audiences and children. Initially intending to be a professional pianist, he switched to the study of composition and conducting at the Vienna Conservatoire, and also studied German language and literature at the University of Vienna, where he earned a D.Phil. in 1929. After graduation, he taught opera at the Volkshochschule, while earning additional income as a music critic and radio broadcaster. He found work, too, as a conductor and lecturer. As a music composer, his original compositions received acclaim and popularity in Europe, and he also established a respected opera studio in Vienna; for younger performers also Pahlen established a number of children's choruses and choirs. With the onset of World War II, however, he fled to Argentina, where he became chief conductor for the Filharmonica Metropolitana and then of the Filharmonia in Rosario. He continued to write music while publishing numerous books in German and Spanish, some of which were for juvenile audiences, including *Manuel de Falla* (1953), *Que es la musica?* (1956), *La musica en la educatión moderna* (1961), *Grösse Meister der Musik* (1968), and *Opera der Welt* (1979). In 1949 he moved to Uruguay, becoming professor of musicology at the University de la Republica in Montevideo and president and chief conductor of the Chorus-Organization. In 1957 he was also hired as manager of the Theatre Colon, an opera house in Buenos Aires. Pahlen returned to Europe in 1972, moving to Mannedorf, Switzerland and obtain-

ing Swiss citizenship in 1982. He continued to lecture and travel abroad, as well as compose operas, songs, choral pieces, and musical theater for children and adults. Honored with such awards as the Great Cross for Culture and Sciences and the Great Cross from the Land of the Salzburgs, his most recent prize was the Gold Medal of Honor for Services to the Republic of Austria, which he received in 2002. Pahlen wrote of his life in his autobiography, *Ja, die Zeit andert viel: Mein Jahrhundert mit der Musik* (2001).

OBITUARIES AND OTHER SOURCES:

PERIODICALS

Independent (London, England), August 6, 2003, p. 18.
Times (London, England), July 31, 2003.

*   *   *

PANTOLIANO, Joe 1951-

PERSONAL: Born Joseph Pantoliano, September 12, 1951, in Hoboken, NJ; son of Dominic (a factory worker and hearse driver) and Mary (a seamstress) Pantoliano; married Morgan Kester (an actress), 1979 (divorced, 1985); married Nancy Sheppard (an artist), February 18, 1994; children: (first marriage) Marco, (second marriage) Melody (stepdaughter), Daniella, Isabella Grace. *Education:* Studied acting under Herbert Bergoff at HB Studio, New York, NY.

ADDRESSES: Agent—United Talent Agency, 9560 Wilshire Blvd., Suite 500, Beverly Hills, CA 90212.

CAREER: Actor on stage, in films, and television. Stage roles include *One Flew over the Cuckoo's Nest; Italian-American Reconciliation; The Death Star; The Off-Season; Visions of Kerouac; Brothers,* 1982; and *Orphans,* 1983. Television appearances include *McNamara's Band,* ABC, 1973; *Free Country,* ABC, 1978; *More than Friends,* ABC, 1978; *From Here to Eternity,* NBC, 1979; *Alcatraz: The Whole Shocking Story,* NCB, 1980; *Hill Street Blues,* NBC, 1984; *Robert Kennedy and His Times,* CBS, 1985; *L.A. Law* (pilot), NBC, 1987; *Destination: America,* ABC, 1987; *The Hitchhiker,* HBO, 1987; *Rock 'n' Roll Mom,* ABC, 1988; *Nighbreaker,* TNT, 1989; *El Diablo,* HBO, 1990; *The Fanelli Boys,* NBC, 1990-91; *One Special Victory,* NBC, 1991; *Civil Wars,* ABC, 1991; *Highlander,* syndicated, 1992; *Through the Eyes of a Killer,* CBS, 1992; *Dangerous Heart,* USA Network, 1994; *The Immortals,* HBO, 1995; *The Last Word,* Showtime, 1995; *NYPD Blue,* ABC, 1995; *The Marshall,* ABC, 1995; *Ed McBain's 87th Precinct: Ice,* NBC, 1996; *EZ Streets,* CBS, 1996; *Natural Enemy,* HBO, 1997; *Top of the World,* HBO, 1998; *Sugar Hill,* 1999; and *The Sopranos,* HBO, 1999-2002. Voiced roles for animated television series, including *Godzilla,* Fox, 1998-99; *Beethoven,* CBS, 1994; *The Lionhearts,* syndicated, 1998; and *Disney's Hercules,* ABC and syndicated, 1998. Appeared in television specials, including *Mr. Roberts,* NCB, 1984; *Dig That Cat . . . He's Real Gone!,* HBO, 1989; and *Super Bloopers and New Practical Jokes,* NBC, 1991.

Film roles include *The Godfather, Part II,* Paramount, 1974; *The Idol Maker,* United Artists, 1980; *The Final Terror,* Comworld/Watershed, 1981; *Monsignor,* Twentieth Century-Fox, 1982; *Risky Business,* Warner Bros., 1983; *Eddie and the Cruisers,* Avco Embassy, 1983; *The Mean Season,* Orion, 1985; *Goonies,* Warner Bros., 1985; *Running Scared,* Metro-Goldwyn-Mayer/United Artists, 1986; *The Squeeze,* TriStar, 1987; *Scenes from the Goldmine,* Hemdale, 1987; *La Bamba,* Columbia, 1987; *Empire of the Sun,* Warner Bros., 1987; *Amazon Women on the Moon,* Universal, 1987; *The In Crowd,* Orion, 1988; *Midnight Run,* Universal, 1988; *Short Time,* Twentieth Century-Fox, 1990; *Downtown,* Twentieth Century-Fox, 1990; *Back-street Dreams,* Vidmark Entertainment, 1990; *The Last of the Finest,* Orion, 1990; *Zandalee,* Live Home Video, 1991; *Used People,* Twentieth Century-Fox,

1992; *Calendar Girl,* Columbia, 1993; *Me and the Kid,* Orion, 1993; *The Fugitive,* Warner Bros., 1993; *Three of Hearts,* New Line Cinema, 1993; *Baby's Day Out,* Twentieth Century-Fox, 1994; *Robot in the Family,* 1994; *Teresa's Tattoo,* Vidmark Entertainment, 1994; *The Flight of the Dove,* New Horizons Home Video, 1994; *Steal Big, Steal Little,* Savoy Pictures, 1995; *Scenes from Everyday Life,* 1995; *Bad Boys,* Columbia, 1995; *Bound,* Gramercy, 1996; *Taxman,* Conterclock Pictures, 1998; *U.S. Marshals,* Warner Bros., 1998; *The Matrix,* Warner Bros., 1999; *The Life before This,* Alliance Atlantis, 1999; *Black and White,* Grey Productions, 1999; *Tinseltown,* Samuel Goldwyn, 1999; *Ready to Rumble,* 2000; *Memento,* 2000; *Pray for the Cardinal,* 2000; *The Adventures of Pluto Nash,* 2002; *A Piece of My Heart,* 2002; *Daredevil,* 2003; and *Bad Boys II.*

MEMBER: Screen Actors Guild (member of board of directors), Creative Coalition.

AWARDS, HONORS: DramaLogue awards, best actor, for *Orphans* and *Italian American Reconciliation.*

WRITINGS:

(With Travis Malloy, and director) *Just like Mona* (screenplay), 2001.
(With David Evanier) *Who's Sorry Now: The True Story of a Stand-up Guy,* Dutton (New York, NY), 2002.

SIDELIGHTS: Joe Pantoliano is best known for his many character roles on television and in films, most notably his recurring role as Ralph Cifaretto on *The Sopranos.* Born and raised in New Jersey, Pantoliano enjoys portraying villains and tries to infuse even his most evil characters with recognizable humanity. "The basic training for an actor is to get to know yourself and use yourself to tell the story—your own rage, humor, and history to make it real for what you're doing," Pantoliano told Luaine Lee in the *Knight Ridder/Tribune News Service.* "And I love it every day. It's a gift, getting a job and going to work."

Pantoliano recalls his childhood in Hoboken, New Jersey, in his memoir *Who's Sorry Now: The True Story of a Stand-up Guy,* co-authored with David

Evanier. In his book Pantoliano candidly recalls growing up poor with a mother who ran numbers and a father who drove a hearse for a funeral home. Also central in Pantoliano's life was an ex-convict named Florio Isabella, a small-time mobster who became Pantoliano's stepfather and mentor. It was Florio who encouraged Pantoliano to act in school plays and to perfect his reading skills in order to prepare for an acting career.

After graduating from high school, Pantolino moved first to Manhattan and then to Los Angeles, working his way up from Off-Broadway to national touring companies and guest appearances on television shows. His feature film work has brought him connection to some of the most important producers and directors in Hollywood, including Steven Spielberg, Taylor Hackford, Christopher Nolan, and Andy Davis. He was also approached early on about taking a starring role on *The Sopranos,* but he actually joined the cast for the second season, which began filming in 1999. His character, Ralphie, had few redeeming qualities, to say the least. *Daily Variety* correspondent Phil Gallo wrote: "Pantoliano has finessed Ralph into one of 'The Sopranos' darkest characters, rising from a violent and smarmy knucklehead to a thorn-in-the-ass who has so penetrated the Soprano-run world that his dismissal is next to impossible. There are signals that his demise is possible." Indeed, Pantoliano's character's violent death was one of the climactic moment of the show's fourth season in 2002.

In his memoir, Pantoliano concentrates on his unconventional boyhood rather than his more predictable career ascent. His days of petty juvenile crime and his parents' penchant for gambling also provide the grist for his film *Just like Mona,* which marked his directorial debut. In his *Booklist* review of *Who's Sorry Now,* David Pitt called the book "downright fascinating," while noting that Pantoliano "writes in a style that will be instantly familiar to his fans: tough, outspoken, but with a charming side, too." A *Publishers Weekly* contributor concluded: "The once-dyslexic 'Joey Pants' writes with energy, humor and honesty, and his passionate closing chapter . . . is icing on the cake."

BIOGRAPHICAL AND CRITICAL SOURCES:

BOOKS

Contemporary Theatre, Film, and Television, Volume 24, Gale (Detroit, MI), 2000.

Newsmakers, Issue 3, Gale (Detroit, MI), 2002.

PERIODICALS

Booklist, October 15, 2002, David Pitt, review of *Who's Sorry Now: The True Story of a Stand-up Guy,* p. 374.
Boston Globe, April 1, 2001, p. M9.
Cape Cod Times, November 2, 2002, Frazier Moore, "'Joey Pants' Makes Good Playing Bad."
Christian Science Monitor, October 1, 1999, p. 20.
Daily Variety, September 12, 2002, Phil Gallo, review of *The Sopranos,* p. 7.
Entertainment Weekly, November 15, 1996, p. 55; October 4, 2002, Bruce Fretts, review of *Who's Sorry Now,* p. 148.
Hollywood Reporter, July 3, 2001, p. 12.
Knight-Ridder/Tribune News Service, July 2, 2001, Luaine Lee, interview with Pantoliano, p. K4954.
Los Angeles Times, February 15, 1991, p. 9.
People, November 19, 1990, p. 89; May 21, 2001, Michael A. Lipton, "All in the Family: Joe Pantoliano's Childhood Reads like a Script from the Sopranos," p. 75; July 30, 2001, p. 102.
Publishers Weekly, September 9, 2002, review of *Who's Sorry Now,* p. 54.
USA Today, August 18, 1993, p. 2D; February 7, 2001, p. D4.

ONLINE

Joey Pants Web site, http://www.joeypants.com/ (May 22, 2003).*

*   *   *

PARENTI, Christian

PERSONAL: Born in rural New England. *Education:* Attended New School for Social Research; London School of Economics, Ph.D. (sociology).

ADDRESSES: Home—San Francisco, CA. *Office*—New College of California, 777 Valencia St., San Francisco, CA 94110.

CAREER: Author, journalist, and educator. New College of California, San Francisco, professor of modern history, political economy, and criminal justice; Open Society Institute Center on Crime and Communities, senior fellow. Radio journalist in Central America, New York, and California.

WRITINGS:

Lockdown America: Police and Prisons in the Age of Crisis, Verso (New York, NY), 2000.
The Soft Cage: Surveillance in America from Slavery to the War on Terror, Basic Books (New York, NY), 2003.

Contributor to several publications, including *Christian Science Monitor, In These Times, Nation, New York Newsday, Progressive, Salon.com, San Diego Union Tribune,* and *Washington Post.*

SIDELIGHTS: In his book *Lockdown America: Police and Prisons in the Age of Crisis,* professor, journalist, and author Christian Parenti examines the penal system in the United States. Specifically, he traces political and ideological developments that have occurred since the end of the civil rights movement of the 1960s, in order to uncover reasons for America's high rates of incarceration: although the United States only represents five percent of the world's population, the country has twenty-five percent of the world's prisoners.

In his book Parenti theorizes that during the 1960s capitalist economic policies undermined working-class power by raising corporate costs, lowering profits, increasing unemployment rates, and creating a surplus workforce. The migration of inner-city industrial jobs—traditionally held by minorities and the working-class—to locations where workers could be hired for lower rates of compensation devastated cities by leaving many workers unemployed, thus increasing rates of homelessness and crime. These conditions made inner-city life unpleasant, which led to an attempt to contain or remove the targeted source of the problem—identified as the African-American and Hispanic communities, both associated with the welfare system and crime. Parenti argues that as a result, at the turn of the twenty-first century, the United States imprisoned black males at four times the rate of

South Africa's apartheid system, creating a ratio of seven African American men for each Caucasian male imprisoned. In the last section of the book, Parenti looks inside the prison system and reports on the appalling conditions in which inmates survive, including how prisoners are often kept in solitary confinement for years, and how rape—of both males and females—is encouraged and participated in by guards as a means of isolation and control.

Lockdown America was widely praised by reviewers. *Monthly Review* writer David Gilbert called the book "an analytical gem" and said, "Its forte is laying bare the driving forces behind the burgeoning of the criminal justice system." Theodore Hamm, in the *Nation,* commented, "As Parenti makes painfully clear, prisons today are about everything but individual reform." Phil Scraton, in a review for *Race and Class,* called the book "stunning, evocative and brilliantly written" and concluded that it is "in the best tradition of investigative journalism, has the pace of a fine novel and carries the authority of meticulous academic research." J. W. Mason, in the *American Prospect,* said it "at least combats the strong societal tendency to avert our eyes from what the American criminal justice system has become." *Progressive* reviewer Craig Aaron commented that what separates Parenti's book from others on the subject "are his gripping descriptions of gang sweeps, border raids, and jailhouse violence." Vivien Miller, in the *Times Literary Supplement,* concluded, "Conservatives will find this study to be polemical, sensationalist and scaremongering; liberals will find that it confirms their worst fears about economic and social reform." However, Matthew Yeomans of the *Voice Literary Supplement* pointed out that most of the material had been thoroughly documented in earlier sources, and that Parenti's argument places blame on the "police, politicians, and the faceless captains of capitalism."

Parenti's second book, *The Soft Cage: Surveillance in America from Slavery to the War on Terror,* looks at the evolution of the U.S. government's ability to monitor its citizens during the past two centuries. Slave passes, fingerprinting, immigrant identification cards, driver's licenses, automated teller machine cards, credit cards, toll passes, and parolee tracking devices are all analyzed to chart the progression of the government's increasingly powerful ability to monitor individuals—all with the consent of its citizens. Richard Seamon, in the *United States Naval Institute*

Proceedings, quoted Parenti as saying, "We are not 'being watched' so much as we are voluntarily 'checking in' with authorities." A contributor to *Kirkus Reviews* concluded that the author "reminds us that privacy protects, as democracy is meant to, the marginalized, the outcast, and the different." However, a *Publishers Weekly* contributor found that Parenti's "lens is too sharp and his antigovernment animus too apparent."

BIOGRAPHICAL AND CRITICAL SOURCES:

PERIODICALS

American Prospect, January 3, 2000, J. W. Mason, review of *Lockdown America: Police and Prisons in the Age of Crisis,* p. 63.

Kirkus Reviews, July 15, 2003, review of *The Soft Cage: Surveillance in America from Slavery to the War on Terror,* p. 955.

Monthly Review, March, 2001, David Gilbert, review of *Lockdown America,* p. 45.

Nation, October 11, 1999, Theodore Hamm, "Our Prison Complex," p.23.

Progressive, December, 1999, Craig Aaron, "The Theatrics of Force," pp. 41-42.

Publishers Weekly, July 14, 2003, review of *The Soft Cage,* p. 68.

Race and Class, July-September, 2000, Phil Scraton, review of *Lockdown America,* p. 89.

Sun, October, 2000, D. B. Jensen, "Crimes of Punishment: An Interview with Christian Parenti."

Times Literary Supplement, November 12, 1999, Vivien Miller, review of *Lockdown America,* p. 37.

United States Naval Institute Proceedings, August, 2003, Richard Seamon, review of *The Soft Cage,* p. 86.

Voice Literary Supplement, September 21, 1999, Matthew Yeomans, review of *Lockdown America,* p. 86.

ONLINE

Ampersand, http://www.mprsnd.org/ (November 5, 2003), Christopher J. Carley, "Sometimes Politics Leaves You Feeling Dirty" (interview).

Independent Films, http://www.independentfilms.com/ (November 5, 2003), "Parenti, Christian."

New College of California Web site, http://www.newcollege.edu/ (November 5, 2003), "Christian Parenti."*

* * *

PARKER, Marjorie Blain 1960-

PERSONAL: Born March 2, 1960, in Edmonton, Alberta, Canada; daughter of William Ross (a lawyer), and Sandra Joan (a language arts teacher; maiden name, McDonald) Blain; married Jay Gordon Parker (a gas and electric distribution designer), September 27, 1986; children: Steven Maxwell, Casey Blain, Rachel Faye. *Ethnicity:* "Caucasian." *Education:* University of Calgary, bachelor of commerce (management information systems), 1982. *Religion:* Catholic. *Hobbies and other interests:* Walking, cooking, reading, traveling, skiing.

ADDRESSES: Home—9194 East Evans Pl., Denver, CO 80231 *Agent*—Melanie Colbert Agency, 17 West St., Holland Landing, Ontario L9N 1L4, Canada. *E-mail*—jandmparker@comcast.net.

CAREER: Arthur Andersen, Calgary, Alberta, Canada, information systems consultant, 1982-86; Price Waterhouse, Denver, CO, information systems consultant, 1986-88; Software AG, Denver, technical software support, 1988-2002.

MEMBER: Authors' Guild, Society of Children's Book Writers and Illustrators, Canadian Society of Children's Authors, Illustrators, and Performers, Colorado Council of the International Reading Association.

AWARDS, HONORS: Henry Bergh Children's Book Award, American Society for the Prevention of Cruelty to Animals, Mr. Christie's Book Award Silver Sea, both 2002, and KIND Children's Book Award, National Association for Humane and Environmental Education, 2003, all for *Jasper's Day.*

WRITINGS:

Jasper's Day, illustrated by Janet Wilson, Kids Can Press (Toronto, Ontario, Canada), 2002.

Ice Cream Everywhere!, illustrated by Stephanie Roth, Scholastic (New York, NY), 2002.

Hello, School Bus!, illustrated by Bob Kolar, Cartwheel Books (New York, NY), 2004.

Hello, Fire Truck!, illustrated by Bob Kolar, Cartwheel Books (New York, NY), 2004.

Hello, Freight Train, illustrated by Bob Kolar, Cartwheel Books (New York, NY), 2004.

Contributor to children's magazines.

WORK IN PROGRESS: If I Could Be, illustrated by Cyd Moore, for Dutton (New York, NY), publication expected 2005; *A Paddle of Ducks,* illustrated by Wendy Bailey, for Kids Can Press (Toronto, Ontario, Canada), publication expected 2005.

SIDELIGHTS: After Marjorie Blain Parker won her first ribbon for a poem published in the school bulletin during third grade, she became hooked on writing. Yet many years passed before this native Canadian returned to creative writing. After graduating from college with a business degree, she worked for an accounting firm, and in 1986 she moved to Denver, Colorado, with her American husband. Shortly thereafter, she took a correspondence course in writing for children. "I needed a hobby since I had to leave all my friends and family behind in Canada," Parker wrote on her Web site. "I really enjoyed the writing and many of my pieces were published in children's magazines."

Parker's commitment to writing decelerated with the arrival of each of their three children, but once the kids were all of school age, she resumed her professional writing career. "In 1999, inspired by a writer friend, I decided to go for it," she continued. "My goal was to get a manuscript accepted before I turned forty." To this end she wrote stories, joined a critique group, and attended writers' conferences. Her first children's work *Jasper's Day,* an award-winning picture book about boy's last day with his beloved dog, appeared in 2002. The family of Jasper, a golden retriever suffering from cancer, celebrates the day with meaningful activities before taking him to the veterinarian to be put to sleep and later interring him in the backyard. Several reviewers suggested that *Jasper's Day* would be useful for bibliotherapy, including a *Kirkus Reviews* contributor, who remarked favorably upon the author's "exquisite sensitivity" in telling the story. Finding "the difficult situation . . . described gently, but realistically," *School Library Journal* critic Lucinda Snyder Whitehurst thought the story might help children experiencing similar situations. Whitehurst also expressed concern that children with healthy pets might find the story "upsetting" and thus recommended that parents consider this before sharing the book with their children. Writing in *Booklist,* Ilene Cooper thought that the author expressed clearly the difficulty in seeing a pet die, but noted that the book offers "a celebration of life that will remind children to make the most of every moment with those they love."

With more books on the way, Parker once noted that she "loves the writing life" and "hopes to establish a body of work worthy of the respect of book lovers and the literary community."

BIOGRAPHICAL AND CRITICAL SOURCES:

PERIODICALS

Booklist, December 15, 2002, Ilene Cooper, review of *Jasper's Day,* p. 769.

Kirkus Reviews, September 15, 2002, review of *Jasper's Day,* pp. 1397-1398.

Resource Links, October, 2002, Heather Hamilton, review of *Jasper's Day,* p. 8.

School Library Journal, January, 2003, Lucinda Snyder Whitehurst, review of *Jasper's Day,* p. 110.

ONLINE

Marjorie Blain Parker Home Page, http://www. marjorieblainparker.com (July 7, 2003).

*   *   *

PATTERSON, Carolyn Bennett 1921-2003

OBITUARY NOTICE—See index for *CA* sketch: Born April 12, 1921, in Laurel, MS; died of cirrhosis of the liver July 7, 2003, in Washington, DC. Editor and author. Patterson was a former editor for *National Geographic* magazine. After earning a B.A. from Louisiana State University in 1942, she worked as a crime reporter for the *New Orleans State* newspaper and then for the American Red Cross during World War II. She moved to Washington, D.C., with her husband, and applied to work as a file clerk for *National Geographic.* Instead of becoming a clerk, however, she was placed in an editorial position in 1949, becoming a news-service writer in 1950 and a caption and magazine writer in 1953. In 1960 Patterson was made assistant legend (caption) editor, and four years later she was promoted to legend editor, thus becoming the first woman to be given a credit on the *National Geographic*'s masthead. Unlike with many magazines, captions in the *National Geographic* are considered to be as important as the articles themselves, and Patterson found herself traveling all over the world to do the research necessary to write accurate legends; she also wrote articles for the magazine and became a rugged outdoorsperson as she hiked terrain from Brazil to Australia. After also being appointed senior assistant editor in 1973, Patterson retired in 1986. Her book about her experiences with the magazine, *Of Lands, Legends, and Laughter: The Search for Adventure with "National Geographic,"* was published in 1998.

OBITUARIES AND OTHER SOURCES:

PERIODICALS

Los Angeles Times, July 12, 2003, p. B21.
Washington Post, July 11, 2003, p. B6.

*   *   *

PATTILLO, Donald M. 1940-

PERSONAL: Born August 15, 1940, in Tallassee, AL; married Sharon Bennett, August 22, 1970; children: Duncan. *Ethnicity:* "Anglo-Saxon." *Education:* University of Alabama, B.S., 1962; Georgia State University, M.B.A., 1970, Ph.D., 1976. *Politics:* "Centrist." *Religion:* Protestant. *Hobbies and other interests:* Classical music.

ADDRESSES: Home—1171 Fords Lake Place, Acworth, GA 30101. *Office*—U.S. Peace Corps, Atinska 4, Skopje, Macedonia. *E-mail*—donpatilo@yahoo.com.

CAREER: Educator, consultant, and author. Professor of business and economics, c. 1970s-80s; academic consultant and writer, c. 1990s; U.S. Peace Corps, beginning 1999. *Military service:* U.S. Air Force, 1962-66, first lieutenant.

WRITINGS:

A History in the Making: Eighty Turbulent Years in the American General Aviation Industry, McGraw-Hill (New York, NY), 1998.
Pushing the Envelope: U.S. Aircraft Industry, University of Michigan Press (Ann Arbor, MI), 1998.

WORK IN PROGRESS: A fictional work on the Wright brothers. Conducting research on revisions of published books.

*   *   *

PEEK, Dan William 1945-

PERSONAL: Born August 29, 1945, in Omaha, NE; son of George (a broom and hammer-handle peddler) and Clarica Faye (a practical nurse; maiden name, Manes; present surname, Earhardt) Peek; married Joy Lynn Williams (a microbiologist), July 1, 2000; children: Rachael Cailliach, Sarah Perez. *Education:* Attended Central Missouri State College (now University), 1963-64, and Boston University, 1973-74. *Politics:* "Unreconstructed liberal." *Religion:* Presbyterian. *Hobbies and other interests:* Old-style five-string banjo, golf, fishing.

ADDRESSES: Home—4802 North Roemer Rd., Columbia, MO 65202. *E-mail*—dpeek@socket.net.

CAREER: Consultant, entrepreneur, musician, and author. U.S. Industries, New York, NY, internal auditor, 1978-81; Alpha Business Center, Inc., Derry, NH, franchise owner, 1981-84; VR Business Brokers, Inc., Boston, MA, consultant, 1984-87; Franchise Objectives, Inc., Boston, president and chief executive officer, 1987-92; writer, 1992—. Musician; member of Celebrated Renaissance Band.

WRITINGS:

To the Point: The Story of Darts in America, photographs by Bill Batty and Kathryn Cunningham, Pebble Publishing (Rocheport, MO), 2001.

Contributor of articles, essays, and reviews to periodicals, including *American Way, Games Annual,* and *Journal of American Folklore.*

WORK IN PROGRESS: A book on "some of the processes and practices, myths, and manipulations that drive the American commercial culture," publication by Pebble Publishing expected in 2003; *Rasta Pasta,* a novel.

SIDELIGHTS: Dan William Peek told *CA:* "I have been a writer all of my adult life. In addition to mountains of marketing and advertising copy, I have written articles, essays, and reviews. However, it was not until I experienced a lengthy bout of heart disease, hospitalizations, and surgeries in the mid-1990s that I made the decision to get serious about writing books. I had a wealth of material: not only had I by then lived on the planet for over half a century, I had been taking notes. What I had lacked to that point was the clear focus that a near-fatal illness can bring to human understanding. I no longer lack that focus.

"My general objective in writing books is to describe some of the complexities of American culture in plain language and simple structure of the sort exemplified by the writings of Robert L. Heilbroner and Henri Pirenne. In terms of voice and narrative structure, I have been influenced by the work of contemporary Irish writers, notably Tim Pat Coogan, and 'creative nonfiction' American writers, in particular the author and folklorist Keith Cunningham.

"I write most willingly about activities which seem to have meaning beyond their immediate cultural impact; for example, the sport of darts in America. But I do not limit the scope of my subjects. In the past few years, I have discovered some very fundamental things about writing: writers write and do so for the same reasons that fish swim and dogs bark; writers may not always publish, but they always write; and writing is about the truth. The truth is fascinating and unlimited in scope.

"I am still taking notes."

*   *   *

PETERSON, Mendel (Lazear) 1918-2003

OBITUARY NOTICE—See index for *CA* sketch: Born March 18, 1918, in Moore, ID; died July 30, 2003, in McLean, VA. Historian and author. Peterson was a museum curator who was especially interested in the

undersea exploration of shipwrecks, and he became known to colleagues as the "father of underwater archaeology." He initially studied English in college, earning a bachelor's degree from the University of Southern Mississippi in 1938 and a master's degree from Vanderbilt University the next year. He then found work with the Civilian Conservation Corps as a camp educational adviser. It was during World War II, when he was in the U.S. Navy serving in the Pacific theater, that Peterson learned to be a deep-sea diver and he became fascinated by underwater exploration. Returning to the states, he studied textile engineering at Lowell Technical Institute and then got a job designing and testing foul-weather gear for the Navy in Antarctica. The Smithsonian Institute hired him in 1948 as curator of their department of history. This position provided Peterson with the opportunity to study naval archives, and he became an expert in underwater archaeology, leading many dives to explore shipwrecks, especially in the Caribbean. One such venture led Peterson and his colleagues to discover the true location where Christopher Columbus first set foot in the New World; it turned out not to be the island of San Salvador, as was originally believed, but rather a small island in the Caicos archipelago. Peterson was made chair of the department of armed-forces history at the Smithsonian in 1956, curator of the division of historical archaeology in 1969, and director of underwater exploration in 1973. He was also vice president of the Explorers Research Corporation for Underwater Exploration. Continuing to work as a consultant even after retirement, Peterson was the author of a number of books on his favorite subject, including *History under the Sea* (1965; third edition, 1969), *Buried Treasure beneath the Spanish Main* (1972), and *Funnel of Gold: Commerce and Warfare in the West Indies* (1975).

OBITUARIES AND OTHER SOURCES:

PERIODICALS

Washington Post, August 28, 2003, p. B4.

*   *   *

PHELPS, O(rme) Wheelock 1906-2003

OBITUARY NOTICE—See index for *CA* sketch: Born July 5, 1906, in Hobart, OK; died July 3, 2003, in Claremont, CA. Educator and author. Phelps was a former professor of economics and dean at Claremont

McKenna College. A graduate of the University of Chicago, where he earned his doctorate in 1945, he remained at Chicago as an assistant professor and dean until 1947, when he became one of the first faculty members of the newly founded Claremont Men's College and Graduate School (later Claremont McKenna College). He was senior professor of economics there and served as dean from 1970 to 1974, when he retired but remained active at Claremont McKenna for many more years. Phelps was the author of *Introduction to Labor Economics* (1950; fourth edition, 1967), which was a required textbook at many universities for years, and *Discipline and Discharge in the Unionized Firm* (1959), as well as penning monographs and contributing to professional journals.

OBITUARIES AND OTHER SOURCES:

PERIODICALS

Los Angeles Times, July 6, 2003, p. B17.

*   *   *

PILNIAK, Boris Andreyevich
    See VOGAU, Boris Andreyevich

*   *   *

PILNJAK, Boris
    See VOGAU, Boris Andreyevich

*   *   *

PILNYAK, Boris
    See VOGAU, Boris Andreyevich

*   *   *

PINES, Dinora 1918-2002

PERSONAL: Born December 30, 1918, in Lutsk, Russia (now Poland); died February 26, 2002; daughter of doctors; married Anthony Lewison (an attorney), 1947; children: two sons. *Education:* Attended University College London and London School of Medicine for Women and Royal Free Hospital, 1940-45; trained as psychoanalyst, 1959-65.

CAREER: Psychoanalyst and physician. Physician in private practice, beginning 1945; psychoanalyst in private practic, beginning 1965; Elizabeth Garrett Anderson Hospital, staff physician. Taught in Germany and Greece.

MEMBER: British Psychoanalytic Society.

WRITINGS:

A Woman's Unconscious Use of Her Body, Yale University Press (New Haven, CT), 1994.

Contributor of scholarly papers on psychoanalytic topics to journals.

SIDELIGHTS: Psychoanalyst Dinora Pines was born in 1918 in Lutsk, Russia (now Poland). Her parents were both doctors; her father was a well-known ophthalmic surgeon. When Pines was born, the Russian Revolution was raging, and her father was serving as a medical officer in the Tsarist Russian forces.

When Pines was eighteen month old, her family moved to Antwerp, Belgium, and then to London, England. Her father had heard that he could work as a physician in England, but after they moved there he found that English authorities would not accept his qualifications. He had to take his examinations again, and because he spoke little English, he took them in Latin, and passed. He then worked as a general practitioner in the East End of London. Pines grew up speaking Russian at home, and English at school and with friends.

Pines attended the City of London School for Girls and University College, London. She studied modern languages, learning French, German, and Spanish; she later learned Italian and Greek, so that with her Russian and English, she eventually spoke seven languages.

In 1940, during World War II, Pines decided that the world needed doctors more than it needed linguists and, like her brothers, she decided to study medicine. She enrolled at the London School of Medicine for Women and completed her clinical training at the

Royal Free Hospital in London. She became qualified as a physician in 1945 and began working at the Elizabeth Garrett Anderson Hospital.

Pines noticed that some patients who were not cured by medicine alone often responded when they were treated with kindness and emotional understanding. This was particularly true for patients who were in excruciating pain; they often felt better when they were able to share their feelings with Pines.

At the Anderson Hospital, Pines met Hilda Abraham, who was the daughter of one of psychoanalyst Sigmund Freud's colleagues. They became close friends, and through Abraham, Pines became fascinated with Freud's theories of psychoanalysis.

In 1945, at the close of World War II, Pines was recruited for a secret relief mission to the Nazi concentration camp at Auschwitz. Pines had many relatives who had died in concentration camps, so she was eager to help the people who had suffered in them, but for some reason the mission was abandoned. She later worked with survivors of the Holocaust and wrote many scholarly papers on the topic.

In 1947 Pines married Anthony Lewison, a lawyer; they eventually had two sons. She moved to general practice with an office in her home, so she could be there for her children, but when they grew older she decided to become a psychoanalyst. She entered training in 1959, completing it in 1965, and opened a private practice of psychotherapy. She also worked briefly at the Brent Consultation Centre, where she did research on young women who were sexually promiscuous.

Pines became a training psychoanalyst for the British Psychoanalytic Society. She often traveled to speak at meetings in the United Kingdom and in other countries, and taught in Germany and Greece. She was also a cofounder of a psychoanalytic group in St. Petersburg, Russia.

Pines was the author of *A Woman's Unconscious Use of Her Body,* which examines how women express their inner conflicts through their bodies, as well as how women's physical experiences affect their psyches. Deeply rooted in traditional psychoanalytic theory, the book collects over two decades' worth of papers by Pines in which she distils her observations of her patients. She notes that when patients could not express their feelings, or when they didn't even consciously know their feelings, they often suffered rashes, pains, asthma, and other physical problems. The final chapter of the book examines the effect of the Holocaust on women survivors and their daughters. In *New Statesman,* Adrianne Blue called the book "jargonistic but fascinating."

When Pines was not working, she enjoyed hosting visitors at her home, and engaged in travel and following advancements in archeology. Pines died on February 26, 2002, at the age of eighty-three.

BIOGRAPHICAL AND CRITICAL SOURCES:

PERIODICALS

New Statesman, July 23, 1993, Adrianne Blue, review of *A Woman's Unconscious Use of Her Body,* p. 41.
Publishers Weekly, April 4, 1994, review of *A Woman's Unconscious Use of Her Body,* p. 68.

OBITUARIES:

ONLINE

Times (London, England), http://www.the-times.co.uk/ (March 22, 2002).*

*   *   *

PLIATZKY, Leo 1919-1999

PERSONAL: Born August 22, 1919, in Salford, England; died May 4, 1999; son of a tailor; married Marian Jean Elias, 1948 (died 1979); children: one son, one daughter. *Education:* Corpus Christi College, Oxford degree (classics; first class honors), 1939, advanced degree (philosophy, politics, and economics; first class honors), 1946.

CAREER: Fabian Society, London, England, research secretary, 1946-47; British Civil Service, London, England, Ministry of Food, staff member, 1947-50, Ministry of the Treasury, staff member beginning 1950, then undersecretary, 1967, deputy secretary, 1971, and second permanent secretary, 1976, permanent secretary of Department of Trade, 1977-79; retired 1980. Board member of British Airways, 1980-84; Associated Communications Corporation Ltd., director 1980-82; Central Independent Television, board member, 1981-89; Ultramar, board member, 1981-90. Chair of Industry Working Party on Production of Television Commercials, 1986-89; visiting professor at City University, 1980-84; associated fellow, London School of Economics, 1982-85; senior resident fellow, Policy Studies Institute, 1983-84; History of Parliament Trust trustee, 1982-99, treasurer, 1983-94; governor of Charles Dickens Primary School, 1996-97. Actively supported Camphill Village Trust (residential charity for the mentally handicapped). *Military service:* Served with Royal Army Ordnance Corps and Royal Electrical and Mechanical Engineers, in Egypt and Italy, 1940-45 (mentioned in dispatches).

MEMBER: Reform Club.

AWARDS, HONORS: Knighted, 1972; made Knight Commander of the British Empire, 1977; honorary fellow, Corpus Christi College, Oxford, 1980; D.Litt., Salford University, 1986.

WRITINGS:

Getting and Spending: Public Expenditure, Employment, and Inflation, Blackwell (Oxford, England), 1982, revised, 1984.
Paying and Choosing: The Intelligent Person's Guide to the Mixed Economy, Blackwell (New York, NY), 1985.
The Treasury under Mrs. Thatcher, Blackwell (New York, NY), 1989.

Associated with report by Industry Working Party on Production of Television Commercials, 1987.

SIDELIGHTS: During a career in the British Civil Service that spanned more than three decades, Leo Pliatzky served in the Ministry of Food and Depart-ment of Trade. However, as a London *Times* contributor remembered, "Pliatzky's reputation as one of Whitehall's most formidable figures had been forged over a quarter of a century at the Treasury."

"The part he played in the [mid-1970s International Monetary Fund] negotiations is regarded by some friends as his finest hour, but he is best remembered in Whitehall for his introduction of cash limits and the battles which were subsequently fought with the big spending ministries," stated the *Times* contributor, who described Pliatzky as "a formidable force . . . loyal, honest friend . . . [and] generous family man" that had "a first-class brain . . . total self-belief . . . intransigence and [a] low boiling-point." Following his retirement from the British civil service, Pliatzky wrote three books on finance that were published during the 1980s: *Getting and Spending: Public Expenditure, Employment, and Inflation; Paying and Choosing: The Intelligent Person's Guide to the Mixed Economy;* and *The Treasury under Mrs. Thatcher.* In addition to writing these books, Pliatzky's post-career activities during the 1980s included chairing the Industry Working Party on Production of Television Commercials; working as a visiting professor at City University, serving as an associated fellow at the London School of Economics, and as a senior resident fellow at the Policy Studies Institute. In addition, he assumed leadership positions on the boards of various organizations.

BIOGRAPHICAL AND CRITICAL SOURCES:

PERIODICALS

Banker November, 1985, p. 177.
Director, May, 1982, p. 20.
Economist, June 5, 1982, p. 94.
Public Administration, summer, 1990, p. 276.

OBITUARIES:

PERIODICALS

Times (London, England), May 17, 1999.*

*   *   *

POLÈSE, Mario 1943-

PERSONAL: Born November 7, 1943, in the Netherlands; citizenship, Canadian; son of Julius (a translator) and Kate (a cook; maiden name, Gross) Polèse; married Céline Hallé, July 11, 1971; children: Geneviève,

Caroline. *Education:* City University of New York, B.A., 1965; University of Pennsylvania, M.A., 1967, Ph.D., 1972; postdoctoral study at Université d'Aix-Marseille, 1972-73.

ADDRESSES: Home—4174 Harvard, Montréal, Québec, Canada H4A 2W7. *Office*—Institut National de la Recherche Scientifique-Urbanisation, Université du Québec, 3465 Durocher, Montréal, Québec, Canada H2X 2C6; fax: 514-499-4065. *E-mail*—mario.polese@inrs-urb.uquebec.ca.

CAREER: Brome County Rural Development Agency, Brome County, Québec, Canada, assistant manager, 1967; University of Montréal, Montréal, Québec, lecturer at Urban Institute, 1969-70; University of Québec, Montréal, professor and researcher in urbanization at National Institute for Scientific Research-Urbanization, 1970—, director of the institute, 1984-89. University of Toronto, associate of Centre for Urban and Community Studies, 1992—; McGill University, senior adjunct professor, 1995—; guest lecturer at other institutions, including Universidad Autónoma de Puebla, Mexico, University of Geneva, Erasmus University, Université de Bourgogne, University of California, Los Angeles, Université Laval, and Université du Quebec à Trois Rivières. Statistics Canada, member of advisory committee on service statistics, 1988—; International Baccalaureat, Geneva, Switzerland, chief examiner for economics, 1989-91; Montréal Inter-University Group, director of urbanization and development, 1989—; Towards Socially Sustainable Cities, international project coordinator, 1995-98; Engineering Institute of the West Indies, co-team leader of Caribbean regional infrastructure study, 1995-96; Partnership in Urban Development, coordinator, 1997—. Québec Department of Immigration, special advisor to deputy minister's office, 1975-76; Office de Planification et de Dévelopement du Québec, special advisor to deputy chief executive officer, 1979-80; Canadian Social Science Federation, member of board of directors, 1980-83; Canadian Department of External Affairs, member of Canadian committee, International Institute for Applied Systems Analysis, 1981-87; Québec Department of the Environment, ad hoc commissioner for Bureau d'audiences publiques sur l'environnement, 1984; Government of Québec, committee member, Conseil de la science et de la technologie, 1987-88; Federal Economic Development Bureau, special advisor to deputy minister, 1992-93; consultant to auditor general of Canada, Québec Department of Transport, and Major & Martin, Inc.

MEMBER: Canadian Regional Science Association (president, 1980-81; executive vice president, 1982-88), Association de Science Régionale de Langue Française (vice president, 1981-97).

WRITINGS:

(With B. Bonin) *À propos de l'association économique Canada-Québec,* École Nationale d'Administration Publique (Québec City, Québec, Canada), 1980.

(Editor, with W. J. Coffey) *Still Living Together: Recent Trends and Future Directions in Canadian Regional Development,* Institute for Research on Public Policy (Montréal, Québec, Canada), 1987.

(With W. J. Coffey, Bailly, and A. Paelinck) *Spatial Econometrics of Services,* Ashgate Publishing (Aldershot, England), 1992.

Économie urbaine et régionale, Economica (Paris, France), 1994.

(Editor with J. Wolfe) *L'urbanisation des pays en dévelopement,* Economica (Paris, France), 1995.

(Editor with S. Pérez) *Modelos de analysis y de planificacion urbana: estudios sobre la evolucion y tendencias de la ciudad de puebla,* Plaza y Valdez (Mexico City, Mexico), 1996.

(Editor with M. Lungo, and contributor) *Economía y desarollo urbana en Centramérica,* FLACSO (San José, Costa Rica), 1998.

Economía urbana y regional: introducción a la relación entre territorio y desarollo, Libro Universitario Regional (Cartago, Costa Rica), 1998.

(Editor, with R. Stren, and contributor) *The Social Sustainability of Cities: Diversity and the Management of Change,* University of Toronto Press (Toronto, Ontario, Canada), 2000.

Contributor to books, including *Local Development: The Future of Isolated Cultural Communities and Small Economic Regions,* University of St.-Anne Press (Church Point, Nova Scotia, Canada), 1986; *The Canadian Economy: A Regional Perspective,* edited by D. Savoie, Methuen (Toronto, Ontario, Canada), 1986; *The Canadian Economy: Problems and Policies,* edited by G. C. Ruggeri, Gage (Toronto, Ontario, Canada), 1987; *Parting as Friends: The Economic Consequences for Québec,* edited by J. McCallum and C. Green, Institut C. D. Howe (Toronto, Ontario, Canada), 1991; and *Community Economic Development: Perspectives on Research and Policy,* edited by B. Calaway and J. Hudson, Thomson Educational

Publishing (Toronto, Ontario, Canada), 1994. Contributor to professional journals, including *Regional Studies, International Regional Science Review, Environment and Planning, Canadian Journal of Development Studies, Canadian Geographer, Environments, Urban History Review, Economic Geography,* and *Review of Urban and Regional Development Studies.* Editor, *Canadian Journal of Regional Science,* 1982-88; member of editorial board, *Annals of Regional Science,* 1982- 88, *Revue d'Économie Régionale et Urbaine,* 1982—, *Economic Development Quarterly,* 1990—, and *Région et Dévelopement,* 1996—.

SIDELIGHTS: Mario Polèse told *CA:* "I am an academic. Thus my writing is basically motivated by the needs of students and the need to disseminate research results to fellow researchers and the community at large."

R

RADIN, Beryl A(viva) 1936-

PERSONAL: Born November 15, 1936, in Aberdeen, SD; daughter of Norman (in business) and Sophie (a homemaker; maiden name, Edelman) Radin. *Education:* Antioch College, B.A., 1958; University of Minnesota, Twin Cities, M.A., 1963; University of California, Berkeley, Ph.D., 1973. *Politics:* Democrat. *Religion:* Jewish.

ADDRESSES: Office—University of Baltimore, 1304 St. Paul St., Baltimore, MD 21202. *E-mail*—bradin@ix.netcom.com.

CAREER: Educator and author. University of Texas, Austin, assistant professor of public policy, 1973-78; University of Southern California, professor of public administration, 1978-94; University of Baltimore, Baltimore, MD, professor of government and public administration, 2002, State University of New York, Albany, professor of public administration, 2002—. U.S. Department of Health and Human Services, consultant to assistant secretary for management and budget. Bellagio Study and Conference Center resident scholar, summer, 1998. Member of board, Holdeen Indian Program and Human Services Research Institute. *Journal of Public Administration Research and Theory,* managing editor, beginning 2000.

MEMBER: Association of Public Policy Analysis and Management (president, 1995-96, 2001—), Public Management Research Association (member of board, 2001—), American Political Science Association.

WRITINGS:

Implementation, Change, and the Federal Bureaucracy: School Desegregation Policies in HEW, 1964-1968, Teachers College Press (New York, NY), 1977.

(With Willis D. Hawley) *The Politics of Federal Reorganization: Creating the U.S. Department of Education,* Pergamon Press (New York, NY), 1988.

(With others) *New Governance for Rural America: Creating Intergovernmental Partnerships,* University Press of Kansas (Lawrence, KS), 1996.

Beyond Machiavelli: Policy Analysis Comes of Age, Georgetown University Press (Washington, DC), 2000.

The Accountable Juggler: The Art of Leadership in a Federal Agency, C.Q. Press (Washington, DC), 2002.

Contributor to books, including H. George Frederickson and Yong-Hyo Cho, editors, *The White House and the Blue House: Government Reform in the United States and Korea,* University Press of America, 1997; *Federalism: Comparative Perspectives from India and Australia,* Manohar Press (New Delhi, India), 1999; Dall W. Forsyth, editor, *Quicker, Better, Cheaper: Managing Performance in American Government,* Rockefeller Institute Pres (Albany, NY), 2001; and *Making Government Manageable: Executive Organization and Management in the Twenty-first Century,* Johns Hopkins Press, 2002. Contributor of articles and reviews to periodicals, including *Publius, Journal of Politics, American Political Science Review, New York Times Book Review, Journal of Public Administration*

Research and Theory, Journal of Comparative Policy Analysis, Public Administration Review, Journal of Policy Analysis and Management, Public Administration Quarterly, International Review of Public Administration, Administration in Mental Health, Policy Analysis, Public Welfare, Race, and *Evaluation.*

BIOGRAPHICAL AND CRITICAL SOURCES:

PERIODICALS

American Political Science Review, March, 1989, Garry D. Brewer, review of *The Politics of Federal Reorganization: Creating the U.S. Department of Education,* p. 297.

American Review of Public Administration, December 2002, Harvey Averch, review of *Beyond Machiavelli: Policy Analysis Comes of Age,* pp. 471-478.

Choice, November, 2002, C. T. Goodsell, review of *The Accountable Juggler: The Art of Leadership in a Federal Agency,* p. 554.

Journal of Policy Analysis and Management, fall, 1989, Lorraine M. McDonnell, review of *The Politics of Federal Reorganization,* p. 688; spring, 1997, Rosemary O'Leary, review of *New Governance for Rural America,* p. 319; spring, 2002, Ted Marmor, review of *Beyond Machiavelli,* p. 316

Policy Studies Journal, autumn, 1996, Kenneth E. Pigg, review of *New Governance for Rural America,* p. 515.

Political Science Quarterly, spring, 1989, Charles O. Jones, review of *The Politics of Federal Reorganization,* p. 169.

Public Administration Review, July-August, 2002, Larry Luton, review of *Beyond Machiavelli,* p. 504.

Publius, summer, 1996, Alvin D. Sokolow, review of *New Governance for Rural America,* p. 201.

*   *   *

RAFFEL, Dawn 1957-

PERSONAL: Born September 10, 1957, in Milwaukee, WI; daughter of Mark Joseph Raffel (a furniture salesman) and Francine Leonore (Bern) Goldfarb; married Michael Evers, July 13, 1985; children: Brendan, Sean. *Education:* Brown University, A.B., 1979.

ADDRESSES: Home—Hoboken, NJ. *Office*—O, The Oprah Magazine, 1700 Broadway, New York, NY 10019.

CAREER: Magazine editor and author. *Seventeen,* New York, NY, fiction editor, 1981-83; freelance writer, 1983-85; *Redbook,* New York, NY, associate fiction editor, 1985-86, senior associate fiction editor, 1986-90, fiction editor, 1990-91, books and fiction editor, 1991-97, senior editor, 1997-99, deputy editor, 1999; *O,* New York, NY, deputy editor, beginning 1999, then executive editor. Teacher at West Virginia University and at writers' conferences.

MEMBER: American Society of Magazine Editors.

AWARDS, HONORS: Hob Broun prize for fiction, *Quarterly,* 1991.

WRITINGS:

In the Year of Long Division (short stories), Knopf (New York, NY), 1995.
Carrying the Body (novel), Scribner (New York, NY), 2002.

Contributor to anthologies, including *Micro Fictions, The One You Call Sister, I've Always Meant to Tell You: Letters to Our Mothers,* and *Wild Women;* contributor to periodicals, including *Iowa Review, New Letters, Los Angeles Times, Quarterly, Epoch, Interview,* and *Conjunctions.*

SIDELIGHTS: Long-time magazine editor Dawn Raffel began her fiction career penning short stories, placing many in national magazines and ultimately publishing the critically praised short-fiction collection *In the Year of Long Division.* Released in 1995, the debut work prompted *Los Angeles Times Book Review* contributor Erika Taylor to call Raffel "a writer of such obvious and extreme talent that even her lesser stories are well worth reading." Seven years later she expanded achieved publishing success with a longer work, the 126-page novel *Carrying the Body.* Based in New York City, Raffel worked her way up the editorial ranks at *Redbook* before moving to a top editorial post at *O,* a periodical created by popular television talk-show host Oprah Winfrey.

In *Carrying the Body* readers meet Elise, a woman returning with her sick young son James to her family's shabby home where her father and younger sister have been living since Elise's mother's death. Readers quickly learn that it was the mother who served as the family's mortar; since her death Elise's father and sister have become as run-down as the house they inhabit. Elise's sister, resentful of her role as caretaker to her aging father, drowns her anger in gin, but despite her troubled state proves to be the only character capable of positive action.

A *Kirkus* reviewer, bemoaning Raffel's "sonorous and deliberately overwrought" narration, called the novel "virtually unreadable." Patricia Gulian however, concluded otherwise, noting in her *Library Journal* review that although *Carrying the Body* is neither "easy" nor "pleasant" to read, it nonetheless is "worth the disquietude it creates" for the readers. In *Booklist* Mary Ellen Quinn also favored the work, noting that "there is no denying the power of the language" in Raffel's "cryptic but oddly compelling novel."

BIOGRAPHICAL AND CRITICAL SOURCES:

PERIODICALS

Booklist, September 1, 2002, Mary Ellen Quinn, review of *Carrying the Body,* p. 59.
Kirkus Reviews, November 15, 1994, review of *In the Year of Long Division,* pp. 1491-1492; July 15, 2002, review of *Carrying the Body,* p. 988.
Library Journal, September 1, 2002, Patricia Gulian, review of *Carrying the Body,* p. 215.
Los Angeles Times Book Review, January 8, 1995, Erika Taylor, review of *In the Year of Long Division,* p. 6.
O, October, 2002, Cathleen Medwick, review of *Carrying the Body,* p. 90.
Publishers Weekly, November 28, 1994, review of *In the Year of Long Division,* p. 43; September 2, 2002, Melissa Mia Hall, interview with Raffel and review of *Carrying the Body,* p. 51.
Review of Contemporary Fiction, spring, 2003, Gregory Howard, review of *Carrying the Body,* p. 160.*

*   *   *

RAINE, Kathleen (Jessie) 1908-2003

OBITUARY NOTICE—See index for *CA* sketch: Born June 14, 1908, in Ilford, Essex, England; died July 6, 2003, in London, England. Author. Raine was a prize-winning British poet, critic, editor, and translator who was an authority on nineteenth-century writers William Blake and William Butler Yeats. Educated at Girton College, Cambridge, where she studied psychology and the social sciences and earned a master's degree in 1929, she worked various jobs after graduation and became interested in Celtic culture and spiritualism. Her interest in spiritualism and philosophy imbues much of her poetry, beginning with the collection *Stone and Flower: Poems, 1935-1943* (1943). Raine continued her verse writing, publishing the books *The Pythoness and Other Poems* (1948) and *The Hollow Hill and Other Poems, 1960-1964* (1965), but she also built a reputation for her scholarly nonfiction work, including *William Blake* (1969) and the seminal two-volume study *Blake and Tradition* (1968, second edition, 2002, as *Blake and Antiquity*). After writing for several decades, Raine's popularity as a poet suddenly rose in the 1970s. Building on this success she founded the Temenos Academy of Integral Studies, where students were instructed in the philosophies and religions of Christianity, Judaism, Islam, Buddhism, and Hinduism; in conjunction with this institution she also founded and edited the journal *Temenos* from 1981 to 1992. Honored with prizes that included the Cholmondeley Award, the French foreign-book prize, and the Edna St. Vincent Millay Prize, Raine's many other works include the poetry collections *The Lost Country* (1971), *The Oracle in the Heart, and Other Poems, 1975-1978* (1980), and *Living with Mystery: Poems, 1987-1991* (1992); the nonfiction works *Blake and the New Age* (1979), *Poetry and the Frontiers of Consciousness* (1985), and *W. B. Yeats and the Learning of the Imagination* (1999); and the autobiographical *Faces of Day and Night* (1972), *Farewell Happy Fields: Memories of Childhood* (1973), and *The Land Unknown* (1975). Raine was also an editor and translator of numerous other works. For her many literary contributions, she was named a fellow of the Royal Society of Literature, a commander of the Order of the British Empire, and commander of the French Ordré des Arts et des Lettres.

OBITUARIES AND OTHER SOURCES:

BOOKS

Writers Directory, 18th edition, St. James Press (Detroit, MI), 2003.

PERIODICALS

Independent (London, England), July 8, 2003, p. 16.
Los Angeles Times, July 12, 2003, p. B20.

New York Times, July 10, 2003, p. C14.

Times (London, England), July 8, 2003.

Washington Post, July 12, 2003, p. B7.

*   *   *

RAMA RAO, K.V.S. 1967-

PERSONAL: Born September 14, 1967, in Guntur, Andhra Pradesh, India; son of K. Sankara Rao and K. Sarojini (a homemaker); married K. Kalyani (a homemaker), October 12, 1997; children: K. Kasaratha Sankara Sai (son), K. Manasvi (daughter). *Hobbies and other interests:* "Serving my guru," devotional poetry.

ADDRESSES: Agent—c/o Author Mail, Minerva Press Pvt., Ltd. 5-E, Rani Jhansi Rd., Jhandewalan Extn., New Delhi, India. *E-mail*—kvs_rama_rao@yahoo.com.

CAREER: Poet.

WRITINGS:

The Light of Devotion, of Knowledge, of Brahma (poetry), Minerva Press (New Delhi, India), 2001.

WORK IN PROGRESS: A second volume of poetry.

SIDELIGHTS: K.V.S. Rama Rao told *CA:* "My guru Kanhayya Ram Nath—also known as Guru Siddha Nath—transformed me from mortal to immortal. After meeting my guru for the second time, poetry poured out from my heart. Hence, as an offering to my guru's lotus feet, I write poetry.

"I am indebted to my guru for showing me the enlightened path by which one's life becomes meaningful. My works are my guru's greatness. I am only an instrument in his hand."

BIOGRAPHICAL AND CRITICAL SOURCES:

PERIODICALS

Sadhu Vaswani Mission East and West Series, June, 2002, review of *The Light of Devotion, of Knowledge, of Brahma.*

RAPLEY, Robert 1926-

PERSONAL: Born 1926.

ADDRESSES: Home—Ottawa, Ontario, Canada. *Agent*—c/o Author Mail, McGill-Queen's University Press, 3430 McTavish St., Montreal, Quebec H3A 1X9, Canada.

CAREER: Independent scholar.

WRITINGS:

A Case of Witchcraft: The Trial of Urbain Grandier, Manchester University Press (Manchester, England), 1998.

Also the author of scholarly articles.

SIDELIGHTS: Robert Rapley is an independent scholar living in Ottawa, Canada, and the author of *A Case of Witchcraft: The Trial of Urbain Grandier.* Rapley helps to explicate the bizarre case of witchcraft and possession of the Ursuline nuns in Loudun, France, in the early seventeenth century, an incident that writer Aldous Huxley dramatized in his 1952 *The Devils of Loudun,* and that was further popularized by a play, an opera, and a movie. Rapley focuses on the handsome, worldly Catholic priest Urbain Grandier, who was both influential and controversial in the Loudun community. As David Longfellow noted in *Journal of Church and State,* Grandier's "intelligence, penchant for politics, acid tongue, and impregnation of a city magistrate's daughter earned him powerful enemies in Loudun." Such enemies extended beyond the community: his support for the governor of Loudun earned him the enmity of Cardinal Richelieu and Louis XIII, who were involved in a battle to centralize power in Paris. The sudden rash of satanic possession among Loudun's nuns, as well as an outbreak of the plague, provided Grandier's enemies with the opportunity they sought to bring him down. Accused of having brought about the visions and hallucinations of the nuns through witchcraft, Grandier was ultimately condemned to death by burning at the stake; he went to his fate protesting his innocence.

Rapley brings some new evidence to the historical reconstruction and also uses Grandier as the focal point of the affair in an account that won critical praise from reviewers in England and North America. Robin Briggs, writing in the *Times Literary Supplement,* felt that Rapley creates a "clear and judicious narrative of an exceptionally complex sequence of events." Briggs went on to call the book "an admirable piece of historical craftsmanship" and to praise its author for "unquestionably succeed[ing] . . . in conveying the grim fascination of this haunting story." William Monter, reviewing *A Case of Witchcraft* for the *American Society of Church History,* commented that Rapley "narrates Grandier's exploits and his death far more carefully and, in the end, more persuasively than did Huxley." Longfellow also commended Rapley's "thorough account" and noted that it "fills an important gap" in the historical record. The *New Yorker's* John Banville had further praise for the title, calling it a "superb unravelling of the story of Grandier," and a "work of impeccable scholarship" written with the "verve and narrative drive of a first-rate historical novel."

BIOGRAPHICAL AND CRITICAL SOURCES:

PERIODICALS

American Society of Church History, June, 2000, William Monter, review of *A Case of Witchcraft: The Trial of Urban Grandier,* pp. 432-434.
Journal of Church and State, summer, 1999, David Longfellow, review of *A Case of Witchcraft,* pp. 609-610.
New Yorker, November 1, 1999, John Banville, review of *A Case of Witchcraft,* pp. 115-117.
Times Literary Supplement, November 5, 1999, Robin Briggs, review of *A Case of Witchcraft,* p. 28.

ONLINE

McGill-Queen's University Press Web site, http://www. mqup.mcgill.ca/ (November 7, 2003), "Robert Rapley."*

*   *   *

REEKIE, Jocelyn (Margaret) 1947-

PERSONAL: Born 1947, in Regina, Saskatchewan, Canada; daughter of Robert M. (a lawyer) and Mary Elizabeth (a homemaker) Barr; married William David Reekie (a facilities manager), September 4, 1968; children: Stephanie Mary Reekie Christensen, Christo-

pher David. *Ethnicity:* "Caucasian." *Education:* University of Regina, B.A. (English and psychology), 1969. *Hobbies and other interests:* Painting and drawing, crafts, hiking, canoeing and kayaking, horseback riding, animals of all kinds, swimming.

ADDRESSES: Home and office—P.O. Box 267, Quathiaski Cove, British Columbia V0P 1N0, Canada. *E-mail*— jreekie@connected.bc.ca.

CAREER: Writer, 1983—. Worked as a swim instructor and coach of synchronized and speed swimming in Regina, Saskatchewan, Dawson Creek, British Columbia, and Campbell River, British Columbia, Canada, 1965-83. CJDC-Radio, copywriter, 1971-72; *Peace River Block News,* staff journalist, beginning 1972. Worked as a substitute teacher in Dawson Creek, 1972-79; storyteller and creative writing teacher at schools, 1983—. Quadra Children's Center, board member, 1997-2000; Quadra Island Cultural Committee, member, 2001; Campbell River Arts Council, board member, 2003—.

MEMBER: Children's Writers and Illustrators of British Columbia, Federation of British Columbia Writers.

WRITINGS:

(Coeditor with Annette Yourk) *Shorelines: Memoirs and Tales of the Discovery Islands,* Kingfisher Publishing (Quathiaski Cove, British Columbia, Canada), 1995.
Tess (young-adult historical novel), Raincoast Books (Vancouver, British Columbia, Canada), 2002.

Contributor to periodicals, including *Vancouver Sun, Campbell River Mirror,* and *Gulf Islands Gazette.*

WORK IN PROGRESS: The Savage Years, a sequel to *Tess,* and an untitled novel, both for Raincoast Books (Vancouver, British Columbia, Canada).

SIDELIGHTS: Jocelyn Reekie told *CA:* "Born the fifth of nine children—seven of us girls—I became interested at a very early age in survival of the fittest. I believed that to survive childhood in my house I would need a titanium interior and a sponge-rubber exterior. I had neither, but got through anyway. Part of my modus operandi of survival was to become adept at creating fiction, often to the dismay of my parents.

"Beyond survival, there was Grandpa. My father's father suffered from crippling arthritis, but that didn't stop him from painting watercolors and from loving to be outdoors. From the time I was small, I accompanied him on Sunday sojourns to the various city parks, where he would show me different birds and flowers and tell me about statues, monuments, or the politicians whose pictures hung in the rotunda of the legislature. When we returned home he would sit in a big chair and pat the arm. 'Do you want to hear a story?,' he'd say. Of course I did. When I learned to read he started bringing books and asked me to read to him. Eventually I told him stories of my own.

"As a child I cherished my Sunday afternoons with Grandpa. As an adult I can feel and smell and taste and hear them still. They will be delicious all my life. And the love of story Grandpa nourished in me will go on and on."

BIOGRAPHICAL AND CRITICAL SOURCES:

PERIODICALS

Booklist, March 1, 2003, Carolyn Phelan, review of *Tess,* p. 1207.
Canadian Materials, January, 2003, Lisa Doucet, review of *Tess.*
Resource Links, December, 2002, Victoria Pennell, review of *Tess,* p. 48.

* * *

REID, Robin (Nicole) 1969-

PERSONAL: Born December 17, 1969, in Milwaukee, WI; daughter of Norman Sylvester (a contractor) and Lunnette Elfreda (a homemaker) Reid; married Jon Gunnar Rygh (a marketing director), January 25, 1996. *Ethnicity:* "African American." *Education:* Oberlin College, B.A. (economics).

ADDRESSES: Home—New York, NY. *Office*—Cataland Films, 450 West 15th St., Suite 602, New York, NY 10011. *Agent*—c/o Author Mail, Simon Spotlight, 1230 Avenue of the Americas, New York, NY 10020. *E-mail*—robin.reid3@verizon.net.

CAREER: Independent producer. Arts Engine (nonprofit documentary filmmakers company), member of board of directors.

WRITINGS:

The Big Storm ("Little Bill" series; based on the characters from Bill Cosby's *Little Bill* television series), illustrated by Kirk-Albert Etienne, Simon Spotlight (New York, NY), 2002.
Thank You, Dr. King ("Little Bill" series; based on the characters from Bill Cosby's *Little Bill* television series), illustrated by Dan Kanemoto, Simon Spotlight (New York, NY), 2003.

WORK IN PROGRESS: Little Cab, Big City, about a New York City Chinatown cab.

SIDELIGHTS: Independent producer Robin Reid has contributed two titles to the "Little Bill" series of books adapted from the television series of the same name created by comedian Bill Cosby. Reid told *CA:* "Writing for 'Little Bill' gives me much joy. Since the television series emphasizes family and community relationships, as well as self-reliance, I am able to use themes to create stories that are dear to me." *The Big Storm,* the fourth book in the series, was praised as a "light and humorous story" by Lynda Jones in the *Black Issues Book Review.* When a nighttime thunderstorm frightens Little Bill, his family devises imaginative ways to cheer him. The picture book also features brightly-colored paper cutout illustrations to complement the story.

"I try my best to speak from a child's perspective," Reid continued, "to respect a child's point of view on the world that they live in. In a world that is requiring children to become adults very quickly, I hope to provide a space that is exclusively for them."

BIOGRAPHICAL AND CRITICAL SOURCES:

PERIODICALS

Black Issues Book Review, September-October, 2002, Lynda Jones, review of *The Big Storm,* p. 60.

RICE, Patty

PERSONAL: Raised in MD; children: Tonja, Pamela. *Education:* Attended George Washington University.

ADDRESSES: Home—Lanham, MD. *Agent*—Nina Graybill, Graybill & English, LLC, 1875 Connecticut Avenue NW, Suite 712, Washington, DC 20009.

CAREER: Poet and novelist. George Washington University, Washington, DC, office staff; newsletter assistant editor.

MEMBER: My Sister Writers (cofounder).

WRITINGS:

Somethin' Extra (novel), Simon & Schuster (New York, NY), 2000.
Reinventing the Woman (novel), Simon & Schuster (New York, NY), 2001.

Also the author of the poetry chapbook *Manmade Heartbreak.*

WORK IN PROGRESS: Writing a third novel.

SIDELIGHTS: Novelist Patty Rice writes what she terms "self-help fiction," about African-American women who overcome abuse and their feelings of helplessness to build fulfilling lives for themselves. "I want women to understand that we are viable people," Rice told *Metro Connection* interviewer Sharee Brooks. "We tend to define ourselves by whether we have a man or whether we have children. We just need to know that we are good enough just standing alone."

In Rice's first novel, *Somethin' Extra,* the protagonist is twenty-five-year-old Genie Gatlin. Genie's mother committed suicide because of her father's infidelity, and from this Genie has drawn the conclusion that men are not to be trusted. She habitually becomes involved with married men, which prevents her relationships from becoming too serious. Her strategy works, until one man leaves his family for her, only to decide that he wants to return to his family, leaving

Genie shattered. *Booklist* reviewer June Hathaway-Vigor wrote, "The pages will fly as readers find out how [Genie] builds a healthy, whole life out of the wreckage."

Rice, a long-time resident of the Washington, D.C., suburb of Prince George's County, Maryland, used that area as a setting both for *Somethin' Extra* and her second novel, *Reinventing the Woman.* At the beginning of *Reinventing the Woman,* the main character, Camille, ends her relationship with her boyfriend of seven years, unable to endure any more of his abusive attacks. With nowhere else to go, Camille leaves the home she shared with her boyfriend in New Jersey and moves in with her older sister, Melanie, who lives in suburban Maryland, where the sisters were raised. Moving back to Maryland forces Camille to confront the conflicts that led her to leave home in the first place—primarily that her mother, Catherine, always favored Melanie. When Catherine helps Camille get a job with "Reinventing the Woman," a business owned by motivational speaker Nora Jordan, Camille begins to develop confidence in herself, which leads her to build a better life for herself. "The heroine's psychological breakthrough is neatly accomplished," a reviewer commented in *Publishers Weekly.*

BIOGRAPHICAL AND CRITICAL SOURCES:

PERIODICALS

Black Issues Book Review, March, 2001, Erica Woods Tucker, review of *Reinventing the Woman,* p. 23.
Booklist, December 1, 1999, June Hathaway-Vigor, review of *Somethin' Extra,* p. 685.
Essence, January, 2001, review of *Reinventing the Woman,* p. 60.
Library Journal, November 15, 1999, Molly Gorman, review of *Somethin' Extra,* p. 100; November 1, 2000, Ann Burns and Emily Joy Jones, review of *Reinventing the Woman,* p. 102.
Prince George's Journal (Prince George's County, MD), February 15, 2000, Sherree Price, interview with Rice, p. A6.
Publishers Weekly, November 6, 2000, review of *Reinventing the Woman,* p. 68.

ONLINE

Berkley Jove Authors Web site, http://berkleyjoveauthors.com/ (November 13, 2003), "Patty Rice."

G.R.I.T.S. Online Reading Club, http://www.thegrits. com/ (November 13, 2003), review of *Reinventing the Woman.*

Metro Connection, http://www.blackindc.com/ (November 13, 2003), Sharee Brooks, "Feeling the Pages with Patty Rice."

Penguin Putnam Web site, http://www.penguinputnam. com/ (November 13, 2003), "Patty Rice."

Washingtonian Online, http://www.washingtonian.com/ (November 13, 2003), Courtney Porter Martin, review of *Reinventing the Woman.*

Ye Olde Font Shoppe, http://www.webcom.com/yeolde/ (November 13, 2003), "Manmade Heartbreak by Patty Rice."*

*   *   *

RICH, Harvey L. 1944-

PERSONAL: Born 1944; married. *Education:* Attended Georgetown University Medical School.

ADDRESSES: Home—Washington, DC, and Paris, France. *Office*—c/o American Psychoanalytic Foundation, 9 Breakers Island, Dana Point, CA 92629. *E-mail*—hlrich2101@aol.com.

CAREER: Psychoanalyst and author. Clinical psychiatrist/psychoanalyst in private practice in Washington, DC, beginning c. 1970. American Psychoanalytic Foundation, founder and former president; cofounder of Coalition for Patients' Rights. Former faculty member, Georgetown University School of Medicine, Washington School of Psychiatry, Washington Psychoanalytic Institute, Wilford Hall Medical Center at Lackland Air Force Base, and Uniformed Services University of Health Sciences. Consultant to World Bank. Teacher and lecturer, appearing at schools and on National Public Radio.

MEMBER: American Psychiatric Association, American Psychoanalytic Association.

WRITINGS:

(With Teresa H. Barker) *In the Moment: Celebrating the Everyday,* Morrow (New York, NY), 2002, published as *In the Moment: Embracing the Fullness of Life,* Morrow (New York, NY), 2003.

Contributor to *Washington Post.*

SIDELIGHTS: Psychoanalyst Harvey L. Rich, M.D. has seen the effects of the fast pace of modern life through his work as a clinical psychiatrist in private practice. After thirty years treating patients in the Washington, D.C., area, Rich decided to deal with what he saw as a growing problem on a more-than-one-to-one basis. Together with Teresa H. Barker, he has authored *In the Moment: Celebrating the Everyday* as a way of helping people truly experience the emotional, spiritual, and physical facets of events that would otherwise be forgotten as meaningless. Drawing on his own life, his reflections on the terrorist attacks of September 11, 2001, as well as his expertise as a professional, Rich maintains that "celebrating life's moments is an important antidote to what is poisoning our very humanity." While disagreeing with some of Rich's points, a *Publishers Weekly* contributor nonetheless praised *In the Moment* as a book that, through a philosophy that "has its merit" and examples that "are appropriate," can help readers looking for meaning "gain new perspective." In a *Library Journal* review, Douglas C. Lord commended Rich's effort as "genuine" and "heartfelt".

As Rich noted in an interview with Mike Carruthers for *Something You Should Know,* truly experiencing such things as minor achievements, the pain of a loss, or a serious conversation with a friend or family member are among the things people live through without truly understanding or appreciating their significance. "We are rushing past the little moments," he explained to Carruthers, "and we're losing the texture of life. It's those little moments [shared with others that give] . . . texture to our lives."

BIOGRAPHICAL AND CRITICAL SOURCES:

PERIODICALS

Library Journal, January, 2003, Douglas C. Lord, review of *In the Moment: Celebrating the Everyday,* p. 137.
Publishers Weekly, September 16, 2002, review of *In the Moment,* p. 56.

ONLINE

Harvey L. Rich Home Page, http://www.harveyrich. com (October 16, 2003).

*   *   *

RIPLEY, C. Peter 1941-

PERSONAL: Born 1941, in ME. *Education:* Florida State University, B.A., 1966, Ph.D., 1973.

ADDRESSES: *Office*—Florida State University, 401 Bellamy Building, Tallahassee, FL 32306-2100.

CAREER: Historian and author. Florida State University, Tallahassee, professor of history, 1973—.

WRITINGS:

Slaves and Freedmen in Civil War Louisiana, Louisiana State University Press (Baton Rouge, LA), 1976.
(Editor with John W. Blassingame) *The Speeches of Frederick Douglass,* Yale University Press (New Haven, CT), 1979.
(Editor with others) *The Black Abolitionist Papers,* five volumes, University of North Carolina Press (Chapel Hill, NC), 1985-1992.
Richard Nixon, Chelsea House (New York, NY), 1987.
(Editor with Roy E. Finkenbine, Michael F. Hembree, and Donald Yacovone) *Witness for Freedom: African-American Voices on Race, Slavery, and Emancipation,* University of North Carolina Press (Chapel Hill, NC), 1993.
Conversations with Cuba, University of Georgia Press (Athens, GA), 1999.

Contributor of reviews and articles to journals, including the *American Historical Review.* Contributor to *The African-American Experience in Louisiana: Part B: From the Civil War to Jim Crow,* edited by Charles Vincent, Center for Louisiana Studies/University of Louisiana (Lafayette, LA), 2000.

SIDELIGHTS: A professor of history at Florida State University, C. Peter Ripley has focused on America in the 1960s and on African-American history. His works

as researcher, writer, and editor have helped to change the historical perspective on slavery, abolition, and the struggle for emancipation. Such works include *Slaves and Freedmen in Civil War Louisiana, The Black Abolitionist Papers,* and *Witness for Freedom: African American Voices on Race, Slavery, and Emancipation.* He has also dealt with the American presidency in 1987's *Richard Nixon,* and in 1999's *Conversations with Cuba* he takes a new look at a thorny foreign policy issue through the lives of ordinary citizens of Fidel Castro's Cuba.

In his first book, *Slaves and Freedmen in Civil War Louisiana,* Ripley examines both slavery as an institution in that state and also the Union policy pursued in Louisiana after the state's early occupation. Ripley contends in his study that these federal policies presented a "rehearsal for Reconstruction" and largely failed in securing equality for African Americans. Peter Kolchin, writing in the *Journal of American History,* praised the study as "thorough, informative, and based on extensive research," but at the same time found that its "deficiencies stem from the author's excessively moralistic approach to his subject." For Kolchin, the author is too eager to "assign blame for the failure to achieve this equality." Despite reservations about certain "errors and omissions" in the work, Louis S. Gerteis, writing in the *American Historical Review,* thought Ripley's book is "useful and, perhaps, important" because of his discussion of such themes as the relationship between slave and master. And a critic for *Choice* felt that "Ripley's work should encourage similar studies."

Between 1985 and 1992 Ripley coedited the five volumes of *The Black Abolitionist Papers,* a collection of voices from the African-American community speaking out on slavery and abolition in England, Canada, and the United States. These documents were culled from a seventeen-reel microfilm collection that contained letters, newspapers, speeches, essays, and pamphlets in the United States, Canada, and England. The first volume deals with speeches and writers who attempted to influence the population in Great Britain between 1830 and 1865. Richard Blackett, writing in the *Journal of American History,* thought that Ripley and his fellow editors do a "masterful job" in avoiding repetition by being "highly selective" of the contributors and also by presenting a broad range of voices from the era. For Blackett, this is a "volume that will have to be consulted whenever the Atlantic abolitionist movement is examined." The editors, Blackett concluded, "are to be commended both for their investigative talents . . . and for their skilled arrangement of the documents."

Reviewing the second volume of *The Black Abolitionist Papers,* which focuses on Canada, Waldo E. Martin, Jr., writing in the *Journal of American History,* found it a "fascinating collection" that "offers invaluable insight into Canada's black community." Martin also praised the "excellent variety of the documents" and further commented that volume two "continues the exemplary editorial standards" found in the first. Ripley turns to the United States in the last three volumes, which have been similarly commended by reviewers. A critic for *American Visions* thought the third installment is a "valuable reference supplement," while Ravonne A. Green in *Library Journal* called it an "impressive and invaluable aid." A reviewer for the *Virginia Quarterly Review* commented that, in spite of the "one noticeable gap" in the collection—the absence of material from Frederick Douglass—the third volume is "essential . . . for anyone interested in early 19th-century African American History."

Ripley continues in a similar vein with his "splendid" *Witness for Freedom,* a "respectful examination of African American participation in the antislavery movement," according to Marton L. Dillon in the *African American Review.* Selected from the five-volume work, the documents in *Witness for Freedom* are intended as a more-accessible, one-volume approach. As such, the book is "fashioned to reveal the course of Northern black antislavery activities from 1817 to 1865," as Dillon commented, in so doing showing "African Americans shaping the crusade against slavery at many points." Dillon went on to note that this "valuable collection" should serve to turn readers to the larger five-volume work. One of the important issues this collection highlights, according to Michael A. Cooke in the *Mississippi Quarterly,* is "the growing militancy and frustration of black abolitionists with white Northerners who were willing to compromise certain principles for the sake of preserving the Union." For Janet Harrison Shannon, reviewing *Witness for Freedom* in the *Journal of American History,* the work is an "excellent introduction to black abolitionism," and has, as one of its strengths, the "inclusion of obscure sources and individuals." Shannon additionally felt that the book "will appeal to a wide audience." And writing in the

New York Review of Books, David Brion Davis felt that the efforts of Ripley and others in the field "lead us out of the Plato's cave of Civil War legend." For Davis, the documentary and research work of Ripley and others puts modern readers in touch with the real and actual voices of the time, allowing us to "hear the aspirations, the pain, the rage of African Americans."

From racial themes, Ripley turns to politics in his concise biography *Richard Nixon.* Ripley is "nonjudgmental," according to Joyce Whitson in *School Library Journal,* as he takes the reader through Nixon's career, from his California beginnings, to his years as vice president under President Dwight Eisenhower, to his own term as thirty-seventh U.S. president, and concluding with his resignation as a result of the Watergate scandal. Whitson further commended the short history for being both "detailed" and "well balanced."

Politics also informs Ripley's *Conversations with Cuba,* but here the author attempts to show the human face of ordinary Cubans with whom he came into contact on his five visits to the island between 1991 and 1997. Through such individual stories, he shows the changing economic situation of the country. Ripley includes profiles of teachers, a gold trader, and others caught in the maw of history, as well as his own personal observations. Avia Chomsky, reviewing the book in the *Times Literary Supplement,* felt "Ripley is at his best in recounting conversations with individual Cubans." Chomsky further noted that the book "offers a satisfying glimpse into today's Cuba." *Library Journal*'s Mark L. Grover found the same book "well written and informative" if not "entirely objective." Wendy Gimbel, however, writing in the *Los Angeles Times* thought that "the strength of [Ripley's] writing is that it is simply observational, it values the search for objectivity." According to Gimbel, Ripley "makes the case for reconciliation" between the two countries.

BIOGRAPHICAL AND CRITICAL SOURCES:

BOOKS

Ripley, C. Peter, *Slaves and Freedmen in Civil War Louisiana,* Louisiana State University Press (Baton Rouge, LA), 1976.

PERIODICALS

African American Review, winter, 1995, Merton L. Dillon, review of *Witness for Freedom: African-American Voices on Race, Slavery, and Emancipation,,* pp. 673-676.

American Historical Review, June, 1977, Louis S. Gerteis, review of *Slaves and Freedmen in Civil War Louisiana,* pp. 747-748.

Booklist, October 1, 1999, Joe Collins, review of *Conversations with Cuba,* p. 342.

Choice, February, 1977, review of *Slaves and Freedmen in Civil War Louisiana,* p. 1658.

Journal of American History, September, 1977, Peter Kolchin, review of *Slaves and Freedmen in Civil War Louisiana,* pp. 443-444; June, 1985, Richard Blackett, review of *The Black Abolitionist Papers, Volume I,* pp. 402-403; December, 1988, Waldo E. Martin, Jr., review of *The Black Abolitionist Papers, Volume II,* pp. 936-937; December, 1994, Janet Harrison Shannon, review of *Witness for Freedom,* pp. 1314-1315.

Library Journal, February 15, 1991, Ravonne A. Green, review of *The Black Abolitionist Papers, Volume III,* pp. 206-207; October 15, 1999, Mark L. Grover, review of *Conversations with Cuba,* p. 87.

Los Angeles Times Book Review, March 12, 2000, Wendy Gimbel, review of *Conversations with Cuba,* p. 6.

Mississippi Quarterly, fall, 1994, Michael A. Cooke, review of *Witness for Freedom,* pp. 693-695.

New York Review of Books, November 4, 1993, David Brion Davis, review of *Witness for Freedom,* pp. 6-11.

School Library Journal, December, 1987, Joyce Whitson, review of *Richard Nixon,* p. 108.

Times Literary Supplement, October 29, 1999, Avia Chomsky, review of *Conversations with Cuba,* p. 33.

Virginia Quarterly Review, autumn, 1991, review of *The Black Abolitionist Papers, Volume III,* p. 116.

ONLINE

Florida State University Web site, http://www.fsu.edu/ (November 7, 2003) "Dr. C. Peter Ripley."*

*   *   *

RITTER, (William) Scott, Jr. 1960-

PERSONAL: Born 1960, in FL; married. *Education:* Franklin and Marshall College, B.A. (Soviet history).

ADDRESSES: Agent—c/o Greater Talent Network, Inc., 437 Fifth Avenue, New York, NY 10016; c/o Author Mail, Context Books, 368 Broadway, Suite 314, New York, NY 10013. *E-mail*—info@greatertalent.com.

CAREER: Weapons inspector, writer, and lecturer. United Nations, New York, NY, weapons inspector in Iraq, 1991-98. News analyst for CNN and NBC television networks. Producer of documentary film *Shifting Sands: The Truth about Iraq,* 2000. *Military service:* U.S. Marine Corps; attained rank of major.

WRITINGS:

Endgame: Solving the Iraq Problem—Once and for All, Simon & Schuster (New York, NY), 1999.

(With William Rivers Pitt) *War on Iraq: What Team Bush Doesn't Want You to Know,* Context Books (New York, NY), 2002.

Frontier Justice: Weapons of Mass Destruction and the Bushwhacking of America, Context Books (New York, NY), 2003.

SIDELIGHTS: Scott Ritter, a former United Nations weapons inspector in Iraq, has lectured and written on the U.S.-led invasion of that country and expressed his criticism of the reasoning that led to the overthrow of the Saddam Hussein regime in 2003. In *Endgame: Solving the Iraq Problem—Once and for All, War on Iraq: What Team Bush Doesn't Want You to Know,* and *Frontier Justice: Weapons of Mass Destruction and the Bushwhacking of America,* Ritter criticizes Iraq policy as waged by both President Bill Clinton and President George W. Bush.

Born into a military family in Florida in 1960, Ritter grew up at postings around the world. After earning a bachelor's degree in Soviet history, he joined the armed forces, working in military intelligence in the former Soviet Union, where he met his wife. During the 1991 Gulf War, he served at Marine Central Command headquarters in Saudi Arabia under General Norman Schwarzkopf. At the end of that conflict, Ritter left the military service and joined the United Nations Special Commission (UNSCOM) on weapons inspection in Iraq. Between 1991 and 1998, when he resigned, Ritter participated in fifty-two inspection missions, heading fourteen of those. In 1995 he and his team were responsible for tracking down missile guidance systems in Iraq purchased from Russia via a Palestinian intermediary. Three years later Ritter and his team were denied entrance to sensitive sites; the Iraqis accused him of being a U.S. spy. After months of repeatedly being denied access, and feeling that he lacked the support of the U.S. State Department or the United Nations, Ritter publicly resigned his position, indicating that weapons inspection in Iraq was more illusion than reality.

Thereafter, Ritter began lecturing and writing about the situation in Iraq. In the 1999 title *Endgame,* he writes of his experiences as a weapons inspector in Iraq, detailing the history of the Hussein regime and arguing for a Marshall Plan-style solution to the Iraq problem in which mutual cooperation might replace open antagonism between that country and the international community. The book was published at a highly politicized time, following close upon President Clinton's Operation Desert Fox, a limited military response to Hussein's noncompliance. Reviewing Ritter's book for *Middle East Policy,* Michael V. Deaver wrote that the former Marine offers "many interesting revelations." Deaver specifically felt that Ritter's "detailed descriptions of the organizational structures and responsibilities of the Iraqi concealment mechanism" are a "valuable" contribution to the literature. However, Deaver also complained of what he saw as Ritter's "reliance on loose logic and insinuation" in the author's explanation of why Iraq "chose to develop" weapons of mass destruction.

Reviewing *Endgame* for *Commentary,* Bret Louis Stephens found that Ritter "writes colorfully about what inspections were actually like." Further, Stephens noted that though Ritter "tells a riveting story, and paints throughout a grim picture of the Iraqi menace, the prescriptions [he] draws from his observations and experiences are disappointing and utterly unconvincing." Ritter observed in his book that, lacking an international coalition, a military response to Hussein was not practical; therefore, a diplomatic solution involving promised aid for disarmament should be sought. The *Nation*'s William M. Arkin was equally skeptical of such a solution and also found fault with Ritter's portrayal of UNSCOM's activities. "The greatest damage Ritter does in his flawed book," wrote Arkin, "is in understating UNSCOM's achievements, thus also overstating Iraq's current potential for weapons of mass destruction." For a reviewer in the

Economist, however, the "real strength" of the book is its "extraordinary reporting." According to the same reviewer, "Amid his snooping, Mr. Ritter unearths a wealth of detail about the workings of Mr. Hussein's police state." Writing in *RUSI Journal,* Neil Patrick also had praise for *Endgame,* calling it an "exciting read, a veritable airport lounge pot boiler full of high drama." Patrick, however, had little faith in Ritter's proposed solutions, as did Tim Weiner in the *New York Times Book Review.* Weiner felt that Ritter's *Endgame* "is a map without a key," a book that "reads like a sputtering argument written in anger, laid out in fits and starts." Weiner did, though, find "several impassioned yet reasoned passages indicting aspects of American policy in Iraq." These include descriptions of the cost that sanctions on Iraq had on the most vulnerable of the population there, killing tens of thousands of children through lack of food and medicine. Weiner also noted that "some secrets are spilled here." These included the fact that many of those on the U.N. inspection teams were CIA operatives gathering information on Iraq.

With the buildup to renewed war in Iraq in 2003, Ritter became a vocal critic of President Bush's policies, seemingly turning against his own former hard-line policy regarding that country. He repeatedly argued that weapons of mass destruction in Iraq had successfully been dealt with by inspectors. Speaking with Massimo Calabresi of *Time Online,* he rejected the notion that he changed his mind about Saddam Hussein and his nuclear stockpiles. "I have never given Iraq a clean bill of health," he told Calabresi. "Never! Never! I've said that no one has backed up any allegations that Iraq has reconstituted weapons capability with anything that remotely resembles substantive fact." As reported by *BBC News Online,* Ritter observed, "'My government is making a case for war against Iraq that is built upon fear and ignorance.'" In *War on Iraq,* Ritter provides essentially a lengthy interview in which he further argues that Iraq was no threat to its neighbors and that over ninety percent of the country's weapons had been destroyed since 1991. Ritter also argues against any ties between the Hussein regime and the terrorist group al-Qaeda, which was responsible for the September 11, 2001, attacks on the United States. A reviewer for *New Statesman* felt that Ritter "states quite clearly what the war is and is not about."

In 2003, with Hussein toppled and American troops in Iraq, Ritter renewed his criticisms of U.S. Iraq policy in *Frontier Justice,* in which he points out the failure to locate weapons of mass destruction in Iraq and takes the Bush administration to task for leading the nation to war, as he contends, in support of a lie. A contributor for *Publishers Weekly* found it "no surprise" that Ritter's book is considered "controversial." Despite Ritter's strong arguments, the same contributor found the author's "tone" to be "tiresome." Pointing to such phrases as "Ranger Bush and his west Texas lynch mob" that Ritter uses in his book, the same reviewer commented that such descriptions "may be amusing at first, but not after the umpteenth use." Ritter, the former military man, also notes in his book that he has become involved in a group called SAVE! which hopes to solve such conflicts in the future by "adopting a non-threatening posture."

BIOGRAPHICAL AND CRITICAL SOURCES:

BOOKS

Ritter, Scott, *Frontier Justice: Weapons of Mass Destruction and the Bushwhacking of America*, Context Books (New York, NY), 2003.

PERIODICALS

Boston Globe, July 20, 2002, Scott Ritter, "Is Iraq a True Threat to the US?"

Commentary, July, 1999, Bret Louis Stephens, review of *Endgame: Solving the Iraq Problem—Once and for All*, p. 86.

Economist (U.S.), May 1, 1999, review of *Endgame*, p. 80.

Europe Intelligence Wire, October 5, 2002, review of *War on Iraq: What Team Bush Doesn't Want You to Know*.

Foreign Affairs, July-August, 1999, Eliot A. Cohen, review of *Endgame*, p. 132.

Guardian, October 5, 2002, Steven Poole, review of *War on Iraq*, p. R31.

Maclean's, September 7, 1998, "Weapons Furor," p. 33.

Middle East Economic Digest, September 11, 1998, Toby Ash, "Iraq: UNSCOM in Crisis," p. 24.

Middle East Policy, October, 2002, Michael V. Deaver, review of *Endgame*, p. 180.

Nation, May 17, 1999, William M. Arkin, review of *Endgame*, pp. 31-34.

New Statesman, October 7, 2002, review of *War on Iraq*, p. 59.

New York Times Book Review, April 11, 1999, Tim Weiner, review of *Endgame*, p. 26.

Publishers Weekly, October 7, 2002, review of *War on Iraq*, p. 22; August 4, 2003, review of *Frontier Justice: Weapons of Mass Destruction and the Bushwhacking of America*, p. 71.

RUSI Journal, August, 1999, Neil Patrick, review of *Endgame*, pp. 91-92.

ONLINE

BBC News Online, http://www.bbc.co.uk/ (September 9, 2002), "Profile: Scott Ritter."

Greater Talent Network Web site, http://www.greatertalent.com/ (November 7, 2003), "Scott Ritter."

NewsHour with Jim Lehrer Online, http://www.pbs.org/newshour/ (August 31, 1998), transcript of interview with Ritter.

Time Online, http://www.time.com/ (November 7, 2003), Massimo Calabresi, "Scott Ritter in His Own Words."*

*   *   *

RODGERS, Gordon 1952-

PERSONAL: Born 1952, in Gander, Newfoundland, Canada. *Education:* Attended Memorial University of Newfoundland; University of British Columbia, M.F.A.

ADDRESSES: Agent—Creative Publishing, P.O. Box 8660, 36 Austin Street, St. John's, Newfoundland, A1B 3T7, Canada.

CAREER: Writer and practicing psychologist; formerly university lecturer and government research assistant.

WRITINGS:

Floating Houses (poems), Creative Publishers (St. John's, Newfoundland, Canada), 1984.

The Phoenix (novella), Creative Publishers (St. John's, Newfoundland, Canada), 1985.

Pyrate Latitudes (poems), Creative Publishers (St. John's, Newfoundland, Canada), 1986.

A Settlement of Memory (novel), Killick Press (St. John's, Newfoundland, Canada), 1999.

Former poetry editor of *Prism International.* Contributor to literary journals and magazines; work included in *Choice Poems from the Newfoundland Quarterly,* edited by Everard H. King, Harry Cuff Publications, 1981.

SIDELIGHTS: Although he may be best known as a poet, Gordon Rodgers has also written some notable works of prose inspired by the history of his native Canadian province of Newfoundland. In his first novella, *The Phoenix,* the crash of a Czechoslovakian passenger plane in Newfoundland during the 1960s—an accident that actually occurred and killed thirty-seven people—is told through the eyes of thirteen-year-old Michael, who lives in the province. As Michael traverses a bog where the plane crashed in Gander, Newfoundland, he "takes his first steps towards a mature understanding of life and death," Cathy Simpson explained in *Books in Canada.* Simpson also noted that Rodgers's background as a poet is apparent due to his "cunning interweaving of thematic images" in this book.

Rodgers's first full-length novel, *A Settlement of Memory,* was inspired by Newfoundland's union history. The protagonist of *A Settlement of Memory,* Tom Vincent, is a labor organizer modeled on historical figure William Coaker, the man who organized the Fisherman's Protective Union in Newfoundland in 1908. In Rodgers's novel, Vincent attempts to rent an office for the union on Water Street, the main street of St. John's, the major city of Newfoundland, in 1913. The businessmen who own the office spaces on Water Street refuse to rent to him, but Vincent is undeterred in his quest to break the control of the owners. *A Settlement of Memory* "is backed by extensive research," Diana Brebner commented in *Books in Canada,* which forms "the skeleton for a consistent and authentic narrative."

BIOGRAPHICAL AND CRITICAL SOURCES:

PERIODICALS

Books in Canada, June, 1986, Cathy Simpson, review of *The Phoenix,* p. 20; October, 1999, Diana Brebner, review of *A Settlement of Memory,* pp. 35-36.

Canadian Literature, autumn-winter, 2001, Colin Hill, review of *A Settlement of Memory,* pp. 236-238.

Newfoundland Quarterly, fall, 1988, review of *The Phoenix* and *Pyrate Latitudes,* p. 42.

Quill and Quire, August, 1999, review of *A Settlement of Memory,* p. 32.

ONLINE

Creative Publishers Web site, http://www.nfbooks.com/ (October 27, 2003), "Gordon Rodgers."*

* * *

ROGERS, Chris 1944-

PERSONAL: Born 1944, in Houston, TX; married, c. 1958 (divorced, 1973); children: four. *Education:* Attended University of Houston.

ADDRESSES: Home—Hilltop Lakes, TX. *Agent*—c/o Random House/Bantam Books, 1745 Broadway, New York, NY 10019. *E-mail*—crnovelist@aol.com.

CAREER: Crime novelist and book illustrator. Art design and production business owner; marketing consultant; certified practitioner of neurolinguistic programming; writing instructor at "Unboggle Your Mind" master class and Rice University School of Continuing Studies; speaker at national conferences, associations, schools, and libraries; 2001 delegate to White House Conference on Small Business.

AWARDS, HONORS: Best Unpublished Mystery Novel, Golden Triangle, 1992, for "Wicked Step Daughter"; Ten by Ten Competition, Scriptwriters Houston, 1995, for stage play *The Tip;* Empire Screenplay Competition, 1997, for screenplay *Mirror's Edge.*

WRITINGS:

"DIXIE FLANNIGAN" SERIES

Bitch Factor, Bantam Books (New York, NY), 1998.
Rage Factor, Bantam Books (New York, NY), 1999.

Chill Factor, Bantam Books (New York, NY), 2000.

Also author of "Dixie Flannigan" novel *Slice of Life,* published in installments on the author's home page.

OTHER

(Illustrator) Vickie Milazzo, *Create Your Own Magic for CLNC Success,* Vickie Milazzo Institute, 2003.

Also author of unpublished novel, "Wicked Step Daughter." Author of short play, *The Tip,* produced by Scriptwriters Houston at Stages Repertory Theatre, 1995, as well as screenplays *Mirror's Edge* and *Invite the Devil In,* the latter published as a short story in *Deep South Writers Conference Chapbook,* University of Southwestern Louisiana, 1996. Contributor of stories to *Alfred Hitchcock Mystery Magazine.*

SIDELIGHTS: Chris Rogers grew up in a working-class family in Houston, Texas, never attended high school, married at the age of fourteen, and raised four children. She taught herself to be a writer by studying how-to books, attending writing conferences, and reading her favorite authors. Apart from winning several awards for her writings, she now teaches and lectures on the subject.

After a divorce, Rogers—who had been a homemaker during her marriage—opened her own art-design and production business. However, she ultimately realized it was not the career she wanted for the rest of her life. After writing several travel brochures and pondering the possibility of opening a bed-and-breakfast inn, she turned her hand to fiction writing. While mysteries were—and are—her favorite reading material, she had little confidence in her ability to write complex, compelling plotlines. So she decided to try romance novels. Her first four attempts were rejected—one publisher commented that her manuscript contained too much mystery for a romance novel. Then she won a regional competition for best unpublished mystery novel. "That kind of showed me I did need to focus on mystery," Rogers told Fritz Lanham during an interview for the *Houston Chronicle.* After her first mystery novel, *Bitch Factor,* was published, it received four-and-a-half stars out of a possible five by—ironically—*Romantic Times* magazine, "and it wasn't intended to be a romance," she commented. *Bitch Factor* became the first in Rogers's "Dixie Flannigan" series of books.

Rogers discovered the protagonist for her "Dixie Flannigan" series while on a taxi ride in Houston. She asked the driver if tending the taxi was his full-time job and he told her no, he was also a bounty hunter. Rogers was intrigued. During the ensuing discussion, she pondered the idea of a female bounty hunter, and out of this conversation grew the character of Dixie Flannigan, a prosecutor turned bounty hunter. "I decided she would be a mature woman—she's 39," Rogers told Lanham. "She would be single. Why? Because she's still figuring out what she wants to be, which is why she's bounty hunting."

In *Bitch Factor,* Flannigan is tracking down Parker Dann, a man accused of the drunk-driving, hit-and-run death of eleven-year-old Betsy Keyes. Dann, professing innocence, had fled to South Dakota. Flannigan tracks and eventually captures him, but shortly after she does so, a blizzard strikes and the pair becomes stranded. During their time together, Flannigan comes to believe in the charming Dann's innocence, especially after discovering that Keyes's younger sister had died in an earlier accident. Flannigan sets out to investigate both accidents.

A reviewer for *Publishers Weekly* pointed out that, while there are "some glaring flaws" in the story, the "snappy dialogue and memorable characters" make for "pleasurable entertainment." In *Library Journal,* Laurel A. Wilson called Rogers' work "masterful from beginning to end" and Flannigan "the best new heroine to come along in years."

Alicia Graybill commented in *Library Journal* that while *Bitch Factor* received critical acclaim, in *Rage Factor*—her second Flannigan mystery—Rogers "has surpassed herself." After capturing sexual sadist Lawrence Coombs, who stands trial for rape, Flannigan is shocked when the jury acquits him. Shortly thereafter, Coombs is found bound, beaten, and sexually assaulted in a local park. The attack is blamed on the Avenging Angels, an all-woman vigilante group Flannigan suspects one of her friends belongs to. Coombs, however, blames Flannigan for his attack and seeks revenge. There are also several subplots in the novel, one of which includes a famous Hollywood actress who is being stalked and who hires Flannigan as a bodyguard for her daughter. Flannigan also deals with a budding relationship with Parker Dann, who first appeared in *Bitch Factor*. A *Publishers Weekly* reviewer commented that while this novel suffers from "slow-moving subplots . . . the climactic showdown scene between Dixie and Coombs is a knockout." And Graybill called the book "a page-turner, nearly impossible to put down."

While reviewing the next book in the Flannigan series for the *Chicago Tribune*, Linda DuVal noted that while *Rage Factor* "left some of [Rogers'] fans reeling from the graphic violence," she "tone[d] it down" for *Chill Factor*. In the third book, Flannigan happens to be in a bank when Edna Pine, her friendly, little-old-lady, next-door neighbor walks in and pulls off a robbery, escaping with a significant sum of money. After hiding the haul, Pine is gunned down by the local police. Mass confusion ensues as shortly after Pine's death, the police who shot her are found murdered. Pine's son Marty—also Flannigan's high-school sweetheart—becomes the prime suspect in the policemen's death; he asks Flannigan to find out what possessed his mother to become a bank robber. Broadening the plot is what a *Publishers Weekly* reviewer called "a manipulative, blackmailing sociopath" called the "Shepherd of the Light."

While the *Publishers Weekly* reviewer concluded that the book's "overheated plot leaves readers in the cold," Jenny McLarin wrote in *Booklist* that "Dixie is one of the most likable female protagonists in mystery fiction" and that *Chill Factor* "is a definite heartwarmer." DuVal noted that Rogers' "rapid-fire storytelling style relies largely on crisp, decisive language and short, quick chapters." Graybill commented in *Library Journal* that "A small degree of sex and violence will make this book a bit too hard-boiled for some readers," but concluded that fans of Rogers' previous books will also enjoy this one.

BIOGRAPHICAL AND CRITICAL SOURCES:

PERIODICALS

Booklist, January 15, 1999, Emily Melton, review of *Rage Factor,* p. 840; December 15, 1999, Jenny McLarin, review of *Chill Factor,* p. 760.

Chicago Tribune, February 28, 2000, Linda DuVal, "Plenty of Thrills without the Chills in Rogers' New Mystery," p. 3.
Houston Chronicle, March 29, 1998, Fritz Lanham, "Mystery Woman" (interview with Rogers), p. 26.
Library Journal, January, 1998, Laurel Wilson, review of *Bitch Factor,* p. 144; January, 1999, Alicia Graybill, review of *Rage Factor,* p. 158; January, 2000, Alicia Graybill, review of *Chill Factor,* p. 162.
Publishers Weekly, January 18, 1999, review of *Rage Factor,* p. 331; January 24, 2000, review of *Chill Factor,* p. 295.

ONLINE

Chris Rogers' Home Page, http://www.chrisrogers.com (November 14, 2003).*

*   *   *

ROGOVIN, Anne 1918-2003

OBITUARY NOTICE—See index for *CA* sketch: Born August 4, 1918, in Buffalo, NY; died of brain cancer July 7, 2003, in Buffalo, NY. Educator and author. Rogovin was a teacher of mentally handicapped children who also wrote books on child rearing. Attending the New York State College for Teachers (now Buffalo State College of the State University of New York), she earned a B.A. there in 1940. However, when she refused to sign a loyalty oath for the Buffalo public school system, no one would hire her there as a teacher. She consequently found employment at the city's Board of Cooperative Educational Services and began teaching mentally impaired students. She went on to earn her master's degree in special education from her alma mater in 1963. Through her work with special-needs children she developed the philosophy that youngsters learn best by doing things for themselves; this led to her development of "learning boards" containing activities that stimulate a child's senses of touch, smell, and sight. Rogovin's learning boards were later included in two exhibitions at the Buffalo Gallery: "Learning by Doing" (1971) and "Please Do Touch" (1977). Rogovin, who as a social activist marched in numerous peace rallies and was blacklisted for supporting accused communist spies Julius and Ethel Rosenberg, also conducted workshops for parents on child rearing. Her books include *Learning by Doing: An Illustrated Handbook for Parents and Teachers of Children Who Learn Slowly* (1971; second edition, 1977), *Let Me Do It!* (1980), *1,001 Wonderful Wonders: Activities for All Children* (1992), and *Turn off the TV and...* (1995). In 1993 she was named Buffalo News Citizen of the Year, and in 2003 was given the Distinguished Alumna Award by Buffalo State College.

OBITUARIES AND OTHER SOURCES:

PERIODICALS

Buffalo News, July 8, 2003, p. C6.
New York Times, July 20, 2003, p. A25.

*   *   *

ROSENBLATT, Kathleen Ferrick 1947-

PERSONAL: Born 1947. *Education:* Canisius College, 1968; postdoctoral research in French studies.

ADDRESSES: Home—Los Angeles, CA. *Agent*—c/o State University of New York Press, 90 State St., Suite 700, Albany, NY 12207-1707.

CAREER: Author. Doctor of homeopathy and oriental medicine.

WRITINGS:

René Daumal: The Life and Work of a Mystic Guide, State University of New York Press (Albany, NY), 1999.

SIDELIGHTS: Kathleen Ferrick Rosenblatt's book *René Daumal: The Life and Work of a Mystic Guide* is the result of twenty years of research and interviews with several people who knew the subject of the book personally. Daumal (1908-1944) was the author of several essays on topics as diverse as surrealism and Hindu esthetics; a book of poetry; and two allegories, *A Night of Serious Drinking* and *Mount Analogue*—the latter a classic work of esoteric spiritual fiction.

He was also founder of the avant-garde journal *Le Grand Jeu,* named after a literary group he formed in his teens with two like-minded peers. "They wanted political, psychological, and metaphysical revolution," explained Erik Davis in a review of Rosenblatt's book for the *Village Voice.* "Anticipating the 1960s, they explored automatic handwriting, astral travel, sensory deprivation, and drugs."

The young Daumal, who would die in Paris at the age of thirty-six from tuberculosis, was highly intellectual and is considered a seminal author of the metaphysical avant garde. A satirist, poet, essayist, and deeply spiritual ascetic, he taught himself Sanskrit at the age of sixteen. He combined the converging influences of Surrealism, Marxism, Hinduism, Freudianism, and parapsychology in his struggle for a more personal understanding of spirituality; he is credited with being the first to find a connection between classical Hindu poetics and the revolutionary, spiritual teachings of G. I. Gurdjieff. Daumal's contact with Gurdjieff instigated a radical life change in the young man that fostered a revolutionary approach to the workings of the inner human being and the entire cosmos.

Rosenblatt translated Daumal's works from their original French, and her book is the first comprehensive investigation into all aspects of his life and work. In her review of *René Daumal* for *Parabola,* Fran Shaw praised the "enthusiastic style" employed by Rosenblatt as a catalyst for a heightened appreciation of Daumal's works.

BIOGRAPHICAL AND CRITICAL SOURCES:

PERIODICALS

Parabola, February, 2000, Fran Shaw, review of *René Daumal: The Life and Work of a Mystic Guide,* pp. 132-136.
Publishers Weekly, December 7, 1998, Jonathan Bing, review of *René Daumal,* p. 48.
Village Voice, September 21, 1999, Erik Davis, review of *René Daumal,* p. 87.*

*   *   *

RYERSON, Eric
See COFFEY, Wayne

S

SAFRAN, Nadav 1925-2003

OBITUARY NOTICE—See index for *CA* sketch: Born August 25, 1925, in Cairo, Egypt; died of cancer July 5, 2003, in State College, PA. Educator and author. Safran was a professor of government at Harvard University and an expert on the Middle East. Although his family did not actively practice Judaism, Safran rediscovered his religious roots as a teenager and joined a kibbutz in what was then still Palestine in 1946. In 1948 he fought for Israel as a lieutenant in that country's war for independence. After the armistice was signed in 1949, he moved to the United States, earned a B.A. from Brandeis University in 1954 and a Ph.D. from Harvard in 1956. He remained at Harvard to teach government for two years and then worked as a research fellow at the university's Center for Middle East Studies. Safran eventually became director of the center, but had to resign in 1985 when it was discovered that he had accepted grant money from the Central Intelligence Agency (CIA) without properly informing the university. The scandal compromised the reputation of American learning institutions, as people in the Middle East came under the erroneous impression that U.S. schools were funded by the CIA. Despite the scandal, Safran remained respected by his colleagues, and he stayed at Harvard as a professor until his retirement in 2002. His writings about politics in the Middle East were highly regarded and include such books as *Egypt in Search of Political Community* (1961), *Israel Today: A Profile* (1965), *Israel: The Embattled Ally* (1981), and *Saudi Arabia: The Ceaseless Quest for Security* (1985), the last which he couathored with John C. Campbell.

OBITUARIES AND OTHER SOURCES:

PERIODICALS

Boston Globe, July 10, 2003, p. B7.
New York Times, July 27, 2003, p. A25.

*   *   *

SAMUELS, Gertrude 1910(?)-2003

OBITUARY NOTICE—See index for *CA* sketch: Born c. 1910 in Manchester, England; died July 2, 2003, in New York, NY. Journalist, photographer, and author. Samuels was an award-winning reporter who spent over thirty years with the *New York Times*. She was brought to the United States by her parents when she was fourteen years old, and she eventually attended the Busch Conservatory of Music and George Washington University. However, when she was offered a job at the *New York Post* in 1937 she left school to work as a journalist. During World War II she also worked for *Newsweek* and *Time* before joining the *New York Times* staff as a writer for the paper's Sunday magazine in 1943, becoming a writer and photographer in 1947 and editor in 1972. She left the newspaper in 1975 to become a freelancer, and she returned to school to complete her B.A. in English at New York University in 1982, followed by an M.A. in 1983. During her career, Samuels reported on events from around the world, often in dangerous locations such as Middle East refugee camps and war-torn Korea. She also wrote and photographed stories about crime and drugs in America's inner cities. For her work, she won the Front Page Award from the American Newspaper Guild, and the George Polk Award, which she earned in 1955 for her stories about school desegregation. Samuels turned some of her reportage into books, including *Report on Israel* (1960) and *The Secret of Gonen: Portrait of a Kibbutz on the Border in a Time of War* (1969). She was also a novelist, publishing such fiction as *Run, Shelley, Run!* (1974) and *Adam's Daughter* (1977), as well as writing several plays, among them *Judah the Maccabee and Me* (1970), *The Assignment* (1974), and *Of Time and Thomas Wolfe* (1980).

OBITUARIES AND OTHER SOURCES:

BOOKS

Ward, Martha E., and others, editors, *Authors of Books for Young People,* third edition, Scarecrow Press (Metuchen, NJ), 1990.

PERIODICALS

New York Times, July 5, 2003, p. A13.
Washington Post, July 6, 2003, p. C10.

*   *   *

SANDERS, Mark A. 1963-

PERSONAL: Born 1963. *Education:* Brown University, Ph.D.

ADDRESSES: Office—Department of African American Studies, Emory University, Atlanta, GA 30322. *E-mail*—msander@emory.edu.

CAREER: Author and professor. Emory University, Atlanta, GA, associate professor of English and director of program of African-American studies.

WRITINGS:

(Editor with J. V. Brummels) *On Common Ground: The Poetry of William Kloefkorn, Ted Kooser, Greg Kuzma, and Don Welch,* Sandhills (Ord, NE), 1983.

Before We Lost Our Ways, Hurakan Press (Texas City, TX), 1996.

(Editor and author of foreword) Sterling Allen Brown, *A Son's Return: Selected Essays of Sterling A. Brown,* Northeastern University Press (Boston, MA), 1996.

Afro-Modernist Aesthetics and the Poetry of Sterling A. Brown, University of Georgia Press (Athens, GA), 1999.

SIDELIGHTS: In his foreword to *A Son's Return: Selected Essays of Sterling A. Brown,* Mark A. Sanders explains that the collection of reviews, essays, and lectures present in the book provides an introduction to the life and work of Brown, a renowned African-American poet, folklorist, and literary critic. Brown's work has been deemed essential for an accurate understanding of early twentieth-century African-American art and politics; indeed, he is often referred to as the "Dean of American Negro Poets."

In a *Publishers Weekly* review, Maria Simpson commented that, upon his death in 1989, Brown left behind a "legacy of criticism for which modern commentators of African American culture should remain eternally grateful." She complimented Sanders for the collection presented in *A Son's Return,* which she saw as the "most representative of [Brown's] work on literature, history, folklore and music" and also stated that the book "underscores Brown's weakness as a critic." In his review for *Library Journal,* Charles L. Lumpkins wrote that the sixteen essays selected by Sanders for the book "present a tantalizing sampler . . . that leaves the reader wishing for a complete collection of the writer's publications."

In *Afro-Modernist Aesthetics and the Poetry of Sterling A. Brown,* Sanders closely examines the historical context of Brown's three collections of poetry and traces the manner in which the poet called for a revisionist perspective of the Harlem Renaissance, black identity, and artistic expression. In his review for the *Mississippi Quarterly,* literary critic William J. Maxwell wrote: "Sanders complements and challenges black vernacular literary theory with recent revisionist histories of an internally riven aesthetic modernism, for his book aims to demonstrate how Brown's verse reshapes grand, temporally sweeping concerns [about] 'black being' and the 'prevailing discourses defining American culture'—in the sometimes brutally fractured historical context of modernist culture." Concluding his lengthy review, Maxwell wrote: "'Fundamentally,' Brown once said . . . 'I'm a teacher. I took teaching seriously. I got the papers back to the people. . . . Sometimes I was called the red ink man.' Despite the mental red ink inspired by Sanders's uneven account of Brown's historical attachments and circumstances, the fluent readings of *Afro-Modernist Aesthetics* will help to elevate the teaching of a remarkable poet nearer to his own high pedagogic standard. . . . Sanders's book is vital equipment for grasping the post-modernist meaning of perhaps thc lcast-known most important American poet."

BIOGRAPHICAL AND CRITICAL SOURCES:

PERIODICALS

Library Journal, September 15, 1996, Charles L. Lumpkins, review of *A Son's Return: Selected Essays of Sterling A. Brown,* p. 68.
Melus, winter, 1998, D. K. Campbell, review of *A Son's Return,* pp. 196-199.
Mississippi Quarterly, spring, 2000, William J. Maxwell, review of *Afro-Modernist Aesthetics and the Poetry of Sterling A. Brown,* pp. 301-306.
Publishers Weekly, October 7, 1996, Maria Simpson, review of *A Son's Return,* p. 67.
Western American Literature, winter, 1985, James R. Saucerman, review of *On Common Ground: The Poetry of William Kloefkorn, Ted Kooser, Greg Kuzma, and Don Welch,* pp. 326-327; fall, 1998, Shaun T. Griffin, review of *Before We Lost Our Ways,* p. 307.

ONLINE

Emory University Web site, http://www.emory.edu/ (November 17, 2003), profile of Mark A. Sanders.*

*   *   *

SAURET, Martine

PERSONAL: Female. Education: Sorbonne, University of Paris III, license, 1980, certificate (commerce), 1982; Université du Langues Orientales (Paris, France), diploma (Russian language and civilization), 1980; University of Minnesota, M.A., 1984, Ph.D. (with honors), 1991.

ADDRESSES: Home—1604 Northrop La., Minneapolis, MN 55403. *Office*—Department of Foreign Languages and Literatures, Western Michigan University, Kalamazoo, MI 49008. *E-mail*—MSauret@aol.com.

CAREER: Educator and author. University of Minnesota Language Center, Minneapolis, instructor in French and German, 1984-85; Association Henzel, Paris, France, English teacher, 1985-86; University of St. Thomas, Minneapolis, instructor in French, 1988-89; St. John's University, Collegeville, MN, instructor, 1990-91, assistant professor of French, 1991-92; Western Michigan University, Kalamazoo, assistant professor, 1992-97, associatc professor of French, 1997—, director of program in Besançon, France, 1999—. Speaker at educational institutions, including Purdue University, University of Virginia, University of Toronto, and University of Missouri—Columbia; teacher of English as a second language. Ambassade de France aux Éats-Unis, New York, NY, committee member, 1999—.

MEMBER: Modern Language Association of America, Société Française des Études du Siezième Siècle, Alliance Française of Kalamazoo, Pi Delta Phi.

AWARDS, HONORS: National Endowment for the Humanities grant, 1998; Newberry Library fellow, 1998.

WRITINGS:

"Gargantua" et les délits du corps, Peter Lang (New York, NY), 1997.
(Translator into French) Tom Conley, *The Graphic Unconscious in Early Modern French Writing,* Presses Universitaires de Vincennes (Vincennes, France), 2000.

Contributor to books, including Christopher Baker, editor, *Absolutism and the Scientific Revolution, 1600-1720,* Greenwood Press (Westport, CT), 2000. Contributor of articles to periodicals, including *French Women in the Renaissance Newsletter, Nouvelle Revue du 16e Siècle, Renaissance Quarterly, Renaissance News and Notes, Sixteenth Century Studies,* and *Substance.*

WORK IN PROGRESS: A book, *Voies cartographiques.*

SIDELIGHTS: Martine Sauret told *CA:* "I like to write to understand things, to develop thoughts in a more materialistic way, analyze and synthesize my thoughts. My work is influenced by discussions, newspapers, philosophers, and critics; sometimes by a very bad book, in which case I write to mention what is wrong.

"After reading material, I start on the computer and write notes. Sometimes I use a fountain pen. I love to organize my ideas in a very specific notebook with clarity, and this visual aid enhances my writing.

"Who inspired me? My writing is inspired by two of my former professors—and now friends—who have helped and supported me in writing about authors who were hard to decipher but extremely fascinating to me. What inspires me? When I was a child, I was fascinated by maps. My new book deals with imagination and maps."

*   *   *

SAVAGE, Thomas 1915-2003

OBITUARY NOTICE—See index for *CA* sketch: Born April 25, 1915, in Salt Lake City, UT; died July 25, 2003, in Virginia Beach, VA. Novelist. Savage was a popular author of Western novels that often drew on his own experiences as a ranch hand. In his early career, he also worked as a wrangler, welder, plumber's assistant, and railroad brakeman. In 1940 Savage finished his undergraduate studies at Colby College; he published his first novel, *The Pass,* four years later and found work as an English instructor at Suffolk University two years after that. Struggling at first to make a living and support his family, Savage saw his fortunes take a turn for the better when Columbia Pictures purchased the film rights for his second book, *Lona Hanson* (1948). Although a film was never produced, Savage enjoyed a successful career as a writer after that, publishing thirteen novels in all. He also continued to teach English, moving to Brandeis University in 1949, where he remained until 1955, and also teaching at Vassar College and Franconia College. Among his other novels are *The Power of the Dog* (1967), *A Strange God* (1974), *I Heard My Sister*

Speak My Name (1977; published as *The Sheep Queen,* 2001) and *The Corner of Rife and Pacific* (1988), the last of which was nominated for a PEN/Faulkner Award and won a Pacific Northwest Booksellers Association Award.

OBITUARIES AND OTHER SOURCES:

PERIODICALS

International Herald Tribune, August 26, 2003, p. 4.
New York Times, August 25, 2003, p. A19.

*   *   *

SCANLAN, Patricia 1956-

PERSONAL: Born 1956, in Ballygall, Dublin, Ireland.

ADDRESSES: Home—Dublin, Ireland. *Agent*—c/o Author Mail, Poolbeg Press, 123 Baldoyle Industrial Estate, Baldoyle, Dublin 13, Ireland.

CAREER: Novelist. Worked as a librarian for Dublin Public Libraries, beginning 1974; part-time editorial consultant for Hodder Headline Ireland, beginning 2003.

WRITINGS:

Apartment 3B, Poolbeg Press (Dublin, Ireland), 1992.
City Girl, Poolbeg Press (Dublin, Ireland), 1992.
Finishing Touches, Poolbeg Press (Dublin, Ireland), 1992, Dell (New York, NY), 1994.
City Woman, Poolbeg Press (Dublin, Ireland), 1993.
Foreign Affairs, Poolbeg Press (Dublin, Ireland), 1995.
Promises Promises, Poolbeg Press (Dublin, Ireland), 1996.
Mirror Mirror, Poolbeg Press (Dublin, Ireland), 1997.
City Lives, Poolbeg Press (Dublin, Ireland), 1999.
Ripples, New Island Books (Dublin, Ireland), 1999.
Francesca's Party, Poolbeg Press (Dublin, Ireland), 2001, Thomas Dunne Books (New York, NY), 2002.

Also author of poetry collections *Three-dimensional Sin*, 1988, *Yell Ow*, 1988, and *Selected Poems*, 1993. Coauthor and editor for New Island's "Open Door" literacy series.

ADAPTATIONS: City Girl was adapted for audio cassette, read by Kate Forbes, ISIS Audio Books, 1990/1999; *Mirror, Mirror* was adapted for audio cassette, ISIS Audio Books, 2000; *City Woman* was adapted for audio cassette, ISIS Audio Books, 2000.

SIDELIGHTS: Patricia Scanlan worked for many years as a librarian for the Dublin public libraries before she began publishing novels. Her romantic fiction has been very popular in her native Ireland and has a growing audience in the United States. The novels feature entertaining stories about smart, sexy Irish women who are capable of surmounting substantial economic, domestic, and romantic challenges.

One of Scanlan's earlier novels is *City Girl*, a story about entrepreneur Devlin Delaney, who opens a lavish women's health club in Dublin. But Devlin's promising career is contrasted by a troubled past. Her good friends Caroline and Maggie are supportive when Devlin decides to keep the baby she gives birth to out of wedlock. In turn Caroline struggles with substance and spousal abuse, and Maggie discovers that her husband is cheating on her. The ultimate success of these three "lusty and larger-than-life heroines" was described by a *Publishers Weekly* writer as "mildly entertaining" and exceedingly sweet.

A trio of friends is also the focus of *Finishing Touches*, a novel about women who first met at school in Port Mahon, Ireland. The central figure is Cassie, who is fettered by the responsibility of caring for her mother. Her chums Aileen and Laura move away from home and give their friend insight into a more glamorous life in Dublin and London. A *Publishers Weekly* reviewer enjoyed the "study of contrasts" that this plot allowed, and concluded that the book would "have readers cheering both for the heroine and the author."

Scanlan's most widely reviewed novel is *Francesca's Party*, in which a forty-year-old Dublin housewife dramatically reconfigures her life after discovering that her husband is having an affair. Francesca begins by confronting the lovers in a hotel and returns home

to mourn the loss of a seemingly perfect life. She had been quite happy with her banker husband, their two loving sons, comfortable home, and social position. In time, she breaks with the past by asking her husband for a divorce, finds new friends, and starts her own career.

Reviews of *Francesca's Party* described the novel as an enjoyable read that explored the highs and lows of the heroine's existence, blending humor and heartache. A *Kirkus Reviews* writer particularly enjoyed the scene when Francesca catches her philandering husband in the act, noting that "the victory of that moment for all wronged women is nearly worth the price of admission." Overall, the novel was judged to be "compelling enough to hold you till the end." In a review for *Library Journal*, Heather McCormack recommended the book to "fans of women's fiction and authors like Maeve Binchy." *Emigrant Online* contributor Pauline Ferrie called the novel "another eminently readable tale of love lost and found" and a "convincing story."

BIOGRAPHICAL AND CRITICAL SOURCES:

PERIODICALS

Kirkus Reviews, July 1, 2002, review of *Francesca's Party*, p. 914.
Library Journal, August, 2002, Heather McCormack, review of *Francesca's Party*, p. 146.
Publishers Weekly, July 20, 1992, review of *City Girl*, p. 244; September 26, 1994, review of *Finishing Touches*, p. 61.

ONLINE

Emigrant Online, http://www.bookviewireland.ie/ (March 17, 2003), Pauline Ferrie, review of *Francesca's Party*.*

*   *   *

SCHAFFNER, Ingrid 1961(?)-

PERSONAL: Born c. 1961. *Education:* Mount Holyoke College, B.A., 1983; New York University Institute of Fine Arts, M.A.

ADDRESSES: Home—20 Clinton St., No. 6E, New York, NY 10002.

CAREER: Curator and author. Independent curator based in New York NY; University of Pennsylvania Institute of Contemporary Art, Philadelphia, adjunct curator, 2001—.

AWARDS, HONORS: Whitney Museum Helena Rubinstein curatorial fellow.

WRITINGS:

(Editor, with Matthias Winzen) *Deep Storage: Collecting, Storing, and Archiving in Art,* Prestel (New York, NY), 1998.
(Editor, with Lisa Jacobs) *Julien Levy: Portrait of an Art Gallery,* MIT Press (Cambridge, MA), 1998.
The Essential Henri Matisse, Harry N. Abrams (New York, NY), 1998.
The Essential Vincent Van Gogh, Harry N. Abrams (New York, NY), 1998.
The Essential Andy Warhol, Harry N. Abrams (New York, NY), 1999.
The Essential Pablo Picasso, Harry N. Abrams (New York, NY), 1999.
Salvador Dalí's Dream of Venus: The Surrealist Funhouse from the 1939 World's Fair, photographs by Eric Schaal, Princeton Architectural Press (New York, NY), 2002.
Hannelore Baron: Works from 1969 to 1987, Smithsonian Institution Traveling Exhibition Service (Washington, DC), 2001.
The Essential Joseph Cornell, Harry N. Abrams (New York, NY), 2003.

Contributor of essays to exhibition catalogues.

SIDELIGHTS: Ingrid Schaffner prepared for her career as a curator by participating in the Whitney Museum of American Art's independent study program. Her writings have explored the work of curators, detailed the history of an art gallery, described an example of surrealist architecture, and provided introductions to several important artists.

As coeditor of *Deep Storage: Collecting, Storing, and Archiving in Art,* Schaffner reflects on the commonalities between the work of curators and the work of art-ists: while the museum makes choices about what to collect and retain, each individual piece of artwork itself involves choices by the artist from among collected materials and experiences.

While the importance of curators in art history has been acknowledged and documented, the contributions of art dealers largely has not, according to Francis M. Naumann in an *Artforum International* review of *Julien Levy: Portrait of an Art Gallery.* Naumann pointed out that the book, coedited by Schaffner, works to redress this omission in art history scholarship. Schaffner's own essay, included in the collection, "provides the most complete account yet of Levy's activities during the years in which his gallery was open," according to Naumann. Levy began his career selling photographs in a Madison Avenue storefront gallery he opened in 1931. Several months later he held New York's first exhibition dedicated to surrealism, and over the next seventeen years he showed the work of, among others, Jean Cocteau, Joseph Cornell, Salvador Dalí, Paul Delvaux, René Magritte, Pablo Picasso, and Yves Tanguy. *Julien Levy* was intended to serve as a catalogue to the art exhibition of the same title organized by Schaffner and co-curator Lisa Jacobs at New York City's Equitable Gallery; the book, like the exhibit, loosely follows the thematic organization Levy employed in his own writings on surrealism.

Schaffner returns to the topic of surrealism in her next work, *Salvador Dalí's Dream of Venus: The Surrealist Funhouse from the 1939 World's Fair.* Here Schaffner centers her text on a series of photographs taken of the structure designed by Salvador Dalí and erected in New York for the 1939 World's Fair. The "funhouse"—long since torn down—featured a two-story reproduction of Botticelli's painting "Birth of Venus" and various sculptures of female torsos and legs protruding from the building's pink-and-white exterior. Inside were the "living liquid ladies," topless women wearing mermaid costumes and swimming in tanks. This display created much controversy, some of it captured by Schaffner in quotes taken from newspaper articles of the time. Eugene Burt, in a review of *Salvador Dalí's Dream of Venus* for *Library Journal,* noted that Schaffner's is "the only book to document this little-known creation."

In addition to her work on overlooked areas in art, Schaffner has produced a number of guides to the art-world's best-known figures. Her books on Vincent van

Gogh, Pablo Picasso, and others for the "Essential . . ." series present readable, colorful texts on these major artists.

BIOGRAPHICAL AND CRITICAL SOURCES:

PERIODICALS

Artforum International, February, 1999, Francis M. Naumann, review of *Julien Levy: Portrait of an Art Gallery,* pp. 19-21.
Library Journal, February 15, 2003, Eugene C. Burt, review of *Salvador Dalí's Dream of Venus: The Surrealist Funhouse from the 1939 World's Fair,* p. 135.
School Arts, December, 1999, Ken Marantz, review of "Essential . . ." series, p. 48.

ONLINE

Mount Holyoke College Web site, http://www. mtholyoke.com/ (June 9, 2003).*

* * *

SCHAPPELL, Elissa

PERSONAL: Married Ron Spillman; children: two. *Education:* New York University, M.F.A. (creative writing).

ADDRESSES: Home—Brooklyn, NY. *Agent*—c/o Author Mail, Morrow/HarperCollins, East 53rd St., 7th Floor, New York, NY 10022.

CAREER: Writer and editor.

AWARDS, HONORS: Best Book of the Year, *Los Angeles Times,* 2000, for *Use Me.*

WRITINGS:

Use Me (fiction), Morrow (New York, NY), 2000.

Vanity Fair, New York, NY, contributing editor; *Tin House,* founding coeditor; contributor to numerous magazines, including *GQ, Vogue, Bomb, Bookforum,* and *Spin.*

WORK IN PROGRESS: A second novel.

SIDELIGHTS: A longtime editor and freelance magazine writer, Elissa Schappell collected ten interrelated stories in her first book, *Use Me.* The book focuses primarily on Evie Wakefield, a woman who defines herself by her need for a man's love. The book traces her life from the time she is a young woman on through her thirties, when she marries and becomes a mother. Evie's relationship with the opposite sex and especially her father, who is waging a losing battle against cancer, are the pivotal themes that thematically drive the stories. "The narrative presents a world in which all love has its sexual element, and in which the relationship between a father and daughter can define the daughter's entire life," wrote a reviewer in *Publishers Weekly.*

The book also features Evie's college friend Mary Beth McEvoy, who, unlike Evie, has a tenuous and unfulfilling relationship with her parents. In many ways, Mary Beth acts as a counterpoint to Evie. For example, whereas a teenager Evie is depicted as somewhat innocent, the wild and sophisticated Mary Beth had three abortions before she was eighteen years old. Furthermore, her uncaring mother taught her how to purge after eating so that she can maintain a slim figure. Nevertheless, just like Evie, Mary Beth also needs a man's love to fill the emptiness she feels inside.

Some reviewers commented that Schappell provides a stereotypical and traditional view of women. Writing in *Washington Post Book World,* Carolyn See said, "*Use Me* is utterly traditional; it goes back 50 years, straight to Salinger's *Uncle Wiggly in Connecticut,* where loveless women have nothing to do but get roaring drunk on a dark suburban afternoon. What else could they possibly do?" Nevertheless, See noted that the stories are "beautifully written." Several other reviewers also praised Schappell's writing. Commenting on the story "Try an Outline," *Library Journal* contributor Nancy Pearl noted that "the writing is evocative and the narrative voice rings true." Emily Eakin, writing in *Us,* said that Schappell "layers Evie's story poetically." In the *New York Times Book Review,* Cathleen Schine noted, "Schappell's prose is agile and deft, and her sentences sound like the riffs of a recklessly funny friend." *Salon.com* contributor Stephanie Zacharek praised Schappell as "artful at integrating the story's multiple layers." Zacharek concluded, "Lively without ever stumbling over its own cleverness, funny without being smart-alecky, *Use Me* is a story about growing up that's written for grown-ups—the kind who realize that getting there wasn't even half the battle."

Schappell says that some of Evie's story is based on her own life in that she had a loving family and her father died. Nevertheless, she stresses that the book is not autobiographical and warned that, in general, readers can draw more from a novel when they don't concern themselves with a book's possible autobiographical elements. "People like to think things are autobiographical," Schappell said in an interview with Ron Hogan on the *Beatrice* Web site. "But I also think it stops readers from becoming completely engaged in the work."

BIOGRAPHICAL AND CRITICAL SOURCES:

PERIODICALS

Booklist, March, 2000, Michelle Kaske, review of *Use Me,* p. 1197.
Library Journal, March 15, 2000, Nancy Pearl, review of *Use Me,* p. 130.
New York Times Book Review, April 9, 2000, Cathleen Schine, review of *Use Me,* p. 10.
People, April 24, 2000, David Cobb Craig, review of *Use Me,* p. 49.
Publishers Weekly, January 24, 2000, review of *Use Me,* p. 290.
Us, April 10, 2000, Emily Eakin, review of *Use Me,* p. 48.
Village Voice, March 28, 2000, Kera Bolonik, review of *Use Me,* p. 62.
Washington Post Book World, February 25, 2000, Carolyn See, review of *Use Me,* p. C8.

ONLINE

Beatrice, http://www.beatrice.com/ (November 17, 2003), Ron Hogan, interview with Elissa Schappell.

Salon.com, http://www.salon.com/ (March 14, 2000), Stephanie Zacharek, review of *Use Me.**

*   *   *

SCHIFFMAN, Stephan

PERSONAL: Male.

ADDRESSES: Office—DEI Management Group, 888 Seventh Avenue, 9th Floor, New York, NY 10010. *E-mail*—contactus@dei-sales.com.

CAREER: Business consultant and author. DEI Management Group, New York, NY, founder and president. Speaker on radio and television programs.

WRITINGS:

The Consultant's Handbook: How to Start and Develop Your Own Practice, B. Adams (Boston, MA), 1988.
Power Sales Presentations: Complete Sales Dialogues for Each Critical Step of the Sales Cycle: Qualifying, Interviewing, Presentation, Closing, B. Adams (Boston, MA), 1989.
Cold Calling Techniques That Really Work, B. Adams (Boston, MA), 1987, fourth edition, 2000.
The Twenty-five Sales Habits of Highly Successful Salespeople, B. Adams (Holbrook, MA), 1991.
Stephan Schiffman's Telemarketing, B. Adams (Holbrook, MA), 1992, revised as *Stephen Schiffman's Telesales,* Adams Media (Avon, MA), 2002.
Closing Techniques That Really Work!, B. Adams (Holbrook, MA), 1994, third edition, 2004.
The Twenty-five Most Common Sales Mistakes—And How to Avoid Them, Adams Publishing (Holbrook, MA), 1995.
High-efficiency Selling: How Superior Salespeople Get That Way, Wiley (New York, NY), 1997.
Make It Your Business: The Definitive Guide to Launching, Managing, and Succeeding in Your Own Business, Pocket Books (New York, NY), 1998.
The Twenty-five Sales Strategies That Will Boost Your Sales Today!, Adams Media (Holbrook, MA), 1999.

Make It Happen before Lunch: Fifty Cut-to-the-Chase Strategies for Getting the Business Results You Want, McGraw-Hill (New York, NY), 2000.

Getting to "Closed," Dearborn Trade (Chicago, IL), 2002.

Sales Just Don't Happen: Twenty-six Proven Strategies to Increase Sales in Any Market, Dearborn Financial (Chicago, IL), 2002.

Twenty-five Sales Skills They Don't Teach You at Business School, Adams Media (Avon, MA), 2002.

The Young Entrepreneur's Guide to Business Terms, Franklin Watts (New York, NY), 2003.

The Twenty-five Most Dangerous Sales Myths, Adams Media (Avon, MA), 2004.

Author of sales-related videos and audiobooks, including *Getting Through: Cold Calling Techniques to Get Your Foot in the Door,* 1994. Contributor of articles to periodicals.

SIDELIGHTS: Stephan Schiffman is a certified management consultant who has become one of the top corporate sales trainers in the United States. Schiffman is the author of a number of books, videos, and audiobooks that focus on effective selling techniques, including *Cold Calling Techniques That Really Work!, Twenty-five Sales Skills They Don't Teach You at Business School,* and *Stephan Schiffman's Telesales.* Commenting on Schiffman's audiobook *Getting Through: Cold Calling Techniques to Get Your Foot in the Door,* Nancy Spillman explained in a *Booklist* review that "Schiffman projects vitality and enthusiasm as he relates to aspiring salespeople his proven strategies for increasing income, sales, and promotions."

A reviewer for the *Dallas Business Journal* said that while little enthusiasm exists for cold-calling business prospects, Schiffman's *Cold Calling Techniques That Really Work!* "simplifies the basic techniques aimed to warm staff to the art of cold calling." Schiffman believes that in the future, most cold calls will be made over the telephone, and he outlines the five steps to success in this area. Among Schiffman's suggestions is to keep the conversation on a positive note by asking the potential customer questions that will elicit a "Yes" answer.

Reviewers complemented the style, strategies, and comprehensive information found in *Cold Calling Techniques That Really Work!* Jeffrey D. Smith noted

in *Sales and Marketing Management* that Schiffman "also includes sound advice on overcoming objections, reaching the decision maker, and self-motivation, as well as an appendix containing complete scripts for phone techniques." Smith concluded that "If you really want to sell, this book will provide you with a wealth of ideas to improve your cold-calling techniques."

BIOGRAPHICAL AND CRITICAL SOURCES:

PERIODICALS

Booklist, January 15, 1994, Nancy Spillman, review of *Getting Through: Cold Calling Techniques to Get Your Foot in the Door* (sound recording), p. 955.
Dallas Business Journal, January 28, 2000, review of *Cold Calling Techniques That Really Work!,* p, 69.
Library Journal, Mark Guyer, November 1, 1998, review of *Make It Your Business,* p. 137.
Philadelphia Business Journal, November 23, 2001, review of *Cold Calling Techniques That Really Work!,* p. 21.
Sales and Marketing Management, November 1991, Jeffrey D. Smith, review of *Cold Calling Techniques That Really Work!,* p. 118.

ONLINE

DEI Management Group Web site, http://www.dei-sales.com (November 16, 2003).*

*   *   *

SCHNEIDER, Herman 1905-2003

OBITUARY NOTICE—See index for *CA* sketch: Born May 31, 1905, in Kreschov, Poland; died July 31, 2003, in Boston, MA. Educator and author. Schneider is best remembered as the author of dozens of science books for children and teenagers. After immigrating with his family to America from Poland, he was educated at the Free Academy (now City College of the City University of New York), where he earned a B.S. in 1928 and an M.S. in 1930. He began teaching in New York City public schools in 1928, becoming a science supervisor in 1948, and from 1941 to 1946 he was also an instructor at Bank Street College. Schneider began publishing science books for children in the 1940s, many of them cowritten with his wife, Nina. Among these titles are *How Big Is Big?: From Stars to Atoms, a Yardstick for the Universe* (1946; revised edition, 1959), *Rocks, Rivers, and the Changing Earth: A First Book about Geology* (1952), *Science around You* (1966), and *Secret Magnets* (1979). He also wrote a number of books by himself, such as *Everyday Machines and How They Work* (1950) and *Laser Light* (1978), the latter winning the award for best science book for teenagers from the New York Academy of Sciences. In addition to teaching and writing, Schneider served as a consultant for filmstrips published by University Films, Inc.

OBITUARIES AND OTHER SOURCES:

PERIODICALS

Los Angeles Times, August 7, 2003, p. B13.
New York Times, August 6, 2003, p. A17.

*   *   *

SCHOEMAKER, Paul J. H. 1949-

PERSONAL: Born 1949, in Deventer, Netherlands; son of Paul (an entrepreneur) and Betty Vaessen (a homemaker) Schoemaker; married Joyce A. Maggiore (a microbiologist, educator, and writer), July 14, 1973. *Ethnicity:* "Caucasian." *Education:* University of Notre Dame, B.S., (magna cum laude), 1972; Wharton School, University of Pennsylvania, M.B.A. (finance), 1974, M.A. (management), Ph.D. (decision sciences). *Politics:* "Compassionate Conservatism." *Religion:* Catholic (non-practicing). *Hobbies and other interests:* Piano playing, tennis, and golf. Enjoy ethnic cuisines with good intellectual conversation.

ADDRESSES: Office—Department of Marketing, The Wharton School, University of Pennsylvania, 700 Jon M. Huntsman Hall, 3730 Walnut Street, Philadelphia, PA 19104-6340. *E-mail*—schoemak@Wharton.upenn. edu.

CAREER: University of Pennsylvania, Philadelphia, Emerging Technologies Management Research program, instructor and director, 1974—; University of

Chicago, Chicago, IL, professor in graduate school of business, 1980s; Decision Strategies International, Inc., West Conshohocken, PA, founder, chairman, and CEO, 1990—; Visiting professor, London Business School; consultant. Member of board for OmniChoice, RealHome, TLContact, Open, and VS Holdings.

AWARDS, HONORS: American Assembly for Collegiate Schools of Business Annual Western Electric Fund Award; S.S. Huebner Foundation for Insurance Education grant; National Science Foundation, Decision and Management Program grant; Best Paper Prize of the Strategic Management Society, 2000.

WRITINGS:

Experiments on Decisions under Risk: The Expected Utility Hypothesis, Martinus Nijhoff Publishers (Boston, MA), 1980.
(With J. Edward Russo) *Decision Traps: Ten Barriers to Brilliant Decision-making and How to Overcome Them,* Doubleday/Currency (New York, NY), 1989.
(With Paul R. Kleindorfer and Howard C. Kunreuther) *Decision Sciences: An Integrative Perspective,* Cambridge University Press (New York, NY), 1993.
(Editor with George S. Day and Robert E. Gunther) *Wharton on Managing Emerging Technologies,* Wiley (New York, NY), 2000.
(With J. Edward Russo) *Winning Decisions: Getting It Right the First Time,* Currency (New York, NY), 2002.
(With Robert E. Gunther) *Profiting from Uncertainty: Strategies for Succeeding No Matter What the Future Brings,* Free Press (New York, NY), 2002.

Contributor, *The Quest for Optimality,* edited by Jean H. P. Paelinck, Gower Publishing Company (Brookfield, VT), 1984. Author of more than seventy academic and applied papers in such publications as *Harvard Business Review, Journal of Mathematical Psychology, Management Science,* and *Journal of Economic Literature.*

SIDELIGHTS: Paul J. H. Schoemaker, with a doctorate in decision sciences, has specialized in strategic planning and executive development. His books on decision making have attracted wide notice and contributed to his reputation as a creative thinker on the subject of uncertainty in business.

For twelve years, Schoemaker taught seminars at the University of Chicago's Center for Decision Research. At that time, in the 1980s, his book *Experiments on Decisions under Risk: The Expected Utility Hypothesis,* was, according to *Fortune* contributor Ira Horowitz, "probably the best book-length guide for managers trying to get a handle on the promises and pitfalls of EU." Horowitz explained that "EU", or "expected utility," was then the main topic of debate at most business schools. EU is concerned with the question: "How can one go about making optimal decisions in situations characterized by risk and uncertainty?" In his book, as R. K. Sarin pointed out in *Engineering Economist,* Schoemaker discovers that "people's choices often violate the principles of expected utility theory" and concludes that the theory might not work in the real world because individuals do not necessarily act rationally when thinking about risk. So although the theory makes for lively classroom discussions, it might not work in life as well as it is predicted to do.

In 2000 Schoemaker, then a professor at the Wharton School at the University of Pennsylvania and director of the school's Emerging Technologies Management Research program, helped edit *Wharton on Managing Emerging Technologies.* The book makes clear that new technologies will demand new business skills. "Whether they like it or not," wrote LaRoi Lawton for *Journal of Organizational Excellence,* the book shows that business managers and executives are going to have to get not only used to, but competent with, the technologies of the Internet and the emerging field of biotechnologies. "Since the game is different, a different set of management skills, outlines, and plans are needed," wrote Lawton. Although he found the book to be "coldly written," Justin Koherty wrote in *Telecomworldwire* that "This book teaches the reader how to grasp and ride the mechanical bronco bull that is emerging technologies."

Schoemaker co-authored his next book, *Winning Decisions: Getting It Right the First Time,* with J. Edward Russo, a business school professor at Cornell University. In this publication, Schoemaker attempts to break decision making down to four major steps: framing the decision; gathering information about that decision; coming to conclusions; and finally analyzing the experience. Schoemaker draws on case studies to

highlight the individual steps, and includes worksheets that readers can use to work through the steps themselves. This is "an outstanding book" that "makes a comprehensive analytical tool," wrote a reviewer for *Booklist.* In a review for *Inc.* Paul B. Brown referred to the book as "one of the few business books published in 2001 that's worth the cover price."

In *Profiting from Uncertainty: How to Succeed No Matter What the Future Brings,* written with Robert E. Gunther, Schoemaker points out that "Uncertainty cannot be pinned down or coaxed into cages." In other words, in the fast-changing world of contemporary business, executives must learn to live with uncertainty. Schoemaker helps them make the best of it by advising them to plan for multiple future scenarios. He author also states that up to fifty percent of the successes of most businesses is due to general economic and industry conditions; that is, things that are beyond the control of management. Although Schoemaker admits that managers cannot predict the future, he does state that they can better prepare themselves for uncertainty. Rather than looking to business models of the past, managers must plan for many possible futures, giving them a better chance to succeed. They must be fully aware of the uncertainties of their businesses and know how they can best profit from them.

"Obstacles create opportunities, in his view," wrote Stephanie Overby for *CIO.com.* Overby concluded that Schomaker's book is "requisite reading for corporate decision makers." The book outlines four steps that can help managers to make the most of their decisions. First they must prepare for the unknown. Then they must create a clear vision of how the company will compete in all the possible future scenarios. Next, managers must build flexibility into their plans. Their companies must be able to adjust quickly to the inevitable changes in the economy and in the market. And finally, managers must be aware of what those potential changes might be. In an article posted on the *WallStraits Web site,* a reviewer stated: "If you are interested in learning how to build visions of multiple futures to help take advantage of an uncertain future for your business . . . this book will give you a solid foundation to build on with concrete ideas and methods to explore."

BIOGRAPHICAL AND CRITICAL SOURCES:

PERIODICALS

Booklist, November 1, 2001, review of *Winning Decisions: Getting It Right the First Time,* pp. 451-452.

Choice, March 1981, review of *Experiments on Decisions under Risk,* p. 994.

Engineering Economist, winter, 1983, R. K. Sarin, review of *Experiments on Decisions under Risk,* pp. 170-171.

Fortune, April 19, 1982, Ira Horowitz, review of *Experiments on Decisions under Risk,* pp. 201-202, 204.

Inc., February 1, 2002, Paul B. Brown, review of *Winning Decisions.*

Journal of Organizational Excellence, spring, 2001, LaRoi Lawton, review of *Wharton on Managing Emerging Technologies,* pp. 99-100.

Publishers Weekly, November 5, 2001, review of *Winning Decisions,* p. 56; June 3, 2002, review of *Profiting from Uncertainty: How to Succeed No Matter What the Future Brings,* p. 77.

Research-Technology Management, September, 2000, review of *Wharton on Managing Emerging Technologies,* p. 61.

Telecomworldwire, October 12, 2000, Justin Doherty, review of *Wharton on Managing Emerging Technologies.*

ONLINE

CIO.com, http://www.cio.com/ (January 7, 2002), Stephanie Overby, "The Upside of Uncertainty."

WallStrait Web sites, http://www.wallstraits.com/ (January 7, 2003), review of *Profiting from Uncertainty.*

*   *   *

SCHONBERG, Harold C(harles) 1915-2003
(Newgate Callendar)

OBITUARY NOTICE—See index for CA sketch: Born November 29, 1915, in New York, NY; died July 26, 2003, in New York, NY. Editor, critic, and author. Schonberg was a nationally renowned, Pulitzer Prize-winning music and literary critic who wrote for the *New York Times* for three decades. He was a graduate of Brooklyn College, where he earned his A.B. in 1937, and of New York University, where he received his master's degree in 1938. Schonberg's love of music began at a very young age; he was just four years old when he began to learn to play the piano and soon discovered that he could easily remember entire pieces after hearing them only once. Athe age of twelve he

was mesmerized by his first trip to the Metropolitan Opera, where he watched a performance of Richard Wagner's *Meistersinger.* He later declared that it was on that day that he decided to pursue a career as a music critic, a plan that first saw reality when he was an undergraduate student writing reviews for the *Musical Advance.* After completing his master's degree, he became assistant editor of *American Music Lover* (later renamed *American Record Guide*). With the onset of World War II, Schonberg enlisted in the U.S. Army Signal Corps, where he was a decoder and later a parachutist. He returned to civilian life in 1946 to become a contributing editor to *Musical Digest* and assistant music critic for the *New York Sun;* he was also a contributing editor and columnist for *Musical Courier* from 1948 to 1952. Schonberg joined the *New York Times* staff in 1950 as a music and record critic, becoming senior music critic from 1960 until his retirement in 1980. As a music critic, he lent his prodigious knowledge of the musical world to his articles, though he modestly maintained that music criticism should always be considered a matter of the writer's (hopefully educated) opinion and not the authoritative, final word on a piece of music or a performance. Schonberg's spare, to-the-point style was clear, informative, and unembellished when writing reviews, but more leisurely when writing longer pieces on a particular area of music for the newspapers Sunday column. For his excellence in criticism, he was awarded the 1971 Pulitzer Prize. In addition to music, Schonberg was very knowledgeable about chess, and he reported on the famous Boris Spassky vs. Bobby Fisher match in 1972 and the Garry Kasparov vs. Anatoly Karpov match in 1984. He also wrote many literary reviews for the *New York Times* under the pen name Newgate Callendar. Schonberg completed eleven books during his career, including *The Great Pianists* (1963; revised edition, 1987), *The Great Conductors* (1967), *Grandmasters of Chess* (1973; revised edition, 1981), and *The Virtuosi: Classical Music's Great Performers from Paganini to Pavarotti* (1988). After his retirement from the *New York Times,* he continued to contribute reviews to the newspaper, as well as to such publications as *American Record Guide* and *Classical Record Reviewer.*

OBITUARIES AND OTHER SOURCES:

BOOKS

Ward, Martha E., and others, editors, *Authors of Books for Young People,* third edition, Scarecrow Press (Metuchen, NJ), 1990.

Writers Directory, 18th edition, St. James Press (Detroit, MI), 2003.

PERIODICALS

Los Angeles Times, July 28, 2003, p. B9.
New York Times, July 28, 2003, p. A18.
Times (London, England), August 4, 2003.
Washington Post, July 28, 2003, p. B5.

* * *

SCHROTH, Richard J.

PERSONAL: Male. *Education:* Western Illinois University, B.A., University of Illinois, M.A., Indiana University, Ph.D.

ADDRESSES: Office—c/o Perot Systems, 2300 West Plano Parkway, Plano, TX 75075. *Agent*—c/o Rhoda Dunn, Random House (Crown Books), 1745 Broadway, New York, NY 10019.

CAREER: Management consultant and technology strategist. Marriott Corporation, senior vice president and chief technology officer; Index Vanguard, founding member; CSC Research, senior vice president; Index Research and Advisory Services, senior vice president; Executive Insights, Ltd., president and CEO; Executive Viewpoints, Inc, president and CEO; Perot Systems Corporation, chief technology officer, 2001—. Member, A.T.& T. Executive Education faculty; Net-Base Corporation, member of board of directors, 2000—.

AWARDS, HONORS: Western Illinois University, Outstanding Alumni of the Year, 1989; Indiana University, Outstanding Alumni of the Year, 1996; Aresty Institute, Wharton School, University of Pennsylvania, senior fellow.

WRITINGS:

(With A. Larry Elliott) *How Companies Lie: Why Enron Is Just the Tip of the Iceberg,* Crown Publishers (New York, NY), 2002.

SIDELIGHTS: Richard J. Schroth has worked as a management consultant and technology strategist for more than thirty years, advising and directing some of the world's top executives of the largest international companies. Among his customers are General Electric, Pfizer Pharmaceuticals, Monsanto Corporation, Bank One Corporation, and Royal Dutch/Shell. One of his first positions was with the Marriott Corporation. Later, he founded his own company and most recently has joined Ross Perot's company, Perot Systems Corporation, as chief technology officer. Schroth is well known as a leading nationwide consultant of emerging technologies and is well informed on the topic of how businesses succeed and fail. With this background, he has joined with co-author A. Larry Elliott and produced *How Companies Lie: Why Enron Is Just the Tip of the Iceberg,* a book that teaches investors how to evaluate those corporations.

In the late 1990s few Americans knew who or what Enron was, but within only a few years Enron was synonymous for corporate greed and corruption. It was one of the first companies to be exposed as having lied about its profits in order to secure investors. Using deceitful accounting practices, Enron inflated its worth to lure investors, then abruptly announced bankruptcy. Investors lost everything. Subsequent investigations showed that other companies were employing the same fraudulent accounting systems. Investors began to ask who they could trust.

According to a *Publishers Weekly* writer, Schroth argues that many corporations have so manipulated investors' perceptions of their worth "that the stock market has become little more reliable than a casino." Enron was not the first company to do so, and according to Schroth, it will hardly be the last. He states that since almost fifty percent of American households buy stock in large corporations, it is essential to restore trust to the practice of investing. Yet a remedy, Schroth writes, will be difficult to achieve. "Lies and deception at their basest level help the inner circle achieve personal goals of greed and cover up their incompetence as executives," he writes, citing dishonest accounting practices in such companies as Cendant, Waste Management, Sunbeam, Global Crossing, and Tyco International.

To help investors, Schroth offers a checklist of indicators that might signal financial corruption of a particular company. These include an abrupt turnover at key executive positions of the company; insider stock trading in large volumes; restatements of earnings; reduction in shareholder equity; elaborate compensation and stock option plans; sudden downgrades in credit ratings; and withdrawals of hedge funds. However, Schroth points out that no checklist will provide foolproof evidence. He states that fraudulent companies will adjust their plans to make their false accounting practices less easily detected. "Keeping up with the indicators of lies and deception," write Schroth, "is like trying to paint a moving train." To balance this out, he suggests that investors need to ask "hard, even rude, questions."

BIOGRAPHICAL AND CRITICAL SOURCES:

PERIODICALS

Publishers Weekly, June 3, 2002, review of *How Companies Lie: Why Enron Is Just the Tip of the Iceberg,* p. 82.

ONLINE

Frontline Web site, http://www.pbs.org/ (April 15, 2003), "Question Investors Need to Ask."*

*   *   *

SCHWARTZ, Herman 1931-

PERSONAL: Born December 19, 1931, in Brooklyn, NY; son of Jacob and Rose Schwartz; married Mary Cahn, November 20, 1960; children: Susan, Daniel (deceased). *Education:* Harvard University, A.B. (magna cum laude), 1953, J.D., 1956. *Religion:* Jewish. *Hobbies and other interests:* Reading, opera, music.

ADDRESSES: Home—4619 Chevy Chase Blvd., Chevy Chase, MD 20815. *Office*—American University, Washington College of Law, 4801 Massachusetts Ave., Washington, DC 20016. *E-mail*—hschwar@wcl.american.edu.

CAREER: Professor of law, Constitutional scholar, and human rights activist. Admitted to the Bar of the State of New York, 1957; State University of New York,

Buffalo, professor of law, 1966-77; State of New York Commission of Correction, Albany, chairman, 1975-76; U.S. Senate, Washington, DC, chief counsel of Citizen's Subcommittee, 1977-78; U.S. Treasury, Washington, DC, chief counsel of revenue sharing, 1978-79; U.S. Senate Antitrust Subcommittee, Washington, chief counsel, 1979-80; American University, Washington College of Law, Washington, DC, professor of law, 1982—, codirector of Human Rights Center. Advisor and consultant; member of U.S. delegations to United Nations human rights commission conferences on human rights; member of boards, including the Foundation for a Civil Society, Congressional Human Rights Foundation, Chair, national Law Center on homelessness and poverty, 2001-2003; Executive Committee Justice Initiative, Open Society Institute, 2002—; and Helsinki Watch.

MEMBER: American Civil Liberties Union (founder, of prisoners' rights project, 1969), American Law Institute.

AWARDS, HONORS: American Civil Liberties Union-Niagara Frontier Award for civil liberties work, 1972; William Conable Award for civil rights, 1974; award for outstanding work in the field of corrections, New York State Bar Association, Criminal Justice Section, 1976; Medgar Evers Award, National Association for the Advancement of Colored People, Buffalo, NY, for contribution to integrated education, 1976; certificate of commendation for community contribution, City of Buffalo, 1977; Citizens Counsel for Human Rights Award, Buffalo, 1982.

WRITINGS:

(Editor and author of introduction) *The Burger Years: Rights and Wrongs in the Supreme Court, 1969-1986,* Viking (New York, NY), 1987.
Packing the Courts: The Conservative Campaign to Rewrite the Constitution, Scribner (New York, NY), 1988.
The Struggle for Constitutional Justice in Post-Communist Europe, University of Chicago Press (Chicago, IL), 2000.
(Editor) *The Rehnquist Court: Judicial Activism on the Right,* Hill and Wang (New York, NY), 2002.

Author of reports, including, with wife, Mary C. Schwartz, *Prison Conditions in Poland,* 1988; with Mary C. Schwartz, *Prison Conditions in Czechoslova-*

kia, 1989; with Robert Kushen and Abner J. Mikva, *Prison Conditions in the Soviet Union: A Report of Facilities in Russia and Azerbaidzhan,* 1991; with Joanna Weschler, *Prison Conditions in Poland: An Update,* 1991; all Human Rights Watch (New York, NY); and *Property Rights and the Constitution: Will the Ugly Duckling Become a Swan?* Washington Institute Press (Washington, DC), 1987. Contributor to journals and periodicals, including *Harvard Law Review, Yale Law Journal, Michigan Law Review, University of Chicago Law Review, Los Angeles Times, Newsday,* and the *New York Times.*

WORK IN PROGRESS: Right Wing Justice, due spring, 2004.

SIDELIGHTS: Herman Schwartz is a professor of law, a Constitutional scholar, and a strong proponent of civil and human rights, including prisoners' rights. In 1971, he acted as an observer at the Attica Prison riot, and he served on the Commission of Corrections of New York State. Schwartz is the author and editor of a number of volumes that focus on his field of interest, particularly Constitutional law. He has advised numerous former Soviet-bloc nations and others in Africa and Central America on constitutional and legal reform and drafting.

As editor of *The Burger Years: Rights and Wrongs in the Supreme Court, 1969-1986,* he presents fifteen retrospective essays by various authors who study the work of the U.S. Supreme Court during Warren E. Burger's seventeen years as chief justice. Rodney A. Smolla wrote in the *New York Times Book Review* that "what the essays reveal is that the Burger Court has been for many years the Rehnquist Court," and commented that Schwartz, "in an excellent opening essay, sets the tone for the pieces that follow, a tone decidedly antagonistic to the Edwin Meese-William Rehnquist axis of jurisprudence. Mr. Schwartz and his contributors treat the Constitution as a document intended to invite what Representative Thaddeus Stevens in 1866 called the 'advancing progress of a higher morality.'"

One chapter concerns the court-access decisions of the Burger Court. Four chapters address First Amendment rights, and there are three on equality, three on criminal justice, and four are concerned with economic regulation. Decisions handed down by the Burger Court include those on abortion and others that reached

into the bedroom and the workplace. A *Kirkus Reviews* contributor wrote that "the record proceeds to assaults upon the *Miranda* warning, freedom of the press, the wall between church and state, and minority rights. It's generally dismal, according to the articulate libertarian experts." These include Sidney Zion and Yale Kamisar.

American Political Science Review critic Charles Lamb called the essays collected by Schwartz "well-written liberal critiques of conservative Supreme Court policy." "As would be expected," wrote Lamb, "they typically conclude that during the seventeen years under Chief Justice Burger, major strands of Warren Court policy tended to survive—although at times severely battered or altered. The two areas of legal policy identified as experiencing the most dramatic shift to the Right are access to federal courts and national security." The contributors also make predictions as to the trends they expect to see in the Rehnquist Court.

In *Packing the Courts: The Conservative Campaign to Rewrite the Constitution,* Schwartz studies appointments by President Reagan's judge pickers, not only to the U.S. Supreme Court, but also to trial and appellate courts, of those who shared his conservative views on such issues as school prayer, abortion, criminal justice, economic regulation, and the rights of criminal defendants, and how these appointments increased after the appointment of Edwin Meese as attorney general. Schwartz argues that Reagan used strict guidelines, choosing appointees whose positions against a woman's right to choose and for school prayer, for example, could be predetermined. *Choice* reviewer R. A. Carp noted that Schwartz "is extremely well-qualified to prepare this text."

Schwartz notes the inconsistencies of the legal agenda of Meese and other conservatives and how they ignored the original intent of the framers of the Constitution with regard to states' rights. Stuart Taylor, Jr. wrote in the *New York Times Book Review* that Schwartz "is on target with many criticisms. . . . This ideological filter not only broke with the long-established view that federal judges have a special duty to protect minorities against the abuses of majority rule, it weeded out some highly qualified Republican judicial candidates, awarded nominations to some mediocre candidates, and produced a tilt toward white males."

A *Kirkus Reviews* contributor called *Packing the Courts* "an unusually accessible book about the interplay of law and politics—and one that makes a persuasive case against the appointment of judges who ascend to the bench with heavy ideological baggage."

The Struggle for Constitutional Justice in Post-Communist Europe was called "a superior piece of research" by *Choice* reviewer A. R. Brunello. Schwartz provides an accounting of the role of the constitutional courts in reforming the political structures of such countries as Russia, Poland, Hungary, Bulgaria, and Slovakia. James L. Gibson wrote in *Law and Politics Book Review* that "those who are interested in understanding the behavior of constitutional courts in transitional regimes cannot afford to ignore this important book. . . . Professor Schwartz's analysis is carefully detailed and documented, comprehensive, informed by theory, and just simply fascinating."

Schwartz is editor of a collection of essays by seventeen Constitutional scholars that was published as *The Rehnquist Court: Judicial Activism on the Right,* further documenting the changes in the Supreme Court since the liberal Court of Chief Justice Earl Warren. The liberal essays were also published in *Nation* magazine. The most noteworthy decision that is discussed is the Court's five to four ruling in December 2000, giving the presidency to George W. Bush over Al Gore, Jr. Essayists include Susan Estrich, Charles Ogletree, Stephen Bright, Norman Redlich, and journalist Tom Wicker. *Library Journal's* Steven Puro called the volume an "excellent critical overview."

Topics include the free exercise of religion and church-state separation, the narrowing of the rights of the accused, gay rights, abortion, and freedom of speech. Scott Christianson reviewed the volume for *Empire Page* online, noting that "how the Court has dealt with the environment and civil rights is sufficient to curl your hair. We also lean how the tilt toward business interests and the retreat from corporate and securities regulation has opened the door to global abuses such as Enron and you-name-it. In the process, we get to see how internal inconsistencies and contradictions pop up between one area of law and another. Ultimately, the politics of it all obliterates any pretense of judicial independence, fairness, or justness."

BIOGRAPHICAL AND CRITICAL SOURCES:

PERIODICALS

American Political Science Review, March, 1988, Charles Lamb, review of *The Burger Years: Rights and Wrongs in the Supreme Court, 1969-1986,* pp. 304-305.

Booklist, July, 1988, review of *Packing the Courts: The Conservative Campaign to Rewrite the Constitution,* p. 1766; December 1, 2002, Vernon Ford, review of *The Rehnquist Court: Judicial Activism on the Right,* p. 633.

Choice, January, 1989, R. A. Carp, review of *Packing the Courts,* p. 875; January, 2001, A. R. Brunello, review of *The Struggle for Constitutional Justice in Post-Communist Europe,* p. 980.

Kirkus Reviews, March 15, 1987, review of *The Burger Years,* p. 461; May 15, 1988, review of *Packing the Courts,* pp. 750-751; September 15, 2002, review of *The Rehnquist Court,* p. 1372.

Law and Politics Book Review, December, 2000, James L. Gibson, review of *The Struggle for Constitutional Justice in Post-Communist Europe,* pp. 630-632.

National Catholic Reporter, February 7, 2003, Robert Drinan, review of *The Rehnquist Court,* p. 26.

New York Times Book Review, June 21, 1987, Rodney A. Smolla, review of *The Burger Years,* p. 18; December 11, 1988, Stuart Taylor, Jr., review of *Packing the Courts,* p. 33.

ONLINE

Empire Page, http://www.empirepage.com/ (January 14, 2003), Scott Christianson, review of *The Rehnquist Court.*

*   *   *

SCHWARTZ, Leslie (A.) 1962-

PERSONAL: Born 1962; daughter of Harvey and Mary Schwartz; married; children: a daughter. *Education:* University of California, Berkeley, B.A. (with honors), 1984. *Religion:* Jewish.

ADDRESSES: Home—2000 Riverside Dr., Los Angeles, CA 90026. *Office*—UCLA Extension Westwood, 1010 Westwood Blvd., Los Angeles, CA 90039. *Agent*—Henry Duncan, 27 West 20th St., New York, NY 10010. *E-mail*—LSchwartz62@earthlink.net.

CAREER: Novelist, journalist, and teacher. Council of Literary Magazines and Presses, reporter, 1990—; story analyst/script coverage consultant, 1992—; freelance editor, 1995—; University of California, Los

Angeles (UCLA), extension program, fiction writing instructor; PEN Center West's Emerging Voices, master class instructor; PEN in the Classroom, poetry instructor.

MEMBER: PEN Center West.

AWARDS, HONORS: Hedgebrook Writer's fellowship, 1994 and 1996; James Jones Literary Society Award for best first novel, 1999 for *Jumping the Green; Kalliope* Woman Writer of the Year, 2004.

WRITINGS:

Jumping the Green (novel), Simon & Schuster (New York, NY), 1999.
Angels Crest (novel), Doubleday (New York, NY), 2004.

Jumping the Green has been translated into several languages, including Hebrew and German. Contributor of numerous short stories and articles to magazines, including *Good Housekeeping, Los Angeles Times,* and *Self.*

SIDELIGHTS: Leslie Schwartz is an award-winning author and writing teacher whose first novel, *Jumping the Green,* examines love and loss within the family. The story revolves around up-and-coming sculptress Louise Goldblum, who comes from a dysfunctional family with alcoholic and abusive parents. When her beloved sister Esther is murdered, Louise seeks solace with a fellow artist, Zeke, who abuses Goldblum sexually and emotionally. Schwartz tells Louise's tale through alternating looks at the present and the past, including incidents when the younger Louise had to deal with her parents' emotional detachment and was exposed to violence and sex at a very young age. The adult Louise, who is also involved in drugs and drinks heavily, struggles as she realizes she is on a road to self-destruction that threatens not only her promising career but also her life.

Writing in *Library Journal,* Robin Nesbitt noted that the novel's depiction of sexual and physical abuse is "not for the weak of heart." Nesbitt went on to comment, "Erotic, sad, and thought-provoking, this intense story of love and families gone bad is a compelling

yet disturbing read." A contributor to *Publishers Weekly* commented that Schwartz handled the flashback chapters well and said that they "infuse the plot with a page-turning momentum, without sacrificing the elegance of Louise's gradually more penetrating introspection." Writing in the *Washington Post,* Laurie Foos generally praised the book and concluded, "It is a testament to Schwartz's gifts as a writer that the novel transcends clichés of violence and ultimately becomes a tale of survival, even in the most harrowing of circumstances."

Schwartz told *CA:* "I was always interested in writing. I always wrote, even as a little girl. Writing seemed natural to me, easier than trying to talk to people for sure. Nothing in particular made me decide one day that I wanted to be a writer. It was just something I always did.

"My students are my biggest influence on my work. They are so good and open and unscathed yet by the business of publishing. They write from such a raw and open-wound kind of place that it can't help but keep me honest. They remind me why I do it in the first place.

"My writing process has evolved over the years. At first I would write secretly in my room and never, ever, ever show anyone anything. But eventually I started to see the uselessness of that and after I 'came out' as a writer, I began to get more serious about how often I wrote. Now I try to write at least an hour every day, in the morning when it's the most still and quiet. And I walk every day in the hills behind my house with the dog, so I do a lot of writing there, working plot points out and discovering my characters. I don't believe in writers block. Sometimes, I just stop writing for a while. It's not a big, dramatic thing. I just need time away. I do require utter and complete silence when I write, though, which makes it hard sometimes in Los Angeles. If I even hear the slightest, tiniest sounds of music or conversation coming from a neighbor's house, I can't concentrate at all and I start eavesdripping or getting distracted and angry and wishing I lived deep in the unexplored forest. So I guess you could say my process requires silence. Also, I show my work to people. I have a group of trusted writers who read my pages in progress and critique my work. And usually before I sit down to write, I thank my creator for my talents and especially for my lack of talent. And I pray for help. Otherwise it feels too lonely.

"The most surprising thing I have learned as a writer . . . hmmm, there are so many. I think when I realized that gender is bunk, I could finally write from a man's point of view. I stopped thinking in generalitites and asked myself what do we all want? To be loved, to be unafraid, etc., etc. If you write from the point of view of an individual, gender doesn't matter. A man can cry just as much as a woman can throw a punch, that sort of thing. I've learned that sterotypes mean certain death for writers. I also realized that my imagination is fertile and alive and trustworthy, so I don't do much research anymore, which has been particularly freeing. I learned that working with young writers is enormously instructive for me. It keeps me humble. There is so much raw, undiscovered talent out there. It's amazing, really. I've learned not to be jealous or covetous of other people's talents. There's room for all of us."

BIOGRAPHICAL AND CRITICAL SOURCES:

PERIODICALS

Booklist, October 1, 1999, Nancy Pearl, review of *Jumping the Green,* p. 344.

Entertainment Weekly, November 19, 1999, Charles Winecoff, review of *Jumping the Green,* p. 139.

Library Journal, October 15, 1999, Robin Nesbitt, review of *Jumping the Green,* p. 108.

Los Angeles Times, November 14, 1999, Mark Rozzo, review of *Jumping the Green,* p. 10.

Publishers Weekly, August 9, 1999, review of *Jumping the Green,* p. 344.

Washington Post, December 12, 1999, Laurie Foos, review of *Jumping the Green,* p. 4:1.

ONLINE

Leslie Schwartz Home Page, http://www.leslieschwartz.com (November 18, 2003).

Writer's Register, http://www.writersregister.com/home.phtml (November 18, 2003), "Leslie Schwartz."*

*   *   *

SCHWARTZ, Ruth L. 1962-
(Judith Joyce)

PERSONAL: Born February 22, 1962, in Geneva, NY; daughter of George Schwartz (a physician and author) and Loretta Schwartz Nobel (an author). *Education:* University of Michigan, M.F.A., 1985; Wesleyan University, B.A., 1983.

ADDRESSES: Home—6035 Majestic Avenue, Oakland, CA 94605. *E-mail*—Ruthpoet@aol.com.

CAREER: San Mateo County AIDS Program, San Mateo, CA, program coordinator, 1992-94; Northern California Cancer Center Cancer Information Service, Union City, CA, cancer information specialist, 1994-96; Susan Ireland's Resume Service, Oakland, CA, resume writer, 1996-98; Cleveland State University, Cleveland, OH, assistant professor, 1998-2000; California State University—Fresno, assistant professor, 2000—.

AWARDS, HONORS: Associated Writing Programs competition winner, 1994, for *Accordion Breathing and Dancing;* Pablo Neruda Prize, *Nimrod* magazine, 1999; Anhinga Press Prize in Poetry, 2000, for *Singular Bodies,* and 2001, for *Edgewater.*

WRITINGS:

POETRY

Accordion Breathing and Dancing, University of Pittsburgh Press (Pittsburgh, PA), 1996.

Singular Bodies, Anhinga Press (Tallahassee, FL), 2001.

Edgewater, HarperCollins (New York, NY), 2002.

Some works published under pseudonmym Judith Joyce.

SIDELIGHTS: Ruth L. Schwartz told *CA:* "The theme of the body and its transformations—through eros, illness, disability, and death—figures prominently in my work. My ten years in AIDS and cancer education, and my close personal experience with kidney failure and transplantation, have profoundly informed my writing; so has my visceral awareness of the violence and alienation so prevalent in urban American life at the close of the twentieth century. Still, my belief in joy—and in the redemptive capacities of sexuality and love—is at the core of my poetry."

*   *   *

SCHWED, Peter 1911-2003

OBITUARY NOTICE—See index for *CA* sketch: Born January 18, 1911, in New York, NY; died July 31, 2003, in New York, NY. Editor, publisher, and author. Schwed was a former executive editor and publisher for Simon & Schuster. He attended Princeton University for two years, but left in his junior year to help support his family during the Great Depression. Getting a job at the Provident Loan Society of New York, he rose to the position of assistant vice president there. During World War II he joined the U.S. Army and fought in Europe, earning a Bronze Star and achieving the rank of captain. He left the military in 1945 to join Simon & Schuster as an editor. At the New York publishing house he was promoted to vice president and executive editor in 1957, publisher of trade books in 1966, and chair of the editorial board in 1972. Schwed was chair emeritus from 1982 to 1984 before leaving the company. While at Simon & Schuster, he earned a reputation as an editor who worked closely with authors such as P. G. Wodehouse and David McCullough, carefully shepherding their books through to publication. As an athlete who enjoyed playing tennis, he also published many books on sports by such stars as Jack Nicklaus, Ted Williams, and Björn Borg. Schwed was also the author of over a dozen books himself, including *Sinister Tennis: How to Play against and with Left-Handers* (1975), *Overtime!: A Twentieth-Century Sports Odyssey* (1987), *How to Talk Tennis* (1988), *Plum to Peter: Letters of P. G. Wodehouse to His Editor* (1996), and *Say, Could That Lad Be I?* (1998). He also wrote the autobiography *God Bless Pawnbrokers* (1975) and the fiction work *The Common Cold Crusade: A Novel Not to Be Sneezed At* (1994).

OBITUARIES AND OTHER SOURCES:

PERIODICALS

Los Angeles Times, August 6, 2003, p. B11.
New York Times, August 5, 2003, p. C13.

SCOTT, Harvey W(hitefield) 1838-1910

PERSONAL: Born February 1, 1838, near Peoria, IL; died August 7, 1910, in Baltimore, MD; son of John Tucker (a farmer) and Anne (Roelofson) Scott; married Elizabeth Nicklin, 1865 (died); married Margaret McChesney, 1876; children: (first marriage) two sons; (second marriage) three children. *Education:* Pacific University, B.A. (first degree ever awarded), 1863.

CAREER: Worked a variety of jobs to put himself through school, including woodcutting, team driving, and school teaching; *Portland Oregonian* (newspaper), editor, 1865-1910, owner from 1877; collector of customs in Portland, 1872-77; director of Associated Press, 1900-10. *Military service:* Washington Territory Volunteers, 1855-56, fought in the Yakima War.

MEMBER: Oregon Historical Society (president, 1898-1901); Lewis and Clark Exposition (president, 1903-04)

WRITINGS:

History of Portland, Oregon, D. Mason (Syracuse, NY), 1890.
Religion, Theology, and Morals, 2 volumes, compiled by Leslie M. Scott, Riverside Press (Cambridge, MD), 1917.
History of the Oregon Country (newspaper articles), 6 volumes, compiled by Leslie M. Scott, Riverside Press (Cambridge, MD), 1924.
Shakespeare (newspaper articles), compiled by Leslie M. Scott, Riverside Press (Cambridge, MD), 1928.

SIDELIGHTS: Harvey W. Scott was the most powerful newspaper owner and editorialist on the West Coast during the forty-five years he oversaw publication of the *Portland Oregonian,* from 1865 until his death in 1910. A lifelong habit of wide and voracious reading, together with a dedication to educating the pioneers of Oregon in matters of literature, religion, ethics, and history informed Scott's strongly opinionated daily editorials. Among his accomplishments is counted the transformation of Oregon from a Democratic into a predominantly Republican state; his editorials also championed the gold standard, opposed suffrage for blacks and women, fought the organization of labor and protective legislation for workers, and argued against the legal prohibition of alcohol.

Scott was one of nine children born in rural Illinois to farmers who valued the written word and encouraged their children to keep diaries. In 1852, the Scott family made the arduous journey west along the Oregon Trail, losing one of the children and Scott's mother to death along the way. They cleared land for a farm in the Willamette Valley of Oregon then moved to Puget Sound, Washington, in 1854, where another farm was established. Harvey Scott helped his father clear land, plant and harvest crops, and went to school in his spare time. For eight months, at the age of seventeen, he fought with the Washington Territory Volunteers against native Americans in the Yakima War of 1855-56, then enrolled in a college preparatory school. By 1859 he had finally earned enough credits to enroll in Pacific University, where, in 1863, he was awarded the first bachelor's degree bestowed there. Scott put himself through school by working as a teacher, team driver, and woodcutter. After graduation he continued for a time as a schoolteacher before moving to Portland, Oregon, to study law under Judge E. D. Shattuck and work as the first city librarian for the frontier town. When Shattuck was asked to write an editorial for the *Portland Oregonian,* he passed the job on to Scott, who wrote an impassioned diatribe on the subject of the assassination of President Abraham Lincoln. This early piece, which appeared April 17, 1865, "showed both his verbal strength and his youthful immoderation," wrote Lauren Kessler in the *Dictionary of Literary Biography.* Scott's experiences farming the frontier land, supporting himself through his education by dint of hard labor, his terms as schoolteacher and librarian exhibiting his love of learning and of books, are all themes that present themselves in analyses of Scott's editorial contributions to the *Oregonian* during the decades when he owned and ran the newspaper.

During his lifetime, Scott spoke movingly about the duty of newspapers to present their readers with facts about events of the day, but in practice he took little interest in the news section of the *Oregonian.* Kessler observed that "although he wrote of the responsibility of a newspaper to gather news and report on daily intelligence, Scott clearly regarded the news function of his paper as subordinate to his department, criticism and opinion." Scott's mission for his "department" of

the paper revealed itself over the decades primarily taking off from his self-appointed role as educator of a barely literate pioneer readership with little access to printed materials. "His job was to contribute to the cultural education of his pioneer readers by freely instructing them in morals, philosophy, theology, literature, and history," Kessler remarked. Furthermore, Kessler continued, "Scott's early pioneer experiences forged in him a rugged individualism which translated into a host of political beliefs he expounded for more than four decades." With an apparently indomitable belief in his own opinions, Scott expounded on subjects of his choosing in the only newspaper of consequence in the American Northwest, and did so without significant editorial opposition until the turn of the twentieth century.

Among Scott's favorite topics was regional history, which he hoped would help his readers "develop pride in their own past and grasp what for Scott was the ultimate historical lesson: hard work leads to success." In 1890 Scott edited and contributed to a *History of Portland, Oregon.* After his death, a son, Leslie M. Scott, collected his father's editorials, essays, and speeches on the history of Oregon into six volumes, titled *History of the Oregon Country.* Leslie Scott collected two volumes of his father's writings on religion in *Religion, Theology, and Morals,* and another volume full of Harvey Scott's writings on Shakespeare. Scott's outspokenness on these topics was matched by his opinionated stance on politics—local, state, and national. In the half century he wrote on the topic, he unfailingly supported the Republican ticket on matters of the day, speaking out for American expansionism, against Chinese immigration, against the organization of labor into unions and the institution of laws protecting workers, against the prohibition of alcohol—as detrimental to business interests—and for what was called "sound money," that is, adherence to the gold standard, an issue he fought over and over for three decades and for which he is attributed with carrying Oregon, alone among the western states.

By the turn of the twentieth century, however, Scott's opinions, particularly on political matters, were beginning to seem out of step with what a significant number of Oregonians believed. A rival newspaper, the *Oregon Journal,* with a Democrat at the helm, became the first serious competition Scott's *Oregonian* had ever experienced under his editorship. Scott came out strongly on issues such as initiative and referendum—which allowed ordinary citizens to place petitions on the ballot for the general populace to vote on—and direct primaries, both of which Scott opposed as detrimental to the interests of the Republican party and both of which were instituted in Oregon in the early years of the twentieth century. Scott was also against the enfranchisement of women, and through the power of his paper was able to see an amendment to the state constitution on the issue defeated in 1884, 1900, 1906, 1908, and 1910. The amendment passed in 1912, two years after Scott's death. Ironically, the crusade for the women's vote in Oregon was led by Scott's elder sister, Abigail Scott Duniway, who wrote, edited, and published a weekly pro-suffrage newspaper from 1871 to 1887 called the *New Northwest.* Her powerful brother's unstinting opposition to her cause, or, just as damaging, his refusal to comment on the issue in his paper at all, was inspired by his belief that women voters would support the kinds of government aid—for example in the form of workman's compensation—that Scott abhorred, and perhaps by a sense of competition he felt with an older sibling and fellow newspaper publisher. Despite some defeats in later years, at the time of his death in 1910, Scott "was the undisputed leader of Oregon journalism," Kessler wrote. In later years the editorialist was offered the prospect of several political positions, but, acknowledging the unprecedented power he held in print, would not consider stepping down into a post of mere political influence.

BIOGRAPHICAL AND CRITICAL SOURCES:

BOOKS

Dictionary of Literary Biography, Volume 23: *American Newspaper Journalists, 1873-1900,* Gale (Detroit, MI), 1983.
Downs, Robert B., and Jane B. Downs, *Journalists of the United States,* McFarland (Jefferson, NC), 1991.
Gaston, Joseph, *The Centennial History of Oregon, 1811-1912,* S. J. Clarke (Chicago, IL), 1912.
Horner, Joseph B., *Oregon History and Early Literature,* J. K. Gill (Portland, OR), 1919.
Notson, Robert C., *Making the Day Begin: A Story of the Oregonian,* Oregonian Publishing Co. (Portland, OR), 1976.
Portrait and Bibliographic Record of the Willamette Valley, Oregon, Chapman (Chicago, IL), 1903.

Turnbull, George S., *History of the Oregon Newspapers,* Binford & Mort (Portland, OR), 1939.

PERIODICALS

Journalism Quarterly, January, 1929, pp. 1-10; December, 1938, pp. 359-369.
Oregon Historical Quarterly, June, 1913, pp. 87-133; September, 1937, pp. 251-264; September, 1969, pp. 197-232.*

*   *   *

SEIDMAN, Richard

PERSONAL: Married. *Education:* State University of New York at Binghamton, B.A. (English); Lewis and Clark College, M.Ed. (teaching the deaf). *Hobbies and other interests:* World religions, environmental issues.

ADDRESSES: Home—924 Garden Way, Ashland, OR 97520. *E-mail*—info@oracleofkabbalah.com.

CAREER: Author and teacher of the deaf. Worked as a college writing instructor, technical writer, janitor, farm hand, and ice-cream pushcart vendor. Friends of Trees, founder, 1989, and advisory board member; advisory board member, Hawaii Ho'olau Hou, 1994-2002.

AWARDS, HONORS: Urban Forestry Medal, National Urban Forest Council; Community Hero, City of Portland, OR.

WRITINGS:

The Oracle of Kabbalah: Mystical Teachings of the Hebrew Letters, St. Martin's Press (New York, NY), 2001.

SIDELIGHTS: Richard Seidman's life has been a journey toward spiritual fulfillment. He spent many years as a practitioner of Zen Buddhism, although he was raised Jewish in Brooklyn, New York. For a while Seidman rejected Judaism, feeling it was limited and unsatisfying. Eventually he revisited the faith he had known as a child and began to see it in a different light. Seidman was drawn especially to the Kabbalah, a source of Jewish mysticism and in 2001 authored the book *The Oracle of Kabbalah: Mystical Teachings of the Hebrew Letters.*

During the 1990s, after an enlightening experience at a friend's seder meal, Seidman began studying with Rabbi Aryeh Hirschfield, a renown musician, song-writer, and expert on Jewish mysticism. Hirschfield helped Seidman renew his interest in the teachings of the Jewish faith. In an online interview with the *Jewish Review,* Seidman explained that he started to see Judaism as "fresh, vibrant, and spiritually satisfying." To Seidman, "Aryeh was living proof that an enlightened, humane, humorous and deeply spiritual Judaism is possible."

In 1997 Seidman turned his attention to the symbolism of the Aleph Beit, the Hebrew alphabet. Jews believe that these letters hold mystical powers that enlighten people in search of answers from the divine. Seidman wrote *The Oracle of Kabbalah: Mystical Teachings of the Hebrew Letters* as a manual for both Jewish and non-Jewish readers. Designed as a book and card set, *The Oracle of Kabbalah* explains the meanings behind the letters and allows readers to use the cards to gain new perspectives on troubling situations.

Although the book is called an oracle, Seidman makes it clear that the cards have no psychic abilities and are not meant to be used to forecast future events. In an interview on the *Oracle of Kabbalah* Web site, Seidman commented that the cards "provide a perspective on your present situation and show consideration to keep in mind as you weigh possible courses of action." The teachings about the letters are adapted from the Jewish faith, but Seidman also draws on his studies of Zen and Native American religions to explain themes in the book. In a review for *New Connexions,* Jenny Swanpool said that "Richard borrows from other traditions, especially Zen, to clarify and amplify his themes, which allowed me to feel included in the Universal family even though I am not Jewish and have little exposure to the Jewish tradition."

BIOGRAPHICAL AND CRITICAL SOURCES:

ONLINE

Jewish Review, http://www.oracleofkabbalah.com/ (November, 2001), Paul Haist, review of *The*

Oracle of Kabbalah: Mystical Teachings of the Hebrew Letters.

New Connexions, http://www.oracleofkabbalah.com/ (September/October, 2002), Jenny Swanpool, review of *The Oracle of Kabbalah.*

Oracle of Kabbalah Web site, http://www.oracleofkabbalah.com/ (June 16, 2003), Interview with Seidman.*

*   *   *

SHAFFER, David R. 1946-

PERSONAL: Born February 4, 1946, in Watsonville, CA; son of Herbert (an electrician) and Gerrie Shaffer; married Garnett Stokes, June 6, 1981 (divorced, August, 1987); companion of Gail Williamson. *Ethnicity:* "German/French." *Education:* Attended Cabrillo College, 1963-65; Humboldt State University, A.B., 1967, M.A., 1968; Kent State University, Ph.D., 1972. *Politics:* Democrat.

ADDRESSES: Home—365 Riverbend Circle, Royston, GA 30662. *Office*—Department of Psychology, University of Georgia, Athens, GA 30602. *E-mail*—dshaffer@ arches.uga.edu.

CAREER: Educator and author. Kent State University, Kent, OH, assistant professor of psychology, 1972-73; University of Georgia, Athens, assistant professor, 1973-76, associate professor, 1976-82, professor of psychology, 1982—. *Military service:* U.S. Marine Corps Reserve, active duty, 1970-72.

MEMBER: American Psychological Association, Society for Research in Child Development.

AWARDS, HONORS: Josiah Meigs Award for Instructional Excellence, University of Georgia, 1990; research prize, American Association of Trial Consultants, 2000.

WRITINGS:

Social and Personality Development, Wadsworth Group (Belmont, CA), 1979, 4th edition, 2000.

Developmental Psychology: Childhood and Adolescence, Wadsworth Group (Belmont, CA), 1985, 6th edition, 2002.

(With Carol Sigelman) *Life-span Human Development,* Wadsworth Group (Belmont, CA), 1991, 2nd edition, 1995.

(With Gail Williamson and Patrick Parmelee) *Physical Illness and Depression in Older Adults: A Handbook of Theory, Research, and Practice,* Plenum, 2000.

(Editor with Bruce D. Waslick) *The Many Faces of Depression in Children and Adolescents,* American Psychiatric Publishing (Washington, DC), 2002.

Paid in Full, Alabaster Books (Kernersville, NC), 2003.

Contributor of nearly 100 articles to professional journals. Associate editor, *Personality and Social Psychology Bulletin,* 1975-79, *Journal of Personality and Social Psychology,* 1979-80, and *Journal of Personality,* 1980-86.

Shaffer's books have been translated into Chinese and Spanish.

WORK IN PROGRESS: Developmental Psychology, 7th edition; research on the effects of sport participation on the psycho-social development of adolescent families.

SIDELIGHTS: David R. Shaffer told *CA:* "My primary motivation for writing textbooks is to have up-to-date volumes on the subjects I teach. Since the texts have been successful, I continue to revise them.

"I have also authored more than ninety refereed articles in professional journals on such topics as attitudes and social influence processes, self-disclosure among acquaintances, psychological influences on jury decision-making, and mental health outcomes for people providing care to sick or disabled family members, to name a few. These are topics that motivated me to conduct the research that resulted in my books."

BIOGRAPHICAL AND CRITICAL SOURCES:

PERIODICALS

Adolescence, winter, 1990, review of *Developmental Psychology: Childhood and Adolescence,* 2nd edition, p. 1001; winter, 1996, review of *Developmental Psychology,* 4th edition, p. 996.

New England Journal of Medicine, March 1, 2001, Samuel Barondes, review of *Physical Illness and Depression in Older Adults: A Handbook of Theory, Research, and Practice,* p. 694.

*   *   *

SHARMA, Arun K. 1950-

PERSONAL: Born August 22, 1950, in Jodhpur, Rajasthan, India; son of Devdutt (an engineer) and Chandrakala (a homemaker) Sharma; married December 25, 1979; wife's name Rajlaxmi (divorced); children: Samidha. *Education:* BSMC & H, B.S., 1980. *Religion:* Atheist. *Hobbies and other interests:* Music, painting, reading, social work.

ADDRESSES: Home—Shivaji Marg, Mount Abu, Rajasthan, India. *Agent*—Shanker Banerjee, Flower Literary Agency, Alipore Rd., Calcutta, India. *E-mail*—asharma@datainfosys.net.

CAREER: Physician, musician, and poet. Physician in private practice, Mount Abu, Rajasthan, India; founder of free health clinic, c. 1985. People for Animals, founder of Mount Abu chapter. Vocalist and musician; recordings include *Tu Hi Hai,* Plus Music, 1998.

MEMBER: Indian Medical Association.

AWARDS, HONORS: MCCP, College of Chest Physicians, 1993; award from Millennium International Hindi Conference, 2000, for service to Hindi language; International Society of Poets Editors' Choice award, 2001, for poem "Ritualistic Rape"; Trivani Award, Rotary Club of Mount Abu, 2002.

WRITINGS:

POETRY

In Search of a Song, Vanguard Publications (Jodhpur, India), 1986.

Chup Kyon Ho Koi Baat Karo (in Hindi), Do, 1991.

Terracotta Sutra, Do, 1994.

Nirvana and the Cybergod: The Singapore Poems, Do, 1995.

Saanp to Saanp Hi Hota Hai (in Hindi), Do, 1996.
Success Is a Journey, Do, 1997.
The Rosary of the Rain, Do, 2003.

Also author of poetry collections *Basant Behose Ho Jata Hai* (in Hindi), *Indra Dhanushi Ganlion Men Kanbatian Foolon Ki* (in Hindi), and *Moods of the Love Lake.* Author of song lyrics. Contributor of poetry to *Journal of Poetry Society* (India), *Vaataayan, City Courier, Samajh, Indian Literature, Yardbird Reader, Poetry.com,* and *Rosedog.com.*

BIOGRAPHICAL AND CRITICAL SOURCES:

ONLINE

Yardbird Reader Online, http://www.yardbird.com/ (November 16, 2003), "A. K. Sharma."

*   *   *

SHENTON, James P(atrick) 1925-2003

OBITUARY NOTICE—See index for *CA* sketch: Born March 17, 1925, in Passaic, NJ; died of complications following heart surgery July 25, 2003, in Paterson, NJ. Educator and author. Shenton was a history professor at Columbia University who specialized in nineteenth- and twentieth-century American history. After serving in the U.S. Army Medical Corps in Europe during World War II, he attended Columbia, where he earned his Ph.D. in 1954. After completing his master's degree there, though, he was already on the university's faculty as an associate professor of history; and he was promoted to full professor of American history in 1967. A pacifist who supported the civil rights movement, Shenton participated in the 1965 march in Selma, Alabama, and in 1968 was accosted by police for trying to keep officers away from protesting students. Shenton's love and concern for his students was obvious throughout his tenure, and he spent more hours in the classroom than most of his academic colleagues, teaching during the summer and also lecturing for a lengthy course on U.S. history broadcast on television as *The Rise of the American Nation.* Shenton was the author or editor of several books in his field, among them *History of the United States to 1865* (1963), *History of the United States from 1865 to the*

Present (1964), and *These United States* (1978). When he was not in the classroom, Shenton could be found conducting walking tours of New York City, educating the interested public in the history of sites such as Ellis Island.

OBITUARIES AND OTHER SOURCES:

BOOKS

Writers Directory, 12th edition, St. James Press (Detroit, MI), 1996.

PERIODICALS

New York Times, July 28, 2003, p. A19.

*   *   *

SHIELDS, Carol (Ann) 1935-2003

OBITUARY NOTICE—See index for *CA* sketch: Born June 2, 1935, in Oak Park, IL; died of complications from breast cancer July 16, 2003, in Victoria, British Columbia, Canada. Author. Shields was an author of novels, short stories, and poetry who celebrated the life of ordinary people in such books as the 1993 Pulitzer Prize-winning novel *The Stone Diaries.* After graduating from Hanover College with a B.A. in 1957, she married and spent most of the next two decades raising a family. Though much of her early life was occupied with taking care of her five children, she still managed to squeeze in time to write stories and poems, collecting the latter in *Others* (1972) and *Intersect* (1974). Returning to school when her children were older, she completed her master's degree at the University of Ottawa in 1975, and published *Susanna Moodie: Voice and Vision* (1976), which was based on her thesis. Her first novel, *Small Ceremonies* (1976), is about a woman writing a thesis on Susanna Moodie. Shields went on to write several more fairly conventional, at times self-consciously derivative, novels about ordinary people in modern times, including *The Box Garden* (1977) and *A Fairly Conventional Woman* (1982), as well as the short-story collections *Various Miracles* (1985) and *The Orange Fish* (1989). *Various Miracles* marked the beginning of a more experimental period in her writing in which she played more with narrative and point of view. Having lectured at the University of Ottawa from 1976 to 1977 and at the University of British Columbia for the two years after that, in 1980 Shields accepted a position as professor at the University of Manitoba. Her years as a teacher were also productive as a writer: she completed such novels as *The Republic of Love* (1992); *The Stone Diaries* (1993), which also received the Governor General's Award for English-language Fiction, a National Book Critics Circle Award, and a Booker Prize shortlist; and *Larry's Party* (1997), as well as the poetry collection *Coming to Canada* (1992), the play *Anniversary* (1998), written with David Williamson, and the short-story collection *Dressing up for the Carnival* (2000). Shields served as chancellor at Manitoba from 1996 until 2000, retiring two years after learning she had breast cancer. Despite her illness, she continued to write, completing the biography *Jane Austen* (2001), which won a Charles Taylor Prize, and the novel *Unless* (2002), the second of her books to be shortlisted for the Booker Prize. Shields was working on another novel when she passed away.

OBITUARIES AND OTHER SOURCES:

BOOKS

Contemporary Novelists, seventh edition, St. James Press (Detroit, MI), 2001.

PERIODICALS

Chicago Tribune, July 18, 2003, section 3, p. 12.
Los Angeles Times, July 18, 2003, p. B12.
New York Times, July 18, 2003, p. A19.
Times (London, England), July 18, 2003.
Washington Post, July 18, 2003, p. B7.

*   *   *

SIDMAN, Joyce 1956-

PERSONAL: Born June 4, 1956, in Hartford, CT; daughter of Robert J. Von Dohlen (an architect); married May 31, 1981; husband, a doctor; children: two sons. *Ethnicity:* "Causasian." *Education:* Wesleyan University, B.A. (German), 1978; Macalester College, teacher's license, 1983. *Hobbies and other interests:* Gardening, bird watching, environmental issues.

ADDRESSES: Agent—c/o Houghton Mifflin, 222 Berkeley, Boston, MA 02116-3764. *E-mail*—mailbox@joycesidman.com.

CAREER: Writer. *St. Paul Pioneer Press,* St. Paul, MN, columnist, 1996-2000; freelance columnist, 2000—. COMPAS Writers & Artists in the Schools, St. Paul, writer-in-residence, 1997—. Volunteer in public schools and at Children's Hospital, Minneapolis, MN.

MEMBER: Society of Children's Book Writers and Illustrators, Children's Literature Network, Cooperative Children's Book Center-Net, Loft Literary Center (Minneapolis, MN).

AWARDS, HONORS: New Women's Voices Award, Finishing Line Press, 1999, for *Like the Air;* Showcase Book citation, Children's Book Council, best book of the year citation, Infolink, 2000, and Children's Literature Choice List citation, 2001, all for *Just Us Two: Poems about Animal Dads;* Best Book of the Year citation, Bank Street College, and nonfiction honor list citation, *Voice of Youth Advocates,* 2002, both for *Eureka!: Poems about Inventors;* Poetry Pick, *Voice of Youth Advocates,* 2002, and Best Books for Young Adults selection, American Library Association, both for *The World according to Dog: Poems and Teen Voices.*

WRITINGS:

Like the Air (chapbook; poetry for adults), Finishing Line Press (Georgetown, KY), 1999.
Just Us Two: Poems about Animal Dads (for children), illustrated by Susan Swan, Millbrook Press (Brookfield, CT), 2000.
Eureka!: Poems about Inventors (for middle-graders), illustrated by K. Bennett Chavez, Millbrook Press (Brookfield, CT), 2002.
(Editor) *Good Morning Tulip* (anthology of student writing), illustrated by Dhan Polnau, COMPAS Books (St. Paul, MN), 2002.
(With others) *The World according to Dog: Poems and Teen Voices,* illustrated by Doug Mindel, Houghton Mifflin (Boston, MA), 2003.
Song of the Water Boatman: Pond Poems, illustrated by Beckie Prange, Houghton Mifflin (Boston, MA), 2004.

When I Am Young and Old (poetry), illustrated by Elivia Savadier, Millbrook Press (Brookfield, CT), in press.

Contributor of essays and poems to books, including *Gifts from Our Grandmothers,* edited by Carol Dovi, Crown (New York, NY), 2000; *Stories from Where We Live: The Great North American Prairie,* edited by Sara St. Antoine, Milkweed (Minneapolis, MN), 2001; and *Line Drives: 100 Contemporary Baseball Poems,* edited by Brooke Horvath and Time Wiles, Southern Illinois University Press (Carbondale, IL), 2002. Contributor of numerous poems and stories to *Cricket* and *Cicada;* of occasional columns and reviews to *Riverbank Review;* and of numerous poems for adults to various journals, including *Christian Science Monitor, Cream City Review, ArtWorld Quarterly,* and *North Coast Review.*

WORK IN PROGRESS: A book of poems about meadow creatures; poems about physics in nature; a picture book of concrete poetry; a nonfiction book on symmetry.

SIDELIGHTS: Poet Joyce Sidman has written several books of verse for children and teenagers, including *Just Us Two: Poems about Animal Dads, Eureka!: Poems about Inventors,* and *The World according to Dog: Poems and Teen Voices. Just Us Two* was praised by *Christian Science Monitor* contributor Karen Carden for the way that Sidman's eleven poems about animal families "capture the tenderness evident in the father-child relationship." The poems are also scientifically accurate: Sidman did extensive research into animal behavior before writing her poems, and she lists facts about her subjects, which range from wolves to penguins and frogs, in prose form at the back of the book.

Sidman's next book of poetry, *Eureka!,* "celebrat[es] that combination of creative insight and steadfastness that characterizes the successful inventor," John Peters explained in *Booklist.* Each of Sidman's sixteen poems "invites readers inside the head of an individual who, through imagining, laboring, investigating, testing, and persevering, in some way transformed the world for generations to come," Martha Davis Beck wrote in *Riverbank Review.* Those individuals cover a range of time, from the prehistoric woman who first used clay to make a bowl to Tim Berners-Lee, the father of the

World Wide Web, and a range of fields, from science (Marie Curie, the discoverer of radiation) to recreation (Walter Frederick Morrison, the inventor of the Frisbee).

In *The World according to Dog,* Sidman combines her own poems about life with a dog with essays by various teenagers about their own pets. The combination is "sure to engage dog fanciers," Margaret Bush wrote in *School Library Journal,* but, according to *Booklist*'s Gillian Engberg, "even teens who prefer cats will appreciate Sidman's tight lines, sincere emotion, and clever humor."

Sidman told *CA:* "I was a verbal kid who loved school but ended up being sent out in the hallway a lot because I couldn't help talking to my neighbor. The temptation for whispered, smart-aleck comments was just too great. I loved to draw, too, and remember creating a series of illustrated comic books with a friend about four girls from different countries (the character representing me was from Egypt, for some reason or other). My attitude toward writing was transformed by a sixth-grade teacher who brought different, wacky pictures each week as story-starters. She liked what I wrote, often reading my work aloud. (My favorite books at about this period were British-style mysteries: *The Diamond in the Window,* by Jane Langton, and the books of Joan Aiken—*The Wolves of Willoughby Chase,* etc.). As an adolescent, I gravitated toward poetry, which has remained my favorite mode of expression—I love its vivid, metaphorical, condensed language.

"I was blessed with a top-notch education that exposed me to all kinds of literature, and teachers who expected first-rate writing out of me. A long-suffering high school English teacher was an ongoing mentor, reading my poems and kindly commenting on them. At Wesleyan University, I was lucky enough to study with poets Richard Wilbur and F. D. Reeve, and became a total snob about hanging out with exciting 'creative' people vs. boring 'pre-med' people. Fate had the last laugh, however: I married a doctor (a former Peace Corps worker) and have come to find his work fascinating. My husband is an avid reader and often helps me with my work.

"My children have had a profound influence on my writing life. Their personalities and interests have both broadened and inspired me. Seeing the world through their eyes was what drew me once more into children's literature. I loved those days when we would write and draw our own books together! My college-age son is now studying cosmology—the origins of the universe—and discussions with him are mind-boggling. My younger son is very interested in the writing process, and we often compare our work.

"The teaching I do (week-long poetry-writing residences in local K-8 schools) definitely informs my work. Turning kids on to poetry and its power is a thrill. Watching them respond to the written word—and seeing what they write about themselves—constantly reminds me of their depths and emotions. My students help me see the world in a new way, every single day I teach.

"Lately, I find myself more and more interested in science. The natural world is central to my life, and I am eager to find out more about its workings. After writing for several hours in the morning, I walk in the woods daily with my dog, Merlin—inspiration for *World according to Dog*—watching the seasons progress. For me, nature and creativity are firmly entwined. With books like *Just Us Two* and *Song of the Water Boatman*, I hope to help young readers delve into the world outside their four cozy walls.

"At this point in my life, I don't feel much different from my eleven-year-old self: an imaginative blabber-mouth who likes to explore the woods with a friend, play in the mud, and scribble in a tiny notebook."

BIOGRAPHICAL AND CRITICAL SOURCES:

PERIODICALS

Booklist, October 15, 2002, John Peters, review of *Eureka!: Poems about Inventors,* pp. 403-404; April 1, 2003, Gillian Engberg, review of *The World according to Dog: Poems and Teen Voices,* pp. 1405-1406.
Bulletin of the Center for Children's Books, March, 2003, review of *The World according to Dog.*
Children's Book Review Service, November, 2000, review of *Just Us Two: Poems about Animal Dads.*
Christian Science Monitor, October 26, 2000, Karen Carden, review of *Just Us Two,* p. 21.
Kirkus Reviews, February 1, 2003, review of *The World according to Dog,* p. 239.
Reading Teacher, March, 2003, Cyndi Giorgis and Nancy J. Johnson, review of *Eureka!,* pp. 582-590.
Riverbank Review, winter, 2000-2001, Christine Alfano, review of *Just Us Two,* p. 55; spring, 2002, Joyce Sidman, "Touching the World," pp. 25-27; winter, 2002-2003, Martha Davis Beck, review of *Eureka!,* pp. 56-57.
School Library Journal, December, 2000, Carolyn Angus, review of *Just Us Two,* p. 136; January, 2003, Susan Oliver, review of *Eureka!;* May, 2003, John Peters, review of *Eureka!,* p. 103, and Margaret Bush, review of *The World according to Dog,* p. 177.

ONLINE

Children's Literature Network Web site, http://www.childrensliteraturenetwork.com/ (June 30, 2003), "Joyce Sidman."
Joyce Sidman Home Page, http://www.joycesidman.com (September 26, 2003).

*   *   *

SIEGEL, Jan
    See ASKEW, Amanda Jane

*   *   *

SINHA, Manisha 1962-

PERSONAL: Born November 2, 1962, in Patna, India; naturalized U.S. citizen; daughter of S. K. (a provincial governor) and Premini (Verma) Sinha; married Karsten R. Stueber (a professor), December 27, 1988; children: Sheel K. *Ethnicity:* "Asian Indian." *Education:* Delhi University, B.A. (with honors), 1984; State University of New York at Stony Brook, M.A., 1985; Columbia University, M.Phil., 1988, Ph.D., 1994. *Politics:* "Liberal/Left." *Religion:* Hindu.

ADDRESSES: Home—20 Whittemore Rd., Sturbridge, MA 01566. *Office*—W. E. B. DuBois Department of Afro-American Studies, 325 New Africa House, University of Massachusetts, Amherst, MA 01003; fax: 413-545-0628. *E-mail*—mashinha@afroam.umass.edu.

CAREER: Harvard University, Cambridge, MA, fellow at W. E. B. Du Bois Institute for Afro-American Research, 1992-94; University of Massachusetts, Amherst, assistant professor, 1994-2000, associate professor of history, 2000—. University of North Carolina at Chapel Hill, fellow in humanities, 1994-95; lecturer at colleges and universities, including University of Münster, 1998, Mount Holyoke College, 1996, Harvard University, 2000, the Citadel, 2000, and Indiana University—Bloomington and Stanford University, 2001; speaker at Smithsonian Institution and local historical societies.

MEMBER: American Historical Association, Organization of American Historians, Association for the Study of African American Life and History, Southern Historical Association.

AWARDS, HONORS: Whiting fellow in humanities, 1992-93; grant from American Council of Learned Societies, 1994; Rockefeller fellow, 1994-95; grant from American Philosophical Society, 1999.

WRITINGS:

The Counterrevolution of Slavery: Politics and Ideology in Antebellum South Carolina, University of North Carolina Press (Chapel Hill, NC), 2000.
(Editor, with John H. Bracey, Jr.) *African Americans: A Documentary History from the African Slave Trade to the Twenty-first Century,* two volumes, Prentice-Hall (New York, NY), 2001.

Contributor to books, including *Feminist Nightmares, Women at Odds: Feminism and the Problem of Sisterhood,* edited by Susan Ostrov Weisser and Jennifer Fleischner, New York University Press (New York, NY), 1994; *Red Badges of Courage: Wars and Conflicts in American Culture,* edited by Biancamaria Pisapia, Ugo Rubeo, and Anna Scacchi, Bulzoni (Rome, Italy), 1998; and *Black Imagination and the Middle Passage,* edited by Maria Diedrich, Henry Louis Gates, Jr., and Carl Pedersen, Oxford University Press (New York, NY), 1999. Contributor of articles and reviews to periodicals, including *Civil War History.*

WORK IN PROGRESS: The Triumph of American Radicalism: African Americans and the Movement to Abolish Slavery, 1775-1865; research on black abolitionists.

SIDELIGHTS: Manisha Sinha told *CA:* "As a historian, I am primarily interested in writing books that will change and inform our historical knowledge. I am inspired by the subject of my works, particularly the African-American struggle for equality in this country. I have also been inspired by some of the foremost chroniclers of black history, such as Eric Foner, Barbara J. Fields, Lawrence Levine, Henry Louis Gates, and of course the great W. E. B. Du Bois.

"I tend to research my topics exhaustively first. I read all author/historians who have written on the topic and all 'primary documents'; in archives and libraries. As a rule, I write continuously for a year to complete a project. The civil rights movement and my interest in race led me to my topics."

BIOGRAPHICAL AND CRITICAL SOURCES:

PERIODICALS

Choice, May, 2001, J. Z. Rabun, review of *The Counterrevolution of Slavery: Politics and Ideology in Antebellum South Carolina,* p. 1682.

*   *   *

SKLANSKY, Amy E(dgar) 1971-

PERSONAL: Born February 7, 1971, in Chattanooga, TN; daughter of R. Allan (a federal judge) and Gail (a teacher; maiden name, Martin) Edgar; married Joseph J. Sklansky (an attorney), August 9, 1997; children: Phoebe Edgar. *Ethnicity:* "Causasian." *Education:* University of Virginia—Charlottesville, B.A. (English and American studies).

ADDRESSES: Home—259 Beacon St., Apt. 61, Boston, MA 02116. *Agent*—Judy Sue Goodwin Sturges, Studio Goodwin Sturges, 146 West Newton St., Boston, MA 02118. *E-mail*—sklansky@mindspring.com.

CAREER: HarperCollins Children's Books, New York, NY, editor, 1993-98; Studio Goodwin Sturges, Boston, MA, editor, 1998—.

WRITINGS:

(Compiler) *ZOOMzingers: Fifty+ Body and Brain Teasers from the Hit PBS TV Show,* Little, Brown (Boston, MA), 1999.
(Compiler) *ZOOMfun with Friends; Fifty+ Great Games, Parties, Recipes, Jokes, and More from the Hit PBS TV Show,* Little, Brown (Boston, MA), 1999.
ZOOMfun Outside: Fifty + Outrageous Outdoor Games, Experiments, and More from the Hit PBS TV Show, Little, Brown (Boston, MA), 2000.
ZOOMjournal, Little, Brown (Boston, MA), 2000.
ZOOMdos You Can Do: Fifty+ Things You Can Craft, Bake, and Build, Little, Brown (Boston, MA), 2000.
(Adapter) Richard B. Stolley, editor, *Life: Our Century in Pictures for Young People,* Little, Brown (Boston, MA), 2000.
From the Doghouse: Poems to Chew On, illustrated by Karla Firehammer and others, Henry Holt (New York, NY), 2002.
Skeleton Bones and Goblin Groans: Poems for Halloween, illustrated by Karen Dismukes, Henry Holt (New York, NY), 2004.

WORK IN PROGRESS: From Egg to Chick (nonfiction), illustrated by Pam Paparone, for HarperCollins (New York, NY), publication expected in 2005.

SIDELIGHTS: After working for five years as an editor at HarperCollins, Amy E. Sklansky began writing her own books for children. Her first titles are a handful of companion books to the television series *ZOOM,* created by Public Broadcasting Station WGBH in Boston, Massachusetts. For them she compiled and created activities, experiments, crafts, recipes, and projects based on various themes. With editor Richard B. Stolley, Sklansky adapted the best-selling adult work *Life: Our Century in Pictures* for children. When *Life* rolled off the presses in 2000, it was to good reviews. Remarking favorably on "this superb collection of carefully chosen, powerful images with pithy captions," a *Publishers Weekly* contributor dubbed it "a visual treasure trove." It was chosen a *Publishers Weekly* best children's book of the year.

In 1998 Sklansky joined the Studio Goodwin Sturges, a studio founded in Boston's South End in 1989 by Judy Sue Goodwin Sturges, a professor of illustration at the Rhode Island School of Design and a former art director. The first title Sklansky authored there was *From the Doghouse: Poems to Chew On,* a collection poems from a dog's eye view. "Dogs come in so many different sizes, shapes, colors, and personalities that I thought it would be interesting to think like one for awhile," she commented in a Studio Goodwin Sturges publicity brochure. "I asked myself, 'What kinds of things do dogs think about every day? What kinds of things do they dream about?'"

Sklansky enjoys poetry and admits to having always had one or more dogs while growing up, so verse was a natural choice, as was a first-person voice. Also, as she explained in her brochure, "I like that poetry is a puzzle—that you have to wrestle with words and really chew on them before you can spit them out into a poem that works." To illustrate *From the Doghouse,* a team of four illustrators sewed nearly 120,000 tiny beads onto cloth, creating pictures. Some of the artists' own dogs inspired several illustrations. *From the Doghouse* caught reviewers' attention. *School Library Journal*'s Shawn Brommer found the poems suitable for young children, stating "New readers will feel comfortable with the easy rhyme and bouncy rhythm."

BIOGRAPHICAL AND CRITICAL SOURCES:

PERIODICALS

Kirkus Reviews, August 1, 2002, review of *From the Doghouse: Poems to Chew On,* p. 1144.
Publishers Weekly, October 30, 2000, review of *Life: Our Century in Pictures,* p. 77; July 22, 2002, review of *From the Doghouse,* p. 117.
School Library Journal, August, 2002, Shawn Brommer, review of *From the Doghouse,* p. 180.

OTHER

A Conversation with Amy E. Sklansky (publicity brochure), Studio Goodwin Sturges, c. 2002.

*   *   *

SKLENICKA, Carol 1948-

PERSONAL: Born December 11, 1948, in San Luis Obispo, CA; daughter of Robert Jame (a produce broker) and Dorothy (a secretary and educator; maiden name, Johnston) Sklenicka; married R. M. Ryan (a writer), June 21, 1979; children: Katherine Snoda,

Robert Lewellin. *Education:* California State Polytechnic University, B.A. (English), 1971; Washington University, St. Louis, M.A. (English), 1978, Ph.D. (English), 1986. *Politics:* "What have you got." *Religion:* "Buddhist Episcopalian." *Hobbies and other interests:* Hiking, cooking, reading, travel.

ADDRESSES: Office—1422 East Albion St., Milwaukee, WI 53202. *Agent*—Deborah Schneider, Gelfman & Schneider, 250 West 57th St., New York, NY 10107. *E-mail*—sklen@mixcom.com.

CAREER: Writer.

MEMBER: Authors' Guild, D. H. Lawrence Society of North America.

AWARDS, HONORS: Annual Best Story Award, *Sou'wester,* 1979, for "Room Changes"; fiction fellowship, Wisconsin Arts Board, 1982, for "Clearance"; Summer grant, National Endowment for the Humanities, 1988; Wisconsin Arts Board travel fellowship, 1998.

WRITINGS:

D. H. Lawrence and the Child (literary study), University of Missouri Press (Columbia, MO), 1991.

Stories, essays, and reviews published in *Sou'wester, Confrontation, South Atlantic Quarterly, Iowa Woman, Military Lifestyle, Willow Springs, Clackamas Literary Review, Village Voice, America, Metro, Milwaukee,* and *Transactions.*

WORK IN PROGRESS: Acting Our Age (novel about Vietnam); research for a literary biography of Raymond Carver.

SIDELIGHTS: Carol Sklenicka told *CA:* "My fiction has been inspired by the desire to put quiet lives in the forefront of a story, to play with point of view and glimpse things from an unusual perspective. My book about D. H. Lawrence focuses on his little-discussed child characters, while my novel, *Acting Our Age,* will tell the story of Vietnam from a homefront girl's

perspective. In this one aspect I have been inspired by the stories and poems of Raymond Carver, though I would not presume to any claim to be in his league. I have admired his work since I first read it in the 1970s, and am now engaged in research toward a biographical study of his work."

*   *   *

SLOAN, Mark

PERSONAL: Male.

ADDRESSES: Home—Charleston, SC. *Agent*—c/o Author's Mail, Quantuck Lane Press, 145 East 16th St., Suite 20A, New York, NY 10003.

CAREER: Curator, photographer, and author. Light Factory, Charlotte, NC, executive director, 1985-86; San Francisco Camerawork, San Francisco, CA, associate director, 1986-89; State University of New York, Potsdam, director of Roland Gibson gallery, 1992-94; College of Charleston, Charleston SC, director of Halsey gallery, 1994—, and associate professor of arts management. *Exhibitions:* Photography included in "Tabula Rasa" series, touring U.S. cities and Paris, France, and at Detroit Institute of Arts, 1985.

WRITINGS:

(With Roger Manley and Michelle Van Parys) *Hoaxes, Humbugs, and Spectacles: Astonishing Photographs of Smelt Wrestlers, Human Projectiles, Giant Hailstones, Contortionists, Elephant Impersonators, and Much, Much More!,* Villard Books (New York, NY), 1990.
(And editor with Roger Manley and Michelle Van Parys) *Dear Mr. Ripley: A Compendium of Curioddities from the Believe It or Not! Archives,* Little, Brown (Boston, MA), 1993.
(With Roger Manley) *Self-made Worlds: Visionary Folk Art Environments,* Aperture (New York, NY), 1997.
Wild, Weird, and Wonderful: The American Circus, 1901-1927, as Seen by F. W. Glasier, Photographer, Quantuck Lane Press (New York, NY), 2003.

WORK IN PROGRESS: Rarest of the Rare: Stunning Specimens at the Harvard Museum of Natural History, for HarperCollins, 2004.

SIDELIGHTS: Mark Sloan is an artist and curator with a bent toward the unusual. He has served as director of the Halsey Gallery in Charlotte, North Carolina, since 1994, and is an associate professor of arts management at the College of Charlotte. Sloan is also a successful artist whose work has appeared in exhibitions both in the U.S. and in France.

Sloan's first book, *Hoaxes, Humbugs, and Spectacles: Astonishing Photographs of Smelt Wrestlers, Human Projectiles, Giant Hailstones, Contortionists, Elephant Impersonators, and Much, Much More!*, written with Roger Manley and Michelle Van Parys, collects unusual historical photographs. Noting that the photos included "seem like dramas condensed into a single intriguing moment," Ralph Novak pointed out in a review of the book for *People* that "the events [these photographs] recorded were once real phenomena—current, hip entertainment."

Sloan rejoins Manley and Van Parys in continuing their examination of oddities in *Dear Mr. Ripley: A Compendium of Curioddities from the Believe It or Not! Archives.* The book compiles photographs from the files of Robert LeRoy Ripley, whose name has become synonymous with the strange and unbelievable. Ripley, a newspaper cartoonist, used these pictures as the basis for many of his cartoons, yet the photographs themselves are "breathless, Barnum-esque, . . . graphically simpler and stronger, emotionally more complex" than the cartoons, suggested Eric Levin in *People.*

In the photographs collected as *Self-made Worlds: Visionary Folk Art Environments* Sloan and Manley shift focus to the world of folk artists. Donna Seaman, reviewing the 1997 work for *Booklist,* commented that the chosen photos "all have an aura of sanctity, or ritualized creativity and devotion." She continued, "Manley, Sloan, and their contributing photographers have done a great service here by preserving these precious, out-of-the way, and very fragile sites."

Wild, Weird, and Wonderful: The American Circus, 1901-1927, as Seen by F. W. Glasier, Photographer features promotional photographs of circus life taken by Glasier, a commercial photographer. "As a sustained document of circus life at this time, there is no known equivalent" notes Sloan of Glasier's work. David Bryant, reviewing *Wild, Weird, and Wonderful* for *Library*

Journal, called the photos "profoundly sad," but noted that they "testify to the circus's multiple functions as art, culture, and lifestyle, as a working zoo or a window on human deformity."

BIOGRAPHICAL AND CRITICAL SOURCES:

PERIODICALS

Booklist, December 15, 1997, Donna Seaman, review of *Self-Made Worlds: Visionary Folk Art Environments,* p. 679; February 15, 2003, Ray Olson, review of *Wild, Weird, and Wonderful: The American Circus, 1901-1927, as Seen by F. W. Glasier, Photographer,* p. 1029.
Entertainment Weekly, February 21, 2003, Chris Nashawaty, review of *Wild, Weird, and Wonderful,* p. 154.
Library Journal, April 15, 1998, Judith Yankielun Lind, review of *Self-made Worlds,* p. 72; February 15, 2003, David Bryant, review of *Wild, Weird, and Wonderful,* p. 131.
People, January 21, 1991, Ralph Novak, review of *Hoaxes, Humbugs, and Spectacles,* p. 32; September 6, 1993, Eric Levin, review of *Dear Mr. Ripley,* p. 26.
Publishers Weekly, January 13, 2003, review of *Wild, Weird, and Wonderful,* p. 52.*

*   *   *

SMOLIN, Lee 1955-

PERSONAL: Born June 6, 1955 in New York, NY. *Education:* Hampshire College, Massachusetts, B.A., 1975; Harvard College, M.A., 1978, Ph.D. (physics), 1979.

ADDRESSES: Home—London, England. *Office*—Department of Physics, Pennsylvania State University, 320 Osmond Lab, University Park, PA 16802. *E-mail*—lx33@psu.edu.

CAREER: Physicist and professor. Institute for Theoretical Physics, University of California-Santa Barbara, postdoctoral fellow, 1980-81; Institute for Advanced Study, Princeton University, fellow, 1981-

83; Envico Frumi Institute, University of Chicago, postdoctoral fellow, 1983-84; Yale University, New Haven, CT, assistant professor, 1984-88; Syracuse University, New York, associate professor, 1988-91, professor, 1991-93; Pennsylvania State University, University Park, professor, 1993—. Visiting scientist, Institute for Theoretical Physics.

WRITINGS:

The Life of the Cosmos, Oxford University Press (New York, NY), 1997.
Three Roads to Quantum Gravity, Basic Books (New York, NY), 2001.

SIDELIGHTS: Physicist Lee Smolin has long been known in his field as a maverick. Even fellow scientists who respect his work acknowledge that much of it is controversial and often speculative. His main research interest for much of his career has been quantum gravity, or the search for a theory that could link together the quantum theory of subatomic particles and the theory of general relativity, usually applied to large bodies such as galaxies or the universe. In such books as *The Life of the Cosmos* and *Three Roads to Quantum Gravity,* Smolin has attempted to make his speculations available to the non-scientist reader. He presents physics from a personal perspective, addressing philosophical questions and telling the story of his own development as a physicist.

Smolin's early educational path did not suggest that he would eventually become a leader in the field of quantum gravity. As a high school student he was a mediocre performer, eventually dropping out and playing with his short-lived rock band, Ideoplastos. Smolin was also an admirer of Buckminster Fuller, and he attempted to make a business selling geodesic dome pool covers based on Fuller's ideas. The mathematics involved in the structure of the domes led him to the tensor calculus and to Albert Einstein, who had based his theory of relativity on the same type of math. Then Smolin came to Hampshire College, not to enroll himself, but to drive his girlfriend to an admissions interview. While there he chatted with a physics instructor and was inspired to apply. Eventually Smolin earned his Ph.D. from Harvard and began a string of postdoctoral fellowships at prestigious universities across the United States before starting as an assistant professor at Yale University.

In 1986 Smolin made an important connection, meeting Indian physicist Abhay Ashtekar at a workshop on quantum gravity at the Institute for Theoretical Physics. Ashtekar was a leader in the field, developing equations that began building a bridge between Einstein's equations for general relativity and the mathematics of quantum mechanics. Smolin began working with Ashtekar, coming to Syracuse University, where Ashtekar was also a professor, in 1988. Carlo Rovelli came from Italy to work with the pair, and soon the three were drawing attention due to the potential of their theory to alter the way scientists think of space. Marcia Bartusiak summarized the trio's work for *Discover* magazine in 1993: "What is emerging from their initial explorations is a tantalizing picture of what space might look like on the tiniest levels. Instead of a space-time structure that's immeasurably smooth, their calculations hint that it might have a fine-grained structure, a texture that resembles a carpet woven out of an endless series of ultrasmall loops, interlinked in every direction." Where there are no loops—in the tiny spaces between the threads—there is no time or space. The challenge for their theory was its wholly speculative nature. Speaking to Bartusiak in *Discover,* professor Bryce DeWitt, also a researcher in quantum gravity, said "They have to tie their method to something that could, at least in theory with some sort of thought experiment, be observed in the real world."

In 1997 Smolin published his first book attempting to explain the potential for connecting relativity theory and quantum theory, aimed at engaging not only his fellow physicists but also interested laypeople with little background in the subject. With *The Life of the Cosmos,* Smolin asks how the universe came into being and how it came to support life, using his links between the properties of subatomic particles and the properties of stars and galaxies as the foundation for his answers. The crux of Smolin's argument is his theory of self-generating universes, comparable to the biological reproduction of life forms like humans. John Maddox, reviewing *The Life of the Cosmos* for *New Statesman,* explained Smolin's thesis: "Smolin's crucial supposition is that inside each black hole is another universe, closely resembling the one from which it springs (not least in the kind of matter it contains), but with properties that are, by chance, slightly but significantly different. Then, given successive generations of universes inside the black holes of their parental universes, there will be a tendency for the ensemble of all the universes to be dominated by those that produce lots of black holes." Effectively, Smolin proposes a kind of natural selection on a universal scale, so that the kinds of universes most likely to dominate will be the kinds most likely to generate and support life. Smolin is also careful to explain that his theory is unproven and, as yet, unprovable. Though his theories were far from the mainstream of scientific thought, response to his book was generally positive. Reviewing the book for *Astronomy,* Jennifer Birriel wrote, "*The Life of the Cosmos* may not offer satisfactory answers to all of its readers, but the questions it raises are worth contemplation." Joseph Silk criticized Smolin's knowledge of astronomy, but nonetheless concluded, "I must admit, finally, that the book is worth reading."

Smolin pursues his theory further in *Three Roads to Quantum Gravity,* in which he presents the history of relativity theory and quantum theory, and the efforts to link the two in a "theory of everything," for the general reader. The "three roads" of the title refer to possible approaches to forging this link: string theory, the loop approach forged by Smolin, and a third path that is not yet clear, requiring a new understanding of space and time not yet developed. The third path would contain both quantum theory and general relativity as limited explanations in particular circumstances. Michael Redhead, in his review for the *London Review of Books,* wrote that although Smolin's discussion of that third path is "wildly speculative," it is nonetheless compelling, with ideas that are "remarkable and provocative." Reviewing the book for the London *Guardian,* Mark Buchanan said Smolin writes with "impressive clarity," and "a talent for explaining the core ideas behind the bewildering details." Reviewers also noted the need for more research to back up these ideas: physics professor Michael Riordan suggested in the *New York Times* that, "without objective ways to verify their revolutionary claims, these imaginative theories of quantum gravity will remain rooted only in the misty realms of metaphysics." Smolin predicts in *Three Roads to Quantum Gravity* that these objective ways may come about as soon as 2010. Professor Paul Renteln responded to that claim in *American Scientist,* noting that Smolin is "one of a small handful of physicists around the world who have been able to make genuine progress on an extraordinarily difficult problem that has stumped some of the world's finest minds for eighty years." Whether or not his predictions bear out, Renteln said, "One has to admire his intrepid spirit and utopian vision."

BIOGRAPHICAL AND CRITICAL SOURCES:

PERIODICALS

American Scientist, January-February, 2002, Paul Renteln, "Quanitizing the Universe," pp. 76-78.
Astronomy, March, 1998, Jennifer Birriel, review of *The Life of the Cosmos,* pp. 100-101.
Discover, April, 1993, Marcia Bartusiak, "Loops of Space," pp. 60-68; July, 1997, Tim Folger, review of *The Life of the Cosmos,* pp. 120-121.
London Review of Books, May 23, 2002, Michael Redhead, "Spin Foam," pp. 30-31.
New Statesman, June 6, 1997, John Maddox, review of *The Life of the Cosmos,* pp. 44-45.
New York Times Book Review, August 19, 2001, Michael Riordan, "Space-Time Is of the Essence," p. 11.
New York Times Magazine, July 13, 1997, Dennis Overbye, "The Cosmos according to Darwin."
Omni, October, 1992, Thomas R. McDonough and David Brin, "The Bubbling Universe," pp. 84-89.
Publishers Weekly, June 25, 2001, review of *Three Roads to Quantum Gravity,* p. 60.
Science, August 1, 1997, Joseph Silk, review of *The Life of the Cosmos,* p. 644.
Times Higher Education Supplement, June 13, 1997, Ayala Ochert, "Can This Man Go Where No Physicist Has Gone Before?," p. 20.

ONLINE

2think.org, http://www.2think.org/ (October 22, 2002), review of *The Life of the Cosmos.*
Guardian Online, http://books.guardian.co.uk/ (February 17, 2001), Mark Buchanan, "Quantum Leap."
NTLWorld Web site, http://homepage.ntlworld.com/ (October 22, 2002), Anthony Campbell, review of *The Life of the Cosmos,* review of *Three Roads to Quantum Gravity.*
Oxford University Press Web site, http://www.oup-usa.org/ (October 22, 2002), description of *The Life of the Cosmos.*
Physics Web, http://physicsweb.org/ (December, 2000), Michael Duff, "A Maverick's Quest for Quantum Gravity."
Tech Directions, http://www.techdirections.com/ (October 22, 2002), review of *Three Roads to Quantum Gravity.**

SNIECHOWSKI, James

PERSONAL: Married third wife, Judith Sherven (a psychologist), 1988. *Education:* Earned Ph.D. (human behavior). *Religion:* Roman Catholic.

ADDRESSES: Home—Windham, NY. *Agent*—c/o Author Mail, St. Martin's Press, 175 Fifth Ave., New York, NY, 10010. *E-mail*—jksjes@hotmail.com.

CAREER: Therapist. Men's Health Network, Washington, DC, cofounder, 1992; Menswork Center, Santa Monica, CA, founder and former director; The Magic of Differences (relationship training and consulting firm), NY, cofounder with wife, Judith Sherven; Westside Gender Reconciliation Workgroup, cofounder. With Sherven, conductor of training seminars, workshops, lectures, and corporate consultations; cohost, with husband, of *Wisdom* radio show.

WRITINGS:

WITH WIFE, JUDITH SHERVEN

The New Intimacy: Discovering the Magic at the Heart of Your Differences, Health Communications (Deerfield Beach, FL), 1997.
Opening to Love 365 Days a Year, Health Communications (Deerfield Beach, FL), 2000.
Be Loved for Who You Really Are, Renaissance Books (Los Angeles, CA), 2001, published as *Be Loved for Who You Really Are: How the Differences between Men and Women Can Be Turned into the Source of the Very Best Romance You'll Ever Know,* St. Martin's Griffin (New York, NY), 2003.

Coauthor, with Sherven, of audiobooks, including *Embracing Intimacy, Breaking through Resistance, Mothering the Girl Within, Fathering the Boy Within, Womanhood: Power, and Identity, Calling Men to Community, Sons and Fathers* (three-tape series), *You Are the Healer, The Healing Power of Relationships,* and *Preventing Domestic Violence.* Coauthor of online column for Wisdom Networks, and of articles for periodicals and Web sites, including *Chinese Women Today, Lightworks, Backlash!, Los Angeles Times,* and *Mensight.*

SIDELIGHTS: When counseling couples and writing about relationships, therapists James Sniechowski and wife Judith Sherven draw from their own experiences as a happily married couple as well as from their professional expertise. Sniechowski and Sherven are well known for their books and articles about relationships and for their many radio and television appearances. The husband-and-wife relationship counselors are also the founders of The Magic of Differences, a consulting firm.

Their first book, *The New Intimacy: Discovering the Magic at the Heart of Your Differences,* is a guide to appreciating the differences between men and women and learning how to use them to enrich a relationship. In an interview with Bert H. Hoff and Scott Abraham for *Men's Voices,* Sniechowski shared some of his thoughts about the book. Being very involved in the men's movement, he explained that he "wanted to do something about relationships that would honor men, not protecting them when they didn't deserve it, but not bashing them out of hand." Sniechowski also noted that when he and his wife run seminars and counseling sessions, half of their audience is usually composed of men, which is unusual in their field. "We have said something, we've done something, we've organized it in such a way that men are finding it attractive, either consciously or unconsciously," he told Hoff and Abraham. As cofounder of the Men's Health Network, Sniechowski has a vested interest in men's thoughts, feelings, and concerns about relationships. Sniechowski and Sherven, unlike many relationship counselors, target their books toward this often overlooked gender.

Opening to Love 365 Days a Year, the couple's second book, contains an affirmation for every day of the year that readers can reflect upon. For example, the book begins on January 1 with the advice that "when you can remember your partner's feelings, beliefs, behaviors are just as important and valid as yours are, then you start off with the possibility of building a passionate, successful love between equals." J. Steven Svoboda, a reviewer for *Everyman,* observed that *Opening to Love* "addressed countless subjects that would normally be omitted from a guide to loving well, and yet are critically important to creating three-dimensional love."

According to *Library Journal* reviewer Margaret Cardwell, in *Be Loved for Who You Really Are* the couple presents "a blueprint for what they call 'the arc of love.'" Providing the foundation for the book are stories from their own marriage as well as incidents taken from their patients. Cardwell also noted that the book is full of suggestions for couples, and it has a "spiritual, New Age flavor." Readers learn to explore differences and use them to their advantage instead of allowing these dissimilarities to alienate them from their partner.

Sniechowski and Sherven have devoted nearly two decades to helping people understand that honesty, trust, and acceptance are key ingredients in the recipe for a successful relationship. "Long-term relationship is a voyage of discovery and an exciting way of being alive, as opposed to a process that one just settles into, accommodates, and ultimately is consumed by," reflected Sniechowski in his *Men's Voices* interview with Hoff and Abraham. "It really becomes an adventure in life, an adventure in what we call 'practical spirituality' and a meditation on daily loving. That's part of the pay-off."

BIOGRAPHICAL AND CRITICAL SOURCES:

BOOKS

Sherven, Judith, and James Sniechowski, *Opening to Love 365 Days a Year,* Health Communications (Deerfield Beach, FL), 2000.

PERIODICALS

Everyman, March-April, 2000, J. Steven Svoboda, review of *Opening to Love 365 Days a Year.*
Library Journal, September 15, 2001, Margaret Cardwell, review of *Be Loved for Who You Really Are,* p. 99.
Men's Voices, spring, 1998, Bert H. Hoff and Scott Abraham, interview with James Sniechowski and Judith Sherven.

ONLINE

Mensight Online, http://mensightmagazine.com/ (June 30, 2003), J. Steven Svoboda, interview with Sherven and Sniechowski.

New Intimacy: Sherven-Sniechowski Web site, http://www.thenewintimacy.com (November 16, 2003).*

*   *   *

SOJOURNER, Mary

PERSONAL: Born in northern PA.

ADDRESSES: Home—Flagstaff, AZ. *Office*—c/o University of Nevada Press, Mail Stop 166, Reno, NV 89557. *E-mail*—KALI11440@aol.com.

CAREER: Environmentalist, author, and teacher.

WRITINGS:

Sisters of the Dream: A Novel, Northland Publishers (Flagstaff, AZ), 1989.
Delicate: Stories of Light and Desire, Nevermore Press (Flagstaff, AZ), 1999.
Bonelight: Ruin and Grace in the New Southwest, University of Nevada Press (Reno, NV), 2002.

SIDELIGHTS: Mary Sojourner moved from the northeast to the southwest, concerned for the plight of the natural landscape there and committed to preserving it. As an environmental activist, Sojourner has fought against the increasing development of land in Arizona and been arrested for protesting at a uranium mine. But she has also sought to use her writing as part of her activism, encouraging readers to see the beauty of the land around them and to feel concern for its loss. In both her 1989 novel, *Sisters of the Dream,* and her 2002 collection of nonfiction essays, *Bonelight: Ruin and Grace in the New Southwest,* Sojourner has written about the strength and dignity of the Southwestern landscape and the people who live closest to it.

Sisters of the Dream tells the story of Liz Morrigan, a character who follows the pattern of Sojourner, moving from the East Coast to Flagstaff, Arizona, to make a new life. Morrigan makes a circle of powerful women friends and is initiated into the life and rituals of the Hopi Indians. In her dreams, Liz travels back to the Hopi culture of the twelfth century, which

Sojourner recreates with historical detail. Reviewers found the strength of the book in the relationships between the women friends. Susan E. Davis, in *New Directions for Women,* said *Sisters of the Dream* "vibrantly affirms life and women's struggles to live it to the fullest." A critic for *Publishers Weekly* wrote that although the dream sequences sometimes slowed the pace with excessive detail, "Sojourner effectively communicates the unquenchable strength of her beleaguered heroines."

The collection *Bonelight* is a compilation of essays, including columns for *Writers on the Range* and commentaries for National Public Radio. Most of the essays are very short, some only half a page, depicting Sojourner's growing relationship with the landscape of her adopted home. The poet Maxine Kumin reviewed *Bonelight* for *Women's Review of Books,* remarking on the passion and pain evident in Sojourner's writing. Kumin wrote, "Sojourner is not afraid to be personal, to express grief for her dead father, a kind of pride for having left her old life behind, fear for her mortality as she comes into menopause . . . and pure rage at the developer she faces across the table for a session of pseudo-partnership and compromise." Martin Naparsteck, a reviewer for *Salt Lake Tribune,* suggested that some of Sojourner's emotions were too easy or simple, and some of her arguments no more than "bumper sticker" slogans. Naparsteck found a sense of superiority in some of Sojourner's diatribes against developers and suburban sprawl, saying "Looking down on other people isn't insight. It's arrogance." Of other pieces, Naparsteck said, "When she is gutsy or confessional, Sojourner is a fine writer."

Sojourner has written that in her fiction and essays she tries to give back to the land that has given her so much. On her Web site, she wrote, "I write and teach from this simple perspective: our stories, our poems, our best works are inextricably drawn from and linked with the land on which we live."

BIOGRAPHICAL AND CRITICAL SOURCES:

PERIODICALS

New Directions for Women, November, 1989, Susan E. Davis, review of *Sisters of the Dream,* p. 25
Publishers Weekly, June 30, 1989, review of *Sisters of the Dream,* p. 85; April 1, 2002, Judith Rosen, "Self-pubbed Author Opens Doors for UP," p. 21.

Western American Literature, winter, 1990, James B. Hemesath, review of *Sisters of the Dream,* pp. 389-390.
Women's Review of Books, July, 2002, Maxine Kumin, "Enough Is Enough," pp. 31-32.

ONLINE

High Country News online, http://www.hcn.org/ (April 15, 2002), Renee Guillory, review of *Bonelight.*
Mary Sojourner Web site, http://www.magictails.com/marysojourner (October 22, 2002).
Salt Lake Tribune online, http://www.sltrib/com/ (June 16, 2002), Martin Naparsteck, "*Bonelight* Has Biting Essays and a Few Bumper Stickers."
University of Nevada Press Web site, http://www.nvbooks.nevada.edu/ (October 22, 2002).*

*   *   *

SOPER-COOK, JoAnne (M.)

PERSONAL: Born in Hant's Harbour, Newfoundland, Canada; married Paul Cook. *Education:* Memorial University of Newfoundland, B.A. (honors), 1998, M.A., 2003.

ADDRESSES: Agent—c/o Breakwater Books, P.O. Box 2188, 100 Water St., St. Johns, Newfoundland A1C 6E6, Canada.

CAREER: Writer and editor. Highland College, St. John's, Newfoundland, Canada, instructor in technical writing and business communications, for two years; Memorial University, St. John's, Newfoundland, Canada, peer tutor at the Writing Centre, 1995-98 and 2001, substitute English professor, 2001, program coordinator and writing instructor for the Summer Bridging Program, 2002; Jesperson Publishing, managing editor/editor-in-chief, 1997-99; Themestream Publications, leader of writing workshops, 1999-2000. Actor in play *A Breath of Spring,* 1994; actor, director, and writer of play *The Dark Night of the Soul,* 1995; led theater workshops for Phoenix Theatre Group, 1995, and Performing Arts Group. Advisor to Newfoundland and Labrador Publishers Association, 1998-99; Canada Council, jury member (writing and publishing section), 2001.

MEMBER: Atlantic Publishers Marketing Association (treasurer, 1998, secretary, 1999).

WRITINGS:

(And director) *The Dark Night of the Soul* (play), produced in St. John's, Newfoundland, Canada, 1995.

Walking the Messiah (novel), Breakwater Books (St. John's, Newfoundland, Canada), 1999.

The Wide World Dreaming (novel), Breakwater Books (St. John's, Newfoundland, Canada), 2000.

A Cold-blooded Scoundrel (novel), Moonlit Books (Auckland, New Zealand), 2001.

Waterborne (novel), Goose Lane Editions (Fredericton, New Brunswick, Canada), 2002.

Writer of editorials for Robinson-Blackmore Newspaper Group, 1987; contributor of poems, short stories, and nonfiction to periodicals, including *Newfoundland Lifestyle Magazine, TickleAce, Carbonear Compass, Muse, Rant, Waxing and Waning,* and *Essays in Canadian Writing;* frequent book reviewer for *Essays in Canadian Writing.* Work featured in anthologies, including *Genger Evocations,* Memorial University, 1995; *Rhapsody on Leroux,* 1998; and *Land, Sea and Time,* Breakwater Books, 2001. Also author of unproduced, unpublished stage plays *Full Moon and Samhain* and *The Dead Man's Clothes.*

WORK IN PROGRESS: The Paragon of Animals: An Inspector Devlin Mystery, for Moonlit Books; *Hauling down the Moon; The Summer People.*

SIDELIGHTS: Canadian writer JoAnne Soper-Cook's works cover a wide range of themes. Her first novel, *Walking the Messiah,* is about a woman named Moriah who is suffering from multiple personality disorder. The title of the book refers to one of Moriah's personalities, a masculine entity that speaks Aramaic—the language spoken in Palestine two thousand years ago—and claims to be Jesus. Moriah has murdered her father and is incarcerated in a mental institution. During Moriah's confinement, the story of her troubled childhood is told by her various personalities, each in the first person, culminating in an explanation of what drove her to kill her father. The result can be difficult to follow, a reviewer commented in *Books in Canada:* "Time is supple and disorienting; the voices blend and merge with each other."

Soper-Cook's next novel, *The Wide World Dreaming,* delves into the realm of historical fiction, telling the story of Napoleon, emperor of France during the early nineteenth century, from his own perspective. The book *A Cold-blooded Scoundrel* is a murder mystery based on the historical serial killer Jack the Ripper, told from the point of view of a British inspector named Phillip Devlin. The gruesome nature of the murders and the suspense that Devlin may be targeted as a victim is balanced by the book's humorous cast of characters.

Waterborne, like *Walking the Messiah,* is the story of an adult woman who is still tortured by a horrendous childhood and the mysteries of her family. The main protagonist is Stella Maris Goulding, a reclusive author who lives in Elsinore, an isolated fishing village in Newfoundland, Canada. The other voices present in this novel are those of Stella's mother—a woman with a secret that could expose why she has hated her only child—and grandmother, a wise and comforting Scottish woman. "Soper-Cook moves effortlessly from one voice to the next," Elizabeth Mitchell commented in *Quill and Quire,* and "the women and their intricately entwined lives are deftly realized."

BIOGRAPHICAL AND CRITICAL SOURCES:

PERIODICALS

Books in Canada, October, 1999, review of *Walking the Messiah,* p. 36.

Globe and Mail, July 13, 2002, Dannette Dooley, review of *Waterborne.*

Quill and Quire, August, 2002, Elizabeth Mitchell, review of *Waterborne.*

ONLINE

AuthorsDen.com, http://www.authorsden.com/ (November 11, 2003), reviews of *Walking the Messiah, The Wide World Dreaming, A Cold-blooded Scoundrel,* and *Waterborne.*

Breakwater Books, http://www.breakwater.nf.net/ (February 7, 2000), "JoAnne Soper-Cook."

JoAnne Soper-Cook Home Page, http://www.geocities. com/magdalene_the_harlot (October 27, 2003).*

SPENCER-FLEMING, Julia

PERSONAL: Born in Plattsburgh, NY; daughter of an Air Force pilot; married; husband's name Ross Hugo-Vidal; children: Victoria, Spencer, Virginia. *Education:* Earned J.D. *Religion:* Episcopalian.

ADDRESSES: Home—Buxton, ME. *Agent*—c/o St. Martin's Press, 175 Fifth Avenue, New York, NY 10010. *E-mail*—julia@juliaspencerfleming.com.

CAREER: Attorney and novelist.

AWARDS, HONORS: St. Martin's Press Malice Domestic award, 2002, Anthony Award for best first novel, 2003, both for *In the Bleak Midwinter.*

WRITINGS:

In the Bleak Midwinter, St. Martin's Minotaur (New York, NY), 2002.
A Fountain Filled with Blood, St. Martin's Minotaur (New York, NY), 2003.

SIDELIGHTS: Julia Spencer-Fleming completed her first novel, *In the Bleak Midwinter,* just days after giving birth to her third child. A few months later, Fleming found herself lacking enough time to find an agent and a publisher. Instead, she entered her manuscript in St. Martin's Press's Best First Novel contest. Only months after that, *In the Bleak Midwinter* won the award and was published in 2002.

Spencer-Fleming has written two novels in the series, which features a female Episcopalian priest and a local police chief who share an unacknowledged attraction for each other. The novels take place in Millers Kill, an upstate-New York town Spencer-Fleming modeled after her own hometown of Plattsburgh, New York. She explained on her Web site that she chose this setting because "That part of New York, where poor farms and Saratoga money and the mountains all come together, has always held a bone-deep fascination for me."

In the Bleak Midwinter revolves around a mystery involving an abandoned baby and the baby's recently deceased mother. The second in the series, *A Fountain*

Filled with Blood, has the duo arguing about a recent rash of gay bashings in their town. Both novels use the harsh northern weather as a challenging background to the conflicts.

Rex E. Klett, reviewing Spencer-Fleming's debut novel in *Library Journal* recommended *In the Bleak Midwinter* for all collections for Fleming's "superb skill, exact detail, and precise diction, [which] highlights credible personal conflicts." A *Publishers Weekly* contributor called the novel "a riveting pageturner from start to finish with characters who are well developed and believable." *A Fountain Filled with Blood* builds on the popularity of the first mystery with "even more action and plot twists" than Spencer-Fleming's "notable debut," according to a *Kirkus Reviews* critic. Sue O'Brien noted in *Booklist* that "serious issues such as gay bashing and contamination of the town's water supply . . . add depth to the story." Reviewing *A Fountain Filled with Blood* in *Publishers Weekly,* a critic called the novel "every bit as riveting as the first." The mystery has "eloquent exposition and natural dialogue," the critic added, noting that Spencer-Fleming's "precisely constructed plot moves effortlessly to its dramatic conclusion."

BIOGRAPHICAL AND CRITICAL SOURCES:

PERIODICALS

Booklist, February 15, 2003, Sue O'Brien, review of *A Fountain Filled with Blood,* p. 1055.
Kirkus Reviews, December 15, 2001, review of *In the Bleak Midwinter,* p. 1726; February 15, 2003, review of *A Fountain Filled with Blood,* p. 274.
Library Journal, February 1, 2002, Rex E. Klett, review of *In the Bleak Midwinter,* p. 136.
Publishers Weekly, February 11, 2002, review of *In the Bleak Midwinter,* p. 164; February 24, 2003, review of *A Fountain Filled with Blood,* p. 55.

ONLINE

Julia Spencer-Fleming Web site, http://www.juliaspencerfleming.com (May 20, 2003).*

*   *   *

SPINELLA, Marcello 1970-

PERSONAL: Born September 3, 1970, in Passaic, NJ; son of Philip and Catherine (Palermo) Spinella; married Pamela Karin Rodsniak (a paralegal), July 27, 2002. *Ethnicity:* "Caucasian." *Education:* Earned

Ph.D. *Hobbies and other interests:* Drawing, music, reading, writing fiction.

ADDRESSES: Home—537 Lakeside Dr. N., Forked River, NJ 08731. *Office*—Division of Social and Behavioral Sciences, Richard Stockton College of New Jersey, P.O. Box 195, Jim Leeds Rd., Pomona, NJ 08240-0195. *E-mail*—mspinella_phd@hotmail.com.

CAREER: Educator and author. Richard Stockton College of New Jersey, Pomona, assistant professor of psychology, 1999—.

WRITINGS:

The Psychopharmacology of Herbal Medicine: Plant Drugs That Alter Mind, Brain, and Behavior, MIT Press (Cambridge, MA), 2001.

WORK IN PROGRESS: Herbal Medicines for the Mind and Brain, for Haworth Press; *The Pharma Sutra,* a work of fiction.

SIDELIGHTS: Marcello Spinella told *CA:* "My primary motivation for writing is an extension of my sense of curiosity. I'm a neuropsychologist and college professor, so I'm lucky enough to have found my way to an occupation that encourages, if not requires, me to learn and discover. Writing is essentially a way to organize my thoughts and findings, and then to communicate my findings to others. While the goal of any scientific writing is to persuade the reader of the conclusions drawn, the best writing makes those conclusions seem merely apparent. Instilling a sense of clarity in the reader is always my goal while I'm writing. One writer who impressed that upon me was Daniel Goleman, the author of *Emotional Intelligence.* He took a relatively unknown area of research and turned it into a household word without ever raising an eyebrow. Research results in psychology can be complicated and infested with jargon, but Goleman has a way of expressing it in a way that makes intuitive sense.

"The idea for my book stemmed from a personal interest in herbal medicines. I realized how popular they were and had always been interested in the medicinal use of plants. In an age where medicines usually come in the form of a manufactured tablet, the idea of using a plant as a medicine seems a novelty, which is ironic since plants were the original source of most drugs for most of human history. In graduate school, I happened across a few research articles on the pharmacological effects of herbal medicines and realized that some of them work in a manner similar to conventional drugs. After finding a few such articles, I wondered if anyone had compiled all of the research available on psychoactive herbs, and I soon found out that apparently no one had. Millions of people take psychoactive herbal medicines, and there was no one authoritative source to guide the general public or health care professionals.

"My general areas of interest for research include psychopharmacology, or the study of psychoactive drugs, and executive functions, which are mental abilities that include impulse control, planning, organization, flexible thinking, judgment, and decision-making. The intersection of these two interests lies in addiction, where certain drugs are able to hijack a person's executive functions and make him or her act in a way that is harmful and destructive. So my research focuses on showing the relationships between those two.

"I've also taken a stab at fiction, writing a novel called *The Pharma Sutra.* It's about a pharmaceutical company that develops a drug to stimulate the oxytocin system of the brain, which strengthens social and emotional bonds. While the anticipated use was for marriage counseling, the company unleashes another potently addicting drug on the public, as so many other pharmaceutical companies have done in the past. It's basically a book about how people manage their lives and manage their emotions, and the pitfalls about doing that with a drug."

BIOGRAPHICAL AND CRITICAL SOURCES:

PERIODICALS

Library Journal, September 1, 2001, Natalie Kupferberg, review of *The Psychopharmacology of Herbal Medicine: Plant Drugs That Alter Mind, Brain, and Behavior,* p. 216.
Quarterly Review of Biology, September, 2002, Elaine D. Mackowiak, review of *The Psychopharmacology of Herbal Medicine,* p. 366.

SPINKA, Penina Keen 1945-

PERSONAL: Born February 5, 1945, in Brooklyn, NY; daughter of Jack (a shoemaker) and Yetta (a salesperson) Keen; married Barry A. Spinka (an underwriter), December 23, 1984; children: Rasha Nechama Aberman, Warshaw, Tzivia Leah Aberman Wasserman. *Education:* Attended Queens Hospital School of Nursing and Nassau Community College. *Politics:* "Honesty-Fairness Party (my own)." *Religion:* "Jewish-Earthist." *Hobbies and other interests:* Hiking, gardening, sightseeing, reading.

ADDRESSES: Home—Glendale, AZ. *Agent*—c/o Dutton Publicity, 375 Hudson St., New York, NY 10014.

CAREER: Writer. City of Los Angeles Municipal Reference Library, Los Angeles, CA, library clerk; word-processing operator for title insurance reports. Served as a volunteer providing library service to homebound residents.

MEMBER: National Fantasy Fan Federation, Society of Children's Book Writers and Illustrators, Parents of North American Israelis, Woman's American O. R. T., Hudson Valley Writers' Guild.

WRITINGS:

White Hare's Horses (young adult), Atheneum (New York, NY), 1991.
Mother's Blessing (young adult), Atheneum (New York, NY), 1992.
Picture Maker, Dutton (New York, NY), 2002.
Dream Weaver, Dutton (New York, NY), 2003.

SIDELIGHTS: Penina Keen Spinka's first books were young-adult historical novels about Native American culture. She became interested in learning more about America's first tribes when she lived in southern California and was introduced to the tribes of the West Coast, particularly the Chumash and the Aztec. She learned that the Chumash had been forced into slavery by Spanish missionaries who invited them to a feast, then sprinkled them with holy water and forced them to submit to the Christian religion. On her Web site, Spinka compares them to the Jews who were similarly oppressed during the Spanish Inquisition. "I began to understand why it was important for the Chumash to keep their culture," she says.

White Hare's Horses is set in 1522, in what would become southern California, and is about a Chumash girl whose village is raided by Aztecs riding horses they have stolen from the Spanish conquistadors. It is also an historical account of how horses were introduced into North America. White Hare's dying grandfather had warned her of "foreign places and strange people who can cross vast distance," and to save her village, she must free the horses, which she does by imitating the call of a colt in distress, and then leading the horses over the Santa Monica Mountains. *School Library Journal*'s Margaret A. Chang believed that "although Spinka clearly respects the Native Americans she describes, she does not create convincing characters, and the dialogue is too often anachronistic." "Especially appreciated is Spinka's ability to project a sense of Indian history yet to come, as well as admiration for this nonviolent people," wrote Rosie Peasley in *Voice of Youth Advocates.*

Mother's Blessing, a prequel to *White Hare's Horses,* is also set in southern California and takes place some 500 years before the arrival of the Spanish conquistadors and missionaries. The protagonist is Child, a Chumash girl who accompanies her mother into exile after her father disowns her at birth because she is not male. They find refuge with a wise older woman in another village. As Child grows, she becomes a confident New Woman, skilled in the use of the bow. In search of her spirit guide, she travels to what is now New Mexico, where she finds her guide and discovers that she is the true *wot* (leader) of her people. *School Library Journal*'s Patricia Dooley called this part of the story "the novel's strong point."

New Woman is introduced to new wonders, such as clay and metal pots and new forms of agriculture. When she learns that her people are starving, she returns with the corn that has been grown in the east and brings together three villages to show them how to plant the crop that will save them. Peasley noted that "Spinka tactfully handles such natural parts of Indian life as the first menstruation, a young brave's invitation for Child to share his bed, and the ritual of vision-inducing drugs." Kathryn Jennings of the *Bulletin of the Center for Children's Books* called New Woman "a true heroine—charming, intelligent, and brave." A *Kirkus Reviews* contributor wrote that this second novel "further establishes the author's skill as a fluent storyteller who is well-versed in North American legend."

When Spinka moved to the Hudson Valley region of upstate New York, she investigated the histories of New York tribes, and her adult novel *Picture Maker* is set in the Northeast in the fourteenth century. Picture Maker, of the Ganeogaono tribe, draws pictures that foretell the future, a talent that saves her people, but she is captured by the Algonquins and sold as a slave. Her name is now Little One, and at age thirteen, she becomes pregnant when she is raped by the violent Feather Hawk. She kills him and escapes and eventually settles in a Naskapi village in eastern Canada. She is accepted into the tribe but is traded to an Inuit tribe who call her Mikisoq. Her newborn girl is then killed, as is the Inuit custom in times of famine. When a group of Inuit split off into another group, she joins them and meets a Norseman who names her Astrid. Together they cross the Labrador Sea to Greenland, only to encounter further attacks against her husband's way of life and her special gift.

A *Kirkus Reviews* contributor noted that "the history is complete and unforgiving but sometimes takes precedence over character." *Library Journal*'s Jane Baird wrote that "Exhaustive research of the peoples of eastern North America, Canada, and Greenland provides the real heart of this novel," while a reviewer for *Publishers Weekly* said Spinka has "uncovered native traditions and beliefs in primitive North America and brought them to life through the eyes of her courageous young heroine."

BIOGRAPHICAL AND CRITICAL SOURCES:

PERIODICALS

American Indian Quarterly, summer, 1992, Clifford E. Trafzer, review of *White Hare's Horses,* p. 381.
Book Report, November-December, 1992, Holly Wadsworth, review of *Mother's Blessing,* p. 45.
Bulletin of the Center for Children's Books, June, 1991, Zena Sutherland, review of *White Hare's Horses,* p. 251; July, 1992, Kathryn Jennings, review of *Mother's Blessing,* p. 306.

Kirkus Reviews, May 1, 1992, review of *Mother's Blessing,* p. 617; October 1, 2001, review of *Picture Maker,* p. 1391; November 1, 2002, review of *Dream Weaver,* p. 1566.
Library Journal, October 1, 2001, Jane Baird, review of *Picture Maker,* p. 144; December, 2002, Jane Baird, review of *Dream Weaver,* p. 181.
Publishers Weekly, November 5, 2001, review of *Picture Maker,* p. 40; January 13, 2003, review of *Dream Weaver,* p. 42.
School Library Journal, April, 1991, Margaret A. Chang, review of *White Hare's Horses,* p. 124; May, 1992, Patricia Dooley, review of *Mother's Blessing,* p. 134.
Voice of Youth Advocates, April, 1991, Rosie Peasley, review of *White Hare's Horses,* p. 36; August, 1992, Rosie Peasley, review of *Mother's Blessing,* p. 170.

ONLINE

Penina Keen Spinka Web site, http://www.peninakeenspinka.com (April 27, 2002).*

*   *   *

STERRY, David Henry 1957-

PERSONAL: Born June 2, 1957 in Dover, NJ; married Michael Amy Cira (divorced); married Arielle Eckstut, July, 5, 2002. *Education:* Reed College, B.A. (English). *Politics:* "Everyone should have enough to eat and a warm place to sleep." *Religion:* "Humanistic Neo-Pagan." *Hobbies and other interests:* Reading, baseball, team handball, eradicating sexual exploitation of children, stopping world hunger, ending homelessness, acting, soccer, table tennis, golf, movies, laughing, music, Popeye, photography.

ADDRESSES: Home—112 Auburn St., San Rafael, CA 94901. *Agent*—Mark Reiter, IMG, New York, NY. *E-mail*—sterryhead@earthlink.net.

CAREER: Writer and actor. Has worked for HBO, A.T. & T., Isuzu, Levi's, the television show *Fresh Prince of Bel Air;* screen writer for Disney Studios and Twentieth Century-Fox. Also worked variously as a cherry picker, soda jerk, limo driver, marriage counselor, cartoon character, voice artist and pitch doctor.

MEMBER: Screen Actors Guild, American Federation of Television and Radio Artists, Writers Guild of America.

AWARDS, HONORS: Four Clio Awards; named Cabaret Performer of the Year.

WRITINGS:

Satchel Sez, Random House (New York, NY), 2001.
Chicken: Self-Portrait of a Young Man for Rent, Regan Books/HarperCollins (New York, NY), 2002.

Contributor to periodicals, including *Private Dancer, Madison Review,* and *Long Island Review.*

WORK IN PROGRESS: Master of Ceremonies: A True Story of Love, Murder, and Chippendale's, and *Working Stiffs: Men in the Sex Business.*

SIDELIGHTS: David Henry Sterry is a writer and actor who has had a varied background. In addition to working in theater and television, and performing a number of odd jobs in his lifetime, Sterry was employed as a sex worker in the 1970s. His memoir *Chicken: Self-Portrait of a Young Man for Rent* chronicles his year as a male prostitute in Hollywood.

When Sterry arrived for his first year of college in California, he realized that there were no dorms to live in and ended up wandering the streets. He was soon enticed by a man offering him a steak dinner, and woke up hours later in a scary and abusive situation. The man had stolen all of his money. Soon thereafter Sterry was hired to work at Hollywood Fried Chicken; a week later his boss helped him become a gigolo: a well-paid, teenaged escort servicing love-hungry women in Beverly Hills. The next year of his life is detailed in *Chicken,* which, Sterry explained in an online interview with *Book Browser,* he wrote in order to answer the question "How did a nice boy like me, from a nice family, with a good education, end up in this strange, savage, and abusive world, as a young man for rent?"

The memoir describes Sterry's painful, yet sometimes hilarious encounters with men and women in the prostitution scene of Los Angeles, all juxtaposed against his double-life as a student at a Catholic college, complete with a girlfriend and philosophy classes. Ted Leventhal in *Booklist* commented that while Sterry's story is, in places, "too concise and literary . . . the horror and incredulity of his lost years are not lost on the reader." A *Publishers Weekly* reviewer felt that while "Sterry doesn't seem to trust its basic appeal and relies on a gimmicky . . . prose style . . . the material here is fascinating."

Sterry made *Chicken* into a "1-Ho Show," which he performed in San Francisco and planned to take to the Edingburgh Fringe Festival. *Chicken* has also been optioned for film.

Sterry has also published a book with his wife, Arielle Eckstut, titled *Satchel Sez: The Wit, Wisdom, and World of Leroy "Satchel" Paige.* The book includes trivia about Paige's life, and lots of quotes from the famous player, along with a collection of snapshots. David Marasco of *TDA Book Review* called this volume "a wonderful little book."

Sterry told CA: "I've been writing since before I can remember. My wife says I have a writing disorder.

"Woody Allen says there are only two things in life you can control: art and masturbation. I like to combine these activities whenever possible. I write for hours and hours while I watch movies (*Bottle Rocket, Trainspotting, Gone with the Wind, The Godfather,* etc.) and sports—English premier soccer is the best.

"My influences are Mark Twain, Oscar Wilde, Irvine Welch, Jerry Stahl, Anthony Burgess, Buster Keaton, Satchel Paige, Kurt Vonnegut, Nick Drake, John Mantyn, Willie Dixon, Earl Fatha Hines, Reverend Gary Davis, Van Morrison, Roberto CLemente, Ernie Banks, Popeye, Casey Stengel, Christopher Guest, etc.

"I wrote *Satchel Sez* because he was my hero. I wrote *Chicken,* my memoir, to save my life."

BIOGRAPHICAL AND CRITICAL SOURCES:

PERIODICALS

Booklist, January 1, 2002, Ted Leventhal, review of *Chicken: Self-Portrait of a Young Man for Rent,* p. 785.

Library Journal, February 1, 2002, Rachel Collins, review of *Chicken,* p. 118.

Publishers Weekly, November 26, 2001, review of *Chicken,* p. 48.

ONLINE

Book Browser, http://www.bookbrowser.com/ (August 12, 2002), interview with Sterry.

TDA Book Review Web site, http://www.thediamondangle.com/ (April 9, 2003), David Marasco, review of *Satchel Sez.*

* * *

STEYER, James P(earson)

PERSONAL: Born in New York, NY; married; wife's name Elizabeth; children: Lily, Kirk, Caroline. *Education:* Stanford University, B.A., 1978, J.D., 1983.

ADDRESSES: Home—San Francisco, CA. *Office*—Stanford University Center for Race and Ethnicity, Bldg. 240, Stanford, CA 94305-2152. *E-mail*—jim@theotherparent.com.

CAREER: Entrepreneur, activist, and author. California Supreme Court, law clerk, then prosecuting attorney, c. 179; National Association for the Advancement of Colored People Legal Defense Fund, former civil-rights attorney; East Palo Alto Community Law Project, founder and former chairperson, 1984; Stanford University School of Education and Department of Political Science, lecturer 1987—; Children Now, cofounder, 1988; JP Kids (media company), founder and CEO, 1996-2002; Common Sense Media, chairman and CEO, 2003—. Volunteer teacher since 1980s; host of weekly television segment *Kids and the Media,* KPIX Channel 5. Member of board of trustees, Stanford Alumni Association, Children Now, National Parenting Association, and San Francisco Free Clinic.

MEMBER: Phi Beta Kappa.

AWARDS, HONORS: Stanford University Walter J. Gores award for excellence in teaching, 1982-83; Children Now Voice for Children Leadership Award, 1998.

WRITINGS:

The Other Parent: The Inside Story of the Media's Effect on Our Children, Atria Books (New York, NY), 2002.

Contributor of articles and columns on civil rights, education, and children's issues to periodicals.

SIDELIGHTS: James P. Steyer is an author and award-winning faculty member at Stanford University who is also an expert on children's media in the United States. After graduating from Stanford, Steyer worked as a civil rights attorney specializing in cases dealing with poverty. He gained recognition as founder of the East Palo Alto Community Law Project, a legal office serving low-income families unable to afford to hire proper council. Despite his promising legal career, Steyer was haunted by memories of children he had once tutored in New York City's ghetto schools, and in 1988 he founded Children Now, a national advocacy and media organization.

As the father of three children, Steyer had a vested interest in the media and children's television programming. In 1996 he founded JP Kids, a family media company credited with creating successful television series for children such as the Disney Channel's *The Famous Jett Jackson.* Steyer also founded Common Sense Media, a nonprofit organization that serves both children and their parents as a resource for locating quality children's media.

Steyer's book *The Other Parent: The Inside Story of the Media's Effect on Our Children* is an in-depth examination of the media's role as the "other parent" to many U.S. young people. Leroy Hommerding, reviewing the book for *Library Journal,* concluded that "without demonizing the media, Steyer offers an in-depth look at the effects of TV, video games, and the Internet on today's kids and explains the lack of social responsibility in many media companies as they cater to stockholders over children." In an interview with *Stanford* magazine, Steyer cited the lack of educational programming for children as one of his major concerns about contemporary media. "In the media world, we have stripped away the very rules created both to protect kids and to enhance their lives," he explained, adding that this state leaves children "almost entirely to the profit-driven manipulations of a largely unregulated free market." Praised by industry experts for his initiative, passion, and insight, Steyer's book was described by Hommerding as a "balanced and stimulating study" that provides "practical strategies for parents, educators, and even the government."

BIOGRAPHICAL AND CRITICAL SOURCES:

PERIODICALS

Library Journal, June 1, 2002, Leroy Hommerding, review of *The Other Parent: How the Media Shapes Kids' Lives,* p. 169.
Stanford, November-December, 2002, "Spoiling Our Kids" (interview).

ONLINE

Common Sense Media, http://www. commonsensemedia.com/ (June 9, 2003), "James P. Steyer."
Stanford University Web site, http://www.stanford.edu/ (June 9, 2003).
The Other Parent Web site, http://www.theotherparent. com/ (November 16, 2003), "James P. Steyer."*

*   *   *

STŘÍBRNÝ, Zdeněk 1922-

PERSONAL: Born October 1, 1922, in Bystřce p. Hostýnem; son of Josef (a cabinetmaker) and Jindîška (a household and shop manager) Stîíbrný; married, 1952; wife's name Mariana (a translator); children: Jan. *Ethnicity:* "Czech." *Education:* Charles University, Prague, M.A., 1949, Ph.D., 1951, C.Sc., 1957, Dr.Sc., 1965. *Politics:* Social Democrat. *Hobbies and other interests:* Music, both classical and jazz, sports (only televised now).

ADDRESSES: Home—Kcérvenému Vrchu 678, 16O OO Prague 6-Vokovice, Czech Republic. *Office*—Charles University, College of Liberal Arts, Department of English and American Studies, Náměstí J. Palacha 2, 116 38 Prague 1, Czech Republic.

CAREER: Educator and author. Czechoslovak Academy of Sciences and Arts, Prague, researcher, 1952-61, consultant, 1989-92; Charles University, Prague, professor of English and American literature and head of English department, 1961-70, 1990—; research professor in computer center, 1971-88.

MEMBER: International Shakespeare Association (member of executive committee, 1991—), Deutsche Shakespeare-Gesellschaft (honorary member), Shakespeare Society (Prague; honorary chairman, 1997—), Shakespeare Association of America, Franz Kafka Society, Circle of Modern Philologists, Prague (chairman, 1990—, honorary chairman, 1996—).

AWARDS, HONORS: Prize of the Czechoslovak Academy, 1960, 1988; D.Litt., University of Leicester, 1991.

WRITINGS:

Shakespeare's History Plays (in Czech with English summary), Czechoslovak Academy (Prague, Czechoslovakia), 1959.
Shakespeare's Predecessors (in Czech with English summary), Charles University Press (Prague, Czechoslovakia), 1965.
A History of English Literature (in Czech), two volumes, Czechoslovak Academy (Prague, Czechoslovakia), 1988.
Shakespeare in Eastern Europe, Oxford University Press (New York, NY), 2000.

WORK IN PROGRESS: A volume of Shakespearean essays with an autobiographical preface, for University of Delaware Press; another volume of Shakespearean essays written in Czech for Charles University Press.

SIDELIGHTS: Zdeněk Stříbrný told *CA:* "When I was asked by the two editors of the new series *Oxford Shakespeare Topics* to write on Shakespeare and Eastern Europe, I immediately felt that this was a work I was born to do. I remembered vividly the most exciting course for me at my alma mater, Charles University in Prague, after the liberation of Czechoslovakia in May 1945. It was a seminar on Anglo-Russian literacy relations conducted by Professor Otakar Vočadlo right after his return from the Nazi concentration camp at Buchenwald. Still pale and thin, he overwhelmed us by a flood of linguistic, historical, and literary data, inviting us to connect them by our own effort. Under his stimulating supervision, I started to probe into Shakespeare's influence on A. S. Pushkin, whom I loved best of all Russian authors. Ever since then I have been hooked on Shakespeare as well as his impact on Slavonic and other East European countries. I have been convinced that a full survey of Shakespeare's influence on European culture should include important East European writers, translators, critics, actors, directors, designers, filmmakers, composers, and other artists who creatively responded to Shakespeare's spell. Owing to word limit I had to be highly selective, so that my book should be considered as the first, basic attempt at covering the vast field both historically and geographically. I expect that it will be evaluated and elaborated by more detailed studies.

"So far I have received letters of thanks and appreciation from as far as St. Petersburg, Sofia, Bonn, London, Los Angeles, etc. The most encouraging recent letter was from Stephen Greenblatt of Harvard University, saying: 'It is a wonderful, fascinating and important book.' Linda Dean, director of education at the Alabama Shakespeare Festival, wrote in an e-mail to her friends: 'It's extremely well researched and wonderfully readable. . . . The closing chapters focus on Shakespeare behind the Iron Curtain and Post-Communist Shakespeare. These chapters should help us realize how precious artistic and political freedom are.'"

BIOGRAPHICAL AND CRITICAL SOURCES:

PERIODICALS

Times Literary Supplement, June 16, 2000, Jonathon Bate, review of *Shakespeare in Eastern Europe.*

*   *   *

SUZUKI, Shunryu 1904-1971

PERSONAL: Born 1904, in United States; died December 4, 1971, in California; son of a Soto Zen priest. *Education:* Graduated from Komazawa Buddhist University. *Religion:* Soto Zen Buddhist.

CAREER: Soto Zen priest in Japan, 1930s; director of two kindergartens in Japan, late 1940s and early 1950s; Sokoji Soto Zen temple, San Francisco, CA, interim director after 1959; Zen Center of San Francisco, founder, mid-1960s; also founder of Zen Mountain Center, Tassajara Springs, CA, 1967.

WRITINGS:

Zen Mind, Beginner's Mind, edited by Trudy Dixon with an introduction by Richard Baker, Walker/Weatherhill (New York, NY), 1970.
Branching Streams Flow in the Darkness: Zen Talks on the Sandokai, edited by Mel Weitsman and Michael Wenger, University of California Press (Berkeley, CA), 1999.
Not Always So: Practicing the True Spirit of Zen, HarperCollins (New York, NY), 2002.

SIDELIGHTS: Shunryu Suzuki, who died in 1971, provided much of the foundation for the rise in popularity of Zen Buddhism in the late twentieth-century United States as founder of the San Francisco Zen Center. Suzuki was a well-known teacher and religious figure who, as interest in alternative religions was burgeoning inside the Californian counterculture, helped explain the concepts and tenets of this Eastern faith to Western-trained minds.

Born in 1904, Suzuki was the son of a Soto Zen priest in Japan, and followed his father's career choice as a young man. He did not study with his parent, however, as was customary, and during the tense years of World War II and Japanese aggression, became involved in the pacifist movement. In 1959 Suzuki immigrated to the United States after the Japanese-American membership of the Sokoji Soto Zen temple in San Francisco invited him to lead their group.

During the mood of disillusionment and reevaluation that was characteristic of progressive Western intellectual thought in the 1960s, more young people began coming to Suzuki's temple in search of a new form of spiritual fulfillment. In response, he began to hold lecture series and classes for those who wished to pursue Buddhism seriously. Suzuki taught an entire generation of Westerners the core Soto Zen practice of *zazen,* or meditation. In 1967, he founded the first Zen Buddhist monastery in the United States, the Zen Mountain Center in Tassajara Springs, California.

Suzuki's first book, *Zen Mind, Beginner's Mind,* is a collection of speeches he gave at the San Francisco Zen Center. First published in 1970, the book and its contents provide instructions for seekers of spiritual enlightenment in zazen and other key Soto Zen concepts. Throughout the text, Suzuki's talents as a teacher—along with his dry sense of humor—are evident. A quarter-century later, the work remained perennially popular, and was in its thirtieth printings.

Another work authored by Suzuki was published many years after his 1971 death. The 1999 volume *Branching Streams Flow in the Darkness: Zen Talks on the Sandokai,* edited by Mel Weitsman and Michael Wenger, is a transcript of sessions led by Suzuki at the height of his career. Here, Suzuki discusses the "Sandokai," an eighth-century poem that is the cornerstone of Zen thought; it is recited daily in Buddhist temples. Its twenty-two couplets point out dichotomies in the universe, such as light and dark, and rough and smooth. Suzuki examines the poem line by line, and answers questions from students. "Readers of his precious book will be familiar with his earthy, clear, intense style," noted a *Publishers Weekly* reviewer.

BIOGRAPHICAL AND CRITICAL SOURCES:

BOOKS

Chadwick, David, *Crooked Cucumber: The Life and Zen Teaching of Shunryu,* Suzuki Broadway Books, 19.
Religious Leaders of America: A Biographical Guide to Founders and Leaders of Religious Bodies, Churches, and Spiritual Groups in North America, second edition, Gale (Detroit, MI), 1999, pp. 549-550.

PERIODICALS

Booklist, October 1, 1999, p. 324.
Library Journal, November 1, 1970, pp. 3783-3784.
Los Angeles Times Book Review, April 2, 1995, p. 9.
Publishers Weekly, October 11, 1999, p. 69.*

T

TAYLOR, Gillian F. 1967-

PERSONAL: Born January 2, 1967, in Hethersett, Norfolk, England. *Education:* Sheffield University, B.A. (with honors; archaeology, ancient history), 1988; Computeach International, diploma, 2001. *Religion:* "Heathen." *Hobbies and other interests:* Role-playing games, wine-making, sewing, knitting, annoying the cats, gardening, collecting pony stories.

ADDRESSES: Home—99 Harcourt Rd., Sheffield, South Yorkshire S10 1DH, England. *E-mail*—gftay@rockingw.freeserve.co.uk.

CAREER: Novelist and clerical worker. Sheffield University film unit, volunteer, 1988-96; volunteer for local Oxfam shop, 1994-98; clerical worker, beginning c. 2002.

WRITINGS:

NOVELS: "BLACK HORSE WESTERN" SERIES

Rocking W, Robert Hale (London, England), 1993.
The Paducah War, Robert Hale (London, England), 1996.
The Horseshoe Feud, Robert Hale (London, England), 1998.
Cullen's Quest, Robert Hale (London, England), 1999.
Darrow's Law, Robert Hale (London, England), 1999.
San Felipe Guns, Robert Hale (London, England), 2000.
Darrow's Word, Robert Hale (London, England), 2001.

Hyde's Honour, Robert Hale (London, England), 2001.
Navajo Rock, Robert Hale (London, England), 2002.
Darrow's Badge, Robert Hale (London, England), 2003.

WORK IN PROGRESS: Research into carnivals and fairgrounds of the late Victorian era in the United States.

SIDELIGHTS: Gillian F. Taylor told *CA:* "I always loved to watch westerns on the telly as a child, partly because of the horses. . . . Creating characters and stories came naturally to me. I wrote my first novel at about age fourteen. I could never think of anything else I could really want to do, other than write books, and I still can't.

"After graduation, I tried writing science fiction and fantasy, which I love. My efforts recieved very little attention from agents and publishers. When I saw the movie *Young Guns* I was inspired to write a western based on those characters, even though I knew westerns are deeply unfashionable amongst publishers. I found a publisher who took westerns, and although my first offering was rejected—the main reason was length—the rejection letter asked to see future work, giving details of their requirements. I tried again, was rejected, . . . edited *Rocking W* again, and was accepted!

"I've learned to write a strong, clear plot where the hero must take action to resolve the situation. There's nothing to beat a good villain, someone the reader can enjoy and understand. I like to include a range of ethnic types in my books; the West was populated by a mass of immigrants, so I have included Swedish, German, English, and Dutch settlers, along with Irish and Ukrainian cowhands. Spanish-American and coloured characters occur wherever it would be logical.

"I have used 'Indian attacks' against characters, but I take care to explain their motivation, and to portray their actions and beliefs with accuracy.

"When I am writing, I aim to write around two pages a day. I like to have the overall outline of a novel developed before I start, and I'll probably have imagined several scenes in advance. I develop the main characters, noting clothing, tastes and quirks. Once I have finished a manuscript, I go back and read it again. I always have to do some rewriting, as I have to write to a standard length of 45,000 words and I'm never on spot first time. I'm never afraid to throw out whole scenes and completely rewrite the course of a plot. Editing a book is the most important thing an author can do.

"The more westerns I write, the more ideas I have. Once I have created a good character, I want to know what else happens to them. I daydream as I walk to work, do the washing up, and as I remove the endless cat fur from furniture and carpets. Those daydreams, the people I create, who take on lives of their own, have to be set down for others to share. No one else can put down on page the people and places in my imagination. I'm proud of my work, which goes beyond straight-forward 'cowboys and Indians' stories. With perseverence and time, I may be able to give up the day job!"

BIOGRAPHICAL AND CRITICAL SOURCES:

ONLINE

Gillian F. Taylor Web site, http://www.geocities.com/freyni (October 2, 2003).

*   *   *

TORRANCE, E(llis) Paul 1915-2003

OBITUARY NOTICE—See index for *CA* sketch: Born October 6, 1915, in Milledgeville, GA; died of complications from pneumonia July 12, 2003, in Athens, GA. Psychologist, educator, and author. Torrance was a psychology professor who became famous for developing the Torrance Tests of Creative Thinking. His teaching career began even before he was out of college, when he taught for a year at the Midway Vocational High School in his hometown from 1936 to 1937. His interest in student creativity began at Georgia Military College, where he was a teacher, counselor, and principal from 1937 to 1944. At Georgia Military he noticed that some teenagers who were not academically successful were actually very creatively intelligent; he consequently developed his first creativity test in 1943 to measure this correlation. The next year he earned a master's degree from the University of Minnesota. While working on his Ph.D. at the University of Michigan, he worked as a counselor at Kansas State University, becoming director of its Counseling Bureau from 1949 to 1951. After completing his doctorate in 1951, he was director of the U.S. Air Force's Survival Research Field Unit for six years, and it was while there that Torrance further developed his creativity test. Some have criticized the test because it de-emphasizes knowledge in favor of creativity, while others have even blamed the test for lowering students' SAT scores. However, many educators consider it a useful tool, especially when used in conjunction with other intelligence-measuring tests. Torrance became a professor of educational psychology at the University of Minnesota in 1958, then joined the faculty at the University of Georgia, where he eventually retired in 1984. In addition to his creativity test, he developed the Future-Problem-Solving program in 1974; this program organizes some 300,000 students from around the world in performing tasks involving creative problem-solving. As an author, Torrance published dozens of books, including *Guiding Creative Talent* (1962), *Creative Learning and Teaching* (1970), *Search for Creativity* (1979), *Mentor Relationships* (1984), and *The Manifesto: A Guide to Developing a Creative Career* (2002). He was honored in 1984 when the University of Georgia named the Torrance Center for Creative Studies after him; among his many other honors, he was also named to the Hall of Fame of the National Association for Creative Children and Adults.

OBITUARIES AND OTHER SOURCES:

PERIODICALS

Atlanta Journal-Constitution, July 16, 2003, p. B6.
Los Angeles Times, July 18, 2003, p. B13.

TORTELLA CASARES, Gabriel 1936-

PERSONAL: Born November 24, 1936, in Barcelona, Spain; son of Gabriel Tortella Oteo (a publisher; in business) and Maria Teresa Casares Sanchez (an archivist); married Clara Eugenia Núñez, December 21, 1985. *Education:* University of Wisconsin, Ph.D., 1972; Universidad de Madrid, Ph.D., 1973.

ADDRESSES: Home—Conde de Cartagena 5, No. 6C, 28007 Madrid, Spain. *Office*—Facultad de ciencias economicas, Universidad de Alcala, 28802 Alcala de Henares, Madrid, Spain; fax: 3491-885-4206. *E-mail*—gabriel.tortella@uah.es.

CAREER: University of Pittsburgh, Pittsburgh, PA, associate professor, 1967-80; Universidad de Alcala, Alcala de Henares, Madrid, Spain, catedrático, 1981—.

MEMBER: European Association for Banking History (chair of academic advisory council), Academia Europaea, Asociacion de Historia Economica (president), Economic History Society, Economic History Association.

AWARDS, HONORS: Premio Rey Juan Carlos, Bank of Spain, 1994.

WRITINGS:

Los orígenes del capitalismo en España, Tecnos (Madrid, Spain), 1973.
(With others) *La banca española en la restauración,* Volume 1: *Política y finanzas,* Volume 2: *Datos para una historia económica,* Banco de España (Madrid, Spain), 1974.
(With Jordi Nadal) *Agricultura, comercio colonial y crecimiento económico en la españa contemporánea,* Ariel (Barcelona, Spain), 1975.
Banking, Railroads, and Industry in Spain, 1829-1874, Arno Press (New York, NY), 1977.
(With Juan Carlos Jiménez) *Historia del banco de crédito industrial,* Alianza (Madrid, Spain), 1986.
Introducción a la economía para historiadores, Tecnos (Madrid, Spain), 1986.
(With others) *Education and Economic Development since the Industrial Revolution: A Study in Comparative History,* Generalitat Valenciana (Valencia, Spain), 1990.

(With Clara Eugenia Núñez) *La maldición divina: ignorancia y atraso económico en perspectiva histórica,* Alianza (Madrid, Spain), 1993.
(With José Luis García Ruiz) *Una historia de los bancos central e hispano americano, 1901-1991: Noventa años de gran banca en España,* privately printed (Madrid, Spain), 1994.
El desarrollo de la españa contemporánea: historia económica de los siglos XIX y XX, Alianza (Madrid, Spain), 1994, translation by Valerie Herr published as *The Development of Modern Spain: An Economic History of the Nineteenth and Twentieth Centuries,* Harvard University Press (Cambridge, MA), 2000.
(Editor with Richard Sylla and Richard Tilly, and contributor) *The State, the Financial System, and Economic Modernization,* Cambridge University Press (New York, NY), 1999.
La revolución del siglo XX: capitalismo, comunismo y democracia (essay; title means "The Twentieth-Century Revolution: Capitalism, Communism, and Democracy"), Editorial Taurus (Madrid, Spain), 2000.
(With Alfonso Ballestero and José Luis Díaz Fernández) *Del monopolio al libre mercado: la historia de la industria petrolera españa,* Lid (Madrid, Spain), 2003.

Contributor to books, including *How to Write the History of a Bank,* edited by Martin M. G. Fase, Gerald Feldman, and Manfred Pohl, Scholar Press (Aldershot, England), 1995; *The Industrial Revolution in National Context: Europe and the USA,* edited by Mikulas Teich and Roy Porter, Cambridge University Press (New York, NY), 1996; *Challenges of Economic History: A Volume in Honour of Ivan T. Berend,* edited by Buza János, Csató Tamás, and Gyimesi Sándor, [Budapest, Hungary], 1996; *Banking, Trade, and Industry: Europe, America, and Asia, from the Thirteenth to the Twentieth Century,* edited by Alice Teichova, Ginette Kurgan-Van Hentenryk, and Dieter Ziegler, Cambridge University Press (New York, NY), 1997; and *Economic Change and the National Question in Twentieth-Century Europe,* edited by Alice Teichova, Herbert Matis, and Jaroslav Pátek, Cambridge University Press (New York, NY), 2000. Contributor to academic journals, including *Economic History Review, Economistas, Revista de Occidente, Información Comercial Española, España Económica, Expansión,* and *Revista de Historia Económica.*

WORK IN PROGRESS: Una historia de los bancos central e hispano americano (1900-2000): Un siglo de gran banca en España, with José Luis García Ruiz; *Historia de campsa: los primeros veinte años, 1927-1947,* with Mercedes Cabrera and Sebastián Coll; research on banking and monetary history, education, and economic growth.

SIDELIGHTS: Gabriel Tortella Casares told *CA:* "One writes because one wants his work to be known by others. Since I was a child I wanted to write because I liked to read, I admired workers, and I thought intellectual life was the highest activity possible for a human being. I write history because I am interested in explaining modern society, and I think it cannot be understood without turning to the past. When we go to the doctor we are asked about our medical history and even that of our parents. The social scientist does the same thing to his patient, society.

"I grew up in Spain, then a backward country ruled by a dictator who seemed destined to live forever. My main questions were: why is Spain backward? And, is backwardness related to dictatorship? I thought the answers were in the past and in the great synthesizers of history: Karl Marx, Joseph Schumpeter, Adam Smith. I also read John Maynard Keynes and many other economists whose writings had a bearing on history and the general understanding of modern society. For Spanish history the writings of Jaime Vicens Vives, Antonio Ramos Oliveira, and Raymond Carr were most illuminating. These are probably the greatest influences on my work.

"Most of my writings are the product of research. This implies setting a problem and reading about it in books and archives until a satisfactory answer seems to be formed: writing then is just putting all this in a certain order. Sometimes my research involves quantitative analysis. Usually I start writing a preliminary essay about what the problem is and outlining the main hypotheses. This helps me to organize the research work, and then the end product develops and modifies the blueprint.

"I find myself writing more and more essays, which are the product of reflection from my own work and from discussions and readings. These essays sometimes take years to develop in my head. Sometimes I have produced short articles about ideas which, in the end, became a longer essay. This is the case with my recent *La revolución del siglo XX: capitalismo, comunismo, y democracia,* which is an essay on the history of the twentieth century and is the product of many years of developing some ideas and trying to give answers to some problems."

*   *   *

TREADWELL, Theodore R. 1916-

PERSONAL: Born August 5, 1916, in Arlington, NJ; son of Theodore R., Sr. (a teacher) and Rebecca C. (a musician) Treadwell; married April 7, 1945; wife's name Elizabeth Ann (marriage ended, April 16, 1984); married March 12, 1988; wife's name, Elizabeth C.; children: Lucinda, Nancy Treadwell Moore, Daniel, Andrew, Theodore III. *Ethnicity:* "Caucasian." *Education:* Rutgers University, A.B., 1940; Harvard University, M.B.A., 1942. *Politics:* Independent. *Religion:* Protestant. *Hobbies and other interests:* Naval research, photography.

ADDRESSES: Home—35 Valerie Lane, Danbury, CT 06811. *E-mail*—diodor@aol.com.

CAREER: W. R. Grace and Co., distribution manager for Cryovac Division for eighteen years. Member of local Chamber of Commerce; community volunteer. *Military service:* U.S. Naval Reserve, active duty as commander during World War II; served in South Pacific; became lieutenant; received five battle stars.

WRITINGS:

Splinter Fleet: The Wooden Subchasers of World War II, Naval Institute Press (Annapolis, MD), 2000.

WORK IN PROGRESS: A Taste of Salt, a naval biography; research on the submarine chasers of World War I and World War II.

SIDELIGHTS: Theodore R. Treadwell told *CA:* "Too little is known about the class of naval warships known as 'subchasers.' The parts they played in World War II have been ignored or overlooked in history. They had a significant role in all theaters of the war, not only for anti-submarine patrol, but for landing control, shallow water minesweeping, search and rescue, gunboats, convoy screening, and harbor patrol.

"My writing process is agonizingly slow and methodical, in an effort to make the finished product clear and easy to read."

*   *   *

TSURU, Shigeto 1912-

PERSONAL: Born March 6, 1912, in Tokyo, Japan; son of Noburo and Iyo (Shida) Tsuru; married Masako Wada, 1939. *Ethnicity:* "Japanese." *Education:* Harvard University, A.B., 1935, M.A., 1936, Ph.D., 1940. *Hobbies and other interests:* Playing the games of chess and go.

ADDRESSES: Home—8-11-1 Akasaka, No. 211, Minato-ku, Tokyo 107-0052, Japan.

CAREER: Economist and author.

AWARDS, HONORS: LL.D., Harvard University, 1985.

WRITINGS:

Essays on Economic Development, Kinokuniya Bookstore (Tokyo, Japan), 1968.
(Editor with Helmut Weidner) *Environmental Policy in Japan,* Sigma (Berlin, Germany), 1989.
Institutional Economics Revisited, Cambridge University Press (New York, NY), 1993.
Selected Essays of Shigeto Tsuru, Edward Elgar (Brookfield, CT), Volume I: *Economic Theory and Capitalist Society,* 1994, Volume II: *The Economic Development of Modern Japan,* 1995.
Japan's Capitalism: Creative Defeat and Beyond, Cambridge University Press (New York, NY), 1996.
The Political Economy of the Environment: The Case of Japan, University of British Columbia (Vancouver, British Columbia, Canada), 1999.

*   *   *

TSYPKIN, Leonid 1926-1982

PERSONAL: Born 1926, in Minsk, Russia; died of a heart attack, 1982, in Moscow, Russia; children: one son.

CAREER: Doctor and medical researcher. Institute for Poliomyelitis and Viral Encephalitis, Moscow, Russia, research scientist.

WRITINGS:

Summer in Baden-Baden, translated by Roger and Angela Keys, with an introduction by Susan Sontag, New Directions (New York, NY), 2001.

SIDELIGHTS: Leonid Tsypkin wrote about Russian author Fyodor Dostoyevsky in his only published book, *Summer in Baden-Baden,* a "fiercely imagined, impeccably researched little novel," according to *Washington Post Book World* critic Marie Arana. Tsypkin, a native of Russia, originally finished the work in 1980 but held little hope of seeing it published; he had a tense relationship with government officials. Tsypkin had been demoted from his job at a research institute in Moscow, quite possibly as punishment for his son's immigration to the United States as well as his own unsuccessful efforts to obtain an exit visa. Tsypkin also kept his writings private, refusing to publicize his work. Still, *Summer in Baden-Baden* was smuggled out of Russia in 1981 and was scheduled to be published, in installments, in a weekly Russian-language newspaper in New York City. In the spring of 1982, shortly after the first installment appeared, Tsypkin died of a heart attack. He never saw his work in print. *Summer in Baden-Baden* received little notice until 2001, when a translated version was published in the United States.

Summer in Baden-Baden is "partly autobiography, partly a travelogue and partly a reimagining of Dostoyevksy's life," according to Vassily Aksyonov in the *New Leader.* The tale begins as an unnamed narrator travels by train to Leningrad to visit the Dostoyevsky Museum. The narrator carries a diary by Anna Grigoryevna, Dostoyevsky's second wife, that details the couple's turbulent summer in Baden-Baden, Germany, in 1867. Tsypkin intertwines two stories: that of the narrator and his passionate admiration of Dostoyevsky, the other of Dostoyevsky's months in Baden-Baden, during which he gambled compulsively, suffered epileptic fits, and wrestled with feelings of intense self-loathing. As David Bergman remarked in the *Review of Contemporary Fiction,* "Tsypkin's account is unsparingly frank. As a specialist in cancer's response to lethal viruses, Tsypkin approaches Dostoyevsky's self-destruction with the same unflinching, clinical fascination."

Critics observed that *Summer in Baden-Baden* is a challenging yet rewarding read. Steve Harris, reviewing the work for the online journal *Samsära Quarterly,* noted that "Tyspkin moves freely and confusingly through time, blurring the lines between the narrator's life and Dostoyevksy's life." In *America* Peter Heinegg stated that the work "is written in a breathlessly reeling, feverish style, with sentence-paragraphs that hectically spin and swirl, sometimes for pages, without pausing for a period." Yet, as Shaazka Beyerle wrote in *Europe,* Tsypkin's "prose is emotive without being flowery—it brings to life people, places, feelings, and impressions." Arana remarked that *Summer in Baden-Baden* "stands to change the way we think of twentieth-century Russian fiction. It is, in more ways than one, a chronicle of fevered genius." And Harris concluded, "Armed with some Dostoyevsky basics . . . the patient reader will be rewarded not only with a fine modernist meditation on one of Russian literature's greatest writers but also the story of one writer's devotion to the writing life."

BIOGRAPHICAL AND CRITICAL SOURCES:

PERIODICALS

America, February 18, 2002, Peter Heinegg, review of *Summer in Baden-Baden.*

Europe, May, 2002, Shaazka Beyerle, review of *Summer in Baden-Baden.*

New Leader, November-December, 2001, Vassily Aksyonov, review of *Summer in Baden-Baden.*

New York Times Book Review, June 2, 2002, review of *Summer in Baden-Baden.*

Publishers Weekly, August 13, 2001, review of *Summer in Baden-Baden.*

Review of Contemporary Fiction, summer, 2002, David Bergman, review of *Summer in Baden-Baden.*

Washington Post Book World, January 13, 2002, Marie Arana, review of *Summer in Baden-Baden.*

ONLINE

Samsära Quarterly, http://www.samsaraquarterly.net/ (November 17, 2003), Steve Harris, review of *Summer in Baden-Baden.**

V

VALDATA, Patricia 1952-

PERSONAL: Born October 16, 1952, in New Brunswick, NJ; daughter of William and Ethel (Kovaks) Valdata; married Robert Schreiber (a computer systems architect), April 21, 1979. *Education:* Douglass College, B.A. (mass communications), 1974; Rutgers University, B.A. (English), 1977; Goddard College, M.F.A. (writing), 1991. *Hobbies and other interests:* Soaring, boating.

ADDRESSES: Office—Cloudstreet Communications, 36 Gina Court, Elkton, MD 21921. *E-mail*—pvaldata@ cloudstreetcomm.com.

CAREER: Writer and educator. Technical writer and editor, 1975-89; University of Delaware, Newark, adjunct instructor, 1990-94, assistant professor of English, 1994-97; Cloudstreet Communications, Elkton, MD, founder and president, 2000—. AstraZeneca, Wilmington, DE, writer and project manager.

MEMBER: International Association of Business Communicators (president of Delaware chapter, 2001), Women Soaring Pilots Association (founding member and former president), American Women Pilots.

AWARDS, HONORS: Joseph C. Lincoln Award, Soaring Society of America, 1994, for story "Just like a Hawk"; First Prize, *International Icarus,* for poem "Directions to Bombay Hook"; First Prize, Eastern Shore Regional Poetry Competition, 2000, for "Fluid Dynamics"; Individual Artist Award for Poetry, Maryland State Arts Council, 2001.

WRITINGS:

Crosswind (novel), Wind Canyon, 1997.
Looking for Bivalve (poetry chapbook), Pecan Grove Press (San Antonio, TX), 2002.

WORK IN PROGRESS: Two more novels.

SIDELIGHTS: Patricia Valdata told *CA:* "I come from a blue-collar background where participation in the arts was not encouraged. It took me a long time to take myself seriously as a writer, and so I was well into my forties before my first novel was published. I hope to make up for lost time now, and I urge anyone who wants to write to do so regardless of their background or environment."

*   *   *

VAZIRANI, Reetika 1962-2003

OBITUARY NOTICE—See index for *CA* sketch: Born August 9, 1962, in Patiala, Punjab, India; committed suicide July 16, 2003, in Chevy Chase, MD. Educator and author. Vazirani was considered a promising new poet whose first two books were award winners. She came to the United States with her family in 1967, graduating from Wellesley College with a B.A. in 1994 and earning her M.F.A. from the University of Virginia three years later. She was working as an instructor at the University of Virginia when her first poetry collection, *White Elephants,* was released in 1996. The book earned the Barnard New Women Poets Prize that year; her second book, *World Hotel* (2002), won the Anisfield-Wolf Book Award. Vazirani's poetry often speaks of her childhood and the experience of being an immigrant in the United States. She was employed as a writer-in-residence at Sweet Briar College from 1998 to 2000, and in 2002 became writer-in-residence at William and Mary College. Shortly before her death she accepted a position with the faculty at Emory University, which she was scheduled to assume in the fall of 2003. Vazirani, who was reportedly engaged in a troubled marriage to Pulitzer Prize-winning poet Yusef Komunyakaa, apparently killed her fifteen-month-old son and then committed suicide, according to investigators.

OBITUARIES AND OTHER SOURCES:

BOOKS

Writers Directory, 18th edition, St. James Press (Detroit, MI), 2003.

PERIODICALS

Atlanta Journal-Constitution (Atlanta, GA), July 18, 2003, p. F6.
Times (London, England), July 19, 2003, p. 22.
Washington Times, July 24, 2003, p. B2.

*   *   *

VOGAU, Boris Andreyevich 1894-1938
(Boris Pilnyak; Boris Andreyevich Pilniak; Boris Pilnjak)

PERSONAL: Born October 11, 1894, in Mozhaisk, Moscow Province, Russia; died in Stalin's labor camps April 21, 1938 (some sources say 1941); son of a veterinarian; married Maria Sokolova, 1917 (marriage ended); married Olga Scherbinovskaia, 1925 (marriage ended); married Kira Andronikashvili (an actress), 1933; children (first marriage): one son, one daughter. *Education:* Attended University of Kolomna; Moscow Commercial Institute, degree in economics, 1920.

CAREER: Writer from 1915. Arrested during Stalinist purges, 1937.

MEMBER: All-Russian Writer's Union (president 1929).

WRITINGS:

S poslednim parokhodom i drugie rasskazy (title means "With the Last Steamer and Other Stories"), 1918.
Ivan-da-Mar'ia (stories; title means "Ivan and Mary"), 1922.
Byl'e (stories; title means "Bygones"), 1922.
Golyi god, 1922, translation by Alec Brown published as *The Naked Year,* 1928, translated by A. R. Tulloch, 1975.
Nikola-na-Posadiakh (stories; title means "As It Was"), 1923.
Povesti o chernom khlebe (title means "Stories about Black Bread"), 1923.
Mashiny i volki (title means "Machines and Wolves"), 1923-1924.
Mat'syra zemlia (title means "Mother Earth"), 1924.
Angliiskie rasskazy (title means "English Tales"),1924.
Tales of the Wilderness (includes "The Snow," "A Year of Their Lives," "A Thousand Years," "Over the Ravine," "Always on Detachment," "The Snow Wind," "Wind," "The Forest Manor," "The Bielokonsky Estate," "Death," "The Heirs," and "The Crossways"), translated by F. O'Dempsey, 1925.
Rasskazy (short stories), 1927, 2nd revised edition, 1933.
Povest' nepogashennoi luny, 1927, translation by Beatrice Scott published as *The Tale of the, Unextinguished Moon,* 1967.
(With A. Rogozina) *Kitaiskaia sud'ba cheloveka,* 1927, translation by Vera T. Reck and Michael Green published as *Chinese Story and Other Tales,* 1988.
Ivan-Moskva, 1792, translation by A. Schwartzman published as *Ivan Moscow,* 1935.
Raplesnutoe vremia. Rasskazy (title means "Spilled Time: Stories"), 1927, reprinted, 1966.
Krasnoe derevo (novella), 1929, translation published as "Mahogany," in *Mother Earth and Other Stories,* 1968.
Shtoss v zhizn (title means "A Chance on Life"), 1929.
Volga vpadaet v Kaspiiskoe more, 1930, translation by Charles Malamuth published as *The Volga Falls to the Caspian Sea,* 1931, published as *The Volga Flows to the Caspian Sea,* 1932.
Rasskazy (stories), 1932.

Rozhdenie cheloveka (novella; title means "The Birth of Man"), 1935.

Izbrannye rasskazy (selected stories), 1935.

Sozrevanie plodov (title means "The Ripening of Fruit"), 1936.

Mother Earth and Other Stories, translated by Vera T. Reck and Michael Green, 1968.

Dvoiniki (title means "Doubles"), 1983.

Romany (title means "Novels"), 1990.

Zashtat (title means "Back of Beyond"), 1991.

OTHER

Sobranie sochinenii (collected works), 3 volumes, 1923.

Korni iaponskogo solntsa (title means "Roots of the Japanese Sun"), 1926.

Kamni I korni (title means "Stones and Roots"), 1927.

Sobranie sochinenii, 8 volumes, 1929-1930.

O'kei: amerikanskii roman (title means "OK: An American Novel"), 1932.

Izbrannye proizvedeniia (selected works), edited by V. Novikov, 1976.

Tselaia zhizn': Izbrannaia proza (title means "A Whole Life: Selected Prose"), 1988.

Chelovecheskii veter (title means "Human Wind"), 1990.

Rasskazy, povesti, romany, (includes complete version of *Solianoi ambar),* Sovetskii Pisatel, 1990.

Tret'ia stolitsa (title means "The Third Capital"), 1992.

SIDELIGHTS: Published under the name Boris Pilnyak, Boris Andreevich Vogau's chaotic, romantic fiction derives from Russia's tumultuous revolutionary period; in it, he describes the confused personal experience of a grand historical shift. As Trotsky explained in *Literature and Revolution:* "Pilnyak takes the Revolution in its periphery, in its back yards, in the village, and mainly in the provincial towns. His Revolution is a small-town one . . . A vital part of [it] is grasped with a keen eye, but as if in a hurry, as if rushing past. . . . The meaningless dreary life of a filthy provincial philistine perishing in the midst of the October storm, is painted by Pilnyak . . . as a series of bright spots . . . The general impression is always the same—a restless dualism."

Vogau was born on September 12, 1894, in a town of the Moscow province. His father was a country veterinarian and a Volga German, and both parents were Populists during the 1880s and 1890s. Vogau's work was influenced not only by his experiences in small Russian towns, but also by his experience of revolutionary fervor and his study of literature. As Michael Falchicov remarked in *The Reference Guide to World Literature:* Vogau "belongs to that transitional generation of Russian writers whose work and life were fundamentally determined by the Bolshevik Revolution and its outcome. Born into the radical intelligentsia and brought up in central Russian provincial towns, [his] earliest influences were the mystical modernists Belyi and Remizov and, more distantly, Dostoevskii and Leskov."

Vogau became a writer early in life—he was first published at the age of twenty-one, and by age twenty-eight he published *Golyi god,* his renowned civil war novel. The novel traces the effects of the revolution on Russia's provincial areas, where the delicate moral and social fabric of life easily unravels. Falchikov noted: "The striking features of *Golyi god* are its verbal and stylistic inventiveness and its extraordinary atmosphere of bold youthful enthusiasm and horror and suffering. There is little plot and no obvious heroic figure-unless it is Russia." Irving Howe, writing in the *New Republic,* was more skeptical: "*Golyi god* is aggressively experimental, and now suffers from the fact that few things in literature date more than the bold experiment of yesterday." The novel was extremely popular, however, and its romantic view of the revolution placed Vogau in difficult straits with Soviet authorities.

Howe explained that Vogau "had a fine gift for getting into trouble. His eye for social and moral fissures led him to themes of danger. As a man, he seems to have been rather timorous, again and again recanting the 'heresies' that his imagination could not resist. . . . Whereas the Bolsheviks saw Russia through the prism of revolution, . . . [Vogau] saw the Revolution through the prism of Russian history." Vogau's success, then, led him into struggles with the Soviet government; Howe later explained: "Not in command of a coherent ideology, [he] exposed himself guilelessly to the ideologies swirling across Russia in the years before Stalin shut everything down."

Following Vogau's success in the early 1920s, he wrote prolifically in the complicated, literate style Soviets dubbed "Pilnyakism." Evelyn Bristol, in the *Encyclopedia of World Literature,* described this approach:

"The complex and unconventional style . . . features the liberal use of such devices as the frame story, the flashback, enigmatic narrative transitions, lyrical digressions, leitmotifs, symbols, insertions of documents, dialectical renderings, wordplay, and typographical peculiarities." This complex style, filled with chaotic shifts, further angered the Soviets, who insisted that Vogau describe Russia in a more synthesized, orderly fashion. Only by representing Russian life more coherently, moving toward the happy conclusion of Communism, could Vogau continue his art.

Vogau continued to write in his own way, however, and his writing increasingly angered authorities. In the title story of *Povest' nepogashennoi luny* (1927, "Tale of the Unextinguished Moon"), Vogau writes about a military leader who undergoes surgery for the Party and dies in the process. Falchikov explained: "The conflict between science and nature is an important theme in this story, but most critics detected a thinly fictionalized account of the circumstances surrounding the death of army commander M. F. Frunze, widely rumoured to be the Stalin regime's first 'medical murder.'" Howe remarked, incredulously: "'The Unbending Man' [the politician of Vogau's story], clearly a facsimile of Stalin, is shown as a heartless, paranoid dictator, while the simple, decent victim, Gavrilov, bears a close resemblance to Frunze. How [Vogau] . . . , who by then had already experienced the bitterness of political gang-ups, could have permitted himself to write this story, and how [the journal] *Novy Mir* could have risked printing it, I do not understand." Vogau quickly recanted, calling the story "the grossest of errors," but his fate with the regime was sealed.

When Beatrice Scott translated *Tale of the Unextinguished* into English in 1967, Americans enjoyed Vogau's boldness. J. K. Davidson, writing in the *New York Times Book Review,* commented: Vogau "is a masterly stylist" who "describes society at the moment when it has no system and is uncertain of its values. . . . his stories are somber, not melancholic; but they have the effect of creating in us an almost unbearable melancholy at the thought of what upheaval meant 50 years ago in Russia and what it would mean again, in another time, in another place." Howe, reviewing the translation for *Harper's,* wrote: "Though a literary modernist, [Vogau] . . . also had something in him of the ancient tribal bard. He was a marvelous storyteller, a spellbinder, an enchanted

rhetorician. . . . Some of his stories are simply magnificent." The reviewer went on to note that the title story "is one of the most terrifying pieces ever written in the Soviet Union." Stalin arrested Vogau during the purges in 1937, after the author has published more of his work abroad. Accused of "anti-Soviet activities," Vogau was taken into the Soviet work camps; some believe he was assassinated in 1938, though some sources claim he died after several years in the camps.

Perhaps most disturbing about Vogau's turbulent career—and ultimate martyrdom—is that his complicated, chaotic, allusive writing style reflected his supposed political stance. Vogau's writing not only exposed political crimes, but also linguistically evoked the experience of political displacement. His crime—or virtue—was in what he allowed others to feel.

BIOGRAPHICAL AND CRITICAL SOURCES:

BOOKS

Encyclopedia of World Literature in the Twentieth Century, St. James Press (Detroit, MI), 1999.
Reference Guide to World Literature, St. James Press (Detroit, MI), 1995.*

*   *   *

VOLANSKI, John J. 1956-

PERSONAL: Born May 13, 1956, in Geneva, OH; son of John L. and Rita (Oliva) Volanski; married April 2, 1986; wife's name Christie; children: Mitch Wilson, Joshua Wilson. *Education:* Ohio State University, B.S. (electrical engineering), 1979, M.B.A., 1987. *Hobbies and other interests:* Audio recording, martial arts, volleyball, music.

ADDRESSES: Agent—c/o Author Mail, Pacific Beach Publishing, P.O. Box 90471-A002, San Diego, CA 92169. *E-mail*—soundadvice@johnvolanski.com.

CAREER: Engineer and technical writer. Employed as an electrical engineer by aerospace and defense industry. Holds U.S. patent on "console for providing virtual reality environments."

AWARDS, HONORS: Product of the Year award, Securities Industry Association, 2000, for Integra Digital Video Time-lapse Recorder.

WRITINGS:

Sound Recording Advice, Pacific Beach Publishing (San Diego, CA), 2002.

Contributor of articles to periodicals, including *Avionics, Electronic Musician, Aftertouch,* and *Keyboard.*

SIDELIGHTS: John J. Volanski explained in an interview posted on his Web site that *Sound Recording Advice* began as a series of articles he published in *Electronic Music* magazine. "I wrote quite a bit of it, then lost interest and put it on the shelf for several years. then I started thinking that I should link all these articles together and write a book on home studio recording. . . . I finally decided to put together an instruction manual that discusses all of the basic aspects of home recording studios, including what equipment to buy and where to get it."

An electrical engineer, Volanski has operated a home recording studio since the early 1980s, and has designed and developed many electrical and audio systems for entertainment, as well as surveillance and avionic applications. As he explained in his interview: "Being an electrical engineer with an audio engineering background, I approach the subject of home recording from the technical side, rather than the musician's side. The trick is to explain technical subject such as grounding, power conditioning, acoustics, and other related issues in a factual yet simplified way so as to not turn off the musicians who are really only interested in recording their own music. I wrote the book from a do-it-yourself viewpoint, so that the home studio owner would not just buy equipment off the shelf but also really be involved with the inner workings of the studio."

BIOGRAPHICAL AND CRITICAL SOURCES:

ONLINE

John J. Volanski Web site, http://www.johnvolanski. com (November 20, 2003).

W-Z

WALKER, Alexander 1930-2003

OBITUARY NOTICE—See index for *CA* sketch: Born March 22, 1930, in Portadown, Armagh, Northern Ireland; died July 15, 2003, in London, England. Journalist and author. Walker was a renowned film critic for the London *Evening Standard* who also wrote several actor biographies and other books about film. He inherited a love for the cinema from his mother, who began taking her son to the movies when he was only four years old. When, during World War II, she broke her glasses and could not see the screen, Walker went to see the pictures for her and then reported to her on what happened in what would become his earliest practice as a critic. As a teenager, he fell in love with classic movies such as *Citizen Kane* and began writing, selling a radio play to the British Broadcasting Corp. when he was only fifteen years old. He received a B.A. from Queen's University, Belfast and later attended the College d'Europe, in Bruges, Belgium, and the University of Michigan, where he taught philosophy and comparative government from 1952 to 1954. While in Michigan he met the owner of the London *Evening Standard,* who promised him a job if he came back to England. When Walker decided to take the job offer, the publisher reneged. Nevertheless, Walker found a job in England as a features editor for the *Birmingham Gazette,* followed by three years as film critic for the *Birmingham Post.* In 1960 he managed to get his foot back in the door at the *Evening Standard,* and from then until his death he was a regular feature-writer in that newspaper. Walker, who was named Critic of the Year in 1970, 1974, and 1998 by the British Press, gained a reputation as a fair, sometimes painfully frank critic although he could also be ebulliently effusive about the films he enjoyed.

Making friends with a number of actors and directors—he was especially close to Peter Sellers and director Stanley Kubrick, whose *2001: A Space Odyssey* and *A Clockwork Orange* Walker much admired—the critic at one point famously rankled director Ken Russell, who punched Walker during a television program after receiving a bad review. In addition to his work for the *Evening Standard,* Walker was a columnist for *Vogue* from 1974 to 1986 and often appeared on radio and television programs. He also was the author of movie-star biographies and general books on film, including *Stanley Kubrick Directs* (1971), *Garbo: A Portrait* (1980), *National Heroes: British Cinema in the Seventies and Eighties* (1985), *"It's Only a Movie, Ingrid": Encounters on and off the Screen* (1988), *Fatal Charm: The Life of Rex Harrison* (1993), and *Audrey: Her Real Story* (1994). Among his honors, Walker was named a chevalier of the French Ordre des Arts et des Lettres in 1981.

OBITUARIES AND OTHER SOURCES:

BOOKS

Writers Directory, 18th edition, St. James Press (Detroit, MI), 2003.

PERIODICALS

Daily Post (London, England), July 16, 2003, p. 11.
Daily Telegraph (London, England), July 16, 2003.
Guardian (London, England), July 16, 2003, p. 23.
Independent (London, England), July 16, 2003, p. 16.

Los Angeles Times, July 17, 2003, p. B13.
Times (London, England), July 16, 2003, p. 27.

* * *

WALKER, Richard L(ouis) 1922-2003

OBITUARY NOTICE—See index for *CA* sketch: Born April 13, 1922, in Bellefonte, PA; died of cancer July 22, 2003, in Columbia, SC. Educator, diplomat, and author. Walker, a professor of international relations and an expert on the Far East, was a former ambassador to South Korea. After graduating from Drew University in 1944 and studying Chinese at the University of Pennsylvania, he served as an interpreter during World War II at the U.S. Army's Pacific headquarters. He then went back to school to earn a Ph.D. from Yale University in 1950. That same year he joined the faculty at Yale, where he was an assistant professor of history until 1957, when he moved to the University of South Carolina. He spent most of the rest of his career with that institution as a professor of international relations, heading the department from 1957 to 1972. Walker also founded the Institute of International Studies in 1961. In 1981 President Ronald Reagan selected Walker to be U.S. ambassador to South Korea, a position Walker held until 1986, when he returned to the University of South Carolina, retiring as professor emeritus in 1992. During his career Walker lectured around the world, including at schools in Taiwan, Japan, and China. He was the author or editor of over a dozen books about Asia, among them *China under Communism: The First Five Years* (1955), *The China Danger* (1966), *The Human Cost of Communism in China* (1971), and *Korean Remembrances* (1998).

OBITUARIES AND OTHER SOURCES:

PERIODICALS

Los Angeles Times, July 25, 2003, p. B15.
New York Times, July 24, 2003, p. A21.
Washington Post, July 26, 2003, p. B7.

* * *

WALL, William 1955-

PERSONAL: Born July 6, 1955, in Cork, Ireland; son of Michael (a farmer) and Margaret (a shopkeeper; maiden name, Regan) Wall; married Elizabeth Kirwan (a teacher), June 30, 1979; children: Illan, Oisin. *Ethnicity:* "Irish." *Politics:* "Liberal/Left." *Religion:* "None."

ADDRESSES: Home—County Cork, Ireland. *Agent*—Gill Coleridge, 20 Powis Mews, London W11 1JN, England. *E-mail*—kirwall@eircom.net.

CAREER: Poet and novelist.

WRITINGS:

Mathematics and Other Poems, Collins Press (Cork, Ireland), 1997.
Alice Falling (novel), Norton (New York, NY), 2000.
Minding Children (novel), Hodder/Sceptre (London, England), 2001.
The Map of Tenderness (novel), Hodder/Sceptre (London, England), 2002.

Work represented in anthologies, including *Phoenix Irish Short Stories,* 1998 and 2001. Contributor of short stories and poetry to periodicals.

WORK IN PROGRESS: A fourth novel.

SIDELIGHTS: William Wall told *CA:* "I've been writing something or other since the age of seven or eight, but I know I became a writer at age twelve when I fell seriously ill with Still's Disease. The continuous presence of this disease in my life, even forty years later, has probably contributed to darkening my work. Shakespeare did his work, too—the book that has most influenced me could well be *King Lear.* University exposure to existentialism is an additional factor. This dark side of my writing has provoked some controversy, and my friends keep urging me to write something gentle. No doubt I will some day.

"Despite all that I love writing and am rarely completely happy unless I'm working on something. I've written lots of stories and poems and won prizes and publication, given readings and all the usual stuff, but the greatest charge of all is sitting down in front of my Apple iBook knowing there's a set of characters that has a life of its own, and it's my job to chronicle those lives—at least the tiny segment of their existence that happens in my world.

"We live, in relative isolation, just outside Cork City, Ireland. There are green fields in front and behind the house. We're only twenty minutes from the sea. Still we're close enough to the cinema, galleries, theaters, cafés, and restaurants to feel we're living in a city, and to benefit from the advantages that brings. E-mail and the Internet bring the world even closer."

WALLACE, (Richard Horatio) Edgar 1875-1932

PERSONAL: Born April 1, 1875, in London, England; died of pneumonia February 10, 1932, in Beverly Hills, CA; son of Richard Edgar (an actor) and Polly Richards (an actress); married Ivy Maud Caldecott, 1901 (divorced 1911); married Violet King, 1921; children: (first marriage) two daughters, two sons; (second marriage) one daughter.

CAREER: Writer. Worked various jobs, including as a factory worker and merchant seaman; South African correspondent, Reuters, 1899-1902; *Daily Mail,* London, England, South African correspondent, 1900-02, reporter, 1903-07; *Rand Daily News,* Johannesburg, South Africa, editor, 1902-03; *Standard,* London, reporter, 1910; *Week-End* (later *Week-End Racing Supplement*), London, 1910, began as racing editor, became editor; *Evening News,* London, racing editor and special writer, 1910-12. Chair of board of directors, British Lion Film Corporation. *Military service:* Royal West Kent Regiment, 1893-96; Medical Staff Corps, 1896-99; worked at War Office during World War I.

MEMBER: London Press Club (chair, 1923-24).

WRITINGS:

"INSPECTOR ELK" CRIME NOVELS

The Nine Bears, Ward, Lock (London, England), 1910, revised edition published as *The Other Man,* Dodd, Mead (New York, NY), 1911, revised as *Silinski, Master Criminal,* World (Cleveland, OH), 1930, published as *The Cheaters,* Digit (London, England), 1964.

The Fellowship of the Frog, Ward, Lock (London, England), 1925, Doubleday (New York, NY), 1928.

The Joker, Hodder & Stoughton (London, England), 1926, published as *The Colossus,* Doubleday (New York, NY), 1932.

The Twister, Long (London, England), 1928, Doubleday (New York, NY), 1929.

The India-Rubber Man, Hodder & Stoughton (London, England), 1929, Doubleday (New York, NY), 1930.

White Face, Hodder & Stoughton (London, England), 1930, Doubleday (New York, NY), 1931.

OTHER CRIME NOVELS

The Four Just Men, Tallis Press (London, England), 1906, revised edition, 1906, Small, Maynard (Boston, MA), 1920, with a new introduction by Alan Weissman, Dover Publications (New York, NY), 1984.

Angel Esquire, Holt (New York, NY), 1908.

The Council of Justice, Ward, Lock (London, England), 1908.

Captain Tatham of Tatham Island, Gale & Polden (London, England), 1909, revised edition published as *The Island of Galloping Gold,* Newnes (London, England), 1926, published as *Eve's Island,* 1926.

The Fourth Plague, Ward, Lock (London, England), 1913, Doubleday (New York, NY), 1930.

Grey Timothy, Ward, Lock (London, England), 1913, published as *Pallard the Punter,* 1914.

The River of Stars, Ward, Lock (London, England), 1913.

The Man Who Bought London, Ward, Lock (London, England), 1915.

The Melody of Death, Arrowsmith (Bristol, England), 1915, Dial Press (New York, NY), 1927.

The Clue of the Twisted Candle, Small, Maynard (Boston, MA), 1916.

A Debt Discharged, Ward, Lock (London, England), 1916.

The Tomb of Ts'in, Ward, Lock (London, England), 1916.

The Just Men of Cordova, Ward, Lock (London, England), 1917.

Kate Plus Ten, Small, Maynard (Boston, MA), 1917.

The Secret House, Ward, Lock (London, England), 1917, Small, Maynard (Boston, MA), 1919.

Down under Donovan, Ward, Lock (London, England), 1918.

The Man Who Knew, Small, Maynard (Boston, MA), 1918.

The Green Rust, Ward, Lock (London, England), 1919, Small, Maynard (Boston, MA), 1920.

The Daffodil Mystery, Ward, Lock (London, England), 1920, published as *The Daffodil Murder,* Small, Maynard (Boston, MA), 1921.

Jack o' Judgment, Ward, Lock (London, England), 1920, Small, Maynard (Boston, MA), 1921.

The Book of All Power, Ward, Lock (London, England), 1921.

The Angel of Terror, Small, Maynard (Boston, MA), 1922, pubished as *The Destroying Angel,* Pan (London, England), 1959.

Captains of Souls, Small, Maynard (Boston, MA), 1922.

The Crimson Circle, Hodder & Stoughton (London, England), 1922, Doubleday (New York, NY), 1929.

The Flying Fifty-five, Hutchinson (London, England), 1922.

Mr. Justice Maxell, Ward, Lock (London, England), 1922.

The Valley of Ghosts, Odhams Press (London, England), 1922, Small, Maynard (Boston, MA), 1923.

The Clue of the New Pin, Small, Maynard (Boston, MA), 1923.

The Green Archer, Hodder & Stoughton (London, England), 1923, Small, Maynard (Boston, MA), 1924.

The Missing Million, Long (London, England), 1923, published as *The Missing Millions,* Small, Maynard (Boston, MA), 1925.

The Dark Eyes of London, Hodder & Stoughton (London, England), 1924, Doubleday (New York, NY), 1929.

Diana of Kara-Kara, Small, Maynard (Boston, MA), 1924, published as *Double Dan,* Hodder & Stoughton (London, England), 1924.

The Face in the Night, Long (London, England), 1924, Doubleday (New York, NY), 1929.

Room 13, Long (London, England), 1924.

Flat 2, Garden City (New York, NY), 1924, revised edition, Long (London, England), 1927.

The Sinister Man, Hodder & Stoughton (London, England), 1924, Small, Maynard (New York, NY), 1925.

The Three Oaks Mystery, Ward, Lock (London, England), 1925.

Blue Hand, Ward, Lock (London, England), 1925, Small, Maynard (Boston, MA), 1926.

The Daughters of the Night, Newnes (London, England), 1925.

The Gaunt Stranger, Hodder & Stoughton (London, England), 1925, published as *The Ringer,* Doubleday (New York, NY), 1926.

The Hairy Arm, Small, Maynard (Boston, MA), 1925, published as *The Avenger,* Long (London, England), 1926.

A King by Night, Long (London, England), 1925, Doubleday (New York, NY), 1926.

The Strange Countess, Hodder & Stoughton (London, England), 1925, Small, Maynard (Boston, MA), 1936.

The Three Just Men, Hodder & Stoughton (London, England), 1925, Doubleday (New York, NY), 1930.

Barbara on Her Own, Newnes (London, England), 1926.

The Black Abbot, Hodder & Stoughton (London, England), 1926, Doubleday (New York, NY), 1927.

The Day of Uniting, Hodder & Stoughton (London, England), 1926, Mystery League (New York, NY), 1930.

The Door with Seven Locks, Doubleday (New York, NY), 1926.

The Man from Morocco, Long (London, England), 1926, published as *The Black,* Doubleday (New York, NY), 1930.

The Million-Dollar Story, Newnes (London, England), 1926.

The Northing Tramp, Hodder & Stoughton (London, England), 1926, Doubleday (New York, NY), 1929, published as *The Tramp,* Pan (London, England), 1965.

Penelope of the Polyantha, Hodder & Stoughton (London, England), 1926.

The Square Emerald, Hodder & Stoughton (London, England), 1926, published as *The Girl from Scotland Yard,* Doubleday (New York, NY), 1927.

The Terrible People, Doubleday (New York, NY), 1926.

We Shall See!, Hodder & Stoughton (London, England), 1926, published as *The Gaol Breaker,* Doubleday (New York, NY), 1931.

The Yellow Snake, Hodder & Stoughton (London, England), 1926.

Big Foot, Long (London, England), 1927.

The Feathered Serpent, Hodder & Stoughton (London, England), 1927, Doubleday (New York, NY), 1928.

The Forger, Hodder & Stoughton (London, England), 1927, published as *The Clever One,* Doubleday (New York, NY), 1928.

The Hand of Power, Long (London, England), 1927, Mystery League (New York, NY), 1930.

The Man Who Was Nobody, Ward, Lock (London, England), 1927.

The Ringer (adapted from Wallace's play), Hodder & Stoughton (London, England), 1927.

The Squeaker, Hodder & Stoughton (London, England), 1927, published as *The Squealer,* Doubleday (New York, NY), 1928.

Terror Keep, Doubleday (New York, NY), 1927.

The Traitor's Gate, Doubleday (New York, NY), 1927.

Number Six, Newnes (London, England), 1927.

The Double, Doubleday (New York, NY), 1928.

The Thief in the Night, Readers Library (London, England), 1928, World Wide (New York, NY), 1929.

The Flying Squad, Hodder & Stoughton (London, England), 1928, Doubleday (New York, NY), 1929.

The Gunner, Long (London, England), 1928, published as *Gunman's Bluff,* Doubleday (New York, NY), 1929.

The Golden Hades, Collins (London, England), 1929.

The Green Ribbon, Hutchinson (London, England), 1929, Doubleday (New York, NY), 1930.

The Terror, Detective Story Club (London, England), 1929.

The Calendar, Collins (London, England), 1930, Doubleday (New York, NY), 1931.

The Silver Key, Doubleday (New York, NY), 1930, published as *The Clue of the Silver Key,* Hodder & Stoughton (London, England), 1930.

The Lady of Ascot, Hutchinson (London, England), 1930.

On the Spot, Doubleday (New York, NY), 1931.

The Coat of Arms, Hutchinson (London, England), 1931, published as *The Arranways Mystery,* Doubleday (New York, NY), 1932.

The Devil Man, Doubleday (New York, NY), 1931, published as *The Life and Death of Charles Peace,* 1932.

The Man at the Carlton, Hodder & Stoughton (London, England), 1931, Doubleday (New York, NY), 1932.

The Frightened Lady, Hodder & Stoughton (London, England), 1932, Doubleday (New York, NY), 1933.

When the Gangs Came to London, Doubleday (New York, NY), 1932.

The Road to London, edited by Jack Adrian, Kimber (London, England), 1986.

OTHER NOVELS

The Duke in the Suburbs, Ward, Lock (London, England), 1909.

Private Selby, Ward, Lock (London, England), 1912.

1925: The Story of a Fatal Peace, Newnes (London, England), 1915.

Those Folk of Bulboro, Ward, Lock (London, England), 1918.

The Books of Bart, Ward, Lock (London, England), 1923.

The Black Avons, Gill (London, England), 1925, published in four volumes as *How They Fared in the Times of the Tudors, Roundhead and Cavalier, From Waterloo to the Mutiny,* and *Europe in the Melting Pot,* 1925.

CRIME STORY COLLECTIONS

Sanders of the River, Ward, Lock (London, England), 1911, Doubleday (New York, NY), 1930.

The People of the River, Ward, Lock (London, England), 1912.

The Admirable Carfew, Ward, Lock (London, England), 1914.

Bosambo of the River, Ward, Lock (London, England), 1914.

Bones, Being Further Adventures in Mr. Commissioner Sanders' Country, Ward, Lock (London, England), 1915.

The Keepers of the King's Peace, Ward, Lock (London, England), 1917.

Lieutenant Bones, Ward, Lock (London, England), 1918.

The Adventures of Heine, Ward, Lock (London, England), 1919.

Bones in London, Ward, Lock (London, England), 1921.

The Law of the Four Just Men, Hodder & Stoughton (London, England), 1921, published as *Again the Three Just Men,* Doubleday (New York, NY), 1933.

Sandi, the King-Maker, Ward, Lock (London, England), 1922.

Bones of the River, Newnes (London, England), 1923.

Chick, Ward, Lock (London, England), 1923.

Educated Evans, Webster (London, England), 1924.

The Mind of Mr. J. G. Reeder, Hodder & Stoughton (London, England), 1925, published as *The Murder Book of Mr. J. G. Reeder,* Doubleday (New York, NY), 1929.

More Educated Evans, Webster (London, England), 1926.

Sanders, Hodder & Stoughton (London, England), 1926, published as *Commissioner Sanders,* Doubleday (New York, NY), 1930.

The Brigand, Hodder & Stoughton (London, England), 1927, Academy (Chicago, IL), 1985.

Good Evans!, Webster (London, England), 1927, published as *The Educated Man—Good Evans!,* Collins (London, England), 1929.

The Mixer, Long (London, England), 1927.

Again Sanders, Hodder & Stoughton (London, England), 1928, Doubleday (New York, NY), 1929.

Again the Three Just Men, Hodder & Stoughton (London, England), 1928, published as *The Law of the Three Just Men,* Doubleday (New York, NY), 1931, published as *Again the Three,* Pan (London, England), 1968.

Elegant Edward, Readers Library (London, England), 1928.

The Orator, Hutchinson (London, England), 1928.

Again the Ringer, Hodder & Stoughton (London, England), 1929, published as *The Ringer Returns,* Doubleday (New York, NY), 1931.

The Big Four, Readers Library (London, England), 1929.

The Black, Readers Library (London, England), 1929, expanded version, Digit (London, England), 1962.

The Cat Burglar, Newnes (London, England), 1929.

Circumstantial Evidence, Newnes (London, England), 1929, World (Cleveland, OH), 1934.

Fighting Snub Reilly, Newnes (London, England), 1929, World (Cleveland, OH), 1934.

For Information Received, Newnes (London, England), 1929.

Forty-eight Short Stories, Newnes (London, England), 1929.

Four Square Jane, World Wide (New York, NY), 1929.

The Ghost of Down Hill, World Wide (New York, NY), 1929.

The Governor of Chi-Foo, Newnes (London, England), 1929, World (Cleveland, OH), 1934.

The Iron Grip, Readers Library (London, England), 1929.

The Lady of Little Hell, Newnes (London, England), 1929.

The Little Green Man, Collins (London, England), 1929.

Planetoid 127, Readers Library (London, England), 1929.

The Prison-Breakers, Newnes (London, England), 1929.

Red Aces, Hodder & Stoughton (London, England), 1929, Doubleday (New York, NY), 1930.

The Reporter, Readers Library (London, England), 1929.

Killer Kay, Newnes (London, England), 1930.

The Lady Called Nita, Newnes (London, England), 1930.

Mrs. William Jones and Bill, Newnes (London, England), 1930.

The Stretelli Case, and Other Mystery Stories, World (Cleveland, OH), 1930.

The Guv'nor, and Other Stories, Collins, 1932, published as *Mr. Reeder Returns,* Doubleday (New York, NY), 1932, and as *The Guv'nor and Mr. J. G. Reeder Returns* (two volumes), Collins (London, England), 1933-34.

Sergeant Sir Peter, Chapman & Hall (London, England), 1932, reprinted as *Sergeant Dunn C. I. D.,* Digit (London, England), 1962.

The Steward, Collins (London, England), 1932.

The Last Adventure, Hutchinson (London, England), 1934.

The Woman from the East, and Other Stories, Hutchinson (London, England), 1934.

Nig-Nog, World (Cleveland, OH), 1934.

The Undisclosed Closet, Digit (London, England), 1962.

The Man Who Married His Cook, and Other Stories, White Lion (Oxford, England), 1976.

Unexpected Endings, Edgar Wallace Society (Oxford, England), 1980.

Two Stories, and The Seventh Man, Edgar Wallace Society (Oxford, England), 1981.

The Sooper and Others, edited by Jack Adrian, Dent (London, England), 1984.

The Dead Room: Strange and Startling Tales, edited by Jack Adrian, Kimber (London, England), 1986.

OTHER SHORT-STORY COLLECTIONS

Smithy, Tallis Press (London, England), 1905, revised edition published as *Smith, Not to Mention Nobby Clark and Spud Murphy,* Newnes (London, England), 1914.

Smith Abroad: Barrack Room Sketches, Hulton (London, England), 1909.

Smith's Friend Nobby, Town Topics (London, England), 1914, published as *Nobby,* Newnes (London, England), 1916.

Smithy and the Hun, Pearson (London, England), 1915.

Tam o' the Scouts, Newnes (London, England), 1918, published as *Tam of the Scoots,* Small, Maynard (Boston, MA), 1919, published as *Tam,* Newnes (London, England), 1928.

The Fighting Scouts, Pearson (London, England), 1928.

VERSE

The Mission That Failed! A Tale of the Raid, and Other Poems, Maskew Miller (Cape Town, South Africa), 1898.
Nicholson's Nek, Eastern Press (Cape Town, South Africa), 1900.
War!, and Other Poems, Eastern Press (Cape Town, South Africa), 1900.
Writ in Barracks, Methuen (London, England), 1900.

PUBLISHED PLAYS

The Terror (adapted from Wallace's novel *Terror Keep*; produced in 1927), Hodder & Stoughton (London, England), 1929.
The Man Who Changed His Name (produced in 1928), Hodder & Stoughton (London, England), 1929.
The Squeaker (adapted from Wallace's novel; produced in London, England, 1928; produced in New York, NY as *Sign of the Leopard,* 1928), Hodder & Stoughton (London, England), 1929.
The Flying Squad (adapted from Wallace's novel), Hodder & Stoughton (London, England), 1929.
The Calendar (also directed; produced in London, England, 1929), Samuel French (London, England), 1932.
The Case of the Frightened Lady (produced in London, England, 1931), Samuel French (London, England), 1932, published as *Criminal at Large* (produced in New York, NY, 1932), Samuel French (New York, NY), 1934.
The Green Pack (produced in London, England, 1932), Samuel French (London, England), 1933.
The Forest of Happy Dreams (produced in London, England, 1910), in *One-Act Play Parade,* Allen & Unwin (London, England), 1935.
An African Millionaire (produced in South Africa, 1904), Davis Poynter (London, England), 1972.
The Mouthpiece (produced in London, England, 1930), Chivers (London, England), 1994.

OTHER PLAYS

Dolly Cutting Herself, 1911.
(With others) *Hullo, Ragtime,* 1912.

(With others) *Hullo, Tango!,* 1912.
Hello, Exchange!, 1913, produced as *The Switchboard,* 1915.
The Manager's Dream, 1913.
(With others) *Business as Usual,* 1914.
(With Wal Pink and Albert de Courville) *The Whirligig* (includes music by Frederick Chappelle), 1919, produced as *Pins and Needles,* 1922.
M'lady, 1921.
(With Albert de Courville) *The Looking Glass* (includes music by Frederick Chappelle), 1924.
The Mystery of Room 45, 1926.
Double Dan (adapted from Wallace's novel), 1926.
A Perfect Gentleman, 1927.
The Yellow Mask (musical), music by Vernon Duke, lyrics by Desmond Carter, 1927.
The Lad, 1928.
Persons Unknown, 1929.
On the Spot, 1930.
Smoky Cell, 1930.
Charles III (adapted from a play by Curt Götz), 1931.
The Old Man, 1931.

SCREENPLAYS

Nurse and Martyr, 1915.
The Ringer, 1928.
Valley of the Ghosts, 1928.
The Forger, 1928.
Red Aces (also directed), 1929.
The Squeaker (also directed), 1930.
Should a Doctor Tell?, 1930.
(With V. Gareth Gundrey) *The Hound of the Baskervilles* (adapted from Arthur Conan Doyle's novel), 1931.
The Old Man, 1931.
(With others) *King Kong,* 1933.

OTHER

Unofficial Despatches, Hutchinson (London, England), 1901.
Famous Scottish Regiments, Newnes (London, England), 1914.
Field Marshall Sir John French and His Campaigns, Newnes (London, England), 1914.
Heroes All: Gallant Deeds of War, Newnes (London, England), 1914.

The Standard History of the War (four volumes), Newnes (London, England), 1914-16.

War of the Nations, Volumes 2-11, Newnes (London, England), 1914-19.

Kitchener's Army and the Territorial Forces: The Full Story of a Great Achievement (six volumes), Newnes (London, England), 1915.

The Real Shell-Man, Waddington (London, England), 1919.

People: A Short Autobiography, Hodder & Stoughton (London, England), 1926, Doubleday (New York, NY), 1929.

This England, Hodder & Stoughton (London, England), 1927.

My Hollywood Diary, Hutchinson (London, England), 1932.

Winning Colours: Selected Racing Writings of Edgar Wallace, edited by John Welcome, Bellew (London, England), 1991.

Columnist, *Star,* London, England, 1927-32, and *Daily Mail,* London, England, 1930-32. Drama critic, *Morning Post,* London, England, 1928. Contributor to periodicals, including Birmingham *Post* and *Thompson's Weekly News.* Editor, *Town Topics,* 1916, and *Sunday News,* 1931. Founded *Bilbury's Weekly, R. E. Walton's Weekly,* and *Bucks Mail.*

SIDELIGHTS: Edgar Wallace produced more than 200 works—including over 170 novels—in a career that flourished during the first three decades of the twentieth century. "The typical Edgar Wallace book is a straight-forward crime novel or thriller in which the plot is the most significant point," wrote J. Randolph Cox in the *Dictionary of Literary Biography.* He added that Wallace "was not a great writer" but "a great storyteller who appealed mainly to his own generation." Louis J. McQuilland lauded Wallace in *Bookman* as "a great serial writer," and noted that Wallace professed pride in what he called "my big output."

Wallace began his literary career while working as a journalist in Africa. His first book, *The Mission That Failed!, A Tale of the Raid, and Other Poems,* was published in 1898, and additional verse volumes appeared during the next few years. His first thriller, *The Four Just Men,* was appraised by Cox as "the highly improbable story of a plot against the English foreign secretary," and though it failed to prove profitable, its

heroes, three vengeful friends, appeared in two sequels and a collection of tales, and eventually managed to bring about the deaths of more than fifteen criminals while expressing what Armin Arnold, writing in the *International Fiction Review,* described as an "instinct for justice."

Notable among Wallace's ensuing novels are *The Angel of Terror,* a 1922 publication summarized by a *New York Times Book Review* contributor as "well made and well told," and *The Clue of the New Pin,* which was described in the same publication as the work of "an author who possesses a flair for satire and a certain amount of dry humor." Another novel, *The Hairy Arm,* concerns a series of grisly decapitations, and it was acknowledged by a *New York Times Book Review* critic as "entertaining reading." *The Sinister Man,* meanwhile, impressed a *New York Times Book Review* critic as "an interesting story about dope smuggling in England." Still another tale, *The Girl from Scotland Yard,* won recognition in the *New York Times Book Review* as "a puzzle that should baffle even the most skilled of those who pride themselves upon being able to guess the guilty party in the first chapter or two."

Among Wallace's other publications are a series of novels featuring the resourceful Inspector Elks. Wallace also produced various collections of short stories, including *Sanders of the River* and *Bosambo of the River,* recounting the exploits of Commissioner Sanders, an English colonialist who wields considerable power among natives in western Africa. "The stories about Sanders may represent Wallace's strongest contributions to English literature," wrote Cox, who added that the tales were derived from the author's "experiences and knowledge gained in Africa, fortified by research and his own fertile imagination." Similarly, a contributor to the *St. James Guide to Crime and Mystery Writers* observed, "To a certain extent Wallace was more convincing in the short story medium." The writer hailed Wallace's shorter works as "stunning examples of a lost art" and described them as "pithy, tightly-plotted, neatly contrived, with twists in their tails."

Wallace died in 1932, when he was only fifty-six years old and was still enjoying considerable popularity. A year earlier, H. Douglas Thomson had written in *Masters of Mystery: A Study of the Detective Story,* "To many people detective fiction is nowadays synonymous with the novels of Mr. Edgar Wallace." Upon Wallace's death, Francis D. Grierson lamented in *Bookman* that "the world has lost a great man," and E. C. Bentley declared in the *English Review* that Wallace's "death will be regretted as long as some millions of us live."

In the ensuing years, however, some critics questioned the quality of Wallace's extensive output. George Jean Nathan, as early as 1935, contended in *Passing Judgements* that "much of [Wallace's] work was popular, but none of it had the slightest artistic reason for being," and Colin Watson, writing in *Snobbery with Violence: Crime Stories and Their Audience,* conceded that "trying to assess Wallace's work in literary terms would be as pointless as applying sculptural evaluation to a load of gravel." Watson added, though, that Wallace "wrote as well as he needed to write in satisfaction of a voracious but uninstructed public appetite."

BIOGRAPHICAL AND CRITICAL SOURCES:

BOOKS

Dictionary of Literary Biography, Volume 70: *British Mystery Writers, 1860-1919,* Gale (Detroit, MI), 1988.

Nathan, George Jean, *Passing Judgements,* Alfred A. Knopf (New York, NY), 1935.

St. James Guide to Crime and Mystery Writers, 4th edition, St. James Press (Detroit, MI), 1996.

Thomson, H. Douglas, *Masters of Mystery: A Study of the Detective Story,* Collins (London, England), 1931.

Twentieth-Century Literary Criticism, Volume 57, Gale (Detroit, MI), 1995.

Watson, Colin, *Snobbery with Violence: Crime Stories and Their Audience,* Eyre & Spottiswoode (London, England), 1971.

PERIODICALS

Bookman, March, 1926, Louis J. McQuilland, "The Bookman Gallery: Edgar Wallace," pp. 301-304; March, 1932, Francis D. Grierson, "Edgar Wallace: The Passing of a Great Personality," p. 3101.

English Review, March, 1932, E. C. Bentley, "Edgar Wallace: The Great Storyteller," p. 3114.

International Fiction Review, July, 1976, Armin Arnold, "Friedrich Dürrenmatt and Edgar Wallace," pp. 142-144.

New York Times Book Review, April 12, 1922, review of *The Angel of Terror,* p. 11; April 15, 1923, review of *The Clue of the New Pin,* pp. 22, 24; July 19, 1925, "The Head Hunter," p. 13; January 24, 1926, "London Dope Runners," p. 9; June 19, 1927, "A Girl Detective," p. 24.

ONLINE

Official Edgar Wallace Web site, http://www.edgarwallace.org (October 14, 2003).*

*   *   *

WALLENSTEIN, Peter 1944-

PERSONAL: Born May 22, 1944, in East Orange, NJ; son of Crandall R. and R. Carol (Van Duyne) Wallenstein; married Sookhan Ho, 1986. *Education:* Columbia University, B.A., 1966; Johns Hopkins University, Ph.D., 1973.

ADDRESSES: Office—Department of History, Virginia Polytechnic Institute and State University, Blacksburg, VA 24061-0117. *E-mail*—pwallens@vt.edu.

CAREER: Sarah Lawrence College, Bronxville, NY, assistant professor of history, 1970-75; University of Toronto, Toronto, Ontario, Canada, visiting assistant professor of history, 1975-77; University of Maryland in East Asia, assistant professor of history, 1979-82; Virginia Polytechnic Institute and State University, Blacksburg, began as assistant professor, 1983, became associate professor.

MEMBER: Organization of American Historians, Southern History Association.

AWARDS, HONORS: American History Association fellowships, 1983, 1991; Virginia Foundation for the Humanities fellowship, 1989, 1992; Virginia Historical Society fellowships, 1990, 1991; McClung Award from East Tennessee Historical Society, 1992; Mario D. Zamora Distinguished Service Award, Virginia School Science Association, 1996.

WRITINGS:

From Slave South to New South: Public Policy in Nineteenth-Century Georgia, University of North Carolina Press (Chapel Hill, NC), 1987.

Virginia Tech, Land Grant University, 1872-1997: History of a School, a State, a Nation, Pocahontas Press (Blacksburg, VA), 1997.

(Editor with Paul Finkelman) *The Encyclopedia of American Political History,* CQ Press (Washington, DC), 2001.

Tell the Court I Love My Wife: Race, Marriage, and Law: An American History, Palagrave (New York, NY), 2002.

Contributor of articles and chapters to books, including Paul Finkelman, editor, *His Soul Goes Marching On: Responses to John Brown and the Harper's Ferry Raid,* University Press of Virginia (Charlottesville, VA), 1995; Catherine Clinton and Michele Gillespie, editors, *The Devil's Lane: Sex and Race in the Early South,* Oxford University Press (New York, NY), 1997; Kenneth W. Noe and Shannon H. Wilson, editors, *Appalachia in the Civil War,* University of Tennessee Press (Knoxville, TN), 1997; and Elna C. Green, editor, *Before the New Deal: Essays in Southern Social Welfare History, 1830-1930,* University of Georgia Press (Athens, GA), 1998. Contributor to scholarly periodicals, including *Chicago-Kent Law Review, Virginia Magazine of History and Biography,* and *Virginia Social Science Journal.*

SIDELIGHTS: Peter Wallenstein's *From Slave South to New South: Public Policy in Nineteenth-Century Georgia* uses tax records from the state of Georgia to draw conclusions about public services to the citizenry before, during, and after the U.S. Civil War. The author sees government fiscal policy as a barometer of social change during the nineteenth century, and he argues that the Civil War itself, and not Reconstruction, serves as the benchmark for sweeping changes in taxation and social services for Georgians. In her *Journal of American History* review of the work, Priscilla Ferguson Clement praised Wallenstein's "thoroughly argued thesis" and concluded that the book provides "a very useful and provocative analysis of one southern state during the nineteenth century." A *Virginia Quarterly Review* contributor felt that *From Slave South to New South* offers "a refreshing redrawing of the map of Southern history." In *American Historical Review,* Bar-

ton C. Shaw wrote: "This is an insightful book. It is well argued and well researched, and it squeezes considerable sense from the arcanum of Georgia's tax records. Best of all, the book is written in clear and often felicitous English. It will serve as a model for similar studies of other states."

Virginia Tech: Land Grant University 1872-1997: History of a School, a State, and a Nation charts the history of Virginia Polytechnic Institute and State University decade by decade, from its founding in the nineteenth century throughout thc twentieth century. Wallenstein began writing the book prior to teaching a course on the subject at Virginia Polytechnic, and as he perused the topic he brought in more general information about the land-grant system, racial and gender issues, and the changing educational goals of the institution. In a review for *Virginia Magazine of History and Biography,* Melissa Kean noted that the book is "infused with obvious affection for the institution" while it "displays broad understanding of the issues that are at the heart of the school's development." Kean concluded: "Wallenstein's approach has yielded a rarity—an institutional history that is neither parochial nor bogged down in detail." *Journal of Southern History* reviewer Robert F. Durden likewise felt that the work "does shed considerable and quite interesting light on all of Virginia's tax-supported colleges and universities and on the nation's highly diverse land-grant educational institutions."

Wallenstein is also author of *Tell the Court I Love My Wife: Race, Marriage, and the Law—An American History.* This study focuses on laws restricting interracial marriage and the way such legislation impinged upon issues of identity and culture. In *Booklist,* Vernon Ford observed that the work "compellingly traces the legal intersection between race and sex." The book also explores legal definitions of blackness and whiteness and the variations in laws from state to state. Thomas J. Davis in *Library Journal* called *Tell the Court I Love My Wife* a "compelling analysis" and "superb legal history" that succeeds at "filling a remarkable void in the literature."

BIOGRAPHICAL AND CRITICAL SOURCES:

PERIODICALS

American Historical Review, number 4, 1988, Barton C. Shaw, review of *From Slave South to New South: Public Policy in Nineteenth-Century Georgia,* pp. 1120-1121.

Booklist, September 1, 2001, review of *The Encyclopedia of American Political History,* p. 149; November 15, 2002, Vernon Ford, review of *Tell the Court I Love My Wife: Race, Marriage, and the Law—An American History,* p. 552.

Choice, September, 1987, F. Petrella, Jr., review of *From Slave South to New South,* p. 189.

Journal of American History, September, 1988, Priscilla Ferguson Clement, review of *From Slave South to New South,* pp. 603-604.

Journal of Southern History, November, 1999, Robert F. Durden, review of *Virginia Tech, Land Grant University, 1872-1997: History of a School, a State, a Nation,* pp. 894-896.

Library Journal, May 15, 2001, Thomas J. Baldino, review of *The Encyclopedia of American Political History,* p. 108; November 1, 2002, Thomas J. Davis, review of *Tell the Court I Love My Wife,* p. 108.

Virginia Magazine of History and Biography, winter, 2001, Melissa Kean, review of *Virginia Tech, Land Grant University, 1872-1997,* pp. 108-109.

Virginia Quarterly Review, winter, 1988, review of *From Slave South to New South,* p. 14.*

*   *   *

WALLER, Maureen 1950-

PERSONAL: Born 1950; daughter of John Gamble (a physician) and Margaret Mary (Gorman) Waller; married Brian MacArthur (a journalist). *Education:* Queen Mary College, London, master's degree (British and European history, 1660-1714). University College, London, B.A., 1972. *Religion:* Christian. *Hobbies and other interests:*Visiting historic houses and churches; travel in Greece, Turkey, India, Italy, and France; reading history, biography, and fiction; theatre; art and antiques.

ADDRESSES: Home—London, England. *Agent*—Jonathan Lloyd, Curtis Brown Group, Haymarket, London W1, England. *E-mail*—maureenwaller@ onetel.com.

CAREER: Historian and author. Has worked as an editor at several publishing houses, including Book Club Associates, London, England, 1973-2000.

WRITINGS:

Seventeen Hundred: Scenes from London Life, Four Walls Eight Windows (New York, NY), 2000.

Ungrateful Daughters: The Stuart Princesses Who Stole Their Father's Crown, Hodder and Stoughton (London, England), 2002, St. Martin's Press (New York, NY), 2003.

London 1945: Life in the Debris of War, J. Murray, 2004.

WORK IN PROGRESS: A documentary about demythologising William of Orange for BBC Northern Ireland and accompanying Web site.

SIDELIGHTS: In *Seventeen Hundred: Scenes from London Life,* historian Maureen Waller provides a vivid portrait of a city that would in time become the veritable capital of the world. But in 1700 the English capital was still an essentially medieval city, with open sewers, foul-smelling streets, rampant disease, and appalling rates of infant mortality. It was also the birthplace of epochal ideas and discoveries, thanks to the likes of Isaac Newton, John Locke, and Edmund Halley.

In *Seventeen Hundred,* which a reviewer in *Booklist* called "a superbly written portrait of a city on the cusp of greatness," Waller set out, in her own words, "to hold up a mirror to catch a reflection of the daily life of Londoners. . . . Their voices well up from letters and court documents . . . as if for three centuries they have been waiting for an audience." Richard Wunderli in *History: Review of New Books* quoted Waller on this point and noted the organization of chapters around topics such as "Childbirth," "Death," "Food and Drink," "Prostitution and Vice," and "Religion and Superstitions." Wunderli commented that "This method is valuable for introducing readers to the daily life, the sights, sounds, and smells of London, as if we had just walked into a William Hogarth print."

Sheryl Fowler in *School Library Journal* called *Seventeen Hundred* "An enlightening and, in most cases, disgustingly good read," observing that while its value as a work of history is unquestionable, it would also be intriguing to teenage readers fascinated with such topics as tattooing or deformities in humans or animals. A reviewer in *Publishers Weekly* described *Seventeen Hundred* as a "radiant book" and noted that "this rigorous, informative, and entertaining text deserves a wide readership."

Waller's book *Ungrateful Daughters: The Stuart Princesses Who Stole Their Father's Crown* focuses on events leading up to and following the Glorious

Revolution of 1688, in which Dutch nobleman William of Orange and his English wife Mary restored the English throne to Protestant control. This restoration ended what had become by then an aberration, with a Catholic in power; moreover, it displaced an unpopular monarch, James II (Mary's father), in favor of a couple who enjoyed popular support. Historians have tended to treat the Glorious Revolution as a virtual inevitability and to speak of it in the terms used by its supporters, but as Waller shows in *Ungrateful Daughters,* there is far more to the story.

James had two daughters, Mary and Anne, by a Protestant and commoner named Anne Hyde. In 1673, after Anne's death, James—who had never been very appealing and was now a man of forty, an advanced age at the time—married fifteen-year-old Maria Beatrice Eleanor d'Este of Modena. Maria burst into tears when she saw him, and for the first few years of her marriage, she cried virtually every time she saw her husband.

On June 9, 1688, after fifteen childless years, Maria presented the king with what he most wanted: a male heir. However, this event led to the ouster of James by his elder daughter Mary and her husband William, who assumed power in a bloodless coup assisted by Mary's sister, now Princess Anne of Denmark; James and his second wife and son fled to France and the protection of the Catholic monarch there. While history regards the Protestant restoration as a success, Waller offers a much different account of the story on a personal level. Mary and Anne, as Waller's title indicates, come across in the narrative as ungrateful daughters whose father, though far from a charming personality, had loved them and was deeply hurt by their betrayal, and whose stepmother had showed them nothing but kindness.

Waller makes it clear that James was far from lovable. As observed by Lucy Moore in the *New Statesman,* she begins the book with an incident that penetratingly illustrates his personality and the reasons why—aside from religious conflict and the treachery of his daughters—he came to the pass that he did. Apprehended by sailors while trying to flee across the English Channel on a cold night in December 1688, James was taken to a tavern where one of the sailors, recognizing the king, bowed before him and asked for a blessing. Wrote Moore, "As Waller observes, James's late brother, Charles II, would have turned this scene into a triumph. 'The most charming and accessible of kings, he would have allowed them all to kiss his hand, he would have called for a round of drinks and told them stories, and asked about their lives and women. Before long they would have been carrying him back to Whitehall and throwing out the Dutch invader.' But James thrust the man aside, called for paper and ink, and sat distant and desperate by the fire, brooding on what and who had brought him to this fate."

"Waller's fluent narrative is solidly grounded," Robert C. Jones wrote in *Library Journal,* lauding the extensive bibliography and notes as well as sixteen pages of illustrations. A reviewer in *Publishers Weekly* called the book "a highly readable, thoroughly researched family saga that shows vividly how the personal and the political interacted to produce one of the seminal events in British history." A commentator in *Kirkus Reviews* called *Ungrateful Daughters* a "lively, instructive history," and Sarah Bradford in the *Spectator* concluded that "Waller's interpretation is unusual and fascinating."

BIOGRAPHICAL AND CRITICAL SOURCES:

PERIODICALS

Booklist, May 1, 2000, Jay Freeman, review of *Seventeen Hundred: Scenes from London Life,* p. 1648.

History: Review of New Books, spring, 2000, Richard Wunderli, review of *Seventeen Hundred: Scenes from London Life,* p. 115.

Kirkus Reviews, November 1, 2002, review of *Ungrateful Daughters: The Stuart Princesses Who Stole Their Father's Crown,* p. 1604.

Library Journal, February 15, 2003, Robert C. Jones, review of *Ungrateful Daughters: The Stuart Princesses Who Stole Their Father's Crown,* p. 153.

New Statesman, Lucy Moore, "The Girl Pretenders," May 20, 2002, p. 51.

New York Times Book Review, February 23, 2003, T. H. Breen, "A Serpent's Tooth," section 7, p. 19.

Publishers Weekly, April 17, 2000, review of *Seventeen Hundred: Scenes from London Life,* p. 65; November 25, 2002, review of *Ungrateful Daughters: The Stuart Princesses Who Stole Their Father's Crown,* p. 52.

School Library Journal, June, 2001, Sheryl Fowler, review of *Seventeen Hundred: Scenes from London Life,* p. 188.

Spectator (London, England), May 18, 2002, Sarah Bradford, "Two Marble-hearted Fiends," p. 42.*

*   *   *

WANG, Annie 1972-

PERSONAL: Born Rui Wang, 1972, in Beijing, China; immigrated to United States, 1993, naturalized citizen, 2000; daughter of a newspaper editor and an author. *Ethnicity:* "Chinese." *Education:* Graduated from University of California, Berkeley, 1996.

ADDRESSES: Home—Hong Kong, and San Francisco. *Agent*—c/o Pantheon Publicity Department, 1745 Broadway, New York, NY 10019.

CAREER: Writer. Worked at *Washington Post* Beijing bureau, Beijing, China; U.S. State Department, contract interpreter. Cofounder, with sisters Wei Wang and Fei Wang, of Chinese Culture Net, San Francisco, CA, 1997—.

WRITINGS:

Lili: A Novel of Tiananmen, edited by Dan Frank, Pantheon Books (New York, NY), 2001.

Contributor to periodicals, including the *South China Morning Post, Time* (Asia), and *Washington Post;* author of books published in China.

SIDELIGHTS: Annie Wang left China in 1993 to study at the University of California at Berkeley and later took a position as a contract interpreter for the U.S. State Department, a move that helped her become a United States citizen in 2000. The following year she published *Lili: A Novel of Tiananmen,* set around the massacre of prodemocracy demonstrators in Tiananmen Square in 1989. Wang acknowledges that the book is an emotional, rather than a political, view of the events of that period. A *Publishers Weekly* contributor said her version, "at once convincing and

utterly foreign, both attracts and terrifies." Wang lives in Hong Kong and San Francisco, and has previously published a number of books in China.

Wang grew up a member of the privileged class of the Chinese Communist Party. In 1989, as a sixteen-year-old academic prodigy, she was named one of China's ten outstanding students. Wang hosted radio shows for teens, wrote, and dreamed of studying in the United States. Her father was a newspaper editor, and she enjoyed capitalist luxuries such as telephones, movies, and books, some of which were banned and inaccessible to the majority of the people. Thomas Crampton wrote in the *International Herald Tribune* that "to evade rules prohibiting Chinese from entering Beijing's luxury hotels, Wang and her autograph-seeking teenage friends hid outside the entrance in a senior official's borrowed Mercedes, waiting for foreign musicians to greet fans. Many of Wang's friends cashed in their connections for the wealth and power brought by joining investment banks like Morgan Stanley. Wang, however, turned to writing."

Wang's novel was born on a May day in 1989, as she pedaled her bicycle through Tiananmen Square, and it took her ten years to complete. "The result," wrote Sorina Diaconescu of the *Los Angeles Times,* "is a kaleidoscopic view of 1980s China, seen through the eyes of Lili, a street-smart heroine who turns tricks on the sidewalks of Beijing as an easy fix to boredom." *Booklist*'s Elsa Gaztambide described Lili as "brimming with angst and rebellion, as refreshing as she is disagreeable."

Lili is arrested for "hooliganism" and sentenced to three months of re-education in the country. After she is raped by a party official, she runs away and returns to the city, where she lives on the edge, in a world populated by gangs and filled with violence. Lili brings further humiliation on her family by falling in love with a Chinese-speaking American journalist named Roy, who takes her along as he travels across China. It is then that Lili begins to understand her country, as she compares the lives of poor villagers and the lush accommodations of foreign diplomats and businessmen. Like Wang, Lili witnesses the student revolt and massacre by the People's Liberation Army in Tiananmen Square. In a *Library Journal* review, Shirley N. Quan called Wang's writing "clear, full of imagery" and noted that "she describes the oppression of free-spirited and free-thinking women in China."

Diaconescu wrote that "the narrative hopscotches in a series of snapshots capturing the poverty and indignity of China's provincial backwaters, the snug comforts party officials enjoy, the materialism of a new urban generation, and the tension between Chinese values and the transplanted cultural heritage of the West."

BIOGRAPHICAL AND CRITICAL SOURCES:

PERIODICALS

Booklist, May 1, 2001, Elsa Gaztambide, review of *Lili: A Novel of Tiananmen,* p. 1669.
Economist, August 11, 2001, review of *Lili,* p. 73.
International Herald Tribune, June 5, 2001, Thomas Crampton, "A Novel of Sex, Violence, and Tiananmen Square."
Library Journal, June 1, 2001, Shirley N. Quan, review of *Lili,* p. 219.
Los Angeles Times, June 21, 2001, Sorina Diaconescu, "A Kaleidoscopic View of China from a Street-smart Whiz Kid," p. E1.
Ms., October-November, 2001, Mai Hoang, review of *Lili,* p. 71.
Publishers Weekly, June 11, 2001, review of *Lili,* p. 58.
Times Literary Supplement, February 22, 2002, Frances Wood, "An Untamed Soul," p. 23.
Washington Post Book World, July 22, 2001, Lisa See, "Interesting Times," p. T04.

ONLINE

ChineseCulture.net, http://chineseculture.net/ (April 30, 2002).*

*　　*　　*

WARD, Peter D(ouglas) 1949-

PERSONAL: Born 1949. *Education:* McMaster University, Ph.D., 1976.

ADDRESSES: Office—University of Washington, Department of Earth and Space Sciences, 63 Johnson Hall, P.O. Box 351310, Seattle, WA 98195-1310. *E-mail*—ward@ess.washington.edu.

CAREER: Paleontologist. University of Washington, Seattle, department of earth and space sciences, adjunct professor of geological sciences.

WRITINGS:

(With David J. Bottjer and Carole Jean Stentz Hickman) *Mollusks: Notes for a Short Course,* University of Tennessee (Knoxville, TN), 1985.
The Natural History of Nautilus, Allen & Unwin (Boston, MA), 1987.
In Search of Nautilus: Three Centuries of Scientific Adventures in the Deep Pacific to Capture a Prehistoric, Living Fossil, Simon & Schuster (New York, NY), 1988.
(Editor, with Virgil L. Sharpton) *Global Catastrophes in Earth History: An Interdisciplinary Conference on Impacts, Volcanism, and Mass Mortality,* Geological Society of America (Boulder, CO), 1990.
On Methuselah's Trail: Living Fossils and the Great Extinction, illustrations by Linda Krause, W. H. Freeman (New York, NY), 1992.
The End of Evolution: On Mass Extinctions and the Preservation of Biodiversity, Bantam Books (New York, NY), 1994.
The Call of Distant Mammoths: Why the Ice Age Mammals Disappeared, Copernicus (New York, NY), 1997.
Time Machines: Scientific Explorations in Deep Time, Copernicus (New York, NY), 1998.
(With Donald Brownlee) *Rare Earth: Why Complex Life Is Uncommon in the Universe,* Copernicus (New York, NY), 2000.
Rivers in Time: The Search for Clues to Earth's Mass Extinctions, Columbia University Press (New York, NY), 2000.
Future Evolution, images by Alexis Rockman, foreword by Niles Eldredge, New York Times Books (New York, NY), 2001.
(With Donald Brownlee) *The Life and Death of Planet Earth: How the New Science of Astrobiology Charts the Ultimate Fate of Our World,* Times Books (New York, NY), 2002.

WORK IN PROGRESS: Gorgon: The Greatest Catastrophe in Earth's History, Viking (New York, NY), 2004.

SIDELIGHTS: While working, teaching, and publishing in the field of paleontology, Peter D. Ward has written many books that make current scientific discoveries accessible to the general reader. With research interests in analytical geochemistry, astrobiology, and paleontology, his writings include discussions on the nautilus and its fossilized relations, extinction theories, the question of whether advanced life forms are likely to exist outside of Earth, and where the Earth stands within its lifecycle. These works present complex, highly technical material to non-scientists and provide insight into the imaginative and adventurous aspects of scientific research. In some cases, Ward is reporting on the work of others, but often he relates his own personal experiences. Recently his research has focused on the Cretaceous-Tertiary extinction event and ammonites, as well as on the living cephalopods nautilus and sepia.

Two of Ward's early books are about the nautilus, *The Natural History of Nautilus* and *In Search of Nautilus: Three Centuries of Scientific Adventures in the Deep Pacific to Capture a Prehistoric, Living Fossil.* This chambered cephalopod is the only remaining link to the once-numerous fossil nautiloids and ammonoids, and has mystified investigators for hundreds of years. Because of the creature's deep sea habitat, longstanding misconceptions about the nautilus were not challenged until the 1960s. Ward's second book on this subject was described in *Appraisal* as "an enjoyable account of the history, study, and current knowledge of one of Earth's longest lived and most curious creatures." In *Booklist,* a critic wrote that the information is "absorbingly recounted in an excellent contribution to both single-genus studies and scientific history."

The mass extinction of ammonites is the subject of Ward's *On Methuselah's Trail: Living Fossils and the Great Extinction.* He questions why the nautilus has survived, when the very similar ammonites disappeared sixty-five million years ago, and determines that in fact the nautilus's history supports Darwinian theory. As *New Scientist* writer Jeff Hecht commented, "Dinosaurs are the rage among the extinct. . . . Yet . . . the study of marine invertebrates can yield crucial insights into the larger evolution." Philip Morrison commented in *Scientific American* that it is also material for an engaging read, calling *On Methuselah's Trail* "a wonderful small book. . . . lively with reminiscence, gossip, and sharp argument."

Ward treats a perhaps more familiar subject in *The Call of Distant Mammoths: Why the Ice Age Mammals Disappeared.* Large mammals such as giant ground sloths, saber-toothed tigers, and mammoths were part of a mass extinction 10,000 years ago that the author believes was caused by a catastrophic event. Reviewers approved of his writing style and analytical methods. In *Science Books & Films,* Donald J. Blakeslee commended the book for "both its writing and . . . comparative approach." *Library Journal's* Gloria Maxwell noted that Ward's style is "conversational and dynamic" and that "his facts are stunning." In *Publishers Weekly,* a writer remarked that Ward "clearly loves his work, and writes about it capably and with passion."

Another of Ward's books focuses on the methods and materials that give paleontologists a view to prehistoric creatures, events, and conditions. *Time Machines: Scientific Explorations in Deep Time* explains sediment stratigraphy, radioactive and magnetic dating analysis, and biophysical reconstructions, among other technical tools of the trade. Calling the book a "must read," *American Scientist* writer Tom Paulson commented that Ward is "an excellent storyteller with an insider's license to occasionally poke fun at his own profession." Ted Nield commented in *New Scientist* that Ward's revelations about how a scientist's imagination can help draw information from a seemingly insignificant bit of rock are "exhilarating."

One of Ward's most widely reviewed books is *Rare Earth: Why Complex Life Is Uncommon in the Universe,* in which he and coauthor Robert Brownlee consider the likelihood that there is intelligent extraterrestrial life. This endeavor includes a discussion of recent studies that underscore the complex evolutionary process that has taken place on earth. It also challenges the idea popularized by late scientist Carl Sagan that our galaxy could hold a million other civilizations. Reviewers found the authors' work to be substantial and persuasive. In *Astronomy,* Robert Naeye was troubled by "careless factual errors" in the book, but he still found that it "provides a comprehensive overview of current developments in astrobiology and the history of life on Earth." Naeye concluded that the authors "marshal enough valid arguments to cast double on Sagaesque optimism." A reviewer for *R & D* called the book "an excellent reference work" and "an admirable and timely overview of the latest ideas and works-in-progress." *Science's* Christopher P. McKay found that "*Rare Earth* provides a sobering and valuable perspective in just how difficult it might be for complex life and intelligence to arise." And *American Scientist* writer Tim Tokaryk called it "a stellar example of clear writing on a complex issue."

Ward and Brownlee also worked together on *The Life and Death of Planet Earth: How the New Science of Astrobiology Charts the Ultimate Fate of Our World.* This work focuses on the likely future of the earth and human race, predicting dramatic changes in land formation and climate, the eventual sterilization of the environment, and later, the loss of the entire planet into a red giant. While contemporary issues are dwarfed by larger forces and a time frame of billions of years, the authors do show human treatment of the planet as speeding this process. Ward and Brownlee succeed in making this information interesting and understandable, according to many reviewers. A *Publishers Weekly* reviewer judged that the authors "don't make an airtight case," but concluded that "they do deftly bring together findings from many disparate areas of science in a book that science buffs will find hard to put down." Similarly, a *Kirkus Reviews* writer wrote they "too quickly shift from solid scientific fact to their own extrapolations." But the writer also noted, "anyone who wants to see just how the cards are stacked ought to be reading this." Gilbert Taylor noted in *Booklist* that the book presents a "compellingly grim scenario" and is "creative but scientifically grounded." *Library Journal*'s Denise Hamilton remarked that the authors "effectively communicate their knowledge and sense of wonder while making the scientific evidence clear to readers of even limited science backgrounds."

BIOGRAPHICAL AND CRITICAL SOURCES:

PERIODICALS

American Scientist, March, 1999, Tom Paulson, review of *Time Machines,* p. 180; March, 2000, Tim Tokaryk, "Life Issues: Its Origin, Rarity and Sometimes Artful Arrangement," p. 168.

Appraisal, winter-spring, 1989, review of *In Search of Nautilus,* pp. 89-90.

Astronomy, August, 2000, Robert Naeye, review of *Rare Earth,* p. 105.

Booklist, August, 1988, review of *In Search of Nautilus,* pp. 1874-1875; December 15, 2002, Gilbert Taylor, review of *The Life and Death of Planet Earth,* p. 715.

Kirkus Reviews November 15, 2002, review of *The Life and Death of Planet Earth,* p. 1683.

Library Journal April 1, 1997, Gloria Maxwell, review of *The Call of Distant Mammoths,* p. 119; December, 2002, Denise Hamilton, review of *The Life and Death of Planet Earth,* p. 170.

New Scientist, February 15, 1992, Jeff Hecht, review of *On Methuselah's Trail,* p. 56; February 6, 1999, Ted Nield, review of *Time Machines,* p. 49.

Publishers Weekly March 17, 1997, review of *The Call of Distant Mammoths,* p. 71; November 18, 2002, review of *The Life and Death of Planet Earth,* p. 53.

Research and Development, August 2000, "Rare Moon," p. 11.

Science April 28, 2000, Christopher P. McKay, review of *Rare Earth,* p. 625.

Science Books & Films, November, 1997, Donald J. Blakeslee, review of *The Call of Distant Mammoths,* p. 237.

Scientific American May, 1992, Philip Morrison, review of *On Methuselah's Trail,* p. 140.*

*   *   *

WARD, Terence 1953?-

PERSONAL: Born c. 1953, in Boulder, CO; son of Patrick (an economic adviser) and Donna Ward; married; wife's name, Idanna. *Education:* University of California, Berkeley, graduated; University of Geneva International Management Institute, M.B.A.; Emory University, Ph.D.

ADDRESSES: Home—New York, NY, and Florence, Italy. *Office*—Inter-Change Consultants, 255 West 108th St., Ste. 6C1, New York, NY 10025. *E-mail*—wardnyc@aol.com.

CAREER: Management consultant, Inter-Change Consultants, New York, NY. Worked for the Hay Group, New York, NY, and Middle East Industrial Relations Counselors, Athens, Greece.

WRITINGS:

Searching for Hassan: An American Family's Journey Home to Iran (memoir), Houghton Mifflin (Boston, MA), 2002.

SIDELIGHTS: Terence Ward is a management consultant who conducts programs and seminars internationally. His focus is on motivation, leadership, team building, communications, and decision-making, and his clients include many *Fortune* 500 companies and large foreign corporations. He speaks Greek, Italian, Indonesian, Arabic, and Farsi, and advises governments and corporations in the Islamic world. Ward holds dual citizenship in the United States and Ireland.

Ward was born in Colorado but spent his childhood in Saudi Arabia and moved to Iran in 1960. His father was an economic adviser to the National Iranian Oil Company during the period when Shah Mohammed Reza Pahlavi was in power. The Ward family lived a privileged life in Tehran and were served by Hassan Ghasemi, whom Ward and his three brothers called their "Persian father." Hassan and his wife, Fatimeh, cooked and cared for the Ward family and the house, but also became close friends. The Wards left Tehran in 1969. After the fall of the shah in 1979, they had no way of staying in touch with Hassan, and it was not until after the reign of the Ayatollah Khomeini and the Iran-Iraq war that they were able to return to Iran to find their friend. Ward describes this journey in his book, *Searching for Hassan: An American Family's Journey Home to Iran.*

Published in January 2002, the book served an unexpected and important purpose because Ward's narrative highlights the achievements and beauty of historical Islamic culture. Many Americans were first exposed to Iran with the 1980 hostage crisis and the rule of Khomeini, and in light of the terrorist attacks on the United States on September 11, 2001 (Ward and his wife witnessed the collapse of the World Trade Center from their New York apartment), the inaccurate perception that the world of Islam is only a haven for radicals was too often perceived as being factual.

As the family began their pilgrimage in 1998, they were unclear even as to the name of Hassan's village, but they did eventually find him. "Amazingly," wrote Stephen Lyons in a *USA Today* online review, "the family traveled freely throughout Iran, without incident, accompanied by drivers and guides, including a colorful and inept Armenian named Avo. Not your typical American tourists, the Wards possess many advantages, including a working knowledge of Farsi. Ward's own command of Iranian culture and history is evident as he eloquently guides the reader through a rich culture dating back 2,500 years to Cyrus the Great."

Adam Goodheart wrote in a *New York Times Book Review* article that Ward "too often . . . trips over himself in his eagerness to spill out each new episode of the journey, and in his puppyish affection for his own family and for the Ghasemis. Still, his enthusiasm propels you along. In Ward's telling, the journey becomes a search not just for Hassan but for the Iran he remembers and loves—a country not of black-robed mullahs but of cherry orchards, sitar music, and saffron-flavored ice cream. For thousands of years, he reminds us, the very word 'Persia' suggested a realm of pleasure, color, and light, inspiring Westerners as diverse as Goethe, Whitman, and Emerson."

A *Kirkus Reviews* contributor maintained that the "best sections" of the book are those that provide historical material. *Library Journal*'s Mary V. Welk called *Searching for Hassan* "a powerful memoir that plumbs the depths of Iranian culture and tradition." A *Publishers Weekly* reviewer said Ward "succeeds in his loving portrait of a constantly changing, complex land." "Readers will feel a part of the family," wrote Christine C. Menefee in *School Library Journal*, "learning how the strengths of each individual contributed to the success of the quest."

In an interview published on the *Houghton Mifflin Web site*, Ward commented, "My family's search was a path of rediscovery. Uniting with our long-lost Persian friends closed a circle in all our lives. On the journey, we learned that the artistic face of Iran—cinema, music, and the masterpieces of Persian poetry—still resonates in the hearts of the people, far more than the bullhorns of the mullahs. Iranian culture is 2,500 years old. It is refined, rich, and enduring. And above all, it is filled with hospitable courtesy, humor, and friendship."

BIOGRAPHICAL AND CRITICAL SOURCES:

BOOKS

Ward, Terence, *Searching for Hassan: An American Family's Journey Home to Iran,* Houghton Mifflin (Boston, MA) 2002.

PERIODICALS

American Scholar, spring, 2002, Tara Bahrampour, "Persian Pleasure Trip," p. 154.
Kirkus Reviews, November 15, 2001, review of *Searching for Hassan: An American Family's Journey Home to Iran,* p. 1604.

Kliatt, July, 2003, Edna M. Boardman, review of *Searching for Hassan,* p. 50.

Library Journal, January, 2002, Mary V. Welk, review of *Searching for Hassan,* p. 136.

Los Angeles Times, March 11, 2002, Mary Rourke, "An American Puts a Different Spin on Iran's 'Axis' Image," p. E1.

Middle East Journal, summer, 2003, review of *Searching for Hassan,* p. 526.

New York Times Book Review, March 10, 2002, Adam Goodheart, "Pilgrims from the Great Satan: An Account of a Family's Search for Old Friends in Iran," p. 26.

Publishers Weekly, November 19, 2001, review of *Searching for Hassan,* p. 54.

School Library Journal, February, 2002, Christine C. Menefee, review of *Searching for Hassan,* p. 157.

Washington Post Book World, February 24, 2002, Gelareh Asayesh, "Lost Paradise," p. 13

ONLINE

Houghton Mifflin Web site, http://www.houghtonmifflinbooks.com/ (April 18, 2002), "A Conversation with Terence Ward, Author of *Searching for Hassan.*"

USA Today online, http://www.usatoday.com/ (January 24, 2002), Stephen Lyons, "Journey Back to Iran Finds Change in Spirit."*

*   *   *

WARGIN, Kathy-jo 1965-

PERSONAL: Born 1965, in Tower, MN; married Ed Wargin (a photographer). *Education:* Studied music at University of Minnesota—Duluth.

ADDRESSES: Home—Northern Michigan. *Agent*—c/o Author Mail, Sleeping Bear Press, 300 North Main St., P.O. Box 20, Chelsea, MI 48118.

CAREER: Writer. The Wargin Company, Petosky, MI, co-owner, with husband.

AWARDS, HONORS: Official Children's Book of Michigan, Michigan House of Representatives, 1998, and Children's Choice Award for Best Picture Book,

Capital Area District Library, both for *The Legend of the Sleeping Bear;* Children's Book of the Year Award, Great Lakes Booksellers Association, 1999, for *The Legend of Mackinac Island.*

WRITINGS:

Scenic Driving Michigan, photographs by Ed Wargin, Falcon Press (Helena, MT), 1997.

The Legend of Sleeping Bear, illustrated by Gijsbert van Frankenhuyzen, Sleeping Bear Press (Chelsea, MI), 1998.

Michigan: The Spirit of the Land, photographs by Ed Wargin, Voyageur Press (Stillwater, MN), 1999.

The Legend of Mackinac Island, illustrated by Gijsbert van Frankenhuyzen, Sleeping Bear Press (Chelsea, MI), 1999.

The Michigan Counting Book, illustrated by Michael Glenn Monroe, Sleeping Bear Press (Chelsea, MI), 2000.

The Legend of the Loon, illustrated by Gijsbert van Frankenhuyzen, Sleeping Bear Press (Chelsea, MI), 2000.

The Great Lakes Cottage Book, photographs by Ed Wargin, Sleeping Bear Press (Chelsea, MI), 2000.

L Is for Lincoln: An Illinois Alphabet, illustrated by Gijsbert van Frankenhuyzen, Sleeping Bear Press (Chelsea, MI), 2000.

The Legend of the Lady's Slipper, illustrated by Gijsbert van Frankenhuyzen, Sleeping Bear Press (Chelsea, MI), 2001.

The Michigan Reader for Boys and Girls, illustrated by K. L. Darnell, Sleeping Bear Press (Chelsea, MI), 2001.

The Legend of the Voyageur, illustrated by Gijsbert van Frankenhuyzen, Sleeping Bear Press (Chelsea, MI), 2002.

The American Reader, illustrated by Kathryn L. Darnell, Sleeping Bear Press (Chelsea, MI), 2002.

The Legend of Leelanau, illustrated by Gijsbert van Frankenhuyzen, Sleeping Bear Press (Chelsea, MI), 2003.

The Edmund Fitzgerald: Song of the Bell, Sleeping Bear Press (Chelsea, MI), 2003.

V Is for Viking: A Minnesota Alphabet, Sleeping Bear Press (Chelsea, MI), 2003.

Contributor of poems to *M Is for Mitten: A Michigan Alphabet,* by Annie Appleford, illustrated by Michael G. Monroe, Sleeping Bear Press (Chelsea, MI), 1999.

Contributor to *Voices of Michigan,* Volume II: *An Anthology of Michigan Authors,* edited by Jane Winston, Mackinac Jane's Publishing Company (Warner Robbins, GA), 2000.

SIDELIGHTS: Northern Michigan resident Kathy-jo Wargin has found a niche writing about the natural beauty, Native-American legends, and history of the Great Lakes region. She has written picture book versions of legends about such animals as bears, loons, and turtles, and about such places as Mackinac Island, the Leelanau Peninsula, and Lake Superior, the watery grave of the ore carrier *Edumund Fitzgerald.* "I like to retell old legends because of the wonderful messages they offer," she told Julia Durango of the Ottawa *Daily Times.* "I also believe it's important we keep history alive by remembering the stories passed down for generations through the oral tradition."

Nature and music have long been a part of Wargin's life. Born in Tower, Minnesota, she grew up in Grand Rapids, and later studied music at the University of Minnesota in Duluth. She parlayed her interest in the music of instruments into the music of words in her picture books. After teaming up with her husband, photographer Ed Wargin, to create *Scenic Driving Michigan,* she authored *The Legend of Sleeping Bear,* which was the first children's book for Michigan-based Sleeping Bear Press. In it, she retells the Native-American tale of the great sleeping bear who waits for her cubs, which have been turned into the Manitou Islands, in Lake Michigan, west of the Leelanau Peninsula. This was the first of many Wargin titles to be illustrated by Gijsbert van Frankenhuyzen, a Dutch artist who came to the United States because of its natural beauty, serving as an art director for *Michigan Natural Resources* magazine before embarking on a picture book-illustrating career. With more than 200,000 copies sold, *The Legend of the Sleeping Bear* became a mainstay of Sleeping Bear Press and was named the Official Children's Book of Michigan in 1998.

Following up on this success, Wargin wrote about several other Michigan legends, including *The Legend of Mackinac Island.* Pronounced "Ma-ki-naw," this island lies east of St. Ignace in the Straits of Mackinac and has long played a role in Michigan history. In Wargin's retelling of a Native-American creation tale, the painted turtle Makinauk and his animal friends

discover land in an ancient time when all the earth was covered with water. Several of Wargin's subsequent picture books feature Native-American girls. For instance, *The Legend of the Lady's Slipper,* which Cathy Collison of the *Detroit Free Press* called a "lovely story," recounts the tale of young Running Flower, who must make a desperate dash through the forest in an attempt to save the people of her village. And in *The Legend of Leelanau,* young Leelinau enters the forbidden Spirit Wood, where, not wanting to grow up, she plays with the Pukwudijinees, or tiny fairies. In *Kirkus Reviews,* a critic praised Wargin's version of the Leelinau legend, calling it "a fluid retelling that even young listeners will comprehend and older readers will enjoy."

Among Wargin's other books are educational alphabet primers about the states of Michigan, Illinois, and Minnesota; *The Michigan Reader for Boys and Girls,* full of stories and activities for readers of various ages; and *The Edmund Fitzgerald: Song of the Bell,* about the sinking of the famous ore freighter in 1975.

BIOGRAPHICAL AND CRITICAL SOURCES:

PERIODICALS

Daily Times (Ottawa, IL), February 20, 2001, Julia Durango, "Kathy-jo Wargin's Illinois Alphabet."
Detroit Free Press, June 10, 2001, Cathy Collison, review of *The Legend of the Lady's Slipper,* p. 5; October 21, 2001, Janis Campbell, review of *The Michigan Reader for Boys and Girls,* p. 5.
Kirkus Reviews, April 15, 2003, review of *The Legend of Leelanau,* p. 613.
Tribune Books (Chicago, IL), January 7, 2001, Mary Harris Russell, review of *L Is for Lincoln: An Illinois Alphabet,* p. 5.*

*   *   *

WELD, John 1905-2003

OBITUARY NOTICE—See index for *CA* sketch: Born February 24, 1905, in Birmingham, AL; died June 14, 2003, in Dana Point, CA. Journalist, editor, publisher, and author. Weld had a colorful career that began after he attended Alabama Polytechnic Institute in the early

1920s. He made a go of working in vaudeville and even tried out for the U.S. Olympic diving team before moving west to Hollywood, where his experiences as a stuntman from 1923 to 1926 he later wrote about in *Fly away Home: Memoirs of a Hollywood Stunt Man* (1991). On the advice of well-known gossip columnist Louella Parsons, Weld next became a writer for the *New York American* and was stationed in Paris in 1927 as a reporter for the *Paris Times,* an adventure he wrote about in *Young Man in Paris* (1985). Weld also wrote for the *New York World* and *New York Herald* during the early 1930s, then briefly tried his hand at screenwriting for Columbia Pictures. He worked as a freelance writer in 1935 before moving to Laguna Beach, California, where he ran a Ford dealership and was hired as a copy writer for the Ford Motor Company. During the 1940s he was also editor of the *Consolidated News* for Consolidated Aircraft Corp. and became publications director for Ford from 1944 to 1949. In 1951 Weld and his wife began editing and publishing the *Laguna Beach Post,* which they ran until the mid-1960s. He also worked as a documentary movie producer of such films as *Freightboat round the World* (1963), *Ireland from a Gypsy Caravan* (1965), and *The Basque Sheepherder* (1972). When he was not occupied in one of his many commercial ventures, Weld wrote fiction and nonfiction books, including the novels *Don't You Cry for Me* (1940) and *Mark Pfeiffer, M.D.* (1943), his autobiographies, a collection of newspaper columns titled *Laguna, I Love You: The Best of "Our Town"* (1996), and the biography *September Song: An Intimate Biography of Walter Huston* (1998).

OBITUARIES AND OTHER SOURCES:

PERIODICALS

California Newspaper Publishers Association Bulletin, July 14, 2003, p. 4.
Los Angeles Times, July 22, 2003, p. B10.

*   *   *

WESTERFELD, Scott

PERSONAL: Married Justine Larbalestier (a researcher and writer).

ADDRESSES: Home—New York, NY; Sydney, Australia. *Agent*—c/o Tor Books, 175 Fifth Avenue, New York, NY 10010.

CAREER: Writer, composer, and media designer.

AWARDS, HONORS: Philip K. Dick Award special citation, 2000.

WRITINGS:

SCIENCE-FICTION NOVELS

Polymorph, Penguin (New York, NY), 1997.
Fine Prey, Penguin (New York, NY), 1998.
Evolution's Darling, Four Walls Eight Windows (New York, NY), 1999.
The Killing of Worlds, Tor (New York, NY), 2003.
The Risen Empire, Tor (New York, NY), 2003.

Also author of short stories.

FOR CHILDREN

The Berlin Airlift, Silver Burdett (Englewood Cliffs, NJ), 1989.
Watergate, Silver Burdett (Englewood Cliffs, NJ), 1991.
Blossom vs. the Blasteroid, Scholastic (New York, NY), 2002.
Diamonds Are for Princess, Scholastic (New York, NY), 2002.
Rainy Day Professor, Scholastic (New York, NY), 2002.

WORK IN PROGRESS: The novel *The Secret Hour,* for Eos.

SIDELIGHTS: Scott Westerfeld is a writer, composer, and media designer. His musical compositions have been performed in dance productions both in the United States and in Europe. He has also created numerous educational software programs for children. He has worked as a ghostwriter, and has published children's books, as well as short stories and novels for adults.

Reviewers have characterized Westerfeld's science-fiction novels as "space opera," which Gerald Jonas of the *New York Times,* defined as "far-future narratives that encompass entire galaxies and move confidently among competing planets and cultures, both human and otherwise." In an interview on the *Penguin Web site,* Westerfeld defined science fiction as "a way of writing (and of reading) which utilizes the power of extrapolation. It expands both the real world . . . and the literary. In regular fiction, you might be alienated. In [science fiction], you're an alien."

Westerfeld's first science-fiction novel, *Polymorph,* explores identity and sexual issues with a title character who is able to change gender and appearance. In his *Penguin* interview Westerfeld explained how his move to New York City inspired the idea for the story. "When I first moved to New York in the 1980s, I was amazed that it was such a richly textured city: layers of graffiti, legacies of immigrant influences, overlapping strata of big money and extreme poverty. To explore it all, you'd have to be a polymorph." Praising *Polymorph,* John Mort in *Booklist* called Westerfeld "a writer to watch."

Evolution's Darling, which earned its author a Philip K. Dick Award special citation, and Notable Book status from the *New York Times,* tells the story of Darling, an artificial intelligence who evolves into a sentient being through a relationship with a teenage girl. The reader follows Darling as the character becomes a galactic art dealer and develops a relationship with Mira, a high-tech killer. Trevor Dodge, in a review for the *Review of Contemporary Fiction,* stated that Westerfeld challenges the reader to "ponder if a machine can be made human, and if so, what purpose humanity would serve."

Discussing Westerfeld's work within the context of the challenges inherent in writing science fiction, Jonas commented in the *New York Times* that "to master such material and still bring to life characters with recognizable emotions and aspirations is a challenge few writers care to take on. Westerfeld succeeds admirably."

BIOGRAPHICAL AND CRITICAL SOURCES:

PERIODICALS

Booklist, December 1, 1997, John Mort, review of *Polymorph,* p. 612; February 15, 2003, Regina Schroeder, review of *The Risen Empire,* p. 1060.

Fantasy and Science Fiction, review of *Polymorph,* p. 46.

Kirkus Reviews, January 15, 2003, review of *The Risen Empire,* p. 118.

Library Journal, April 15, 2000, review of *Evolution's Darling,* p. 128.

New York Times, June 18, 2000, Gerald Jones, review of *Evolution's Darling,* p. 22; April 27, 2003, Gerald Jones, review of *The Risen Empire,* p. 23.

Publishers Weekly, April 17, 2000, review of *Evolution's Darling,* p. 57; January 20, 2003, review of *The Risen Empire,* p. 61.

Review of Contemporary Fiction, fall, 2000, Trevor Dodge, review of *Evolution's Darling,* p. 151.

School Library Journal, December, 1989, Ann Welton, review of *The Berlin Airlift,* p. 127.

Science Fiction Chronicle, February-March, 2003, Don D'Ammassa, review of *The Risen Empire,* p. 54.

ONLINE

Analog Science Fiction, http://www.analogsf.com/ (July 6, 2003), Tom Easton, review of *The Risen Empire.*

Baltimore City Paper Online, http://www.citypaper. com/ (July 12, 2000), Adrienne Martini, review of *Evolution's Darling.*

Penguin Web site, http://Penguin.com/ (1998), interview with Westerfeld.

Sci-Fi.com, http://www.scifi.com/ (July 6, 2003), Thomas Myer, review of *Polymorph;* (January 1, 2002) Paul Witcover, review of *Evolution's Darling;* (2002) Steven Sawicki, review of short story "Non-Disclosure Agreement"; (2003) Donna McMahon, review of *Fine Prey;* Paul Witcover, review of *The Risen Empire.**

*   *   *

WESTMORELAND, Timothy A. 1966-

PERSONAL: Born 1966, in Dallas, TX; married; wife's name Debbie. *Education:* University of Texas, Austin, B.A. (English), 1992; University of Massachusetts, Amherst, M.F.A. (creative writing).

ADDRESSES: Agent—c/o Author Mail, Harcourt, 15 East 25th St., New York, NY 10010.

CAREER: Writer. University of Texas, Arlington, astronomy instructor; University of Massachusetts, Amherst, writing instructor.

AWARDS, HONORS: Writing scholarships from Bennington College, Mount Holyoke College and Bread Loaf.

WRITINGS:

Good as Any (stories), Harcourt (New York, NY), 2002.

Work represented in anthologies, including *Scribner's Best of the Fiction Workshops* and *Best New American Voices 2001.* Contributor of short fiction to literary journals, including *Indiana Review.*

WORK IN PROGRESS: Gathering, a novel.

SIDELIGHTS: Timothy A. Westmoreland, who was diagnosed with diabetes when he was seven, studied astronomy but turned to writing and teaching writing after his vision worsened. He had begun to lose his sight at age eighteen, and in spite of dozens of eye surgeries, Westmoreland will eventually be unable to see. His diabetes has also left him with only thirty percent of his kidney function.

Westmoreland grew up near Dallas, Texas, in a family that did not value his intellectual abilities. The rural landscape of Texas figures in his collection *Good As Any,* as does New England, home to Amherst College, where he teaches creative writing in the school's Excel program. A *Publishers Weekly* contributor called the eight short stories in his debut collection "bleak, powerful. . . . Though Westmoreland's spare, elegant and highly textural prose provides some relief, the sadness that permeates almost every one of these stories can be overwhelming."

The stories are about men who have suffered, most through injury and illness, but also emotionally, with the result being that they are intensely lonely and long for someone with whom they can connect. Diabetes afflicts several, and one has a steel rod in his leg. These are working-class people who understand and enjoy fishing and shooting and who eat red meat. But

they can also be poetic when they describe something in nature, such as geese flying in formation overhead or the stars in the night sky. The love of a woman is central in some stories, but more often the object of these men's affections is a dog.

In "They Have Numbered All My Bones," Buckley Miller is a dying man who recalls the woman he loved long ago. The man in "The Buried Boy" is a diabetic who watches numbly, unable to function, as a boy buried in the sand by his friends is abandoned and panics with the incoming tide. The male character in "Blood Knot" suffers from diabetic delirium while on a fly fishing trip. In the title story, Mitch abandons everything, including his girlfriend Delilah, to care for Rose Marie, his beloved dog who is dying from a terminal illness.

"Darkening the World," also included in *Best New American Voices 2001,* is about Straw, a happy but unemployed paper-mill worker whose morning laughter annoys his roommate Pork, who thinks Straw needs to experience some negative feelings. Murphy is dying in "Strong at the Broken Places," and his friends want to help him but do not know how. *Library Journal's* Jim Coan wrote that without expressing sentimentality, Westmoreland "illuminates the world of extreme conditions, but a deep sense of compassion and sympathy for the characters comes through." In a *Booklist* review, Warrell Beth noted that the final story, "Winter Island," in which characters claim to have seen flying pigs, is an example of the way in which Westmoreland "uses seemingly imaginary events to heighten the sense of disconnection his characters feel from others, from themselves, and from life."

An *Austin Chronicle* reviewer wrote that Westmoreland "imbues his stories with enough sly humor and hope, however muffled, to make his characters' sad fates fascinating and unexpectedly illuminating." Katherine Wolff said in the *New York Times Book Review* that *Good as Any* asks the difficult questions "about human yearning . . . the meaning of home, and perhaps most essentially, about why men love dogs. Answers lie in Westmoreland's taut scenes and the finality of a few well-aimed guns."

BIOGRAPHICAL AND CRITICAL SOURCES:

PERIODICALS

Austin Chronicle, February 15, 2002, review of *Good as Any.*

Booklist, November 15, 2001, Warrell Beth, review of *Good as Any,* p. 549.

Library Journal, January, 2002, Jim Coan, review of *Good as Any,* p. 156.

Los Angeles Times Book Review, January 27, 2002, Mark Rozzo, "First Fiction," p. R10.

New York Times Book Review, February 3, 2002, Katherine Wolff, review of *Good as Any.*

Publishers Weekly, August 6, 2001, Judith Rosen, "Keeping It Short," p. 52; November 5, 2001, review of *Good as Any,* p. 38.*

ONLINE

UTA Magazine, http://utamagazine.uta.edu/ (October 14, 2003), Sherry Wodraska Neaves, "Fiction with Feeling."*

*   *   *

WETZEL, David

PERSONAL: Education: University of Chicago, Ph.D. (history), 1976.

ADDRESSES: Office—University of California, Berkeley, Business Services, 192 University Hall, Berkeley, CA 94720-1110. *E-mail*—dwetzel@uclink4.berkeley.edu.

CAREER: Author and historian. University of California, Berkeley, administrative analyst, 1986—.

WRITINGS:

The Crimean War: A Diplomatic History, East European Monographs (Boulder, CO)/Columbia University Press (New York, NY), 1985.

(With Francine Haber and Kenneth R. Fuller) *Robert S. Roeschlaub: Architect of the Emerging West, 1843-1923,* Colorado Historical Society (Denver, CO), 1988.

(Editor) *From the Berlin Museum to the Berlin Wall: Essays on the Cultural and Political History of Modern Germany,* Praeger (Westport, CT), 1996.

(Editor with Theodore S. Hamerow) *International Politics and German History: The Past Informs the Present,* Praeger (Westport, CT), 1997.

A Duel of Giants: Bismarck, Napoleon III, and the Origins of the Franco-Prussian War, University of Wisconsin Press (Madison, WI), 2001.

SIDELIGHTS: David Wetzel received his doctorate in history in 1976, at about the time funding of the humanities decreased in favor of technical fields. Wetzel took a full-time administrative position at the University of California, Berkeley, but has not abandoned his academic interests. He has written a number of volumes, beginning with *The Crimean War: A Diplomatic History.* Being multilingual in French, German, Italian, Russian, and Spanish, as well as English, Wetzel has been able to fully explore primary source documents in his research. For *The Crimean War,* he drew on archives and private papers in Britain, Austria, and France. Believing that diplomacy during the war can be studied by itself, without constant reference to actions on the battlefield, he writes about campaigns only when they impact ministerial decision making. In the early chapters, Wetzel elaborates on the various elements that brought on the war. *Choice*'s G. H. Davis wrote that "Wetzel's coverage of French foreign minister Drouyn de Lhuys and his Austrian counterpart, Count Buol, is especially strong." *Slavonic and East European Review* contributor D. W. Spring said Wetzel "avoids the minutiae of diplomacy which bedevil clarity of exposition in this genre, yet he reveals the substance of the various phases of negotiations with a sure grasp of their complexity."

Wetzel is coauthor with Francine Haber and Kenneth R. Fuller of *Robert S. Roeschlaub: Architect of the Emerging West, 1843-1923.* Roeschlaub was born in Germany and came to the United States as an infant, and his educated parents provided an atmosphere of liberalism, literature, music, and the arts in their Quincy, Illinois, home. Roeschlaub rose to the rank of captain in the Eighty-fourth Illinois Volunteer Infantry and was awarded several medals of honor. He then studied architecture, and in 1873, he moved his family to Denver, where he became the state's first licensed architect. His notable buildings include approximately fifty schools he designed for Denver and the surrounding area, and his love of the Rocky Mountains is reflected in the rough-cut stone he used in his designs. A good example of this style can be seen in the Central City Opera House, built in 1878. Harold Kirker wrote in *Pacific Historical Review* that "this finely researched and attractively produced monograph . . . will interest readers of this journal less as biography or architectural history than as a chronicle of the growth of a city and a profession on the American frontier in the initial period of maturation." *Western Historical Quarterly*'s Carroll Van West called *Robert S. Roeschlaub* "a book sure to be enjoyed not only by Denver architects, historians, and preservationists, but by all scholars interested in the architectural development of the American West."

With *From the Berlin Museum to the Berlin Wall: Essays on the Cultural and Political History of Modern Germany,* Wetzel honors German history scholar Gordon Craig. The book includes essays by such scholars as Henry Ashby Turner, Diethelm Prowe, Theodore S. Hamerow and Fritz Stern. Wetzel's own contributions include an essay about the breach of the Berlin Wall and another on Bismarck and South Germany.

Wetzel and Hamerow, an emeritus historian at the University of Wisconsin, edited *International Politics and German History: The Past Informs the Present,* and Wetzel and Prowe provide the introductory chapter which addresses eighteenth- to twentieth-century Europe and Germany's role therein. Richard L. Merritt wrote in *Perspectives on Political Science* that Paul W. Schroeder's "Does the History of International Politics Go Anywhere?" is "the book's centerpiece." Other chapters include Paul Gordon Lauren's "The Diplomatic Revolution of Our Time," David E. Barclay's "Monarchy, Court, and Society in Constitutional Prussia," Hermann-Josef Rupieper's "Der Bund für Burgerrecht: Transnational Relations and the Problem of Democratization in West Germany, 1949-1954," and Gaines Post, Jr.'s "Reflections on the German Question." Merritt maintained that "historians and advanced graduate students will welcome this book," which he described as "less a tightly spun argument than a richly textured tapestry of knowledge and thinking."

Wetzel's *A Duel of Giants: Bismarck, Napoleon III, and the Origins of the Franco-Prussian War* is the first work in English on the subject in nearly four decades. Wetzel notes that neither Otto von Bismarck nor Napoleon III were strongly in favor of war and explains how it could have been avoided, had not a variety of lesser players been so impassioned as the various European powers vied for position. *Booklist*'s

Allen Weakland called the volume a "truly important work in its refocusing of attention on a diplomatic struggle that has long been ignored."

BIOGRAPHICAL AND CRITICAL SOURCES:

PERIODICALS

American Historical Review, October, 1986, Norman Rich, review of *The Crimean War: A Diplomatic History,* p. 909.
Booklist, October 15, 2001, Allen Weakland, review of *A Duel of Giants: Bismarck, Napoleon III, and the Origins of the Franco-Prussian War,* p. 379.
Choice, July-August, 1986, G. H. Davis, review of *The Crimean War,* pp. 1725-1726.
English Historical Review, January, 1989, F. R. Bridge, review of *The Crimean War,* p. 230.
German Studies Review, October, 2000, Matthias Zimmer, review of *International Politics and German History: The Past Informs the Present,* p. 637.
Journal of Military History, April, 2002, Terry Strieter, review of *A Duel of Giants,* p. 578.
Pacific Historical Review, February, 1991, Harold Kirker, review of *Robert S. Roeschlaub: Architect of the Emerging West, 1843-1923,* pp. 106-107.
Perspectives on Political Science, summer, 1998, Richard L. Merritt, review of *International Politics and German History,* p. 173.
Publishers Weekly, October 1, 2001, review of *A Duel of Giants,* p. 51.
Reference & Research Book News, February, 1997, review of *From the Berlin Museum to the Berlin Wall: Essays on the Cultural and Political History of Modern Germany,* p. 16; February, 1998, review of *International Politics and German History,* p. 20.
Slavonic and East European Review, July, 1987, D. W. Spring, review of *The Crimean War,* pp. 471-472.
Western Historical Quarterly, November, 1989, Carroll Van West, review of *Robert S. Roeschlaub,* p. 460.

ONLINE

H-Net Reviews, http://www2.h-net.msu.edu/reviews/ (January 17, 2002), Peter Fritzsche, review of *From the Berlin Museum to the Berlin Wall: Essays on the Cultural and Political History of Modern Germany.**

WOELFLE, Gretchen 1945-

PERSONAL: Born January 30, 1945, in Dunkirk, NY; daughter of Arthur (a business executive) and Ruth (a homemaker; maiden name, Godden) Woelfle; formerly married; children: Cleo, Alice. *Education:* University of California—Berkeley, B.A. (English), 1966; Union College, M.A. (American studies), 1972; Vermont College, M.F.A. (writing for children), 2000. *Politics:* Green Party. *Religion:* "Buddhist/Quaker." *Hobbies and other interests:* Urban agriculture, hiking, camping, singing.

ADDRESSES: Home—Los Angeles, CA. *Office*—c/o Author Mail, Candlewick Press, 2067 Massachusetts Ave., Cambridge, MA 02140. *E-mail*—gwoelfle@aol.com.

CAREER: Editor, teacher, and freelance writer, 1966-98; interactive multimedia educational scriptwriter, 1988-98; children's author, 1992—. Artistic residencies at Hedgebrook Writer's Colony, 1992, Villa Montalvo, 1994, Dorset Colony House, 1995, Ragdale Foundation, 1996, 1997, 2001, 2002, and Byrdcliffe Art Colony, 1997.

MEMBER: Society of Children's Book Writers and Illustrators, Authors Guild, Authors League, Quaker Bolivia Link (member, board of directors), Phi Beta Kappa.

AWARDS, HONORS: Magazine Merit Award for Fiction, Society of Children's Book Writers and Illustrators (SCBWI), 1997, for "Sail by the Moon"; Anna Gross Giblin nonfiction research grant, SCBWI, 1997; *The Wind at Work* named to Children's Literature Top Choice List, 1998; *Katje, the Windmill Cat* was Children's Book of the Week selection, London *Sunday Times,* and shortlisted for Children's Book Award (England), 2001.

WRITINGS:

The Wind at Work: An Activity Guide to Windmills, Chicago Review Press (Chicago, IL), 1997.
Katje, the Windmill Cat, illustrated by Nicola Bayley, Candlewick Press (Cambridge, MA), 2001.

Bees Make Honey and Robins Give Singing Lessons: How Animals Help Each Other, NorthWord Press (Chanhassen, MN), 2004.

Also author of "Sail by the Moon." Contributor to *Stories from Where We Live: The North Atlantic Coast,* 2000; *Stories from Where We Live: The Great North American Prairie,* 2001; *Stories from Where We Live: The California Coast,* 2002; and *Stories from Where We Live: The Great Lakes,* 2003, all edited by Sara St. Antoine, Milkweed Editions (Minneapolis, MN). Contributor of fiction and essays to children's periodicals, including *Cricket, Spider, Cicada, Faces,* and *Highlights for Children,* as well as features, travel articles, and art reviews to national and international publications.

Katje, the Windmill Cat has been translated into five languages, including Dutch, Chinese, and Japanese.

WORK IN PROGRESS: A middle-grade novel and biographies.

SIDELIGHTS: Gretchen Woelfle did not figure out her true vocation—writing children's books—until she was well into her forties. Even then, it took a job layoff to set her on her path. She was writing for educational multimedia projects, a job she enjoyed, but one day in 1992 when one project ended, no new project materialized. Fortuitously, her mother-in-law sent her a tape recording of some old family stories from eighteenth- and nineteenth-century Maine and from Gold Rush California. Upon hearing these tales, Woelfle thought some would make good stories for kids. Having a bit of time on her hands, the author decided to transform them into works for children. "It took me a while to learn the difference between anecdotes and stories, but several of these family stories finally appeared in *Cricket, Spider,* and *Cicada* magazines," Woelfle confided to *CA.*

Growing up in Dunkirk, New York, a small town on the Lake Erie shore, Woelfle enjoyed the out of doors but also read avidly. "Every summer I joined the library reading club," she recalled on her Home page, "and one year the librarian questioned me every day when I returned to take out four new books. She didn't believe I could read that much. I was insulted!" Later after earning a college degree in English, she wrote for magazines in London, New England, the Midwest, and California. She married and had two daughters in whom she inspired a love of reading.

Woelfle's first book for children, *The Wind at Work: An Activity Guide to Windmills,* grew out of her concern for America's dependence on fossil fuels. She explained, "I wanted to tell kids about renewable energy, particularly wind power. But as I began to research the subject, I got caught up in the human-interest side of windmills. How they changed people's lives in the past. How windmills inspired a folk culture of their own. How people's needs and ingenuity changed windmills themselves. And, of course, how windmills can help create a more sustainable energy future."

"Since I love research as much as I love writing—sometimes more!—," Woelfle told *CA,* "I went after people, places, and things to write the windmill story. I visited windmills and windmillers in the Netherlands, I drove across the American West, I toured a wind-turbine factory in California, and I spoke to engineers, historians, and windmill restorers and collectors." Although Woelfle did extensive research and planned a nonfiction overview of the devices, when she found a publisher, the publisher wanted an extensive series of activities relating to wind power and windmills as well. So Woelfle designed many activities—science and nature experiments, arts and crafts projects, musical activities, cooking and sewing projects, and story-writing, energy conservation, and community action projects—which a *Children's Digest* reviewer found "very interesting." Then the author compiled an extensive list of places to visit restored and working windmills, and finally embarked on illustration research, as she recalled, "Again, it was an adventure through time and space to obtain drawings, paintings, photographs, and charts that illustrate one thousand years of windmill history." According to *Booklist*'s Susan Dove Lempke, Woelfle's work paid off in "this attractive volume [that is] enhanced by thoughtfully selected photographs and reproductions."

Even after *The Wind at Work* appeared in 1997, Woelfle could not get windmills out of her mind. When she read about how a cat rescued a baby in a cradle during a flood nearly six hundred years ago, she thought it a great adventure. But it needed a story to frame it, and because she could not find the historical facts about the event, she invented a tale. "Since I had

windmills on my brain, the story became *Katje, the Windmill Cat,*" the author said. In this picture book, Katje the cat and Nico the miller live happily together; that is, until Nico brings home a wife, Lena. Katje loves the couple's new baby Anneka, but when Lena shoos Katje away, she takes up residence in the mill. It takes a near-disaster and heroic rescue to restore family harmony.

To illustrate the tale, Nicola Bayley, an award-winning English illustrator famous for her cats, created a series of pastel-pencil miniatures inspired by Dutch Renaissance paintings. *Katje, the Windmill Cat* elicited praise from reviewers. In a starred review in *Publishers Weekly,* the writer called the tale "an engaging story" portrayed "with warmth and imagination." Other admirers of the work include a *Kirkus Reviews* contributor, who described Woelfle's as "a stately storyteller's voice," and Grace Oliff of *School Library Journal,* who dubbed the book a "gentle, charming tale" with "simple, graceful prose [that] is a pleasure to read aloud."

Katje, the Windmill Cat has been translated into five languages, including Chinese and Japanese. Woelfle is pleased that children in Asia get glimpses of old-fashioned windmills via Bayley's illustrations. *Katje* has returned home, in Dutch, to the Netherlands. Woelfle added, "It tickles me that the Dutch edition changes Katje's name (which means 'Kitty') to Bontje ('soft and furry')."

Woelfle's environmental interests again emerge in her picture book *Bees Make Honey and Robins Give Singing Lessons: How Animals Live Together.* This book was inspired by a scientific article claiming that the theory of cooperation in nature is challenging the theory of competition. Woelfle furthers the cause by demonstrating the concepts of cooperation in parents, families, and communities of twelve wild animal species.

A few of her family stories also found a home in *Stories from Where We Live,* a series of anthologies published by Milkweed Editions that combines two of Woelfle's passions—literature and the environment. Each volume of *Stories from Where We Live* focuses on one North American bio-region and contains stories, essays, and poems that incorporate the landscape, flora, and fauna into the heart of the piece.

Woelfle said, "I was pleased to coauthor one essay, 'Fire in the Chaparral!,' with my daughter Cleo, who has begun her publishing career far earlier than her mother."

Since her children have grown up and left home, Woelfle has become an inveterate traveler, visiting many continents and cultures. Woelfle told *CA:* "My travel inevitably informs my writing. My life has been deeply enriched by other cultures, and I want to pass that on. Our world is connected by technology today, and I hope we can deepen that connection to include tolerance and appreciation of each other and the natural environment. That is why I write stories."

BIOGRAPHICAL AND CRITICAL SOURCES:

PERIODICALS

Booklist, September 1, 1997, Susan Dove Lempke, review of *The Wind at Work: An Activity Guide to Windmills,* p. 121; February 1, 2000, Ellen Mandel, review of *Katje, the Windmill Cat,* p. 940.
Children's Digest, September, 2000, review of *The Wind at Work,* p. 26.
Kirkus Reviews, August 15, 2001, review of *Katje, the Windmill Cat,* p. 1223.
Publishers Weekly, September 10, 2001, review of *Katje, the Windmill Cat,* p. 92.
School Library Journal, October, 1997, Steven Engelfried, review of *The Wind at Work,* p. 158; November, 2001, Grace Oliff, review of *Katje, the Windmill Cat,* p. 139.

ONLINE

Gretchen Woelfle Home Page, http://www.gretchenwoelfle.com (July 1, 2003).

*   *   *

WOOLFOLK, William 1917-2003
(Winston Lyon)

OBITUARY NOTICE—See index for *CA* sketch: Born June 25, 1917, in Centermoriches, NY; died of congestive heart failure July 20, 2003, in Syracuse, NY. Author. Though he never won a major literary award,

Woolfolk forged a successful writing career for himself that ranged from comic-book stories to novels and nonfiction. He graduated from New York University with a B.A. in 1938 and then worked for two years as a copywriter before becoming a freelance magazine writer. Serving in the U.S. Army during World War II, he returned home to write for comic books during what is generally considered that medium's Gold Age. Woolfolk did not create any new comic-book heroes, but he was in high demand to write stories about Batman, Captain Marvel, Superman, and other popular characters. One claim to fame he had, however, was in inventing the expression "Holy Moley" for Captain Marvel. During this time, Woolfolk also founded and briefly ran O. W. Comics. He earned ten times the average comic-book writer's salary, but when the era of the comics waned, he decided to move on. He became a contributor of stories to magazines such as *Scene* and *Shock* during the 1950s and early 1960s; meanwhile, the 1950s also saw the beginning of his long career as a novelist beginning with 1953's *The Naked Hunter.* His *My Name Is Morgan* (1963) was a Literary Guild selection and was followed by *Criminal Court* (1966), which Woolfolk published under the pseudonym Winston Lyon. Woolfolk also wrote two novels under the Lyon pen name that were based on the Batman character: *Batman vs. Three Villains of Doom* (1966), which was based on the television series, and *Batman vs. the Fearsome Foursome* (1967), a novelization of a "Batman" film. Beginning in 1961, Woolfolk started writing for the television series *The Defenders* and is credited with penning two screenplays that were nominated for Emmy awards. He also continued to write novels, among them *Maggie: A Love Story* (1971), *The President's Doctor* (1975), *The Sendai* (1981), and his last novel, *The Adam Project* (1984). Woolfolk wrote two books about parenting, too: *The Great American Birth Rite* (1975), which he wrote with his wife, and *Daddy's Little Girl: The Unspoken Bargain between Fathers and Their Daughters* (1982), which he wrote with his daughter, Donna Woolfolk Cross. Although Woolfolk made a good living writing books, he is often best remembered for his early comic books; in 2002 Comic-Con International awarded him its Inkpot Award for his contributions to the genre.

OBITUARIES AND OTHER SOURCES:

PERIODICALS

Los Angeles Times, August 10, 2003, p. B17.

New York Times, August 9, 2003, p. A12.
Washington Post, August 11, 2003, p. B5.

*   *   *

ZEISES, Lara M. 1976-

PERSONAL: Surname rhymes with "vices;" born January 20, 1976, in Philadelphia, PA; daughter of Nancy Stone. *Ethnicity:* "Caucasian." *Education:* University of Delaware, B.A. (English, with journalism concentration; with advanced honors), 1997; Emerson College, M.F.A. (creative writing), 2001.

ADDRESSES: Home—Wilmington, DE. *Agent*—George Nicholson, Sterling Lord Literistic, 65 Bleecker St., New York, NY 10012. *E-mail*—zeisgeist@aol.com.

CAREER: Writer. Worked as an intern for *Baltimore Sun* and *News Journal;* also worked briefly as a features reporter in Indiana and Delaware.

MEMBER: Society of Children's Book Writers and Illustrators.

AWARDS, HONORS: Honor book award, Delacorte Press Contest for First Young-Adult Novel, 2001, and Best Book for the Teen Age selection, New York Public Library, 2003, both for *Bringing up the Bones.*

WRITINGS:

Bringing up the Bones (young-adult novel), Delacorte Press (New York, NY), 2002.
Contents under Pressure (young-adult novel), Delacorte Press (New York, NY), 2004.

Coauthor of play produced by Delaware Theater Company. Contributor of fiction and nonfiction to periodicals, including *Jewish Education News* and *Kliatt.*

WORK IN PROGRESS: Anyone but You, a young-adult novel, publication expected in 2006.

BIOGRAPHICAL AND CRITICAL SOURCES:

PERIODICALS

Booklist, November 15, 2002, Gillian Engberg, review of *Bringing up the Bones,* p. 596.
Publishers Weekly, October 7, 2002, review of *Bringing up the Bones,* p. 74.
School Library Journal, November, 2002, Susan W. Hunter, review of *Bringing up the Bones,* p. 178.

ONLINE

Lara M. Zeises Official Web page, http://www.zeisgeist.com/(July 1, 2003).

*   *   *

ZURLO, Tony 1941-

PERSONAL: Born October 7, 1941, in Takoma Park, MD; married Vivian Wei Lu (an educator). *Ethnicity:* "One-half Italian, a quarter Nigerian, and a quarter Chinese." *Education:* State University of New York—Stony Brook, M.A. (liberal arts), 1974; University of Texas—Arlington, M.A. (history), 1975; Texas A&M—Commerce, Ed.D. (English), 1980. *Politics:* Democrat. *Hobbies and other interests:* Politics, music.

ADDRESSES: Office—Tarrant County College—Southeast Campus, 2100 Southeast Pkwy., Arlington, TX 76018-3144. *E-mail*—libai@comcast.net.

CAREER: Wright State University—Lake Campus, Celina, OH, assistant professor of English, 1986-89; Hebei Teachers' University, Shijiazhuang, People's Republic of China, visiting professor of English, 1990-91; Tarrant County College, Arlington, TX, professor of English, 1992—. Former Peace Corps volunteer in Nigeria. Member of board of advisors, *New Texas* journal; member of board of directors, Dallas Soccer. *Military service:* U.S. Army, 1967-70; became first lieutenant.

MEMBER: National Council of Teachers of English, Friends of Nigeria, Returned Peace Corps Volunteers, World Affairs Council of Greater Fort Worth, Fort Worth Sister Cities International.

AWARDS, HONORS: Numerous first place and finalist awards in regional and state fiction and poetry contests; Minnie Stevens Piper Teaching Award nomination; National Institute for Organizational Development Excellence Award.

WRITINGS:

Japan: Superpower of Pacific, Dillon Press (New York, NY), 1991.
China: The Dragon Awakes, Dillon Press (New York, NY), 1994.
West Africa, Lucent Books (San Diego, CA), 2001.
Life in Hong Kong, Lucent Books (San Diego, CA), 2001.
China ("Nations in Transition" series), Greenhaven Press (San Diego, CA), 2002.
Japanese Americans, Lucent Books (San Diego, CA), 2003.
Vietnam ("Nations in Transition" series), Greenhaven Press (San Diego, CA), 2004.
Filipino Americans, Lucent Books (San Diego, CA), 2004.

Contributor of poems and short stories to magazines and journals, and book reviews to *Peace Corps Writers.* Former editor of *Friends of Nigeria* newsletter.

SIDELIGHTS: Poet, short-story writer, and nonfiction book writer Tony Zurlo has written a handful of books for children. As he told *CA:* "My writing career is directly connected to teaching as a Peace Corps volunteer in Nigeria and as a visiting professor in China later in my career. From these experiences I learned first-hand that people round the world are fundamentally alike." After publishing poems and short stories based on his personal impressions of and adventures in Africa and Asia, he expanded his work in the nineties to writing nonfiction for children. These works, most of which form part of several series, include books about life in Japan, China, and Vietnam, as well as an overview of life in West Africa. "I believe that the key to promoting peace and harmony in the world is by learning about and deepening our understanding of other cultures," he explained, "and by writing I try to share my insights with others." His knowledge of Asian culture is evident in these works, claim critics. Reviewing *China: The Dragon Awakes, Booklist*'s April Judge dubbed the volume "informative" and "interesting." Diane S. Marton of *School Library Journal* also praised Zurlo for "the clear, informative text," as well as the personal anecdotes and observations in his 2001 title *Life in Hong Kong.*

BIOGRAPHICAL AND CRITICAL SOURCES:

PERIODICALS

Booklist, April 15, 1995, April Judge, review of *China: The Dragon Awakes,* p. 1497.
School Library Journal, April, 1992, John Philbrook, review of *Japan: Superpower of the Pacific,* p. 144; June, 2002, Diane S. Marton, review of *Life in Hong Kong,* p. 171; January, 2003, Diane S. Marton, review of *China,* p. 173.